LAND USE LAW FOR SUSTAINABLE DEVELOPMENT

This book surveys the global experience to date in implementing land use policies that move us further along the sustainable development continuum. The international community has long recognized the need to ensure that ongoing and future development is conducted sustainably. While high-level commitments toward sustainable development such as those included in the Rio and Johannesburg Declarations are politically important, they are irrelevant if they are not translated into reality on the ground. This book includes chapters that discuss the challenges of implementing sustainable land use policies in different regions of the world, revealing problems that are common to all jurisdictions and highlighting others that are unique to particular regions. It also includes chapters documenting new approaches to sustainable land use, such as reforms to property rights regimes and environmental laws. Other chapters offer comparisons of approaches in different jurisdictions that can present insights that might not be apparent from a single-jurisdiction analysis.

Nathalie J. Chalifour is an assistant professor in the Faculty of Law at the University of Ottawa in Ontario, where her teaching and research interests fall in the areas of environmental law, property law, and international environmental law and policy. She holds a Doctorate of Law and a Master of Law from Stanford University, where she completed a research fellowship as a Fulbright Scholar. She has written numerous works in the field of environmental law and policy, including book chapters on environmental taxation and articles on the nexus between international trade rules and forest conservation. Professor Chalifour is contributing editor of the looseleaf service *The Canadian Brownfields Manual* (2005).

Patricia Kameri-Mbote is an associate professor of Law and Chair of the Department of Private Law, Faculty of Law at the University of Nairobi. She holds a Doctorate in Law and a Master of Law from Stanford University, a Master of Law in Law and Development from Warwick University, and a Postgraduate Diploma in Women's Law from the University of Zimbabwe. Her teaching and research interests fall in the areas of environmental law, law, science and technology, intellectual property rights, land law, and feminist jurisprudence. She has published widely in the areas of international environmental law, biotechnology, women's rights, and property rights.

Lin Heng Lye is an associate professor in the Faculty of Law at the National University of Singapore and Deputy Director of the Faculty's Asia-Pacific Centre for Environmental Law. She chairs the University's interdisciplinary Executive Committee for the Masters in Environmental Management program and is Visiting Associate Professor at the Yale School of Forestry and Environmental Studies. She holds Master's degrees in Law from Harvard University and the University of London and an LLB from the University of Singapore. She is an Advocate and Solicitor of the Supreme Court of Singapore and was Vice-Dean and Director of the Law Faculty's graduate programs. Her teaching and research interests lie in property law and environmental law.

John R. Nolon is a professor of Law at Pace University Law School. He received his JD degree from the University of Michigan Law School, where he was a member of the Barrister's Academic Honor Society. Professor Nolon has been appointed Visiting Professor of Environmental Law at the Yale School of Forestry and Environmental Studies and named Director of the Joint Center of Land Use Studies formed by Yale and Pace University Law School. He served on the Editorial Advisory Board of the *National Housing and Development Reporter* and is a member of the Editorial Board of *The Land Use and Environmental Law Review*. He has worked extensively on sustainable development in South America as a Fulbright scholar.

Land Use Law for Sustainable Development

Edited by

NATHALIE J. CHALIFOUR
University of Ottawa

PATRICIA KAMERI-MBOTE
University of Nairobi

LIN HENG LYE
National University of Singapore

JOHN R. NOLON
Pace University

with a Message from Kofi A. Annan,
Secretary-General of the United Nations

CAMBRIDGE
UNIVERSITY PRESS

CAMBRIDGE UNIVERSITY PRESS
Cambridge, New York, Melbourne, Madrid, Cape Town, Singapore, São Paulo

Cambridge University Press
32 Avenue of the Americas, New York, NY 10013-2473, USA

www.cambridge.org
Information on this title: www.cambridge.org/9780521862165

© IUCN Academy of Environmental Law 2007

First published 2007

Printed in the United States of America

A catalog record for this publication is available from the British Library.

Library of Congress Cataloging in Publication Data

ISBN-13   978-0-521-86216-5 hardback
ISBN-10   0-521-86216-7 hardback

Contents

Contributors

Patryck de Araújo Ayala Attorney of Mato Grosso State; Law PhD student, Federal University of Santa Catarina, Brazil

Mekete Bekele Assistant Professor, Faculty of Law, Addis Adaba University, Ethiopia

Karen Bubna-Litic Senior Lecturer in Law in the Faculty of Law at UTS, Australia

Nathalie J. Chalifour Assistant Professor, Faculty of Law, University of Ottawa, Ontario, Canada

Ed Couzens Attorney, RSA, and Senior Lecturer, Faculty of Law, University of KwaZulu-Natal, Durban, South Africa

Heline Sivini Ferreira Law PhD student, Federal University of Santa Catarina, Brazil

Nyokabi Gitahi Legal Associate, African Wildlife Association, Kenya

Jose Juan Gonzalez President of the Mexican Institute for Environmental Law Research and Professor of Environmental Law at the Universidad Autonoma Metropolitana, Mexico

Ian Hannam Member, IUCN Commission on Environmental Law; Chair, IUCN CEL Specialist Working Goup on Sustainable Soil; Environmental Law and Policy Specialist, Asian Development Bank, Beijing, China

Parvez Hassan Senior Partner, Hassan & Hassan, Lahore, Pakistan, and President, Pakistan Environmental Law Association

David R. Hodas Professor of Law, Widener University School of Law, Wilmington, Delaware, USA

Michael I. Jeffery Professor of Law and Director, Centre for Environmental Law, Macquarie University, Sydney, Australia; Deputy Chair of the IUCN Commission on Environmental Law

Patricia Kameri-Mbote Associate Professor and Chair, Department of Private Law, Faculty of Law, University of Nairobi, Kenya

Nuntapol Karnchanawat Thailand

Emmanuel Kasimbazi Senior Lecturer, Faculty of Law, Makerere University Uganda, and Partner, Kasimbazi & Co. Advocates, Uganda

Michael Kidd Professor of Law, University of KwaZulu-Natal, Pietermaritzburg, South Africa

Kheng-Lian Koh Faculty of Law, National University of Singapore; Director, Asia-Pacific Centre for Environmental Law; IUCN CEL Regional Vice Chair for South and East Asia

W. J. Kombe Professor of Urban Land Management and Planning at the University College of Land and Architectural Studies, Dar es Salaam, Tanzania

Louis J. Kotzé Faculty of Law, North-West University, Potchefstroom Campus, South Africa

Muhammed Tawfiq Ladan Head, Department of Public Law, Faculty of Law, Ahmadu Bello University, Zaria, Kaduna State, Nigeria

José Rubens Morato Leite Professor of the Undergraduate and Postgraduate Courses, Federal University of Santa Catarina, Brazil

Lin Heng Lye Associate Professor and Deputy Director, Asia-Pacific Centre for Environmental Law, Faculty of Law, National University of Singapore; and Visiting Associate Professor, Yale School of Forestry and Environmental Studies, USA

Sunee Mallikamarl Professor of Law, Chulalongkorn University, Bangkok, Thailand

Linda A. Malone Marshall-Wythe Foundation Professor of Law, William and Mary Law School, Williamsburg, Virginia, USA

Akio Morishima Chair of the Board of Directors, Institute for Global Environmental Strategies, Japan

Albert Mumma Associate Professor, Faculty of Law, University of Nairobi, Nairobi, Kenya

John R. Nolon Professor of Law, Pace University School of Law, and Counsel to the Law School's Land Use Law Center; Visiting Professor, Yale School of Forestry and Environmental Studies, USA

Charles Odidi Okidi University of Nairobi, Nairobi, Kenya

George Okoth-Obbo United Nations High Commissioner for Refugees (UNHCR) for Kenya, Nairobi, Kenya

H. W. O. Okoth-Ogendo Professor of Public Law, University of Nairobi, Nairobi, Kenya

Bibobra Bello Orubebe Faculty of Law, Delta State University Abraka, Nigeria

Amber Prasad Pant Professor of Law, Tribhuvan University, Faculty of Law, Nepal Law Campus, Kathmandu, Nepal

Gabriella Pavon L.L.M., Pace University School of Law, USA

Willemien du Plessis Professor of Law, Faculty of Law, North-West University, Potchefstroom, South Africa

Michel Prieur   Professor of Environmental Law, Limoges University, and President of the International Center of Comparative Environmental Law, France

Du Qun   Professor, Research Institute of Environmental Law, Law School of Wuhan University, Wuhan City, Hubei Province, China; Member, IUCN Commission on Environmental Law; and Deputy Chair, IUCN CEL Specialist Working Group on Sustainable Soil

Lana Roux   North-West University, Potchefstroom, South Africa

Nchunu Sama   Executive Director of the Foundation for Environment and Development in Cameroon and Part-Time Lecturer in environmental law at the Regional College of Agriculture Bambili, Cameroon

Juan Rodrigo Walsh   Senior Partner at Estudio Walsh, Consultares Ambientales, Buenos Aires, Argentina

UNITED NATIONS **NATIONS UNIES**

THE SECRETARY-GENERAL

MESSAGE TO THE SECOND COLLOQUIUM
OF THE IUCN ACADEMY OF ENVIRONMENTAL LAW
Nairobi, 4 October 2004

It gives me great pleasure to send my greetings to everyone who has gathered at the University of Nairobi for this timely colloquium of the IUCN Academy of Environmental Law on the theme of land use and environmental law.

Land use is at the heart of our hopes of achieving truly sustainable development. Yet in urban and rural areas alike, the pressures are immense.

According to the latest projections of UN-Habitat, the world's urban slums will double in population over the next 30 years, meaning that in just one generation, we could see 2 billion people living in conditions that deny their inhabitants the basic dignities of housing, health care, sanitation, education, transport, and employment. Already, nearly half the developing world's urban population lives in unplanned squatter settlements.

The challenges in rural areas are just as formidable. Deforestation and desertification are threatening ecosystems, biodiversity, and food security. Nearly 2 billion hectares of land are affected by human-induced degradation of soils, putting the livelihoods of nearly 1 billion people at risk. Safeguards must be put in place to ensure that intensification of agricultural production and increased use of agrochemicals, needed to satisfy the growing population in many developing countries, do not lead to further decline in environmental quality. Moreover, there is a need to regularize the tenure of the rural poor so they have the long-term security that comes with living on titled land.

Environmental law has a special role to play in addressing these issues. Law professors and legal experts can help national and local authorities devise legal regimes that enhance sustainable development instead of hindering it. You can help map out realistic and concrete land law reforms. You can share best practices and successful legal models. And through your teaching you can instill in new generations of legal practitioners an appreciation for the rule of law and its essential place in human affairs.

Both the Earth Summit in Rio de Janeiro and the World Summit on Sustainable Development in Johannesburg recommended strengthening the law for environment and development. I would like to thank you for your support of this cause, and also for timing your meeting to coincide with this year's observance of World Habitat Day. Please accept my best wishes for a successful colloquium.

Kofi A. Annan

Foreword

Human settlements have been both the home and the hallmark of civilization since the first human beings congregated. This history of each part of the Earth is told through the cultural, economic, and social settings of cities, towns, and villages. City states continue to this day, and often the commercial and political life of large cities defines the policies of states. The world's cultural heritage is bound up in its human settlements. So, too, is the world's future.

In the latter years of the 20th century, the emergence of megacities signaled a reshaping of all aspects of both national life and international relations. There are models of planned urban growth, such as the brilliant development of the Pudong New Area in Shanghai, China, or the transformation of Singapore after the Second World War into a clean and green city, with extraordinary provisions guaranteeing the well-being of its citizens. These examples demonstrate that the environmental and social and economic pillars of sustainable development can be coordinated and advanced in tandem. Unfortunately, these examples are the exceptions. Many of the megaconurbations of millions of city inhabitants lack clean water, sewage systems, decent housing, educational opportunities, jobs, and parks and recreation. Despite major social and urban planning programs in cities across Brazil, favelas persist and grow in many states. Slums and shantytowns are a defining feature of major cities in many African, Asian, and South American nations.

Megaconurbations today produce air pollution, chronic health problems, water pollution, and a host of inevitable social problems. Their demand for electricity, food, potable water, and shelter extends deeply into the countryside. No city can be deemed self-sufficient, even if its local laws stop at its borders. Its economy imports most of what it needs to exist and is dependent on the effectiveness of laws in other localities that protect the watersheds that feed its water supply, or the farms that feeds its people, or the fuel that supplies its energy. Such urban centers export their chemical and hazardous wastes, their air pollutants, and their social problems far beyond their borders.

In a world of global trade, communications, and interdependent environmental needs, all regions have a shared stake in understanding how to guide land use and development so that it becomes sustainable. Yet, our regimes of nation states and intergovernmental relations mean that each stakeholder usually ignores the land use and environmental problems of other stakeholders. We live with a legal fiction that each nation must solve its own environmental degradation issues of its cities. Since land use laws are essentially national and local, and traditionally law has always been the principal instrument governing land use decisions, most legal scholarship about land use and cities is national. Little attention is paid to instances where the legal infrastructure is overwhelmed by rapid migration into slums or the emergency of civil strife. Little comparative legal analysis exists to let governments in one nation learn from the successes of others.

Environmental law encompasses the law that governs the uses of land, water, soils, air, forests, and all the natural resources that urban settlements require. The contributors to this book examine legal issues that are common across all nations. They inaugurate here a comparative environmental law analysis of the law of land use for sustainable development.

This volume contains reflections from scholars representing the legal systems from all regions of the world. The authors gathered, along with many other environmental law scholars whose papers and contributions could not be published in this volume, at the University of Nairobi, in Kenya, for the Second Colloquium of the IUCN Academy of Environmental Law. Without prompting, these legal experts volunteered papers that cover land use comprehensively. Topics include land use planning, settlement, implications of climate change, and food security. Although addressing land use locally, clearly these titles indicate that this book provides what amounts to a careful scholarly analysis of issues central to planetary sustainability.

The chapters of this book, and the primary materials published in its companion volume, ably edited by John Nolon, provide guidance for attaining the Millennium Development Goals adopted by the United Nations. Its themes illuminate how states can use legal tools to help realize the Millennium Development Goals of poverty alleviation and environmental sustainability. The book at the same time contributes to the foundations of learning and education about the law of land use for sustainable development.

Kenya and Africa broadly know well the need to enhance land use planning as a foundation for economic, social, and environmental development. The University of Nairobi selected the theme for the Second Colloquium, and the Planning Committee reached out to scholars in each part of Africa and around the world to make the Colloquium a solid success. There are many who deserve thanks for making this book possible. We were honored that Wangari Maathai, as Assistant Minister of the Environment of Kenya, opened the Colloquium; by the final day of our deliberations, she had become the Nobel Peace Prize Laureate for that year. The UN-Habitat program and the United Nations Environment Programme were key sponsors, whose financial and expert support is much appreciated. The fine support and cooperation of the Government of Kenya included the Kenya Wildlife Services, National Environment Management Agency, and other offices. The Vice Chancellor of the University of Nairobi, the Principal of the College, and the environmental experts on the Faculty of Law were strong and steadfast supporters of the Colloquium during the two years of time that went into preparing it. Their contributions are gratefully acknowledged. The assistance of the African Wildlife Foundation and that of the International Union for the Conservation of Nature and Natural Resources (IUCN) Environmental Law Centre were essential to the success of the colloquium. Above all, thanks are due to the many individuals from Kenya on the University of Nairobi organizing committee and the host committee, including Dr. Patricia Kameri-Mbote. Space precludes commending the many additional contributions. Their support underpins this book, without which it would not be.

This book, then, is a forceful message to every level of readership in all regions of the world. Its publication underscores the credibility and growing legitimacy of the IUCN Academy of Environmental Law as a learned society, filling what has hitherto been a special gap, the absence of a global network of scholars engaged across all regions in the development of environmental law.

It has been a privilege to have cochaired the Second Colloquium of the IUCN Academy of Environmental Law on the Law of Land Use for Sustainable Development and to extend these heartfelt thanks to all involved.

Charles Odidi Okidi
University of Nairobi
Kenya

Nicholas Adams Robinson
Chair, IUCN Academy of Environmental Law
Pace University, New York

Acknowledgments

The editors would like to thank and acknowledge the help of the following people. Without their contributions, the conference and book would not have been possible.

- Professor Crispus Kiamba, then Vice Chancellor of the University of Nairobi, along with his deputies, Professor George Magoha and Professor J. T. Kaimenyi
- The Principal of the University of Nairobi, Professor Isaac Mbeche
- Professor James Odek, the Dean of the Faculty of Law, University of Nairobi, and Professor Dorothy McCormick, Director of IDS, University of Nairobi
- Academics from the University of Nairobi who loyally attended the colloquium with or without papers together with seventy academic colleagues and students who volunteered their time to ensure that the Colloquium succeeded
- Ms. Elizabeth Mbebe and Professors Mohamed Jama, Isaac Nyamongo, and Priscilla Kariuki, of the University of Nairobi, who headed planning and logistics
- Ms. Winni A. Mbeche and the Secretariat staff who took care of all the conference details with great diligence
- Katerina Sarafidou, CEL Liaison Office, IUCN Environmental Law Centre, Bonn, Germany
- Katrina Anders, Sean Bawden, Gilles Comeau, Celine Délorme, Dereck Eby, Jahmiah Ferdinand-Hernandez, Preet Gill, John Georgakopoulous, Martin Kreuser, and Yolanda Saito, all students at the Faculty of Law, University of Ottawa, for their help with editing
- Susan Moritz, Research Consultant to the Land Use Law Center at Pace University School of Law, for her help in editing

INTRODUCTION

Nathalie J. Chalifour, Patricia Kameri-Mbote, Lin Heng Lye,
John R. Nolon, and Charles Odidi Okidi

As human populations grow and land and natural resources come under greater pressure, land use planning has been an increasingly important subject of policy discussion at the national level. Governments, communities, and indeed all stakeholders are being forced to recognize the importance of not only rationalizing the *use* to which land is put, but even more importantly ensuring that land and resources are stewarded ecologically for future generations. Rooted in the inherently logical yet incredibly complex notion of sustainable development, intelligent land use and stewardship policies are being implemented in different regions of the world. The progress, however, is far too slow to bridge the gap between current development patterns and existing resources effectively. For example, urban growth continues unabated, while cities are unable to provide basic levels of sanitation, employment, health, and education for current residents.

This book is an attempt to survey the global experience to date in implementing land use policies that move us further along the sustainable development continuum. Its chapters include diagnoses of the challenges of implementing sustainable land use policies that appear in different parts of the world. These chapters reveal that some problems are common to all jurisdictions, while others appear unique to particular regions. The book also includes chapters documenting new and emerging approaches such as reforms to property rights regimes and environmental laws. Other chapters offer comparisons of approaches in different jurisdictions that can present insights that might not be apparent from a single-jurisdiction analysis. The chapters are described further in the following sections.

The book is the second in a series of publications issued by Cambridge University Press in connection with the International Union for the Conservation of Nature and Natural Resources (IUCN) Academy of Environmental Law's annual colloquia on topics relating to sustainable development. The second such colloquium, held in Nairobi, Kenya, in October 2004, centered on the theme of land use for sustainable development. In addition to providing an excellent venue, holding the colloquium in Nairobi was significant in several ways. By attracting some 160 scholars from around the world, it helped bolster the University of Nairobi's global reputation as a place for discussions of an academic issue of global significance. The colloquium also provided an important boost for environmental law and policy teaching in Africa. For example, many African professors have since requested that the University of Nairobi provide leadership in founding an African association of environmental law professors. The theme of the colloquium also resonated strongly with many participants from African countries, given the importance of land use issues to environmental sustainability, food security, and poverty eradication. In a wonderful coincidence, during the colloquium Professor Wangari Mathai, who gave the opening address, was announced as the first ever environmental advocate to receive a Nobel Prize.

As editors, we had to make the difficult decision of choosing how best to organize the wealth of information contained within the chapters of the book. We had two basic choices – to organize the book by substantive themes that recurred within various chapters or to organize the book by region. While both approaches had merit, we chose the latter because we considered it important to emphasize the truly global representation of the materials contained within this work. As is immediately apparent from a glance at the contents, the book includes chapters from every major region of the world. We felt it was important to showcase this diversity to encourage readers to take the opportunity to learn about both the familiar and the unique challenges faced by countries in different regions of the world. In the rest of this introduction, we briefly summarize the themes that recur within various chapters in order to help guide a reader's journey through the book toward a particular topic of interest.

The chapters in the book break down loosely into two main themes. First, a number of the chapters offer assessments of constraints or challenges to sustainable land use management in different countries and regions. Second, a number of the chapters discuss emerging approaches to help advance sustainable land use. All of these major themes have subthemes within them. To bridge the themes and provide some context to the conference, Akio Morishima graced the conference with a series of distinguished lectures entitled *Challenges of Environmental Law – Environmental Issues and Their Implications to Conventional Jurisprudence.* This series of lectures, reproduced in the book, recounts how environmental problems in Japan have compelled challenges to traditional legal systems and theories and have been instrumental in the evolution of new jurisprudence and environmental laws. Professor Morishima traces the evolution of environmental law through the courts, particularly through four major lawsuits on pollution in Japan. He addresses new environmental issues such as increased risks with increasing industrial pollution and the multitude of stakeholders, particularly in the urban context. He calls for a new system of rights for this shift in social paradigms, as societies move toward sustainability.

A group of the chapters within the "constraints and challenges" theme consider the issue of finding a path for sustainable development in the context of the ever-growing urban landscape. Parvez Hassan, for example, examines the links between urbanization and environmental challenges in Pakistan, while Muhammed Tawfiq Ladan in the chapter "Environmental Law and Sustainable Land Use in Nigeria" illustrates the inadequacies of Nigeria's laws relating to mining forestry and town planning in addressing environmental problems. Another series of chapters within the "constraints and challenges" theme offer diagnoses of national policies relating to land management. Amber Prasad Pant's chapter "Nepal's Legal Initiatives on Land Use for Sustainable Development" examines the history, policies, and laws relating to land use planning, proposing suggestions for improvement. George Okoth-Obbo examines the environmental impact of the large-scale refugee presence in Kenya, arguing that it is important to develop a national governance structure (including changes to environmental laws) to plan and manage refugee activity, including the ecological impacts.

Several chapters examine the challenge of reforming existing laws in ways that better reflect local community customs and values, and that involve communities directly in sustainable land management activities. Ed Couzens's chapter, for instance, examines the challenge of translating Western-styled philosophies of elephant preservation and ivory trade restrictions with the need to find viable conservation solutions for local communities that share the landscape with elephants. In the chapter "Land Use Planning in Mexico," Gabriella Pavon and Juan Jose Gonzalez explore how to develop a sustainable urban system within an environmental land use plan to help overcome poverty and achieve effective social development. Mekete Bekele examines Ethiopia's national legal framework for implementing some of the principles and operative provisions of the Convention on Biological Diversity relating to communities' access to the genetic resources found in their backyards. In the chapter "Managing Land Use and Environmental Conflicts in Cameroon," Nchunu Sama emphasizes the importance of reforming land use laws in order to address inequities caused in part by the imposition of colonial land policies on indigenous traditions such as communal land tenure.

Several chapters address the tool of environmental impact assessment (EIA), stressing the role that well-designed EIA policies can and should play in helping move policies toward sustainable land use planning. This subtheme in essence provides a bridge between the evaluation of constraints and challenges and the discussion of new and emerging approaches. In the chapter "Environmental Impact Assessment: Addressing the Major Weaknesses," Michael I. Jeffery provides a comparative analysis of the EIA implementation process in Australia and Canada, highlighting the importance of procedural fairness in environmental decision making and the need to facilitate public participation as a way of achieving that goal. Evaluating the use of EIA in South Africa, Michael Kidd similarly emphasizes the importance of procedural fairness. Kidd focuses on the "four Ps" – provisions, process/procedure, people, and politics – that he argues are central to the operation of EIA. Lana Roux and Willemien du Plessis in "EIA Legislation and the Importance of Transboundary Application" analyze the EIA processes in South Africa, Namibia, and Swaziland, pointing out the similarities and differences in the requirements and processes in these countries. In a chapter comparing the application of EIA in the Nigerian and U.S. oil and gas industries, Bibobra Bello Orubebe argues that EIA laws must be strengthened to take into account the power of large, multinational corporations such as those that exist in the oil and gas industry. In a related chapter, Sunee Mallikarmal and Nuntapol Karnchanawat evaluate the use of environmental management plans to help balance conservation and exploitation of natural resources. Their chapter evaluates in some detail the adaptation of Denmark's spatial and environmental management planning in Thailand's Khon Kaen Province. Juan Rodrigo Walsh in his chapter "Argentina's Constitution and General Environment Law as the Framework for Comprehensive Land Use Regulation" examines the impact of minimal standards legislation that resulted from Argentina's constitutional reform in 1994, looking in particular at the link between rural and urban land use policies and the need to integrate conservation policies into the broader policy framework.

The second theme of "emerging approaches" also includes several subthemes. One group of chapters explore reforms of property rights regimes and governance structures. With respect to property rights, Patricia Kameri-Mbote examines how changes to property rights structures can facilitate effective wildlife management, while Nyokabi Gitahi makes the case for the need to provide incentives for wildlife management through environmental easements provided for under the Environment Management and Coordination Act, 2000. In terms of reform of governance regimes, Louis J. Kotzé proposes a governance model that breaks out of the "line department" model and moves toward a more lateral regime that incorporates environmental issues into other dimensions of decision making. W. J. Kombe examines environmental planning and management in Tanzania, which has moved from bureaucratic-controlled to stakeholder-driven urban planning and management. After providing a historical review of the development of land use laws within different levels of government in the United States, John R. Nolon argues that while the flexibility of land use mechanisms helped achieve sustainable land use policies in the United States over the course of its history, there are now opportunities to reform land use policies strategically to provide some cohesion to the modern system. In her chapter "Land Use Planning, Environmental Management, and the Garden City as an Urban Development Approach in Singapore," Lin Heng Lye demonstrates how the city-state transformed its economy in a short time frame without sacrificing environmental quality, in large part because of the help of strong land use planning and environmental laws.

As so many other writers in this field do, mainly for the lack of a better term, we and many of the authors in this book have used the term *land use planning* in a way that is meant to include not only land and soil, but freshwater and salt water as well. A number of the chapters in the book consider how to incorporate effective land use planning and stewardship in the realm of water. In her chapter, Linda A. Malone considers the implications of the 2004 U.S. Ocean Commission report for land use reform to improve ocean water quality by taking an ecosystem-based approach, coordinated at the national level with international cooperation. Ian Hannam and Du Qun analyze the legal framework of a partnership program in China designed to help control land degradation. Karen Bubna-Litic looks at the management of irrigated land in Australia. Emmanuel Kasimbazi in the chapter "The Development of Environmental Law and Its Impact on Sustainable Use of Wetlands in Uganda" effect of environmental law on wetlands in Uganda.

Another two chapters focus on the role of protected areas in successful land use management. The chapter "Protection of Natural Spaces in Brazilian Environmental Law" by José Rubens Morato Leite, Heline Sivini Ferreira, and Patryck de Araújo Ayala discusses natural areas protection in Brazil, taking into account the context of the risk to society, the global environmental crisis, and obstacles that emergent countries face in reaching a satisfactory level of environmental protection. Koh Kheng-Lian's chapter "ASEAN Heritage Parks and Transboundary Biodiversity Conservation" examines the opportunity for achieving conservation by working in a regional, transboundary model.

Albert Mumma examines the role of administrative tribunals in the sustainable management of land use, looking in particular at Kenya's Environment Tribunal. Mumma's chapter argues that Kenya possesses institutional arrangements for resolving environmentally and land use–related disputes and for facilitating sustainable land use, but notes that significant administrative obstacles remain.

A chapter by Nathalie J. Chalifour explores a whole set of alternative policy instruments – economic instruments – that she argues have the potential to help policymakers implement sustainable land and resource decisions. She provides a theoretical overview of these instruments, which range from taxes and fees to subsidies and trading systems, and discusses some of the challenges involved in implementing them at the national policy level.

A series of chapters examine the potential for advancing sustainable land use management through international and regional initiatives. In his chapter "Climate Change Adaptation and Mitigation: Exploring the Role of Land Reforms in Africa," H. W. O. Okoth-Ogendo argues that a land reform process that included policy changes, tenure reform, redesign of land use structures, and reconceptualization of land administration functions could provide opportunities for the creation of an adaptive threshold and mitigation interventions in the management of climate change effects in Africa. David R. Hodas argues that climate change offers African countries an enormous sustainable development opportunity, by allowing nations in the region to avoid the errors of highly fossil-fuel-dependent countries and move directly into the development of renewable energy resources. Michel Prieur examines the European Landscape Convention, which is the first regional convention exclusively dedicated to land use planning. The Convention's main innovation is to take landscape into account as a permanent and ordinary component of daily life – an element of the human environment that needs special and continuous attention independent of its value or beauty.

The international community has long recognized the need to ensure that ongoing and future development is conducted sustainably. Participants at the Rio Conference in 1992 affirmed, and reaffirmed in Johannesburg in 2002, their commitment to pursuing sustainable development, mapping out specific action plans and emphasizing the need for a global partnership on sustainable development. These high-level commitments are politically important, but irrelevant if they are not translated into reality on the ground. We hope this book will help to accomplish this objective by providing information and analysis to the global community about what is working, where challenges remain, and how to chart a way forward.

Challenges of Environmental Law – Environmental Issues and Their Implications to Jurisprudence

Akio Morishima

The theme of my lectures in the next three days, in brief, is "The Challenges of Environmental Law to Conventional Jurisprudence." This is because there is a need for conventional jurisprudence to catch up with changing environmental issues. I will address such questions as the following:

- What is presented as a new issue of law
- How environmental law studies as a new form of jurisprudence have dealt with this issue
- What are the issues to be solved by environmental law and environmental law studies at this moment, and
- What issues environmental law should deal with and what strategies it should employ in the future

I was asked to adopt one theme for each lecture, if possible, and to make the three lectures into one coordinated "Distinguished Lecture on Environmental Law." In response to this difficult request, I would like to structure the lecture as follows: In Lecture I on the first day, which is titled "Land Use and Environmental Law," I would like to explain why and how a new system of laws is needed to solve a variety of social issues caused by environmental issues that goes beyond the conventional laws and jurisprudence on land use. In Lecture II, I would like to focus on "The Courts and Environmental Law." Here, I will discuss what role the Courts (Judiciary) can play in setting up new principles of environmental law and of environmental legislation. On the last day, in Lecture III, I would like to discuss "New Approaches of Environmental Law."

As will be mentioned in Lectures I and II, matters that were not dealt with in conventional law studies, including risk management of chemical substances and coordination of interests between different stakeholders with different values, have become serious problems in dealing with environmental issues. Environmental law had to take them as priority issues and, using new concepts and rules, solve them in actual lawsuits. Then, as global environmental issues came to be considered as urgent issues, environmental law had to be involved in the transformation process of social systems, seeking a new legal system to support the paradigm shift from the current system of multiproduction and multiconsumption to a sustainable and recycling-based society. This has just started, and there are many things to be done in the future. In Lecture III, I would like to explain the future direction of environmental law and the steps for environmental law to take in realizing a sustainable society.

In this lecture, I will talk about environmental issues in Japan and the development of environmental law in Japan, in which I have been deeply involved in the past 30 years, but it is not for the purpose of explaining specific cases from Japan to you. It is partly because I have detailed and correct information on Japanese cases, but mainly because I believe that the Japanese experience will be of some help to the construction of a new system of laws in other countries as well. According to my old esteemed friends from other countries, environmental laws in their countries, like those in Japan, were developed through challenges against traditional legal systems and theories. Despite the differences between the Common Law and Civil Law, or the differences in court proceedings and in lawmaking, or in legal techniques, the lawyers in each country, I believe, try to deal with environmental issues with common concern and equal recognition. We will be facing further challenges of environmental issues in the future and have to resolve those issues. In doing so, if Japan's experience could provide some assistance in building up innovative theories on environmental law through the wisdom and intellect of those present today, I should say it is my utmost pleasure and honor as a lawyer from Japan to have helped in this process.

∾

LECTURE I: LAND USE AND ENVIRONMENTAL LAW

1 LAND USE AND ENVIRONMENTAL ISSUES

Basically, changes in the environment are caused by natural phenomena. However, the large (over 250 percent) increase in global population from 2.5 billion in the middle of the 20th century to 6 billion by the end of the century, has brought the realization that various human-related activities taking place in various parts of the world are affecting the global environment in various ways, one of which is deforestation. Human activities are conducted in connection with some form of land use – industrial activities are carried out at each industrial facility built on an industrial site, and urban life is made possible by the use of land for residences, offices, roads, and parks. Needless to say, farmland is used for agriculture and forests are for forestry. Even activities on the sea, such as fishery and maritime transportation, need land for ports and harbors as well as for anchoring sites. Furthermore, rivers, lakes, and swamps all inevitably use land in a variety of ways. Human activities that take place on a particular land site will have a direct effect on the land on which the activities take place, and possibly also on neighboring areas. However, such activities may also indirectly affect land and areas farther away. For example, the cutting of trees in the upper stream area of a river will dry up the groundwater in the downstream area or have an adverse effect on fishery resources around the mouth of the river. Thus, it can be seen that various forms of land use affect the environment both directly and indirectly. Moreover, pollution generated from human activities diffuses into the air and water, leading to environmental pollution.

To prevent any further degradation of the environment, it is important to curb extensive land use. It is true that the ultimate cause of environmental degradation stems from inappropriate land use, but it is the actual human activities on the land that affect the environment very widely, for example, deforestation, development of farmland, construction of roads, agriculture, construction of buildings, production of chemicals, and generation of wastes (fumes and sewerage). Moreover, a variety of entities, both public and private, are involved in these activities. Under these circumstances, restrictions on land use will not be effective unless the activities conducted by specific entities are restricted.

2 OBJECTS AND CONTENTS OF ENVIRONMENTAL LAW

The purpose of environmental law is to restrict human activities so that the land can be used without inflicting adverse effects on the environment and good environmental conditions can be maintained. However, considering the wide range of stakeholders and the wide variety of human activities, the environmental law system should go beyond the conventional legal system of land use, which regulates only the activities of land users, which are mainly composed of landowners. Environmental law is a unique field of law in that it covers all stakeholders whose activities have impacts on the environment – these include national and local governments, businesses and companies, nongovernmental organizations (NGOs), and citizens. Environmental law can take appropriate legal measures to deal with actual impacts on the environment caused by the various activities of these stakeholders. As a legal system, environmental law should step over the concept of restricting land use to deal with such public property as air, quality of water, and ecosystems, or with such extensive and complex environmental conditions as climate change. As a result, environmental law is required to set up a new legal area with its own system and logic different from the conventional jurisprudence that has been dealing with individual human beings and property.

Every country has started building its environmental law systems only recently, and so, compared with the long history of traditional legal studies in Europe, environmental law is still in its infancy. According to conventional views, environmental law might be defined as a system of law that aims to maintain the order of human society by taking some social measures to alleviate various effects on the environment caused by human activities. Here, environmental preservation has been regarded in a passive way, as law for preventing and alleviating environmental degradation. However, at the World Summit for Sustainable Development (WSSD) in 2002, the concept of sustainable development (SD) was expanded to cover not only environment and development (business) issues but also society itself. It was considered that the concept of sustainable development involves a paradigm shift to a recycling-oriented society, showing a great conceptual transformation of the environment itself. This means that the object and the goal of environmental law could further expand in the future, and environmental law would be expected to play a more active role in covering not only such traditional environmental issues as those issues relating to air, water, and nature, but also socioeconomic systems themselves, including the environment.

So far, the object of environmental law has been changing in accordance with the changes in human activities that affect the environment. For example, in the course of industrialization, air and water pollution were identified, and the object of environmental law at that time was to control the pollution. The destruction of nature and erosion of land as a result of extensive development of forestry and farmland became the subject at issue. Then, the issues of excessive consumption of fossil fuels, acid rain, and climate change drew people's attention. What is worse, all these human activities are not conducted independently but are related to each other. For example, extensive land development, industrialization, and increased consumption of fossil fuels are interlinked or are conducted as a part of the other activities. In environmental law, we have to deal with all these related issues in a systematic and integrated manner. As for the content of environmental law, it has to cover interdisciplinary areas in addition to those traditional areas of public law, private law, international law, and the constitution. On top of that, environmental law is now requested when seeking legal solutions to various social issues that conventional laws were not intended to deal with, such as risk management of chemical substances for which reliable scientific data have not been obtained. Moreover, for the realization of a sustainable society through the transformation of social structures, even issues that take place in the atmosphere or the protection of the benefits of future generations come under the ambit of environmental law.

3 CHALLENGES TO THE TRADITIONAL LAW SYSTEM

Since the Industrial Revolution started in England in the 18th century, parts of Europe have become gradually industrialized, but they did not realize until the early 20th century the need for building up a new legal system to protect the environment against pollution caused by industrialization. In the conventional legal system, consideration of the environment took the form of limitation of land use by landowners, which generated a few rules in private law such as nuisance laws to adjust land use between neighboring landowners, and in public law, limitation rules on the use of real estate such as zoning in city planning and building codes. In the 20th century when industrialization expanded rapidly and globally, in most Western developed societies, people became aware of the serious destruction of the natural environment, and its expansion and escalation. In the international community, this concern was first expressed at the Conference on the Human Environment held in Stockholm in 1972. Little by little, it became clear that conventional legal systems could not deal with these issues. To seek practical solutions to the environmental problems that societies were facing, challenges to the conventional legal system and jurisprudence arose gradually in the 1970s, aiming to develop new philosophies and techniques for environmental law.

In the conventional legal system of Western society and other developed countries, the right to exercise land ownership was secured, and landowners could freely use, profit from, and dispose of their land. There are, in principle, no restrictions on the use of land except for a few limitations of land use in compliance with city planning. According to the traditional idea of law, the acts of public authorities, including the public authority on private ownership, should be minimized. Factory owners considered that the emission of fumes into the air and the discharging of sewage from drains into rivers were acts arising from the ownership of land and within their legitimate right as owners. Economists took it for granted that owners did not need to pay for the pollution, naming it as an externality. Owners of forest land cut trees growing on their land and sold them by right of their ownership, which was the right thing to do according to traditional laws of land ownership and land use. However, as environmental issues were being recognized as social issues and it was becoming clear that the traditional law was not capable of dealing with these social issues, challenges to the traditional legal system started in various classes of society in various ways. Direct campaigns by citizens against companies that caused pollution, legal actions against governments and businesses, requests for new laws to lawmaking bodies, and changes in voting patterns: all these were part of the challenges to the traditional legal system. New concepts of environmental law were suggested, and some of the traditional legal concepts were rejected, leading us to the evolution and development of a new environmental law system. In spite of these efforts, environmental issues are becoming serious much faster than the development of environmental law, and especially in the area of climate change, we have not even had clues for solutions. Under the circumstances, we have not found solid environmental law systems, or the future direction of environmental legal studies, but it is still in motion, changing day by day, to follow the changes in the nature of environmental issues.

4 ENVIRONMENTAL ISSUES IN JAPAN

To help you understand my lecture, I would like to start by explaining briefly about environmental issues in Japan and their social and economic backgrounds just after World War II. In 1945, Japan was defeated in the U.S.–Japan war. The repeated air raids during World War II burned most of the major cities down to the ground, and industries were totally destroyed. For the government of Japan in the 1950s and 1960s, the priority was put on reconstruction of the economy. First of all, dams were constructed to develop electric power resources, and with the energy shift to petroleum after the 1950s, industrial sites (petrochemical industrial complexes) were developed in various places in Japan. The government of Japan at that time gave most importance to economic growth and ignored environmental conservation in policymaking processes. This resulted in a number of cases of health damage in the late 1960s among those who were living around the industrial sites. These cases were suspected to be related to air and water pollution and became serious social problems. However, legal systems to deal with environmental pollution were not developed smoothly because of the lack of knowledge of chemical substances that polluted the environment, the difficulties of identifying the source of pollution that was diffused into the air and water, and the broad extent of citizens living in a wide range of areas affected. The laws to deal with environmental pollution have to manage "risks" that are different from those presumed in conventional laws, which made it more difficult to develop pollution-related laws, especially when the Japanese government was not active in regulating pollution.

In 1952, Japan was liberated from U.S. occupation. In the 1960s, demands for more direct participation in the policymaking process increased among the general public, which were symbolically reflected in the series of demonstrations in 1960 against the revision of the Japan–U.S. Security Treaty, when tens of thousands of citizens demonstrated in front of the Diet Building. At the same time, many grassroot campaigns against environmental pollution were seen in various parts of Japan. A period of turmoil on university campuses occurred in the late 1960s, triggering a breakdown of psychological barriers for young people in challenging traditional authorities that had long reigned over Japanese society. It seems to me that this social and historical background has had some effect on the attitudes and psychology of young lawyers who challenged conventional interpretation of the law to establish innovative theories of environmental law. This will be mentioned in Lecture II.

Also, as will be mentioned in Lecture II, various cases of pollution suits and citizens' movements against pollution in the 1960s led to the Basic Law for Environmental Pollution Control enacted in 1970 and to subsequent laws for controlling air and water pollution. The Japanese government introduced the world's severest standards for emission control at that time. As regards the effects of these regulations and controls in the 1960s, the Organization for Economic Co-operation and Development (OECD) report on Japanese environmental policy review in 1977 (*Environmental Policies in Japan*) concluded that Japan had won the battle for pollution control although it was still fighting the war for better quality of the environment and its amenities. Health damage from industrial pollution was no longer the largest policy issue in the 1970s and 1980s, as rightly pointed out in this report, but as urbanization progressed concurrently with economic development, urban environmental issues became more serious and arose from numerous and varied sources such as air pollution, noise from motor traffic, urban sewage disposal, waste disposal, and destruction of nature through suburban sprawl. When there are numerous and varied sources generating environmental problems, end-of-pipe regulations (direct control methods) for large-scale plants are not appropriate measures. Rather, it is necessary to conduct environmental assessment of urban development in advance and regulate numerous stakeholders by using a variety of techniques systematically. Economic incentives such as tax benefits and subsidies were introduced to lead people to employ environmentally friendly methods.

In the 1990s, global environmental issues were being recognized in the international community, and Japan actively participated in the Earth Summit (United Nations Conference on Environment and Development, UNCED) held in Rio de Janeiro in 1992 and ratified the Framework Convention on Climate Change and the Convention on Biological Diversity. In Japan, the Basic Law for Environmental Pollution Control was amended to enact the Basic Environment Law in 1993, aiming to establish a sustainable society as a follow-up to the Rio Declaration on Environment and Development, and the Basic Environment Plan was established in 1994 to implement the Basic Environment Law. After that, laws to promote energy saving and recycling were enacted, and in 2000 the Basic Law for Establishing a Recycling-Based Society was enacted. The system of laws for a sustainable society is different from laws for pollution control and those for urban environmental management in every way – in terms of its purpose, contents, and methods. Lecture III will deal with the legal system required for the paradigm shift from a mass-production and mass-consumption society to a recycling-based society.

5 CHALLENGES OF ENVIRONMENTAL LAW

In this section, I would like to summarize new issues for the law brought about by industrial pollution, issues of the urban and natural environment, and global environmental issues in Japan and in the world after the 20th century.

The first issue is risk. Because of the introduction of various new chemical substances in our lives and large-scale and radical changes in natural and ecological systems as a result of human activities, there was an extensive outbreak of new phenomena that were not well understood scientifically. They caused a variety of social issues that required judicial settlements. In the conventional legal system, where the contents and range of rights and duties of every entity are clear, it was not easy to deal with these uncertainties and risks. In presenting evidence in a lawsuit, risks present difficult considerations. The second issue is the wide variety of objects to be regulated under environmental laws. As typically observed in the issue of global warming, there are a number of human activities that generate greenhouse gases, and we cannot name all of them. They include such large-scale activities as the combustion of heavy oil at industrial plants and smaller-scale activities such as driving cars and heating houses. The conventional legal technique of regulating activities of a certain facility or a certain activity by setting a standard does not function effectively in this context. In environmental law, new legal techniques should be introduced. The third issue is the wide variety of stakeholders, which is the natural consequence of the variety of objects to be dealt with in environmental law. Since there are a number of stakeholders involved in a case, the law needs to consider their diverse interests. The conventional legal system regulates rights and duties of individuals on an equal footing, and those of the nation vis-à-vis individual persons. On the other hand, environmental law is required to take into account such complicated interests as those of future generations. In environmental law, participation in the policymaking and decision-making processes, as well as in the implementation process, is an issue that must be considered.

The fourth issue is the most difficult. When there is a paradigm shift toward a recycling-based society in the 21st century, how and with what jurisprudence can we reform the free-market economy and private ownership (the prerequisites of our current society and legal system), so that the Polluter Pays Principle (PPP), the Extended Producers Responsibility (EPR), and the Precautionary Principle are widely accepted to realize a recycling-based society? It seems that environmental law is now faced with this difficult question.

LECTURE II: THE COURTS AND ENVIRONMENTAL LAW

In my lecture today, I would like to present a few lawsuits that took place in Japan and describe how Japanese courts, in their efforts to deal with new issues raised by environmental conflicts, created laws through legal interpretations in the litigation to respond to social needs, and how these judgments affected lawmakers in a later period. I would also like to talk about the limitations of the courts, which have to make judgments under the framework of written law. Especially in the case of Japan, a lawsuit against the government has its own limitations, and I would also like to talk about this.

1 DAMAGE SUITS – FOUR MAJOR POLLUTION LAWSUITS

In the 1960s, many industrial complexes such as petrochemical industrial complexes were constructed in various parts of Japan, and people living in adjacent areas started to suffer from health problems such as asthma and organic mercury poisoning. At that time, there were big social debates on whether air and water pollution were the causes of those health problems. As I have stated, government policies in those days put the emphasis on economic growth, and no efficient pollution control measures were taken either in the legislature or in the administration, except for a few government surveys on areas suffering from pollution. In fact, there were many victims of health hazards, but in each case, the management of the factories concerned denied that there was a relationship between these health hazards and pollution, because of the lack of scientific knowledge at that time. In some cases of damage to fisheries caused by water contamination, fishermen's groups resorted to force to fight against industrial plants, but most of those who suffered from health hazards caused by air and water pollution were isolated and weak. If the victim or plaintiff attempts to claim compensation from the plant, that defendant is required (according to the Japanese rule of damage compensation, Article 709 of the Civil Code) to prove the "causal relationship" between the damage and the activities of the industrial plant suspected of causing the pollution, as well as to prove the "negligence" of the plant. If several plants are related to the pollution, plaintiffs have to prove that defendants acted jointly (Article 719 of the Civil Code). The conventional legal system assumes that the social and economic status of the victims and the tortfeasors are "equal" and there is no substantial difference in their ability to access evidence. However, most of the victims of these health hazards were fishermen, their wives (who were homemakers), and ordinary citizens with no special resources, and it was almost impossible (therefore they were not equal from the beginning) for them to verify a causal relationship based on such high-level scientific knowledge or to prove the negligence of large companies with which they had no contact.

No public system had been established for the relief of victims of pollution until the Law Concerning the Relief of Pollution-Related Health Damage was established in 1969, with the exception of the case in Yokkaichi City, where, under the strong leadership of the Mayor, health checks for public elementary and middle-school students were conducted and health insurance payments for asthma patients were subsidized by the city. It should be noted that this 1969 Law was not at all satisfactory as a system of compensation, since only medical expenses not covered by social insurance were paid to the victims. As I will later explain, it was only after the enactment of the Pollution-Related Health Damage Compensation Law in 1973 that loss of income and other damage were included in the compensation. Against this background, young and highly motivated lawyers in the large cities around those polluted areas formed groups and decided to file lawsuits against companies that caused such health hazards as Minamata disease in Kumamoto and Niigata, Itai-itai disease in Toyama, and asthma in Yokkaichi.

At the beginning, they did not seem to have much chance of winning, as it was quite difficult for the poor victims to file a lawsuit, with the difficulties of proving causal relationships, negligence of factories, and so on. The groups of lawyers, however, pursued the lawsuits not only to provide relief for individual victims of pollution, but also to change the attitude toward pollution control of central and local governments as well as business and society. They tried to do so by revealing in the lawsuits the economic and political structure that generated the pollution and by drawing public attention to the mechanisms of pollution. From this perspective, they were supported by antipollution groups of citizens and other support groups and were able to engage in the lawsuits although they could not expect rewards from them. The efforts of these lawyers can be seen as an attempt to realize the ideal of citizens' participation in social reforms through lawsuits, as explained in Lecture I. All those lawsuits were filed between 1967 and 1969, and judgments were pronounced in the first instances (district courts) between 1971 and 1973 (decisions by Toyama District Court on 30 June 1971, Niigata

District Court on 29 September 1971, Yokkaichi Branch of Tsu District Court on 24 July 1972, and Kumamoto District Court on 20 March 1973). They were collectively called "the Four Major Pollution Lawsuits" in Japan.

The major point of controversy in those lawsuits was the "causal relationship" between the pollution and the health hazards. Most cases of pollution showed an unclear relationship between the two, because health damage was caused by continued exposure to very low levels of chemicals in the environment (in some cases, even the nature of the chemicals was not known). Scientific knowledge of causal relationships was limited, and in many cases (especially in the case of nonspecific diseases), it was difficult to distinguish the problems arising from health hazards from other diseases. Therefore, requesting plaintiffs to show a "preponderance of evidence" (more likely than not) in accordance with the burden of proof in the traditional law system would literally mean there was no relief for the victims. Especially in the case of nonspecific problems, it was almost impossible for each patient to prove the cause of his or her disorder. The Court of Yokkaichi, stretching the conventional theory of causal relationships, made a judgment that if a relationship between the pollutant and the disease was epidemiologically (statistically) proved, a specific causal relationship was inferred unless the defendant, the factory, produced counterevidence for each case that the disease had another cause.

As regards "negligence," conventional law requires the plaintiff to prove that due care was not taken by the defendant in preparing for predictable risks at the time of the operation. Therefore, whether the factory neglected this duty or not was the decisive factor in the judgment. In the case of the Minamata disease in Kumamoto, inorganic mercury was used as a catalyst in the course of the production process. In this case, it was contested whether the factory could predict the health hazards caused by inorganic mercury at the time of operation. The court decided that even though the factory could not predict the specific disease (organic mercury poisoning), it was still negligent because it had neglected to pay due attention to security, stating that every chemical factory was required to examine all potential risks of chemicals to be used before starting its operations, since there were various kinds of hidden risks in the chemical industry. Some scholars evaluate the sentence as a "no-fault judgment dressed as negligence."

"Joint liabilities" were referred to in the judgment of the Yokkaichi Court, which stated that factories located in one petrochemical industrial complex were jointly related in an objective way notwithstanding that they did not have any subjective close relationship with each other in terms of management and production. It ordered that since all defendants were jointly and severally responsible under Article 719 of the Civil Code, unless each factory verified the degree of its contribution to the damages, it had to be responsible for all damage jointly and severally.

The Four Major Pollution Lawsuits (the Itai-itai Cadmium case, the Yokkaichi Asthma case, the Minamata and Niigata Mercury poisoning cases) had a great impact not only on the development of tort legal theory, but also on damage assessment theory. As mentioned, the courts in these cases developed the compensation theories of causal relationship, negligence, and joint tort liability. The new methods of assessment of damages also had impacts on subsequent lawsuits such as consumer product liability lawsuits.

All these lawsuits were civil suits, in which victims of health hazards claimed damages against business enterprises, the polluters. The process of these lawsuits drew the attention of society, and, through the mass media, as the social and economic structures behind the pollution were made clear, eventually public criticism of the government's slow action resulted. Besides relieving victims, which was the original function of civil suits, the lawyers who filed those lawsuits intended to use the trials strategically and, by putting social pressure on the legislature and the administration, to give political impetus to the formulation of pollution-control policies. In this respect, their goal was fully achieved. As a result of these successful lawsuits, especially after the 1972 victory in the case of the Yokkaichi Petrochemical Industrial Complex, which had a direct relationship with other industrial complexes in Japan, several important laws against pollution were enacted. For example, the government amended the Factory Location Law in 1973 to tighten regulations on factory construction, and the Air Pollution Control Law in 1974 to strengthen regulations against air pollution by introducing total pollutant load control of sulfur dioxide. In addition, the Pollution-Related Health Damage Compensation Law was enacted in 1973 to introduce an epidemiological approach of indemnifying victims of health hazards caused by air and water pollution, including living and medical allowances. This was the first case of systematizing compensation by using the idea of the Polluter Pays Principle (PPP), and it was later referred to when the U.S. Compensation and Liability Act (often referred to as the Superfund Act) was enacted. After the victory of the victims in the Four Major Pollution Lawsuits, damage suits against health hazards were filed one after another in industrial sites in various parts of Japan, and so were injunction suits against waste disposal sites, roads, and power generation plants.

2 CIVIL INJUNCTION SUITS

Although victims of health hazards caused by pollution were able to win the Four Major Pollution Lawsuits, overcoming the limits of conventional damage compensation theory, it was too late to take relief measures to deal with existing problems caused by health hazards. It is very important to take preventive measures to preclude such damage. Injunction suits may be used to prevent the construction and operation of facilities that have the capacity to generate pollutants. In the 1970s, as a gradually increasing number of damage suits succeeded in challenging the conventional legal framework, the number of injunction suits filed increased. In the Japanese legal system, there is no written rule of injunction in the civil law, so the common law is referred to in making judgments. However, conventional ideas of injunction are more restricted in the civil law than in the compensation law. We have to consider the legal basis of the claim for injunctions and how to justify the balancing of interests between the parties.

Regarding the legal basis of injunction suits, human rights could be the basis if we deal with environmental pollution from the perspective of health hazards. It is acceptable in conventional law and is generally referred to as a legal basis for requesting suspension. In one case, property right was the basis of the injunction suit, stating that landownership would be violated by the pollution generated by the defendant. Although this case was based on conventional legal theory, in many cases, infringements or the possibility of infringements of human health were the basis of injunction suits.

What is worth noting are the cases in which a right to the environment was brought about as a legal basis for injunctions. The Japan Bar Association advocated the right to the environment in 1970 on the occasion of an international pollution symposium in Osaka, Japan, just before the idea of this right was presented in the Statement for Human Environmental Quality in Stockholm in 1972. The right to the environment, since then, has been discussed among scholars in Japan, but the courts to this day have not admitted it as a right in private law, saying that it is difficult to assume that people in the community share a common exclusive controlling right. This environmental right was claimed in several cases, including a lawsuit requesting the suspension of construction of a thermal power plant, which was filed by citizens not only from surrounding areas but from distant places. However, the court did not approve the request on the ground that there was no legal basis. In another example, an action was filed to suspend a proposed land development, because of loss of fauna and flora, but this has not been successful as yet. In civil trials, where private rights are to be claimed, it is difficult to claim interests related to the right to the environment since they are not directly related to private rights.

In judging the appropriateness of claims for suspension of projects, the importance of the violated interests or interests to be violated (its nature and contents) and the usefulness of the act of violation will be compared. More precisely, the courts decide whether the request for suspension can be filed by balancing the impacts of the suspended activity on the community, the possibilities of pollution generated by the facility concerned, the seriousness of the damage expected, the preventability of damage, and the benefits and/or detriments for those concerned. When the violated interests are health hazards, the Japanese courts tend to approve the suspension rather easily, but in cases of infringement of daily life whose symptoms are seldom apparent, the usefulness of the act of violation is compared with the infringement on daily life.

Especially in the case of public facilities, a major point of discussion is how to deal with the public nature of the facility (social utility). Most of the activities today that have a major impact on the environment involve the construction of such public facilities as waste disposal plants, sewerage treatment plants, roads, dams, and estuary weirs. In most cases, claims for injunction are filed against these public facilities. In some cases, actions have been brought against existing public facilities, such as the Shinkansen bullet trains and international airports in various parts of Japan. The Japanese courts, except when there are high possibilities of health hazards to many citizens, tend to assign more importance to the public nature of the facility and seem to be reluctant to suspend the operation of the facility. Injunction suits have been filed by people who live along major highways, who asked that pollutants be suspended above a certain level and that only a certain number of cars be allowed on the roads, but only one case, in which a health hazard of lung disease was recognized in one of the residents along the highway, was successful. While requests for injunction were not generally accepted, the court approved the award of compensation for the health hazards of residents living along the highways, on the basis of the National Compensation Law, stating that the construction would be illegal if they suffered from pollution and noise caused by the large number of cars traveling on the highways.

There is also the burden of proof on the claimant in the case of injunction suits. To request suspension of an activity before any environmental damage has occurred, the person who files the suit has to claim and prove that damage would be caused by that activity. As regards environmental risks, it is quite difficult for ordinary citizens to prove such risks, because of lack of scientific knowledge. To resolve this difficulty, a court has decided that the injunction would be approved on the basis of proof to be established by the claimant of the probability (reasonable doubt) of the damage, unless the polluter proved that damage was highly improbable. In this way, the court alleviated the burden of the claimant to prove a causal relationship. There are several cases similar to this.

It should be noted that, prior to the enactment of the Environmental Assessment Law, there were several cases in which injunctions were ordered; the decisions stated that the environmental assessments conducted before construction were insufficient. In one case, the construction of a sewage disposal plant was suspended because of the lack of an appropriate level of environmental assessment prior to the construction. The other case involved an action for an injunction against the construction of a waste incineration plant, in which a full year on-site survey of air pollutants was requested, in order that sufficient environmental assessment could be made in advance.

3 ADMINISTRATIVE LITIGATION

Lawsuits against the government are filed according to the Administrative Case Litigation Law. Probably in every country, including Japan, national laws impose severe constraints on filing lawsuits against the public administration. The first is the standing to sue, in which it is prescribed that only those who have legal interests in the administrative measures taken by the government can file lawsuits against the government. Usually, these are people who have received an administrative enforcement. If this idea is interpreted precisely, neighboring citizens who bear only the impact of the environmental pollution to be caused by the construction of waste disposal centers are not considered to have legal interests in this context. In the past, for administrative litigation filed by residents for the protection of the environment, district courts have not approved their standing to sue. However, in an administrative litigation in which revocation of the night flight schedules of airlines was requested by residents around the Osaka Airport because of the noise generated by aircraft, the Supreme Court approved in 1988 the standing to sue of those who "will be severely disturbed by the noise of the aircraft," although the request for revocation itself was denied. It drew public attention as the first case in which a third party's standing to sue was approved, although the third party was still highly restricted. On the other hand, a 1999 decision of the Supreme Court did not approve the residents' standing to sue in an administrative litigation for revocation of administrative action since they had an opportunity to submit their comments to the government before the urban road planning was finalized. There was another decision in which citizen groups were denied standing to sue in a lawsuit against forest development. In Japan, unlike in the United States, environmental groups have not been considered to have standing to sue in administrative litigation.

The second restriction is the ripeness of administrative actions. In a decision on an industrial site development plan or a railroad construction plan, if a plaintiff tries to file a lawsuit to protect the environment, the plaintiff must have standing to sue, and there should be "actions that reach the 'ripe' stage of an exercise of public authority's enforcement," which can be the object of the administrative revocation suits. Here again, the court employed a rather narrow interpretation of the law and turned down the claim by the public on the ground that the administrative action concerned had not yet reached the final stage of the administrative procedure.

Administrative litigation includes lawsuits by citizens to request corrections of "financially unlawful acts" by local government, in addition to revocation litigation for administrative actions. As mentioned previously, although many restrictions were prescribed in litigation to revoke administrative decisions in Administrative Case Litigation Law, administrative lawsuits by citizens have been used as a tool to protect the environment. There is also an example of a successful administrative lawsuit by citizens, in which citizens on behalf of the prefectural government requested compensation from a paper manufacturing company to pay for the expenses of dredging the sludge discharged by the company into the harbor under the control of the prefectural government, claiming that not charging the expenses to the company would be an illegal accounting procedure (financially unlawful).

4 CREATION OF LAW THROUGH LAWSUITS

The Japanese Constitution stipulates that the judiciary is "bound only by the constitution and laws" (Article 76, Clause 36). However, the judiciary is, in the same way as their counterparts in other countries, contributing to the formulation of laws through the interpretation of laws. Especially when lawmaking cannot catch up with the rapid changes in society, the creativity of lawyers stands out more than ever. As mentioned before, the policy of the government of Japan until the 1960s was to put priority on economic growth, and ever-worsening environmental pollution resulted. With no useful laws to control pollution and no other way to deal with this situation, civil lawsuits requesting compensation for health hazards suspected to be caused by industrial pollution were used as a tool to run an antipollution campaign that was aimed at creating a shift in the attitude of the legislature and the government by revealing the facts of environmental pollution to the public. Through each lawsuit, the cases of environmental pollution were tried and discussed in the framework of civil law and, through innovative interpretation of the law, lawyers, faced with the reality, made every effort to balance the equity of the business enterprises and the victims of the pollution. In this way, lawyers tried to make their way forward by loosening each tight knot in the conventional legal system.

It could be said that environmental law was created through modification of the conventional laws in the course of civil damage and/or injunction suits at each pollution lawsuit. Faced with the actual cases of health damage caused by pollution, the courts drastically modified the conventional laws in damage suits and ordered private companies to pay the damages. However, in actions for injunctions, the courts have to balance the plus and minus aspects of the injunction. Above all, in the cases of an injunction relating to public works, the courts have to step into the decision-making process of the government. Therefore, the courts seem to have been emphasizing the "publicness" of the activity and avoiding the checking of the government's decisions. In addition, in the cases of administrative litigation, because of the framework of Administrative Case Litigation Law, the creation of law by the courts is further restricted. It should be noted that the courts in Japan, compared with the U.S. courts, have not functioned well in checking governmental procedures.

So far, creation of laws has proceeded steadily in the courts. However, the steps taken have not been and will not be easy. The courts have traditionally been trying very hard to protect personal rights including the right to health and security by interpreting and modifying the technical defects of existing laws. It is worth noting how the Japanese courts will function as the creator of laws relating to the conservation of ecosystems as well as the realization of sustainable development.

LECTURE III: THE NEW APPROACHES OF ENVIRONMENTAL LAW

Environmental issues have presented various new considerations that the conventional legal system and jurisprudence have not been able to address. There are some pressing issues mounting in front of us, introducing legal concepts and principles new to the conventional legal system. In today's lecture, I would like to talk about them.

The first issue is how to control risks systematically in a legal system, when such risks are raised with increasing industrial pollution in Japan. The second is how the law should deal with various stakeholders in the context of the many activities that affect the environment, particularly in such areas as urban environmental protection. The third issue is how to envisage a new legal system for this shift in social paradigms – it should include a system of rights, which is emerging as global environmental issues are beginning to be recognized and a shift toward a sustainable society is being sought. As environmental issues become diversified, new approaches are being taken in environmental law. I have already summarized these issues at the end of Lecture I, and so I will discuss the details of this issue in today's lecture.

1 ENVIRONMENTAL RISK CONTROL

As mentioned in Lecture II, Japanese industry until the early 1960s operated without any consideration of the impacts on the environment caused by emissions from industrial plants, which, as a result, brought about numerous health hazards in neighboring areas. In the 1970s, strict regulations were introduced to control pollution. However, because scientific knowledge of chemical substances at that time was limited, people began to think that the "end of pipe control method" against known risks might not be enough, and that the risks of chemical substances should be investigated in advance for better control. The decision in the Minamata mercury disease case in 1973 had a great impact on the discussion of risk control and triggered the establishment of a chemical substance review system, which, however, was not satisfactory.

In the United States, the National Environmental Policy Act (NEPA), on the basis of which the courts developed the Environmental Impact Assessment (EIA) system, was enacted in 1969. This system required the federal government, before it implemented a project, to assess whether it might cause negative effects on the environment. The results of the assessment were publicized and the citizens' reactions were reflected in the final assessment report. If the findings were unsatisfactory, citizens could file a suit to request suspension of the project.

The Environmental Impact Assessment system functioned as (1) a risk assessment system to choose in advance a process with less risk and as (2) an information exchange system between the government and the citizens (stakeholders). Since many environmental issues were not scientifically well investigated, and very often the local knowledge of the residents was more reliable than that of the scholars, the government, through this system, tried to collect information from citizens as well as provide them with new information and to persuade them to exchange it with each other. Under this system, the government (the operating body) had to hear the opinion of the citizens, therefore, citizens took part in the government decision-making process. In such issues as those related to the environment, in which values are diverse, appropriate methods for citizen participation in decision making should be explored to ensure better consensus building.

In Japan, the introduction of EIA was discussed in the late 1970s in terms of prevention, but the industrial sector worried about the antipollution movement that was active at that time, and the effort for EIA legislation was abandoned in 1983 because of the strong objections of the industrial sector. They accepted the technical assessment but did not accept citizens' participation in the decision-making process, fearing the establishment of new businesses might be interfered with by citizen movements. On the other hand, each ministry in the national government had already introduced the technical assessment, and in 1989, a unified system of assessment was decided on at a cabinet meeting. However, for the operating body to implement a business project, they must negotiate with the residents on such matters as land acquisition and therefore have to explain the project to residents and hear their opinions. In many cases, the process was rather confused because of the lack of consistent rules for citizen participation.

Finally, in 1997, the Environmental Impact Assessment Law was enacted to stipulate the citizens' rights to submit comments on the assessment made by the operating body. Its aim is to prevent environmental degradation by promoting multilateral environmental assessment based on input from citizens. For citizens to provide comments, they must be fully and precisely informed about the project and its possible impact on the environment. Therefore, the Environmental Impact Assessment Law requests that business operating bodies publicize their assessment method and their standards to provide enough information to citizens.

Second, I would like to discuss the Pollutant Release and Transfer Register (PPTR). This system, legislated in 1999, was based on the 1996 OECD recommendation (some local governments had introduced the system previously). Under this system, business corporations are requested to register the total amount of chemical emissions and the total amount of waste transferred from one place to another and report them to the national government. The national government then publicizes the data classified according to chemicals and to geographical areas. The purpose of this system is to clarify the process of chemical control, including control of chemicals whose impact on human beings has not been identified. In this system, disclosure of information to citizens is expected to promote and improve voluntary chemical controls by companies. Although it is an indirect method, it is a way to promote risk control by providing information to the public.

Under the conventional legal system, the scope of the rights and duties of an operational body is clearly defined, but in environmental law interests protected by law, including risk management, are not yet very clear. If we focus on our surrounding environment, the scope widens from health hazards and the living environment to amenities; therefore, it is difficult to tell what is to be regulated by laws and what is not. Moreover, it will be our future task to find a better way of building a new legal system that deals with such uncertain issues as climate change and ecological risk management and control.

2 DIVERSITY OF CAUSAL ACTIVITIES

The major problems to be solved in cases of industrial pollution are air and water pollution caused by smoke and effluent from large-scale industrial plants. These are most effectively regulated by a direct end-of-pipe system that restricts the emission of pollutants from plants to below a certain level. The substances to be covered are limited, and it is not technically difficult for large plants to follow the system. From the government's point of view, they can easily control the plants. However, urbanization issues such as automobile transportation and waste disposal are hard to address since cars enter cities from other areas and waste is thrown away in many places. Furthermore, to deal with global warming (climate change) issues, we cannot identify specific sources of greenhouse gases that are generated by varieties of human activities such as the combustion of heavy oil at industrial plans, use of motor vehicles, heating of offices, and use of gas boilers in households. To regulate these activities, the conventional direct system is not effective at all. The activities are too diverse and too numerous for one system to regulate. A new system is being introduced, in which economic methods, including such incentives as subsidies, or such economic burdens as taxes, are used to promote voluntary activities. In addition, the provision of information and education can lead to voluntary activities by citizens. All of these are beyond the scope of the conventional legal system of rights and duties, but environmental law will have to deal with the vast varieties of human activities beyond the simple person-to-person or nation-to-nation relationships to global perspectives such as climate change.

3 VARIETIES OF STAKEHOLDERS

Many people have their interests adversely affected by environmental degradation. On the other hand, our daily life directly affects the environment in issues of the urban environment and the global environment. In this way, wide varieties of people are involved as stakeholders in environmental issues. Depending on their position in society, as policymakers and government officials, business people, citizens, nongovernmental organizations (NGOs), and scholars, they differ in their level of information, their access to information, their values, and their ability to assess information. In the past, government policy was decided through constitutional democracy, whereby representatives of citizens make policies and the administration implements policies decided by the legislature, following majority rule. However, in environmental issues, in which different values confront each other and affect the interests of a number of citizens with a variety of backgrounds, citizens' participation in the decision-making process is considered important and inevitable. Considering the involvement of various stakeholders in the environmental issues of today, it is important to invite participation of all stakeholders in decision making to address issues from their respective standpoints.

As regards the participation of citizens in the decision-making process, information disclosure has been systemized for the past decade, first by local governments, now by the national government, and even discussions of government councils are publicized as a common practice. Public hearings are widely implemented, but still few of them are obligatory in Japan. In the area of the environment, the Environmental Impact Assessment Law (1997) and the Revised Waste Disposal and Public Cleansing Law (1997) stipulate the public hearing process as obligatory. Before the government makes a certain decision, various items of information are collected and assessed from various perspectives. In making decisions on environmental issues, information and comments must be collected as widely as possible to cover uncertainties in environmental issues that might be assessed from various points of view. However, no legal system has been established so far to allow citizens to participate directly in the policymaking process.

Citizen participation in not only decision making, but also implementation of policy is important. Environmental issues today vary greatly, from the effects of urbanization to global warming, and the factors related to them are diverse. This makes it difficult for governments to deal with environmental issues by using the traditional direct control method alone. Therefore, it is necessary that all stakeholders actively engage with environmental issues in their own capacities. It is important for citizens to participate in the decision-making process as well as in the implementation of policies.

In the 1990s when environmental issues began to draw public attention, business organizations voluntarily started to take action. Taking the global warming issue as an example, the Japan Business Federation has been pursuing voluntary measures to meet the target set in the Kyoto Protocol. Their efforts cover 80 percent of total CO_2 emissions by the industry sector. These days, many big businesses in Japan are including environmental aspects in their management policies. Obtaining certification of ISO14001, introduction of the environmental management system, and the publication of environmental reports are examples of the efforts of those companies to make their businesses more environmentally friendly.

4 PARADIGM SHIFT TOWARD A SUSTAINABLE SOCIETY

Since the Conference on the Human Environment in Rio de Janeiro in 1992, the realization of a sustainable society has been considered the task for human beings in the 21st century. In Japan, in response to this global initiative, the Basic Environment Law was enacted in 1993, followed by the establishment of the Basic Environment Plan in 1994. The plan clearly states that for the purpose of passing on environmental benefits to the generations to come as a common basis of human life, it is important to reexamine the way of living in our modern civilization and to shift its production–consumption pattern into a sustainable one. The plan specifies a recycling-based society, harmony with nature, public participation, and international partnership as the long-term goals of Japan's environmental policy and, to achieve the goals, presents integrated policy measures that include various kinds of initiatives such as research and development of scientific technologies, provision of research data, and promotion of environmentally friendly activities in various sectors. Some of the measures are not closely related to legal policy measures, but to make a paradigm shift to a sustainable society; these measures should be closely examined from a strategic point of view in an integrated manner.

Of course, the Basic Environment Law describes basic national policy and is not legally enforceable. If a sustainable society is a recycling-oriented society, recycling-related laws would be a set of legal structures directly focused on the paradigm shift toward a recycling-oriented society. The Basic Law for Establishing a Recycling-Based Society was enacted in 2000 to cover the long-term goal of revolution. This law stipulates the principle of "3Rs" (reduce, reuse, recycle), but what is important is that the law also stipulates Expanded Producers Responsibility (EPR) and assigns to producers the responsibility to collect and dispose of the used products. Before the enactment of this law, the Containers and Packaging Recycling Law (1995) and the Law for Recycling of Specified Kinds of Home Appliances (1998) were enacted; the Law for Recycling of Building Materials (2002) and the Law Concerning the Promotion of Recycling Food Cyclical Resources (2000) were enacted at almost the same time as the Basic Law for Establishing the Recycling-Based Society, and the subsequent Law Concerning Recycling Measures of Used Vehicles (2002). All of these laws employ the idea of EPR.

Here, I would like to discuss the new concept of EPR, which is considered to be a basic principle for realizing the 3Rs. However, the liability of producers is to collect waste and dispose of it, and they are not always responsible for covering the cost of disposal. The cost is shouldered by either the person who first purchases the product or the person who disposes of it at the end of the product's life. If so, the concept of EPR may work as an incentive for producers and promote recycling and reusing, since the cost of disposal has been collected from the consumers (or will be collected at the time the product is thrown away) and will ease the burden of producers. It does not work in the same way for reducing materials used in production, since the disposal cost for these materials is added to the price and collected from consumers.

Furthermore, even if a system of recycling each specific product is established, the recycling market may not function well, and, in terms of social structure, the system will not lead to a paradigm shift unless there is a plan to set the ratio of recycling materials against the total amount of materials used in society. Actually, there seem to be problems in that a certain recycling material may fall short in the recycling production procedure or recycled goods may not sell well. A Life Cycle Assessment (LCA) of recycled goods is necessary in order to determine whether they really save resources and energy, taking every element into consideration.

In the same way, the introduction of an environmental tax is being discussed in connection with the Polluter Pays Principle (PPP), emphasizing the effectiveness of economic incentives, especially taxation, in inducing social change in various sectors. In Japan, an administrative relief system (along with the Pollution Control Public Works Cost Allocation Law) was introduced in the 1970s to provide compensation for victims of industrial pollution, whereby business-operating bodies cover indemnification in proportion to the amount of pollutants generated by their factories. The environmental tax, however, has not been introduced at this moment because of objections from the industrial sector. As for the concept of PPP itself, it is not always clear who the polluters are. For example, in the case of the air pollution caused by sulphur oxide discharged from industrial plants, it is clear that the plant caused the pollution. But in EPR, who is the polluter in the case of a car that is to be disposed of (who pays for the disposal cost)? In Japanese law, the person who first purchased the car will shoulder the cost of final disposal, but if so, how are EPR and PPP related to each other? Besides, in the conventional market economy, the principle of liability for negligence is employed to settle the issues, but how does PPP work in this context? If PPP is properly prescribed by law, is it considered an exception to negligence liability?

At any rate, for lawyers who have long been accustomed to the way of thinking that deals with specific rights and duties of individuals, or those between nation and individuals, to seek the establishment of a sustainable society through a paradigm shift will not be easy, and the path toward the construction of a holistic environmental legal system will be far and long.

PART ONE

INTERNATIONAL ISSUES AND LEGAL RESPONSES
TO SUSTAINABLE LAND MANAGEMENT

1 Is Conservation a Viable Land Usage? Issues Surrounding the Sale of Ivory by Southern African Countries

Ed Couzens

1 THE SYMBOL AND THE REALITY

The African elephant is a potent symbol of and for conservation efforts worldwide. However, the true value of wild animal species must be considered not as abstract symbols, but as essential components of their ecosystems. The elephant has been described as a "superkeystone" species.[1] It is truly the landscape architect of the African bush and many physical and biological aspects of its habitat are dependent on its continued presence.

The argument goes even further. In Africa, animals have formed an integral part of the landscape. The *res nullius* of Roman Law finds an interesting expression in the law of property as it is applied in most African legal systems. Traditionally, neither land nor animals are capable of private ownership. Colonial systems of government and the laws that came with them changed this. No Eurasian system of land ownership has been successfully applied in Africa, except to the detriment of Africans. Refinements of the Eurasian- or European-influenced status quo probably would not go far enough in addressing questions of intra- and intergenerational equity – deeper reform is needed. Terms like *investment* and *ecotourism* have the ugly connotation of new colonialism, because new boundaries are created between the land and its people.[2] Elephants are the gentle giants of the planet. Africa is the antithesis of the gentle giant, but it has the potential to represent a new order of coexistence of myriad cultures. Land represents

---

[1] Sources for this proposition are innumerable. Essentially, what it means is that certain species play roles within their ecosystems that are so significant that rapid increases in or removal of the species world be immediately noticeable. Serious depletion of the number of tortoises in an African game reserve, for example, would have an effect on the ecosystem but the impact would not be measurable for a long time. A rapid depletion of elephants, in contrast, would be noticeable almost immediately as elephants alter their ecosystems continually: playing roles in feeding other species, providing refuges for other species, and influencing the nature of vegetative growth and distribution.

[2] Personal comment, 23 April 2004, Professor Jeremy Ridl, School of Law, University of KwaZulu-Natal, Durban.

The author's attendance at the IUCN Conference was assisted by funds received from the NRF in South Africa. The writer would like to acknowledge the valuable comments made during the preparation of this chapter by Professor Jeremy Ridl, School of Law, University of KwaZulu-Natal, Durban; Andrew Blackmore, Head Integrated Environmental Management Conservation Planning Division, Ezemvelo KZN Wildlife; and the reviewer Nathalie J. Chalifour, Assistant Professor, Faculty of Law, University of Ottawa. Where possible, the author has specifically acknowledged suggestions made by these persons – any errors are those of the writer.

a more complex emotional theme. So, too, do animals, especially the large and visible forms.

It is not because there are too many elephants that proponents of increased trade can claim that they are overly destructive. The simple fact that African elephant numbers have dropped to approximately 400,000–600,000, from 1.1–1.3 million in 1979–1981, should end any debate on whether there are "too many" or not.[3] It is natural for an elephant to be destructive – that is its "function" in its ecosystem. It is the epitome of the "land manager" in modern integrated environmental management. It is a critical component in successful ecosystem management (as much a creative as a destructive force, driving important ecological processes). While the resulting landscape may not be aesthetically particularly appealing to a foreign eye, it is a landscape that is interactive with its inhabitants. However, as elephants have been pressed into diminishing conservation areas, it has become impossible to preserve those areas that appeal to the tourist (in other words, to keep them looking as they did when European colonists arrived) unless elephants are removed through active intervention. The alternative would be to allow the elephant to proliferate and eventually decrease in numbers through natural destruction of its own food source until, after many centuries, it recovered in harmony with the land.

Within its natural environment, the elephant is a crucial component for its capacity for land management and by its mere presence. Its natural environment is, however, increasingly taking the form of small pockets of land surrounded by economically depressed areas in which human beings live in poverty – encroaching human settlement means increased competition between humans and elephants over resources. These people – often the original indigenous inhabitants of an African country – need to be convinced of the worth to them of elephants if they are to accept conservation as a viable land use. As is has been put by one commentator, "[e]lephants as sources of pure joy to Africa's visiting tourist are worse than smallpox to the peasant whose crops they have just destroyed."[4]

The struggle that conservationists face, therefore, in ensuring biodiversity is to involve local people and to provide tangible and measurable economic and social benefits from conservation to those people. Practically, there are two ways in which this can be done: either by conserving the elephant as a symbol (of a "flagship species" that draws tourists, thereby creating opportunities for uplifting of these impoverished communities from within) or by making active market usage of elephant products and risking harming the tourism industry. With the first approach currently operative, in the face of the moratorium on the ivory trade, it is becoming apparent that benefits are not reaching local people as effectively as they should. This calls into question the viability of pure preservation as a land use and requires that the alternative be investigated. The first question to be posed and answered, then, is whether opening trade in ivory is viable, controllable, and conducive to biodiversity preservation and whether benefits will indeed reach local people.

---

[3] See, for example, *National Geographic* Vol. 195, No. 2 (February 1999) 104 for the figure of 600,000. Other commentators have suggested that the figure might be closer to 400,000; for instance, personal comment, Daphne Sheldrick, David Sheldrick Conservation Trust, Nairobi, Kenya, 2 October 2004.

[4] Ian Parker, *What I Tell You Three Times Is True: Conservation, Ivory, History and Politics* (Librario) (2004) 381.

2 ISSUES OF SPACE AND ACCESS

South Africa's history of landownership has been one of deprivation and hardship –
and of reservation of land to the elite. Those without access to financial resources have
found themselves increasingly sidelined in terms of access to land.

The issue, however, is not merely one of deciding whether or not to allow previously
marginalized peoples access to land. Another issue that needs further investigation
is the demographic question of the "direction" in which South Africa's population
is heading. South Africa is by a long way the most urbanized country in Southern
Africa – its population by the 21st century neared or had passed the 60 percent urbanized
mark. The migration has conventionally been seen as having been from rural areas
to urban ones. While overall this is undoubtedly accurate, it would be dangerous to
see the drift as being in one direction only. In fact, people move regularly back and
forth between rural and urban areas and this raises unique problems in regard to
conservation.

In game reserves such as uMkhuze, iMfolozi, and Hluhluwe,[5] much poaching[6] is
done by disaffected youths seeking entertainment rather than sustenance. Similarly,
one of the major poaching problems in KwaZulu-Natal generally is that of so-called
taxi hunting in conservation areas or on private farmlands. This involves large groups
of city dwellers traveling by minibus taxi to engage in hunting with dogs. Usually associated with heavy gambling, these hunts are rapacious in the extreme and have caused
much ill feeling between different interest groups. In recent times, however, within the
province of KwaZulu-Natal, efforts have been made to provide for controlled traditional
hunting with dogs.[7] The significance of this development must not be underestimated:
Never before in South Africa's legislative history has there been anything approaching
condoning, let alone approval, of traditional hunting.

This change shows a shift in conservation thinking toward new ways of managing
resources – some of which would have been seen as "heretical" only a few years ago.

The pure preservationist approach (which sees the elephant as a sacrosanct species
entitled to priority to land) is largely a Western construct and has few African champions.
Just as the elephants have been coerced into smaller domains, so too have the African
people. In a deliberate attempt to acculturate, civilize, and educate Africans, colonial
regimes deprived people of a fundamental property right and distanced them from
their land. Hunting has become "poaching," a sport become a crime, in this inherited
form of land management. In a new understanding of our land, there must surely be a
pragmatic accommodation of these "poachers."

That said, the more common and "conventional" problem is that of rural peoples
living alongside or close to the borders of conservation areas, feeling excluded, living
in poverty, and becoming resentful at their exclusion. When animals, elephants in
particular, leave park boundaries and damage crops or injure inhabitants, conservation
authorities have traditionally accepted no responsibility. At the same time, however,

---

[5] All of which are in the province of KwaZulu-Natal and are controlled provincially, rather than nationally.
[6] Not of elephants, but of species such as zebra, and antelope such as impala and duiker.
[7] The KwaZulu-Natal Nature Conservation Management Amendment Act 5 of 1999, promulgated but not
yet in effect. The Act being amended is the KwaZulu-Natal Nature Conservation Management Act 9 of
1997.

the animals are strictly protected against being harmed by local people.[8] In many cases, these people are in fact the traditional inhabitants of the conservation areas – having been evicted from the land in the late 19th or early 20th centuries.

Modern conservation thinking recognizes that there is a need to be more inclusive, and to spread benefits to the immediate borders of conservation areas as well as to the national or provincial coffers. In most cases thus far this has taken the form of fairly low-level community involvement – employing local people inside parks, allowing local people to sell art and crafts from within parks, allowing people access to grass for thatching and wood for firewood, and providing a small levy on gate revenues. (The sale of ivory may provide an opportunity for such revenues to increase substantially.) The gate "community" levy is a controversial thing, however. In KwaZulu-Natal, the fund holding this combined levy has now grown to approximately R20 million, not all of which has been spent. One problem that arises is whether to spend it improving the conditions of communities living near the parks that provided it or, spreading benefits more widely, to assist communities farther afield who are poorer still and live without even the limited advantages of proximity to a conservation area.

Probably some two-thirds of the levy money raised thus far has been spent.[9] In the province of KwaZulu-Natal, Ezemvelo KZN Wildlife follows a policy that money should be allocated to communities closer to the resource (the conservation land) rather than farther – without excluding funding for projects farther afield, if needed. Local communities decide whether people farther away will benefit from money raised from conservation levies. This could be seen as a problem but, in practice, the areas that have access to the funds are large. "Local" communities tend in fact to cover wide areas. In KwaZulu-Natal an Inkosi (or traditional leader) decides where the money is to go, in consultation with a council that consults as an open forum. The management body, Ezemvelo KZN Wildlife, cannot therefore decide on how money will be used – nor even whether the money is to be used for the specific benefit of conservation.[10]

In March 2004, for example, the Makhwela Community near Louwsburg in KwaZulu-Natal, which is close to the Ithala Game Reserve, received five new school classrooms (at a cost of R358,417) through monies generated from levies on tourist accommodation in and entries to the park.[11] The objection might be made that school classrooms are not directly beneficial to conservation. This would, however, be shortsighted. The Makhwela Community now has a visible benefit, which it chose itself, from the use of land as a game reserve.

The "community levy" approach works well in those areas with bigger game reserves, but less well where the area to be protected has significant conservation value but is

---

[8] See, for example, the South African Supreme Court case of *Mbhele v Natal Parks, Game and Fish Preservation Board* 1980 (4) SA 303 (D&CLD), where it was held that the plaintiff had no claim in delict (tort) against the defendant after being injured by a hippo that had left a game reserve under the control of the defendant, since the hippo had not at the time been under the control of the defendant – and that the defendant had no duty to take steps to control the hippo, as the expense of this would have been prohibitive. At the same time, had the roles been reversed and the plaintiff have injured the hippo, he would doubtless have been liable in delict and subject to prosecution.

[9] Personal comment, 1 May 2004, Andrew Blackmore, Head Integrated Environmental Management Conservation Planning Division, Ezemvelo KZN Wildlife.

[10] Ibid.

[11] See http://www.kznwildlife.com/news_archives.htm.

small and not visited on a grand scale. This might be where cross-area funding will become of great importance, with larger conservation areas effectively funding smaller ones.

As scientists argue increasingly that biodiversity needs to be conserved by protecting ecosystems rather than species, so the recognition must follow that humans are increasingly part of those ecosystems and both affect and are affected by them even when not living directly within them. There is no reason why the "ecosystem approach" to conservation area land management should not include human beings as essential components.

In South Africa the issue has become even more fraught as people dispossessed of land in terms of racially biased legislation after 1913 have been afforded the opportunity, by the Constitution[12] and by the Restitution of Land Rights Act,[13] to restitution of the land or to equitable redress. In a number of cases, claims have been laid in respect of land incorporated into sensitive conservation areas. For example, a claim was made on behalf of the Makuleke Community in respect of an area of the northern Kruger National Park. The matter was settled contractually, with the Makuleke accepting limited access and managerial rights over the area that would remain part of the Park. A dispute then arose when the Makuleke announced their intention to sell the rights to shoot elephant to foreign hunters. The matter has not yet been resolved.

It is not uncommon for protected areas to have two or more land claims lodged against them. Approximately 90 percent of the land situated within protected areas in KwaZulu-Natal has claims against it. It is not likely that many of the claimants will get the land back physically, but many will regain some degree of control. Ezemvelo KZN Wildlife will then become the conservation agency to manage the land (and the animals on it) on behalf of the successful claimants.

3 THE CONVENTION ON INTERNATIONAL TRADE IN ENDANGERED SPECIES

The Convention on International Trade in Endangered Species (CITES)[14] is an "old-style" Convention that does not make provision for ongoing monitoring of compliance, does not have a permanent secretariat charged with ensuring that it is operating successfully,[15] and does not make any provision for financial support of signatory countries that face financial costs for implementing the Convention. CITES was signed at Washington, D.C., in 1973, as one of a number of Conventions surrounding the 1972 United Nations Conference on the Human Environment (UNHCE) in Stockholm. CITES regulates international trade in wildlife and has only limited jurisdiction to regulate the internal actions of states.

---

[12] The Constitution of the Republic of South Africa Act 108 of 1996, s25(7).

[13] Act 22 of 1994.

[14] The Convention on International Trade in Endangered Species of Wild Fauna and Flora, 1973, http://www.cites.org/.

[15] A permanent Secretariat (located originally in Lausanne, and now in Geneva, Switzerland) oversees the application of the CITES system, but day-to-day operation is a matter for the national authorities of the parties.

According to one commentator:

> Successful as the Convention may be in providing for strict controls on trade in
> endangered species and their derivative products, it is at least arguable that the
> stated aim of CITES in terms of the protection of endangered species against over-
> exploitation though international trade controls implicitly acts to legitimize such
> trade in fact.[16]

CITES is not designed in itself to protect or conserve endangered species, with the possible exception of species threatened with extinction and listed in Appendix I. Appendix I
species are not available for commercial trade and are thus ostensibly protected against
trade. Despite this ambiguity, regulation of trade through the CITES permitting system
is the closest the world has come to a global conservation monitoring system.

In November 2002 CITES Conference of the Parties (COP) 12 was held in Santiago,
Chile. Southern African countries launched an assault on the effective ivory trade
ban. Zimbabwe did not receive permission for another auction sale, but South Africa,
Namibia, and Botswana successfully proposed amendments to the annotation to the
elephant's Appendix II downlisting. South Africa gained the right to sell most (28,000
kilograms, or 28 tonnes) of its current stockpile (32,000 kilograms, or 32 tonnes). The
decision provided for a

> one-off sale [by South Africa, Namibia, and Botswana to Japan] for non-commercial
> purposes [within the range state] of government stocks declared by African elephant
> range States to the CITES Secretariat within the 90-day period before the transfer to
> Appendix II of certain populations of the African elephant takes place.[17]

This sale was not to take place before the end of May 2004.

Kenya, however, opposed proposals at CITES COP 12 to reopen the ivory trade[18]
and has warned that it will continue to press for increased restriction of the ivory trade.

The International Fund for Animal Welfare reported in March 2004 that

> Kenya, Uganda, Ethiopia, Mali, Cameroon, Tunisia and Ghana are concerned that
> conditions under which the [Southern African] ivory should be sold have not been
> met. These countries said that until the conditions are met, no sales should be allowed
> to take place. The decision was taken at a meeting in Nairobi this week.[19]

The proposed sale of ivory did not, in fact, take place in 2004. According to the South
African Department of Environmental Affairs and Tourism, although South Africa,
Botswana, and Namibia met all of the necessary conditions for international trade, "the
process had been delayed due to lack of data from certain south-east Asian countries."[20]

---

[16] David M. Ong, "The Convention on International Trade in Endangered Species (CITES, 1973): Implications of Recent Developments in International and EC Environmental Law" *Journal of Environmental
Law* Vol. 10 No. 2 (1998) 291 at 294.

[17] Resolution 10.2 CITES COP 12, 2003 "Elephants – Conditions for the Disposal of Ivory Stocks
and Generating Resources for Conservation in African Elephant Range States," http://www.cites.org/
eng/decis/valid12/10-02.shtml.

[18] "Kenya against Ivory Proposal" in *Daily News* 4 September 2002 at 4.

[19] "Pressure on SA to abort ivory sales" in *Natal Witness* 11 March 2004, http://www.witness.co.za/
content/2004_03/22474.htm.

[20] "SA on Track to Sell Ivory Stocks" *Mail & Guardian Online* 24 March 2004, http://www.mg.co.za/
Content/13.asp?ao=33072.

4 CITES AND RURAL PEOPLE: THE EXAMPLE OF THE CHOBE ENCLAVE TRUST

In June 2002, the writer attended a meeting with a community in Botswana – the Chobe Enclave Trust. Also present were various conservation officials from Botswana's Wildlife Department. The Trust area is extremely poor, and little conventional farming is possible as the area has little water and is badly eroded and overgrazed. Botswana has a policy of not culling elephant and there is much conflict between villagers and the species. The villagers are able to raise money every year, however, by selling a quota of elephants to foreign trophy hunters.[21] This money is then ploughed back into the community – apparently fairly successfully in the sense that the vast majority of villagers had opted not to receive individual payouts, but rather to have the money go into common projects.

This model suggests that reopening the international ivory trade could hold significant benefits for similar communities competing with elephants for land – if the money did indeed reach such communities.

However, there are certain attendant problems. The Botswanan government is currently opposed to the culling of elephants, following instead a policy of attracting elite, low-impact tourism. The community on the Chobe Enclave Trust land has reacted with great bitterness to CITES – seeing it as an interfering body that prevented them from offering for sale more than a small number (12 at that time) of elephants per year. This showed a misunderstanding of CITES, which does not regulate wild animals shot for trophies, but showed also that the international convention has not been successful in persuading indigenous communities of its worth. Put another way, while it is possible that the CITES restrictions from 1989 onward have kept elephant numbers from plummeting dangerously low, land users "on the ground" now blame CITES for keeping them poverty-stricken and unable to utilize "their" land as they would like.

There is also a potential problem within the hunting community, attributable to the CITES Appendix I listing. This is the perception that elephants are sacrosanct and not to be hunted. The stigma against hunting the species can be blamed both on Western media/consumer pressure and on the official sanction to the "hands-off" approach given by the Appendix I listing.

Such a misunderstanding is not limited to Southern Africa. Consider, for example, the following extract from a Kenyan newspaper article about villagers in Busi District complaining of the depredations of crocodiles:

> [Her] bitterness and frustration are no doubt the result of her people's helplessness in the face of the marauding man-eaters – thanks to a Government law and the international CITES statute that imposes a ban on the illegal killing and trade in the reptiles.[22]

Once again, CITES can be used to prevent trade in crocodiles and their products, but not to prevent "problem animals" from being killed by domestic authorities.

---

[21] Legitimate sport-hunted ivory trophies may be exported, subject to CITES Appendix I, permitting restrictions such as that they may not be traded commercially after export. See, for instance, http://international.fws.gov/pdf/af.pdf; see also T. Milliken, "African Elephants and the Twelfth Meeting of the Conference Parties, Santiago, Chile, 2002," http://66.249.93.104/search?q=cache:OgxtJVjqWy8J:www.traffic.org/cop12/Elephants_CoP12.pdf+harare+compromise+on+ivory+trade&hl=en.

[22] Oscar Obonyo, "Crocodiles Spread Terror in Village" *Sunday Nation* 3 October 2004 at 16.

5 THE SOUTHERN AFRICAN APPROACH TO REOPENING THE INTERNATIONAL TRADE IN IVORY

The listing of the African elephant on Appendix I of CITES in 1989, giving it complete protection from commercial trade, was done in spite of opposition by Southern African countries, and no provision was made for financial compensation to affected countries.

Effectively, therefore, the developing countries in sub-Saharan Africa are subsidizing other elephant range states and the demands of developed countries in the North. In order to satisfy the current trend in developed countries to stigmatize the use of elephant products, developing countries with well-managed elephant populations are forgoing a potentially lucrative source of revenue. The argument is that countries such as India and those in East Africa benefit from the Appendix I listing as they are currently unable to control the illegal trade in their own (endangered) elephant populations and require a blanket prohibition to prevent laundering, while range states in Southern Africa could control illegal trade in their (nonendangered) populations, but are being required to forgo trade in order to assist range states that cannot. It must be queried, though, whether subsidy provisions would have been the best course. Even were subsidies to be granted, the tusks would still be stockpiled and would still have economic value, and the pressure would still be there to sell them. Equity difficulties would also arise in relation to such payments, the states that would qualify, the states that would contribute, and the precedent value for other species.

The burning of a stockpile of tusks in the Nairobi National Park in July 1989 by the Kenyan Wildlife Service was one of the most significant conservation-related public relations exercises of all time. The symbolic value of Kenya's then president, Daniel Arap Moi's, lighting a pyre of tusks in front of the world's cameras resonates to this day. The act undoubtedly contributed greatly to the public pressure that led to the upgrading from Appendix II to Appendix I at the CITES Conference of Parties in the same year. The act undoubtedly contributed too to Kenya's standing as a tourism destination. Why not, then, continue to burn collated tusks and reap the rewards in public opinion, goodwill, and tourism?

The 1989 burning probably had "once-off stunt" value. Many officials and commentators involved in conservation within Southern Africa denigrate the incident as having been a financial waste that did more harm than good. A second attempt was made in 1992, when Zambia burned a 9,000-kilogram (nine-tonne) ivory stockpile after promises of compensation by international groups. The money raised (allegedly some £3 million) went, however, into a foreign account and was managed by a nongovernmental organization – the Zambian government and conservation authorities were left with no control over the use of the money. In 2002, in its proposal to CITES COP 12 to be allowed to trade in ivory, Zambia argued that it was not known to what extent these funds were use for elephant conservation, nor even how much money remained.[23] The incident therefore made little news worldwide, had no direct influence on public opinion, is barely remembered, does not appear to have benefited Zambia directly, and has had no long-term impact on Zambia's desire to trade ivory. The lesson the experience holds is, therefore, that unless there is a tangible benefit to a land usage, which can be seen and felt by local people, the imposition of foreign conservation ideals can do more harm than good.

---

[23] COP12, Proposal from Zambia (COP12 PROP.9), http://www.cites.org.

In June 1997 the writer was in Harare at the time of the 10th CITES Conference of Parties. It was an interesting place to be, to observe the hysteria and hype that surrounded the issue of resuming trade in elephant products. Approximately 75 proposals to uplist or downlist various species were put forward; however, the main issue in the public eye at the Conference was that of the African elephant and its possible downlisting. The line taken by Southern African countries was fervently in favor of downlisting. Chem Chimutengwende, the Zimbabwean Minister for the Environment, accused some opponents of the downlisting of being

> just racist ... [he said that] they do not like the urbanisation or development of Africa because they like Africa to be one big zoo where they will just come as tourists and see poor blacks practising their traditions and living with wild animals.[24]

Although emotional, and potentially made for political reasons, comments such as this indicated deep resentments. Zimbabwe certainly felt unfairly treated and South Africa, Namibia, and Botswana echoed the position.

In Harare in 1997 South Africa proposed a compromise arrangement,[25] which was initially turned down by the CITES COP. However, out of this refusal arose the formation of an intergovernmental working group that put forward amended proposals. Using a secret ballot, these proposals were adopted with the necessary two-thirds majority.[26]

The elephant was not downlisted worldwide, but a "once-off" test auction of ivory was approved. The sale was to be for a total amount of 59.1 tonnes (of a combined stockpile of more than 150 tonnes), from the three countries (Namibia, Botswana, Zimbabwe); to be sold only to Japan; to be used only for the purpose of the manufacture of *hanko* (personal signet seals); and to take place only after a 21-month moratorium; and after an assessment by a monitoring/investigating committee that was to be set up. This committee was to be called MIKE – "Monitoring Illegal Killing of Elephants." This compromise deal did not go through without opposition and was eventually adopted after the European Union abstained – allegedly because they had failed to reach consensus on the issue, and were frustrated in efforts to postpone the vote.[27]

The elephant issue highlights two different approaches that can be taken to conservation. The "Kenyan model" attempts to maintain elephant populations by ensuring absolute protection from poachers and by banning all trade in elephant products. The approach of the Southern African countries is to manage elephant populations actively, culling animals to provide sufficient habitat, sharing profits with local people, and reinvesting profits in conservation.

6 CAMPFIRE OR "DAMPFIRE"?

Writing of the economic importance of the ivory trade, Parker has suggested that "ivory, [is] not so much a commodity as a currency whose value to Africa ran to millions of

---

[24] See http://www.anc.org.za/anc/newsbrief/1997/news0617.

[25] A selective downlisting limited to a once-off sale, to a single buyer, and to be held after a period of 18 months. The compromise proposal was then adapted to make the eventual sale subject to certain conditions, to be met within the 18-month period, and voted upon.

[26] Jill Gowans, "Africa's View Prevails" *African Wildlife* Vol. 51 No. 4 (July/August 1997) at 14.

[27] See "Global Ban in Ivory Trade Eased for African States" 19 June 1997, http://forests.org/archive/africa/easeban.htm.

dollars annually."[28] It is, according to the same writer, "an integral, inseparable part of general African trade. Ivory profits were not squirreled away in Swiss bank vaults, but recycled vigorously in commerce within the continent."[29]

Zimbabwe has developed a program that aims to reintegrate the lives of rural people with the profits that can be made from wild animals. Essentially, the program rewards rural communities financially from the proceeds of foreign trophy hunting, in return for the locals' participation in conservation.[30] In other words, communities receive a percentage of the amounts paid by safari hunters, which money can go directly into their pockets in proportionate amounts or be spent on community projects such as clinics and schools. In return, the communities protect wildlife in their area.

The the Communal Areas Management Programme for Indigenous Resources CAMPFIRE program has been extremely influential worldwide. For instance, Sri Lanka (where "elephant–human conflict resulted in the deaths of more than 100 elephants and 60 people per year during the 1990's")[31] is implementing a

> community-based project that seeks to fence villagers and their crops in and keep the elephants out. This model was originally pioneered in Zimbabwe by [CAMPFIRE], when it was realized that carving up vast landscapes with linear fences was contrary to the goals of crop protection and wildlife management.[32]

CAMPFIRE has been lauded worldwide as a successful program that has reduced conflict between humans and wild animals over scarce land resources, and that has helped to make conservation a sustainable form of land use.

One problem that arises in the CAMPFIRE model is that communities within communities may find themselves marginalized. In North-Eastern Zimbabwe, for example, an area known as Chapoto Ward has a population of approximately 1,500, divided in a 2:1 ratio between the Chikunda people and the Tembomvura people. The latter complain that their views and needs are not taken into account by the majority, and that because of CAMPFIRE they have been denied access to traditional hunting grounds. One member of the Tembomvura has been quoted as saying that

> CAMPFIRE is a programme for the Chikunda and the Safari people. They are the ones who gain from it. What CAMPFIRE does is to stop us from hunting so that white people can come from far away to kill animals for fun. We have heard that these people pay money but we have never seen any of it.[33]

The thrust of CAMPFIRE is toward people who "own" land in terms of communal tenure, based on a *usufruct* tenure system. Within this system, natural resources (including wildlife) are seen essentially as common property.[34] Within Southern Africa (Zimbabwe in particular), in recent times, the "community-based conservation"

---

[28] Ian Parker, *supra*, note 5 at 222.   [29] Ibid. at 310.

[30] See, for instance, D. H. Chadwick, *The Fate of the Elephant* (Key Porter Books) (1992) at 452.

[31] U.S. Fish & Wildlife Service, "Asian Elephant Conservation Act: *Summary Report 1999–2001*" at 11.

[32] Ibid.

[33] Ravai Marindo-Ranganai and Basia Zaba, "Animal Conservation and Human Survival: A Case Study of the Tembomvura People of Chapato Ward in the Zambezi Valley, Zimbabwe," Centre for Applied Social Studies, University of Zimbabwe, Occasional Paper – NRM Series, 1995.

[34] M. Moyo, "CAMPFIRE: Policy Changes & Legislative Amendments – Programme Impact in the New Millenium," Centre for Applied Social Studies, University of Zimbabwe, Occasional Paper – NRM Series, 2000.

approach has been the most successful in reconciling conservation concerns with the concerns of local people.[35] This approach is characterized by the use of economic incentives, a devolution of authority to communities, and the development of structures that enable communities to control use and distribution.

In recent years, however, CAMPFIRE has effectively collapsed. It is unclear whether this is entirely due to current political events within Zimbabwe, the turmoil of forcible dispossession of land, the collapse of the tourism market, and general social instability, or whether inherent structural problems with CAMPFIRE have contributed. In either case, though, the model is the best example we have seen to date of a practical effort to deal with the conflict between land shortages and conservation with a solution beneficial to both parties.[36]

7 THE CAMPFIRE MODEL FOR LAND AND LAND MANAGEMENT REFORM IN SOUTH AFRICA

In South Africa attempts (through most of the later part of the 20th century) to resolve the land–wildlife access problem focused less on "community-based conservation" than on "protected area outreach" program.[37] This approach sees local communities given certain limited rights of access to conservation areas, and a flow of benefits from conservation revenue – managed for the benefit of the communities. While this gives communities enforceable rights within conservation areas, at a formal level ownership is retained by either the state or provincial authorities.

Changing the approach and giving communities more say in how conservation is achieved face the potential problem of resistance from the authorities at both national and provincial levels. The major criticism of the protected area outreach approach, however, is that it has not in practice made a major difference to the lives of local communities. While such communities are barred from free access to nearby conservation areas, very little money has reached them – and the money that has often been merely remuneration for low-level manual labor.

It is also becoming apparent that community land use projects need to be actively driven, if they are to be viable and sustainable. It is important that implementation mechanisms be inserted from the start of the project. At the macrolevel, CITES has similar needs – and yet the Treaty contains no implementation or enforcement mechanisms. The "communities" under CITES are the States Parties, which are committed to incorporating the Treaty's provisions into their domestic legislation – something that few have done. Even those that have so incorporated the Treaty are often weak when it comes to implementing its provisions. de Klemm, for instance, notes that "[m]ore than two decades after the original Convention, only a small number of the contracting

---

[35] Edmund Barrow and Marshall Murphree, "Community Conservation," in David Hulme and Marshall Murphree (eds.), *African Wildlife & Livelihoods: The Promise & Performance of Community Conservation* (Heinemann/James Currey Ltd.) (2001) 24 at 34.

[36] For further information on the CAMPFIRE program, see S. Metcalfe, "Campfire: Zimbabwe's Communal Areas Management Programme for Indigenous Resources" (1993), http://www.resourceafrica.org/documents/1993/1993_campfire_bg.pdf; D. Hulme and M. Murphree (eds.), *African Wildlife & Livelihoods: The Promise and Performance of Community Conservation* (Heinemann/James Currey Ltd) (2001).

[37] Edmund Barrow and Marshall Murphree, *supra*, note 37 at 32.

parties have . . . enacted specific and relatively comprehensive legislation to implement it."[38]

Within South Africa, the National Environmental Management: Protected Areas Act[39] seeks to obviate such problems by putting into place management programs and agreements. (The Act has been promulgated, but a commencement date has not yet been set.) Within KwaZulu-Natal, provision is made in the KwaZulu-Natal Nature Conservation Management Act (the KZN NCM Act)[40] for local boards for protected areas.[41] The function of these local boards is to assist Ezemvelo KZN Wildlife in its management of protected areas – unlike the management programs provided for by the Protected Areas Act, these are not voluntary bodies but compulsory ones with statutorily prescribed roles. Section 25 of the KZN NCM Act provides that the provincial Minister of Environmental Affairs and Tourism "may" establish a local board in respect of a protected area or areas; once such a board has been established, however, the Minister "must" consult the relevant local board on decisions affecting the area(s).

KwaZulu-Natal is, thus far, the only South African province that has legislated into existence local boards that comprise relevant stakeholders.[42] The significance of this legislative approach for land management is that formal access is given to management, rather than formal tenure.[43] The decision-making process has been broadened as it is no longer merely the conservation authority that is making decisions about resources that affect local communities. This is taken further in the Protected Areas Act, which provides for cooperation agreements to induce communities to assist with specialized aspects.[44] Management plans are provided for – to be established by agreement. These then provide for comanagement of resources, and the regulation of human activities affecting the environment in the relevant areas. This is a significant advance on the traditional Southern African "protected area outreach" program.

An advantage, perhaps, of the KwaZulu-Natal legislative approach is that it puts people on the ground closer to international environmental treaties. The local boards, in terms of their statutory functions and powers, must apply legislation. As this legislation is required to comply with South Africa's international commitments (to CITES, for example), local people gain greater understanding of international law and policy.[45]

8 DIFFERENT APPROACHES TO UTILIZING ELEPHANTS – THE "BATTLEGROUND"

South African National Parks (SANP), supported by the Department of Environmental Affairs and Tourism (DEAT), argues that gradual reductions in South African government funding of SANP have "left the organisation suffering from budgetary deficiencies which could be considerably redressed should the current legal stockpile of ivory be

---

[38] C. de Klemm, *Guidelines for Legislation to Implement CITES* (IUCN Environmental Policy and Law Paper No. 26) (1993) at 5.

[39] Act 57 of 2003.   [40] Act 9 of 1997.

[41] Ibid. s 25.   [42] Andrew Blackmore, *supra*, note 10.

[43] In other words, although tenure over conservation land is not given (or returned, as the case may be), a formal right is given to participate in decision making in respect of the land.

[44] *Supra*, note 41 s 42.   [45] Ibid.

sold."[46] "Revenues," claim SANP and DEAT, "would be used in the interest of elephant conservation."[47]

Kenya, however, opposed proposals at CITES COP 12 to reopen the ivory trade and has warned that it will continue to press for increased restriction. Kenya cited disturbing reports of increases in poaching.[48] Kenya thus wants to reinstate the elephant populations of Botswana, Namibia, and Zimbabwe to Appendix I. The Kenyan position is supported by India.

A report by Traffic and the World Wildlife Fund has singled out Nigeria, Côte d'Ivoire, and Senegal for failing to regulate an illegal ivory trade that is fueling poaching. More than 4,000 kilograms of illegal ivory is on sale in the three countries. As elephant populations in the countries have been nearly wiped out, most illegal ivory is obtained from the surrounding countries.[49] Despite such reports, Tanzania is now considering "breaking ranks" with Kenya and seeking to sell its ivory stockpile (of some 87,000 kilograms, 87 tonnes), in much the same way as the Southern African countries are doing.[50]

The Kenyan government takes utilization of land by wildlife "as a very important aspect of land use, tourism being the largest earner of foreign exchange."[51] Aside from the ecological value of conservation, write Eriksen, Ouko, and Marekia,

> [t]he tourism industry also generates employment and contributes to the growth of other sectors of the economy. Secondary economic activities benefit from tourism, especially in the service industries such as restaurants, car hire companies, curio shops, food and beverage producers and banks. Tourism also generates pressure to improve certain services such as telecommunications, banking and insurance. The growth of hotels has necessitated the provision of goods like furniture and construction material. . . . [w]ildlife offers other direct benefits to local populations such as game meat, forage for domestic animals, timber, fuelwood, honey, medicinal plants and materials for handicrafts and building.[52]

The same writers suggest that

> [l]and tenure regimes have a direct bearing on the management of wildlife. . . . [l]and encompasses a range of resources, whose scope and influence transcend private property boundaries. Statutory law regards land as a single resource to which there may be a variety of rights (use, alienation, etc) whereas customary law tends to recognize a bundle of aggregated rights to the many natural resources associated with

---

[46] Draft Proposal 2, CITES COP 12 Workshop, Department of Environmental Affairs and Tourism, Pretoria, 15 March 2002.

[47] Ibid.

[48] See, for instance, the joint proposal by Kenya and India to CITES COP 12: "Revision of Resolution Conf. 10. 10 (Rev.) on Trade in Elephant Specimens" (COP 12 Doc.34.3), www.cites.org. See also media reports such as "Kenya Up in Arms over Ivory" *news24.com*, 25 February 2003, http://www.news24.com/News24/Africa/News/0,6119,2-11-1447_1325066,00.html.

[49] "More Ivory Than Elephants in Three West African Countries" *Traffic Dispatches* Nr, 22 June 2004, http://www.traffic.org/dispatches/june2004/ivory_markets.html.

[50] Charles Mkoka, "Wildlife Officials Brace for 2004 Ivory Sale" *Mail & Guardian online*, http://www.mg.co.za/articledirect.aspx?area=mg_flat&articleid=33244.

[51] Siri Eriksen, Evans Ouko, and Njeri Marekia, "Land Tenure and Wildlife Management" in Calestous Juma and J. B. Ojwang (eds.), *In Land We Trust: Environment, Private Property and Constitutional Change* (Initiatives Publishers) (1996) 199 at 199–200.

[52] Ibid. at 202.

land.... Where customary tenurial systems have been replaced by modern tenure the flexibility and complexity of rights which can promote sustainable resource management as well as equity are lost.[53]

The last point is significant. Modern "Western" systems of tenure, which tend to prevent communal access to wildlife or its benefits, have the potential to impair conservation in the long term even though in the short term they might be of benefit to conservation and preservation efforts. It is worth noting that in no country that the writer is aware of is it being seriously argued that land should be reserved entirely to wildlife with no financial benefits flowing to local people at all.

9 THE INDIAN/ASIAN ELEPHANT

The "forgotten cousin" of the African elephant faces many of the same problems and raises many of the same issues. This is borne out in a report published in 2003 by the U.S. Fish and Wildlife Service:

> The Asian elephant (*Elephas maximus*) is a keystone species, sharing a land mass with some of the most densely populated and poorest areas in the world. The pressure brought on by these conditions has resulted in the conversion of forest cover to agriculture and villages, fragmenting elephant habitat and populations. While the Asian elephant is the well-known elephant of circuses and elephant rides, the African elephant's plight in the wild has been more successfully popularized by the western media. Relatively few people are aware that the Asian elephant is critically endangered in the wild.[54]

According to the same report, "[d]uring 2001, 31 elephants in Assam were poisoned to death during a 70-day period as retribution for crop raiding. In Sri Lanka, a country with approximately 3,000 elephants, 110–120 elephants are killed each year, most, while crop raiding."[55] Poaching does, however, remain a problem.

> Asian elephant ivory is highly favoured by many ivory traders, and elephant bones and body parts used in the Asian medicinal trade are commodities much in demand by the global marketplace. [It should be acknowledged] that uncontrolled trade in elephant ivory and body parts is a serious threat to the survival of the species... [a]lthough India is estimated to hold as many as 25,000 of the world's wild Asian elephants, it is speculated that about 1,000 of these are mature males (tuskers) of breeding age. The poaching of tuskers is shifting the male Asian elephant population towards the survival of tuskless males (mukhnas).... In January 2001,... five tuskers were poached in the Corbett National Park, in what is widely viewed as one of India's most important and best managed National Parks.[56]

Currently, India sees a need to protect elephants and is therefore opposed to any resumption of the international ivory trade – in this regard India has, in conjunction with Kenya, for many years opposed Southern African attempts to downlist the elephant to CITES Appendix II. However, given the trend toward sustainable utilization and the continual pressure from Indian farmers in their "war" with elephants, it might be that India will

---

[53] Ibid. at 202–203.   [54] U.S. Fish & Wildlife Service, *supra*, note 33 at 3.
[55] Ibid. at 7.   [56] Ibid. at 13.

shift soon toward an approach that sees elephant products traded and the proceeds reinvested into rural areas in order to help resolve land tensions.

10 VALUING THE ENVIRONMENT AND VALUING CONSERVATION AS A LAND USE

It is currently difficult to argue in economic terms against the Southern African position in regard to exploitation of elephant and rhinoceros products. This difficulty arises because against demonstrable tangible (economic) benefits to the countries' economies, and their conservation efforts, is weighed an intangible. The intangible is the value of the elephant as a symbol of conservation, which can attract international tourism and goodwill, and the value of the elephant as a creature with an inherent right to life, as a keystone in its environment, and as a symbol of conservation and environmental protection.

This point goes to issues of how we set about weighing intangibles when making cost–benefit analyses in the environmental field.

At the beginning of this chapter I described the elephant as the "landscape architect" of the African bush environment. In assessing the claims of elephant conservation as a viable land use, it is important to acknowledge that if elephants were to be removed from an environment a surrogate engineering program would be needed to prevent the bush from becoming overgrown and drastically altered. Such programs are extremely expensive. In recent years, for example, elephants (formally eradicated from the area) have been reintroduced to the Greater St. Lucia Wetland Park (a World Heritage site in KwaZulu-Natal). Some 37 elephants have been reintroduced in the hope that they will have an impact on deforested areas (within commercial plantations) where the problem of uniform regrowth within areas harvested for commercial purposes has arisen. Necessary "disruption" can only be caused by biomass (elephants, in this case) as fire would simply destroy uniformly. However, it does still cost money to have the elephants present and the solution, within the eyes of Ezemvelo KZN Wildlife, is to sell ivory.[57]

"African countries," it has been suggested,

> must reconcile the tension between the incentives to preserve elephants and the incentives to reap value from dead elephants. Live elephants can generate substantial tourism revenue and produce additional elephants. Substantial value can also be derived, however, from elephant products.[58]

The sale of ivory, under the auspices of CITES, may be of great significance in solving this conundrum. The trade in elephant products is potentially extremely lucrative and could, if properly utilized, go a long way toward bolstering the incomes of conservation authorities and helping to keep national and provincial parks viable in the face of shrinking funding from central government. However, it is not presently known how the international market for ivory has been affected by the moratorium that has been in effect for almost 15 years.[59] If there is a strong response to the auction, and the stockpiles

---

[57] Andrew Blackmore, *supra*, note 10.

[58] Andrew J. Heimert, "How the Elephant Lost His Tusks" *Yale Law Journal* Vol. 104 (1995) 1473 at 1480.

[59] Since the elephant was listed on Appendix I of CITES in 1989.

are sold for considerable amounts, then the prospect is there that conservation will be given a "shot in the arm" as a legitimate land use.

It appears that there is a strong market in Japan for ivory to be used for the manufacture of *hanko*. However, prior to 1989 a large percentage of the ivory worked in Japan was then sold to the tourism market from the United States and Western Europe. Given the changed mores of the ivory trade, it is uncertain how strong the market is. Perceptions can be extremely important. It might yet become apparent that CITES has gone beyond its mandate (it is, after all, a trade treaty) and in fact "killed off" the industry it was attempting to govern.

It might be that the States Parties to CITES need to reassess the treaty's long-term role and effect within conservation areas – the treaty might even be instrumental, ultimately, in causing certain protected areas to be lost. CITES members need to be cautious not actually to precipitate land use changes on a large scale.

The Southern African ivory sale (permissible after May 2004, subject to certain preconditions, and probably to take place in 2006 once all of these – which had not been satisfied even by COP13 in 2004 – have been satisfied) will raise many important questions relating to land use. For instance, will the economics of resuming the ivory trade (albeit in limited form) have a positive or a negative effect on perceptions of wildlife as a viable form of land use by indigenous peoples? This will depend to a large extent on whether benefits do flow sufficiently and directly to such people, the "competing land users."

Further questions that arise are whether trade will lead to greater acceptance of this form of land use, or whether it will see wildlife "downgraded" to the status of having to "justify" its "occupation of land" in economic terms. If attempts to reopen the ivory trade are not successful, will increased financial and demographic pressure on areas containing wildlife result?

It has been suggested that

> [f]or people in urban, industrial or post-industrial society wildlife has little direct economic significance... and emphasis is placed on its intrinsic or recreational worth. For rural peoples, for whom the presence of wildlife has important economic implications, wildlife valuations tend to be more instrumental, even where their cultures assign an intrinsic value to wildlife.[60]

It is strongly arguable, although not certain (given the influence of Western pressure groups and environmental media), that the opening of the ivory trade to regular sales will begin to shift the urban (and elite) perception of conservation areas as sacrosanct, and inculcate a new recognition of the land as needing turnover to remain viable and sustainable as a conservation area.

Many, if not most, commentators focus on the "need" to educate rural people about conservation. It might be, however, that people in rural areas do already have a good understanding of the true value of the wildlife in their areas – the "need" may then be rather to educate the urban elite as to the realities of conservation costs, and the necessity of using land in financially viable ways. Certainly, the ideal probably lies somewhere between the extremes of preservation for scientific and recreational purposes and consumptive utilization. At present the slant appears to be toward the former, certainly within the perspective of the elite.

---

60 Edmund Barrow and Marshall Murphree, *supra*, note 37 at 29.

To meet its objective, the sale of ivory needs to be handled carefully in terms of public relations. There would seem to be, within the educated, urban, moneyed, largely European population, a high degree of resistance to the use of ivory for ornamental purposes. If conservation land is to utilize ivory effectively as a fund-raising source, then this perception needs to be changed.

Many of the more important decisions relating to conservation are, of course, made in urban areas – within the offices of government departments and influential non-governmental organizations. Arguably, Ezemvelo KZN Wildlife has sought to break this pattern – creating the institution of the local board as a way to import indigenous knowledge into conservation management. The local board then becomes a viable and stable way in which to incorporate indigenous knowledge in decision making.[61]

11 A WORLD CONCERN?

It can be argued strongly that there are certain issues that must transcend national sovereignty, because they are of extreme importance to the global community. The protection of biodiversity in rainforests, the overfishing of the oceans, and the future of important species such as the elephant must be leading examples of these.

Elephants, at first glance, would seem to stand on a different footing from the over-fishing example given earlier – given their position within sovereign borders. The author would like to suggest, however, that in a globalizing world and where the primary end users of elephant products are not located in range states, the sovereignty argument is far more complicated than it initially appears. It is strongly arguable that the international community has rights and interests in controlling trade – and corresponding duties.

These duties are not confined merely to contributing toward increased protection and controlled trade, but must be seen as addressing the fundamental reasons for the need for protection in the first place. While communities local to conservation areas remain unable freely to access such areas, and while adequate benefits are not reaching such communities, there will be resentment of conservation as a land usage and conflict between users.

Southern African countries are moving firmly in the direction of sustainable use in order to fund conservation efforts. The eventual sale of ivory under CITES auspices will go some way toward demonstrating how viable this approach is. Analysis of the effects of the sale will require research into the impact on poaching in other countries (such as Kenya and India), into the effect of the precedent set as countries look to sell their own ivory stockpiles (Tanzania, Zimbabwe, Zambia), and – perhaps the most important of all – into the devolution of benefits from the sale to indigenous/local communities.

12 IN CONCLUSION

Until such time as the Biodiversity Convention[62] and other new environmental treaties have proved to be effective in reconciling the widely divergent approaches to conservation held by important international actors, and by actors with conflicting interests within national borders, there will be tension between the protagonists of preservation

---

[61] Andrew Blackmore, *supra*, note 10.
[62] The Convention on Biological Diversity, 1992, which advocates a more holistic approach to conservation by conserving habitats as much as conserving individual species, http://www.biodiv.org/.

and the advocates of sustainable use.[63] In international law, this tension will be most visible in the inadequacies of those treaties through which countries currently seek to express their environmental views. Inside countries, this tension will be most visible in competition for and over land and access to natural resources.

[63] It should be noted that the conclusions drawn in this chapter are not based on species other than the African elephant; and that even in the case of the African elephant it is not yet clear whether the "sustainable use" view of the Southern African range states or the "Western preservationist" view will prevail. While it seems unlikely that ivory will ever again be traded without severe restrictions, even within the preservationist argument there are concessions to sustainable use (such as the sport trophy exemption, see *supra*, note 22), and the sales of ivory authorized by the CITES COPs of 1997 and 2002 imply strongly that the sustainable use argument is gaining strength.

2 Climate Change and Land Use in Africa

David R. Hodas

1 INTRODUCTION

Sub-Saharan Africa is facing a development crisis. The era of low-cost fossil fuel is coming to an end and with it "business as usual" development built on the bedrock of inexpensive fossil fuel. Simultaneously, climate change driven by fossil fuel use and other human activities is poised to threaten every aspect of human development in Africa, and all of Africa's ecosystems. Africa's contribution to increased green house gases (GHGs) has been minor, but the continent will nevertheless suffer significant adverse effects. This may be unfair, but it is unavoidable reality. However, climate change offers Africa enormous sustainable development opportunities. Successful exploitation of these opportunities, however, can be realized only if African legal systems are designed and those laws are implemented to take advantage of the opportunities. To do this, land use law in Africa must be examined through the lens of climate change, and then, using this new vision, be modified to advance Africa's sustainable development. This chapter first assesses the present world state of petroleum supply and economics and energy use patterns in sub-Saharan Africa. This analysis will reveal the reality that the century-long era of low-cost oil has come to an end and that developing countries can no longer approach development with the assumption that cheap energy will be available to drive the engine of development. The chapter then shifts to evaluating the potential impacts of climate change on Africa and how energy use intersects with the causes of global warming and the adaptation challenges warming will likely pose for sub-Saharan Africa. Finally, the chapter discusses the opportunities that land use–based strategies to mitigate warming present to the region, and the need to reconsider Africa's land use laws to make them compatible with and capable of promoting GHG mitigation projects in sub-Saharan Africa.

2 SUB-SAHARAN AFRICAN ENERGY USE AND THE END OF LOW-COST OIL

The accepted notion that Africa can improve its economic output by following a high-intensity, low-efficiency fossil fuel development path is no longer viable. World market conditions and long-term energy trends do not support any reasonable expectation that oil prices will appreciably drop for any sustained period. On the contrary, all indications point to a steady, inevitable rise, interrupted by short-term, possibly extreme, price spikes, followed by modest price drops. The oil supply facts are stark. In 2004, daily global demand for petroleum rose to 82.4 million barrels per day (mb/day) with supply barely keeping pace, at 84 mb/day.[1] According to the International Energy Agency (IEA), the Organization of Petroleum Exporting Countries (OPEC), driven by petroleum prices above U.S. $50 per barrel, is supplying a record 29.9 mb/day (as a result of renewed Iraq oil production), but OPEC's sustainable spare capacity is very small at less than 1 mb/day.[2] Because short-term demand is highly inelastic, small disruptions in supply, like that caused by Hurricane Ivan in the Gulf of Mexico (which reduced supply by 0.475 mb/day), can trigger rapid increases in the market price.[3]

Moreover, underlying demand for oil is also steadily rising. Quite simply, if the world continues to follow 2004 business-as-usual energy policies, by 2030 the world's energy needs will be almost 30 percent higher than they are now, with two-thirds of the increased demand from developing countries' economic and population growth.[4] China's emerging and voracious appetite for oil, which has grown by 34 percent since 2001, is particularly significant.[5] China's demand is unlikely to diminish: China seeks to double its economic output by 2020 and expand its fledgling car market to 100 million vehicles. In the United States, oil demand is 20.6 mb/day and steadily growing, but its declining domestic production is now only 7.3 mb/day. The result is that the United States is importing 13.3 mb/day, and its imports will rise if its demand growth follows its present path of 2–3 percent per year and its production continues to drop in Alaska,[6] Texas, and California.[7] For oil prices simply to remain at present high levels, around $50–$60 per barrel,[8] the world's oil supply must expand to match growing global demand for oil, and there can be no serious supply disruptions.

Whether supply growth can match projected demand growth by 2030 to 121 mb/day in an ever more fragile world market[9] is debatable, although sustained high prices could

---

[1] International Energy Agency (IEA), *World Energy Outlook 2004* (2004) 4, 12.

[2] Ibid. at 13.

[3] Ibid. at 12; IEA, *Oil Market Report* (12 October 2004) 28–29 (Hurricane Ivan in the U.S. Gulf Coast and labor threats and rebel unrest in the Niger Delta helped drive spot market oil prices over $53 per barrel by early October.)

[4] IEA, *World Energy Outlook 2004* (2004) 29, 31.

[5] China's oil demand, now 6.3 million barrels/day (mb/day), was projected to rise to 6.9 mb/day by late 2005, almost a 50 percent rise in 4 years. However, its domestic oil production is stuck at 3.5 mb/day. Thus, by 2005 China had to import 2.4 mb/day, an amount equal to the entire output of Nigeria or the United Arab Emirates. IEA, *Oil Market Report* (12 October 2004) Tables 1, 3. At this growth rate, China's demand will double in about five years.

[6] Even if the United States were to open the Alaska National Wildlife Refuge to drilling (a highly controversial proposal), it would take about a decade for oil to be produced; median estimates are that the area contains 10.3 technically recoverable reserves (assuming – unrealistically according to most recent reports – no major warming of permafrost), of which 3.2 billion barrels (bbl) are economically recoverable. National Research Council, *Cumulative Environmental Effects of Oil and Gas Activities on Alaska's North Slope* (2003) 56 (available at http://www.nap.edu). Assuming a 40-year life for the field, it would produce only about 0.22 mb/day. At 13.3 mb/day (current U.S. imports) the field would last just 240 days (about 8 months).

[7] *Id.* Tables 2B, 3, and 4.

[8] Roben Farzad, "Shares Take a Heavy Hit as Oil Briefly Touches $60," *The New York Times* (June 24, 2005) http://www.nytimes.com/2005/06/24/business/.

[9] Because the major oil importing countries will increasingly import oil from long-distance suppliers, many of whom may be in politically unstable regions, the world's oil supply market will become more fragile, less elastic, and highly sensitive to any supply disruption, whether from accident, weather, terrorism, labor disputes, political disputes, or even piracy. IEA, *Global Energy Outlook 2004* at 29.

dampen the demand pressure.[10] To meet the world's energy needs in 2030 will require a U.S. $16 trillion investment; the oil supply component of this challenge will be U.S. $3 trillion by 2030 for additional oilfields (mostly to offset production declines in existing oil fields), pipelines, tankers, and refineries.[11] The remaining U.S. $13 trillion will be needed, according to IEA, to expand electricity infrastructure. Although this huge investment will expand developing country electrification, especially in Asia, "the ranks of the electricity-deprived . . . will continue to swell in Africa," and 2.6 billion people will unsustainably rely on traditional biomass fuels for cooking and heating.[12] The economic reality is that Africa's development path cannot follow a business-as-usual model based on low-cost oil and widespread electrification.

This reality is both harsh and unfair. At the same time that Africa seeks, and needs, rapid economic expansion, the world must curtail anthropogenic emissions of greenhouse gases, such as carbon dioxide (CO_2), methane (CH_4), and nitrous oxide (N_2O), which are warming the planet and thereby changing earth's climate. Most of the warming is driven by increased atmospheric concentrations of CO_2, and most of this CO_2 is released by burning fossil fuels. Thus, to limit increases in and ultimately reduce atmospheric CO_2 concentration, fossil fuel use must be reduced. So, not only will high market prices economically limit fossil fuel use in Africa, but environmental imperatives will add to the pressures to reduce fossil fuel use.

Sub-Saharan Africa can legitimately complain that it is utterly inequitable to expect it to sacrifice industrial development to mitigate climate change, when Africa's role in emitting greenhouse gases has been relatively insignificant. However, as Mumma states, that attitude would impair Africa's ability "to develop a vision about its interest on the issue of climate change."[13] Africa's equity argument is supported by past emissions data. From 1800 to 2000, Africa's cumulative CO_2 emissions were just 1.7 percent of the world's total,[14] and in 2002 it contributed only 1.85 percent of global CO_2 emissions.[15] On a per capita basis, CO_2 emissions in Africa average just 0.4 metric ton per year per person (ranging from barely over 0.0 in Ethiopia to 8.1 in South Africa).[16] By comparison, global per capita emissions in 1999 averaged 3.9 tons per person, with the United States emitting 19.5 tons per person.[17] So, the world average is about 10 times greater than sub-Saharan Africa's, and the United States' is almost 50 times greater. As we will see shortly, this disparity in CO_2 emissions is paralleled by the disparity between Africa and the world with respect to the nature of fuel that is used. Conversely, compared to CO_2, sub-Saharan Africa's emissions of the other two major greenhouse gases, methane and nitrous oxide, represent a greater portion of global emissions. Although Africa uses less energy in its agricultural sector than any other region in the

[10] Press Release, IEA, "IEA Director Releases Latest World Energy Outlook, Says Current Energy Trends 'Call for Urgent and Decisive Policy Responses'" (26 October 2004) available at www.iea.org/textbase/press

[11] IEA, *Global Energy Outlook 2004* at 32. The remaining U.S. $13 trillion will be needed, according to IEA, to expand electricity infrastructure.

[12] *Id.* at 30, 36.

[13] Albert Mumma, "The Poverty of Africa's Position at the Climate Change Convention Negotiations," 19 *U.C.L.A. J. Envtl. L. & Pol'y* 181 (2001).

[14] World Resources Institute (WRI), *World Resources 2002–2004: Decisions for the Earth: Balance, Voice, and Power* (2003), Data Table 7, 258–259.

[15] Derived from IEA, *Key World Energy Statistics* (2004) 48–57.

[16] WRI, *World Resources 2002–2004*, Data Table 7, 258–259.

[17] *Id.*

world, its methane emissions are 7.7 percent of the world's emissions; N_2O emissions from Africa are about 10.5 percent of the global total.[18]

   This combination of low fossil fuel energy use and relatively high methane and nitrous oxide emissions (primarily from livestock and agriculture) is symptomatic of sub-Saharan Africa's linked land use and energy problems. It is well understood that in sub-Saharan Africa land is the primary economic resource, and in most sub-Saharan nations agriculture dominates the economy.[19] Unfortunately, most of Africa's energy also is from the land – through inefficient burning of firewood and animal and agricultural waste that is plucked from the land.[20] Not only is this burning inefficient,[21] but it creates enormously unhealthy indoor pollution and is unsustainable.[22] High population growth is intensifying the pressure on all wood from all available sources, for example, encroachment on forests and savannahs for agricultural and pastoral farming, wood fuel, and wood for construction. Forestation, land use conversion, poor topsoil protection practices, fires, urbanization, and inefficient transportation and energy systems account for Africa's methane and nitrous oxide emissions, and much of Africa's carbon dioxide emissions.[23]

   Sub-Saharan Africa's land use and energy crisis is best illustrated and explained by understanding traditional fuel use in Africa. In virtually all of sub-Saharan Africa, with the exception of South Africa, traditional fuels – firewood, crop residue, and biomass – are the single largest source of energy. Overall, traditional fuels account for 59 percent of all sub-Saharan Africa energy.[24] However, if South Africa is excluded from the data, traditional fuels account for 87 percent of all energy in sub-Saharan Africa. By comparison, the average for the entire world is less than 11 percent. The

---

[18] IPCC, *Climate Change 2001: Mitigation* (Bert Metz et al., eds., Cambridge University Press 2001), Fig. 3.14, p. 223. The IPCC carbon equivalent scale defines each ton of methane emissions to have the equivalent greenhouse gas effect of the emission of 23 tons of CO_2; a ton of nitrous oxide is the greenhouse gas equivalent of 296 tons of CO_2. David R. Hodas, "Energy, Climate Change and Sustainable Development," in *Energy Law and Sustainable Development* (Adrian J. Bradbrook and Richard L. Ottinger, eds., IUCN 2003), Table 2.1 at 16.

[19] World Resources Institute, *World Resources 2002–2004* (2003) 246–247. (Africa's percentage of gross domestic product [GDP] from agriculture is nearly three times greater than the world average, and nearly six times greater than Europe's.)

[20] Stephen Karekezi and Waeni Kithyoma, "Renewables and Poverty Reduction in Rural Sub-Saharan Africa," 36 *AFREPREN Newsl.* 2 (African Energy Policy Research Network June 2004), www.afrepren.org ("Biomass energy is the dominant energy form for most African countries.... Biomass is currently used largely in its traditional unprocessed form. The bulk of biomass energy is used for household cooking. Other important end-uses... include small-scale charcoal production, agro-processing and beer brewing").

[21] Improved cook stoves such as the Kenyan Ceramic Jiko reduce daily charcoal to 0.39 kilogram per person per day from 0.67 kilogram per person per day using a traditional stove. In Kenya over 50 percent of urban households use the improved stove, but only about 16 percent of rural households have one. However, dissemination of the stove outside Kenya is still not extensive, so the improved stoves are still not used by most poor Africans. "Kenyan Ceramic Jiko – an Improved Charcoal Stove," 36 *AFREPREN Newsl.* 15 (African Energy Policy Research Network, June 2004).

[22] For instance, Niger consumes around 2 million metric tonnes of firewood annually (wood supplies about 95 percent of its energy needs), but at current rates of consumption Niger will be 3 million tonnes short in its firewood supply by 2010, or "2.5 times the present sustainable supply and [Niger's] forests will disappear." "From Wood to Coal in an Effort to Stop Deforestation," *Africa News* (20 October 2004).

[23] Jason S. Ogala, "Climate Change: Kenya's Response," in 6 *Voices from Africa* (UN NGLS Sustainable Development Part 2) (www.un-ngls.org/documents/publications.en/voices.africa/number6).

[24] WRI, *World Resources 2002–2004*, Data Table 7, 258–259.

Table 2.1. Traditional fuel and electricity

Nation	Energy % from traditional fuels[25]	Electricity consumption per capita (kWh/person)[26]	National grid electrification (percent) (%) (2000–2001 data)[27]
World	11%	2,373	
China	20	1,208	
United States	3	13,228	
Angola	69	116	12%
Benin	78	76	
Cameroon	80	161	
Congo	79	133	
Congo, Dem. Rep.	91	86	
Côte d'Ivoire	91	198	
Ethiopia	93	27	21
Gabon	56	881	
Ghana	73	300	
Kenya	78	121	9
Mozambique	93	347	6
Namibia	15	1,236	
Nigeria	83	72	
Senegal	57	142	
South Africa	11	4,542	66
Sudan	87	75	30
Tanzania	94	65	6
Togo	74	114	
Zambia	81	604	
Zimbabwe	54	827	40

United States (including Puerto Rico) secures only 2.8 percent of its energy by burning traditional "renewables,"[28] while Europe gets only 2.2 percent from these resources. In Asia (excluding the Middle East) the figure is 19 percent; the Middle East and North Africa obtain only 2 percent from traditional sources.[29] In Central America and the Caribbean, the figure is 11 percent, in South America 15 percent, and in Australia and New Zealand only 4.6 percent of energy is obtained from traditional fuels.[30] Overall, developed countries average only 2.6 percent of energy from traditional sources and developing countries outside Africa average 23 percent,[31] whereas sub-Saharan Africa (excluding South Africa) is, tragically, dependent on traditional fuels for 87 percent of its energy.

On a country by country basis, as shown in Table 2.1, the picture of energy use in sub-Saharan Africa is even more stark. Tragically, even in oil-rich sub-Saharan nations,

[25] WRI, *World Resources 2002–2004*, Data Table 7, 258–259.
[26] IEA, *Key World Energy Statistics* (2004) 49–57.
[27] *African Energy Data and Terminology Handbook 2003–2004* (Stephen Karekezi et al., eds., African Energy Policy Research Network 2004) 59.
[28] These sources of energy are renewable only if the wood is not burned faster than trees are actually growing to replace the burned wood.
[29] *Id.*   [30] *Id.*
[31] *Id.*

most people depend upon traditional fuels for their survival. For example, 69 percent of Angola's energy is from traditional fuels, 73 percent of Ghana's, and, most dramatically, 83 percent of all energy use in Nigeria is from traditional fuels even though Nigeria is one of the largest oil producers in the world.[32] Poverty, severe respiratory illness, and environmental destruction parallel these trends.

Electricity and clean modern fuels are limited across Africa. For instance, electricity consumption in Africa (including North Africa) is only 514 kilowatt hours (kWh)/person,[33] whereas sub-Saharan Africa, excluding South Africa, consumed a mere 112.8 kWh per person in 2000.[34] By comparison, the world, on average, consumed 23 times as much electricity per person (2,373 kWh/person), the Organization for Economic Cooperation and Development (OECD) averaged 71 times more person (8,046 kWh/person), and the United States used 117 times the average person in sub-Saharan Africa (excluding South Africa) at 13,228 kWh/person.[35] Even China, with its huge population denominator, consumed more than 10 times the average sub-Saharan nation. Electrification rates in sub-Saharan Africa are also the lowest of any region in the world, at 22.6 percent compared to the world average of 72.8 percent.[36] Electrification in rural Africa is astonishingly low – 2 percent in Ethiopia, 9 percent in Kenya, 6 percent in Uganda, 10 percent in Tanzania, and 12 percent in Angola.[37] Most households in Africa do not have access to electricity.[38] Where electricity is available, it is relatively expensive; generally it is priced at levels similar to United States retail prices.[39] Finally, where fossil fuels are available, they are often in an unhealthy form, such as leaded gasoline[40] and high-sulfur fuels.

3 CLIMATE CHANGE EFFECTS ON SUB-SAHARAN AFRICA

The challenges to sub-Saharan Africa from climate change are also daunting. Global warming is profoundly changing the world's climate. In Africa, the most dramatic and

---

[32] In 2000, Nigeria produced just under 198,000,000 metric tons of oil equivalent, but its population used only 87 kilograms per person (0.0087 ton per person).

[33] IEA, *Key World Energy Statistics* (2004) 49–57.

[34] Stephen Karekezi et al., *Sustainable Energy Consumption in Africa* (African Energy Policy Research Network 2004) 3, www.afrepren.org.

[35] IEA, *Key World Energy Statistics* (2004) 49–57.

[36] Karekezi et al., *Sustainable Energy Consumption in Africa*, 3. Sub-Saharan Africa also has the world's lowest urban electrification rate, 51.3 percent, and rural rate, 7.5 percent, whereas the world average is 91.2 percent urban and 56.9 percent rural. *Id.*

[37] AFREPREN Paper 23 p. 59. The effect of the economic collapse of Zimbabwe, with its abundant hydro-electricity, is tragic since in 2000 84 percent of urban areas and 40 percent of rural areas were electrified. Its current status is unknown.

[38] Karekezi, *supra* note 27.   [39] *Id.*

[40] In most of Africa leaded gasoline is still the standard automobile fuel, and high-sulfur diesel fuel is the usual fuel used by trucks and buses. The cost of removing sulfur from diesel fuel (or buying more expensive low-sulfur oil) or reworking refineries to produce unleaded gasoline is nearly prohibitive. For instance, Kenya's only refinery is able to make only leaded gasoline. Originally built in the 1960s, the refining would now cost more than $181 million to modify for unleaded gas; to convert it into a storage facility for imported unleaded gas would cost $88 million. The health impacts of leaded gas are well known. The inhaled lead stays in the body; at relatively low levels it can impair brain function and nerve development in children and increases the risk of stroke and heart attacks in adults. Marc Lacey, "Belatedly, Africa Is Converting to Lead-Free Gasoline," *The New York Times* (31 October 2004) A3.

visible sign is the shrinking of the glaciers and snow caps on Mount Kilimanjaro and Mount Kenya; 82 percent of Mt. Kilimanjaro's ice has melted since 1912, and about a third has disappeared in about the last decade – at this rate all the ice will be gone by 2020.[41] Glaciers both in the Ruwenzori Mountains in Rwanda and on Mt. Kenya are also rapidly retreating.[42] Recent scientific studies have indicated that the warming of the Indian Ocean results in sub-Saharan droughts; Kenya experienced its worst drought in 60 years during 2001.[43] The surface area of Lake Chad shrank almost 96 percent from 25,000 square kilometers (9,650 square miles) in 1963 to around only 1,350 square kilometers in 2001.[44]

Climate change is also warming the oceans, with serious effects on Africa. All oceans of the world are warmer, having warmed $0.31°C$ ($0.56°F$) in the upper 300 meters (1,000 feet), and $0.06°C$ ($0.11°F$) to a depth of 3,000 meters (10,000 feet) over the past 45 years.[45] The effects of El Niño oscillations in the Pacific Ocean, now more intense and frequent because of global warming, translate into changes in rainfall patterns, droughts, and floods in Africa.[46] The warmest decade in the 20th century in southern Africa was 1985–1995, during which average temperatures increased $0.56°C$ (about $1°F$).[47] The entire continent of Africa warmed $0.5°C$ ($0.9°F$) during the 20th century. Sea-level rise from thermal expansion is already engulfing coastal land on the southern coast of Senegal.[48] Malaria is spreading in Kenya and Tanzania. Coral reefs in the Indian Ocean are bleaching.[49]

It has been broadly assumed across the international community that Africa need not concern itself with global warming because it is only a tiny emitter of greenhouse gases, both in total quantity and per capita. Moreover, because African nations face so many urgent and daunting human development challenges, many, if not most, Africans place climate change very low on their list of policy priorities. However, as political, legal, and economic governance improves in nations across Africa, major economic development will emerge and accelerate rapidly. Climate change will affect the quality

---

[41] L. G. Thompson et al., "Kilimanjaro Ice Core Records: Evidence of Holocene Climate Change in Tropical Africa," 298 *Science* 589–593 (2002), *Ice Caps in Africa, Tropical South America Likely to Disappear within 15 Years*, Ohio State University press release (2001), available at www.acs.osu-state.edu/units/research/archive/glacgone.htm.

[42] L. G. Thompson et al., "Tropical Glacier and Ice Core Evidence of Climate Change on Annual to Millennial Scales," 59 *Climate Change* 137, 152 (2003).

[43] U.S.A.I.D., 1 *Kenya – Drought Information Bull.* (2001), available at www.usaid.gov/hum_response/ofda.

[44] M. T. Coe and J. A. Foley, "Human and Natural Impacts on the Water Resources of the Lake Chad Basin," 106 *J. Geophysical Research (Atmospheres)* 3349–3356 (2001).

[45] J. Levitus, I. Antonov, T. P. Boyer, and C. Stephens, "Warming of the World Ocean," 287 *Science* 2225–2229 (2000).

[46] Andrew C. Revkin, "Ocean Warmth Tied to African Drought," *The New York Times* (24 May 2005) (available at nytimes.com); Martin P. Hoerling et al., "Detection and Attribution of 20th Century Northern and Southern African Monsoon Change" submitted to *Journal of Climate* (20 January 2005) (available at www.cgd.ucar.edu/cas/jhurrell).

[47] J. Arntzen, T. Downing, R. Leemans, J. Malcolm, N. Reynard, S. Ringrose, and D. Rogers, *Climate Change and Southern Africa: An Exploration of Some Potential Impacts in the SADC Region* (World Wildlife Fund, Climatic Research Unit 1996).

[48] K. Dennis, I. Niang-Diop, and R. Nicholls, "Sea Level Rise and Senegal: Potential Impacts and Consequences," 14 *Journal of Coastal Research, Special Issue* 243–261 (1995).

[49] Paul V. Desanker, *Impact of Climate Change on Life in Africa* (2002) (available at www.panda.org/climate). See also Robert W. Buddemaier et al., *Coral Reefs & Global Climate Change: Potential Contributors of Climate Change to Stresses on Coral Reef Ecosystems* (Pew Center on Global Climate February 2004).

and quantity of development and simultaneously will be affected by the accumulated development policy choices made across Africa. With more than a billion people and abundant resources, Africa has the potential to be a major contributor to global warming.

Of the three major GHGs that humans contribute to global warming, carbon dioxide is the most significant to Africa's future, as an opportunity or as an obstacle. Carbon dioxide is emitted from fossil fuel burning and by land use patterns that destroy carbon sinks. One might ask, How can burning fossil fuels in Africa be a problem? After all, as a whole Africa burns little compared to the rest of the world and, except for a handful of countries, produces little. From a traditional development-based perspective, the lack of petroleum and coal burning is a problem, not an opportunity. It is a problem because the high market price of oil and natural gas will further hobble development. Moreover, the price of petroleum is unlikely to drop over time, given the voracious demand from China, which, when added to the enormous oil appetite of the United States, Europe, and emerging economies such as India, pushes demand to the edge of the world's supply envelope, and perhaps beyond.[50] Financially, there is no low-cost, high-carbon development path in Africa's future.

At the same time, Africa is highly vulnerable to the impacts of global warming and must target its adaptation policies to low-carbon opportunities. Thus, land, which Africa has in abundance, must be used wisely both to reduce its vulnerability to climate change and to advance its human development goals. African laws must encourage land use that supports a low-carbon development path and that promotes the creation and preservation of carbon sinks. These sinks that sequester carbon will become valuable economic assets needed by high-carbon economies that will struggle to shift to low-carbon economies. More generally, carbon sequestration will be crucial to a world desperately seeking both to mitigate the effects of past emissions and to reduce net emissions in the future.

Global warming could be an opportunity for Africa – an opportunity to obtain state-of-the-art energy efficiency technology and land use tools, an opportunity to convert both barren land and biologically rich and diverse land into economic assets in a worldwide emission trading market,[51] and an opportunity to obtain funds to advance economic development and to restore and protect key features of its ecosystems. In other words, Africa faces both the necessity and the opportunity to follow the path of sustainable development. However, to exploit these opportunities land use law must be properly designed and implemented in all significant sectors of land use activity – design and use of urban and rural communities, agricultural law, forestry law, transportation, water law, energy use law, public health law, and environmental law.

Climate change is predicted to affect human health and welfare and ecosystem viability adversely across sub-Saharan Africa. The International Panel on Climate Change (IPCC) has identified human health, food security, settlements and infrastructure, natural resource management and biodiversity, and landscapes vulnerable to desertification as the areas in sub-Saharan Africa particularly vulnerable to global warming.[52] The IPCC

---

[50] The world currently uses 82 million barrels of petroleum daily; total current production exceeds daily demand by just 1 percent.

[51] As will be discussed *infra*, carbon sequestration into sinks may emerge as a more conceptually and pragmatically sound source of emission reduction credits than technology-based principles.

[52] Paul Desanker and Christopher Magadza, "Africa," in IPCC, *Climate Change 2001: Impacts, Adaptation, and Vulnerability* (James J. McCarthy et al., eds., Cambridge University Press 2001) 487–531 (hereinafter

believes that Africa is highly vulnerable to climate change because (1) many regions of Africa will be under increased water stress; (2) declines in agricultural production from warming and climate change spikes will jeopardize food security; (3) natural resources and biodiversity could be irretrievably lost or become less productive, causing economic and ecological hardship; (4) warming will expand the regions subject to vector- and water-borne disease to areas previously disease free and will further stress already inadequate health care capability across sub-Saharan Africa; (5) coastal zones vulnerable to sea-level rise will be at risk, and roads, bridges, buildings, and infrastructure in flood zones will be at greater risk from more extreme weather events and flooding.

A few examples of the adverse effects of climate change will help illustrate the scope of the climate change challenge to Africa's future. For instance, in Africa, a high percentage of people live by farming. Agriculture and livestock account for about half of household income and the poorest of rural Africans are the most dependent on agriculture for their economic survival. Agriculture and livestock husbandry are supported to an enormous extent by rainwater, which, in the best of times, is vulnerable to season shifts, weather, and precipitation variability. Sadly, Africa is already the continent with the lowest rate of conversion of precipitation to runoff. Unfortunately, the IPCC projections point to a 0.2°C–0.5°C increase per decade across Africa, with greatest warming over interior Africa, the semiarid regions near the Sahara, and central southern Africa. If the warming is at the low end, then the IPCC anticipates reduced rainfall over most of the Sahel, increased rainfall in east central Africa from December to February but reduced rain from June to August, and decreased growing seasons in southern Africa. If warming is at the upper end (0.5°C), then large portions of Africa will experience rainfall pattern changes significantly beyond changes expected from normal weather pattern variability. This warming will increase evaporation and reduce soil moisture, river basins will see reduced flow and reservoirs will have less water, lakes will shrink, and snow caps and glaciers will disappear. Important sources of freshwater for drinking and river flows will dry up. In Africa, the 300 million people who lived in water-scarce areas in 2000 will grow to about 600 million people who will be living in water-stressed regions. Agricultural output will drop,[53] requiring food imports. Inland fisheries will be at risk from drought, habitat harm, and increased pressure for fish as other agriculture diminishes. Additional demand on ocean fish will further stress fish stocks already endangered by overfishing, bleaching of coral reefs, and stressed coastal marshlands. Moreover, global warming may modify ocean currents, with potential fishery impacts.

Land use changes from population and development pressures will continue to be major drivers of land-cover change in Africa – and climate change will become

Desanker, "Africa," *IPCC Mitigation* [2001]; unless otherwise noted, the following summary of climate change impacts on Africa is taken from this source. The full report is available in print and at www.ipcc.ch/. See also Paul V. Desanker, *Impact of Climate Change on Life in Africa* (World Wildlife Fund 2002), available at www.panda.org.climate.

[53] A recent study suggests that African maize production will drop about 10 percent overall by 2055 as a result of climate change, while food production must double just to meet the basic nourishment needs of the growing poor population. However, local and regional variability will be much greater than 10 percent, with the 130 million poor livestock keepers in sub-Saharan Africa who rely on rain for their livestock feed (maize) at particular risk. Peter G. Jones and Philip K. Thornton, "The Potential Impacts of Climate Change on Maize Production in Africa and Latin America in 2055," 13 *Global Climate Change* 51–59 (2003).

increasingly important by the middle of the 21st century. These changes, exacerbated by climate change, adversely affect distribution and productivity of plant and animal species, water supply, firewood, and other biological services. Increased temperature will extend habitats of disease vectors such as malaria.[54] Increased droughts and flooding in areas with inadequate sanitation will increase epidemics and enteric diseases. Rift Valley fever will spread to areas that experience increased rainfall, increased lake and coastal ocean water temperature could increase cholera epidemics, and increased episodes of heavy rains could expand plague-carrying rodent populations that migrate to human settlements during droughts.[55] Currently inadequate infrastructure – transport, housing, drinking water, sanitation, electricity, and other services – will be stressed by floods, dust storms, and other extreme weather events. Sea level rise, coastal erosion, and saltwater intrusion into wetlands and aquifers will have a significant impact on coastal cities.[56] Semiarid and subhumid woodlands and savannahs are at risk from reduced rainfall, which can cause more fires, and more intense land use due to population pressure. Ecosystem services such as water regulation, carbon sequestration, soil fertility, and habitat formation will be adversely affected, as will domesticated livestock which (other than pigs) tend to be concentrated in semiarid zones of sub-Saharan Africa.[57]

The depth and richness of Africa's biodiversity will also be threatened by climate change, causing both economic and ecological harm. One-sixth of Africa is forested (5 million square kilometers), and trees and shrubs are important part of another 12 million square kilometers. Sub-Saharan Africa contains unique ecosystems whose flora and fauna are at risk from climate change. Critical flora biomes include Cape floral kingdom, Madagascar, Cameroon, and mountain habitats from Ethiopia to South Africa.[58] Desanker further reports that important fauna at risk include savannah and forest species (90 percent of the world's antelope and gazelle species are in Africa) and birds, whose habitat and migratory patterns are threatened by climate change. Biodiversity in Africa is an important source of food, fiber, shelter, fuel, medicine, and income from tourism. Climate change effects on savannahs will alter the major migrations in east Africa and southern Africa, as well as bird migration. Important, heat-sensitive African habitats, such as the mountain habitat that runs from Ethiopia to South Africa at elevations above 2,000 meters and the Cameroon mountain habitats, will be impaired as temperature increases. The South African Cape floral kingdom, with 7,300 species of which about 68 percent exist only there, will be changed by rainfall patterns, warming, and the potential appearance of fires due to reduced rain.[59]

4 CLIMATE CHANGE OPPORTUNITIES FOR AFRICA

Because Africa's capacity to adapt to climate change is low, it must start planning now both to help the world reduce greenhouse gas emissions and to help Africa adapt to the coming climate change effects. But all is not lost. Many important economic

---

[54] M. van Lieshout et al., "Climate Change and Malaria: Analysis of the SRES Climate and Socio-economic Scenarios," 14 *Global Environmental Change* (2004) 87–95.

[55] Desanker, "Africa," *IPCC Mitigation* (2001) 512–513.

[56] *Id.* at 514–516.   [57] *Id.* at 506–507.

[58] *Id.* at 511.   [59] *Id.* at 510.

opportunities to reduce emissions abound in Africa. First, Africa uses fossil fuels so inefficiently that ordinary improvements can have enormous beneficial impacts. For instance, many transportation improvements in sub-Saharan Africa are so beneficial they have negative costs: The benefits of paving roads are so great that they far exceed their costs and significantly reduce carbon emissions at a negative cost of −$41.42 tonnes of carbon (tC).[60] In other words, the economy gains money for each ton of CO_2 emissions eliminated by the improved transportation efficiency flowing from paved roads. Similarly, replacement of old, inefficient motors, boilers, and industrial furnaces with new, efficient, state-of-the-art equipment can be done at a negative or low cost of $/tC.[61] These suggestions are simply the tip of the energy efficiency bounty waiting to be claimed.[62]

Second, although sub-Saharan Africa has not been overly blessed with oil resources or other fossil fuels,[63] it has major untapped sources of renewable energy. These include biomass,[64] particularly agricultural wastes; wind energy;[65] solar (photovoltaic) energy;[66] hydroelectric energy;[67] and some geothermal (principally in the Rift Valley) energy.[68] Africa has 20 percent of the world's potential to generate energy from wind, an amount equal to that of all the so-called Economy in Transition Countries (i.e., Russia and other former Communist bloc nations), exceeded only by North America.[69] As for solar energy, sub-Saharan Africa has 19 percent of the world's potential.[70] However, other than in South Africa and a few countries with significant hydroelectric power, the predominant use of renewable resources, which accounts for about 70 percent of energy used, is the inefficient burning of traditional biomass (wood and charcoal) by the poor for cooking, and not wind or solar energy.

As for fossil fuel, most of its oil is exported from Africa; relatively little is directed to local populations. However, as the world moves forward with reducing greenhouse gas

---

[60] As of June 2005, carbon emission credits were trading in Europe at ° 23.00 (U.S. $27.79)/ton; (see www.pointcarbon.com;), so a project such as this could be worth nearly $70 per ton of carbon emission reductions.

[61] IPCC, *Climate Change 2001: Mitigation* (Bert Metz et al., eds., Cambridge University Press 2001), Table 3.12, 199, 200.

[62] See, e.g., Toru Kubo, Harvey Sachs, and Steven Nadel, *Opportunities for New Appliance and Equipment Efficiency Standards: Energy and Economic Savings beyond Current Programs* (American Council for an Energy-Efficient Economy, September 2001) iv, 5–6 (http://aceee.org). In the United States, just the present appliance efficiency standards will save electricity consumers about $186 billion by 2020; updating current standards to reflect efficiency improvements will save another $19 billion (net present value), and new standards on new products could save yet another $75 billion for equipment purchased through 2020.

[63] IEA, *Oil Market Report*, Table 3. Sub-Saharan Africa produced 5.2 mb/day in late 2004, but without Nigeria and Angola, sub-Saharan Africa produced only 1.77 mb/day. It also possesses significant reserves of oil and natural gas on its west coast, uranium, and 6% of the world's coal reserves. *Energy as a Tool for Sustainable Development for Africa, Caribbean and Pacific Countries* (Ugo Farinelli, ed., UNDP 1999) 23–25.

[64] IPCC, *Climate Change 2001: Mitigation*, Table 3.31, at 244.

[65] *Id.*, Table 3.32, at 246.   [66] *Id.*, Table 3.33a and 3.33b, at 247–248.

[67] *Id.*, Table 3.30, at 243.

[68] *Options for Greenhouse Gas Mitigation in an Integrated East African Power Development* (H. E. Meena, ed., The Centre for Energy, Environment, Science and Technology 2003) 18–19, available at http://uneprisoe.org/reportbooks.htm.

[69] IPCC, *Climate Change 2001: Mitigation*, Table 3.32, at 246.

[70] *Id.*, Table 3.33b, at 248.

emissions, market-based approaches will motivate significant investment in projects in sub-Saharan Africa that improve efficiency or harness renewable energy, thereby creating valuable, tradable carbon emission reduction credits.[71] These credits will emerge from capital invested in efficiency and renewable energy projects. Africa benefits by getting access to renewable energy, reducing its need for fossil fuels, improving the energy efficiency of its economy from agriculture to manufacturing, mitigating climate change, and becoming a region that blossoms from sustainable development.

Third, Africa has enormous capacity to sequester and preserve carbon in biomass – one-sixth of Africa (over 5 million square kilometers) is forested and another 12 million square kilometers is in agricultural land, pasture, and savannah that support large quantities of trees and woody shrubs.[72] Sequestration removes CO_2 from the atmosphere and stores it indefinitely in so-called carbon sinks such as trees, durable wood products, permanent grasslands, or soils.[73] Alternatively, Africa could reduce its future CO_2 emissions by protecting its extensive existing forest from deforestation.[74] Mitigation approaches include reforestation, afforestation, restoration of degraded lands, thickening of savannahs, fire management, sound forest management, agroforestry, slowing of deforestation, community woodlots, forest plantations, watershed management, urban forestry, expansion of durable wood products, and improvement or elimination of the efficiency or use of wood and charcoal for cooking.

5 THE NEED TO RECONSIDER LAND USE LAWS IN SUB-SAHARAN AFRICA

Managing land to conserve carbon involves projects that maintain existing carbon pools by establishing forest reserves, reducing deforestation, managing forests sustainably, developing minimally destructive timber harvest practices, developing fire and pest protection, and preventing forest deterioration from human migration. Beyond merely preserving existing stored carbon, land can also be managed to increase sequestered carbon. Expanding storage can be achieved by land use approaches designed and implemented to capture and store carbon through afforestation, reforestation, agroforestry, enhanced natural regeneration, revegetation of degraded lands, tillage and other agricultural practices to increase soil carbon, and management of forest products to increase in-use lifetimes. Land can also be managed to enhance the use of biomass for energy and as a replacement for use of energy-intensive materials. For instance, biomass could replace materials such as bricks, cement, steel, or plastic, whose manufacture requires large amounts of petroleum (either as an energy source or as raw material). Where energy is needed, sustainable biomass should replace fossil fuels wherever possible.[75]

---

[71] For a discussion of the legal and policy aspects of carbon credit trading see generally M. Lee, *CDM Information and Guidebook* (UNEP 2003) (www.cd4cdm.org); *Joint Implementation Quarterly* (www.jiqweb.org); *Carbon Finance at the World Bank* (carbonfinance.org); and Clean Development Mechanism (cdm.unfccc.int).

[72] IPCC, *Impacts, Adaptation, and Vulnerability* 508.

[73] IPCC, *Climate Change 2001: Mitigation* 303–335.

[74] Reversing current rates of deforestation in the Zaire basin could prevent over 20 billion tons of carbon from escaping into the atmosphere. Willy R. L. Makundi, *Mitigation Options in Forestry, Land-Use Change and Biomass Burning in Africa* (Lawrence Berkeley National Laboratory, Paper No. LBNL-42767, 1998) 3.

[75] http://yosemite.epa.gov/OAR/globalwarming.nsf/content/ActionsInternationalLandUse&Forestry.html.

These actions mitigate climate change and promote sustainable development by simultaneously advancing social, economic, and environmental values. Concrete social, economic, and environmental benefits independently justify undertaking them: Afforestation can create forests in bare land; reforestation returns woody biomass to depleted areas; agroforestry can expand agricultural production by intermixing trees and crops, provide soil and wind protection, improve forestry output, allow pastrosil-viculture for forest and livestock, and promote nontimber tree farms for rubber, tannins, bamboos, and others; urban and community forestry can add shade and wood; and savannah management for biomass storage can help restore and maintain overgrazed areas across Africa.[76] Burning wood or charcoal more efficiently or replacing them with modern fuels or electricity would reduce wood demand and shift burning of biomass to efficient, sustainable technologies.[77] These approaches support community growth, reduce poverty, reduce indoor air pollution and related pulmonary disease, prevent soil erosion and desertification, improve watersheds and river basin systems, promote intergenerational equity, and restore and protect ecosystems and biodiversity.

They can also generate investment capital from the developed world. Under the Kyoto Protocol,[78] every durable, valid, verifiable sequestered ton of carbon can generate a tradable credit that can offset greenhouse gas emissions anywhere in the world. Detailed procedures, rules, and regulations regarding trading at the international level and across Europe are becoming operational, and international institutions, both public and private, are now present to support worldwide carbon emission trading.[79] A global market for tradable credits is now emerging, with clearing prices at about U.S. $10 per ton. Prices are expected to rise substantially as developed countries move up the cost curve of greenhouse gas emission reduction strategies. Prices could rise to U.S. $50–100 per ton. Thus, complying projects under the Clean Development Mechanism (CDM) of the Kyoto Protocol (and such other greenhouse gas trading regimes that subsequently emerge) present enormous opportunity for Africa.

---

[76] Makundi, *Mitigation Options in Forestry*, 6–7.

[77] Sivan Kartha and Eric D. Larson, *Bioenergy Primer: Modernised Biomass for Sustainable Development* (UNDP 2000).

[78] Kyoto Protocol to the United Nations Framework Convention on Climate Change (UN Doc FCCC/CP/1997/L.7/add.1, reprinted in 37 *LLM* (signed 11 December 1997). On November 4, 2004, President Putin signed the bill by which Russia ratified the Kyoto Protocol; the Protocol will enter into effect 90 days after the ratification documents are deposited in the United Nation; Oleg Shchedrov, "Putin Signs Up Russia for Kyoto Pact," *Reuters* (5 November 2004), www.reuters.co.uk. The framework of rules and policies that regulate emission trading and control measures were developed at the Marrakech Conference of the Parties to the UNFCCC. The Marrakech Accords, UN Doc. FCCC/CP/2001?13/Add. 1–4 (2002). For analysis of the Marrakech Accords, see David R. Hodas, "Sustainable Development and the Marrakech Accords" in *The Law of Energy and Sustainable Development* (Adrian J. Bradbrook, Rosemary Lyster, Richard L. Ottinger, and Wang Xi, eds., Cambridge University Press 2005) 56–73; Matthew Vespa, "Climate Change 2001: Kyoto at Bonn and Marrakech, 29 *Ecology L.Q.* 395 (2002); and David A. Wirth, "The Sixth Session (Part Two) and Seventh Session of the Conference of the Parties to the Framework Convention on Climate Change," *American Journal of International Law* (July 2002).

[79] See, e.g., CDM Executive Board and its subsidiary units, cdm.unfccc.int; GHG Protocol Initiative of World Resources Institute and World Business Council for Sustainable Development, cdmwatch.org/; UNEP Risoe Centre on Energy, Climate and Sustainable Development, uneprisoe.org; Carbon Finance at the World Bank, carbonfinance.org/; International Institute for Sustainable Development, www.iisd.ca/; and CDM Watch, cdmwatch.org.

Sequestration and sound agricultural land use can generate carbon reduction credits that can be sold in the emerging market. Sound urban planning can improve transportation efficiency and reduce urban heat island effects. Land use laws should promote and not impede the use of renewable energy such as wind and solar, which generate desperately needed electricity. Land use law must also promote ecosystem and biodiversity protection. Land use laws promoting greenhouse gas emission reductions and sequestration will encourage foreign investment in state-of-the-art technology and renewable energy technology for agriculture, commercial and industrial activity, and transportation.

To seize this opportunity, however, sub-Saharan African must develop land use laws that promote CDM projects and remove legal, institutional, and political barriers to greenhouse gas mitigation. African land use law should promote adaptation to and mitigation of climate change. Climate change occurs (in human terms) relatively slowly, but are very long-lasting. Similarly, the impacts of land use laws emerge slowly, but remain permanently. By reworking African land use law to make it climate change "friendly," land use law can help Africa achieve low-cost adaptation by making climate change part of every land use decision. Decisions today can significantly reduce future harm from climate change. Similarly, land use law can promote greenhouse gas mitigation.

Climate change adds urgency to the project of reconsidering the structure and efficacy of Africa's land use and land tenure laws. Effectively designed land use laws can not only ease the tension between the drive to enhance the immediate economic output of land and the value of sequestering carbon. If policymakers construct and implement land use laws to accommodate carbon trading opportunities that the emerging international climate change laws present, then sub-Saharan Africa can invest in sequestration while enhancing agricultural productivity and food security.

Climate change presents a serious challenge to established land tenure rules throughout sub-Sahara Africa. These laws have produced (particularly as implemented by legal regimes burdened by corruption and lack of effective democratic governance) land use patterns characterized by the extremes of (a) many small, individually owned parcels, subject to state laws and an overlay of traditional community rights, and (b) vast parcels owned by the state and a few individuals. Urban land use planning laws are rare and weak. This system has impaired agricultural improvement.

Land laws must promote improved agricultural and grazing practices that decrease loss of topsoil, improve existing soils, restore and protect grasslands, and restore and protect trees, scrub wood, and forests. Forestry laws need to encourage sensitive harvesting of wood to protect biodiversity and limit greenhouse gas emissions caused by deforestation and soil disruption. Moreover, the land tenure laws must enable landowners to profit by engaging in these sustainable practices and to capture the carbon benefits of sequestration and emissions reduction projects. Legal analysis must identify within each nation's land laws whether the legal system inhibits or promotes carbon sequestration, and then align the legal rules with market incentives for GHG emission reductions and sequestration projects. Land use laws must also discourage land use patterns that increase emissions and inhibit adaptation to climate risk.

Unfortunately, time and space are too limited to address the scope of issues that must be considered in fashioning land use laws to promote sound climate change policy. What is critical, however, is that if lawyers, law professors, and students give to the project the desire to examine land use laws from an informed climate change perspective, legal and institutional solutions will appear, as they already are emerging around the world.[80] Africa has already made a start,[81] but the effort must now proceed in earnest.

---

[80] For example, China recently promulgated the regulation "Interim Measures for the Management of CDM Project Activities in China" to create the legal framework necessary to support foreign investment in CDM projects. *Joint Implementation Quarterly* (October 2004) 2, 5 at www.jiqweb.org.

[81] See, e.g., Stephen Karekezi et al., *Sustainable Energy Consumption in Africa* (African Energy Policy Research Network 2004) www.afrepren.org; *Options for Greenhouse Gas Mitigation in an Integrated East African Power Development* (H. E. Meena, ed., The Centre for Energy, Environment, Science and Technology, 2003) 18–19, http://uneprisoe.org/reportbooks.htm; *African Perspectives on the Clean Development Mechanism*, Papers presented at a regional workshop, New Partnerships for Regional Development: The Clean Development Mechanism under the Kyoto Protocol, Accra, Ghana, 21–24 September 1998 (August 1999) http://uneprisoe.org/CDM/Accra.

3 Climate Change Adaptation and Mitigation: Exploring the Role of Land Reforms in Africa

H. W. O. Okoth-Ogendo

1 THE CLIMATE CHANGE PHENOMENON

1.1 The Link with Anthropogenic Activities

The fact that global climate conditions have been changing beyond natural variability is now well established. Evidence accumulated over the last several decades indicates that this change has intimate links with anthropogenic – that is, human-induced – activities that are essentially responsible for substantially enhanced levels of emission of greenhouse gases (GHGs) into the atmosphere. The Intergovernmental Panel on Climate Change (IPCC), established in 1988, has conducted several assessments, which show that unless deliberate steps are taken to reduce GHG emissions in the coming decades, irreversible changes will occur in the global climate system. Most vulnerable to change are

- Global and regional temperature precipitation and other parameters
- Soil structure and moisture
- Global mean sea levels
- Frequency of extreme events associated with changes in absolute temperatures

The changes will, in turn, lead to a number of adverse effects, on, inter alia

- Ecological systems
- Health and epidemiological patterns
- Hydrological and water resource balance
- Food and fiber production
- Coastal and marine systems
- Human settlements
- Other socioeconomic sectors

This clearly poses an enormous challenge for international and domestic governance.

2 THE GLOBAL FRAMEWORK

2.1 The Climate Change Convention

Confronted with the evidence, the international community has, in the last decade, been involved in discussions about the steps necessary for mitigating or facilitating orderly adaptation to these changes and impacts. An agreement was eventually reached at the Rio de Janeiro Earth Summit in 1992 for a convention to define the strategies necessary for collective intervention into the climate change phenomenon. The United Nations Framework Convention on Climate Change (UNFCCC), which was concluded at Rio, has as its ultimate objective "[the] stabilization of greenhouse gas concentrations in the atmosphere at a level that would prevent dangerous anthropogenic interference with the climate system."[1] The Convention adds that the level envisaged should be achieved within a time frame sufficient to allow ecosystems to adapt naturally to climate change, to ensure that food production is not threatened, and to enable economic development to proceed in a sustainable manner.

Because the available scientific evidence, though substantial, is not entirely free of controversy, the UNFCCC is offered as a "framework" convention to

- Enable parties to build global consensus on what needs to be done to confront the climate change phenomenon
- Facilitate the development of guidelines for the fulfillment of commitments until new and more accurate scientific evidence becomes available
- Provide a flexible mechanism for the enforcement of specific obligations
- Permit its further elaboration through the development of more appropriate protocols on specific issues

In that respect, the UNFCCC must be read together with other international environmental governance instruments, especially those negotiated since Rio, which are, in broad and/or specific terms, concerned, as is the UNFCCC, with the reduction and elimination of unsustainable patterns of development:

- The Convention on Biological Diversity (CBD)
- The United Nations Convention to Combat Desertification (UNCCD)
- The Forest Principles
- Agenda 21

2.2 The Kyoto Protocol

In response to commitments under the UNFCCC, the parties concluded an important protocol in Kyoto, Japan, in December 1997, under which emission reduction targets to 2012 were agreed especially for developed countries.[2] The question of ensuring compliance with the Protocol, however, is one that has not been satisfactorily resolved. Indeed, the Protocol itself does not establish an effective compliance regime and leaves the important question of dispute settlement to the vagaries of bilateral or multilateral negotiation or conciliation. In fact, as of today, the Protocol awaits ratification by either Russia or the United States of America to come into force.

As important a step as the conclusion of that Protocol may have been, its contribution to the management of the climate change phenomenon remains elusive. One must therefore turn to climate change management through domestic policies and programs.

---

[1] United Nations Framework Convention on Climate Change (1992) art. 2, available at http://unfccc.int/2860.php.

[2] The Kyoto Protocol (1997) is available at http://unfccc.int/resource/docs/convkp/kpeng.html.

3 DOMESTIC MANAGEMENT OF CLIMATE CHANGE

3.1 The International Policy Framework

Under Article 4 (1)(f) of the UNFCCC, the parties commit themselves to "take climate change considerations into account . . . in their relevant social, economic and environmental policies and actions." The IPCC, in its Third Assessment Report, issued in 2001, has noted that the capacity of countries to adapt to and mitigate the effects of climate change can be enhanced when climate change policies are integrated into national development policies, "including economic, social and other environmental dimensions."[3]

It is not expected – and it is highly unlikely – that development policies, particularly in Africa, would expressly address climate change issues. What is important is to ensure that those policies should guide decision making toward strategies or capacity development that would permit adaptation to or mitigation of effects of global climate change.

3.2 Adaptation and Mitigation Measures

In addition to commitment to the need to integrate climate change issues into development policy, the UNFCCC expects parties to take precautionary measures to anticipate, prevent, or minimize the causes of climate change and mitigate its adverse effects. That expectation calls for strategic responses at macro- and microlevels that would enable parties to effect measures that would substantially reduce GHG emissions into the atmosphere and that would permit social systems and ecosystems to adapt naturally to adverse consequences of climate change. Parties are, therefore, expected to explore specific adaptation and mitigation options that best suit their particular circumstances.

Adaptation options comprise measures that would enable ecosystems and socioeconomic sectors to adjust in terms of processes, practices, and structures to projected or actual changes in climate parameters. Mitigation options, however, are anthropogenic interventions directed at reducing emissions or enhancing sinks of GHGs.

In order to ensure that adaptation and mitigation options are fully integrated into the policymaking process, it is important that countries

- Identify climate change–induced stress factors in various socioeconomic sectors
- Set targets for reduction of GHG emissions in terms that do not compromise overall development
- Initiate programs for enhancement of sinks
- Protect and conserve natural resources and biodiversity colonies
- Establish mechanisms for periodic review and assessment of the impacts of adaptation and mitigation options

3.3 Capacity Building

The ability to effect adaptation and mitigation measures will depend on a number of parameters, which include

- Existing institutions of economic governance
- The level of technology production and distribution

[3] Intergovernmental Panel on Climate Change, *Third Assessment Report* (Cambridge University Press) (2001).

- Financial resources
- Information exchange

Institutions of economic governance define the overall context in which climate-related anthropogenic activities or policies operate. More specifically, it is these institutions that shape the decision-making processes that generate or limit GHG emissions and other climate change agents, and the availability of resources for policy intervention. Development policy must therefore take account of the nature of the institutions of governance, particularly in sectors that are stress prone, or most likely to destabilize natural climate patterns. Institutions concerned with the control and management of land and land-based resources, energy production and utilization, and human settlements require redesign. Special attention must be directed to the structure and functions of these and similar institutions.

The level of technology production and distribution in any society will determine the speed with which adaptation or mitigation measures can proceed and the quality of their outcomes. In the context of agrarian societies, it is the technology of production and management of land-based resources that one must look to in the design of adaptation and mitigation measures.

Availability of financial resources is always crucial to the success of any development initiative. Depending on the nature of the stress factors induced by climate change in specific sectors, countries require considerable resources to engage in meaningful planning and execution of relevant adaptation and mitigation measures.

The quality of information available for planning and execution of those measures and the rate at which it is available must also be considered. It is information exchange that will determine the extent to which technology and expertise flow into and are used in planning and execution of those measures.

4 EXPLORING THE ROLE OF LAND REFORMS

4.1 The Link between Land Reform and Climate Change

Because Africa is still predominantly agrarian, capacity building for climate change adaptation and mitigation must focus primarily on the control and management of land and land-based resources, particularly in the context of

- Agriculture and related activities
- Forestry and grasslands
- Hydrology and water resources
- Human settlements

The reason is not merely that these remain the primary sources and sinks of GHG in Africa; they are also the most vulnerable to variations in climate parameters. Policies or strategies directed at these sectors are most likely to have a direct effect on climate change. Indeed, as increased food demand due to rapid population growth exerts pressure on land and land resources in Africa, the need for policies and strategies directed at both adaptation to and mitigation of climate change effects will become important. What this implies is that in addition to the more direct measures that individual African countries may well be pursuing, ongoing land reform programs could add significantly to Africa's overall efforts at climate change management. The extent of that contribution will depend on ways specific components of the land reform program in each country are designed and executed.

4.2 Land Reform Processes

Many countries in East, Central, and Southern Africa are in the process of reforming their land sectors in a variety of ways, which include

- Design of new land policies
- Reform of tenure systems
- Reform of land use structures
- Reform of land administration

(a) Design of New Land Policies

Countries that have completed the design of new land policies include the following:

- Tanzania (1995)
- Mozambique (1995)
- South Africa (1996/1997/1998)
- Ghana (1998)
- Zambia (1999)
- Namibia (1999)
- Rwanda (2000)
- Malawi (2001)

The following are in the process of designing policies:

- Zimbabwe
- Swaziland
- Lesotho
- Kenya
- Uganda

The general thrust of these policies is to establish a land system that is economically efficient, socially equitable, environmentally sustainable, and operationally account-able to the people. These policies also seek to establish a normative and institutional framework that would ensure that land and land-based resources are held, used, and managed efficiently, productively, and sustainably. Assessed in terms of their probable contribution to climate change adaptation and mitigation, these policy focuses create a threshold upon which informed decisions on land and land-based resource use can be made. Because their primary objective is to ensure sustainable use of land, the new policies direct particular attention to the economic, social, and environmental sectors most vulnerable to climate change.

(b) Reform of Land Tenure Systems

Beyond the design of land policies, many African countries have initiated far-reaching reforms in land tenure arrangements. That exercise is generally directed at four main objectives.

The first is to facilitate effective exercise of proprietary functions and in particular to facilitate

- Freedom of decision making, including the ability to allocate resources between alternative uses
- Control and management of land resources in the context of declared or implied local and national land policy goals
- Disposition of proprietary resources for similar or alternative uses

The exercise of proprietary functions determines the baseline for resource exploitation and its expected response to or impact on climate change parameters in terms of

- Local adaptive strategies in the light of perceived or actual changes in those parameters
- Specific anthropogenic interventions to arrest adverse consequences of those parameters
- Mitigation of GHG emission potential of particular land uses

Advantage can be taken of that baseline if, in the exercise of those functions, individual land users have the flexibility to convert national climate change policies – where these exist – into cost-effective and economically sound land development options.

The second is to guarantee security of access to the resources to which proprietary rights relate. Such security would relate not only to the physical *solum* itself but also to its products and the stream of economic and social benefits derived from those products. Although security of access has always been central to debates on land tenure reform in Africa, much of this has turned on whether or not certain land tenure models are best suited for that purpose.[4] Whatever position one might take on that issue, what is relevant here is that unless security is guaranteed to both present and future generations of land users, the quality of the resources themselves is unlikely to be sustained over time. The incentive to take account of all parameters that could impact adversely on that quality, including those relevant to climate change, could be considerably reduced if the ultimate objective of secure access to land were merely to guarantee consumptive utilization of resources by the present generation of land users. For climate change adaptation and mitigation purposes, therefore, it is essential that security of access to land and land-based resources be guaranteed in perpetuity *across* generations.

The third is to enhance the intrinsic characteristics of land, both as a resource and as a value. While this is generally considered as a derivative of the special characteristics of particular tenures, reform of land tenure structures in and of itself often reshapes land as an economic, political, and ethical asset. The extent to which such land becomes "liberated" for the market, free from externalities arising from other decision-making centers in the public realm, is usually regarded as important evidence of enhanced value. The other is whether a public ideology about the centrality of land in social relations has developed as a standard with which to evaluate public and private land use decisions. In either case, the expectation is that tenure regimes can be so reformed as to facilitate outcomes that would not jeopardize the essential characteristics of the resource itself.

---

[4] See J. Bruce and S. Migot-Adholla (eds.), *Searching for Land Tenure Security in Africa* (Kendall-Hunt) (1994).

The fourth is to ensure social and political fairness in the allocation of land resources in particular contexts. This is particularly evident in the case of reforms that are distributive or restitutive in nature. In addition to their obvious value as instruments for the redress of economic and social grievances, such reforms enable societies to arrest potential abuse of land resources, especially in marginal and protected areas. Abuses include loss of land cover through indiscriminate invasion of fragile ecosystems or the destruction of forests and water-catchment areas. In addition, distributive or restitutive reforms stimulate productive use of land that would otherwise have remained idle, thus enabling society to add to its stock of food and fiber.

(c) Reform of Land Use Structures

Reform of land tenure systems is usually accompanied by changes in the institutional structures through which national and local policies about the management and performance auditing of particular land uses can be infused into or internalized for land use decision making. Such changes are generally designed to facilitate five objectives.

The first is to provide a framework for standard setting in land use matters. This is particularly important in the context of environmental governance and productivity targeting. The thrust of standard setting is to ensure that the exercise of proprietary functions does not compromise national policy goals, especially those directed at sustainable management of resources. Because of the tendency to approach land use issues on a sector-by-sector basis, however, the result has been for standard-setting institutions to proliferate. Internal conflicts and jurisdictional overlaps are, therefore, common. These have reduced their efficacy as instruments for local decision making.

The second is to enable state or community organs to audit the performance of specific land use requirements. Performance auditing – that is, the ability to direct, monitor, and evaluate land use outcomes or to secure compliance with specific obligations – is clearly fundamental to land use planning and management. In most jurisdictions in Africa, however, this is either totally lacking or simply left to the inefficient province of criminal sanctions. If land use structures are to contribute to sustainable development, simpler and more participatory approaches to performance auditing must be designed.

The third objective of reforming land use structures is to facilitate the control of, or the exercise of trusteeship over, sensitive ecosystems. This, historically, is an area of great controversy, particularly in Africa, where pressure to categorize all land resources under anthropogenic activities remains justifiably strong. That notwithstanding, however, most countries now recognize that certain ecosystems not only are uniquely sensitive to human interference but also constitute a special heritage deserving conservation and preservation for posterity. The fact that such a large number of countries are parties to the Convention on Biological Diversity is one proof of this. The other is the increase, during the last three decades, of national pieces of legislation to protect and manage the environment.[5]

The fourth is to provide infrastructure for the delivery of support services to land use operations generally. It is now established that land tenure changes per se will not provide necessary and sufficient conditions for sustainable land use. Conscious attempts

---

[5] See H. W. O. Okoth-Ogendo and G. Tumushabe, *Governing the Environment: Political Change and Natural Resources Management in Eastern Africa* (ACTS Press) (1999), available at http://www.acts.or.ke/Governing%20-%20contents.htm.

must also be made to create an environment of supplementary services to land users. Institutions set up for this purpose may take a variety of forms. Some consist essentially of mechanisms through which national assistance is channeled to strategic production sectors. Others involve the provision of basic threshold resources necessary for effective land use.

The fifth is to provide a framework for the infusion of new and efficient technologies into land use systems. The relationship between land use systems and technologies of production is complex. While a great deal of information about the impact of technology on land use structures is available, not much has been written on the reverse relationship: that is, the impact of reform of land use structures on technology choices. And yet it seems obvious that particular policy orientations can and do impede the diffusion or adaptation of certain technology options in land use matters. Similarly, particular policy orientations could facilitate such diffusion or adaptation in ways that enable given ecosystems and socioeconomic sectors to respond to the challenges of sustainability.

The starting point for Africa is to ensure that reform of the land sector takes account of indigenous technologies and affords opportunity for their orderly evolution and modernization. The drive toward large-scale mechanized agriculture, supported by expensive imports in the form of machines, fertilizers, and accessories, is not likely, therefore, to strengthen that linkage. Indeed, the widespread collapse of mechanized irrigation systems throughout Africa is clear proof of the danger of bypassing indigenous knowledge systems in agriculture.

Beyond this, it is important that reform of the land sector should permit the use of affordable and adaptable techniques of production, even where productivity gains are not as dramatic as would be achieved with the employment of so-called modern technologies. Experience has demonstrated that the "modern" imported technologies are not only destructive of the environment but also difficult to replicate and domesticate. Consequently, the use of such technologies is not sustainable – as will be discovered long after whatever fund of indigenous knowledge and technology has been forgotten or rendered obsolete.

(d) Reform of Land Administration

Many African countries assume that land administration mechanisms, such as

- Land allocation structures
- Land registration and recordation systems
- Land dispute processing mechanisms
- Land inventory mechanisms

need not be redesigned to take account of the overall objectives of land sector reform. The reason is that these mechanisms are often treated as part of the overall public or political administration function. As such, little attempt is often made to "professionalize" them or to ensure that they are integrated into land reform strategies.[6]

And yet it should be obvious that the performance of land administration institutions is crucial to the overall performance of the land sector, and this for several reasons.

---

[6] See H. W. O. Okoth-Ogendo, *Land Administration: The Neglected Factor in Land Reform in Africa*, paper for the World Bank Regional Workshop on Land Issues in Africa and the Middle East, Kampala, Uganda, 29 April–2 May 2002.

First, land administration mechanisms define the overall governance context in which land operations take place. It is always important to ensure that all functional components of land, as a factor of production, are clearly identifiable and easily accessible. Anthropogenic activities on land cannot be efficiently executed without this qualifier. In recent times, this has become a major issue as organs of civil society seek greater freedom in governance processes at all levels. Second, land administration mechanisms prescribe an important foundation upon which decision-making processes and outcomes in land use are based. This is primarily because the basic information required to make rational land use decisions is often generated by or through these mechanisms. As inputs into land use decision making, therefore, land administration mechanisms also determine the ways development resources to the land sector are allocated. Reform of land administration mechanisms must therefore form part of a comprehensive land reform program.

4.3 Further Climate Management Implications

By creating a new environment for land sector operations consisting, inter alia, of new

- Land policies
- Proprietary systems
- Land use decision-making structures
- Land administration mechanisms

land reform in Africa can assist ecosystems and socioeconomic sectors to adapt to the impacts of climate change in a variety of ways. Land reform can also provide opportunity to build a wide range of mitigation measures into overall land sector operations.

(a) Ecosystem Adaptation

The contribution of land reforms to ecosystem adaptation could occur at three levels. First, they would facilitate the protection of existing land cover through effective management and monitoring of land use change. A set of carefully designed land use rules, for example, could enable society to prevent wanton destruction of forests, watersheds, biodiversity colonies, and grasslands. In addition to ensuring that ecosystems are able to respond naturally and systematically to climate change parameters, the protection of land cover has important climate change mitigation effects through reduced GHG emissions and/or increased availability of sinks and reduction of threats to desertification.

Second, because many reform packages now permit direct community participation in environmental governance, opportunity is now available for the development of civil society networks in ecosystem protection and preservation. Sensitive ecosystems or resources of special heritage can be and in a number of jurisdictions have been put under common management, defined as perpetuated trusteeships designed especially for their preservation across generations. Civil society networks, fired by a new sense of environmentalism, have, in consequence, become important factors in the climate change debate.

Third, because a great deal of emphasis is now placed on systematic land use planning, contemporary land reform packages now provide opportunity to anticipate the consequences of current anthropogenic activities. Even where land use plans at the national and local levels are not strictly observed, the fact that an increased number of them are now available is proof of their importance in ecosystem management.

(b) Socioeconomic Sector Adaptation

Land reforms could assist socioeconomic sectors to adapt to climate change issues by creating the necessary political space in several directions.

First, land reforms can create an environment for efficient use of new and renewable resources and, in particular, exploitation and regeneration of indigenous sources of energy. Where the technology of regeneration is also affordable, socioeconomic sectors may thus be able to support existing ecosystems as well. This balance usually is achieved through land use regulations that require users to ensure that energy sources, such as wood fuel and biomass, are developed and utilized alongside normal agrarian activities. In conditions of intensive population pressure, such provisions are by and large unavoidable.

Second, evidence from Asia indicates that land reforms can trigger demographic responses leading to lower rates of population growth. Such responses could relieve stress on land by encouraging the development of non–land-based enterprises. Alternatively, the adoption of new production technologies in conditions of land scarcity could lead to greater intensity of land use even in the absence of dramatic or demographic responses.

(c) Design of Mitigation Measures

The enactments of new land use and administration institutions could provide opportunity for the design of proactive mitigation strategies, especially in terms of rapid response to extreme events arising from variability in climate parameters. By eliminating excessive protection of private property and increasing the stake of the state and the public in proprietary land use, reform can create legitimacy for the planning and execution of radical measures in emergency situations. This would include capability for

- Early warning
- Emergency response and rapid deployment
- Strategic resource reserve building
- Constant monitoring of trends in the occurrence of those events

Mitigation measures of this kind could thus be executed without resort to lengthy legal tussles.

5 CONCLUSION

This chapter argues that land reform process comprising, inter alia, policy changes, tenure reform, redesign of land use structures, and reconceptualization of land administration functions could provide opportunities for

- The creation of adaptive thresholds
- Mitigation interventions

in the management of climate change effects. The underlying premise of this argument is that the primary goal of land reform is to create macro- and microlevel frameworks for the sustainable management and development of land and land-based resources.

Adaptive thresholds, it is suggested, will be enhanced once proprietary systems and land use and administration structures begin to respond to stress factors induced by climate change. One direct way in which these systems and structures will respond to those factors is by shaping the decision-making processes that generate or limit GHG emissions or other climate change agents. This further provides opportunity for deliberate mitigation strategies in the course of development.

For land reform processes in Africa to contribute fully to climate change adaptations and mitigation, it is important that those parameters be fully integrated into overall development policymaking and planning. The process of integration must be based not only on accurate scientific information but also on accurate assessment of vulnerability of important social and environmental sectors that land reform processes target. It is that assessment that will determine the nature and timing of responses to climate change in any particular context.

Because this chapter offers no empirical data in support of the propositions it makes, it may be useful to explore, through longitudinal studies, precisely how and to what extent various components of land reform can make that contribution. One approach would be to generate data that would demonstrate

- Climate change impacts on specific ecosystems and socioeconomic sectors
- The various ways in which these systems and sectors have adapted over time to those impacts
- Adaptation responses attributable directly or indirectly to the manipulation of specific components of land reform
- Ways some of these components have impeded the adaptive capacities of those systems and sectors
- Interventions, if any, that specific countries have taken to mitigate climate change effects

The results of such a study would enable us to make authoritative statements about the relationship between land reform and climate change adaptation and mitigation in Africa.

4 The Integration of Landscape into Land Use Planning Policy in Relation to the New European Landscape Convention

Michel Prieur

1 INTRODUCTION

The European Landscape Convention is the first regional convention exclusively dedicated to the landscape issue.[1] It was opened for signature in Florence, Italy, on 20 October 2000 and entered into force on 1 March 2004.[2] It had been elaborated by the Council of Europe, which is an international intergovernmental organization set up in 1949, based in Strasbourg, France. Composed of 45 member states from Eastern and Western Europe, the Council has as its main objective the promotion of democracy, human rights, and the rule of law.

In a modern way that is in keeping with the universal principles of the Rio Declaration, the new convention gives practical effect to the Pan-European Biological and Landscape Diversity Strategy,[3] which environment ministries of 55 countries approved in Sofia, Bulgaria, on 25 October 1995, to contribute to the implementation of the Rio Convention of 1992 on biological diversity. Action Theme No. 4 of that European Strategy, entitled "Conservation of Landscapes," had the following aims to be achieved by the year 2000:

> To prevent future deterioration of landscapes and their associated cultural and geological heritage in Europe and to preserve their beauty and identity. To correct the lack of integrated perception of landscapes as a unique mosaic of cultural, natural, and geological features and to establish a better public and policy-maker awareness and more suitable protection status for these features throughout Europe.

In the past, the perception of landscape was strongly linked with that of the conservation of nature. The division of concepts distinguishing and separating culture and nature had predominated for a long time. The reconciliation of the concepts of culture and nature is the fruit of the evolution of ideas and the association of scientific disciplines. Nowadays, landscape as an expression of the perception of space by the people appears not only through natural landscapes, which are in reality designed and worked by humans, but also through artificial landscapes constructed by humans as monumental works of art or in the building of cities. The landscape is not an empty and abstract vision of the countryside but is a working place. Since landscape reflects human activity,

---

[1] "La convention européenne du paysage" (2003), Revue européenne de droit de l'environnement, 3. The text of the Convention is available online at http://conventions.coe.int/Treaty/en/Treaties/Html/176.htm.

[2] The Council of Europe at http://www.coe.int.

[3] Pan-European Biological and Landscape Diversity Strategy at http://www.strategyguide.org/fulltext.html.

both monumental and ordinary, one can speak of cultural landscapes in both rural and urban environments.

In reality, landscape, as the European Convention stresses, is both intrinsically natural and cultural to whoever is contemplating it. Landscape only exists as such because of human perception, which is the reflection of one's culture. But everyone has his or her own perception of landscape. The same landscape is not perceived in the same way by all the people who look at it. Whether they are local peasants, foreign tourists, architects, artists, or commercial travelers, they will not have the same perception of a given space, but they can agree on minimal criteria or preferences for what should be a satisfactory landscape.

What place does the law have in this debate – first in national law and second in international law?

Many States have incorporated landscape concerns into their legal systems, usually in an indirect or implicit way. But in the past few years, everywhere landscape has become an increasing focus of interest. With the entry of the environment into public policies in the 1970s, the landscape became an element or a component of the environment along with water, air, fauna, and flora. As a crossroad concept – with overlapping natural and cultural elements – landscape, having become an object of law, will be implicated in all types of legislative issues concerning environment, urbanism, land use planning, and agriculture. There are generally three categories of States:

- Where landscape legislation is part of legislation on historical monuments and sites, emphasizing the aesthetic and cultural aspects of landscape: Landscape policy depends upon the administration of arts and culture.
- Where landscape legislation is part of legislation on nature protection – placing the emphasis on the natural features of the landscape and its ecological components and including landscape as an element of protected areas policy: Landscape policy depends upon the administration of nature conservation, either as part of agricultural administration or as part of environmental administration.
- Where landscape legislation is part of the legislation on land and urban planning: Landscape policy is part of housing and territorial planning administration.

The European Convention tries to subdivide these divisions so that landscape becomes a common policy for all administrative bodies to express both cultural and natural values.

At the international level, landscape is also naturally attached to three special sectors: historical and cultural heritage, natural environment, and town and country planning. In a critical way, one can notice that Agenda 21 of the Rio Conference on Environment and Development of 1992 contains no express reference to the landscape. Only indirect references are found in Chapter 11 on deforestation and Chapter 36 on public education and awareness raising.[4]

There are few regional conventions that expressly refer to the landscape. We can mention

- The Washington convention of 12 October 1940 on nature protection and wildlife preservation in the Western Hemisphere, which aims to protect scenery of extraordinary beauty

---

[4] United Nations Department of Economic and Social Affairs, Division for Sustainable Development at http://www.un.org/esa/sustdev/documents/agenda21/english/agenda21toc.htm.

- The Benelux convention of 8 June 1982 on conservation of nature and the protection of landscapes
- The Apia convention of 12 June 1976 on conservation of nature in the South Pacific, which provides protection of outstanding landscapes
- The Espoo convention of 25 February 1991 on impact assessment on the environment in a transboundary context, which includes the among the effects of a proposed activity on the environment the activity's effects on landscape as well as on cultural heritage
- The special protocol of 20 December 1994 on the protection of nature and the maintenance of landscapes in the Alps, which indicates protective measures for maintaining alpine landscapes

At the universal level, the famous United Nations Educational, Scientific, and Cultural Organization (UNESCO) convention of 16 November 1972 concerning the Protection of the World Cultural and Natural Heritage mentions landscape as an element of the world heritage, but only landscape of outstanding universal value.[5] The 16th session of the World Heritage Committee, in Santa Fe in 1992, introduced a new category of cultural landscapes.[6]

In all these international instruments, as mainly in national laws, landscape appears always as a space of special value, considered remarkable and recognized and protected as such.[7] The main innovation of the European Convention on Landscape is to take into account the landscape as a permanent and ordinary component of daily life – an element of the human environment that needs special and continuous attention independent of its value or beauty.

We will study the main objectives and principles of the Convention as innovative targets and then present the essential mechanisms of implementation.

2 INNOVATIVE OBJECTIVES AND PRINCIPLES OF THE LANDSCAPE CONVENTION

The European Landscape Convention takes as its starting point the observable fact of landscape deterioration everywhere in terms of landscape quality and diversity. Economic development should not be a factor in deterioration of the quality of life and of the environment. But there is no progress in environmental protection without the education and participation of the public. The environment as the common heritage of the people involves rights and obligations for everyone regarding its management and protection. That is why the Convention's main objectives and principles are concerned with guaranteeing three elements:

- The well-being of all
- Sustainable development
- The promotion of democracy in landscape policy

[5] Convention Concerning the Protection of the World Cultural and Natural Heritage, art. 1, para. 3, available at http://portal.unesco.org/en/ev.php-URL_ID=13055&URL_DO=DO_TOPIC&URL_SECTION=201.html.

[6] See "Cultural Landscapes: The Challenges of Conservation," Ferrara, 11–12 November 2002, UNESCO, 2003.

[7] IUCN, SFDE, "Landscape Conservation Law," IUCN Environmental Policy and Law No. 39, 2000.

Before examining these three elements, it is worth noting the definition and the territorial scope of the Convention, which reflect the modern vision of landscape in public policies.

The Convention gives a broad and abstract definition *of landscape*:

> Landscape means an area, as perceived by people, whose character is the result of the action and interaction of natural and/or human factors.[8]

This definition – which, a priori, does not attribute particular value to landscape (landscape exists without being qualified as remarkable or aesthetic) – takes into account the notion that landscape evolves with time, under the effect of natural forces and the action of human beings. It also emphasizes the idea that the landscape is a complete entity, in which natural and cultural elements are considered simultaneously. To define more completely the Convention's field of territorial application, Article 2 indicates that it applies to natural, rural, urban, and suburban areas. The landscape in question can be land as well as water, inland waters (lakes, ponds), and marine areas (coastal zones, territorial seas). The originality of the Convention lies in its application to ordinary landscapes as well as to outstanding ones, because they all are important for people's quality of life. It even applies to degraded landscapes, inasmuch as they require urgent intervention in order to restore them.

2.1 Landscape as a Key Element of Well-Being for All

Human activity, whether industry, agriculture and forestry, or construction of infrastructure and building for various purposes, has visual as well as physical impacts, modifying the individual's perception of his or her surroundings. It may even cause what some people describe as visual pollution.

The landscape is a familiar part of everyone's daily scene and plays a part in people's sense of belonging to a particular place and a particular community. So on a conscious or even unconscious level it contributes to mental well-being. Unspoiled landscapes probably play a part in combating violence. Those who visit an area, as tourists or for work, take away an impression of a particular identity and a local distinctiveness, leading them to judge their experience of the area positively or negatively. Both local people and visitors will see the landscape as a factor in quality of life.

As mentioned during the meeting of the workshop for the implementation of the European Landscape Convention:

> Research has presented strong evidence of the restorative effect of green spaces in cities, such as green environment for hospitals, schools and other public buildings, urban parks and urban forests, as a resource for mental and physical health. This can be turned into monetary values for society through decreased costs for public healthcare. Such research can better provide convincing arguments for politicians that urban landscapes must contain high quality green spaces for human well-being and the quality of urban life. In this context, the European Landscape Convention

---

[8] European Landscape Convention, *supra*, note 2, art. 1(a).

can also provide a powerful tool to establish the position of the urban design issue as comprising a landscape dimension.[9]

As stated in Article 5(a) of the Convention, landscapes are "an essential component of people's surrounding, an expression of the diversity of their shared cultural and natural heritage, and a foundation of their identity." It is because landscape cannot be separated from people's surrounding that it is "a key element of individual and social well-being," as affirmed in the Preamble to the Convention.

Clearly then, the Convention's purpose is to do everything possible to preserve that individual and collective well-being by means of officially formulated landscape policy, instead of letting landscape take shape and evolve spontaneously.

The fact that landscape involves a sensitive relationship to an area, without any ownership link between the beholder and the beheld, changes landscape into a genuine "common resource," in the words of the Preamble's penultimate paragraph. Because landscape is a common heritage and a shared resource, one should expect that society should take steps to preserve that heritage for present and future generations. The explanatory report to the Convention expresses this very well:

> In their diversity and quality, the cultural and natural values linked to European landscape are part of Europe's common heritage, and so European countries have a duty to make collective provisions for the protection, management and planning of these values.[10]

As landscape is both an essential component of community well-being and a common asset, the individual has rights and duties in respect of that asset; that is ample justification, if any were needed, for the obligation, repeatedly stated in the Convention, to involve the community in landscape policy. The Preamble gives a clear statement of the close link between the individual's rights and duties and concern for well-being:

> The protection, management and planning of landscape entail rights and responsibilities for everyone.

2.2 Landscape Policy and Its Contribution to Sustainable Development

The European Landscape Convention's second main purpose is to help achieve sustainable development.[11]

Landscape is a component of the environment, just as water, air, and biological diversity are. Consequently, landscape policies must be so formulated as to fit in with the objectives of sustainable development. As the explanatory report notes:

> The concern for sustainable development expressed at the 1992 Rio conference makes landscape an essential consideration in striking a balance between preserving

[9] Ingrid Sarlov-Herlin, "New Challenges in the Field of Spatial Planning: Landscapes," in Second Meeting of the Workshop for the Implementation of the European Landscape Convention, Council of Europe, Strasbourg, 27–28 November 2003, T-FLOR 3 (2003)12 Final.

[10] Council of Europe, European Landscape Convention Explanatory Report, paragraph 30, available at http://conventions.coe.int/Treaty/EN/Reports/Html/176.htm.

[11] See "The European Landscape Convention," *Naturopa*, No. 98–2002, Council of Europe, Strasbourg, available at http://www.coe.int/T/E/Cultural_Co-operation/Environment/Resources/Naturopa_Magazine/naturopa98_e.pdf?L=E.

the natural and cultural heritage as a reflection of European identity and diversity and using it as an economic resource capable of generating employment in the context of the boom in sustainable tourism.[12]

This is why the Preamble to the Convention gives prominence to sustainable development as one of the treaty's objectives:

> Concerned to achieve sustainable development based on a balanced and harmonious relationship between social needs, economic activity and the environment. . . .

Sustainable development is now a goal built into all environmental policy, and landscape action is consistently referred to as a factor, of no less significance than others, in sustainable development. It is worth drawing attention here to the two basic principles that shape the concept of sustainable development, Principles 3 and 4 of the Rio Declaration of 1992:

> Principle 3: The right to development must be fulfilled so as to equitably meet developmental and environmental needs of present and future generations.

> Principle 4: In order to achieve sustainable development, environmental protection constitutes an integral part of the development process and cannot be considered in isolation from it.[13]

The conclusion of the Council of Europe seminar of the European Conference of the Ministers responsible for Regional Planning (CEMAT) in Lisbon (26–27 November 2001) on "Landscape Heritage, Spatial Planning, and Sustainable Development" stressed the connection between sustainable development and landscape:

> Agriculture and forestry should not be seen only as economic activities and use of land. They are indispensable tools for landscape management. Their operation methods should be held in line with the goals of prudent and rational use of land and sustainable spatial development.[14]

The fact is that by taking care of the landscape, we simultaneously promote local well-being, safeguard the environment, and protect economic activity. All the ingredients of sustainable development – social, ecological, and economic improvement – are thus involved here. Landscape also adds cultural values, which should be the fourth pillar of sustainable development. The explanatory report to the Convention makes that point several times:

> [T]his [individual, social, and cultural fulfilment] may help to promote the sustainable development of the area concerned, as the quality of landscape has an important bearing on the success of economic and social initiatives, whether public or private.[15]

> These various treatments [of landscapes] may allow an important socio-economic development of the areas concerned.[16]

---

[12] European Landscape Convention Explanatory Report, *supra*, note 11, paragraph 36.

[13] Rio Declaration on Environment and Development (12 August 1992) A/CONF.151/26 (Vol. I), available at http://www.unep.org/Documents/Default.asp?DocumentID=78&ArticleID=1163.

[14] CEMAT, Proceedings, Lisbon, Portugal (26–27 November 2001), available at http://www.coe.int/T/E/Cultural%5FCo%2Doperation/Environment/CEMAT/Publications/ERP66_Lisbon.pdf?L=E.

[15] European Landscape Convention Explanatory Report, *supra*, note 11, paragraph 24.

[16] *Id.*, paragraph 27.

The Preamble of the Convention, which, legally, has the same force as the body of the text, states the economic as well as the social impact of landscape:

> [The landscape] constitutes a resource favourable to economic activity . . . whose protection, management and planning can contribute to job creation.

2.3 Landscape Policy and the Promotion of Active Democracy

Since landscape is considered as an individual and collective heritage, the entire population has the right to be associated with public decisions on that heritage. In the past, landscape as heritage interested only artists, painters, and poets. Then the experts, architects and landscape architects, were the spokespersons for the landscape issue. Today, landscape has become everyone's affair; thus landscape has a role to play in democratic citizenship. The legal treatment of landscape requires democratic procedures for information and participation – something of a leitmotiv in the Convention. As expressed in the explanatory report:

> If people are given an active role in decision-making on landscape, they are more likely to identify with the areas and towns where they spend their working and leisure time. If they have more influence on their surroundings, they will be able to reinforce local and regional identity and distinctiveness and this will bring rewards in terms of individual, social and cultural fulfilment.[17]

To make the exercise of power concerning landscape more democratic, the Landscape Convention is inspired by the principles of the Aarhus Convention of 1998 concerning access to information, public participation in the decision-making process, and access to justice concerning the environment.[18]

Under Article 5(c) of the Landscape Convention, parties have a legal obligation to establish procedures for participation. This means participation not only by the public but also by all parties concerned, including local elected representatives; economic, social, and cultural workers; and experts on landscape.

There are three elements related to participation in landscape policy: the scope of participation, participation arrangements, and participation effects.

The Scope of Participation

The scope of participation is extremely wide in different stages of decision making. First, there is participation in working out landscape policies, with Article 5(c) of the Convention referring to Article 5(b). This is the moment when the principles and strategies of landscape policy are set. It involves national policy as well as local and regional policies. The identification and assessment processes in Article 6(c) are part of it, as is the setting of a landscape quality objective in Article 6(d). Participation here precedes detailed decision making and concerns only planning and strategy.

The second step in participation is related to implementation of policies and plans. It is the step when decisions are to be taken on protection, management, and development

---

[17] *Id.*, paragraph 24.

[18] Convention on Access to Information, Public Participation in Decision-Making, and Access to Justice in Environmental Matters, Aarhus, Denmark, 25 June 1998, available at United Nations Economic Commission for Europe http://www.unece.org/env/pp/documents/cep43e.pdf.

that participation must be provided for. This corresponds to participation in decisions on specific activities of the Aarhus Convention Article 8.

Participation Arrangements

Participation arrangements are not specified in the Landscape Convention, since it is a framework convention. Each State must organize specific participation procedures. The objective is to identify the "aspirations of the public"[19] and "the particular values" that interested parties and the population concerned assign to landscapes.[20] This requires, for instance, consultative bodies, or public inquiries or hearings, or independent mediator intervention, or even local referenda (advisory or with decisive effect). The public must be able to submit comments, information, analyses, or opinions whether written or oral.

Participation Effects

Participation is designed as an aid to decision making, not a substitute for it, except in the case of a direct democratic instrument such as a local referendum. To what extent is participation really able to influence the official decision? While the European Landscape Convention says nothing about this, the Aarhus Convention mentions that the public must be informed of the decision taken and the reasons and considerations on which the decision is based. In other words, the public decision must take due account of public participation. A review before an administrative authority and/or a court will then test whether due account has been taken.

In practice, the success of this participation necessitates prior implementation of all the awareness raising, education, training, and information that the Aarhus Convention foresees in its Articles 6(a) and 6(b).

3 THE ESSENTIAL MECHANISMS OF IMPLEMENTATION OF THE LANDSCAPE CONVENTION

The European Landscape Convention is not very detailed as far as implementation is concerned. Since it is a framework convention, each State is free to choose different tools of implementation. But indirectly one can stress three essential mechanisms of implementation:

- Institutional instruments
- Inventories and education
- Integration instruments

3.1 Institutional Instruments

Although the Convention is silent as to what instruments should be used, the requirement to draw up landscape policy, to recognize landscape in law, and to integrate landscape into other policies calls for specific institutional instruments to perform those functions.

That does not necessarily mean the creation of a specific law on landscape. Giving legal recognition to the landscape issue can be achieved in a constitution or in any

---

[19] European Landscape Convention, *supra*, note 2, art. 1(c).
[20] *Id.*, art. 6-C(1)(b).

piece of legislation on environment or land use planning. But it is necessary to determine which administrative body is in charge of landscape policy. Nowadays there is an undoubted shift toward giving responsibility for landscape to the minister in charge of environment, because landscape is part of the definition of the environment and because landscape, like the environment, is a transsectorial topic. Ensuring that landscape is taken into account by all other administrations requires strong instruments of coordination. The ministry in charge of landscape should be vested with a leadership function and should participate in meetings with other departments on matters potentially affecting landscape. A good coordination instrument is the setting up of a specific national committee on landscape, with the participation of all ministries concerned and of landscape nongovernmental organizations (NGOs). In France, an order of 8 December 2000 set up a national landscape council managed by the Ministry of Ecology and Sustainable Development. Sometimes landscape falls within a specialized agency, as in Switzerland, with a federal office for environment with a landscape protection division.

3.2 Inventories and Education

Drawing up a specific policy on landscape requires both detailed knowledge of landscapes and qualified specialists in landscape sciences.

In order to define a national policy on landscape, inventory mechanisms are necessary. This implies surveys with updates and a special methodology. This also necessitates a multidisciplinary team with landscape specialists and is still too rarely foreseen. Of course the inventory and its organization are conditioned by the policy being followed. The methods and procedures will not be the same if only outstanding and remarkable landscapes are retained, or if, as required by the European Convention, the daily and ordinary landscapes, or even the degraded landscapes, are also retained.

Article 6(c) of the Convention requires the identification of all landscapes throughout the territory. Modern techniques of computerized topography and geographical information systems should be used to reveal the special characteristics of a landscape in rural areas and at the urban level. But after identification there should be an assessment of the landscape identified to analyze the forces and pressures transforming the landscape and to take note of changes. The result should be not a classification but a delicate work of qualification, taking into account the particular values assigned to landscapes by the interested parties and the population concerned. Then the collective determination of what the Convention calls the "landscape quality objectives" will allow the decision makers to adopt concrete measures for protection, management, or development, or a combination thereof, with all the facts in hand.[21]

This work of inventory and assessment must necessarily be carried out by professionals in conjunction with the population. A landscape policy needs to include the serious promotion of training for specialists in landscape appraisal and operations, as well as multidisciplinary programs in schools and universities. Landscape studies should be part of the ordinary training of architects, urbanists, planners, civil servants, lawyers, landscape planners, and landscape designers.[22]

---

[21] Yves Luginbuhl, "Landscape Identification and Assessment and Landscape Quality Objective," in "The European Landscape Convention," *Naturopa, supra*, note 12, at 17.

[22] See the European Council of Landscape Architecture Schools at http://www.eclas.org.

3.3 Integration Instruments and Landscape Planning

As Principle 4 of the Rio Declaration implies, the landscape issue must be an integral part of the development process and cannot be treated in isolation.

Article 5(d) of the Landscape Convention places an integration obligation on parties:

> Each party undertakes . . . to integrate landscape into its regional and town planning policies and its cultural, environmental, agricultural, social and economic policies, as well as in any other policies with possible direct or indirect impact on landscape.

The insertion of landscape into development and town planning programs and other plans is thus necessary through the drafting of specific landscape plans or through a special section on the landscape issue in each town planning instrument. This allows the determination of eventual landscape areas and makes it obligatory for the presence of a well-identified landscape to be taken into consideration. Integration of landscape into planning is a necessity.

According to a Swedish landscape planner:

> The aim of landscape planning and design can simply be expressed as aiming to con-serve and create good outdoor spaces, through the arrangement and composition of landform, water, vegetation and structures. Landscape planning also seeks to look beyond the visual aspects of landscape as scenery to the landscape structures and processes, which are the factors that influence the creation and evolution of land-scapes. A distinguishing feature of landscape planning is its holistic approach, aiming to look beyond some of the thematic "borders" within which many related profes-sions operate. It should cover everywhere and integrate all aspects and viewpoints, combining for example the perspectives and ideas about landscape of ecologists and archaeologists.[23]

Specific attention must be given to urban fringe landscape with industries, business parks, supermarkets, fuel stations, and housing developments: "Those urban fringe areas most clearly succumb to landscape globalization. They are nevertheless everyday landscape for people who live and work there, and perhaps one of the most distinctive cultural landscapes of our time."[24]

The guiding principles for sustainable spatial development of the European conti-nent, which were approved at the Hanover European Conference of Ministers respon-sible for Regional Planning in September 2000 and became an appendix to the Recom-mendation of the Committee of Ministers of the Council of Europe (30 January 2002), are presented as a coherent strategy for integrated development. That is why these guidelines contain a lengthy list of requirements to be met and of factors to be taken into account. One of these requirements sets up the landscape issue as a key element of a sustainable spatial development policy. As one commentator has written: "Spatial development policy, aiming at territorial and social cohesion, is, by characteristic and nature, especially suited to be the framework for the implementation of the Euro-pean Landscape Convention. Landscape policy must thus be an integral component of

---

[23] Ingrid Sarlov-Herlin, "New Challenges in the Field of Spatial Planning: Landscapes," *supra*, note 10, at 111.

[24] *Id.*, at 112.

spatial or territorial development policy. Both have a territorial basis, to be managed for sustainability, and are global and forward-looking."[25]

The urban landscape is becoming an important issue. It provides places of recreation and communication, as well as being a carrier of meaning and a guarantor of the environmental health of the city. Urban open space as part of landscape is becoming an essential component of the urban environment, with special attention to parks and gardens, sports grounds, riverbanks, pedestrian streets, abandoned industrial sites, and suburban areas as a whole. An interesting future research project in the European Union could be the beginning of a European network of cities for the urban landscape. The Landscape Education: New Opportunities for Teaching and Research in Europe (LENOTRE) project brings together 100 universities in Europe involved in teaching and research in landscape planning, design, and management.[26]

Outside the integration of landscape in planning instruments, it is at the level of individual building permits that landscape must be taken into account. Therefore, two legal procedures are necessary: impact studies and building permits. Both should integrate the landscape topic. The European Directive of 27 June 1985 states that impact studies must examine the direct and indirect effects of a project on the environment and therefore on the landscape, which is specially mentioned. The French Environmental Code includes impact on landscape as an element of the general impact study.

But all projects do not always need an impact study. For this reason, a methodology must be set up to control decisions that do not, which are the majority of decisions and which insidiously affect the unprotected landscape. In some national legislation there is always the possibility of refusing a building permit if the project threatens the landscape, even if the landscape is not protected. However, this refusal will only be considered if the landscape has certain aesthetic characteristics. A better legal solution is to require that any request for a building permit include a specific document presenting the effects of the building on the landscape, with graphic and photographic "before" and "after" illustrations. That is the situation in France under the landscape law of 1993. The purpose of this landscape dossier – linked to all building permits in both urban and rural areas – is to oblige the developer to consider the visual impact of a project and to help the public authority responsible for granting the permit consider more thoroughly the effect of all construction on landscape.

EUROPEAN LANDSCAPE CONVENTION

Preamble

The member States of the Council of Europe signatory hereto,

Considering that the aim of the Council of Europe is to achieve a greater unity between its members for the purpose of safeguarding and realising the ideals and principles which are their common heritage, and that this aim is pursued in particular through agreements in the economic and social fields;

---

[25] Maria José Festas, "Landscape and Spatial Planning Synergy," in "The European Landscape Convention," *Naturopa, supra,* note 12, at 14.

[26] Richard Stiles, "A European Network for the Urban Landscape?" in "Towns and Sustainable Development," *Naturopa,* No. 100–2003, at 10, available at http://www.coe.int/T/E/Cultural_Co-operation/Environment/Resources/Naturopa_Magazine/naturopa100_e.pdf?L=E.

Concerned to achieve sustainable development based on a balanced and harmonious relationship between social needs, economic activity and the environment;

Noting that the landscape has an important public interest role in the cultural, ecological, environmental and social fields, and constitutes a resource favourable to economic activity and whose protection, management and planning can contribute to job creation;

Aware that the landscape contributes to the formation of local cultures and that it is a basic component of the European natural and cultural heritage, contributing to human well-being and consolidation of the European identity;

Acknowledging that the landscape is an important part of the quality of life for people everywhere: in urban areas and in the countryside, in degraded areas as well as in areas of high quality, in areas recognised as being of outstanding beauty as well as everyday areas;

Noting that developments in agriculture, forestry, industrial and mineral production techniques and in regional planning, town planning, transport, infrastructure, tourism and recreation and, at a more general level, changes in the world economy are in many cases accelerating the transformation of landscapes;

Wishing to respond to the public's wish to enjoy high quality landscapes and to play an active part in the development of landscapes;

Believing that the landscape is a key element of individual and social well-being and that its protection, management and planning entail rights and responsibilities for everyone;

Having regard to the legal texts existing at the international level in the field of protection and management of the natural and cultural heritage, regional and spatial planning, local self-government and transfrontier co-operation, in particular the Convention on the Conservation of European Wildlife and Natural Habitats (Bern, 19 September 1979), the Convention for the Protection of the Architectural Heritage of Europe (Granada, 3 October 1985), the European Convention on the Protection of the Archaeological Heritage (revised) (Valletta, 16 January 1992), the European Outline Convention on Transfrontier Co-operation between Territorial Communities or Authorities (Madrid, 21 May 1980) and its additional protocols, the European Charter of Local Self-government (Strasbourg, 15 October 1985), the Convention on Biological Diversity (Rio, 5 June 1992), the Convention concerning the Protection of the World Cultural and Natural Heritage (Paris, 16 November 1972), and the Convention on Access to Information, Public Participation in Decision-making and Access to Justice on Environmental Matters (Aarhus, 25 June 1998);

Acknowledging that the quality and diversity of European landscapes constitute a common resource, and that it is important to co-operate towards its protection, management and planning;

Wishing to provide a new instrument devoted exclusively to the protection, management and planning of all landscapes in Europe,

Have agreed as follows:

CHAPTER I – GENERAL PROVISIONS

Article 1 – Definitions

For the purposes of the Convention:
>   a. "Landscape" means an area, as perceived by people, whose character is the result of the action and interaction of natural and/or human factors;

b. "Landscape policy" means an expression by the competent public authorities of general principles, strategies and guidelines that permit the taking of specific measures aimed at the protection, management and planning of landscapes;

c. "Landscape quality objective" means, for a specific landscape, the formulation by the competent public authorities of the aspirations of the public with regard to the landscape features of their surroundings;

d. "Landscape protection" means actions to conserve and maintain the significant or characteristic features of a landscape, justified by its heritage value derived from its natural configuration and/or from human activity;

e. "Landscape management" means action, from a perspective of sustainable development, to ensure the regular upkeep of a landscape, so as to guide and harmonise changes which are brought about by social, economic and environmental processes;

f. "Landscape planning" means strong forward-looking action to enhance, restore or create landscapes.

Article 2 – Scope

Subject to the provisions contained in Article 15, this Convention applies to the entire territory of the Parties and covers natural, rural, urban and peri-urban areas. It includes land, inland water and marine areas. It concerns landscapes that might be considered outstanding as well as everyday or degraded landscapes.

Article 3 – Aims

The aims of this Convention are to promote landscape protection, management and planning, and to organise European co-operation on landscape issues.

CHAPTER II – NATIONAL MEASURES

Article 4 – Division of Responsibilities

Each Party shall implement this Convention, in particular Articles 5 and 6, according to its own division of powers, in conformity with its constitutional principles and administrative arrangements, and respecting the principle of subsidiarity, taking into account the European Charter of Local Self-government. Without derogating from the provisions of this Convention, each Party shall harmonise the implementation of this convention with its own policies.

Article 5 – General Measures

Each Party undertakes:

a. to recognise landscapes in law as an essential component of people's surroundings, an expression of the diversity of their shared cultural and natural heritage, and a foundation of their identity;

b. to establish and implement landscape policies aimed at landscape protection, management and planning through the adoption of the specific measures set out in Article 6;

  c. to establish procedures for the participation of the general public, local and regional authorities, and other parties with an interest in the definition and implementation of the landscape policies mentioned in paragraph *b* above;

  d. to integrate landscape into its regional and town planning policies and in its cultural, environmental, agricultural, social and economic policies, as well as in any other policies with possible direct or indirect impact on landscape.

Article 6 – Specific Measures

Awareness-Raising

Each Party undertakes to increase awareness among the civil society, private organisations, and public authorities of the value of landscapes, their role and changes to them.

Training and Education

Each Party undertakes to promote:

  a. training for specialists in landscape appraisal and operations;

  b. multidisciplinary training programmes in landscape policy, protection, management and planning, for professionals in the private and public sectors and for associations concerned;

  c. school and university courses which, in the relevant subject areas, address the values attaching to landscapes and the issues raised by their protection, management and planning.

Identification and Assessment

  1. With the active participation of the interested parties, as stipulated in Article 5.*c*, and with a view to improving knowledge of its landscapes, each Party undertakes:

  a.

   i. to identify its own landscapes throughout its territory;

   ii. to analyse their characteristics and the forces and pressures transforming them;

   iii. to take note of changes;

  b. to assess the landscapes thus identified, taking into account the particular values assigned to them by the interested parties and the population concerned.

  2. These identification and assessment procedures shall be guided by the exchanges of experience and methodology, organised between the Parties at European level pursuant to Article 8.

Landscape Quality Objectives

Each Party undertakes to define landscape quality objectives for the landscapes identified and assessed, after public consultation in accordance with Article 5.*c*.

Implementation

To put landscape policies into effect, each Party undertakes to introduce instruments aimed at protecting, managing and/or planning the landscape.

CHAPTER III – EUROPEAN CO-OPERATION

Article 7 – International Policies and Programmes

Parties undertake to co-operate in the consideration of the landscape dimension of international policies and programmes, and to recommend, where relevant, the inclusion in them of landscape considerations.

Article 8 – Mutual Assistance and Exchange of Information

The Parties undertake to co-operate in order to enhance the effectiveness of measures taken under other articles of this Convention, and in particular:

a. to render each other technical and scientific assistance in landscape matters through the pooling and exchange of experience, and the results of research projects;

b. to promote the exchange of landscape specialists in particular for training and information purposes;

c. to exchange information on all matters covered by the provisions of the Convention.

Article 9 – Transfrontier Landscapes

The Parties shall encourage transfrontier co-operation on local and regional level and, wherever necessary, prepare and implement joint landscape programmes.

Article 10 – Monitoring of the Implementation of the Convention

1. Existing competent Committees of Experts set up under Article 17 of the Statute of the Council of Europe shall be designated by the Committee of Ministers of the Council of Europe to be responsible for monitoring the implementation of the Convention.

2. Following each meeting of the Committees of Experts, the Secretary General of the Council of Europe shall transmit a report on the work carried out and on the operation of the Convention to the Committee of Ministers.

3. The Committees of Experts shall propose to the Committee of Ministers the criteria for conferring and the rules governing the Landscape award of the Council of Europe.

Article 11 – Landscape Award of the Council of Europe

1. The Landscape award of the Council of Europe is a distinction which may be conferred on local and regional authorities and their groupings that have instituted, as part of the landscape policy of a Party to this Convention, a policy or measures to protect, manage and/or plan their landscape, which have proved lastingly effective and can thus serve as an example to other territorial authorities in Europe. The distinction may be also conferred on non-governmental organisations having made particularly remarkable contributions to landscape protection, management or planning.

2. Applications for the Landscape award of the Council of Europe shall be submitted to the Committees of Experts mentioned in Article 10 by the Parties. Transfrontier local and regional authorities and groupings of local and regional authorities concerned, may apply provided that they jointly manage the landscape in question.

3. On proposals from the Committees of Experts mentioned in Article 10 the Committee of Ministers shall define and publish the criteria for conferring the Landscape award of the Council of Europe, adopt the relevant rules and confer the Award.

4. The granting of the Landscape award of the Council of Europe is to encourage those receiving the award to ensure the sustainable protection, management and/or planning of the landscape areas concerned.

CHAPTER IV – FINAL CLAUSES

Article 12 – Relationship with Other Instruments

The provisions of this Convention shall not prejudice stricter provisions concerning landscape protection, management and planning contained in other existing or future binding national or international instruments.

Article 13 – Signature, Ratification and Entry into Force

1. This Convention shall be open for signature by the member States of the Council of Europe. It shall be subject to ratification, acceptance or approval. Instruments of ratification, acceptance or approval shall be deposited with the Secretary General of the Council of Europe.

2. The Convention shall enter into force on the first day of the month following the expiry of a period of three months after the date on which ten member States of the Council of Europe have expressed their consent to be bound by the Convention in accordance with the provisions of the preceding paragraph.

3. In respect of any signatory state which subsequently expresses its consent to be bound by it, the Convention shall enter into force on the first day of the month following the expiry of a period of three months after the date of the deposit of the instrument of ratification, acceptance or approval.

Article 14 – Accession

1. After the entry into force of this Convention, the Committee of Ministers of the Council of Europe may invite the European Community and any European State which is not a member of the Council of Europe, to accede to the Convention by a majority decision as provided in Article 20.d of the Council of Europe Statute, and by the unanimous vote of the States parties entitled to hold seats in the Committee of Ministers.

2. In respect of any acceding State, or the European Community in the event of its accession, this Convention shall enter into force on the first day of the month following the expiry of a period of three months after the date of deposit of the instrument of accession with the Secretary General of the Council of Europe.

Article 15 – Territorial Application

1. Any State or the European Community may, at the time of signature or when depositing its instrument of ratification, acceptance, approval or accession, specify the territory or territories to which the Convention shall apply.
2. Any Party may, at any later date, by declaration addressed to the Secretary General of the Council of Europe, extend the application of this Convention to any other territory specified in the declaration. The Convention shall take effect in respect of such a territory on the first day following the expiry of a period of three months after the date of receipt of the declaration by the Secretary General.
3. Any declaration made under the two paragraphs above may, in respect of any territory mentioned in such declaration, be withdrawn by notification addressed to the Secretary General. Such withdrawal shall become effective on the first day of the month following the expiry of a period of three months after the date of receipt of the notification by the Secretary General.

Article 16 – Denunciation

1. Any Party may, at any time, denounce this Convention by means of a notification addressed to the Secretary General of the Council of Europe.
2. Such denunciation shall become effective on the first day of the month following the expiry of a period of three months after the date of receipt of the notification by the Secretary General.

Article 17 – Amendments

1. Any Party or the Committees of Experts mentioned in Article 10 may propose amendments to this Convention.
2. Any proposal for amendment shall be notified to the Secretary General of the Council of Europe who shall communicate it to the member States of the Council of Europe, to the others Parties, and to any European non-member State which has been invited to accede to this Convention in accordance with the provisions of Article 14.
3. The Committees of Experts mentioned in Article 10 shall examine any amendment proposed and submit the text adopted by a majority of three-quarters of the Parties' representatives to the Committee of Ministers for adoption. Following its adoption by the Committee of Ministers by the majority provided for in Article 20.d of the Statute of the Council of Europe and by the unanimous vote of the States parties entitled to hold seats in the Committee of Ministers, the text shall be forwarded to the Parties for acceptance.
4. Any amendment shall enter into force in respect of the Parties which have accepted it on the first day of the month following the expiry of a period of three months after the date on which three Council of Europe member States have informed the Secretary General of their acceptance. In respect of any Party which subsequently accepts it, such amendment shall enter into force on the first day of the month following the expiry of a period of three months after the date on which the said Party has informed the Secretary General of its acceptance.

Article 18 – Notifications

The Secretary General of the Council of Europe shall notify the member States of the Council of Europe, any State or the European Community having acceded to this Convention, of:

a. any signature;

b. the deposit of any instrument of ratification, acceptance, approval or accession;

c. any date of entry into force of this Convention in accordance with Articles 13, 14 and 15;

d. any declaration made under Article 15;

e. any denunciation made under Article 16;

f. any proposal for amendment, any amendment adopted pursuant to Article 17 and the date on which it comes into force;

g. any other act, notification, information or communication relating to this Convention.

In witness where of the undersigned, being duly authorised thereto, have signed this Convention.

Done at Florence, this 20th day of October 2000, in English and French, both texts being equally authentic, in a single copy which shall be deposited in the archives of the Council of Europe. The Secretary General of the Council of Europe shall transmit certified copies to each Member State of the Council of Europe and to any state or to the European Community should they be invited to accede to this Convention.

5 EIA Legislation and the Importance of Transboundary Application

Lana Roux and Willemien du Plessis

1 INTRODUCTION

Many countries in Africa either have adopted environmental impact assessment (EIA) legislation or are in the process of doing so. An EIA is one of the available environmental management tools used to facilitate sound integrated decision making where by environmental considerations are explicitly and systematically taken into account in the planning and development process.

Wood and other authors[1] developed EIA evaluation criteria that are essential elements of an effective EIA. The EIA legislation differs from country to country, and different countries use different approaches. Some legislation is process-driven, other is issue-driven. For instance, South Africa, Namibia, and Swaziland are neighbors, but their EIA legislation differs.[2]

In some instances, developments may also have severe consequences outside the boundaries of states. Such transborder consequences are not always addressed in EIA legislation of individual states. The 1992 Declaration and Treaty of the Southern African Development Community (SADC) provides that natural resources and environmental issues of member countries be addressed in a spirit of cooperation,[3] and some of the SADC protocols refer to the fact that transborder EIAs should be undertaken.[4]

In the absence of an agreement or protocol, a transborder development will have to comply with the legislation of all countries in the transborder frontier. There are already several transboundary projects in Africa,[5] some of which are financed by the World Bank.[6] The lack of knowledge concerning the different countries' EIA legislation

---

[1] See Chris Wood, *Environmental Impact Assessment: A Comparative Review* (Longman) (1995).

[2] South Africa's law is the Environment Conservation Act of 1989 (currently under revision), Namibia's is the Environment Management Act (in the process of being adopted), and Swaziland promulgated the Environmental Management Act in 2002.

[3] See Article 21 of http://www.iucnrosa.org.zw/elisa/SADU-protocols/declaration%20treaty.html. Article 24 refers to good working relations and other forms of cooperation such as agreements that are compatible with the Treaty.

[4] See, e.g., SADC Protocol on Wildlife Conservation and Law Enforcement, 1999; SADC Protocol on Forestry, 1999; SADC Protocol on Fisheries, 2001; and revised SADC Protocol on Shared Water Resources, 2001 (original protocol in 1995).

[5] For example, the gas pipeline from Mozambique to South Africa.

[6] For example, the Chad-Cameroon Petroleum Development and Pipeline Project, which is financed by the World Bank, see http://www.worldbank.org/afr/ccproj.

The paper is based on a LLM study by Lana Roux, "Comparison between South African, Namibian and Swaziland EIA Legislation," unpublished, 2003.

and their different applications hampers development projects and conservation of the environment. The United Nations Economic Commission for Europe (UNECE) Convention on Environmental Impact Assessment in a Transboundary Context[7] provides an example of how transborder impacts may be addressed. In North America, the governments of Canada, the United Mexican States, and the United States have an agreement to address cross-border environmental issues;[8] including provisions on assessing environmental impacts, and in Europe a Directive[9] in this regard was issued.[10] The East African Community is also in the process of drafting environmental assessment guidelines.[11] More bilateral or multilateral transborder agreements that specifically address EIAs of different African countries may become even more necessary, especially in the light of the New Partnership for African Development (NEPAD).

The purpose of this chapter is to compare the EIA legislation of South Africa, Namibia, and Swaziland and to measure the legislation against the criteria set by Wood and other authors in order to indicate why a transboundary agreement on environmental impact assessments may be necessary for SADC. We will begin by looking at transboundary EIA agreements and SADC protocols and then compare EIA legislation in South Africa, Namibia, and Swaziland in the light of Wood's criteria. Finally, we will draw some conclusions and make recommendations on the way forward.

2 TRANSBOUNDARY ENVIRONMENTAL IMPACT ASSESSMENT[12]

The term *transboundary*[13] *impact* is defined in the Espoo Convention as "any impacts, not exclusively of a global nature, within the area of jurisdiction of a party caused by a proposed activity the physical origin of which is situated wholly, or in part, within the area of jurisdiction of another party." Apart from the Espoo Convention, other

---

[7] United Nations Economic Commission for Europe (UNECE) Convention on Environmental Impact Assessment in a Transboundary Context, 1991, reprinted at 30 *I.L.M.* 800 (1991) (hereafter the Espoo Convention).

[8] North American Agreement on Environmental Cooperation between the Government of Canada, the Government of the United Mexican States and the Government of the United States of America, 1993, available at www.cec.org/pubs_info_resources/law_treat_agree/naaec/download/naaec-e.doc (hereafter NAAEC).

[9] Directive 85/337/EEC. According to the Directive, member states have to consult other member states if a project has potential transboundary effects. The EIA does not have to include transboundary effects, and consultation with nonmember states is not a necessity. See J. H. Knox, "The Myth and Reality of Transboundary Environmental Impact Assessment," *American Journal of International Law* 96 (2002) 291–319, 299. The so-called Timor Gap Treaty is also an example of a transboundary EIA treaty – see in this regard Dadang Purnama, "Review of Transboundary Environmental Impact Assessment: A Case Study from the Timor Gap," in *Impact Assessment and Project Appraisal* (2004) 17–35 at 22.

[10] Resolution 97–03 on Transboundary Environmental Impact Assessment.

[11] *Supra* note 2.   [12] Hereafter referred to as *TEIA*.

[13] It is important to consider what is meant by "boundaries." The most obvious and commonly recognized physical boundary that comes to mind in this regard is the political border between countries. However, it is important to realize that boundaries within countries, such as states, provinces, municipalities, or other denominations, are also relevant. While boundaries in terrestrial ecosystems might be easier to define and deal with, an understanding of highly dynamic ecosystems such as the marine environment is needed to promote and achieve effective cooperation in all areas. See in this regard the World Conservation Union (the International Union for Conservation of Nature and Natural Resources) [IUCN] and the World Commission on Protected Areas (WCPA) International Symposium on Parks for Peace 12.

conventions such as the Convention on Biodiversity[14] and the Law of the Sea Convention[15] include environmental assessment obligations.[16] The Espoo model provides an excellent example of a convention that could be adopted in a regional context.[17] The Espoo Convention places a general obligation on states to agree to take all appropriate and effective measures to prevent, reduce, and control significant adverse transboundary environmental impacts of proposed activities.[18] The Espoo Convention also sets out the required minimal contents of EIA documentation,[19] as well as provisions for notification,[20] final decisions,[21] and postproject analysis,[22] among others.[23]

2.1 The North American Agreement on Economic Cooperation (NAAEC)

The NAAEC[24] promotes strengthened cooperation among Canada, Mexico, and the United States regarding the conservation, protection, and enhancement of the environment.[25] Article 10(7) of the NAAEC makes provision for the development of recommendations for an agreement on the assessment of environmental impacts of proposed projects likely to cause significant adverse transboundary effects.[26] The contents of the subsequent North American Agreement on Transboundary Environmental Impact Assessment[27] will be discussed briefly.

The North American Agreement initially stipulates that the party of origin must notify any potentially affected parties of the proposed projects.[28] The agreement also stipulates the specific circumstances under which notification must take place. Provision is made under the agreement for time frames within which this notification must take place,[29] including specifications on who is required to notify whom.[30] According to this agreement, notification must take place by means of a record of notification in at least one of the official languages of the party of origin and a translation in the language of the potentially affected parties whenever possible.[31]

The notification of a proposed project should contain sufficient information to apprise a potentially affected party of the nature of the proposed project.[32] Part 1 and

---

[14] Article 29 of the United Nations Conference on Environment and Development: Convention on Biological Diversity, 5 June 1992, reprinted in 31 *I.L.M.* 818 (1992).

[15] Article 206 of the United Nations Law of the Sea Convention 1982, reprinted in 21 *I.L.M.* 1245 (1982).

[16] J. Glazewski, *Environmental Law in South Africa* (Juta) (2004) 274.

[17] Ibid.

[18] The Espoo Convention, *supra* note 7 at Article 2(1).

[19] Ibid. at Appendix 2. [20] Ibid. at Article 5.

[21] Ibid. at Article 6. [22] Ibid. at Article 7.

[23] See Glazewski, *supra* note 16 at 275. A problem is that Espoo applies only to projects that have a significant impact on the environment and that are listed in the appendix to the Convention subject to approval by a competent authority; a *competent authority* is an authority in a member state. According to Knox, *supra* note 9 at 315, the Convention has weak procedural requirements although its requirements are more detailed than those of other similar multilateral agreements.

[24] See Knox, *supra* note 9 at 306–308, as well as the International Law Commission Draft Articles on Prevention of Transboundary Harm (1998) as discussed by Knox, *supra* note 9 at 308–311.

[25] http://www.cec.org/pubs_info_resources/law_treat_agree/pbl.cfm? varla=english.

[26] Ibid.

[27] North American Agreement Resolution 73–03 on Transboundary Environmental Assessment (hereafter referred to as North American Agreement).

[28] Ibid. at Article 2. [29] Ibid. at Article 3.

[30] Ibid. at Article 4. [31] Ibid. at Articles 5 and 6.

[32] Ibid. at Article 7(1).

Part 2 of Appendix 1 stipulate the information that must be included in the notification when the party of origin has decided to conduct a transboundary environmental impact assessment (TEIA). The North American Agreement also makes provision for circumstances in which a notification has not been received. When the potentially affected party has reasonable concerns that its environment would be significantly affected in an adverse manner by a proposed project, such affected party has the right to request information from the party of origin.[33] This is also the case when notification has occurred and additional information is requested.[34]

The North American Agreement also prescribes what content the potentially affected party's response should include.[35] In this regard, the potentially affected party should indicate whether it intends to provide comments or to participate in a TEIA if one is undertaken. If the potentially affected parties indicate that they do not intend to provide comments or to participate in a TEIA, or if they do not respond within the designated period, the party of origin does not have any further obligations for that particular project pursuant to this agreement, unless the potentially affected parties become aware of new information at a later date.[36]

When it is evident that the proposed project is likely to cause significant adverse transboundary environmental impacts on the environment of another party, then the party of origin should ensure that a TEIA is undertaken.[37] This TEIA must comply with all the elements provided for in Appendix 4.[38] The contents of the TEIA are similar to the EIA documentation provided in the Espoo Convention.

The potentially affected parties must be notified of the TEIA and of the elements outlined in Part 2 of Appendix 2, which include additional information on the proposed project, as well as information on the public participation process undertaken by the party of origin.[39] Provisions are also made for elements that the party of origin may use in the process of determining whether a proposed project is likely to cause significant adverse transboundary environmental impacts on the environment of another party.[40]

The party of origin must ensure that any potentially affected parties have a meaningful opportunity to participate and that all relevant information furnished by these parties is taken into consideration.[41] The party of origin must invite close cooperation of any potentially affected parties during the TEIA.[42]

Further, the party of origin must ensure that the public participates in the process. Public participation must occur to the same extent in both the potentially affected

---

[33] Ibid. at Article 8(1).   [34] Ibid. at Article 8(2).

[35] Ibid. at Article 9(1).   [36] Ibid. at Article 9(2).

[37] Ibid. at Article 10(1).

[38] Ibid. at Appendix 4 providing for the basic contents of a TEIA, which include information on the nature of the proposed project, information on the spatial and temporal boundaries of the proposed project, information on the environment likely to be affected, expected adverse transboundary environmental impacts, and proposed mitigation measures.

[39] Ibid. at Article 10(b).

[40] Ibid. at Appendix 3, listing factors for determining significant adverse transboundary impacts, which include context factors such as the potentially affected human population and vulnerable segments of population; geographic extent such as ecological context; unique characteristics of the geographical area; standards regarding the protection of health or the environment as specified in international, national, or subnational legal instruments; probability of occurrence and scientific uncertainty; intensity factor, such as degree and duration.

[41] Ibid. at Articles 11(1) (a) and (b).   [42] Ibid. at Article 11(2).

state party and the party of origin.[43] The party of origin must also submit all the written documentation of any completed TEIA to the potentially affected parties and communicate the decisions made with regard to the proposed project after the review of the TEIA to these parties. Mitigation measures must also be considered as soon as possible during the TEIA and provision must be made for postproject monitoring.[44]

Any party may request consultation regarding any aspects of the operation of these recommendations, including any determination, action, or lack of action taken thereunder.[45] Provision is also made for dispute resolution, but this provision is still to be elaborated upon. It is important that when a TEIA is negotiated, information is exchanged on domestic laws.[46] It becomes more complicated when a project traverses the borders of countries. The conventions on TEIA do not address this question. In such an instance, the proponent–applicant has to comply with the legislation of two or more countries, depending on the project.[47]

2.2 The East African Community (EAC)

The East African Community Treaty[48] (Kenya, Tanzania, and Uganda) has drafted Environmental Assessment Guidelines for Shared Ecosystems in East Africa. The purpose of the guidelines is to harmonize policies, laws, standards, and programs and to promote cooperation among shared ecosystems. The guidelines provide for both EIAs and Strategic Environmental Assessments (SEAs).[49]

2.3 SADC Protocols

Several sector-specific SADC protocols refer to EIAs that have to be done, for example, in the case of development projects within shared watercourse systems.[50] The revised Protocol on Shared Watercourse Systems places an obligation on member states to notify other states on planned measures that may have a significant adverse effect on these states. All technical data and information as well as environmental impact assessments must be made available to the affected states to evaluate the possible effects of the action.[51] The affected state is given six months that may be extended for another six months to react, and additional information must be provided on request. During this period, the planned action may not be implemented without the permission of the affected member states.[52]

According to the Mining Protocol of 1997, member states should encourage "a regional approach in conducting environmental impact assessments especially in relation to shared systems and cross border environmental effects." Member states also

---

[43] Ibid. at Article 12.
[44] Ibid. at Articles 14 and 15.
[45] Ibid. at Article 18.
[46] See Knox, *supra* note 9 at 316.
[47] A practical example is the gas pipeline from Mozambique to South Africa; the applicant had to comply with two different sets of EIA legislation.
[48] Treaty for the Establishment of the East African Community, 1999.
[49] Information obtained from Scott Schang, Environmental Law Institute, Washington, D.C.
[50] Article 5(d) (iii) Protocol on Shared Watercourse Systems of 1995, *supra* note 4.
[51] Ibid. at Article 4(1) (b).
[52] Ibid. at Article 4(1) (c)–(h). Provision is also made for situations in which a member state has reasonable grounds to believe that a shared watercourse may be affected by the action of another state – Article 4(1) (h). Emergency measures are dealt with in Article 4(1) (i).

have to share information on environmental protection and rehabilitation. The Guide-lines for Co-operation of the Protocol on Energy of 1996[53] state that electricity should be developed and utilized in an environmentally sound manner and that electricity projects should be made subject to environmental impact assessments in conformity with agreed basic environmental standards. Several of the Protocols also promote the harmonization and monitoring of legislation and policies dealing with various aspects of the environment,[54] but none of them with the harmonization of legislation dealing with EIAs.

3 COMPARISON OF SOUTH AFRICA, NAMIBIA, AND SWAZILAND

In South Africa, Namibia, and Swaziland each country's EIA system is unique as a result of legal, administrative, and political circumstances specific to each country.[55] In order to compare different countries' EIA systems it is important to compare the particular system in question to a current EIA system that is internationally recognized as good practice as outlined by Wood[56] and is derived from an analysis of the stages in the EIA process.[57]

The EIA process is relatively new in South Africa as well as in Namibia and Swaziland. Indeed in the past, EIA was not a legal requirement for most of the African countries. Most EIAs were conducted on the basis that the project was funded by foreign insti-tutions such as the World Bank, which insisted on EIAs as a requirement of funding. Where property was owned by foreign companies, an EIA was sometimes also required, because of the parent company's code of conduct. These EIAs were more the result of the insistence of the lending agencies than profects driven by a desire to protect the environment.[58]

3.1 Legal Basis of EIA Systems

According to Wood,[59] EIA requirements must be codified in legislation or regulations and must provide for a formal EIA system.[60] The question arises as to whether this legislation and the regulations need to be legally specified or largely discretionary. Although the discretionary EIA system contains certain advantages such as voluntary compliance and absence of judicial involvement, there is a gradual shift toward EIA systems that require both administrative and judicial supervision.[61] In the absence of

---

[53] Ibid., Annexure 1.

[54] See, e.g., Articles 2(d) and 4(2) (b) (ii) Protocol on Shared Watercourse Revised of 2001; item 2(a) (iv) of the Protocol on Energy of 1996. Article 13(8) of the Protocol on Fisheries of 2001 states, "State Parties shall establish standard guidelines and regulations for the application of environmental impact assessments."

[55] See Wood, *supra* note 1 at 11.   [56] Ibid. at 12.

[57] Including consideration of alternatives in project design, screening, scoping, report preparation, review, decision making, monitoring of project impacts, mitigation of project impacts, mitigation of impacts, consultation, and participation. See also C. Wood, "Pastiche or Postiche? Environmental Impact Assess-ment in South Africa" (1999), *South African Geographical Journal* 81 (1999) 52–59 at 53.

[58] P. Tarr and M. Figueira, "Namibia's Environmental Assessment Framework – the Evolution of Policy and Practice" (Unpublished) (September 1999), on file with the author.

[59] See Wood, *supra* note 1 at 72–75.   [60] Ibid. at 72.

[61] The Canadian Federal Government and the New Zealand Government codified their discretionary EIA system into legislation. Ibid. at 74.

mandatory EIA procedures, it is usually difficult to persuade developers that it is in their own interest to conduct one.[62] However, some degree of discretion in the operation of the various steps of the EIA process needs to exist since every eventuality cannot be foreseen in laws and regulations.[63]

South Africa's Constitution includes a right to an environment that is not detrimental to one's health or well-being,[64] while the Namibian Constitution includes a duty on the state to ensure by way of policy that the environment is protected.[65] Swaziland does not have any formal constitutionally entrenched environmental rights. The environmental protection of the country stems from the Swaziland Environmental Action Plan (*EAP*), which provides a holistic perspective and meaningful basis for all kinds of national policy development to ensure sustainable development.[66]

All three countries regulate their EIAs by way of legislation that is specified and mandatory.[67] South Africa's constitution, together with the Environment Conservation Act (ECA),[68] form the main legal framework of environmental legislation in South Africa until the provisions of and the National Environment Management Act (NEMA)[69] come into effect on a date still to be published by the minister in the South African *Government Gazette*.[70]

In Swaziland, the Environmental Audit, Assessment and Review Regulations (EAARR)[71] regulated the process of EIAs[72] until the Environmental Management Act No. 5 of 2002 was passed (hereafter referred to as EMB). This comprises a framework of environmental legislation.[73] Part 4 of the EMB makes provision for an EIA process.[74] Namibia also passed the Environmental Management Act No. 101 of 1998 (EMA),

---

[62] J. Glasson et al., *Introduction to Environmental Impact Assessment* (2nd edition. UCL Press) (1999) 194.

[63] See Wood, *supra* note 1 at 74.

[64] The Constitution of the Republic of South Africa (1996) section 24.

[65] Sections 95(1) and 91(c). The South African Constitution includes a similar obligation in s 24(b).

[66] http://www.swazi.com/government/sz-howgov.html. Swaziland is, however, in the process of adopting the Draft National Environmental Policy of 2000 (hereafter NEP). NEP builds on the analysis and recommendations contained in the EAP and represents the next step in promoting sound environmental management across all areas of decision making. One of the principles in NEP, which provides the people of Swaziland with environmental rights, reads as follows: "Every inhabitant of Swaziland is entitled to live in an environment that is conducive to health and well-being and to have access to the natural environment on an equitable and sustainable basis and to the means enforcing these rights." See http://www.ecs. co.sz/NEP/index.htm.

[67] See P. Tarr, *Environmental Impact Assessment in Southern Africa* (SAIEA) (2003) 147–172, 201–226, 227–242.

[68] Environment Conservation Act No. 73 of 1989.

[69] National Environmental Management Act No. 107 of (1998) (hereafter NEMA). Section 50(2) of NEMA will repeal sections 21, 22, and 26 of ECA as well as regulations GN R1182, 1183, and 1184 issued pursuant to sections 21 and 22 in *GG* 18261.

[70] In a recent case, *Silvermine Coalition v. Sybrand van der Spuy Boerdery and Others*, an unreported judgment by Davis J. in the Cape of Good Hope Provincial Division in the High Court of South Africa (judgment dated 20 June 2001) determined that because sections 21 and 22 of ECA remain in force, when a person seeks authorization to carry out an activity identified under section 21 of ECA, the ECA regulations continue to apply, subject to compliance with section 24(7) of NEMA.

[71] Environmental Audit, Assessment and Review Regulations 58 of 1996.

[72] These regulations were promulgated to give effect to section 18(1) (b) of the Swaziland Environmental Authority Act No. 15 of 1992, which allows the minister to promulgate EIA regulations.

[73] The EMB was accepted in November 2002.

[74] Section 32 of EMB. Throughout the discussion reference will be made to the EAARR as the authoritative source but reference will also be made to the EMB if it includes or explains matters that the EAARR does not include or explain sufficiently.

which is similar to Swaziland's EMB. This act gives statutory effect to Namibia's Environmental Assessment Policy that is set out in Part 4 of the Act and was, in the past, the authoritative source for EIAs.

3.2 Definitions

The term *EIA* is defined in the Swaziland legislation,[75] but not directly in the South African environmental legislation;[76] at this stage South Africa (with GN R1182) and Swaziland limit EIAs to projects. In the Namibian legislation, the term *EIA* is not used. Throughout the legislation the term *Environmental Assessment* (hereafter referred to as *EA*) is used.[77] Wood's[78] definition of EIA is similar to Swaziland's definition in the EAARR but makes provision for the evaluation of policies, plans, and programs.[79]

The term significant impact is used in all three countries' legislation. In the South African NEMA and ECA there is no definition of this term.[80] In the Namibian EMA[81] and in Swaziland's EAARR, Category 3 projects are described as projects that are likely

---

[75] An *EIA* is defined in the EAARR as "the process of predicting and evaluating the likely environmental impacts of a proposed project where the scale, extent and significance of the environmental impact cannot be easily determined."

[76] NEMA does not use the term *EIA* but refers generally to investigation of the environmental impact activities. Section 23 of NEMA (hereafter referred to as IEM) sets out the general objectives of integrated environmental management. One of the objectives is "the identification, prediction and evaluation of the actual and potential impact on the environment, socio-economic conditions and cultural heritage of activities with a view to minimising negative impact, maximising benefits, and promoting compliance with the principles of IEM referred to in section 2. The risks, consequences and alternatives also have to be considered as well as their alternatives and options for mitigation of impacts." When the term *activities* is used in Ch. 5 of NEMA, it includes policies, programs, and projects (which are referred to as *Strategic Environmental Assessment* [SEA]). This definition makes it clear that not only actual activities (for which EIAs are used) are included but also any planning, policy development, and programs. Similarly to NEMA, the ECA does not define EIAs but only refers to environmental impact reports. In GN R1183 (in *GG* 18261 of 1997–09–05 regarding activities identified under section 21(1)), reference is made to environmental impact assessments, but the term is not defined. In the Environmental Impact Management Guideline document of the Department of Environmental Affairs and Tourism EIA Regulations – implementation of sections 21, 22, and 26 of the Environment Conservation Act (April 1998) (hereafter EIA Guideline Document), an *EIA* is defined as "a process of examining the environmental effects of development."

[77] *EA* is defined as "a process of identifying, predicting and evaluating the actual and potential biophysical, social and other relevant effects on the environment of projects prior to their authorisation, or in the case of proposals prior to their implementation, as well as the risks and consequences of projects and proposals and their alternatives and options for mitigation with a view to minimising negative impacts on the environment, maximising benefits and promoting compliance with the principles of environmental management set out in section 6."

[78] See Wood, *supra* note 1 at 1.

[79] Ibid. At this stage none of the three countries' legislation provides for strategic environmental assessments. Although of importance, SEAs are not addressed because of the length of the chapter.

[80] In the EIA Guideline Document (Department of Environmental Affairs and Tourism (DEAT) EIA Regulations Implementation of sections 21, 22, and 26 of ECA, April 1998), the term *significant impact* is described as "an impact that, by its magnitude, duration or intensity alters an important aspect of the environment."

[81] The term *significant effect* means "having, or likely to have, an appreciable qualitative or quantitative impact on the environment, including changes in ecological, aesthetic, cultural, historic, economic and social factors, whether directly, indirectly, immediately or cumulatively."

to have significant adverse impacts on the environment.[82] Wood also uses this term in his discussion but does not define it.[83]

3.3 Activities Requiring an EIA

The coverage of EIA systems refers to both the range of actions subject to EIAs and the range of impacts regarded as relevant.[84] One objective of an EIA is, among others, to ensure that all the environmental impacts of significant actions are assessed prior to implementation. The EIA systems must, therefore, apply to both public and private actions.[85] These actions should not only refer to projects, but must include policies, programs, and plans.[86]

South Africa and Namibia list activities for which an EIA needs to be undertaken.[87] Swaziland has a totally different system from South Africa's and Namibia's. Project categories are distinguished. Category 1 projects are described as unlikely to cause any significant environmental impacts, for example, small-scale developments and renovations. Projects under Category 2 are those projects likely to cause environmental impacts, some of which may be significant, unless mitigation actions are taken. Such projects include those that cause impacts that are relatively well known and easy to predict, and mitigation actions to prevent or reduce the impacts are also well known.[88] This category includes medium-scale projects, including those located near environmentally sensitive areas. Large-scale projects are allocated under Category 3. These projects which include those located in environmentally sensitive areas, are likely to have significant adverse impacts whose which scale, extent, and significance cannot be determined without an in depth study.

Swaziland's approach to categorization of projects according to scale and allocation in both the EAARR and EMB implies that from an early stage it is clear that EIAs are not required for small insignificant projects. A problem with the system in Swaziland, however, is that is that there is no definite standard against which unlisted activities can be measured in order to determine the the scale of the activity. Both South African and Namibian authorities have the power to declare that activities may not be undertaken without their prior consent, even when they are not listed.[89] The Swaziland authority has no similar power under the EAARR or the EMB. Namibia and Swaziland include mining activities as part of their listed activities;[90] South Africa does not.[91]

---

[82] First Schedule under Regulation 7 of EAARR. These significant impacts are further qualified as impacts whose scale, extent, and significance cannot be determined without in-depth study.

[83] See Wood, *supra* note 1 at 1.

[84] Ibid. at 87.   [85] Ibid.

[86] See Wood, *supra* note 57 at 53.

[87] Section 21 of ECA read with GN R1182; section 19–25 of EMA.

[88] *Mitigation* entails the introduction of measurements to avoid, reduce, remedy, or compensate for any significant adverse impacts. See Wood, note 1 at 212, according to whom one of the main purposes of an EIA is to allow the proposed development to proceed, while reducing its impacts to an acceptable level. On the other hand, the secondary purpose is to prevent unsuitable development when it is indicated that certain impacts cannot be mitigated in order to be acceptable.

[89] Section 24(2) of NEMA *supra* note 69; section 19(3) of EMA.

[90] Category 3 of Schedule 1 of EAARR *supra* note 71.

[91] Section 22(4) of the Minerals and Petroleum Resources Development Act 28 of 2004 provides that EIAs should be undertaken when applying for a mining right. The EIAs are approved by the Department of Minerals and Energy.

3.4 Role Players

Relevant Environmental Authorities

Decision making takes place at several stages during the EIA process. The final decision must be made by a body other than the proponent, and it is also important that public participation must be included during this stage. In all three countries, environmental authorities are appointed as decision-making officials[92] and have such mandate unless another sphere of governance is requested to make the decision. In Swaziland and Namibia, one "higher" authority reviews or supervises the decisions of the competent authorities. This is not the case in South Africa, because of the fragmentation of environmental legislation. Wood's categorization does not require the environmental authority to be the decision-making authority. It suffices that the decision be made by a body other than the proponent.[93] This is the case in all three countries.

Applicant

All three countries provide for the roles and responsibilities of applicants or proponents.[94] Wood does not discuss the roles of the applicant–proponent during the EIA process but emphasizes that the decision-making body must not be the proponent.[95]

Consultant

The Swaziland and Namibian legislation does not mention the consultant as a role player in the EIA process. In Namibia, the duty is placed on the proponent to carry out the EA process under EMA,[96] and the competent authority must monitor compliance with the process. In both Namibia and Swaziland, therefore, if a consultant is used, the responsibility of the proponent of the project is to ensure that the EIA or EA is properly done in accordance with the legislation and regulations. In the final instance, the proponent will be the liable person.

In South Africa, Regulation 3(1) of GN R1182 sets out measures for the applicant to appoint an independent consultant who will conduct an EIA on behalf of the applicant. The regulations specify certain requirements that the consultant must comply with. South Africa's NEMA Amendment Act 8 of 2004 includes stipulations for the registration of competent environmental assessment practitioners.[97]

None of the countries accredits consultants as proposed by Wood.[98] He discusses methods of ensuring objectivity during the review of EIA reports; one method is to use EIA consultants during the EIA review stage. He further emphasizes that these

---

[92] The South African Department of Environmental Affairs and Tourism (DEAT) is the implementing authority in terms of both ECA and NEMA. In terms of ECA and NEMA, however, the approval of EIAs can be granted either by DEAT, a Member of the Executive Council of a province, or a local authority, depending on the circumstances – sections 22 and 24 of NEMA; Regulation 4(2) of GN R1183. According to the Swaziland EAARR, the *environmental authority* is the authority that exercises the functions and powers in terms of the Swaziland Environmental Authority Act 15 of 1992. In terms of the Namibian EMA, a *competent authority* (CA) is appointed.

[93] See Wood, *supra* note 1 at 183. See also A. Gilpin, *Environmental Impact Assessment (EIA) Cutting Edge for the Twenty-First Century* (Cambridge University Press) (1996) 24.

[94] Regulation 1, 3 GN R1183; Regulations 4 and 7 EAARR, section 18 EMA.

[95] See Wood, *supra* note 1 at 183.   [96] Section 18(1) of EMA.

[97] Section 24H of NEMA Amendment Act 8 of 2004.

[98] See Wood, *supra* note 1 at 162.

consultants must have the necessary competence to review the EIA reports accurately. He suggests the setting up of an independent review body consisting of experts in the field.[99]

Application

In all three countries, an application must be made in the prescribed format.[100] Wood does not discuss the process of application and registration of a project. It is, however, evident from his discussion that all projects must go through a screening process in order to determine whether an EIA report is necessary for the particular action.[101]

Screening

The process of screening narrows the application of EIA to those projects that may have significant environmental impacts.[102] In the process, it is determined whether or not an EIA report must be prepared for a particular action. The purpose of the screening process is, on the one hand, to prevent unnecessary assessments of a large number of actions that will not have significant environmental impacts and, on the other hand, to ensure that actions with significant adverse environmental impact will be assessed.[103] According to Wood,[104] two broad approaches can be used to establish the significance of the actions. The first is to use a list of actions, thresholds, and criteria in order to determine which actions should be assessed; the second is to establish a procedure for the discretionary determination of which actions should be assessed. In practice, these two approaches are not always strictly applied, but a mixture of both is used in some instances. The required information must be clear and detailed, describing actions, criteria, thresholds, and screening procedures.

From the preceding discussion it is evident that the three countries follow the approach of listing of actions. The list of activities in the South African regulations[105] has very few indications of the lowest level at which the action will have to be assessed in order to eliminate minor activities. The South African regulations do not have a classification in the listed activities of affected environments that can be excluded as nonsensitive areas.[106] The Swaziland EMB and EAARR indicate, in most cases, thresholds in order to eliminate minor activities and provide criteria to determine which actions should be assessed.[107]

Scoping

Scoping is the process of determining the range of issues to be addressed in an EIA report, as well as identifying the significant issues relating to a proposed action. One of the purposes of an EIA is to focus on the most important issues, while ensuring that indirect and secondary effects are not overlooked and irrelevant impacts are eliminated.[108] The

---

[99] Ibid. at 163.
[100] Regulation 4 of GN R1183; Sections 2 and 20 of EMA, Regulation 7 EAARR; Section 32 EMB.
[101] See Wood, *supra* note 1 at 115.
[102] Anon at http://www.ecs.co.sz/env_articles_envassa.htm.
[103] See Wood, *supra* note 1.   [104] Ibid. at 115 and 117.
[105] Schedule 1 of GN R1183.   [106] See Wood, *supra* note 57 at 54.
[107] First schedule of EAARR and sections 32(5) (a) and (b) of EMB.
[108] See Wood, *supra* note 1 at 130.

scoping process can vary considerably from case to case, depending on numerous factors such as complexity of the proposal and the potential effect on the public.[109]

When analyzing the scoping procedures of the three countries according to Wood's criteria,[110] it is evident that the scoping process is mandatory in all three countries. The South African regulations require that the plan of study for scoping must contain an indication of the stages when the relevant authority should be further consulted, and the EIA Guideline Document recommends when these consultations must take place.[111] The South African regulations also require that the scoping report include a description of the public participation process, including a list of interested and affected parties and their comments. The Namibian EMA also makes provision for adequate consultation with the relevant authorities during the scoping process. In fact, the proponent and the competent authority must together determine the form, scope, and content of the EA.[112] Although EMA makes provision for adequate consultation with the relevant authority, it makes no provision for public participation in determining the scope of the EA.

The Swaziland EAARR[113] and EMB[114] also provide for consultation with the relevant authorities after the in-full first Initial Environmental Evaluation (IEE) or project brief (respectively) is accepted. After the respective reports are submitted, interested and affected parties have the opportunity to indicate objections or comments, or make submissions.

South Africa and Swaziland provide public records of the scoping process and all three countries ensure the stakeholders the right of appeal against the decision. It seems as if the new South African EIA regulations will cut out the comprehensive scoping process and conduct screening only to enable the relevant authority to decide whether an EIA is required.

EIA Report Preparation

The preparation of an EIA report can be regarded as the step that makes the EIA process meaningful because it contains the findings related to the predicted impacts of the proposal on the environment.[115] Most countries' EIA regulations specify the minimal regulations required in an EIA report. A problem, however, is that they do not specify a standard for the presentation of this information.[116]

---

[109] See Glazewski, *supra* note 16 at 286. However, Wood, *supra* note 1 at 131–132, sets out certain criteria that are characteristic of a proper scoping procedure. The scoping of impacts must be mandatory in the EIA process. Consultation with the decision-making and environmental authorities and interest groups (such as local communities and any other interested and affected groups or parties) could assist in the identification of all the potentially significant impacts. The consultation with the decision makers and/or environmental authorities provides an opportunity for the relevant authorities to express opinions about the scope of the EIA. The requirement of public participation is important to make the proponents and the decision makers aware of public concerns early in the EIA process. Public meetings may also be conducted because they are the most efficient way to ensure open dialogue on the significance of impacts. Questionnaires and surveys may also be helpful to determine the public's concerns.

[110] See Wood, *supra* note 1 at 33.

[111] EIA Guideline Document 3.2.2.1, *supra* note 80 at 21; see also Regulations 4–6 GN R1883.

[112] Section 23 of EMA.   [113] Regulation 7.

[114] Section 32.   [115] See Wood, *supra* note 1 at 143.

[116] Glasson et al., *supra* note 62 at 172.

Formal published guidance on the preparation of EIA reports is provided in South Africa as part of the EIA Guideline Document.[117] An article on conducting an EIA in Swaziland[118] stipulates some key points to remember during the preparation of an EIA report; it does not, however, contain formally published guidelines. The South African EIA Guideline Document also sets out certain specified EIA methods and techniques that can be employed during this phase.[119] These guidelines are, however, not compulsory by law.[120] Neither Swaziland nor Namibia specifies any EIA methods or techniques to be employed during the preparation of an EIA report. Wood suggests that the preparation of the EIA report requires the use of a wide variety of methods and techniques.[121] He further specifies that these methods and techniques must be described in the EIA report and recommends that clear and readily accessible guidelines on EIA report preparation be made available.[122]

EIA Report Review and Record of Decision

Review of the EIA report is aimed at determining the quality, adequacy, sufficiency, and relevance of the information provided in the report as a basis for decision making. Different countries make use of different procedures during the review process. The fundamental requirement of this stage, according to Wood,[123] is that those bodies with responsibilities and expertise (and the public) have the opportunity to address their concerns regarding the EIA report and the action it describes. These comments should be taken into account by the decision-making or environmental authorities before any decision regarding the action is made.[124] Suitable provisions for public participation are essential in this stage of the EIA process, and it is preferable that this participation precede requests for further information from the proponent.[125] It is also essential that after the formal review is made public all stakeholders have the right to appeal the findings.[126]

When comparing the legislation of the three countries, it is clear that according to Wood's[127] criteria for the review of EIA reports, all three countries make provision for review.[128] The South African EIA regulations, however, do not stipulate the contents of the EIA report review, apart from demanding that the relevant authority consider the

---

[117] EIA Guideline Document 3.2.4.1 *supra* note 111 at 26.

[118] Anon at http://www.ecs.co.sz/em_info.htm.

[119] EIA Guideline Document 3.2.4.1 *supra* note 111 at 26.

[120] See also section 24(4) (b) (iii) of NEMA Amendment Bill.

[121] See Wood, *supra* note 1 at 144.

[122] Ibid. at 148. The relevant authorities in South Africa are, according to Wood, using their approval of the plan of study for EIA to demand the preparation and circulation of a draft EIR. See also Wood, *supra* note 57 at 55. This can be regarded as checks made on the contents of the EIR before it is released, despite the absence of any formal requirement. The Namibian legislation makes provision that after receipt of the EAR, the Ecom can direct that the EAR must be subjected to an independent review at the proponent's expense (section 24[1] [c]) of EMA, and in certain cases convene an ad hoc committee of experts to assist with the review (section 24[1] [d]). This can be regarded as a formal requirement, in certain cases, for checks on the contents of the EAR before it is released. Swaziland's legislation does not make any provision for checks on the contents, form, objectivity, and accuracy of the information presented before publication of the EIA report.

[123] See Wood, *supra* note 1 at 162.

[124] Ibid.

[125] Ibid. at 165.

[126] Ibid. at 166.

[127] Ibid. at 162–166.

[128] Regulations 6, 9–10 GN R1183; Regulations 7–8 and 11 EAARR; section 32 EMB; sections 21–26 EMA.

application after it has received a report that complies with the regulations.[129] NEMA requires that procedures for independent review must be implemented,[130] and the EIA Guideline Document describes this procedure in more detail.[131] The Swaziland EAARR and EMB make provision for a comprehensive review process, in which public involvement plays an extremely important role. The Namibian EMA also makes provision for the review process, but similarly to the South African regulations, it does not provide detail.

With regard to Wood's[132] criteria concerning decision making, it is evident that all three countries' legislation makes provision for decision making after the EIA has been prepared and reviewed. In the respective countries, decision making, however, also takes place earlier in the EIA process, for instance, after a scoping report has been accepted in South Africa;[133] when a project is classified under Category 1 and, in some cases, Category 2 in Swaziland;[134] and after the screening process in Namibia.[135]

In all three countries the EIA legislation gives the decision-making body various powers with regard to the decision they may reach, such as the power to accept the application with or without conditions, to order the proponent to amend the application when necessary, and to refuse the application. The decision-making body in the countries discussed here is a body other than the proponent and these respective bodies are required to issue a record of decision[136] to the proponent. In South Africa, this record of decision will also be made available to other interested parties on request, and in Swaziland and Namibia these records of decision must be published.

EIA Follow-Ups

Monitoring of the EIA system is increasingly necessary in order ensure a successful EIA process. The main purpose of monitoring is the diffusion of EIA practice: the alteration of the EIA system to incorporate feedback from experience and to remedy any weakness identified.[137] Numerous elements of an EIA system can be monitored in order to promote the diffusion of the best EIA practices and to amend the system through feedback from experience.[138]

It is evident that the better the EIA system for monitoring information is, the easier it is to review and implement changes in the EIA system. Consultation and participation, as stipulated throughout the EIA system, are very important in the monitoring process, and adequate provisions must be provided for in environmental legislation.[139]

In comparing the regulations and legislation with Wood's evaluation criteria[140] for the monitoring and auditing of action impacts, monitoring is referred to but not

---

[129] Regulation 9 of GN R1183.   [130] Wood *supra* note 57 at 55.
[131] EIA Guideline Document *supra* note 111 at 3.2.5.2.
[132] See Wood; *supra* note 1 at 181–184.   [133] Regulation 6(3) (a) of GN R1183.
[134] Regulations 7(a) and 7(11) (b) (i) of EAARR. [135] Section 21 of EMA.
[136] In terms of the NEMA Amendment Act 8 of 2004, an environmental authorization will be issued.
[137] See Wood, *supra* note 1 at 241.   [138] Ibid.
[139] Glasson et al., *supra* note 62 at 191. J. Cubitt and R. Diab, "EIA Follow-Up: Current Status and Recommendation," unpublished paper delivered at the South African IAIA Congress 8–10 October 2001 Mapumalanga, 73.1. In Wood's discussion (*supra* note 1 at 197), a distinction is made between the monitoring of individual actions (which is discussed now) and the monitoring of the EIA system as a whole. He also distinguishes among three main types of action monitoring and auditing: implementation monitoring, impact monitoring, and impact auditing.
[140] See Wood, *supra* note 1 at 191–200.

detailed. The Namibian legislation[141] mainly concentrates on the monitoring of projects undertaken by the government. The NEMA Amendment Act 8 of 2004 refers to monitoring but does not specify the provisions.[142] The Swaziland EAARR[143] and EMB[144] make explicit provision for both implementation monitoring and impact monitoring for all projects, by government and by private entities. This legislation also provides for environmental auditing of projects being implemented, as well as already existing projects. The monitoring and auditing procedures are set out in detail in the legislation. Both the Namibian and the Swaziland legislation require that the monitoring arrangements be specified in the EIA report. The South African EIA report, however, does not include such specifications. Swaziland's legislation also stipulates that these auditing results be made available to all interested and affected parties. As discussed, South Africa and Namibia do not provide for auditing reports.

Consultation and Participation

Consultation and participation are integral to the EIA process. They can produce significant benefits for the proponent and for those affected, which may include interested and affected parties from neighboring countries.[145] Democracy is increasingly seen as a continuous and dynamic process in which governments bear the ultimate responsibility, but only with the most careful public scrutiny,[146] which indicates the public's desire to be part of the decision-making process.[147]

The South African EIA regulations make provision for public participation during various stages of the EIA process, including the scoping stage, during the preparation of the EIR, during review of the EIR, and finally during the implementation and monitoring stage.[148] The Namibian legislation has adequate opportunities for public participation throughout the EA process, namely, after the project notification is handed in, during screening, and during preparation and review of the EAR.[149] Swaziland's EAARR[150] and EMB[151] provide that public participation take place only after the required reports are handed in and released for public insight in the case of Category 1 and 2 processes. Category 3 projects, however, require consultation before preparation of an EIA report. It is, therefore, evident that only the Namibian legislation provides for public participation prior to scoping. In all three countries the comments of the interested and affected parties must, however, be taken into consideration during the decision-making process.

Regarding the availability of copies of EIA documents at each stage of the process, all three countries' legislation provides for the availability of copies to interested and affected parties throughout the EIA process. Similarly, in all three countries, the legislation indicates circumstances in which a request for information may be rejected.

In both Namibia and South Africa the roles, responsibilities, and duties of the interested and affected parties are poorly defined.[152] The well-laid-out public participation

---

[141] Section 18 EMA.

[142] Section 24(e) of NEMA Amendment Act 8 of 2004.

[143] Regulation 10 read together with Regulation 5.   [144] Section 33.

[145] See Wood, *supra* note 1 at 225.   [146] Gilpin *supra* note 93 at 63.

[147] See Principles 10 and 17 of the Rio Declaration.   [148] Regulation 3 GN R1183, s 23 NEMA.

[149] Sections 6, 20–21, 24 EMA.   [150] Regulations 8, 11, 13.

[151] Pt. 8.

[152] J. Nel, "Unsustainable EIA Partnerships: Poorly Defined Rights, Roles, Responsibilities and Duties of EIA-Stakeholders," 8 *South African Journal of Environmental Law and Policy* (2001) 105–118.

process of Swaziland, which includes well-defined roles, responsibilities, and duties of the role players in this respect, can serve as a valuable learning point for Namibia and South Africa in order to prevent conflict in the development process.

Access to Information

A successful public participation process is dependent upon adequate access to information.[153] The right to access to information is protected in the South African Constitution,[154] but not in those of Namibia and Swaziland. This constitutional right in South Africa also makes provision for a right of access to information held by private persons, if this information is needed to protect another right. Neither Namibia's nor Swaziland's legislation provides for access to information held by private persons. The Swaziland EMB[155] provides for a very comprehensive and modern system for access to information, including Internet access to this information.[156] This is something both South Africa and Namibia can take note of and consider for inclusion in future legislation.

Reasons and Appeal

Appeal in South Africa should be directed to the minister of the Department of Environmental Affairs and Tourism (DEAT) or to the Member of Executive Council (MEC) of the provincial department who is responsible for authorizing or rejecting the proposed activity.[157] In terms of the South African common law as well as the Constitution,[158] reasons have to be given by the authority for the decisions made by the authority according to the authorization of the project (administrative action).[159] The South African Constitution allows for a broad spectrum of people to seek appropriate relief in respect of any breach or threatened breach of any right provided for in the Bill of Rights.[160] In addition to the *locus standi* clause in the Constitution,[161] NEMA provides that a person may approach the court in the interest of protecting the environment.[162] In terms of the Namibian EMA, any person who feels aggrieved by a decision of the in-full Environmental Commission (EC) under this act, or under powers conferred by regulation, may appeal such decision to the in-full SDC in the prescribed manner, within the prescribed period and upon payment of the prescribed fee.[163]

The EMA makes provision for the same categories of people as the South African Constitution and NEMA as having legal standing in respect of any breach or threatened breach of any provision of EMA, or of any law concerned with the protection of the

---

[153] W. Du Plessis, "Reg op omgewingsinligting in die Europese Gemeenskap," *TSAR* (1998): 222–244 at 222.

[154] Section 32 read with Promotion of Access to Information Act 2 of 2000, section 31 of NEMA, regulation 12 GN R1183. Namibia has similar provisions of the Promotion Act and NEMA.

[155] Sections 50–51. See also Regulations 5 and 11–12 EAARR.

[156] Section 50(3) of EMB.   [157] Regulation 11(1) of GN R1183.

[158] Section 33 of the Constitution of the Republic of South Africa, 1996.

[159] See also South Africa's Promotion of Just Administration Act of 2000.

[160] Section 38 of the Constitution of the Republic of South Africa, 1996, provides that the following people can approach the court: (a) someone acting in his or her own interest, (b) someone who acts on behalf of someone else who is unable to institute such proceedings in his or her own name, (c) someone acting in the interest of or on behalf of a group or class of people, (d) someone acting in the public interest, and (e) an association acting on behalf of its members.

[161] Section 38 of the Constitution of the Republic of South Africa, 1996.

[162] Section 32(f) of NEMA.   [163] S 33(1) of EMA.

environment.[164] Similarly, the EMA, as does the NEMA, gives a person legal standing to act in the interest of the environment.[165] If any person feels aggrieved after the decision made by the SDC in regard to the appeal, he or she may appeal against it to the minister responsible for environment and tourism in the same way as in the first appeal.[166] In terms of the Swaziland EAARR, an appeal may be lodged by any person who has either a substantial interest in the decision of the authority[167] or is aggrieved by its decision[168] and has paid the prescribed appeal fee.[169] The appeal must be directed in writing to the minister responsible for environmental protection in accordance with the prescribed form and within the specified time.[170] The Swaziland EAARR provides a right of appeal for people who have a substantial interest in the decision or who are aggrieved by the authority's decision[171] in respect of legal standing. The EAARR provides a narrower spectrum of access to the court than South Africa[172] and Namibia[173] provide. The EAARR provides that reasons must be given for the decisions that the authority made in writing.[174]

International Implications

In South Africa, provisions are made in NEMA for cases in which an activity will affect the interest of more than one province or traverse international boundaries or cases in which an activity will affect compliance with obligations resting on the Republic in terms of customary or conventional international law.[175] The South African minister responsible for the environment may make regulations in accordance with subsections (3) and (4), which stipulate the procedure to be followed and the report to be prepared in investigating, assessing, and communicating potential impacts. The NEMA Amendment Act 8 of 2004 also includes such provisions.[176] The Namibian EMA does not have a similar provision.

The Swaziland EAARR stipulates that after the authority has received either the Initial Environmental Evaluation (IEE) and Comprehensive Mitigation Plan (CMP) or the EIA report and in-full CMP,[177] and these documents are made available for public review,[178] the authority may also forward the relevant reports and documents to neighboring countries.[179] This process only takes place when the authority believes a project is likely to have a significant impact on the environment of the neighboring country or that country requests the particular documents and reports.[180]

The Swaziland EMB also makes provision for relevant reports and documents to be forwarded to the neighboring country when the project in Swaziland is likely to have a significant adverse effect on that country.[181] The minister shall also invite comments

---

[164] Section 3 of EMA.

[165] Section 3(e) of EMA.

[166] Section 33(2) of EMA.

[167] Regulation 9(1) (a) of EAARR.

[168] Regulation 9(1) (b) of EAARR.

[169] Regulation 9(1) (c) of EAARR.

[170] Section 17(1) of the Swaziland Environmental Authority Act 15 of 1992.

[171] Regulation 9(1) (a)–(c) of EAARR.

[172] Section 38 of the Constitution of the Republic of South Africa, 1996, and s 32 of NEMA.

[173] Section 3 of EMA.

[174] Regulation 8(a) of EAARR.

[175] Section 24(6) of NEMA.

[176] Section 24(6) (a)–(b) of NEMA Amendment Act 8 of 2004.

[177] Regulation 11(6) of EAARR.

[178] Regulation 11(7) of EAARR.

[179] Regulation 11(9) of EAARR.

[180] Regulation 11(9) of EAARR.

[181] Section 32(9) of EMB.

from the neighboring country within a specified period.[182] Before granting an approval, the authority must consider the comments of neighboring countries.[183]

4 CONCLUSION AND RECOMMENDATIONS

The preceding discussion of the South African, Swaziland, and Namibian EIA legislation reveals similarities and differences. When comparing these three countries' EIA legislation, it is important to take into account that the countries' governmental and administrative systems differ. South Africa and Namibia are democratic countries with constitutions as their highest law of the land, while Swaziland is a Kingdom with a fully autonomous government. South Africa is also a larger country with a larger population than Namibia and Swaziland. The legislation must also be evaluated in light of the possibility of transborder agreements or any SADC Protocols that describe procedures for transborder EIAs.

Swaziland provides for a comprehensive EIA process, while Namibia's EIA process is much more streamlined. The Swaziland EIA process may be hailed for its comprehensive description of the project and the public participation process. This is in contradistinction to Namibia's legislation, which merely outlines what the public participation process must include. The Namibian legislation is, however, more realistic, as it provides for a more concise process, and through screening, the authority can determine earlier whether a project will require an EIA.

The Swaziland legislation is an ambitious piece of legislation whose success will be determined by practice. It is important to remember that because all three are regarded as developing countries, there is a the need for EIA processes that address all the issues sufficiently, while keeping the limitations of the country and its people in mind.

Overall, a comparative analysis of the South African, Swaziland, and Namibian legislation offers numerous potential opportunities for improving the current South African EIA legislation. If the three countries' legislation, the Espoo Convention, and the North American Agreement are compared in the light of Wood's criteria, the following similarities are discernible:

- The national legislation and international agreements are based on a legal framework.
- Lists or categories of activities for which an EIA is to be undertaken are given. Swaziland refers also to certain threshold categories.
- Provision is made for consultation and participation.
- Provision is made for appeal.
- The role players are identified.
- The application procedure is described albeit with differing details.

The three countries and the two international conventions differ in the following respects (in terms of Wood's criteria):

- The definitions with regard to EIA differ. Wood includes SEAs, which are not clearly specified in Namibia's and South Africa's EIA legislation or in the two international agreements.

---

[182] Section 32(9) of EMB.   [183] Section 32(10) of EMB.

- The roles and responsibilities of players are not clearly detailed. Wood refers to a specific role for consultants that is not included in Namibian and Swaziland's legislation. The position with regard to the two international agreements is not clear.
- The three countries include screening and scoping. It is not clear what the position is with regard to the two international agreements.
- The procedures with regard to report review are particularly weak in this regard in Namibia and South Africa.
- EIA follow-up and monitoring are poorly described in the South African and Namibian legislation. Swaziland, the Espoo Convention, and the North American Agreement contain explicit provisions in this regard.
- Consultation and participation procedures differ – as do the stages when public participation should be included.
- In South Africa, a right of access to information is granted against both private and public bodies, while Swaziland and Namibia provide such a right only against public bodies. The North American Agreement provides for requests for information.
- The appeal procedure differs.
- South Africa and Swaziland contain provisions for impacts that may have a transborder effect as well as for notification procedures, Namibia does not. The Espoo Convention and the North American Agreement have explicit provisions in this regard.

The three countries more or less comply with Wood's criteria. A careful study of the legislation of these countries, however, reveals certain differences. It is apparent from the discussion of the Espoo Convention and the North American Agreement on TEIA that it is possible to conclude regional agreements with regard to transborder EIAs. It is proposed that a SADC Protocol on EIAs be developed taking into account the legislation of the countries concerned, Wood's criteria, as well as existing transborder conventions and agreements. The protocol should, however, not only focus on the transborder effects of projects undertaken in a specific country, but also make provision EIAs when a project traverses the borders of several states. Specific standards should be set. Member states without EIA legislation will have to conform to the agreement or promulgate EIA legislation that conforms to the standard set by the agreement. Countries with existing legislation should align their legislation with the agreement. As a minimum, the SADC Protocol will have to provide (a) that all national EIA legislation should have a legal basis; (b) that terms related to EIA and SEA are defined; (c) that activities are detailed; (d) that the role and functions of role players are clearly spelled out; (e) that an application procedure is provided for; (f) that there are provision for screening and/or scoping; (g) that there are a report review and a record of the decision; (h) that EIA follow-up and monitoring as well as auditing are ensured; (i) that consultation and participation occur; (j) that access to information is provided; (k) that reasons must be given and mechanisms for appeal must be provided; and (l) that extensive and clear notification and consultation procedures with affected neighboring states are specified. In the case of transborder projects, an EIA procedure should be negotiated by the affected parties. It is important that there be open dialogue between the country of origin and the affected countries. Baseline information, methodologies, and approaches to assessment should also be harmonized to ensure compatibility of results. Joint study groups could be established in this regard and information should be exchanged on a regular basis. A joint decision-making body could also be established and provision made that these further details be dealt with in bilateral or multilateral agreements.[184]

All in all, SADC is a region in need of development, and if development processes are accelerated, they can contribute to poverty alleviation in the region.

---

[184] See in this regard Arctic Environmental Impact Assessment, available at http://finnbarents.urova.fi/ aria/aria_rus/g_trans.asp.

PART TWO

NATIONAL APPROACHES TO LAND USE PLANNING FOR SUSTAINABLE DEVELOPMENT

6 Community Rights to Genetic Resources and Their Knowledge: African and Ethiopian Perspectives

Mekete Bekele

1 INTRODUCTION

Genetic resources are the natural resources of their countries of origin and need both national and international legal protection. There are several legal instruments governing the legal regime of such resources,[1] including the 1992 Convention on Biological Diversity (CBD). The Convention was signed in 1992 and went into force in 1994. It is the belief of some scholars of developing countries that the CBD has certain omissions, among which the *ex situ* collections made prior to the coming into force of the Convention and the failure to recognize intellectual property rights of communities are the major ones.[2] Ever since the adoption of the CBD by the United Nations Conference on Environment and Development (UNCED) between industrialized and nonindustrialized countries about the ownership and access to biological resources arguments have been ongoing.

Access to the biological resources and equitable sharing of benefits emanating from the resources were some of the thorny issues during the negotiations of the Convention and the follow-up activities related thereto.[3] It is evident that source countries of biological resources are developing countries while the developed ones are the most frequent users of the resources. The former are the exporters while the latter are the importers of the resources. Access to natural resources is dependent upon the consent of source countries since the issue touches upon one of the fundamental principles of international law – the principle of national sovereignty over natural resources. Community rights to the natural resources are partly an issue of international law and partly

---

[1] The African Convention on the Conservation of Nature and Natural Resources (1968); Convention for the Conservation of Biological Diversity and the Protection of Priority Wild Areas in Central America; The Convention on the Conservation of European Wildlife and Natural Habitat (Berne Convention) of 1979; South East Asian Agreement on the Conservation of Natural Resources of 1985; Convention on the Conservation of Nature in the South Pacific (Apia) of 1976; and United Nations Convention on the Law of the Sea (UNCLOS) of 1982. The texts of these Conventions can be found in Alexandre Charles Kiss (ed.), *Selected Multilateral Treaties in the Field of the Environment* (Nairobi: UNEP, 1983), and in Iwona Rummel-Bulska and Seth Osafo (eds.), *Selected Multilateral Treaties in the Field of the Environment* (Vol. 2), (Cambridge: Grotius, 1991).

[2] Tewolde Berhan Gebre Egziabher, "Foreword" in Solomon Tilahun and Sue Edwards (eds.), *The Movement for Intellectual Rights* (Addis Ababa: Institute for Sustainable Development, 1996) ix.

[3] Frederic Hendrickx et al., "Convention on Biological Diversity: Access to Genetic Resources – a legal Analysis" *Environmental Policy and Law*, Vol. 23 No. 6 (1993): 250.

one of national laws.[4] Any legal regime that fails to ensure communities' right of access to their biological resources and due recognition of their indigenous knowledge would be a tyrannical regime as far as the communities rights are concerned.

The idea of common utilization of natural resource may not be wholeheartedly welcomed by all States, for it is feared that such practice may put the vital interest of some in jeopardy. Such ideas are viewed with suspicion as trends that would possibly erode the power of States with regard to their sovereignty and control over their natural resources. Most of the developing countries have undergone colonial pillage and have reasonable and legitimate fear given that experience. Encroachment upon the indigenous knowledge and culture of communities[5] may eventually deny them the chance of making decisions as to the use and enjoyment of their natural resources. Sharing certain resources such as transboundary rivers could, however, be a question of necessity rather than of consent of source countries.[6]

2 SOVEREIGNTY OVER NATURAL RESOURCES AND THE NEED FOR CONSERVATION

Black's Law Dictionary defines *natural resources* as "any material in its native state which when extracted has economic value."[7] But the term is not defined by any one of the international legal instruments, though it is included in many of them. One may conclude from the usage of the term that it includes plants and animals. Plants and animals of a given country could be referred to as its biological resources. Ethiopian draft law on "Community Knowledge and Access to Biological Resources" defines the term *biological resource* to "include genetic resources, organisms or parts thereof, populations, or any other component of an ecosystem, including ecosystems themselves, with actual or potential use or value for humanity."[8] The picture is obscured when issues of genetic characters are involved. The emergence and development of genetic engineering and related sciences provided opportunities for individuals and other legal entities to claim proprietary rights over their new species.[9] There is a growing need for the conservation of species and their natural habitat as a result of alarming threats that may lead to the extinction of most of them. Two opposing views, namely, the *anthropocentric* and the *ecocentric*, have emerged, raising the need for a balance to reach consensus on the conservation of the existing biological resources. The anthropocentric approach is concerned with benefits of environmental resources to the present and future generations, while the ecocentric approach is concerned about the intrinsic value of the resources.

---

[4] Nico Schrijver, *Sovereignty over the Natural Resources: Balancing Rights and Duties* (Cambridge: Cambridge University Press, 1997) 36ff.

[5] Vandana Shiva, "A New Partnership for National Sovereignty: IPRS, Collective Rights and Biodiversity," in Solomon Tilahun and Sue Edwards (eds.), *supra* note 2.

[6] Mekete Bekele, "Sharing the Nile Waters: A Quest for Equity among the Riparian States," *NJIWA (Magazine of Eastern Africa Environmental Network)*, Vol. 7 No. 8 (1998): 8

[7] Henry Campbell Black, *Black's Law Dictionary* (St. Paul, Minn.: West Publishing Company, 1991), 713.

[8] Article 2(3) of a draft law entitled "A Proclamation to Provide for Community Knowledge and Access to Biological Resources."

[9] Cyrille de Klemm, *Biological Diversity Conservation and the Law: Legal Mechanism for Conserving Species and Ecosystems* (IUCN – The World Conservation Union, 1993) 2.

The ecocentric view upholds that humanity may use the resources but has no right to destroy them. It seeks to ensure that the life-sustaining systems of the earth and its biosphere are maintained.[10]

Traditionally, the conservation and utilization of natural resources were in the exclusive jurisdictions of States in which they were situated. The principle of national sovereignty over the natural resources has been eroded as a result of recent developments in international law. The ever-increasing environmental degradation led the States and the international community to a consensus that the species and their natural habitats have to be protected.[11] The World Conservation Union (IUCN) has played a pivotal role in bringing about the consensus. The Union, together with other international organizations, managed to organize the international scientific community on the issues of conservation and set three world conservation strategies: the maintenance of essential ecological processes, the preservation of genetic diversity, and the sustainable use of species and ecosystems.[12]

As consensus to conserve biological diversity developed, successive strategies such as "caring for the earth" and "sustainable development" were established. Documents such as the Stockholm and Rio Declarations, the World Charter for Nature, and Agenda 21 (an Action Plan of Rio Earth Summit drawn up by UNCED) have paved the way for actions by States. Many of the principles encapsulated in these documents have already become part of national laws of countries. All these instruments tend to show that there is a firm consensus on the need to conserve biological resources. There were tussles between developed and developing countries as to the ownership and enjoyment of genetic resources. Developing countries were not comfortable with the general notion of the common heritage of humankind with respect to the exploitation of genetic resources as envisaged in instruments such as the United Nations Food and Agricultural Organization's (FAO's) Undertaking on genetic resources.[13] It is a fact that developing countries are resource-rich and developed ones are resource-poor as far as genetic resources are concerned. On the basis of these situations developing countries vehemently negotiated to have the principle of sovereignty over natural resources as one of the guiding principles of the Convention on Biological Diversity.

3 SOVEREIGNTY OVER GENETIC RESOURCES

This section and subsequent sections of the chapter deal with the provisions of the Convention on Biological Diversity on the rights of States and communities over their biological resources, the positions of developing countries with respect to access to genetic resources, and the relationships between the indigenous communities and the collectors of genetic resources. It also addresses community rights realization within federal states.

Article 15 of the Convention deals with the rights and obligations of parties regarding access to genetic resources and their utilization. The Convention recognizes the right of

---

[10] Ibid. at 3.
[12] Ibid.

[11] Ibid.
[13] Frederic Hendrichx et al., *supra* note 3 at 250.

States to determine access to their genetic resources. The first paragraph of this article addresses the access issue as follows:

> Recognizing the sovereign rights of States over their natural resource, the authority to determine access to genetic resources rests with the national governments and is subject national legislation.

According to the preceding excerpt, States that are parties to the convention are expected to create national legislation on access to their genetic resources. This right emanates from the principle of a State's sovereignty over its natural resources. The CBD is the first international instrument to recognize States' sovereignty over their genetic resources. There are, however, arguments by some scholars that Article 15 of the Convention does not grant states proprietary rights over genetic resources, that questions of ownership are not addressed in the Convention, and that the term *their* refers only to the natural resources, not to the State.[14]

The second paragraph of Article 15 of the Convention deals with the obligation of States to facilitate conditions for other Contracting Parties to exploit the genetic resources in question. Though they have the right to determine access, the source countries are obligated not to impose restrictions that may run counter to the objectives of the Convention. A Contracting Party that wants to use the genetic resources is required to employ environmentally sound methods when exploiting the genetic resources of the other Contracting Party. This provision reads as follows:

> Each Contracting Party shall endeavor to create conditions to facilitate access to genetic resources for environmentally sound uses by other contracting parties and not to impose restrictions that run counter to the objectives of this convention.

The obligation not to impose restrictions on exploitation is a hangover from the principle of the common heritage of humankind that was included in the 1983 FAO International Undertaking on Plant Genetic Resources. A grant of free access to a country's genetic resources is not acceptable to the source countries. Accordingly the subsequent annexes to the Undertaking have recognized that nations have sovereign rights over their genetic resources and free access does not mean access free of charge.[15] Paragraph 4 of Article 15 of the Convention says that access to genetic resources shall be subject to prior informed consent (PIC) of the Contracting Parties. We may safely conclude that the CBD adequately provides for the States' sovereignty over their genetic resources. The position regarding genetic resources that were taken out of the country before the coming into force of the Convention is, however, not clear.

Many African countries, including Ethiopia and Kenya, have concerns about the genetic resources that were taken out of their countries and deposited in foreign gene banks.[16] For example, Ethiopia is known for being the country of origin for coffee, but coffee is grown all over the world and in places far away from Ethiopia. The Ethiopian

---

[14] Lyle Glowka et al., *A Guide to the Convention on Biological Diversity* (IUCN – The World Conservation Union, 1994) 76.

[15] Ibid. at 77.

[16] Calestous Juma, "Managing Biological Diversity in Kenya" in Amos Kiriro and Calestous Juma (eds.), *Gaining Ground: Institutional Innovations in Land-Use Management in Kenya*, African Centre for Technology Studies (Nairobi: ACTS Press, 1991) 125–154.

coffee-growing areas are, however, still looked upon as the natural gene banks of indigenous coffee trees. The former U.S. Vice President Al Gore wrote

> The center for diversity of coffee is in the Ethiopian highlands. But coffee is now grown in many countries of the world – the Andes region of Colombia and Brazil is one – and every once in a while, when a new pest or blight cannot be met with genetic resistance from readily available seeds, coffee growers must return to the Ethiopian highlands in search of wild relatives that can combat the new threat. A few years ago, this reliance on coffee's genetic homeland took an ironic twist. As Brazil was coming under international pressure for its tolerance of widespread destruction of the Amazon rain forest a small group of Brazilians went to Addis Ababa to express their concern about the progressive deforestation of areas in Ethiopia vitally important to the future viability of the coffee crop.[17]

Thanks to the Ethiopian indigenous coffee and the multifaceted biotechnologies and genetic engineering, Brazil has recently emerged as a producer of a new brand of coffee that is immune to pests and blight. A number of questions arise here, namely, whether Ethiopia is entitled to claim compensation for either its contribution to the survival of the Brazilian coffee or the unfair coffee market Brazil has created against the country of origin of the coffee crop; whether the Brazilians would be liable for unlawful enrichment by the fact of their exploitation of Ethiopian coffee for the purpose of biotechnology; and whether the coffee-growing rural communities in the Ethiopian highlands are entitled to their intellectual property rights for the preservation or sustainable utilization of the indigenous coffee.

Al Gore made a second reference to the contribution of Ethiopian genetic resource, this time in relation to Californian agricultural report:

> The California Agricultural Lands Project (CALP) recently reported that the Department of Agriculture searched through all 6,500 known varieties of barley and finally located a single Ethiopian barley plant that now protects the entire $160 million California barley crop from yellow dwarf virus. Similar wild genes have contributed to the increase in crop yields – more 300 percent in many crops in the last few decades.[18]

It is obvious that the credit for the preservation by such wild barley genes should, in all fairness, go to the Ethiopian agricultural communities. The former Vice President does not tell us whether Ethiopia or its farming communities should be rewarded for that contribution or not. On the other hand, there are cases in which the genetic resources that have been taken out of the country of origin are no longer available there. There are requests by countries that lost their genetic resources as a result of wanton destruction or systematic expropriation to be compensated for the losses.[19] Do the existing international law principles support compensation for damages and restoration of losses caused by other States?[20]

---

[17] Vice President Al Gore, *Earth in the Balance: Ecology and the Human Spirit* (New Year: Plume, 1994) 133.

[18] Ibid. p. 139.

[19] Edith Brown Weiss, *In Fairness to Future Generations: International Law, Common Patrimony, and Intergenerational Equity* (New York/Tokyo: United Nations University Press, 1993) 79–86.

[20] B. T. Mekete and J. B. Ojwang, "The Right to a Healthy Environment: Possible Juridical Bases" in *South African Journal of Environmental Law and Policy* Vol. 3 No. 2 (1996), 167–170; Mekete Bekele, "The Right to a Healthy Environmental Law: International and National Law Perspectives," in *Indian Journal of*

4 ACCESS WITH PRIOR INFORMED CONSENT (PIC) AND MUTUALLY AGREED TERMS

With regard to access to genetic resources, paragraph 4 of Article 15 of the CBD lays down a condition that it shall be granted on mutually agreed terms and is subject to the provisions of the Convention. One of the provisions of the Convention that needs attention in this respect is paragraph 5 of Article 15, governing issues of prior informed consent. There seems to be mistrust between developing and developed countries with respect to the implications of "mutually agreed terms." The CBD entered into force after negotiations and debates on several issues. The main debate was between the richer genetic-resource-poor North and the poorer genetic-resource-rich South, which took the form of a "North–South Dialogue" on issues of global partnership and common benefit of the Parties to the Convention.[21] The bilateral agreements anticipated may be to the disadvantage of the genetic-rich poor countries of the South. There are arguments that the poorer southerners can sell their genetic resources for throw-away prices as a result of their precarious position in the unfavorable market.

Klaus Bosselmann[22] analyzed the political controversy between the developed countries and the developing countries and observed that the dispute led to the coinage of terms such as "seed war" and "bioimperialism" as a result of its intensity. Developing countries complain that the gene-poor North is robbing the gene-rich South of germplasm as a resource for biotechnology and selling the products to them at exorbitant prices. Developing countries want to have a role in the international genetic resource system and to have access to the gene banks of the developed countries,[23] the gene banks that are mainly stocked by the genetic material from the southern countries. Tewolde Berhan Gebre Egziabher, who uses a parable from the Bible to explain this scenario, depicts this robber and victim relationship of the North and South as follows:

> When good will prevails, such bilateral agreements work well. But in a tussle, the strong party's wish will prevail. The Bible (Exodus 25: 29–34) tells us that Esau, returning hungry from an unsuccessful hunt, sold his birth right as the eldest to his younger brother Jacob for "bread and a pottage of lentils." This is an appropriate parable of our time, as the South could easily sell its biological diversity for a shipload of wheat flour or even less to feed the ever-hungry component of its population.[24]

Apart from weaker bargaining positions of developing countries, Tewolde Berhan argues, there are other processes of disinheritance of the genetic resources: Systematic stealing of the genetic resources is one possibility that cannot be ruled out. Without

---

Politics Vol. 38 Nos. 2 & 3 (2004): 60–64; and Alfred Rest, "New Legal Instruments for Environmental Prevention, Control and Restoration in Public International Law" in *Environmental Policy and Law*, Vol. 23 No. 6 (1993): 260–272.

[21] Klaus Bosselmann, "Plants and Politics: The International Legal Regime Concerning Biotechnology and Biodiversity," in *Colorado Journal of International Environmental Law and Policy* Vol. 7 No. 1 (1995): 111–148.

[22] Ibid. at 132.

[23] Harold J. Bordwin, "The Legal and Political Implications of the International Undertaking on Plant Genetic resources," in *Ecology Law Quarterly* Vol. 12 (1985): 1053–1069.

[24] Tewolde Berhan Gebre Egziabher, *supra* note 2 at 6.

failing to appreciate the provisions of paragraph 5 of Article 15 he suggests the following strategies for the better protection genetic resources:[25]

- All exits from a country should be well guarded to reduce illegal export of germplasm, and laws and their enforcement mechanism should be in place to deal with offenders.
- Southern countries should work together to build up the capacity for tracking germplasm, including the requisite biotechnology, and exchange information.
- Countries should push for the establishment of a worldwide open system for tracking the movement of biological materials.

It is evident from Article 15 of the CBD that the purchasing country has to get prior permission from the source country for the collection of the genetic resources and their exportation. And it is also taken for granted that a providing country that has voluntarily consented to the sale of its genetic resources will be deemed to have known the possible outcome of its transactions. All member countries are expected to formulate their own national legislation as to the procedures of PIC that have to be used. It is becoming common practice for the Parties to require a potential user of the genetic resources to meet the minimal requirements that the collector has to outline and specify the immediate or subsequent user of the resources.[26] The national laws of the providing countries should provide for a legal situation whereby a gene bank that has a large amount of genetic material cannot itself become a provider to compete with the country of origin and kick it out of the market.[27] Countries should be able to control possible illegal export of their genetic resources by enhancing their customs ports and other checkpoints within their national jurisdictions.

5 ETHIOPIAN COMMUNITY ACCESS AND INDIGENOUS KNOWLEDGE APPROACH

The Ethiopian draft law gives the right of ownership of the biological resources to the State and the people of Ethiopia. It prohibits any form of private ownership of such resources and provides for a possibility of access through a government permit. It is stipulated that communities within a defined geographic area can have rights and access to the resources within the area. With respect to consent and access permits by states, the problem is more complicated in federal states such as Ethiopia than in unitary ones. The law defines *access* as the acquisition of biological resources, their derivatives, community knowledge, innovations, technologies, or practices that are authorized by the relevant authority. *Community knowledge* or *indigenous knowledge* is defined as accumulated knowledge, consisting of local practices, innovations, knowledge, or technologies vital for the conservation and sustainable use of biological resources "developed over the years in indigenous/ local communities."[28] Access to the genetic resources of Ethiopia is subject to an access permit (AP) agreement to be made by the applicant and the relevant government agency mandated to grant the permit.[29] The provisions on access permits

---

[25] Ibid. at 7.   [26] Lyle Glowka et al., *supra* note 14 at 81.

[27] Hendrickx et al., at *supra* note 3 at 254.

[28] Paragraphs 1 and 5 of Article 2 of the draft Ethiopian proclamation on Community Knowledge and Access to Biological Resources (2004) (hereafter draft law on access).

[29] Part 6 of the draft law on access.

state that the communities have to be consulted before allowing access to the genetic resources in question.

As a matter of fact Ethiopia is a federal state where the constituent units are accorded the status of a State or a Region.[30] Traditionally, federal state structures are characterized by decentralized administration of the natural resources; therefore, the need for regional environmental laws is very important.[31] Accordingly, the federal draft law adequately provides for the participation of communities in the decision-making process with regard to granting of an AP to the genetic resources' collectors. It is very difficult to have uniform genetic resources laws and regulations for the whole federal arrangement. Every consideration should be made in a federal state before law relating to resources is enacted. The Ethiopian draft law on the access to the resources and the indigenous knowledge of the communities takes into account the existing federal system.[32]

The draft law provides for the limitation of scope of application of the law by stating that it shall not affect the traditional systems of communal knowledge, access to, and sharing of benefits arising out of the bioresources thereof by members of a given community.[33] Objectives of the draft law include the protection of the rights of communities, promotion of their knowledge, guarantee of communities' equitable sharing of the benefits of access, and promotion of food security.[34] All communities have a right to produce, use, sell, transfer, or own as property, in common, any tangible or intangible product. The ownership right of community knowledge is given protection as a communal right and can be exercised communally. There is growing appreciation for the value of knowledge and experience of the local communities in the use and maintenance of the genetic resources in many countries.[35] Until international conventions for the protection of plant genetic resources emerged over the past couple of decades, indigenous communities did not have many problems. It is believed that peasants, particularly the older members of communities, possess a great deal of indigenous knowledge of their productive environment.[36] The indigenous knowledge of the Maasai community[37] in Kenya is considered an asset to the country's sustained world-acclaimed

---

[30] Article 47 of the Constitution of Federal Democratic Republic of Ethiopia of 1995.

[31] Richard B. Stewart, "Introduction: Environmental Regulations in Multi-Jurisdictional Regimes," and Richard L. Revesz, "Federalism and Environmental Regulations: An Overview," in Richard L. Revesz et al. (eds.), *Environmental Law, the Economy and Sustainable Development: The United States, the European Community and the International Community* (Cambridge: Cambridge University Press, 2000) 1–33 and 37–79, respectively.

[32] Paragraph 9 of Article 2 of the draft law on access refers to the competent authorities of either the federal or the regional government.

[33] Article 3 of the draft law on access.   [34] Article 4 of the draft law on access.

[35] Gurdial Singh Nijar, "In Defence of Local Community Knowledge and Biodiversity: A Conceptual Framework and Essential Elements of a Rights Regime" in Solomon Tilahun and Sue Edwards, *supra* note 2 at 73–74; Alison Field-Juma, "Governance and Sustainable Development," in Calestous Juma and J. B. Ojwang (eds.), *In Land We Trust: Environment, Private Property and Constitutional Change* (Nairobi: Initiatives, 1996) 9–38.

[36] Graham Woodgate, "Local Environmental Knowledge: Agricultural Development and Livelihood Sustainability in Mexico," in Michael Redclift and Colin Sage (eds.), *Strategies for Sustainable Development: Local Agendas for the Southern Hemisphere* (West Sussex: John Wiley & Sons, 1994) 133–170.

[37] Joy K. Asiema and Francis D. P. Situma, "Indigenous Peoples and the Environment: The Case of the Pastoral Maasai of Kenya," in *Colorado International Environmental Law & Policy* Vol. 5 (1994): 149–171.

wildlife conservation efforts. Laws of national States should duly recognize and protect such indigenous knowledge.

After recognizing the intellectual property rights of farming and pastoralist communities, the Ethiopian draft law allows individual farmers and pastoralists to use, save, exchange, and sell their animals or farm-saved seeds or use a new breeder's variety, including those from the gene banks. However, the intellectual property rights of individual farmers and pastoralists could be restricted when food security, protection of health, or conservation of biodiversity, or other rights of the farming or pastoral communities are likely to be affected. Another draft proclamation, for the "Administration and Protection of Plant Breeder's Rights," gives exclusive rights to licensees to sell and to license other persons to sell plants or propagating materials of that variety, and such right will be restricted only when found necessary to protect the rights of farmers and pastoralists.[38] Ethiopia's draft law on breeders' rights provides better protection to the communities, in cases of conflict of interest between the individuals and the former.

The National Register of Plant Breeders Rights and the Plant Genetic Resources Centers are some of the newly introduced institutions for the implementation of the rights provided under the law.[39] There are detailed procedures for the application, granting, and withdrawal of plant breeders' rights. Benefit sharing is one of the principles in the draft law aimed at motivating the communities for active participation in the decision-making process on genetic resources.

6 CONCLUSION

The protection and the sustainable use of genetic resources shall only be meaningful if participation of indigenous communities is ensured. Access to genetic resources by the States, communities, individuals, and other entities has to be governed by national laws of the State Parties to the CBD. The existence of detailed domestic laws and regulations on access to the genetic resources and the indigenous community knowledge is of paramount importance for the establishment of a working legal regime for the conservation and sustainable use of the genetic resources.

---

[38] Plant Breeder's Rights as stated in the *Draft Proclamation to Provide for the Administration and Protection of Plant Breeders' Rights* (2004) (hereafter "draft law for breeders").

[39] Article 11 of the draft law on breeders.

7 Easements and Wildlife Conservation in Kenya

Nyokabi Gitahi

1 INTRODUCTION

Wildlife as a resource plays an important role in the economic development of Kenya. It is the main basis of the tourism industry, which contributes greatly to the country's gross domestic product (GDP). Kenya's wildlife is preserved in protected areas in which human settlement is prohibited and land use restricted to wildlife conservation.[1] However, most of these protected areas have been found too small to maintain viable populations and diversity of wildlife in the long term.[2] Over 70 percent of Kenya's wildlife resides outside protected areas.[3] This land provides habitat for wildlife as well as connectivity between various protected areas. While the importance of land outside protected areas to the integrity and viability of protected areas is accepted, the continued availability of wildlife areas outside protected areas is threatened. These lands are rapidly being subdivided, fenced, and converted to other uses such as agriculture and urban development.[4] Unregulated land use change destroys wildlife habitat and migratory routes and threatens the existence of wildlife. It is therefore important to find mechanisms to conserve critical wildlife areas found outside protected areas.

This chapter examines the use of one land conservation mechanism – easements. It traces the history and use of easements in the English Common Law. It discusses the limitations that easements under Common Law present to the use of the easement for wildlife conservation by the requirements for dominant and servient tenement and the rule against easements in gross. Environmental easements under Kenya's Environmental Management and Co-ordination Act 1999 are examined as a means of overcoming the common law constraints on easements and providing for environmental conservation. The example of the use of the environmental easement to conserve wildlife area outside Nairobi National Park is used to illustrate the operationalization of such an easement. In its conclusion, the chapter recommends the crafting of policies and the establishment

---

[1] Wildlife Conservation and Management Act Ch. 376 Laws of Kenya.

[2] W. D. Newmark, *The Role and Design of Wildlife Corridors with Examples from Tanzania* (Royal Swedish Academy of Sciences, Stockholm) (1993), 22: 500–504.

[3] D. Western and M. Pearl, "Conservation without Parks: Wildlife in the Rural Landscape," in D. Western and M. Pearl (eds.), *Conservation for the Twenty-First Century* (Oxford University Press, New York) (1989) 158–165.

[4] See, for example, P. Kristjanson et al., "Valuing Alternative Land-Use Options in the Kitengela Wildlife Dispersal Area of Kenya," *ILRI Impact Assessment Series 10* (A joint International Livestock Research Institute/African Conservation Center) Report (ILRI, Nairobi, Kenya) (2002) 61 pp.

of an institutional framework to support the use of easements for wildlife conservation in Kenya.

The term *wildlife* is used to refer to all types of fauna and flora but does not include domestic animals or plants;[5] this chapter uses the term to refer to wild fauna. Wildlife, as are all living things, are dependent on their environment for food, shelter, and sustenance. The lands upon which wildlife is found provide the necessary environment for their existence; a change in the nature of those lands will affect the wildlife. If the change results in loss of habitat, wildlife may be forced to migrate to other areas or even become extinct.

Kenya's wildlife is of immense diversity, including rare, endemic, and endangered species. This important resource is found mainly in the arid and semiarid areas of the country, which constitute 80 percent of Kenya's total land area.[6] These areas are ecologically fragile and susceptible to frequent droughts. They support approximately 25 percent of the human population and over 50 percent of the country's livestock population. Most of the gazetted protected areas for wildlife use are situated in these arid and semiarid areas. Protected areas designed for the protection of wildlife constitute 8 percent of the country's total land area. They have varying levels of protection and permissible land uses.[7] These areas attract a lot of visitors and are the main basis of the tourism industry, which creates employment and earns foreign exchange.[8]

Tourism's contribution to the overall gross domestic product (GDP) of the country is assessed at nearly 13 percent. This includes all revenue raised from trade, restaurants, and hotels in 2001. Tourism's contribution is far below that of agriculture, which contributed over 24 percent of the overall GDP of the country in 2001.[9]

The disparity between wildlife activities such as tourism and agriculture in their contribution to GDP in Kenya may create an impression that agriculture is a more profitable venture than wildlife-based activities. However, certain government policies have made agriculture appear more profitable than wildlife conservation and reduced the viability of wildlife-based economic activities. In an effort to promote agriculture for food production in the country, the government introduced policies that provided great incentives for agriculture in the country. These included tax exemptions on selected farm machinery and equipment, fertilizers, and most agricultural chemicals. The government also provided subsidized credit facilities to farmers and invested heavily in research and development and protection of the sector from competition from imported commodities.[10] Similar facilitative policies and subsidies were not put in place to encourage wildlife keeping as a land use.

In the arid and semiarid areas, irrigation and other agricultural activities such as development of crops that could resist drought were promoted at the expense of wildlife keeping. The net effect of these measures was to promote agriculture as a more viable land use option than wildlife in the arid and semiarid areas. Wildlife keeping as a land

---

[5] As defined in the Wildlife Conservation and Management Act, *supra* note 1.

[6] Republic of Kenya, *National Development Plan 2002–2008*.

[7] Republic of Kenya, Sessional Paper No. 3 of 1975, *Statement of Future Wildlife Management Policy in Kenya* (1975); UNEP–Government of Kenya, *The Cost Benefit and Unmet Needs of Biological Diversity Conservation in Kenya* (March 1992).

[8] Republic of Kenya *Economic Survey* (2002).   [9] See *National Development Plan, supra* note 6.

[10] Kenya Wildlife Service and African Wildlife Foundation, *Wildlife Utilisation Study* (Report No. 6 – Workshop on Utilisation Policy) (1995).

use must be a viable economic activity if it is to compete against other land use options that are attractive to landowners and users.

2 WILDLIFE HABITAT OUTSIDE PROTECTED AREAS AND CONFLICTING LAND USES

Conservation of lands outside protected areas is critical to wildlife conservation in Kenya because at least 75 percent of wildlife in Kenya is found outside the protected areas, in adjacent lands.[11] These lands are sources of food, and they provide migratory routes for wildlife between protected areas in their seasons.

There are various examples that affirm the importance of lands outside protected areas for wildlife conservation. The Amboseli National Park in Kajiado district is a key wildlife protected area, which generates the highest tourism revenues in Africa.[12] Wildlife species such as wildebeest, zebra, and African buffalo move within the park and adjacent ranches between the wet and dry seasons.[13] In the absence of adjoining ranches, the Amboseli National Park would not survive.[14]

The Longido plains in Tanzania, Amboseli National Park, Chyulu Hills National Park, and Tsavo West National Parks in Kenya are all linked by land that provides migratory routes for elephants between the parks.[15] Open plains to the south of Nairobi National Park also provide grazing and dispersal areas for wildebeest, plains zebra, and eland in the wet season.[16]

Communal ranches bordering Maasai Mara National Reserve serve as dispersal areas for wildlife from the reserve. The reserve adjoins the Serengeti National Park in Tanzania and is famous for the annual migration of wildebeest and attendant predators. Landowners are entitled to utilize their land in any manner that they wish subject to land use regulations, contractual obligations, and the common law rules against nuisance.[17] Kenya has not put in place a comprehensive policy regarding land use, and the existing legislation is disjointed and poorly enforced. Consequently, there is little to ensure that land outside protected areas is used in ways that allow wildlife conservation.

Land use activities modify the characteristics of a landscape, which might result in better or worse quality of habitat for species that are naturally found in such a landscape.

---

[11] UNEP, *supra* note 7; R. A. Kock, "Wildlife Utilisation: Use It or Lose It – a Kenya Perspective," in *Biodiversity and Conservation*, Vol. 4. (1995) 241–256.

[12] Brian Child, "Assessment of Wildlife Utilization as a Land Use Option in the Semi-Arid Rangeland of Southern Africa," pp. 155–175, in Agness Kiss (ed.), *Living with Wildlife: Wildlife Resource Management with Local Participation in Africa*, World Bank Technical Paper No. 130 (Africa Technical Department Series, The World Bank, Washington, D.C.) (1990) 155–175.

[13] David Western, *A Wildlife Guide and a Natural History of Amboseli* (General Printers Ltd., Nairobi) (1983).

[14] David Western, "Ecosystem Conservation and Rural Development: The Case of Amboseli," in David Western et al. (eds.), *Natural Connections; Perspectives in Community-Based Conservation* (Island Press) (1997).

[15] Ian Douglas-Hamilton, "Identification Study for the Conservation and Sustainable Use of the Natural Resources in the Kenya Portion of the Mara–Serengeti Ecosystem" (Ian Douglas-Hamilton & Associates, Nairobi) (1998); D. Western and J. Ssemakula, "The Future of the Savannah Ecosystems: Ecological Islands or Faunal Enclaves?" in *African Journal of Ecology* Vol. 19 Nos. 1&2 (1981) 7–19.

[16] L. Bennun and P. Njoroge, *Important Bird Areas in Kenya* (National Museums of Kenya, Nairobi) (1999).

[17] J. Gaunt and P. Morgan, *Gale on Easements,* 16th edition (Sweet & Maxwell, London) (1997).

This habitat conversion has been identified as a main threat to biodiversity.[18] Although natural causes such as severe drought and other climatic changes cause habitat change, their effect on biodiversity loss is not as alarming as that caused by human activities. Human-induced causes of biodiversity loss, as opposed to natural ones, are persistent and make it difficult for damaged ecosystems to recover.[19]

The factors contributing to habitat conversion include subdivision and fencing of land coupled with inequality in land distribution.[20] Inadequate alternatives to agricultural activities for an increasing population and labor force pose another challenge,[21] in light of government policies and changing environmental as well as socioeconomic conditions that discourage nomadism and encourage sedentary lifestyles in the rangelands. These complex circumstances have resulted in drainage of wetlands, irrigation, farming along riverbanks, and conversion of forest into farmland. The net land conversion for agriculture in arid and semiarid areas was about 7 percent between 1975 and 1993 with most agricultural lands being irrigated.[22]

The rate of land conversion to agriculture is significant because conversions are done at key resource areas such as forested woodland and areas that are the only permanent source of water outside protected areas.[23] Once land is converted to agriculture, there is little chance that it will be converted back to other land use types. Most land use activities encourage the cultivation of one type of crop, thereby simplifying the landscape and causing local extirpation of some species.[24] Overstocking and overgrazing in pastoral areas create competition for pasture between livestock and wildlife and drive away ungulate species. Some rangelands such as those around Amboseli National Park have experienced overstocking and overgrazing with some rangelands carrying more than 50 percent more than recommended livestock numbers.[25]

The migratory nature of wildlife and the dependence of most parks' wildlife numbers on favorable seasons make wildlife vulnerable to habitat conversion outside protected areas. Habitat conversion in the arid and semiarid areas destroys dry season fallback zones for wildlife and limits survival options of wildlife populations.[26] These negative effects are evident in many of Kenya's National Parks and Reserves, including Amboseli National Park,[27] Maasai Mara National Reserve,[28] and Nairobi National Park.[29]

---

[18] A. P. Dobson et al., "Hopes for the Future: Restoration Ecology and Conservation Biology in *Science*" Vol. 277 (1997) 51; see also P. M. Vitousek et al., "Human Domination of Earth's Ecosystems" in *Science* Vol. 277 (1997) 494–499.

[19] Enos E. Esikuri, *Spatio-Temporal Effects of Land Use Changes in Savanna Wildlife Areas of Kenya* (Ph.D. dissertation Faculty of the Virginia Polytechnic Institute and State University, Blacksburg) (1998).

[20] M. Rutten, *Selling Wealth to Buy Poverty: The Process of the Individualisation of Land Ownership among the Maasai Pastoralists of Kajiado District, Kenya, 1890–1990* (Verlag Breintenback Publishers, Saarbrucken) (1992).

[21] See Eskikuri, *supra* note 19   [22] Ibid.

[23] Ibid.   [24] Ibid.

[25] Ibid.   [26] Ibid.

[27] Western and Ssemakula, *supra* note 15, 7–19.

[28] S. N. Wasilwa, "The Change of Land-use Patterns in the Masai Mara and its Impact on the Large Herbivore Populations" (Unpublished Report, World Wide Fund for Nature, Nairobi) (1997).

[29] Imre Loefler, "The Strangulation of a Sanctuary" *Swara* 10(1) (1987) 6–7; see also D. Round-Turner, "Nairobi Zoo?" *Swara* 19(6) and 20(1) (1996) 12–13.

In the event that land use in the lands outside protected areas continues unregulated, the wildlife migratory routes and dispersal areas are under threat of being destroyed. Protected areas could become islands of biodiversity, lacking open lands linking them. This would result in great loss of wildlife species as most protected areas can hardly survive as closed ecosystems,[30] and it would compromise the role of tourism as a key foreign exchange earner in the country.[31]

It is therefore imperative that a mechanism be found to salvage land outside protected areas by protecting it from conversion to agriculture and development. Easements provide an opportunity to do this by limiting land use to activities favorable to wildlife.

3 EASEMENTS AND WILDLIFE CONSERVATION

An easement is one of the specified interests over land recognized by English Law traceable to the Common Law.[32] An interest over land is said to be an easement at common law if it fulfills four essential characteristics: First, there must be a dominant and servient tenement; second, the servient tenement must benefit the dominant tenement; third, the dominant and servient tenements must be owned by different persons; fourth, the interest created by the easement must be specific enough to form the subject matter of a grant. These requirements are discussed further in the context of applying easements for wildlife conservation.

In order to conserve wildlife areas outside protected areas, landowners need to set aside their land for wildlife use and guard it against conversion to uses that are incompatible with wildlife conservation; this means that they have to forgo certain economic activities that might be more economically rewarding. In the absence of any compensation for the opportunity forgone, the burden of wildlife conservation outside protected areas would rest primarily on the landowner. This raises the need for a mechanism to compensate the landowner in return for setting aside land.

The interest created by setting the land aside and probably conveying it to a compensating entity should be one that can last for an agreed period or even in perpetuity and should be binding on subsequent landowners should the ownership of the land change. This kind of arrangement would be akin to an easement, and the rules applicable to easements would apply. Whereas the rules governing easements in property interest support such interests as right of way, they present certain challenges when applied for purposes of wildlife conservation. There is also the question of the validity of such interests. These limitations stem from the history of easements and their evolution as an interest in land.

3.1 Common Law Easement

The Common Law easement was not traditionally used for wildlife conservation, and such purposes as conserving open spaces were considered a matter of delight rather than of necessity.

---

[30] D. Western, "Nairobi Zoo?" *Swara* 19(6) and 20(1) (1996) 19–20.

[31] Republic of Kenya, *Study on the National Tourism Master Plan (Environmental Conservation and Management Plan)* (Draft Final Report Vol. 3) (July 1995).

[32] Ibid.

In England it was held at an early date that, although there can be an easement of light, there can be no easement of prospect (i.e., the right to a view). "[F]or . . . prospect, which is a matter of delight, and not of necessity, no action lies for the stopping thereof. [T]he law does not give an action for such things of delight.[33]

The use of the Common Law easement to restrict use of land for wildlife conservation developed only recently, in Canada and Costa Rica. The approach has been to modify the Common Law easements and create an easement free of the strict common law requirements for use in wildlife conservation. Applying the Common Law easement for wildlife conservation presents the challenge of ensuring that the easement fulfills the requirements of an easement at Common Law.

Two requirements of the Common Law easement must be discussed together, as they are related. The first is the requirement of a dominant and servient tenement; the second is that the two tenements must have different owners. This requires that land use restrictions placed on one parcel of land, called the *servient tenement*, must benefit another parcel of land, the *dominant tenement*. This is to ensure that "diminution of rights incident to the ownership of an estate in a piece of land must be reflected in a corresponding artificial right superimposed on the natural rights incident to another piece of land."[34] The effect of this condition is that the rights of a landowner to use his or her land cannot be restricted by an easement for wildlife conservation unless the restrictions will benefit another parcel of land. "There can be no easement properly so called unless there be both a servient and a dominant tenement."[35]

A landowner who decides to restrict the use of his or her land for purposes of wildlife conservation without identifying another parcel of land to be benefited would create an easement in gross. An easement in gross does not have a dominant tenement. It is a personal interest that is not attached to any estate in land and does not belong to a person by virtue of ownership of an estate in land.[36] As a rule, easements in gross were not recognized in Common Law, and even when they were recognized, they were susceptible to easy destruction by a transfer of the burdened land as they were regarded as a contract over land that is not binding on subsequent holders of title.[37]

An example of an easement in gross that may be created for wildlife conservation is one that names the Kenya Wildlife Service (KWS) (the government entity managing protected areas in Kenya) as a grantee without defining any protected area managed by KWS as the benefited land. While this easement may exist between the contracting parties, it can be defeated by subsequent title holders on the basis that it is an easement in gross and therefore a personal interest to the Kenya Wildlife Service.

The Common Law easement provides a limited opportunity for use to conserve wildlife areas where the land is adjacent to protected areas, as this presents two parcels of land, one of which may be the dominant tenement and the other the servient tenement. In Kenya, for example, an easement may be placed on a parcel of land to maintain a migratory route for wildlife for the benefit of two protected areas by allowing the

---

[33] Cunningham, "Scenic Easements in the Highway Beautification Program" (1968) 45 *Denver L. J.* 167 at 175.

[34] Ibid.

[35] *Rangely v. Midland Railway Company* (1868) 3 Ch. App 306, 310, 311.

[36] *Black's Law Dictionary* (West Publishing Company, St. Paul, Minn.) (1990), 510.

[37] M. Bowles (ed.), *Gale on Easements* (13th ed.) (Sweet & Maxwell, London) (1959), 5.

wildlife to migrate from one protected area to another. In this case, the protected areas become dominant tenements and the migratory route between them are the servient tenement.

In Canada the requirement for a dominant and a servient tenement is overcome by the use of anchor acres. This is done by acquiring a piece of land (the dominant tenement) to be benefited by an easement close to the land that is targeted for protection. The owner of the land sought to be protected (the servient tenement) is requested to place an easement over his or her land for the benefit of the dominant tenement. The process of demarcating land to impose the easement can be lengthy and costly, and sometimes demonstrating the benefit to the dominant tenement is difficult.

In Costa Rica the use of reciprocal easements provides the two tenements. Owners of neighboring lands establish reciprocal easements mutually agreeing to conserve the resources of their respective properties.[38] Over 20 conservation easements protecting over 1,000 hectares of forest land have been established and registered in the National Registry, making them binding upon subsequent landowners.[39] The pitfall with this arrangement is that it relies on current landowners alone to monitor and enforce the easement against one another. If the land changes hands and subsequent title holders are not enthusiastic to monitor the easement, it could fall into disuse and be of no effect.

The third requirement of an easement is that it must "serve and accommodate" the dominant tenement and must be reasonably necessary for the better enjoyment of that tenement. Whereas finding two tenements separately owned might not be a big challenge, it is difficult at all times to show that the easement has a necessary connection with the tenement. It is not enough to show that the easement confers an advantage upon the landowner and makes his or her ownership of the land more valuable. If this is the only proof of easement, the interest created is considered a mere contractual right personal to the parties. It is only enforceable between the two contracting parties.[40] An easement to conserve a wildlife migratory route may easily be seen as connected with the protected area it benefits because wildlife conservation is the natural use of the protected area. It has been held that a right of way for purposes not connected with the land to which it was supposed to be appurtenant did not pass to successive owners of the land.[41]

The fourth requirement for an easement at Common Law is that the right created over land must be specific enough to form the subject matter of a grant. A vague definition of the right created defeats the easement. For example, an easement granting a general right to receive air from adjoining property does not create an easement.[42] In determining whether an easement forms the subject matter of the grant, the question is whether the rights amount to rights of joint occupation or whether they would substantially deprive the property owners of proprietorship or legal possession. Easements do not grant exclusive and unrestricted use of a piece of land.[43] Therefore, a restriction that takes away so many user rights over the property as to grant exclusive use for wildlife conservation for the benefit of another land may not be a valid easement.

---

[38] Stephen A. Mack, "Conservation Easements in Central America," The Environment and Natural Resources Law Center (CEDARENA) (Undated, on file with the author).

[39] Ibid. at 19.
[40] *Re Ellenborough Park* [1956] Ch. 131, 170
[41] *Ackroyd v. Smith* (1850) 10 C.B. 164
[42] Gaunt and Morgan, *supra* note 17.
[43] *Reily v. Booth* (1890) 44 Ch. D. 12. 26

3.2 Statutory Easements

In the Kenyan legal system, the law applicable to easements stems from Common Law of England and statutes enacted by Parliament.[44] The Registered Land Act provides for easements of a character similar to the English Common Law easement in that it requires a servient and a dominant tenement. It defines an *easement* as "a right attached to a parcel of land that allows the proprietor of the parcel either to use the land of another in a particular manner or to restrict its use to a particular extent."[45]

The rights granted by the statutory easement may require the grantor to do something on his or her land or to restrict the doing of something on that land in order to benefit the dominant tenement. This requirement by the statutory easement imports the restrictions of the English Common Law easement discussed previously for purposes of wildlife conservation outside protected areas. As the Common Law easement does, the statutory easement makes no reference to its application for use in matters of wildlife conservation. However, there is no express restriction in adopting the easement for purposes of wildlife conservation provided the requirements of an easement at Common Law are fulfilled. This, as seen earlier, is a difficult task.

Despite innovative efforts to use easements at Common Law for conservation purposes, Common Law frowns on easements that restrict the use of land such as negative rights that restrict a landowner from doing something that otherwise he or she could lawfully do. Instead, these rights are best conferred and acquired by means of restrictive covenants.[46] Although restrictive covenants can restrict almost any use of land, they are not enforceable against a purchaser for value without notice. An easement is valid against subsequent title holders.[47]

Easements that grant negative rights are viewed with caution; the law is reluctant to create any new negative easement.[48] The Common Law easement was not intended for conservation purposes but was limited to necessities such as water, light, way, support, and fences.[49] As expressed by Lord Denning M. R.:

> If such easement were to be permitted, it would unduly restrict your neighbour in his enjoyment of his own land. It would hamper legitimate development . . . we would put a break on desirable improvement. . . . Likewise, every man is entitled to cut down his trees if he likes. Even if it leaves you without shelter from the wind or shade from the sun; there is no such easement known to the law as an easement to be protected from the weather.[50]

The rigidity of common law easements has necessitated law reform to set aside the strict requirements of common law easements and enable the easement to be applied for purposes of conservation.[51] An example of such law reform has taken place in the United States of America resulting in the creation of the conservation easement, as well as in Kenya, with the creation of environmental easements by enacting legislation.

---

[44] The Common Law of England as modified by doctrines of equity is applicable as a source of law for Kenyan courts.

[45] Ch. 300, Laws of Kenya Section 3.

[46] Gaunt and Morgan, *supra* note 17.

[47] Ibid.

[48] *Phipps v. Pears* [1965] 1 Q.B 76

[49] Ibid.

[50] Ibid.

[51] Arlene J. Kwashiak (ed.), *Private Conservancy: The Path to Law Reform, Proceedings and Additional Material from the Environmental Law Centre's Conference on Private Conservancy* (Edmonton, Environmental Law Centre, Alberta) (13 January 1994).

3.3 Environmental Easements

The environmental easement was established in Kenya through the Environmental Management and Co-ordination Act of 1999, a law that came into effect in July 2000. In its provisions relating to the easement, the legislation does away with the Common Law requirements for a dominant and a servient tenement by creating the environmental easement in gross.

> [T]he validity and enforceability of the [environmental] easement shall not be dependent on the existence of a plot of land in the vicinity of the burdened land which can be benefited or, of a person with an interest in that plot of land who can be benefited by the environmental easement.[52]

Whereas one essential feature of the Common Law easement is that it benefits real property, an environmental easement benefits the environment of which land is constituent. The aspect of the environment that benefits from the land use restrictions placed on a parcel of land by an environmental easement is referred to as the *benefited environment*, and the land upon which land use obligations apply under an environmental easement is the *burdened land*.[53]

A unique feature of the environmental easement for wildlife conservation is that it does not entirely rely on the willingness of the landowner to conserve wildlife resources on the land. Anyone in Kenya may petition the court to impose land use obligations on any property for purposes of environmental conservation, which by definition include wildlife resources.[54] The advantage of this provision is that it enables conservation of critical parcels of land outside protected areas such as those containing endangered species. In addition, the landowner may not only be prohibited from carrying out certain activities, he or she may be required by the court to carry out certain activities to achieve the objects of the easement. For example, it may be necessary to require a landowner to take active measures to prevent the spread of an invasive species on a wildlife habitat in order to guarantee availability of pasture for the wildlife.

Environmental easements may be applied to create or maintain migration corridors for wildlife by prohibiting fencing, quarrying, and other activities that might restrict movement of wildlife. They may also be used to preserve scenic view, open space, preserve the quality and flow of water, and preserve any outstanding ecological feature of land.[55] An environmental easement may be imposed in perpetuity, for a term of years, or for an equivalent interest under customary law as the court may determine.[56]

A landowner on whose land an easement is applied is entitled to compensation commensurate with the lost value of the use of the land.[57] The person awarded the easement pays the compensation due to the landowner and is also responsible for enforcing the easement. Should a landowner or his or her agent contravene the provision of an environmental easement, the grantee may apply to court for an environmental

---

[52] Kenya's Environment Management and Co-ordination Act (1999) at section 112(6) and Uganda National Environment Statute (1995) at section 6.

[53] Uganda National Environment Statute (1995) at section 73(2) and Kenya's Environment Management and Co-ordination Act (1999) at section 112.

[54] Kenya's Environment Management and Co-ordination Act, *supra* note 52, at sections 112 and 2.

[55] Ibid. at section 112(4).　　　　　[56] Ibid.

[57] Ibid. at sections 77 and 116, respectively.

Table 7.1. Applying environmental easement to conserve wildlife areas adjacent to Nairobi National Park

The Nairobi National Park is approximately 117 km^2 and was established in 1946 under National Parks Ordinance 9 of 1945. The park serves as a dry season concentration area for wildlife such as zebras and wildebeest and is home to other species including gazelle, impala, eland, giraffe, rhino, buffalo, as well as predators such as lions, cheetahs, leopards, and hyenas. Adjacent to the Park is 2,912 acres of government ranchland that was once used as a breeding ground for sheep and goats. The ranch serves as a wildlife dispersal area and provides unimpeded wildlife migration routes necessary to maintain wildlife populations inside the Park.

An environmental easement has been negotiated to enable the government to grant an easement to the Kenya Wildlife Service (KWS) and the local community jointly and severally. The easement provides that the ranch is retained in open space as one parcel to provide for wildlife habitat, unimpeded wildlife dispersal, and migration to and from Nairobi National Park. It also provides for sustainable open land grazing for livestock by the local community. The easement prohibits cultivation and mining and any other activity that would significantly impair or interfere with the conservation values of the ranch.

KWS and the local community can enforce the provisions of the property in court and have the attendant right to enter upon the property to monitor compliance with the provisions of the easement. The grant of environmental easement has been presented to the Commissioner of Lands for signature as the legal grantor of the easement on behalf of the government.

---

restoration order.[58] Environmental restoration orders enable the courts to grant a wide range of orders to effect the purposes of the environmental easements. The environmental restoration order may be issued to require a landowner to restore the environment as far as possible to its condition before the easement was contravened.[59]

Environmental easements are yet to be implemented in Kenya, and it is likely that some of the provisions of the Environmental Management and Co-ordination Act on environmental easements will need to be interpreted by courts. For instance, the description of land burdened by an environmental easement as "land in the vicinity of the benefited environment"[60] may need to be interpreted should there be disagreement on its exact import. An attempt to apply an environmental easement under the act was made by the Kenya Wildlife Service and its partners to conserve wildlife areas adjacent to Nairobi National Park (see Table 7.1).

4 CONCLUSION

The use of easements for wildlife conservation outside protected areas faces certain challenges from the land and resource tenure system in the country. The government retains wide powers over land and natural resources in Kenya. Wildlife is owned and managed by the government, and wildlife conservation has been carried out through

---

[58] Uganda National Environment Statute, *supra* note 52 at section 75(2), and Kenya's Environment Management and Co-ordination Act, *supra* note 52 at section 114(2).

[59] Kenya's Environment Management and Co-ordination Act, *supra* note 52 at section 108, and Uganda National Environment Statute, *supra* note 52 at section 68.

[60] Uganda's National Environment Statute, *supra* note 52 at sections 2 and 73 (2), and Kenya's Environment Management and Co-ordination Act, *supra* note 52 at sections 2 and 116.

the use of protected areas set up by laws that prohibit access to wildlife resources in the protected areas.

The introduction of individual title to land in Kenya was intended to intensify agricultural development and freeing of land for purposes of obtaining collateral from banks to finance development. Wildlife was seen as a pest and was rapidly driven away to pave the way for agricultural development. Indeed the current land use legislation in Kenya is inadequate to address wildlife conservation outside protected areas. The main legislation that addresses wildlife conservation in Kenya focuses on the management of protected areas and prohibits human habitation or access to the resources enclosed in the protected areas. This, coupled with the lack of a comprehensive land use policy, makes it difficult to impose wildlife conservation as a land use. As a result, there is no guarantee that wildlife areas outside protected areas, some of which are critical to wildlife conservation in the protected areas, will continue to exist in the long term because of economic pressures to develop land in the country.

There are few if any incentives for wildlife conservation outside protected areas in Kenya. Here again, the emphasis on protected areas alone is to blame for the lack of incentives for conservation activities outside protected areas. Other sectors of the economy such as agriculture receive state subsidies to encourage landowners to invest; but none are given for wildlife conservation. This condition results in the loss of wildlife habitat as land is converted to uses that are more lucrative for the landowner. There are some incentives that could be applied, and key among these is the security of tenure over land in the form of both ownership as well as control and access to the resources including wildlife. Others include tourism and consumptive utilization of wildlife resources.

Landowners living near protected areas should be allowed access to the protected areas to graze their livestock and to access and use water and other resources. This provision would reduce the hostility that the landowners have toward wildlife and protected areas and would be a first step in negotiating for wildlife conservation outside protected areas. It would also be a key incentive as the landowners would not have to bear only the costs of wildlife on their land, but also benefit from it.

The government has undertaken the process of formulating a National Land Policy, and it is hoped that most of the issues affecting wildlife conservation will be effectively addressed.[61] Some of the concerns to be taken into account are land tenure and use, including the impact of subdivision of land in rural areas and management of fragile ecosystems as well as human–wildlife conflict. The policy aims to provide for a legal and institutional framework for secure land tenure, including customary tenure and common property resource.[62] Kenya Wildlife Service has also started the process of reviewing Kenya's Wildlife Policy and the Wildlife Conservation and Management Act.

The complex issues relating to the ownership, control, access, and use of land in Kenya need to be resolved urgently as they directly affect wildlife conservation. Incentives should also be devised to encourage wildlife conservation, and these should be applied through institutions that allow the participation of landowners in order for wildlife to continue finding space outside protected areas in future.

---

[61] Republic of Kenya, *National Land Policy Formulation Process: Concept Paper* (Ministry of Lands and Settlement) (March 2004). On file with the author.

[62] Ibid.

Finally, the use of environmental easements in Kenya for conservation has only just begun. In future, the use of these easements on a large scale will require an institutional framework to support its implementation. The institutional framework should ensure the viable function and integrity of natural habitat outside protected areas by using various legal and economic instruments including environmental easements to address land use change in critical environmental conservation areas.

8 Land Tenure, Land Use, and Sustainability in Kenya: Toward Innovative Use of Property Rights in Wildlife Management

Patricia Kameri-Mbote

1 INTRODUCTION

The sustainable management of biological diversity is a major concern of the international community, which now realizes that this diversity is being eroded at an alarming rate due to consumptive uses of species as well as the excessive alteration of habitats through human activities such as cultivation, pastoralism, and urbanization.[1] The increase in human population around the world also accelerates species extinction as such population exerts more pressure on available resources.[2]

Private property right regimes are believed to create incentives for the management of resources. They could, however, also encourage the erosion of the resources.[3] In evaluating the role of property rights in wildlife management, it is imperative to examine critically the laws that have been put in place for the protection of biodiversity and the rights impacting on management activities. Our argument here is that private property rights and current wildlife conservation and management laws and policies in Kenya fail to provide the solution to wildlife biodiversity erosion partly because of their preoccupation with a monolithic system of property ownership favoring the state and individuals and neglecting communities and/or groups.

2 BACKGROUND

Kenya has great faunal and floral diversity, including forests, woodlands, swamps, and grasslands of many different varieties as well as 7,800 plant and animal species.[4] Of all the varieties of plants, 25 percent are shrubs and trees, of which 5 percent are considered endangered while about 8 percent are rare. Kenya's forests, covering no more than 2 percent of the land area, also host many endangered and endemic plant and animal

---

[1] See Rodger A. Sedjo and R. David Simpson, "Property Rights, Externalities and Biodiversity," in Timothy M. Swanson (ed.), *The Economics and Ecology of Biodiversity Decline: The Forces Driving Global Change* (1995).

[2] Richard J. Tobin, *The Expendable Future: US Politics and the Protection of Biological Diversity* (1990).

[3] See, e.g., J. Martinez-Alier, "Ecology and the Poor: A Neglected Dimension of Latin American History," *J. Latin Am. Stud.* 23 (1991), discussing the "tragedy of the enclosure."

[4] See *World Conservation Monitoring Centre, Kenya: Conservation of Biological Diversity and Forest Ecosystems* (1988) and Michael O. Odhiambo, "Liberalisation, Law and the Management of Common Property Resources in Kenya: The Case of Public Land and Forests," (27 March 1996) (mimeographed paper presented at the East African Regional Symposium on Common Property Resource Management, Kampala, 26–28 March 1996, on file with the author).

species.[5] There are 57 prominent mammal species in Kenya, including 33 species of horned animals, 12 large carnivores, and others such as rhinos, elephants, and giraffes.[6] The Kenya Wildlife Service (KWS) manages wildlife on behalf of the state through a system of protected areas.

Kenya lacks major exploitable mineral resources and arable land is scarce. The main economic activities are based on the primary sector, predominantly agriculture,[7] which is both a source of food as well as a revenue earner. The agricultural sector employs over 70 percent of the country's population, and in the 1990s, agricultural products accounted for as much as 25 percent of the gross domestic product (GDP) compared to manufacturing, which contributed 14 percent.[8] The country can be divided broadly into three land categories based on agricultural production and the amount of rainfall received.[9] These are the high-, medium-, and low-potential areas. Over 75 percent of the human population live in the high-potential area to the south and west.

2.1 Population

The total population is currently estimated to be 30 million people. This is expected to double by the year 2025. Only 25.2 percent of this population live in urban areas, the rest live in the rural areas and consequently depend directly on the land for a living.[10] The rural population depends mainly on biological resources as a basis for both subsistence and economic activities.[11] The growth in population has outstripped the agricultural capacity of the land in well-watered areas and resulted in migration to drier, low agricultural potential areas designated in official policy as arid and semiarid lands (ASALs). This has had profound impacts on wildlife management, since 5 percent of KWS's protected areas are in the ASALs, where wildlife and pastoralists compete for range resources. ASALs occupy 88 percent of Kenya's total land area and carry over 20 percent of the total human population and more than 50 percent of the total livestock in the country.[12] Traditional pastoral systems of land use still prevail in these areas and temporary out-migration is common because of climate and insecurity. Pastoralists are, however, increasingly settling permanently because of the interventionist policies of the government, donors, and nongovernmental organizations, which result in the

---

[5] Other estimates put the plant species at 8,000 to 9,000 species. See Kihika Kiambi and Monica Opole, "Promoting Traditional Trees and Food Plants in Kenya," in David Cooper et al. (eds.), *Growing Diversity: Genetic Resources and Local Food Security* (1992) 53.

[6] See G. A. Petrides and Trustees of the Royal National Parks of Kenya, *Kenya's Wildlife Resource and the National Parks* (1955).

[7] For the purposes of this chapter, the term *agriculture* denotes cultivation and livestock keeping. We use the term *settled agriculture* when we discuss areas where livestock keeping is practiced alongside cultivation. This distinguishes zero-grazing from nomadic pastoralism, a distinction that has significant implications for our prescriptions.

[8] See *Republic of Kenya, National Development Plan, 1997–2001* (1996) (hereafter *1997–2001 Development Plan*).

[9] See *Republic of Kenya, Development Plan 1994–1996* (1993) (hereafter *1994–1996 Development Plan*).

[10] See *1997–2001 Development Plan, supra* note 8.

[11] See, e.g., Mansel Prothero (ed.), *People and Land in Africa South of the Sahara: Readings in Social Geography* (1972), noting that most African population is rural.

[12] Republic of Kenya, *Environmental Action Plan for Arid and Semi-Arid Lands in Kenya* (1992).

development of reliable means of communication and permanent water sources that attract pastoralists to settle in central places.[13]

2.2 Value of Wildlife Resources in Kenya

Different biodiversity value judgments were discernible in colonial wildlife conservation policies. While for the native Kenyans, these included direct values associated with the provision of food and clothing, and the promotion of culture, the settler community was concerned with the preservation of wildlife to prevent extinction and thus ensure that wild animal numbers were maintained at such levels as could sustain sport hunting expeditions and wildlife-based tourism. The settler community concerns for preservation were given prominence in wildlife conservation laws and policies while utilization by the native Kenyans to meet their basic needs was proscribed by law. The economic value of wildlife conservation, realized primarily through wildlife-based tourism, remains the primary justification for wildlife conservation in Kenya to date, with emphasis currently placed on popularizing wildlife conservation and management as a profitable land use form.[14]

2.3 Relationship between Property Rights and Wildlife Conservation

Relevant property rights regimes in wildlife conservation comprise private property where wildlife is found on private lands, common property where wildlife is found on communal property or property owned by a group, and government ownership where the government owns wildlife and wildlife protection areas. Open-access situations arise where the land on which wildlife reside is not owned by any person or where common property support structures have disintegrated. Indeed, wildlife raises special problems of ownership since it is a fugitive resource that in its in situ condition cannot be associated with a particular user as its owner.[15] Moreover, wildlife does not recognize property boundaries and its movement cannot be restricted to national parks and reserves. Thus, wildlife invariably avails itself of the space and forage available on private and group land since ecosystem boundaries do not follow the property boundaries. Species are also often found at the boundaries of different parcels of property, which may be no one's land, and seasonal migration necessitates the availability of corridors between different parcels of land.[16]

The definition of *open access resources* as those that can be depleted, are fugitive, and are characterized by rivalry in exploitation aptly fits wildlife in a state of nature since it is subject to use by any person who has the capability and desire to capture and/or harvest it. However, where an individual or group has defined rights over an area in which wildlife is found, such wildlife should be the property of that individual

---

[13] Ibid.

[14] See, e.g., Karen A. Carlson, "The Kenya Wildlife Conservation Campaign: A Descriptive Study of Inter-Cultural Persuasion" (1969) (unpublished Ph.D. dissertation, University of California at Berkeley).

[15] See, e.g., S. V. Ciriacy-Wantrup, *Resource Conservation: Economics and Policies* (1952), for a definition of fugitive resources.

[16] See, e.g., Valentine Udoh James, *Africa's Ecology: Sustaining the Biological and Environmental Diversity of a Continent* (1993) 33.

or group, and it is incumbent upon the group members to regulate the use of the wildlife to ensure that the rates of use do not threaten the existence of the resource by rendering it incapable of reproducing itself.[17] With regard to groups, all the members have simultaneous *ex ante* claims on any unit of the resource, and consequently the harvest of the resource by any one member has to take into account the needs of other members of the community.

Wildlife resources, wherever found, are, however, state property. In general, individual and community landowners have no ownership or use rights over the in situ wildlife resources. Consequently, resources that may have been previously available to all on whose land they appeared are state property. The vesting of the rights thereto in the state, as has happened in many African countries, is tantamount to the appropriation of the rights of the persons or groups upon whose land wildlife resides. The fugitive nature of wildlife resources makes them amenable to capture by nonowners, thus making wildlife management a difficult task for the state.

Wildlife management in protected areas influences and is influenced by adjacent land uses and social values.[18] The refusal of the state to acknowledge the subsidies that individuals and groups provide in sharing their land with wildlife amounts to a taking of the rights of such individuals or groups, who, as property owners, have to forgo benefits such as cultivation, urban development, and livestock keeping and deal with wildlife depredations and transmission of diseases to their livestock. The property rights to wildlife in this case are framed at the wrong level; the state becomes the sole recipient of economic returns accruing from wildlife.

The emphasis on state ownership of wildlife ignores the interaction of different land uses in ecosystems and habitats. The areas that are good for wildlife, namely, those that have permanent water and dry-season grazing, coincide with the areas that the people in the drier parts of Kenya use for their livestock and personal needs. This is the case in Maasai land in Kenya, which hosts many of the national parks and reserves. Consequently, the vesting of property rights to wildlife and the areas they occupy exclusively in the state is likely to impact significantly, for instance, on the Maasai way of life.[19] Where multiple land uses are permitted, as is the case in Amboseli, the challenge is finding a way to guarantee local people's interests in areas that constitute the Park but that they need and previously had unlimited access to and also ensure that wildlife is sustainably managed.

Exclusive state ownership of wildlife also fails to take into account the fact that most wildlife resides on private lands and that reserves and game parks alone cannot ensure the survival of species. Protected areas can easily become "islands" and suffer massive degradation due to the concentration of animals in small areas and the pressure from land users surrounding them. Further, the conversion of public goods into state property for conservation purposes without safeguards to ensure equal access for all may aggravate the situation of communities and individuals that have been long subordinated

---

[17] See Partha Das Gupta and Geoffrey M. Heal, *Economic Theory and Exhaustible Resources* (1979).

[18] See Darryll R. Johnson and James K. Agee, *Introduction to Ecosystem Management*, in *Ecosystem Management for Parks and Wilderness* 3 (Darryll R. Johnson and James K. Agee, eds., 1988).

[19] See Harvey Croze, *Wildlife Resource in Kajiado District*, in *Kajiado District Workshop Report on Wildlife Conservation and Management* 36(FAO & WCMD, No. 34, 1978) 36.

and result in greater poverty and exploitation without the achievement of conservation or equity.[20]

3 LAWS AND POLICIES RELEVANT TO WILDLIFE MANAGEMENT

Kenya's wildlife policy is found in sessional papers, ministerial statements, and development plans. Apart from laws dealing specifically with wildlife, land use, and land tenure laws, local government laws and zoning laws are also relevant. The laws on forests and agriculture also impact on wildlife management, as do the development plans that provide the template upon which the government implements national development policies. Moreover, the Constitution as the supreme law of the land provides the legal context within which wildlife resources are managed. We will critically look at these laws with a view to assessing their efficacy in wildlife management in Kenya.

The Constitution of Kenya contains no direct wildlife protection provisions but includes a provision on the right to life that has been interpreted by some to include the right to a clean and healthy environment.[21] The draft Constitution (2004) contains more explicit environment protection provisions and establishes a National Environment Commission that, inter alia, conducts research on the environment and natural resources and examines and regulates resource use patterns and practices. These normative and institutional provisions have implications for wildlife management in Kenya at the macrolevel. The draft Constitution's provisions on devolution also have direct implications for the management of wildlife resources. Two objectives of devolution are to recognize the right of local communities to manage their own local affairs, form networks, and associations, and ensure equitable sharing of national and local resources. These will impact on the management of areas that provide wildlife habitat, as will the loci for management of devolved local government, namely, district, region, and senate.

3.1 Environment Management and Coordination Act

The Environment Management and Coordination Act (EMCA) provides for the establishment of an appropriate legal and institutional framework for the management of the environment. It also establishes guidelines on cross-sectoral issues such as wildlife conservation. It is expected that all sectoral environmental laws will be revised and harmonized with the provisions of this framework law. This includes the wildlife law. The requirement for environmental impact assessment (EIA) will impact on wildlife management activities in Kenya. The establishment of protected areas requires an EIA. Under EMCA, the Kenya Wildlife Service is mandated to be the lead agency in the country for matters relating to wildlife. The Act also creates the National Environmental Management Authority (NEMA), which is the oversight body for all environmental management matters in the country. At section 6, the Act makes provision for the creation of environmental easements that are not linked to land ownership for the grantor.

---

[20] See, e.g., Todd G. Olson, *Biodiversity and Private Property: Conflict or Opportunity*, in *Biodiversity and the Law* 67 (William J. Snape III, ed., 1996), arguing that an economic system that emphasizes regulation penalizes those who protect biodiversity and noting that there is a need to enlist the cooperation of private property owners interested in protecting their economic interests.

[21] Section 71 of the Constitution.

These can serve as effective mechanisms for enlisting the support of landowners for wildlife management by KWS.

3.2 Land Tenure

The land tenure systems operative in Kenya have been characterized as private/modern, communal/customary, public/state, and open access.[22] These systems overlap in some cases, especially where the tenure reform process is incomplete, as is the case in the trust land awaiting registration, where individuals have rights over land legally vested in local county councils as trustees. Privately owned land constituted 6 percent of the total land area in 1990 while government land (formerly Crown lands) was about 20 percent and included national parks, forest land, and alienated and unalienated land. The most extensive tenure type, however, is trust land (formerly native areas), awaiting smallholder registration that will effectively bring it under the private/modern tenure system. That land constituted 64 percent of total land area in 1990.

Land in Kenya is owned by four different kinds of entities, namely, the government, county councils, individuals, and groups. Different legal instruments govern different categories of land and owners thereof. Further, there are two different systems of registration of land in Kenya, namely, document registration and title registration.[23] The Registered Land Act (RLA) was intended to be the overall land law commitment to the private/modern tenure system. The objective of putting all land in Kenya under this Act has not as yet been achieved. Consequently, we still have a plethora of statutes applying to land. This makes land tenure law in Kenya very complex and in turn impacts on land uses such as wildlife management.

The RLA and the Transfer of Property Act govern individual ownership of land in Kenya. Both statutes confer upon an owner a fee-simple estate to the land in question. The RLA applies to the land formerly held under customary law, namely, native reserves and trust land, which has been registered. The content of property rights one gets under it is absolute and can only be circumscribed, in theory, in exercise of the state's right of compulsory acquisition of land for public purposes after the due process outlined at Sections 75 and 118 of the Constitution has been followed. Sections 27 and 28 of the RLA define the quantum of rights that the registered proprietor has upon registration as absolute ownership of land together with all rights and privileges belonging or appurtenant thereto and not liable to be defeated except as provided for in Section 30 of the Act. Section 30 lists rights capable of overriding the rights of an absolute proprietor. These do not include wildlife conservation. Given the wide latitude given to an owner of land under this statute, the capacity of the state to police all wildlife in Kenya, especially wildlife on private land, effectively is doubtful.

The Transfer of Property Act governs land in settler- and formerly settler-occupied areas, designated during the colonial period as the white highlands, because the aim of including all land under the RLA has not yet materialized. The bundle of rights one gets

---

[22] See, e.g., Peter Ondiege, "Land Tenure and Soil Conservation," in Calestous Juma and J. B. Ojwang (eds.), *In Land We Trust: Environment, Private Property and Constitutional Change* (1996) 117.

[23] See Government Lands Act Chapter 280 of the Laws of Kenya and the Registration of Documents Act Chapter 285 of the Laws of Kenya on document registration and Chapters 281, 282, and 300 (Land Titles Act, Registration of Titles Act, and Registered Land Act, respectively) of the Laws of Kenya on title registration.

under it is the same as what one gets under the RLA, and the Agriculture Act provisions also apply to land held under it.

With regard to government ownership, the taking up of land by the colonial government and the assumption of title to all land in the Crown gave the government the power to assume rights over land and vest them in other holders as it deemed. The precursor to the Government Lands Act, the Crown Lands Ordinance, Chapter 280 of the Laws of Kenya, was originally passed to make provision for regulating the leasing and other disposal of Crown lands. Upon independence, the Crown Lands Ordinance became the Government Lands Act, Chapter 280 of the Laws of Kenya, under which national parks are governed.

As far as groups are concerned, trust land and group ranches are the relevant institutions. Trust land consists of areas that were occupied by the natives during the colonial period and that have not been consolidated, adjudicated, and registered in individuals' or groups' names and native land that has not been taken over by the government. It is governed by the Trust Lands Act and is vested in local authorities designated as Councils. Councils manage all the resources within the trust land under their jurisdiction and control the development of that land. The occupiers of the unregistered land have rights, which are in limbo and awaiting confirmation through registration. These rights are in some cases guaranteed under some form of customary tenure. Conservation responsibilities of the Councils include the protection of trees and forest produce on land that does not fall within a forest area as defined in the Forests Act, Chapter 385 of the Laws of Kenya (forest areas are government land).

It is notable that tenure to trust land is increasingly changing from the trust status to ownership by individuals, legally constituted groups, and the state. The implications of this change are significant. The application of customary law is ousted and the land is removed from the ambit of Council control for conservation and development purposes. In some instances, access thereto for communities previously occupying the land is curtailed significantly, and this impacts negatively on the management of wildlife resources within those areas.[24]

Group ranches are defined as "demarcated area(s) of rangeland to which a group of pastoralists, who graze their individually owned herds on it, have official land rights." The operative statute in this regard is the Land (Group Representatives Act). A *group* for the purposes of the Act is a "tribe, clan, family or other group of persons, whose land under recognised customary law belongs communally to the persons who are for the time being the members of the group, together with any person of whose land the group is determined to be the owner" where such person has, under recognized customary law, exercised rights in or over land that should be recognized as ownership.[25]

Most group ranches are in the areas occupied by pastoral communities in Kenya that coincide with the game reserves. These include Narok, Amboseli, and Samburu. The

---

[24] The Narok area, which hosts Maasai Mara National Reserve, is a telling example.

[25] Each group gets a certificate of incorporation and becomes a body corporate with perpetual succession subject to any conditions, limitations, or exemptions noted on the certificate. They thus have ownership of the land in question in perpetuity and can only cease to be a group by the vote of all members. Group representatives have a duty to hold the property and exercise their powers on behalf and for the collective benefit of all the group members and fully and effectively consult group members in performing their roles. The decision on whether or not a person qualifies for membership in a group is a matter to be determined by the majority of the group members.

composition of group ranches was an attempt at formalizing traditional community structures. The principal idea behind them was to create a land unit smaller than the traditional section but larger than the individual. Group ranches have not worked as well as was hoped for a variety of reasons. First, while the system was meant to capitalize on traditional institutions to institutionalize sustainable resource management, the group representatives lack the authority of traditional leaders.[26] Second, government policy has tended to emphasize individual rights and there is a prevalent view that the group rights would eventually mature into individual ones. Further, despite the fact that 37 percent of Kenyan land is used for pastoralism, as compared to the 9 percent used for agriculture, the latter has received greater attention in policymaking. As in many other parts of the world, pastoralism in Kenya has not been fully recognized as an important land use system.[27]

3.3 Land Use Planning and Zoning Laws

Land use planning and zoning laws are important in wildlife management since they direct the manner in which important areas are to be utilized and thus have the potential to ensure that resources are sustainably managed. General land use planning laws in Kenya fall into two categories, namely, those dealing with urban land and those dealing with agricultural land. In addition to these, we have laws on wildlife and forest conservation, which prescribe rules specifically for these areas.

The Agriculture Act and the Forests Act are relevant in wildlife conservation and management since wildlife found on agricultural land and forests is under the control of the Agriculture and Forests departments, respectively. The Forests Act Cap. 385 provides the legal framework for the conservation of forests. Under it, the Minister responsible for natural resources is empowered to declare any forest area a nature reserve for the purposes of preserving the natural amenities thereof and the flora and fauna therein. The killing of wild animals in a nature reserve is prohibited. The proposed Forests Bill 2004 seeks to amend the Forests Act. It contains provisions that will impact on the management of wildlife in forest areas such as the requirement for formulation of management plans, which requires that an inventory of the forest be taken with a view to determining the true nature of the forest. Such an inventory will include the wildlife resources in the forest and will determine the conditions upon which a management agreement is entered into between the Forests Service or local authorities and other parties. The Bill also allows for the formation of community forest associations to participate in the conservation and management of a state forest or local authority forest. The presence of such associations will impact on the management of wildlife

---

[26] See John Galaty, "The Maasai Group-Ranch: Politics and Development in an African Pastoral Society," in P. Salzman (ed.), *When Nomads Settle: Processes of Sedentarization as Adaptation and Response* (1980) 157. See also John G. Galaty, "Introduction: Nomadic Pastoralists and Social Change – Processes and Perspectives," in John G. Galaty and Philip C. Salzman (eds.), *Change and Development in Nomadic and Pastoral Societies* (1981) 4, and John G. Galaty, "Land and Livestock among Kenyan Maasai: Symbolic Perspectives on Pastoral Exchange, Change and Inequality," in John G. Galaty and Philip C. Salzman (eds.), *Change and Development in Nomadic and Pastoral Societies* (1981) 68.

[27] See, e.g., André Bourgeot, "Nomadic Pastoral Society and the Market: The Penetration of the Sahel by Commercial Relations," in John G. Galaty and Philip C. Salzman (eds.), *Change and Development in Nomadic and Pastoral Societies* (1981) 116, and Charles Lane, *Pastures Lost: Barabaig Economy, Resource Tenure, and the Alienation of Their Land in Tanzania* (1996).

in the forest, and there is need to synchronize the wildlife management functions to prevent conflicting mandates.

Legal regulation of agricultural land use has always been an important facet of Kenya's resource management policies. The basic legislative instrument for that purpose has been the Agriculture Act. Its objectives are, inter alia, to provide for the preservation of the soil and its fertility and to promote and maintain the development of agricultural land in accordance with rules of good husbandry. This legislation covers most of the activities that have contributed to massive land degradation in certain parts of the country. These activities have, however, continued in spite of statutory regulation. The command and control posture of the law ensures that even private property rights owners have very little latitude within which to utilize their rights for the conservation and management of natural resources. The use of criminal law sanctions also creates problems because of the necessity of sufficient policing to detect offenders, which is currently lacking. The holders of private property aim at maximizing the use to which their land can be put, and the capacity of the government machinery to police the use of land is limited by the high costs and lack of funds.

The Physical Planning Act, for its part, makes provision for the preparation and implementation of physical development plans. *Development* for the purposes of the Act is defined to include the making of any material change in the use or density of any land. It makes the preparation of a physical development plan, complying with the requirements of the Physical Planning Liaison Committee, a prerequisite for any land development. Two kinds of plans are provided for, namely, regional and local physical development plans. Among the purposes of regional and local physical development plans is securing suitable provision for the use of land. There is room in these regulations for requirements to be made for sustainable resource management as part of the conditions for land development. It could, for instance, be made a condition that development of land in a wildlife range area result in no more than the minimal and unpreventable number of deaths of the wildlife and that attempts be made to reconcile the imperatives of wildlife conservation with land use. It is surprising that this Act was passed as recently as 1996 but does not address the issue of sustainable biological diversity conservation and management, which has been of concern for some years now. Further, the Act uses existing local authorities, which are based on political as opposed to ecological considerations, as units for management. Consequently, the law does not define new parameters for zoning the country based on sustainable resource management imperatives. Moreover, the Act falls short of providing for area plans based on compatibility of land uses.

3.4 Wildlife Laws and Policies

The first attempt at a comprehensive policy on wildlife management in Kenya is contained in Sessional Paper No. 3 of 1975.[28] This policy was a radical departure from the preservationist policies preceding it. It recognized the value of wildlife both within and outside protected areas. This document identified the primary goal of wildlife conservation as the optimization of returns from wildlife defined broadly to include aesthetic,

---

[28] See Republic of Kenya, *Statement on the Future of Wildlife Management Policy in Kenya* (Sessional Paper No. 3 1975) (hereafter 1975 Policy).

cultural, scientific, and economic gains, taking into account the income from other land uses. Economic gains were specified to derive from both tourism and consumptive uses of wildlife. The need to identify compatible land uses was also cited as an integral part of the policy along with the implementation of such uses and fair distribution of benefits derived therefrom. The need to minimize depredations by wildlife on agricultural land and the need to support tourism were also underscored.

The Policy also recognized that wildlife needed space outside the protected areas if it was to flourish without intensive management and ecological impoverishment. It envisioned that additional space for wildlife management would be secured from landowners willing to accommodate wildlife.[29] Under the Policy, wildlife authorities were to be facilitators, advisers, and assessors working with landowners and residents in wildlife range areas in the country, and not police. The government also undertook the general responsibility of assisting with problem animal control in instances of wildlife impinging adversely on human life and property, within the limits of available resources.

The operative Wildlife (Conservation and Management) Act[30] established the legal provisions for the 1975 Policy. It consolidated the wildlife protection and national parks laws in Kenya and merged the National Parks Organisation with the Game Department. The Act established the Wildlife Conservation and Management Department (WCMD) under the Ministry of Tourism and Wildlife to replace the National Parks Board of Trustees. This department became the overall wildlife management authority for wild animals on state land, trust land, and private land. In particular, it was the responsibility of the department to ensure that wildlife resources gave the best possible returns to individuals and the nation in terms of cultural, aesthetic, and economic gains. In 1990, the Kenya Wildlife Service (KWS) was formed to replace the WCMD. It has been noted that that the word *service* was deliberately used in designating this new body to convey the expectation that this body was to contribute to the welfare of local communities. The new body was charged with the task of ensuring that wildlife resources were sustainably used for national economic development and for the benefit of people living in wildlife areas.[31] It was charged with the task of managing Kenya's 56 conservation units (26 National Parks and 30 National Reserves) and wildlife outside protected areas.

The Act, however, retained most of the provisions on conservation. It vests the powers of management and control of protected areas in a consolidated service of the government, KWS. The stated objective of the statute is to ensure that wildlife is managed and conserved for the benefit of the nation generally and certain areas in particular. The Minister responsible for wildlife is empowered by the Act to declare any area of land a national reserve or game park after consulting the relevant bodies. The law provides for four types of wildlife protected areas, namely, national parks, national reserves, local sanctuaries, and game reserves. The first three are vested in the central government with human activities completely excluded from national parks. Various degrees of human activities are allowed within the national reserves as long

---

[29] Such accommodation would arise as a result of policies encouraging landowners to incorporate wildlife with other forms of land use and reaping the benefits through tourism, cropping for meat and trophies, game ranching, live animal capture for restocking or export, and use of value-added processing of animal products. These uses were to be promoted and regulated by the wildlife authorities in the interest of making a net contribution to Kenya's economic and social development.

[30] Cap. 376, 1976 (amended in 1989).

[31] See section 3A of the 1989 Wildlife (Amendment) Act.

as they are compatible with conservation efforts or requirements. Game reserves are large conservation areas that are vested in local authorities (County Councils) who administer them under the overall guidance and control of the relevant government ministry (Ministry of Local Government). The County Council (which holds it in trust for the residents of the area and also restricts the influx of new immigrants and controls the number of livestock kept on the land) owns the land in the reserves. They are an institution created by the Wild Animals Protection Ordinance of 1951. Section 18(b) of the Wildlife (Conservation and Management) Act (the Wildlife Act)[32] provides for the continued existence of already demarcated game reserves but changes their name to *national reserves*. However, game reserves managed by local authorities have been created with the support of the government. This approach is meant to facilitate local participation both in wildlife conservation measures and in the benefits that accrue from wildlife protection. Further, the law acknowledges the need to take into account varied forms of land use and the interrelationships between these and wildlife conservation but does not lay out the necessary framework for doing so.

Section 29(2) of the Wildlife Act made provision for owners of private land to open up their land for hunting of game. Section 47 authorized game ranching and cropping subject to conditions set out by the Minister responsible for wildlife. However, with increased illegal taking of wildlife and the attendant threat of extinction of species such as rhinos and elephants, the Kenya government, in response to worldwide pressure, banned all game animal hunting in 1977.[33] It also revoked all licenses to trade in wildlife products.[34] This led to the closure of professional hunting companies and shops dealing with game trophies. Wildlife-based tourism was left as the only legal form of utilization. This reduced the value of land for communities that had earned revenue through granting hunting concessions. The government thus appropriated to itself the responsibility for all wildlife in the country including that on privately owned land, departing from measures taken from the late 1940s to the 1970s to enlist the participation of individual and community landowners in wildlife management. Consequently, the public expects the government to pay for wildlife conservation- and management-related costs.

The Wildlife Act, responding to increasing human–wildlife conflicts, provides for compensation to landowners who support wildlife on their land and for properties destroyed by wildlife. Further, KWS implements a scheme for revenue sharing of park entrance fees with rural communities as a way of encouraging those communities to take part in wildlife conservation. It also makes provision for District Compensation Committees to assess compensation claims. However, these Committees do not function effectively.

The Wildlife Act has been widely perceived as inadequate in dealing with wildlife management problems in the light of changed circumstances, and a new law is currently under preparation. Some of the factors necessitating revisions to the law are the ascendance of biodiversity to a position of prime importance, internationally evidenced by

[32] Cap 376.

[33] See Wildlife (Conservation and Management) (Prohibition on Hunting of Game Animals) Regulations, 30 *Kenya Gazette Supplement* (20 May 1977).

[34] See Wildlife (Conservation and Management) (Revocation of Dealer's Licences) Act No. 5 of 1978, 35 *Kenya Gazette Supplement* (23 June 1978).

the coming into force of a plethora of international instruments for its conservation and sustainable use such as the Convention on Biological Diversity,[35] and the continued inability of government agencies to integrate, harmonize, and enforce land use policies and legislation intended to conserve wildlife and other natural resources. The principles of the Convention are relevant to wildlife management and are deposited in the framework environmental law, the Environment Management and Coordination Act 2000. The initiatives taken to create positive incentives for sustainable management of wildlife outside protected areas such as community participation, and the now ended pilot cropping program, are outside its purview and need to be ingrained in new wildlife legislation.

Attempts at Changing the Wildlife Law and Policy
Community participation in wildlife management. In 1992, KWS established the Community Wildlife Service Department, which was charged with ensuring good management of wildlife outside protected areas for the benefit of communities that interact with wildlife, to create trust and dialogue between KWS and those communities, to help communities benefit from wildlife and protect them against losses caused by wildlife, and to initiate collaboration with other sectors concerned with land use. Through it, some of the financial benefits accruing from wildlife conservation are channeled to local communities through the construction of amenities such as schools and hospitals, water supply, and cattle dips. This is in a bid to reduce the conflict between wildlife and humans and to mobilize communities to participate in sustainable wildlife conservation and utilization programs for their own economic gains.

Another mechanism for enlisting landowners' support through the granting of wildlife use rights in pilot wildlife utilization schemes started in some areas in 2002. To obtain wildlife use rights, one had to be a private landowner or a community having rights to a piece of land; provide KWS with a wildlife management plan, a map of the ranch, and results of a recent game count; and indicate the quota applied for. KWS assisted individuals and groups in drawing management plans. Possible proposed uses for wildlife in the ranch include cropping, hunting for home consumption, live animal capture for translocation, bird shooting, game farming (but no sport/safari hunting, which has a higher value and is a lesser damaging use). One could apply for all forms of use. Use rights were granted to individual ranches or associations of ranches that had formed a wildlife management unit. They were granted for an initial five years and could be renewed. Once an application was approved, the land was registered with the KWS – no fee was charged. During the duration of the license, the landowner was obliged to provide KWS with quarterly reports specifying the off-take by species, numbers, and gender and explain the use to which the animals taken were put and the manner in which products such as meat, skins, and horns were disposed. The pilot program continued for 10 years and was discontinued with no alternative incentives being provided to communities and land owners to manage wildlife on their properties. Besides, the operation of the pilot program was within the context of bans on hunting and trade in wildlife products instituted in 1977. This presented problems for croppers who could not sell their trophies and other animal products besides meat.

---

[35] United Nations Conference on Environment and Development: Convention on Biological Diversity – Done at Rio de Janeiro, 5 June 1992, reprinted in 31 I.L.M. 818 (1992).

Attempts at legislative amendment. In an attempt to revise the Wildlife Act, KWS drafted a bill in 1998 that was never published or brought before parliament. The Preamble to the Draft Bill vested KWS, on behalf of the state, with overall wildlife management authority but also acknowledged the need for ensuring the highest and beneficial participation of local communities in wildlife management and conservation. It also pointed to the need to strike a balance between protectionism and unregulated wildlife utilization. Thus it advocated promoting wildlife utilization consistent with scientifically and internationally accepted conservation practices, maximizing biodiversity protection in both protected and unprotected areas, and minimizing human–wildlife conflicts to ensure long-term harmonious coexistence of people and wildlife. The Bill also sought to catalyze the growth of national conservation constituencies and partnerships within the wildlife sector and to streamline community-based and regulated compensation procedures pursuant to damage caused by wildlife, in a bid to create incentives for wildlife management.

The draft Bill did not go as far as to grant rights to wildlife resources to landowners, individuals, and communities. It provided that the ownership of all wildlife found in Kenya, whether on private, trust, or public land, is vested in the state, which may, through KWS, grant wildlife user rights to individuals, groups, or bodies corporate. The draft Bill, however, pointed to the necessity to take varied forms of land use into account and the interrelationship between biodiversity conservation and management and other forms of land use so as to ensure both the compatibility of multiple land uses and the fair distribution of benefits.

More recently, a private member's bill seeking to amend the Wildlife (Conservation and Management) Act has been tabled before Parliament.[36] It seeks principally to fix the levels of compensation for damage caused by wildlife, raising it from the current figure to 1 million Kenya Shillings (Ksh).[37] It also seeks to expand the KWS board of trustees and to provide for licenses for consumptive use of wildlife.

4 PROPERTY RIGHTS AND SUSTAINABLE WILDLIFE MANAGEMENT: A CRITIQUE

4.1 Conceptual and Legal Problems

Most of the laws and policies dealing with wildlife management and the protection of property rights have been in place for a considerable length of time, during which the numbers of some species have declined. In the first instance, policy and legal documents emphasize preservation and conservation while their general objectives are geared toward sustainable management. Further, while the value of wildlife resources seems to have been recognized and realized by the government, some of the established laws and policies that impact on wildlife management are inimical to the enhancement of that value. For instance, the government has promoted the fragmentation of land that is used as dispersal and migration routes by wildlife through land tenure change.[38]

---

[36] The Wildlife (Conservation and Management) (Amendment) Bill 2004.
[37] One U.S. dollar is equivalent to 75 Kenya shillings (Ksh.) at the time of writing.
[38] See Kwame Awere-Gyekye and Kenya Wildlife Service, *National Land Use Patterns and Trends* (1996).

Wildlife Preservation versus Wildlife Management

While Kenya's wildlife policies recognize the need for sustainable management incorporating both conservation and sustainable utilization aspects, wildlife laws are preservationist. The preservationist era was ushered in during colonial rule, when it was sought to protect wildlife from native people. With independence, the government attempted to redress this situation by allowing landowners to sell hunting concessions on their lands and vesting the control of some wildlife areas in local authorities to hold on behalf of the local communities and utilize funds obtained from wildlife management activities to build infrastructure and amenities for the benefit of the locals. The 1975 Sessional Policy Paper was, for instance, intended to give locals more latitude in the management of wildlife resources.[39] These initiatives, however, achieved little success, as a result of, first, the failure of the 1976 Act to give effect to the spirit of the Policy and, second, inadequate funding of the bodies charged with the responsibility of managing wildlife, corruption, and increased poaching.

The ban on hunting put in place in 1977 and the subsequent ban on trade in wildlife products in 1978 reintroduced the previous controls on utilization of wildlife resources. It is remarkable that the preservationist policy initiatives had not stemmed the decline of species. Indeed censuses conducted show that wildlife numbers in most districts declined on average by a third to a half between 1977 to 1993.[40] The few areas where wildlife populations have held their own or increased are Amboseli, Maasai Mara, Laikipia, and Machakos, where utilization programs in one form or another produced economic benefits to landowners. The improved status of large animals in these areas underscores the need to encourage sustainable management through economic incentives, as clearly spelled out in the 1975 paper.[41]

The need to move from preservation of wildlife to sustainable management is further underscored by the fact that the role of human activity in ecosystems is not always negative. It has, for instance, been found that the removal of disturbance factors such as fire, pastoralism, and shifting cultivation can be as negative for resource management as overexploitation, particularly in ecosystems where the human hand has played a shaping role ecologically.[42] This would implement one of the recommendations of the Five Person Review Committee calling for a shift from protectionism, the institutionalization of values that take into account local attitudes and problems, and a move toward sustainable, participatory wildlife management in Kenya.[43]

Lack of Sufficient Incentives for Sustainable Wildlife Management — Limited Value of Wildlife Resources

Kenya's policies with regard to hunting and trading in wildlife products radically changed in the 1970s. Prior to that, the relevant legislation allowed for hunting and

---

[39] See 1975 Policy *supra* note 28. See also The Widlife (Conservation and Management) Act, Cap. 376 of the Laws of Kenya (Act No. 1 of 1976, 8 *Kenya Gazette Supplement* (February 1976) (hereafter the Wildlife Act).

[40] Government of Kenya, *Wildlife Policy* (1996) (hereafter 1996 Wildlife Policy).

[41] Ibid. at paragraph 2.7.   [42] Ibid. at paragraph 2.8.

[43] See Kenya Wildlife Service, Report of the Five-Person Review Committee on Wildlife–Human Conflict released by the Director, Kenya Wildlife Service 25 (December 1995) (on file with the author) (hereafter Wildlife Human Conflict Report).

dealing in wildlife products as long as the relevant authorities issued a valid license. It also made provision for the development of wildlife in privately owned land. Landowners were invited to facilitate the presence of wildlife on their land as one of the forms of economic utilization of wildlife.[44] The only restrictions concerned a few species. These permissive provisions nearly led to the extermination of certain species, particularly the elephant, leopard, and rhinoceros, which were subject to both licensed hunting and poaching on a large scale. The government thus issued regulations in 1977 and 1978 under the relevant legislation, effectively banning hunting and revoking dealers' licenses.

The law currently does not allow for consumptive uses of game even in cases in which the numbers of the particular animals are well beyond potential biological removal levels and are residing outside protected areas. Elephants, which had, for instance, decreased so much in the 1980s that they were included in the list of threatened species under the Convention on International Trade in Endangered Species of Wild Fauna and Flora (CITES),[45] are a good case in point here. The global ban on the sale of ivory has resulted in increased numbers of elephants, which have moved to privately owned lands as a result of congestion within the protected areas.

A related problem is that of market failure. Market failures arise when the necessary or sufficient conditions for market equilibrium fail to hold.[46] In the case of wildlife, poorly defined property rights, markets that are not well developed for both labor and capital, endemic poverty, income constraints, imperfect competition, and high levels of uncertainty all combine to limit the capacity of markets to reflect the full social benefits of wildlife and wild lands. The loss or degradation of wildlife resources and wild lands is thus subsidized and distorted.[47]

Lack of Legal Framework for Involvement of Local Communities in Sustainable Wildlife Management

The law in Kenya lags behind major steps that have been taken to enlist the involvement of communities in sustainable wildlife management. For instance, the ban on hunting remained intact despite the initiatives taken by KWS to grant wildlife use rights to communities who live with wildlife between 1992 and 2002.

Moreover, the state owns all wildlife in Kenya and has maintained strong control over all wildlife management activities. This system creates major problems for many property owners since about 70 percent of wildlife resources in Kenya exist outside protected areas managed by KWS. The owner of the land, though obliged to keep the wildlife on his or her property and bear the costs thereof, has no legal basis for claiming part of the benefits accruing from wildlife conservation and management or appropriating any value of wildlife by dint of owning the property that forms the wildlife range.

---

[44] See section 29(2) of the Wildlife Act.

[45] See Convention on International Trade in Endangered Species of Wild Fauna and Flora reprinted in 12 I.L.M. 1085 (1973).

[46] Robert Bates, "Social Dilemmas and Rational Individuals – an Essay on the New Institutionalism," in James M. Acheson (ed.), *Anthropology and Institutional Economics* 4 (1994) 3 at 45.

[47] See Timothy M. Swanson, "Wildlife and Wildlands: Diversity and Development," in T. M. Swanson and E. M. Barbier (eds.), *Economics for the Wilds* (1992) 1.

One issue of concern to property owners has been the depredations by wildlife. Compensation for this has been inadequate and is provided only for injury to persons and loss of life, not destruction of property. Landowners are thus averse to wildlife management activities in their neighborhood because they devalue their property as settled agricultural, urban, or pastoral land. Such benefits do not necessarily accrue to the local property owners. The fact that the Treasury, a bureaucratic arm of the government, and not KWS, is responsible for paying compensation also alienates the issue of compensation from that of wildlife management. The bases for and amounts of compensation are fixed in an arbitrary manner and do not reflect real cost and benefit assessments.

Conservation an Alien Concept

The setting aside of large tracts of land for conservation coincided with the alienation of land for settler purposes and increases in the population of the natives. Conservation was conceived as a process removed from people, especially the native Kenyans. The values attached to conservation were for the most part removed from the needs and aspirations of native Kenyans, for whom the whole process amounted to both the expropriation of their property rights and the severance of their relationship with their local environment and environmental resources. Potentially helpful projects aimed at benefiting local communities also failed because the needs of those communities were not carefully considered in the formulation of the projects. A good example of such a project is the Kenya Wildlife Management Project, which was set up in Kajiado in 1971 to develop wildlife utilization schemes but ended up concentrating more on sport hunting than on potential benefits that local people could reap from wildlife.[48] A similar problem arose when KWS announced in 1997 that it supported the revocation of the ban on hunting for species that are not threatened with extinction. While the aim of this proposal as originally conceived by the Five Person Review Group was to maximize the benefits of landowners, especially local communities, from wildlife, the potential beneficiaries of such a move now appear to be mainly absentee private owners of ranches who are Kenyan British and rich African residents outside the wildlife areas. The issue of what benefits are to be derived from wildlife conservation remains unresolved.

The state–resource relationship introduced during colonialism that resulted in the stripping of local communities of any powers of management or control of their natural resources, particularly wildlife, also alienates people from conservation. The state has retained close control of wildlife resources and has not always been sensitive to the social and economic needs of sustainable utilization at the local levels and for the most part follows the colonial patterns of mining natural resources to maintain state coffers and benefit the powerful individuals.

Lack of Understanding of the Nature of Private Property Rights

The failure of the colonialists to appreciate the nature of natives' traditional rights led to undue disregard for those rights, which has affected the conceptions of property by the natives to this day. Cronon, for instance, has argued that ownership is a complex

---

[48] See H. Croze, WCMD, UNDP, and FAO, *Aerial Surveys Undertaken by Kenya Wildlife Management Project – Methodologies and Results* (1978).

social institution that varies widely between cultures and therefore only makes sense if the people with whom the property rights holder lives recognize that ownership and vest on that person the rights to impose sanctions against the violation of those rights by anyone else. Since different groups may permit different bundles of rights over the same object, to define property rights is to represent boundaries articulating a set of conscious ecological boundaries between people and things. This delineation of rights underlines what it is that a particular community values and distinguishes the fishers, pastoralists, and agriculturists.[49]

The superimposition of notions of individual property rights' holding and the inflexibility characterized by colonial authorities' contempt for the views of native Kenyans of property as belonging to a community or group and not subject to appropriation by a single individual have contributed significantly to the lack of equilibrium between people and their ecological surroundings. The dualism of notions of property introduced by colonialism continued as the nascent local bourgeoisie was co-opted into the colonial economy. Communities that had enjoyed rights to forest or wildlife resources did not fully comprehend the notion of state and/or individual ownership of those resources and thus continued to harvest the resources notwithstanding legal prohibitions. For the state to exercise property rights to those resources and the land on which they were located, there was a need to police the resources heavily. This explains the military nature of conservation operations in Kenya and other parts of Africa. The machinery of the state has in some instances been outstripped by the incidences of encroachment, leading to the loss of the resources to the state and overharvesting to the detriment of the communities themselves.

The situation is made worse by the fact that most land in Kenya is owned by local authorities as trust land awaiting registration. There have been increasing conversions of trust land to individual ownership in recent years, taking more land outside the purview of the ownership of local authorities, who, at least in theory, hold such land as trustees for the local community. Most of the individuals who have obtained rights to this land are not necessarily members of such communities.

Lack of Proper Planning

Most laws and policies applicable to resource conservation in Kenya are formulated along the lines of specific sectors. Laws on property rights and land use may run counter to those on wildlife management. Notorious examples in this regard include the subdivision of land into individual holdings and the introduction of cultivation and industrial plants in areas that serve as wildlife dispersal and migration areas. Sustainable wildlife management has been adversely affected by both the failure to provide for multiple land uses and the lack of proper management of wildlife-based tourism. The failure to provide for multiple land uses also hampers sustainable wildlife management. That there are no legal provisions for multiple land use areas is evidently appropriate, considering that there are overlaps between human settlements and wildlife habitat.

While it is necessary to preserve unique habitats within national park zones, it is also important to allow wildlife to migrate from and into parks and permit local communities to engage in productive human activities and their traditional way of life alongside the

---

[49] William Cronon, *Changes in the Land: Indians, Colonists, and the Ecology of New England* (Hill and Hang) (2003).

protected areas. This is particularly crucial for communities such as the Maasai, who live in the Mara area and border the Amboseli and Nairobi National Parks. Moreover, the effects of land tenure change have generally not been considered in formulating policies on wildlife conservation. Land uses such as industrialization and cultivation, encouraged by the trend toward individual ownership, have received policy sanctions even in areas where wildlife management would be a more valuable land use.[50] Tenure changes have resulted in irreversible changes to land uses such as pastoralism that are compatible with wildlife conservation. No attempts were made at inception to integrate land uses so as to allow viable interactions between the conservation imperatives and compatible human land uses. The absence of well-thought-out land use plans has resulted in the encroachment of humans into the protected areas, the conversion of those areas into agricultural and settlement areas, and the pushing of wildlife into smaller and drier areas.[51]

Management problems. Besides the problem of systematic encroachment on wildlife habitats by other land use categories, the present forms of wildlife utilization also pose serious management problems. This sector has been conceptualized as a major foreign exchange earner through tourism.[52] Tourism has been promoted as a source of national economic growth without the integration of local level plans with national level policy.[53] Overemphasis on tourism, however, without consideration of the carrying capacity of the parks has caused marked degradation to park ecosystems due, first, to the concentration of lodges, beach hotels, and tented camps in and around the national parks, and second, to the use of motor vehicles within the parks and driving off the road by tour drivers to facilitate wildlife viewing, which have caused stress to sensitive species and degraded the park ecosystem.[54] In the Amboseli National Park, it has been noted that the hunting success of the lion and the cheetah has been reduced by as much as 25 percent as a result of tourist pressure.[55] Further, the presence of off-road tracks in national parks affects grazing land within the parks and surrounding areas and militates against the regeneration of such land.[56] The vulnerability of the tourism

---

[50] See Kwame Awere-Gyekye, *supra* note 38.

[51] Kenya Wildlife Fund Trustees and United Nations Environment Programme, *People, Parks and Wildlife in Kenya: Guidelines for Public Participation in Wildlife Conservation – Case Studies in Kenya* (1988).

[52] See Siri Eriksen et al., "Land Tenure and Wildlife Management," in Calestous Juma and J. B. Ojwang (eds.), *In Land We Trust: Environment, Private Property and Constitutional Change* (1996) 199, noting that the utilization of land by wildlife is an important aspect of land use and that about 27 percent of the revenue earned by the tourism sector can be attributed directly to wildlife and 26 percent indirectly.

[53] See Eddie Koch, "Reality or Rhetoric? Ecotourism and Rural Reconstruction in South Africa," UNRISD Discussion Paper No. 54, 29 (1994).

[54] On the effects of tourism on habitats, see generally H. Cocussis and A. Parpairis, "Tourism and the Environment: Some Observations on the Concept of Carrying Capacity," in H. Briassoulis and Jan Van Der Straaten (eds.), *Tourism and the Environment: Regional, Economic and Policy Issues* (1992) 23. See also H. Briassoulis, "Environmental Impacts of Tourism: A Framework for Analysis and Evaluation," in H. Briassoulis and Jan Van Der Straaten (eds.), *Tourism and the Environment: Regional, Economic and Policy Issues* (1992) 11.

[55] See Wildlife Planning Unit, Ministry of Environment and Natural Resources, *Amboseli National Park Management Plan* (1981).

[56] See David Western and IBRD, *Road Development Plan for Amboseli National Park, Based on the Criteria and Rationale for Reconciling Conservation and Recreational Use* (1974).

sector to competition from other destinations and adverse impacts of travel advisories as a result of the 1998 and 2002 terrorist attacks has negated the capacity of the sector to yield optimal returns.

4.2 Ecological Problems of Protected Areas

Parks can only be the core of conservation and have to be taken along with surrounding ecosystems and land use. The limited size of protected areas cannot guarantee the survival of all species.[57] While knowledge about the interactions between wildlife and their habitats is important in planning protected area management, it is remarkable that little is known, for instance, about the interaction between large herbivores and the savannah they occupy.[58]

Considering that up to 70 percent of wildlife in Kenya is found outside protected areas, it is imperative that such lands are considered in any wildlife conservation and management plans.[59] The tendency to hive off parks from reserves has led to ecological isolation in areas such as Amboseli, where integrated management including surrounding lands would be more beneficial to the entire ecosystem. Further, the delineation of some parks does not take into account the needs for dispersal and migration of animals. Most of such areas are left out of the protected area, which is thus an incomplete ecosystem that does not meet all the needs of the protected species.

The situation may be exacerbated by the ownership of such areas by different nations, individuals, or groups. The Serengeti national park in Tanzania, for instance, does not cover the entire ecosystem used by wildebeests in their natural migrations. The plains used by these migratory species include the Mara region in Kenya and are managed differently from the Serengeti area.[60] It is remarkable that Serengeti is a World Heritage National Park in which no human activities are allowed while Maasai Mara is a national reserve where human activities are permitted, land is owned by different persons, and parts have been converted to plantation farming. This is also the case in Amboseli, where the Maasai group ranches surrounding the park form part of the entire range within which wildlife is found and influence significantly the management of the park. Changes in land ownership and land uses around these protected areas have made the protected areas isolated islands within ecosystems.[61]

Further, some protected areas are not large enough for big mammals and have little land around them to allow for expansion. The size of the Amboseli national park, for instance, is considered very small in relation to the population of wildlife, which includes

---

[57] See Peter Raven, "Wildlife Conservation in Kenya," 280 *Science* (1998) 1510.

[58] See P. Frost et al., "Responses of Savannahs to Stress and Disturbance," *Biology International* (special issue 10) (1986); I. S. C. Parker, "The Tsavo Story: An Ecological Case History," in N. O. Owen-Smith (ed.), *Management of Large Mammals in African Conservation Areas* (1983) 37–49.

[59] See David Western, "Conservation without Parks: Wildlife in Rural Landscapes," in David Western and M. Pearl (eds.), *Conservation for the Twenty-first Century* (1989) 158.

[60] See A. R. E. Sinclair and Peter Arcese (eds.), *Serengeti II: Dynamics, Management, and Conservation of an Ecosystem* (1995), illustrating the fallacious drawing of boundaries that divide ecosystems into parts that cannot be managed together because politically they fall in different nation states and each state has its own rules on how to manage its natural resources. The Serengeti National Park in Northern Tanzania and the Maasai Mara Park in Southern Kenya are one ecosystem but are managed separately by the respective authorities in each country.

[61] See, e.g., David Western, "Wildlife Conservation in Kenya," 280 *Science* (1998) 1507.

large herbivores. Wildlife populations increase once they are accorded protection, but they remain confined by fences and are surrounded in many cases by hostile property owners whose land uses are incompatible with conservation. While in some cases large mammals have been translocated to larger areas, one wonders whether such a strategy is sustainable in the long run given the limited availability of land and the increase in human population.

4.3 Institutional Problems

Because of the close ties between KWS and the government, the former is caught up in some of the bureaucratic procedures of the latter, making it incapable of responding swiftly to conservation problems as they arise. KWS has also not succeeded in developing a strong multidisciplinary research team and maintains a strong-armed wing of military stature that was inherited at independence. KWS has therefore not managed effectively to collect, organize and disseminate information on conservation, and this hampers the efficacy of its policies.[62]

The lack of public involvement in planning and implementing wildlife management projects hampers the success of these projects, which are characteristically imposed on the public.[63] With respect to wildlife conservation, a major hindrance to the government's attempts at conservation is poor interaction between human beings living with neighboring wildlife refuges and the wildlife. The roots of this mismatch can be found in the initial setting up of the refuges by the colonialists, who set aside land that was previously occupied by natives for wildlife conservation purposes. The setting aside did not take into account the interests that the affected communities had in that land. With population increase and consequent need for more land, communities neighboring wildlife refuges have encroached onto the lands set aside for the animals and used them for settled agricultural activities or for rearing of their livestock. In other cases, massive killing of wild animals such as elephants for ivory or rhinos for horns has taken place in the reserves and parks.[64] The benefits derived from wildlife utilization have been limited to wildlife-based tourism and minimal culling by the hotel industry, which supports this tourism. Communities neighboring wildlife refuges may not, however, perceive the trickle down of benefits as worth the constraints placed on them. They look at other African countries such as Zimbabwe and Namibia that have successful wildlife utilization programs.[65] Kenya does not have a legal framework for wildlife utilization and communities neighboring game parks and game reserves, and there are

---

[62] See Evans M. Mwangi and Kenya Wildlife Service, *Protected Area System Coverage* (Kenya Wildlife Service, Nairobi) (1995).

[63] See, e.g., Olawale O. Ajai, "Integrating Biodiversity Conservation in Sectoral Laws and Policies: A Case Study of Nigeria with Considerations for Developing Countries," in Anatole F. Krattiger et al. (eds.), *Widening Perspectives on Biodiversity* IUCN and International Academy of the Environment, Geneva (1994).

[64] See Dhyani J. Berger, *Wildlife Extension: Participatory Conservation by the Maasai of Kenya* (1993) 1, commenting on the negative role that communities neighboring wildlife refuges play as a result of their noninvolvement in conservation activities.

[65] Government of Zimbabwe, *Policy for Wildlife* (1992). This community involvement is believed to have influenced the maintenance of big elephant herds in the late 1980s when their numbers in Eastern Africa significantly dwindled. It also explains the reluctance of the government of Zimbabwe to ratify CITES.

therefore no necessary incentives to contribute positively to wildlife conservation and management.[66]

5 RETHINKING PROPERTY RIGHTS FOR WILDLIFE MANAGEMENT IN KENYA

> Wildlife–human conflicts are not just a litany of specific problems, but a whole unacknowledged perspective on reality. Their solution requires a concept of sustainable wildlife management by and for people on their land, not in spite of them. This approach differs from protectionism, which tends to institutionalize conservation values that take no account of local attitudes and problems.[67]

> Any grandiose plan for the conservation of wildlife without adequate provision for human interests is doomed to fail. Conservation in developing countries often has to be a compromise between scientific idealism and practical reality.[68]

With the declining productivity of land uses such as livestock and cultivation in Kenya, there is need to search for alternative land use options that are economically viable. Sustainable wildlife management should be promoted as one of the alternatives, given the fact that Kenya is endowed with unique wildlife resources. Current wildlife conservation policies emphasizing the setting aside of land for conservation and vesting of such land in the state are not economically or ecologically efficient overall because they do not ensure optimal utilization and management of land and wildlife resources.

Considering the human population's animosity to wildlife and the escalation of this trend as the human and some wildlife species' populations increase, it has become increasingly clear that if wildlife policies are to contribute to sustainable biodiversity management generally, the needs of humans and wildlife have to be taken into account in tandem in framing the policies. Further, these policies have to aim toward sustainable management practices and away from conservation of wildlife resources for conservation's sake.

For sustainable wildlife management to succeed, perceived benefits have to outweigh the benefits of building up the area, using it as pasture, land, or cultivating it. For rural communities, this objective is tied to the satisfaction of basic needs. Conservation imperatives can be harmonized with the aspirations of rural communities through the channeling of benefits derived from wildlife management to such communities and through the stemming of the effects of enclosure of wildlife in parks such as the degradation of park ecosystems and the promotion of wildlife as a viable economic activity for individuals as against cultivation and livestock keeping, which, if uncontrolled, exhaust the soils and ecosystems around them.

In conceptual and legal terms, it is important that the values informing wildlife conservation are revisited. In this regard, market failure, limitations of existing property rights regimes in fostering wildlife management, and failure of law and policy to provide incentives for conservation have to be tackled. On a more practical level, mechanisms

---

[66] Richard E. Leakey, "Kenya's Policy on Wildlife Research and the Commercial Use of Wildlife," in J. G. Grootenhuis et al. (eds.), *Wildlife Research for Sustainable Development* (1991).

[67] See Wildlife–Human Conflict Report *supra* note 43.

[68] See Raman Sukumar, *Ecology of the Asian Elephant and Its Interaction with Man in South India*, Vol. 1, Indian Institute of Science, Bangalore (1985).

should be devised for ensuring that policies are well coordinated and that measures that go beyond the confines of property rights are established to promote conservation. Property rights could more effectively foster the conservation of biological diversity through involving property owners, individuals and communities, in making decisions on conservation and giving them incentives to participate in the activities.

Whether property rights are vested in individuals or in groups, there is need for security of tenure and some measure of political and economic certainty to ensure that property rights' holders can invest in sustainable resource management in the long term without fear of losing their investment.[69] It is difficult to promote tenure incentives in situations in which there are no state-recognized tenurial rights or the state does not accord the tenure holders security of that tenure.[70] While the private property rights institution is recognized in Kenya's laws and policies and different kinds of rights provided for, such rights to property are subject to state appropriation, and in some instances, such appropriation has taken place without the requisite compensation being afforded to the rights holders. Further, the rights of property owners whose land hosts wildlife are subject to state ownership of the totality of the wildlife resources. Such owners of land have incomplete ownership since they cannot enjoy all the rights encapsulated in the grant document and consequently are in no different position from nonowners or people in open access situations insofar as the wildlife resources on their land are concerned.

5.1 Creating New Incentives for Wildlife Management through Law and Policy

Central to the process of rethinking property rights regimes is the need to grant wildlife use rights to landowners be they communities or individuals.[71] Landowners need to have control over and responsibility for wildlife resources if they are to participate meaningfully in management activities.[72] Tenurial security for land and wildlife resources is of the essence in enabling communities and individuals to make management decisions by themselves or as members of larger groups that include all stakeholders. It also makes the enjoyment of property rights to land more meaningful and beneficial and establishes a wildlife–landownership nexus that is necessary in stemming the current apathy toward wildlife conservation.[73]

Incentives for sustainable wildlife management can be created through granting rights to land and wildlife resources to persons best placed to carry out management activities in any given area. While state and private property rights are important and can foster sustainable resource management in certain cases, it should also be appreciated that there are variations thereto that need to be taken into account in framing rights.

---

[69] See T. Panayotou, *The Economics of Environmental Degradation: Problems, Causes and Response* (1989).

[70] See Owen J. Lynch and Janis B. Alcorn, "Tenurial Rights and Community-Based Conservation," in David Western et al. (eds.), *Natural Connections: Perspectives in Community-Based Conservation* (1994) 373.

[71] See, e.g., Siri Eriksen et al., *supra* note 52, arguing that where customary tenure has been replaced by modern tenure, the flexibility and complexity of rights, including community rights, that promote sustainable management as well as equity are absent.

[72] See, "Introduction," in World Wildlife Fund, Dale Lewis, and Nick Carter (eds.), *Voices from Africa – Local Perspectives on Conservation*, World Wildlife Fund, Washington, D.C. (1993) 4.

[73] See Owen J. Lynch and Janis B. Alcorn, "Tenurial Rights and Community-Based Conservation," in David Western et al. (eds.) *Natural Connections: Perspectives in Community-Based Conservation* (Island Press, Washington, D.C.) (1994) 373.

Common property rights, for instance, can be an effective institution for resource man-agement when purely private rights are costly to enforce.[74] Community-based resource management systems need to be strengthened through land tenure arrangements that accommodate the interests of people living in or around protected areas to ensure that they exercise more influence and power over wildlife and other resources than do governments.

The state should also, as far as possible, divest itself of the rights to and control over wildlife resources. These rights should be framed at the right levels to ensure that the rights' holders are the best placed to manage the resources sustainably and have the necessary incentives to do so. In this regard, the state should devolve ownership, control, and management of wildlife resources to individuals, groups, and local authorities. This will increase the self-interest of property owners in managing wildlife and raise their tolerance of wildlife on their property. The role of the state, as the guardian of the public interest, would still subordinate the rights of communities, local authorities, and individuals to the general interests of the country to manage wildlife resources sustainably and entitle the state to intervene in situations in which the property owner's activities threaten the existence of the wildlife resources.

There are, therefore, first, the need for devolution of real power by states and local authorities to local communities and, second, the need to invest in institutional supply within communities through empowerment and removal of the requirement for gov-ernmental involvement in the affairs of the community. With regard to land ownership, the entities best placed to manage wildlife resources should get rights as entities and not be forced to desegregate into individuals or entities closely approximating such. Further, land uses such as pastoralism that are potentially compatible with sustainable wildlife management and are better served by collective rights to land should be pro-moted through law and policy, not perceived as inferior to cultivation and urbanization. Within the collective entities, however, concerns for the equitable sharing of resources among the members should be addressed to prevent situations in which some sections of the community bear the costs of conservation while others receive the benefits, thus replicating the existing ineffective national policies.[75]

Community ownership, where feasible, would provide members with the necessary incentives to look after wildlife, which would, in turn, defuse the acrimonious rela-tionship between humans and wildlife. The community may, in some circumstances, have a greater capacity to police itself more effectively than the state and/or individuals. The members of the community should, however, be well equipped to look after the resources. Since some of the elements of community organization necessary to sustain community wildlife management initiatives have been considerably weakened, there is need for the creation and encouragement of strong and stable local institutions to enable communities to take charge of resource management activities. In this regard,

---

[74] See Elinor Ostrom, *Governing the Commons: The Evolution of Institutions for Collective Action* (1990) 3. See also Glen Stevenson and Carol M. Rose, "The Comedy of the Commons: Custom, Commerce, and Inherently Public Property," 53 *U. Chi. L. Rev.* (1986) 711.

[75] See Kenya Government, *National Development Plan* (1994–1996). Gender considerations have, for instance, been identified as one such factor in many African countries with rural-based economies. Thus, though the rights should be framed at the level of the community, mechanisms should be put in place to ensure that women participate in decision making within the communities.

investments in training such community members would be worthwhile and most beneficial in the long term.[76] The training should build on indigenous systems of local knowledge, natural resource use, and locally supported decision-making structures and initiatives to cut down on costs and secure the confidence of the community. It should also involve the co-optation of traditional institutions to police resource use with limited government intervention. The concept of community should be widened to encapsulate spatial, social, cultural, and economic aspects while recognizing the diversity of interests that exist within and between communities in social and economic spheres. The major unifying factor should be the sustainable management of wildlife resources for the benefit of all the members.

Indirect Rights to Wildlife and Land Resources

Where the imperatives of sustainable wildlife demand that a protected area remain state owned or be held by the local authority as custodian for the local communities and individuals, ways to benefit such local people, particularly landowners, through the management of wildlife resources should be sought. This objective has, however, to be balanced against the need for state involvement in the management of public resources in the context of national development.[77] One way of channeling benefits to local communities is through revenue-sharing programs. In this regard, the nexus between the revenue and sustainable wildlife management should be established to prevent the perception by the communities of such revenue as a windfall unrelated to sustainable management.

Further, in areas where wildlife in a protected area utilizes land owned by individuals or groups, the nature and extent of the contribution of landowners to wildlife management in the entire ecosystem should be worked out so that they get proportionate returns therefrom and those actually providing or sharing pasture with migrating wildlife receive the highest shares.[78]

As a corollary to property ownership, land taxation laws and their impact on wildlife management should be studied, and subsidies or tax credits should be granted to landowners who contribute to the sustainable management of natural resources through, for instance, allowing wildlife normally resident in a protected area to reside on their land. Such a move would not only provide additional income for the landowners but also curb the pressure to expand cultivation and livestock keeping into protected areas.[79] This measure should go along with adequate compensation for life lost and property destroyed by wildlife.[80]

---

[76] International Institute for Environment and Development, *Whose Eden? An Overview of Community Approaches to Wildlife Management* (1994).

[77] D. M. Mbuvi, "The Management, Conservation and Utilisation of Wildlife Resources," in FAO and WCMD, No. 34, *Kajiado District Workshop Report on Wildlife Conservation and Management* (1978) 34 at 35.

[78] See Philip Thresher, "Landowners' Costs of and Returns from Wildlife," in *Kajiado District Workshop Report*, ibid. 38 at 39.

[79] See P. D. Glavovic, "An Introduction to Wildlife Law," *S. Afr. L. J.* (1988) 519.

[80] See Ackim N. Mwenya, "Redefining Conservation in African Terms," in Dale Lewis and Nick Carter (eds.), *Voices from Africa – Local Perspectives on Conservation*, World Wildlife Fund, Washington, D.C. (1993) 193.

Diversification of Wildlife-Based Economic Activities

In considering the best incentives for wildlife management, it is important to consider diversifying the range of legally permissible wildlife-based economic activities. One way of dealing with the conflict between human activities and biodiversity conservation generally would be to find nondestructive ways to use biological resources.[81] It has, for instance, been suggested that consumptive wildlife utilization should be treated in the same way as commercial agricultural operations but that a relationship should be established between utilization and sustainability.

In the realm of wildlife management, the notion of sustainable utilization is increasingly gaining currency in international environmental parlance. The use of wildlife resources is seen as contributing to the regeneration of those resources and enhancing the evolutionary process within the habitats in which the resources are found. The emphasis on tourism needs to be reconsidered, especially in the light of the growing wildlife and human populations and the ensuing competition for land and other resources. More specifically, culling,[82] game ranching, and game cropping[83] should be considered as alternative land use systems. Local communities and landowners should be allowed to participate in these activities, with the KWS playing a supervisory role to ensure that the existence of species is not threatened. Game ranching and cropping have been successfully carried out in Southern Africa on communal lands and on large privately owned farms.[84]

Other possible uses of wildlife include sport hunting, traditional or subsistence hunting, and bird shooting. Landowners, individuals and groups in areas that are not popular tourist areas, have questioned the rationale for limiting wildlife use to tourism and argued fervently for the revocation of the ban on hunting and trade in wildlife products. Such property owners are of the view that tourism and ranching do not produce as much revenue as hunting would. They also believe that hunting is a more beneficial way of controlling wildlife populations than culling. Culling of such species as zebras, impalas, gazelles, elands, giraffes, warthogs, and waterbucks is allowed in Kenya but strictly monitored by KWS. Landowners who currently have culling quotas have sought to have such transformed into hunting permits, arguing that hunting is more economically rewarding than culling.

The issue as to whether or not to lift the ban on hunting is likely to continue over a period of time given the lack of consensus on the form that such hunting should take and the perceptions of property holders on what species they would like controlled.

---

[81] See Victor M. Marroquin-Merino, "Wildlife Utilization: A New International Mechanism for the Protection of Biological Diversity," 26 *Law & Pol'y Int'l Bus.* 303 (1995). See also Barton Thompson Jr., "Endangered Species," *Palgrave Dictionary of Law & Economics* (1998), arguing that one means of addressing overexploitation of endangered species has been to decrease the commercial profitability of taking a species but that this also reduces the incentive to conserve the species' habitat.

[82] The aims of culling are to allow for better management and to generate income from the sale of meat. See D. H. M. Cumming, "The Decision-making Framework with Regard to Culling Large Mammals in Zimbabwe," in Garth Owen-Smith (ed.), *Management of Large Mammals in African Conservation Areas* (Cambridge University Press) (1983) 173–186.

[83] See David Nyeki Musili, *Wildlife Conservation and Tourism in Kenya* (Kenya Wildlife Service, Nairobi) (1993).

[84] Garth Owen-Smith, "Wildlife Conservation in Africa: There Is Another Way," in World Wildlife Fund, Dale Lewis and Nick Carter (eds.), *Voices from Africa – Local Perspectives on Conservation*, World Wildlife Fund, Washington, D.C. (1993) 57 at 64–65.

Most landowners who propose the lifting of the ban favor sport hunting. There are, however, sections of the Kenyan populace who favor only subsistence or traditional hunting and would like sport hunting eliminated. At the center of this controversy is the general feeling that sport hunting is geared toward foreigners only and smacks of colonial conservation biases.

The reintroduction of hunting for whatever purpose without a well-thought-out plan could lead to the resurgence of poaching. Moreover, some property owners would like to be allowed to hunt elephants, which are listed as endangered species under Appendix I of the CITES to which Kenya is a signatory. In the final analysis, the issue of diversifying economic activities based on wildlife goes beyond the purview of landowners. It is a national issue whose consideration entails questions about the overall benefits to be gained from sustainable wildlife management for Kenyans and a determination on whether the costs that Kenyans bear such as forgoing the use of their land for cultivation and livestock keeping are adequately compensated by those benefits. Thus wildlife management policies need to be informed by a broader and more comprehensive understanding of people's true values, needs, and rights and not by a conservation ethos and philosophies informed by "outside" interests.

Allied to the diversification of wildlife-based economic activities is the need to develop local markets for wildlife products and services. This would ensure that the wildlife industry is not predicated on patronage from outsiders, as is currently the case with tourism, but is also informed by local needs and conditions. One way of doing this is through the generation of locally marketable wildlife products such as meat, eggs, skins, and trophies. Further adventure tourism and wildlife-based recreation should be promoted as activities for local Kenyans through education.

Proper Planning and Coordination of Policies

Realizing the true value of wildlife resources in Kenya calls for proper planning of land uses and modes of wildlife management. Land use planning and exercise of property rights to land hosting wildlife resources by different holders should be coordinated to balance the diverse interests of all stakeholders and ensure sustainable management. While there is no need to create leviathan institutions, the balance can only be achieved through the cooperation of different government departments. There should also be collaboration between different departments when the responsibilities of such departments overlap. The Memorandum of Understanding (MOU) of the Forest Department and KWS for wildlife management in forest areas is a good illustration of the benefits to be gained from collaboration.[85]

The proper combination of resource and land use strategies would be another avenue through which a balance between livestock keeping, cultivation, and nomadic pastoralism, on the one hand, and wildlife management, tourism, and other economic opportunities, on the other, could be achieved. This would demonstrate the viability of wildlife management when considered alongside cultivation or livestock keeping. The integration of land tenure and wildlife management policies can be enhanced through the classification of all regions in the country into broad land use categories such as pastoralism, cultivation, forestry, or nature conservation. This would be followed by

---

[85] Kenya Wildlife Service and Forest Department, *Memorandum of Understanding for the Joint Management of Selected Forests* (1991) (on file with author).

formulation of land tenure policies that enhance those purposes in the areas.[86] Zoning is an important way through which the state can intervene to influence the role of private property rights holders in wildlife conservation. Three factors should be considered in the zoning process, namely, wildlife categories, existing land use systems, and the interaction between the two. Other factors to be taken into account include the permissible numbers of people and livestock, the level of cultivation and infrastructure development, changes to the physical and biological resources, and uses of wildlife to be allowed within any given zone.

6 WORKING AROUND THE LIMITS OF PROPERTY RIGHTS: INNOVATIVE USE OF PROPERTY RIGHTS AND SUSTAINABLE WILDLIFE MANAGEMENT

Property rights, whether vested in individuals, groups, local authorities, or the state, can be beneficial for sustainable wildlife management if proper incentives are provided to all parties who bear the costs of management activities.[87] In this regard, it is important to identify feasible forms of organization in instances in which traditional communities have broken down. These kinds of organizations can be based on the commonality of interests in sustainable management of wildlife resources. Common interests will dictate members' adherence to the rules set and stricter and more efficient detection and sanctioning of nonconformers than the state machinery can currently achieve.

6.1 Beyond Private Property Rights' Boundaries

The nature of wildlife resources is such that no single property rights holder is likely to own the entire range within which they are found. Because private or community holdings are likely to host the same wildlife populations at different times, cooperation between different property holders is necessary. The desire to enclose all rights within one parcel of land or in one property holder should be subordinated to the need to manage wildlife resources sustainably where dispersal and migration needs of wildlife demand it.[88] An effective way of operationalizing the collaboration of property rights holders is through the establishment of cooperatives for sustainable wildlife management comprising diverse property rights holders, including state, local authority, individuals, and groups. Such cooperatives should be based on proximity to wildlife resources and the shared interest in the resource as opposed to ethnicity or mode of property holding, which polarizes groups and works against sustainable management imperatives.

Each landowner living in an area that hosts wildlife could, for instance, be a shareholder in a commonly held stock of wildlife that would yield annual dividends to be

---

[86] See Simon Metcalfe, "The Zimbabwe Communal Areas Management Programme for Indigenous Resources (CAMPFIRE)," in David Western et al. (eds.), *Natural Connections: Perspectives in Community-Based Conservation* (Island Press) (1994) 187.

[87] Ibid.

[88] See D. H. M. Cumming, "Conservation Issues and Problems in Africa," in World Wildlife Fund, Dale Lewis and Nick Carter (eds.), *Voices from Africa – Local Perspectives on Conservation*, World Wildlife Fund, Washington, D.C. (1993) 23. See also Barton H. Thompson Jr., "The Endangered Species Act: A Case-Study in Takings and Incentives," 2 *Stan. L. Rev.* (1997) 305, on Habitat Conservation Planning in the United States.

shared out among the members of a cooperative depending on their contribution to wildlife management.[89] The state as the guardian of the public interest and, where applicable, local authorities that own land should also be included as members in the cooperatives. The role of the state should, however, be limited, to preclude the possibility of its monopolizing wildlife management activities. This system would recognize the fugitive nature of wildlife and the big geographic range over which any given species may be distributed. In seeking to operationalize cooperatives for wildlife conservation where the state owns a protected area, however, it is imperative that tenure, in the sense of who owns the land, be divorced from the wildlife resources on that land.[90] Further, cooperation could also take the form of joint land management ventures between the parks administration and group ranchers, local authorities, or individuals. Such ventures can facilitate the change from negative human perceptions of wildlife to appreciation thereof and contribute to the long-term sustainability of wildlife resources.

It should be recognized that wildlife management is one of the many possible land uses. The enjoyment of property rights to wildlife depends on the ability of landowners, public and private, to contract with each other and with other wildlife users to control wildlife stocks and to gain access to them.[91] Memoranda of understanding between different property rights holders can serve as a good basis for collaboration. Such memoranda of understanding would create an atmosphere conducive to sustainable wildlife management and establish bases for contracts among private property owners, groups, local councils, and the state, thus broadening the range of actors in wildlife management.

6.2 Servitudes

Servitudes or rights that a person acquires over another person's land can be used to ensure that private property rights engender sustainable wildlife management.[92] Kenyan laws on property rights to land recognize three main categories of servitudes, namely, easements, profits, and restrictive covenants.[93] *Easements* are defined as rights attached to a parcel of land that allow the proprietor of the parcel either to use the land of another in a particular manner or to restrict its use to a particular extent.[94] They

---

[89] See David Western, "Ecosystem Conservation and Rural Development: The Case of Amboseli," in David Western et al. (eds.), *Natural Connections: Perspectives in Community-Based Conservation* (Island Press) (1994) 50, stating that even in Amboseli, where Community-Based Conservation (CBC) has evolved considerably, it is important to evolve CBC schemes toward individuals but to keep the commonality that is the stock of wildlife from which benefits can be obtained by individuals and members of local communities. This is recognition of the dynamic nature of communities and the forces that are working therein changing the lifestyles from communal to individual among the Maasai. The idea here is to deal with communities as they are and not impose upon them notions that no longer apply.

[90] See H. W. O. Okoth-Ogendo, "Property Theory and Land Use Analysis – an Essay in the Political Economy of Ideas," Discussion Paper No. 209 Vol. 5 (Institute of Development Studies, University of Nairobi) (1974) 291–305.

[91] See Dean Lueck, "Property Rights and the Economic Logic of Wildlife Institutions," 35 *Nat. Resources J.* (1995) 625 at 628.

[92] See Krishna N. Joshi, *Easements and Licenses* (1931), defining a servitude as a real right vested in or annexed to a definite person or piece of land, over some object belonging to another and limiting the enjoyment of that object by that other in a definite manner.

[93] See the Registered Land Act, Cap 300 of the Laws of Kenya.

[94] Ibid. at Preamble.

include, among others, the right of way. For an easement to arise, there must be two adjoining pieces of land owned by two different persons. The land that benefits from an easement is called the *dominant tenement*, while the one over which the right is established is called the *servient tenement*. Further, the easement must be for the benefit of the dominant tenement and cannot be acquired for any other purpose. In the case of wildlife management, the land that hosts wildlife most of the time in a particular area should be designated as the dominant tenement and the land around it that forms part of the habitat necessary for sustainable management should be designated as the servient tenement. Rights of way for the wildlife should be negotiated with the owners of the servient tenements and mechanisms for compensating such owners worked out. Section 6 of EMCA provides specifically for wildlife easements that are not predicated on landownership.

With regard to profits, they may be used to allow persons living with wildlife or neighboring protected areas to take wildlife resources for their benefit, taking into account the need for sustainable wildlife management. *Profits* are rights to go onto the land of another and take a particular substance from that land, whether the soil or products of the soil. The thing to be taken in the case of wildlife management are animals naturally resident on the land. Profits can either be attached to ownership/other interest in land or exist apart from land. Profits are therefore useful in reaching out to people who are affected by wildlife management but do not own land in the area. They can also be used to ensure equitable distribution of proceeds from wildlife resources. People living around a protected area can be allowed to take wildlife from the protected area under regulated conditions that ensure sustainability.

A *restrictive covenant* has the effect of limiting the manner in which a landowner can use his or her land, when such limitation is necessary for the benefit of an adjoining piece of land. It constitutes an important way for landowners to control the use of land. The covenants do not lapse upon the transfer of the land to which they apply and bind subsequent owners who were not party to the agreement. Restrictive covenants can be used by the state to control the uses to which private or group landowners may put their land where such land is part of an ecosystem comprising wildlife range.

6.3 Transferable Development Rights

In cases in which a property owner proposes a kind of development that is not compatible with sustainable wildlife management such as cultivation or building of industries or residential houses on land within an area hosting wildlife resources, the provisions of state acquisition of the property owner's land should be invoked and compensation paid. Compensation could take the form of a grant of land in an area where the proposed use by the property owner can be carried out. In instances in which such land is not available, transferable development rights that the landowner can use elsewhere or sell to others should be given.

9 The Development of Environmental Law and Its Impact on Sustainable Use of Wetlands in Uganda

Emmanuel Kasimbazi

1 INTRODUCTION

Environmental law is a relatively new but rapidly growing and expanding field of law, which aims at protecting the nature, natural resources, and total context within which they exist.[1] Environmental law as it is known today is an amalgam of common law and statutory principles. In recent times, statutory revisions of common law propositions have undergone spectacular growth rates, whether measured by number of cases or actual and potential liabilities – in this case Uganda has been no exception. However, one of the greatest challenges of our age has been achieving sustainable development as defined in the World Commission on Environment and Development (WCED) Report as "development that meets the needs of the present without compromising the ability of future generations to meet their own needs."[2] This definition emphasizes a combination of economic development and protection of the environment.

The old environmental law was inspired by the reductionist reasoning that it could and should stick to its defensive role, in other words, just prevent extremes of ruthless development, without in other respects intervening in economic policy.[3] But in many ways reductionist thinking led to theoretical interpretation of the law and thus became an alibi for continuing ruthless development. Today, there has been a transformation in the international arena to an incorporation of the criteria for the protection of natural, cultural, and social capital in every policy whether public or private and systematic and guided thinking in decision making.[4] All these are instrumental in the development of sustainable development. In essence, environmental law has been developing in a fashion that ensures sustainable use of the environment.

This chapter explores the changing face of environmental law in Uganda in relation to sustainable use of wetlands. It begins by outlining environmental law in the Ugandan context and then looks at the development of laws and policies related to wetlands management. It also considers the institutional framework that supports the legal structure and makes recommendations on the way forward.

---

[1] William H. Rodgers, *Environmental Law* (2nd ed., Hornbook Series, St. Paul, Minn.: West Publishing Company) (1994).

[2] See also the Rio Declaration (1992) and Agenda 21, reprinted in 31 ILM 874.

[3] Decleris Micheal, *The Law of Sustainable Development: General Principles*, European Commission (2000) 4–20.

[4] Ibid.

2 THE NATURE OF THE ENVIRONMENT IN UGANDA

The definition of the term *environment* is broad. *Black's Law Dictionary* defines *environment* as the "totality of physical, economic, cultural, aesthetic, and social circumstances and actors which surround and affect desirability and value of property and which affects the quality of peoples lives."[5] Section 1 of the Ugandan National Environment Act (NEA) defines it as the "physical factors of the surroundings of the human beings including land, water, atmosphere, climate, sound odour taste, the biological factors of animals and plants and the social factor of aesthetics and includes both the natural and the built environment."[6]

From the preceding definitions it may be observed that "environment" involves almost every aspect of life. Therefore, the environment cannot be separated from human actions, ambitions, and needs. It has been observed in the WCED report that environmental stress has often been seen as a result of the growing demand on resources. In that respect natural resources include both living and nonliving resources that if not conserved may be destructible.

3 DEVELOPMENT OF ENVIRONMENTAL LAW IN UGANDA

Law and administration are two main instruments available to society for developing and applying public policy. Law can be defined as a process of decision making, which embodies not merely a set of rules for human conduct, but a system of administrative and judicial mechanisms and conventions, which shape the implementation of the law.[7] Administration, on the other hand, is a form of bureaucratic decision making epitomized by hierarchy specialization of tasks and a strict division of labor through which public policy and legislation are applied.[8] Often law is an adjunct to other policymaking processes such as defining the rights to public participation in decision making. In the wake of the global environmental decline, the international community has increasingly endorsed the use of law and administration as necessary tools for achieving sustainable development in all countries.[9]

Environmental law is one of the new branches of law. This is a body of law that addresses the system of complex and interlocking rules. It seeks to protect the environment from destruction. In specific terms, it is that branch of law that regulates the use, protection, and conservation of the environment and provides rules relating to environmental liability.

For a long time, law did not make a significant contribution to environmental management, including that of wetlands in Uganda. There was a lack of a coherent system of environmental law and administration. Environmental policymaking was not systematic, and government proceeded largely by incremental changes in past assumptions and

---

[5] *Black's Law Dictionary* (6th ed., St. Paul, Minn., West Publishing Company) (1990) 1045.

[6] Chapter 153 of the Laws of Uganda.

[7] Benjamin J. Richardson, *Legal Strategies for Conservation and Management of Wetlands in Kenya and Uganda* (IUCN East African Regional Office, Nairobi) (1990).

[8] Ibid.

[9] World Commission on Environment and Development, *Our Common Future* (Oxford: Oxford University Press) (1987) 310. IUCN, UNEP, and WWF, *Caring for the Earth: A Strategy for Sustainable Living* (IUCN, Gland, Switzerland) (1991) 67–69.

orientations. Uganda had an eclectic and fragmented legal system composed of remnant indigenous customary practices and various ordinances and institutions inherited from colonial authorities.

Prior to the establishment of colonial rule in East Africa, rural communities had evolved various customary rules, which governed use of natural resources, such as forests and wetlands. These indigenous systems of environmental management emerged in a milieu of low population and simple low-energy-demanding technology. Gradually the authority of customary environmental management practices has weakened, eroded by the infusion of new technology and the commercialization of agricultural production coupled with demographic pressures that have intensified exploitation of resources.[10] Where traditional management systems survive, they sometimes suffer from parochialism that prevents the development of a systematic approach capable of addressing larger regional ecological interactions.

The breakdown of indigenous management systems begun in the 19th century with the absorption of the various East African tribes and kingdoms into colonial protectorates established by the British. Besides the destructive economic changes engendered by colonial rule, the system of law and administration founded by the colonial authorities was largely inimical to sound environmental management.[11] The system was elitist and hierarchical with little opportunity for participation by the subjugated indigenous population. The colonial system was geared toward exploitation of natural resources, the benefits of which were not equally distributed among the population. Paradoxically, the colonial system indirectly promoted conservation of some resources such as forest reserves and "big game" wildlife, by limiting their exploitation to people with the appropriate wealth and power. But the preservationist mode of the colonial legislation, especially in the forestry and protected area laws, led authorities largely to ignore wise management of natural resources outside the formally gazetted areas. Although political independence began in East Africa in the 1960s, the structures and institutions set up by the colonial rulers continue to exert a profound influence on contemporary decision making.[12]

Tenure and land use law has a fundamental bearing on the way people perceive their responsibilities to wetlands. Laws on forestry, water resources, and protected areas also influence management practices. In Uganda, this kind of environmental law did not develop until the early 1990s. Since 1990, Uganda has been developing environmental policies based on the principle of sustainable development.[13] Wetland-related policies have been developed in order to ensure sustainable use and management of wetlands.

In 1991, the Ministry of Water, Lands and Environment initiated the Uganda National Wetlands Programme. The first step in implanting this program consisted of taking an inventory of wetlands in the country. By 1993, a project with the main objective of developing a management program and the tools required for such management, including the policy and legislation, was well under way. The policy was approved in

[10] World Commission on Environment and Development, *Our Common Future*, 310.

[11] Patricia J. Deacon and Micheal B. K. Darkoh, "The Policies and Practices behind the Degradation of Kenya's Land Resources – a Preliminary Review" 17 *Journal of East African Research and Development* (1987) 43–48.

[12] John Ntambirweki, "Review of Existing Legislation in the Field of Environmental Legislation" NEAP Secretariat, Kampala (1992) at 2.

[13] See, generally, Uganda Government, the National Environment Action Plan, 1990.

1994, about the same time as the National Environment Action Plan (NEAP). The NEAP incorporates the objectives of wetland conservation and management as well as the guidelines and strategies required for purposes of such conservation and management. Concurrently with the development of the NEAP and the wetlands policy, plans for wetland management were initiated. In 1995, a national wetlands policy that aimed at curtailing the rampant loss of wetland resources and ensuring that benefits from wetlands are sustainable and equitably distributed to the people in Uganda was adopted.

4 THE NATURE OF WETLANDS MANAGEMENT IN UGANDA

4.1 Definition of a Wetland

Wetlands, commonly known as swamps in Uganda, are a resource of considerable importance, as are forests, rangelands, arable land, and open water resources. Uganda's National Policy for the conservation and management of wetland resources defines *wetlands* as "an area where plants and animals have been adopted to temporary or permanently flooding by saline, brackish or fresh water."[14] The National Environment Act defines *wetland* as "areas permanently or seasonally flooded by water where plants and animals have become adopted."[15] Environmental Conventions have also defined the wetlands. For example, the Convention on Biological Diversity defines it as "a complex of plant, animal and micro-organisms communities and their non-living environment interacting as a functional unit."[16] This definition emphasizes that the functional ecological integrity of wetlands should be maintained. A broader definition is given by the Convention on Wetlands of International Importance Especially as Waterfowl Habitat, 1971, which defines *wetlands* as "areas of marsh, fen, peat land, or water, whether natural or artificial, permanent or temporary, with water that is static or flowing, fresh, brackish, salt, including areas of marine water the depth of which at low tide does not exceed 6 meters."[17] This definition adds that wetlands may incorporate riparian and coastal zones adjacent to them.[18] The marine wetlands include sea grass beds and coral reefs and have special characteristics and have quite different management needs from inland wetlands.

One common element in all the definitions is that wetland includes land that is permanently wet and socked with water. Therefore, a wetland is an important resource that involves land and water resources.

4.2 Background to Wetland Management in Uganda

For a long time wetlands have been regarded as *res nullius*. In the Buganda Agreement of 1900, by which Britain acquired the status of a protecting power over the kingdom

---

[14] Republic of Uganda, "The National Policy for Conservation and Management of Wetlands Resources" 1995 at p. v.

[15] NEA, *supra* note 6 at Section 1(o).

[16] Convention on Biodiversity (CBD) (1992) Article 2, reprinted in 31 ILM 1004 (signed 5 June 1992).

[17] Convention on Wetlands of International Importance Especially as Waterfowl Habitat (hereafter Ramsar Convention) Article 1, reprinted in 11 ILM 969 (signed 2 February 1971).

[18] Ibid. at Article 2(1).

of Buganda, wetlands were referred to as "wastelands" and were vested in the Crown.[19] Similar treatment was meted out to wetlands under the other two agreements concluded with Toro in 1900 and Ankole in 1901. The rest of Uganda was declared Crown land.[20] As such wetlands were governed directly by British law applicable in the whole of Uganda in the colonial period. In 1902, the British Crown passed the Uganda Order in Council. Statutes made by the Crown, the common law, and principles of equity were to be the legal regime governing the lives of the people in the protectorate. The Order in Council, however, also permitted the continued application of African customary laws so long as they were not repugnant to morality and natural justice.[21]

The law that was imported into Uganda in 1902 emphasized individual tenure and ownership as its key feature.[22] To buttress individual tenure, the system of land tenure that was introduced emphasized the granting of estates akin to those obtaining in England. Since wetlands had already been alienated to the Crown, individual estates were not granted on them as a matter of policy. Where such grants were made, the essence of ownership entitled the grantee almost unfettered rights of use and abuse, limited only by the eminent domain of the Crown.[23] Both the Crown and its successor, the government of Uganda, did not assign high priority to management of wetlands resources. Their basic concern was with the control of the water resources. It was for this reason that the law provided that

> all rights to the water of any spring, river, stream, watercourse, pond or lake on or under public land whether alienated or not shall be reserved to the Government.[24]

The other resources of the wetlands were not considered valuable. The areas they covered, apart from the water resources they contained, were considered wastelands. If the wetlands contained other valuable resources such as minerals or forests, these could be extracted under the authority of sectoral laws. No controls were placed on the methods for extraction of those resources.

The main legacy of colonialism has been the growth of an overly complex, hierarchical, and centralized system of administration. The national bureaucracies were ill adapted to natural resource management; often they were overpoliticized and sanctions-oriented and functioned without public participation. The legal framework was primarily concerned with the allocation and distribution of rights to exploit resources among the different bureaucratic sectors. These were dealt with under separate laws regulating the exploitation of water, land, forests, minerals, fisheries, wetlands, and so on.[25] In effect, the legislation had a negative orientation, stressing what should not be done. As awareness of the ecological consequences of resource management practices arose, environmental provisions were simply grafted unto the existing legal structure without any attempt to realign the underlying developmental policy of law.[26] The result

---

[19] John Ntambirweki, *The Evolution of Policy and Legislation on Wetlands in Uganda* (Gland, Switzerland, IUCN, 1998).

[20] Ibid. [21] Ibid.

[22] Ibid. [23] Ibid.

[24] Section 27 of the Public Land Act of 1969.

[25] Bondi D Ogolla, "Kenya: Environmental Management Policy and Laws" *Environmental Policy and Law* (1992) 164–175.

[26] Wangu Mwangi, "Kenya Environmental Law Dilemma" *Econews Africa* (1993) 4–5.

is that the law was stretched to implement policies that it was never originally intended to address.

Another legacy of colonialism was the establishment of constitutional representative democracies in the newly independent state. Although there is a modicum of separation of powers by the legislative, executive, and judiciary, in practice, the executive arm of government has played a very dominant role in the policy process and this system has undermined the rule of law.[27] Although a strong executive can readily push through desired legal changes, where sweeping reforms of the law have been attempted such as Amin's Land Reform Decree,[28] the necessary political climate to implement the reforms has been missing.

In addition to the asymmetrical relationship between the executive and other branches of government, colonialism also left an unbalanced relationship between the state and society that is not conducive to effective natural resource management. On the one hand, the state has been capable of pushing through specific development proposals such as a dam or factory where executive decisions were subject to minimal accountability. On the other hand, it has had limited institutional capacity to intervene and actively regulate the environmental activities of rural communities, particularly with regard to diffused activities such as hunting of wildlife or removal of vegetation. The result is an often antagonistic and unconstructive relationship between the government and society.

A new paradigm of environmental law has emerged recently under the aegis of international development and community. This new legal approach has arisen out of the 1972 Stockholm Conference, the World Charter for Nature of 1982, and various international environmental law instruments. The emphasis in environmental law has switched from reactive *command and control* processes to a proactive role embodied in procedures for integrated environmental planning and environmental impact assessment. However, a weakness of this approach is that it has tended to ignore the socioeconomic constraints facing lower-income countries.

The types of environmental laws being promoted often assume the existence of a certain institutional capacity in terms of available financial resources, technical expertise, and bureaucratic competence. In countries lacking basic infrastructure, central government authorities are often unable to implement and enforce effectively their environmental mandates. With regard to wetlands, although the existing laws theoretically provide sufficient power with which to regulate the various uses of the resource, the administrative culture and political economy do not lend themselves to an environmentally enlightened application of the law. Wetlands have never been accorded a legal framework in their own right, but rather have come under the administration of an array of ministries. This has engendered a narrow sectoral approach to the use of wetlands, which have been exploited and managed often for a single purpose that depended on the priorities of the controlling ministry such as agricultural, irrigation, water supply, or flood control. Wetlands have not been perceived as having a variety of functions and values, which could be managed on a multiple-use basis.

---

[27] Y. P. Ghai and J. P. W. McAuslan, *Public Law and Political Change in Kenya: A Study of the Legal Framework of Government from Colonial Times to Present* (London: Oxford University Press) (1970).
[28] Ibid.

4.3 Nature of Wetlands in Uganda

Uganda has over 50 administrative districts and almost all of them have wetlands except a few districts in the dry northern region of Uganda. About 18 percent of Uganda's surface area is open water.[29] Around the extensive and widely distributed lakes and many of the country's rivers, there are elongated tracts of papyrus and grass swamps, especially in the lowland areas bordering the river Nile.[30] The permanent wetland area is estimated to cover an area of 767,400 hectares, representing about 3.7 percent of the country's total land area.[31] There are also about 2,191,500 hectares of seasonal swamps, making the total wetland area just over 15 percent of the land area of Uganda.[32]

There are many types of wetlands in Uganda. Some occur in fringing wetlands along lakeshores; others are found in land fringing rivers or filling old river valleys. The majority contain freshwater; a few are very salty. Most have both inflows and an outflow so water passes through them; a few have inflows or rainfall but no surface outflow. Some contain water permanently; others are seasonal and flood only during the rainy season.[33] A majority of inland wetlands have a permanent central core with seasonal flood plains along the perimeter.[34]

4.4 The Importance of Wetlands to the Ugandan Environment

Uganda's wetlands support a rich diversity of plants and animals. Wetlands also have intrinsic attributes, perform functions and services, and produce goods of local, regional, national, or international importance. Together they represent considerable ecological, social, and economic values. Table 9.1 shows wetland benefits – derived from attributes, functions, goods, and services classified into four categories.

In the rural areas in Uganda, millions of households are engaged in wetland farming, papyrus harvesting, pottery and brick making, and sand mining. About 5 million people, many of them cattle keepers, depend directly on wetlands for their and their livestock's water needs. In urban areas, wetlands purify industrial, commercial, and domestic effluents such as sewerage and the dirt washed down with rainstorms through urban center drainage systems. Wetlands provide social and economic values, through their interaction with human society. The monetary value of wetlands is difficult to determine because some of the values are free public goods such as environmental services. Others are indirect values. For example, the Nakivubo wetland in Kampala alone contributes U.S. $1.7 million to the economy annually as a tertiary wastewater treatment plant. About U.S. $100,000 is estimated to accrue from wetland resources through crop cultivation, papyrus harvesting, brick making, and fish farming. Rural households in Pallisa are estimated to derive about U.S. $200 per hectare per annum from papyrus harvesting.[35]

---

[29] Wetlands Inspection Division, *Wetlands Resource Book* (Kampala, Uganda: National Wetlands Programme) (2001).

[30] Ibid. [31] Ibid.

[32] Jones R. Kamugisha, *Management of Natural Resources and Environment in Uganda: Policy and Legislation Landmarks 1890–1990* (Kampala, Uganda: Regional Soil Conservation Unit/SIDA) (1989).

[33] Ibid. [34] Ibid.

[35] Republic of Uganda, *National Environment Report* (NEMA) 2002.

Table 9.1. Wetland benefits

Direct values	Indirect values	Option values	Nonuse values
Production and consumption of goods and services:	Ecosystem functions and services:	Premium placed on possible future uses and applications:	Intrinsic significance: Cultural value Aesthetic value
Fish	Water quality	Pharmaceutical	Heritage value
Fuel wood	Water flow	Agricultural	Bequest value
Building poles	Water storage	Industrial	
Sand, gravel, clay	Water purification	Leisure	
Thatch	Water recharge	Water use	
Water	Flood control	Gene pool	
Wild foods	Storm protection		
Medicines	Nutrient protection		
Agriculture	Microclimate regulation		
Cultivation	Shore stabilization		
Pasture/grazing	Biodiversity and habitat provision		
Transport			
Recreation			

Source: Government of Uganda, Ministry of Water, *Lands and Environment Wetlands Resource Book,* Kampala, Uganda, 2001a.

Economic valuation of water is difficult but has been attempted by the Wetlands Inspection Division (WID). It is assumed that 1 million families directly depend on wetlands for water, with consumption of five jerrycans (each 20 liters) per family, each at Uganda shillings (Ush) 20.[36] This implies that the value of water alone is (Ush) 100 million per day (about U.S. $50,000). For 30,000 square kilometers of wetland area, this translates to U.S. $8/hectare/year in terms of the value of water for domestic purposes alone. Another valuation based on 5 million users has put the value at U.S. $25 million per year. Wetlands contribute to water supply for both the neighboring communities and the whole population through groundwater storage and water purification.

4.5 Problems Affecting Uganda's Wetlands

For many years wetland use was largely limited to activities that did not alter the ecosystem in a permanent way. However, as a result of increased population, coupled with diminishing available agricultural land, reduced soil fertility, and continuing urbanization, pressure on wetlands is building rapidly. Many people turn to wetlands to provide agricultural and industrial land, domestic and industrial water, and a dumping ground for waste.

In some areas these activities have resulted in serious consequences such as lowered water tables, changes in microclimate, and loss of biological diversity. Although pressure on wetlands is widespread in Uganda, wetland loss and degradation are greatest in the southwestern region of the country, where by 1992 nearly 40 percent of wetlands in Kabale and Kisoro had been converted mainly into dairy pastures.[37] In the east, the conversion of seasonal wetlands to rice cultivation is spreading rapidly in Pallisa, Iganga,

---

[36] This is the equivalent of one cent in U.S. dollars.   [37] *Wetlands Resource Book, supra* note 29.

and Tororo. The districts of Iganga and Bugiri alone account for a quarter of all the wetlands lost in Uganda, while the eastern region accounts for around 75 percent of the total converted countrywide.

The ongoing degradation of the urban wetlands, especially in Kampala (20 percent by 1992) and Masaka, is causing increasing concern to environmental managers.[38] In urban areas wetland conversion is seriously threatening the vital water supply functions of flow regulation and purification. Until recently, official policy supported and even encouraged the drainage of swamps, termed *reclamation,* for agricultural uses.[39] By 1964, some 1,620 hectares had been drained. It is estimated that nearly 3,000 hectares have been reclaimed through drainage, in most cases through excavation of a main drainage channel in the center of the swamps.

Wetlands are threatened by uncontrolled conversion to other types of land uses. The destruction and misuse of wetlands are largely results of increasing human population and changing needs; agricultural expansion; environmentally harmful management, which includes excessive harvesting of wetland plants; swamp fisheries; overgrazing; and inappropriate waste disposal.[40] The impact of the loss and degradation of wetlands takes the form of siltation and pollution of wetlands, damage to wildlife habitat and loss of biological diversity, loss of water supply, and a general deterioration of the quality of life and reduction of options for rural development.

5 MAJOR ELEMENTS OF SUSTAINABLE USE OF A WETLAND

The *sustainable use* of wetlands was defined by the Regina Conference as "human use of a wetland so that it may yield the greatest continuous benefit to present generations while maintaining its potential to meet the needs and aspirations for the future."[41]

One of the elements of sustainable use of wetland is that they must be used wisely. The concept of wise use was also defined in the Regina Conference as the sustainable utilization for the benefit of humankind in a way compatible with the maintenance of the natural properties of the ecosystem. Further, the Uganda wetlands policy provides a more specific definition of sustainable use of a wetland: "utilization which ensures that the products or services from that use are available at the same level for the foreseeable future."[42]

To implement sustainable use of wetlands in legislation a number of tools have to be employed. These include environmental impact assessment, planning, monitoring, and auditing. It is also necessary to employ certain management-specific measures:

a. Zoning of wetlands according to appropriate uses, taking into account the physical, chemical, and biological components of the wetland: In particular, where strict natural reserves are established in wetland areas it may be necessary to establish a buffer zone between the highly protected areas and those intensively used for human activities. The buffer zones would represent a balanced mix of use and conservation and shield the strictly protected areas from encroachment.

---

[38] Ibid.

[40] Benjamin J. Richardson, *supra* note 7.

[42] Republic of Uganda, *supra* note 14.

[39] Ibid.

[41] Ibid.

b. Prohibition of unsustainable uses: This is a matter that depends on circumstances, local conditions, and public knowledge of the particular use of wetland.

c. Control of access of wetlands and their resources: This ensures that the wetlands are not depleted by promiscuous use. In this regard, it becomes necessary to institute a system of permits and licenses to control and limit access to wetlands. Permits and licenses can be used to discriminate between desirable and undesirable activities, giving preference to the latter. If the permits or licenses must be renewed, they can give sufficient oversight to the controlling authority to ensure that poor performers are not granted renewals of their licenses. Permits or licenses can also be coupled with fees to enable the controlling authority to charge higher fees for undesirable activities as a deterrent measure. Permits could also be used to protect specific species in wetlands such as waterfowl by denying permits for activities that target rare and endemic species. In such cases the permits will be issued for specific seasons of the year.

d. Prohibition of the introduction of alien species and eradication of species if they have already been introduced: This requirement is included in the Convention on Biological Diversity.[43]

e. Prohibition of drainage, dredging, or filling of wetlands: If it is conceded that wetlands are a vital ecosystem, it necessarily follows that drainage, dredging, or filling of wetland is inconsistent with that presumption. In any case, it would be impossible to maintain the natural properties of the ecosystem if any of these acts were permitted.

f. Restoration of wetlands: Legislation should provide for the restoration of damaged wetlands. Restoration may be a duty of either a public body or on individual land user. Because of problems of enforcement of public duty, it is often necessary to make restoration the duty of the individual land user in accordance with the well-accepted polluter pays principle. Restoration can be enforced by providing for an environmental restoration order within the legislation on wetlands.

g. Establishment of standards: Legislation should provide for the establishment of various criteria and standards for the management of wetlands. Because each wetland has its own peculiar ecological characteristics, such standards have to be set at the local level as parameters for measuring desirable performance.

h. The wise use of migratory stocks of waterfowl:[44] Although the convention specifies this requirement, there is little authoritative guidance as to the scope of this obligation. However, after carefully scrutiny, one finds that it imposes an obligation that states ensure that the law of taking is confined within the parameters of sustainability. Legislation should ensure that taking of waterfowl must be within its capacity to regenerate and its migratory nature.

6 THE ENVIRONMENTAL POLICY IN UGANDA

Environmental concerns in Uganda were not considered a priority until the coming to power of the National Resistance Movement (NRM) government in 1986 and the establishment of the Ministry of Environmental Protection.[45] This Ministry was charged

---

[43] CBD, *supra* note 16.

[44] Republic of Uganda, *National Environment Action Plan (NEAP)* Report (1993).

[45] Ibid.

with the responsibility of coordinating and enhancing natural resource management, harmonizing the interests of the resource users, monitoring pollution levels, and advising government on policy and legislative reforms. In the ministry, the responsibility of environmental management was given to the Department of Environmental Protection. In addition, there were other sectoral institutions that were concerned with the environment but were highly centralized, resulting in a high level of bureaucracy. Specifically, the government imposed a ban on large-scale drainage in 1986 to protect wetlands in order to avert the negative consequences of such drainage, which had already been observed in southwestern Uganda. This was followed in 1989 by the establishment of the National Wetlands Conservation Programme, which was charged with the formulation of the national wetlands policy.[46]

In general, however, environmental monitoring, coordination, supervision, and management were essentially ad hoc and sector based with considerable duplication of effort, conflicts in responsibility, and rivalry in management of resources.[47] In this context, the National Environment Action Plan (NEAP) process was initiated. The main objective of the NEAP was to review the existing institutional system in order to propose an integrated multisectoral approach, which could provide a realistic comprehensive mechanism for ensuring active participation and interaction in the management of the environment.

One of the NEAP Task Forces considered the issues of water resources and aquatic biodiversity. It reviewed, with regard to wetlands law and policies, the following sectors: fisheries, water resource management, irrigation, and traditional harvesting of wetlands produce. The Task Force undertook consultations at district and national levels and presented its findings and recommendations deploring the state of legislation on the conservation of wetlands.[48]

There were two important results of the NEAP process: the National Environment Management Policy and the National Environment Act.

6.1 National Environment Management Policy (NEMP), 1994

The overall policy goal of the NEMP is sustainable social and economic development that maintains and enhances environmental quality and resource productivity to meet the needs of the present generation without compromising the ability of future generations to meet their own needs. The policy seeks, inter alia, to

a. Provide a broad policy framework for harmonization of sectoral and cross sectoral policy objectives, principles, and strategies
b. Transform existing environmental management systems to establish an integrated and multisectoral approach to resource planning and management by creating NEMA
c. Provide a basis for the formulation of a comprehensive environmental legal framework
d. Provide positive behavioral change
e. Establish an effective monitoring and evaluation system

---

[46] Ibid.   [47] Ibid .

[48] NEAP Secretariat, *Water Resources and Aquatic Biological Diversity* (Ministry of Natural Resources, Kampala) (1993).

The key policy objectives are to enhance the quality of life of all people in Uganda and promote long-term sustainable socioeconomic development through sound environmental and natural resource management and use; integrate environmental concerns in all development policies, planning, and activities at national, district, and local levels with full participation of the people; conserve biological diversity; and raise public awareness.

The NEMP was the first step to ensuring that sustainable development would be implemented through the establishment of an appropriate institutional and legal framework. As a result, the National Environment Act was passed as a mechanism for the implementation of NEMP.

6.2 The National Wetlands Policy, 1995

The National Wetlands Conservation and Management Programme was launched in 1989 with a prime objective of formulating a national policy for wetlands protection and utilization that would lay the basis for environmentally sound management and maximal sustainable productive use of the wetlands systems. As an interim measure, the ministry issued a directive to all district administrators suspending further large-scale drainage of wetlands, pending formulation of national policy and development of guidelines for assessing drainage proposals. This directive exempted subsistence level drainage and some ongoing agricultural projects. In 1995, a National Policy for the Conservation and Management of Wetlands was adopted in order to promote the conservation of wetlands so as to sustain their value for the present and future well-being of people.[49]

The National Wetlands Policy sets five goals: to establish the principles by which wetland resources can be optimally used now and in the future, to end practices that reduce wetland productivity, to maintain the biological diversity of natural and semi-natural wetlands, to maintain wetland functions and values, and to integrate wetland concerns in the planning and decision making of other sectors.

The policy aims at ensuring that no drainage occurs unless more important environment management requirements supersede; ensuring that only nondestructive uses are carried out in and around wetlands; ensuring that wetland developments are subject to environmental impact assessment, audit, and maintenance the optimal diversity of uses and users and consideration for other stakeholders when using a wetland.

7 INSTITUTIONAL FRAMEWORK

There are two institutions responsible for the management of wetlands in Uganda. The institution responsible for the overall management of the environment is the National Environmental Management Authority (NEMA).[50] It is established under the Act and is a corporate body.[51] It implements NEA as far as the management of wetlands is concerned. NEMA is also responsible for issuing wetlands permits and approval of environmental impact assessment (EIA) in relation to any activities in the wetland.[52] Increasingly NEMA has invoked its powers to issue and enforce environmental restoration orders. Currently, the constitutionality of NEMA's powers is subject to a petition.[53]

---

[49] Republic of Uganda, *supra* note 14. Also available at http://www.ramsar.org/wurc_policy_uganda.htm
[50] Ibid.   [51] NEA, *supra* note 7 at Section 5.
[52] Ibid. at Section 36.
[53] See "Nyakaana Sues NEMA for House," *New Vision* (18 April 2005).

The Wetlands Inspection Division (WID) in the Ministry of Water, Lands and Environment is the lead agency for wetland management in Uganda. The mandate of WID is to sustain the biophysical and socioeconomic values of wetlands for the present and future generations. Through the National Wetlands Programme (NWP), WID is in the process of developing policies and legislation, establishing a national inventory of all wetlands, creating national awareness of wetlands, and developing resource management and systems management principles for all wetlands in Uganda.

8 LEGISLATIVE FRAMEWORK

Since there is no comprehensive legislation that specifically protects or conserves wetlands, limited protection may be indirectly achieved through other nonwetland statutes such as the Constitution, the National Environment Act, the Wildlife Act, the Water Act, the Land Act, the Local Government Act, and the Forest Act.

8.1 The Constitution of Uganda, 1995

The constitution is the supreme law of Uganda. It has binding force on all authorities and persons throughout Uganda and has provisions that are relevant to environment and national resource management.[54]

In the National Objective and Directive Principle of State Policy the Constitution provides principles that are important for sustainable wetlands management. The Constitution imposes seven obligations on the Government of Uganda to ensure sustainable management of all natural resources. The first obligation is that the government is obliged to protect important natural resources such as land, water, wetlands, minerals, soil, fauna, and flora on behalf of the people of Uganda.[55] Second, it is required to take all practical measures to provide good water management systems at all levels. Third, it is required to promote sustainable development and public awareness of the need to promote land, air, and water resources in a balanced and sustainable manner for the present and future generations. Fourth, it is required to take all possible measures to prevent or minimize damage and destruction to land, air, and water resources resulting from pollution or other causes. Fifth, it is required to promote and implement energy policies that will ensure that people's basic needs and those of environmental preservation are met; finally, both the central government and local government are required to create and develop parks, reserves, and recreation areas; ensure the conservation of natural resources; and promote the rational use of natural resources so as to safeguard and protect the biodiversity of Uganda.

The Constitution makes wetlands resources subject to public ownership under the trusteeship of the central government or local governments. Thus, Article 237 provides that:

> the government or a local government as determined by parliament by law, shall hold in trust for the people and protect, natural lakes, rivers, *wetlands,* forests reserves, game reserves, national parks and any land to be reserved for ecological and touristic purposes for the common good of all citizens.[56]

---

[54] The Constitution of Uganda, 1995 Art. 2.
[55] Ibid. at Principle VIII of the National Objectives and Guidelines.
[56] Ibid. at Art. 237 (2).

Those provisions that reflect the importance of wetlands should also be seen in the context of the entire constitutional framework on the environment in general. Article 39 provides for every Ugandan a right to a clean and healthy environment.

Article 245 obligates parliament to provide by law measures for the management of the environment to prevent its abuse, pollution, and degradation in order to promote sustainable development and to produce environmental awareness. This provision reflects national policy that requires the state to promote sustainable development and public awareness of the need to manage land, air, and water resources in a balanced and sustainable manner for the present and future generations.

The Constitution under Article 26(1) gives every person a right to own property either individually or in association with others. However, Article 26(2) provides that the State or Local Government can acquire and take possession of land if it is necessary for public use or in the interest of defense or public safety. This authority can be used to acquire land for preservation of wetlands. Under Article 189(3), District Councils shall have the responsibility for any functions and services not specified in the sixth schedule to the Constitution. Under the schedule, wetlands are not under the Central Government; therefore, they should be under the management of local governments.

8.2 The National Environment Act

The National Environment Act is the major Statute that deals with environmental management in Uganda. The aim of the Act is to provide sustainable management of the environment and establish the National Environment Authority (NEA) as a coordinating, monitoring, and supervisory body for environmental management in Uganda.[57]

The Act has key provisions that are relevant to wetlands management. Wetlands, although looked at as part of the environment in general, were given specific treatment in part VII of the Act. Sections 36 and 37 address the management of wetlands and put restrictions on their use. Section 36 specifically restricts reclamation, drainage, or construction or demolition of any structure on the wetland. All activities that may have an effect on wetlands are restricted. The Authority is also empowered to make an investigation it considers necessary, including an environmental impact assessment to determine the effect of an activity on the wetland and the environment in general. The Authority together with the lead agency is required to establish guidelines for the identification and sustainable management of all wetlands in Uganda.

The authority shall, with the assistance of the local environment committees and lead agency, identify wetlands of local, national, and international importance as ecosystems and habitat of species of fauna and flora and compile a national register of wetlands. The authority may in consultation with the lead agency and the District Environmental Committee declare any wetland to be a protected wetland, thereby excluding or limiting human activities in that wetland.

All these provisions stress the need for environmental impact assessment for activities and developments in wetlands. This necessity is more concretely expressed by Section 19, which require that environmental impact assessment be undertaken by the developer where the lead agency in consultation with the executive director is of the

---

[57] NEA, *supra* note 6.

view that the project may or is likely to affect the environment. At the same time the law governing the wetlands must be seen within the total context of the Environment Act in general, especially the provisions relating to pollution, environmental restoration orders, environmental easements, public awareness, and enforcement of the law.

8.3 The Local Government Act

The Local Government Act provides for the decentralization of all levels of government to ensure, inter alia, good governance, democratic participation, and controlled decision making by all the people of Uganda. The Second Schedule of the Act gives the district and city councils more substantiated powers with regard to wetland management; this, however, does not mean that districts "own" wetlands. The decentralized services and activities with regard to natural resources include land surveying, administration, physical planning, and forest and wetland management. The Act further requires city and municipal councils to devolve wetland-related management functions to divisions. It is important to note that the decentralized functions related to natural resources need to be monitored to ensure that the local governments do not abuse the use of natural resources.

8.4 The Water Act

The Act mainly provides for the use, protection, and management of water resources and supply. Water is defined under Section 2 to include water flowing or situated upon the surface of any land; flowing or contained in any river, stream, watercourse or other natural course of water; any lake, pan, swamp, marsh, or spring, whether or not it has been altered or artificially improved; groundwater; and such other water as the ministry may from time to time declare to be water.

The objectives of the Act include allowing for the orderly development and use of water resources other than domestic use, such as the watering of livestock; irrigation and agriculture; industrial, commercial, and mining uses; generation of hydroelectric or geothermal energy; navigation; fishing; preservation of flora and fauna; and recreation in ways that minimize harmful effects to the environment; controlling pollution; and promoting the safe storage, treatment, discharge, and disposal of waste that may pollute water or otherwise harm the environment and human health. The Water Act therefore emphasizes the trustee relationship that government holds all water resources in trust for all the citizens.

8.5 The Land Act

The Land Act deals with tenure, ownership, and management of land in Uganda. Land tenure is specified by the legal system, which determines and regulates the manner in which land is owned, occupied, and used. It is fundamental because it remains the major means of production and of agriculture, the main economic activity.[58] Wetlands fall under several types of tenure in Uganda. These include freehold, mailo, customary, and leasehold. Section 23(1) is in line with the doctrine of public trust as it provides

---

[58] John Araka et al., "Finding Land for All," *African Farmer* (1990) 13–21.

that an association may, when requested by the community on whose behalf it holds land, set aside one or more areas of land for common use by members of the group. The land may be set aside for common use of grazing and watering of livestock, hunting, gathering of wood fuel and building materials, and gathering of honey and other *forest* resources for food and medicinal purposes, as well as other purposes that are traditional in the community using the land. Under Section 42 government may acquire land in accordance with the provisions of the Constitution, and Section 43 provides that a person who owns or occupies land shall manage and utilize land in accordance with the Forest Act, The National Environment Act, the Water Act, and any other law.

According to Section 44 the government shall hold in trust for the people and protect national lakes, rivers, groundwater, natural ponds, natural streams, wetlands, forest reserves, national parks, and any other land reserved for ecological and tourist purposes for the common good of the citizens of Uganda. A Local Government may upon request to the government be allowed to hold in trust for the people and the common good of other citizens of Uganda any resources, including wetland resources. These provisions are intended to enhance the doctrine of public trust in the management of natural resources, but they are narrow in scope and content, making difficult the enforcement of the public trust doctrine, especially taking into account the complex nature of wetlands.

8.6 The Wildlife Act

The Wildlife Act provides for sustainable management of wildlife and consolidates the law relating to wildlife management. *Wildlife* is defined under Section 2 as any wild plant or wild animal of species native to Uganda and includes wild animals that migrate through Uganda. The purposes of the Act among others include the conservation of wildlife throughout Uganda so that the abundance and diversity of their species are maintained at optimal levels commensurate with other forms of land use, in order to support sustainable utilization of wildlife for the benefit of the people of Uganda.

Under Section 3 the ownership of wild animals, including those existing in the wild plant habitat in Uganda, is vested in the Government on behalf of and for the benefit of the people of Uganda. Section 17 provides that the Minister may, after consultation with the Local Government Council in whose area proposed wildlife conservation falls and with approval of parliament signified by its resolution, by instrument, declare an area of land or water a wildlife conservation area. Most of the protected wildlife areas in Uganda have wetlands; therefore, this Act plays a fundamental role in the protection and use of wetlands in those areas.

8.7 The National Environment (Wetlands, Riverbanks and Lakeshores Management) Regulations, 2000

The objectives of these Regulations[59] are as follows:

a. To provide for the conservation and wise use of wetlands and their resources in Uganda
b. To give effect to the public trust doctrine under the Constitution and Land Act

---

[59] Statutory Instrument No. 1 of 1999.

c. To ensure the sustainable use of wetlands for ecological and tourism purposes for the common good of all citizens

d. To ensure that wetlands are protected as habitats for species of fauna and flora

e. To provide for the regulated public use and enjoyment of wetlands

f. To enhance research and research-related activities

g. To minimize and control pollution

In line with Wetlands Policy, the Regulations set out the following principles: that wetlands are utilized in a sustainable manner, compatible with the continued presence of wetlands and their hydrological functions and service; that Environmental Impact Assessment as required under NEA is mandatory for all activities in wetlands likely to have an adverse impact in the wetland; that special measures are essential for the protection of wetlands of international, national, and local importance as ecological systems and habitat for fauna and flora species and for cultural and aesthetic purposes as well for hydrological functions; and that the wise use of wetlands is incorporated in national and local approaches to the management of resources through awareness campaigns and dissemination of information.

The Regulations empower the Technical Committee on Biodiversity Conservation to advise the Board and Executive Director of NEMA on the wise management and conservation of wetland resources.[60] These Regulations also set out the functions of District and Local Environment Committees. The District Environment Councils are responsible for coordinating and advising the District Councils on all aspects of wetlands resource management.[61]

The Regulations that specify the functions of the Local Government Council include regulating activities in a wetland, advising the Council on which area is to be declared a wetland, authorizing research activities, issuing local guidelines and directives to ensure wise use of wetlands, directing that an EIA be carried out on a project that involves use of a wetland or an area within 10 meters of the edge of a wetland, declaring a wetland to be closed for some activities or all activities for the purpose of regeneration, formulating by laws for the management of wetlands, and performing any other assigned duty.[62] The Local Environment Committees are the implementing organ in conservation and management of wetland resource.[63]

The Regulations also specify the procedure for declaring of a specifically protected area. They also make provisions for the inventory of wetlands, resource use permits, and implied covenants in all the issued permits. Effectively implemented, the wetland Regulations have the capacity to ensure sustainable utilization of wetlands. However, the implementation of these Regulations remains difficult, especially in highly populated areas where there is land shortage.

9 UGANDA'S RESPONSE TO INTERNATIONAL OBLIGATIONS OF WETLAND MANAGEMENT

Uganda is a party to the Convention on Wetlands of International Importance Especially as Water Fowl Habitat (Ramsar Convention), which was signed in 1971 and went

---

[60] Ibid. Regulation 6.

[62] Ibid.

[61] Ibid. Regulation 7.

[63] Ibid. Regulation 7.

into force in 1975. It aimed at creating international recognition of the fundamental ecological functions of wetlands and their economic, cultural, scientific, and recreational legislation. Article 2(1) of the Ramsar Convention outlines the obligations of contracting states, which include the designation of wetlands for inclusion on the list of wetlands of international importance. According to Article 2(2), wetlands are to be inscribed on the list according to their international significance in terms of ecology, botany, zoology, limnology, or hydrology.

This convention obliges parties to promote the conservation of critically important wetlands. It requires signatory countries to designate wetlands that are outstanding examples of a region, highly productive communities valuable for educational or scientific purposes, or valuable areas that constitute crucial wildlife habitat. Such wetlands are to be included on the list of the wetlands of international importance. It also requires state parties to give due consideration at national levels by formulating national land use polices in their countries so as to promote conservation of the wetlands; this means that countries have an obligation to prevent domestic activities from harming the environment in other states. This is a good start because it creates international liability for environmental damage. Whereas it recognizes states' sovereign right to exploit their resources, it also requires states to prevent activities within their jurisdiction from causing environmental harm beyond its borders.

Uganda ratified the Convention in 1988. Since then, it has taken several measures to implement its obligations as a party. In 1988, a National Wetlands Conservation and Management Programme was set up to develop the National Policy for the Conservation and Management of Wetland Resources. In 1995, the National Environment Policy and Act were adopted. These two provide measures for implementing the Ramsar Convention.

Uganda has begun to implement the specific requirement of identifying the wetlands of international importance by identifying Lake George and the surrounding swampland.[64]

10 CONCLUSION AND RECOMMENDATIONS

It is important that any measures taken to conserve wetlands be an integral part of the overall environmental law and policy. Therefore, conservation of wetland should be perceived as an important component of the overall conservation strategy. The following recommendations can be made for the sustainable management of wetlands in Uganda:

a. Legal reform and institutional arrangement: Wetlands have been marginalized and regarded as "wastelands." They, therefore, need a strong government institutional arrangement and legislation in order to reverse the high rate of degradation and to ensure sustainable management. Since wetlands are a multisectoral resource, there is a need to create and establish an appropriate institutional arrangement. Although there are sectoral laws that refer to some aspects of wetlands such as water, land, or pollution, there is no comprehensive law for management of wetlands as an ecological entity. Therefore, there is a need to complete the proposed wetlands bill by emphasizing the public trust doctrine in the management of wetlands. As well,

---

[64] See Statutory Instrument No. 1 of 1999, Schedule 3 of the Regulations.

there is need to establish a strong interinstitutional policy implementation institution that coordinates wetlands inspection, monitoring, assessment, restoration, and improvement.

b. Development of public awareness through environmental education: Very often wetlands are degraded because the public either is not fully aware or does not appreciate the diversity of values and functions of wetlands. Moreover, most people are not familiar with environmental laws and policies. Public awareness is, therefore, essential in creating a committed and positive attitude toward conservation and sustainable utilization of wetland resources through environmental education, campaigns, and seminars. Government should, therefore, promote public awareness and understanding of wetland resource by encouraging participation by the public, central and local government authorities, policymakers, and nongovernmental organizations (NGOs). This recognizes the fact that the implementation of any policy and law depends on whether it is realistic in terms of social acceptability and technical feasibility.

c. Environmental impact assessment and monitoring: Development activities in general tend to impact upon natural resources and the environment in various ways. Assessment and evaluation of such impacts help to minimize the economic and social costs by preventing damage, as compared to restoring a degraded wetland. Since EIA is a legal requirement, it should be emphasized in order to minimize wetland degradation.

d. No drainage of wetlands: Uganda has experienced massive drainage of wetlands for human development activities. The effects of this drainage are visible in many parts of the country. Therefore, the law should be implemented vigorously to discourage further drainage of wetlands.

e. Land tenure reform: Wetlands have in many instances been referred to as "wastelands." In order to elevate wetlands from this status and to recognize them as a useful resource there is a need for the government to continue to control their management. All wetlands should continue to be taken as a public resource controlled by the government on behalf of the people of Uganda. There should be no leasing of any wetland to any person or organization in Uganda at any time in the foreseeable future. However, communal use should be permitted, but only if environmental conservation and sustainable use principles and strategies are observed. All future land tenure documents including maps and layouts should indicate whether the area contains a wetland and accordingly exclude wetlands from tenure. Governments should include wetland conservation considerations in the national land use plan so as to maintain the ecological character of wetlands.

f. Recovery of previously drained wetlands: Many wetlands have been drained or modified, especially in southwestern and eastern Uganda. Government should require that wetlands that have already been drained be allowed to regenerate. The government may make a specific policy that aims at restoring soil hydration so as to reestablish wetland vegetation as far as ecologically possible. Such operations may range from rehabilitation of wetlands under leasehold to those where the users have no leases.

g. Research and inventory: Demand-driven research is critical for understanding natural resources. Since wetlands are still being degraded under the current legal framework, there is need to do research to assess gaps and overlaps in the law.

h. Capacity building: Among the reasons for unabated degradation of wetland are weak enforcement mechanisms of environmental law. There are indeed a few cadres knowledgeable in the area of environmental law. Training to develop capacity for enforcement of environmental law is important to the management of wetlands.

i. Promotion of international actions: Wetland resources have transboundary significance. They serve as habitats of migratory water flora and other fauna and, therefore, inevitably require regional and global approaches. Governments should promote and actively participate in regional and international efforts to conserve and sustainably utilize wetlands and encourage the involvement of other countries in the conservation of wetland resources. The government should continue to promote participation in the Ramsar Convention and other treaties related to wetland conservation. It should, therefore, designate more areas as wetlands of international importance. In addition, the government should endeavor to maintain the character of those wetlands that have been declared wetlands of international importance.

10 EIA and the Four Ps: Some Observations from South Africa

Michael Kidd

1 INTRODUCTION

Land use is central to development in Africa; as such, it should be regarded as an issue of public interest[1] and not something to be determined solely by the landowner.[2] Commitment to sustainable development dictates that land and its fruits should be conserved, and one of the most important conservation tools is environmental impact assessment (EIA). This chapter is concerned with the law and practice of EIA in South Africa and makes observations that, it is hoped, may inform the way EIA is practiced in other developing countries.

From my observation of the operation of environmental impact assessment in South Africa, it can be boiled down to four interrelated components beginning with P – the four Ps: provisions, process/procedure, people, and politics. These components are pivotal to the EIA process. There are, however, many aspects to the four Ps that can raise obstacles to the successful operation of EIA, many of which can be observed from the South African experience.

This chapter will commence by examining the way in which EIA has been implemented thus far in South Africa. This initial analysis will be followed by an examination of the four Ps and their subcomponents, using examples from South Africa to illustrate. Current EIA practice in South Africa, as will be revealed, suffers from several flaws. The South African government's proposed amendments to the system will be scrutinized to illustrate how effective they will be in solving these problems. My conclusion is that, although the proposed changes will bring about some positive consequences, there are retrogressive steps that take the practice of EIA in South Africa backward instead of forward.

2 EIA – WHAT IS IT?

For the purposes of this chapter, EIA is defined as a process whereby the impact on the environment of a project is determined, where the environment is defined to include not only the biophysical environment, but also the social.[3] This definition restricts the

---

[1] This chapter describes the law as of 1 November 2004.
[2] See Calestous Juma and J. B. Ojwang (eds.), *In Land We Trust* (Nairobi: ACTS Press) (1996).
[3] See Jan Glazewski, *Environmental Law in South Africa* (2000) at 272.

discussion to the assessment of projects, as opposed to plans and programs, which are beyond the scope of this chapter.

3 CURRENT SOUTH AFRICAN EIA LEGISLATION

The Environment Conservation Act Number 73 of 1989 (ECA) provides for the Minister of Environmental Affairs and Tourism[4] to identify those activities that in his/her opinion may have a substantial detrimental effect on the environment, whether in general or in respect of certain areas.[5] An identified activity may not be undertaken without authorization from the relevant competent authority,[6] in most cases the Member of the Executive Council (MEC) in the province concerned, but where the activity in question is of national importance or has impacts likely to be felt in more than one province, the Minister is the competent authority. Authorization may only be made after consideration of "reports concerning the impact of the proposed activity and of alternative proposed activities on the environment."[7] The Minister is also empowered to make regulations relating to environmental impact reports, including the scope and content of the reports and the relevant procedure to be followed.[8]

In 1997, the Minister promulgated a list of identified activities and "general EIA regulations" setting out the procedure to be followed by developers seeking authorization for their activities. The list of identified activities, which has been amended several times, included the "construction, erection or upgrading" of a variety of items, including nuclear reactors, roads and railways, dams, and "public and private resorts and associated infrastructure"; changes of land use; concentration of livestock, aquatic organisms, poultry, and game in a confined structure for the purpose of commercial production; intensive husbandry of, or importation of, any plant or animal that has been declared a weed or an invasive alien species; release of any organism outside its natural area of distribution that is to be used for biological pest control; genetic modification of any organism with the purpose of fundamentally changing the inherent characteristics of that organism; reclamation of land from the sea and inland waters; waste disposal sites (requiring authorization under s 20 of the Act as well); scheduled processes in terms of the Atmospheric Pollution Prevention Act;[9] and cultivation or any other use of virgin ground (land that has not been cultivated during the previous 10 years).[10]

The Minister has also identified certain geographical areas where identified activities may not take place without authorization,[11] but these constitute a minute portion of the total sensitive areas in South Africa that would benefit from such measures.

The general EIA regulations, which accompany the list of identified activities, set out the process to be followed by the applicant or developer.[12] In short, this requires the applicant to hire an independent consultant to carry out the procedure, which entails the submission of a plan of study for scoping including a description of the activity to be undertaken, the tasks to be performed during scoping, and the method by which

---

[4] Hereafter referred to as "the Minister."   [5] Section 21.
[6] Section 22(1).   [7] Section 22(2).
[8] Section 26.   [9] Act 45 of 1965.
[10] GN R1182 in *GG* 18261 of 5 September 1997, as amended.
[11] The Outeniqua sensitive coastal area and the Pennington/Umtamvuna sensitive coastal area: provided for in GN R1526–1528 and GN R1529–1531 in *GG* 19493 of 27 November 1998, respectively.
[12] GN R1183 in *GG* 18261 of 5 September 1997, as amended.

environmental issues and alternatives will be identified, followed by a scoping report. The scoping report must contain a brief project description, a brief description of environmental issues identified, a description of all alternatives identified, and an appendix containing a description of the public participation process followed, including a list of interested parties and their comments.

On receipt of the scoping report, the authority may decide the matter on the basis of the information supplied in the scoping report or determine that such information must be supplemented by an EIA focusing on the identified alternatives and environmental issues. A plan of study for the EIA must be carried out, followed by the environmental impact report, which must contain a description of each alternative, including the particulars on the extent and significance of each identified environmental impact and the possibility for mitigation of each identified impact; a comparative assessment of all the alternatives; and appendices containing descriptions of the environment concerned, the activity to be undertaken, the public participation process followed, including a list of interested parties and their comments; any media coverage given to the proposed activity; and any other information included in the accepted plan of study.

The relevant authority may then decide to authorize the activity with or without conditions or to reject the application, and this decision, together with certain other prescribed information, must be provided in a record of decision (ROD). The decision may be taken on appeal to the Minister or provincial authority within 30 days from the date of issue of the ROD. This is the only time limit provided for in the regulations.

These regulations, which still largely govern the practice of EIA in South Africa, had been in effect for little over a year when the National Environmental Management Act 107 of 1998 (NEMA) was enacted, to go into effect on 1 January 1999. Chapter 5 of NEMA, headed Integrated Environmental Management (IEM), sets out the general objectives of IEM and provides for implementation in section 24. This section provides that the potential impact on the environment, socioeconomic conditions, and the cultural heritage of activities that require authorization or permission by law and may significantly affect the environment, must be considered, investigated, and assessed prior to their implementation and reported to the organ of state charged by law with authorizing, permitting, or otherwise allowing the implementation of an activity.[13] This basic approach may be supplemented by listing specific activities and geographic areas within which activities require authorization. The section also provides for the making of regulations relating to procedure, and so forth, and provides for certain minimal requirements to be observed in the procedures for investigation, assessment, and communication of the potential impact of activities.[14]

NEMA, which repeals most of the ECA, repeals sections 21, 22, and 26 of that Act and all regulations thereunder regulating environmental authorization and EIAs, but this repeal is to take effect only upon a date to be published by the Minister after regulations under s 24 of NEMA have been promulgated and the Minister is satisfied that the legislation to be repealed "has become redundant."[15]

While section 24 of NEMA requires regulations to be fully effective, it is nevertheless operational; that means that there are two parallel regulatory regimes for EIAs: the ECA procedures and s 24 of NEMA. Apparently, the authorities are using the ECA for

---

[13] Section 24(1).   [14] Section 24(7).

[15] Section 50(2).

"identified activities" (as they are required to do) and are applying section 24 of NEMA to those activities that may significantly affect the environment and are not identified activities in terms of the ECA.

Despite the fact that the NEMA regulations relating to EIAs have not yet been promulgated, a recent amendment to NEMA has changed some central aspects of its treatment of environmental authorizations.[16] At the time of writing, recently published proposed draft regulations on EIAs appear, on an initial assessment, likely to dilute significantly the scope and operation of EIAs in South Africa. Since the regulations are not yet in force, they will not be discussed here.

The existing legislative framework for an EIA appears to be, at first glance, relatively comprehensive on paper. It is in a somewhat of transitionary stage of development, with the operative ECA regime expected to be replaced by a new regime under NEMA. The extent to which the new regime will be significantly different from the old is not clear, although the draft regulations suggest that there will be significant differences.

Having described the situation in South Africa, let us now examine the EIA law and practice in South Africa in the light of the four Ps proposed in the introduction.

4 THE PROVISIONS

The manner in which the legislature provides for EIA is fundamental in two respects: first, the scope of EIA's application and, second, the ease of interpretation of the provisions. A third related aspect is that of the extent to which there is coordination with other legislation.

4.1 Scope of Application

The scope of application of EIAs entails two questions: First, what is assessed? Second, which activities are covered by the regulatory requirements and which are not?

What is understood by the term *environmental assessment*? Does assessment of a development's impact include consideration of the social and economic impacts of that development? The ECA empowers the Minister to make regulations relating to EIAs, which may include "the identification of the economic and social interests which may be affected by the activity in question and by the alternative activities"[17] and "the estimation of the nature and extent of the effect of the activity in question and the alternative activities on the social and economic interests."[18] There is, however, no explicit reference to social or economic impacts in the regulations, although the guidelines on EIA issued by the Department of Environmental Affairs and Tourism (DEAT) do provide that "the effects on human health, socio-economic conditions, physical and cultural resources should be included."[19]

NEMA, as originally promulgated, was more explicit. It stated clearly that EIA is concerned with the "potential impact on the environment, socio-economic conditions

---

[16] National Environmental Management Amendment Act 8 of 2004. The Act has not yet taken effect although it has been enacted (the date of commencement is to be proclaimed by the President and had not, at the time of writing, yet been proclaimed).

[17] Section 26(a)(iv).   [18] Section 26(a)(v).

[19] DEAT, *EIA Regulations: Implementation of Sections 21, 22 and 26 of the Environment Conservation Act* Guideline Document (1998) at 23.

and the cultural heritage."[20] Curiously, however, the Amendment Act removes the references to socioeconomic conditions and the cultural heritage. The significance of this removal is, in part, tempered by close consideration of the definition of *environment* in the Act:

> the surroundings within which humans exist and that are made up of –
>   i. the land, water and atmosphere of the earth;
>   ii. micro-organisms, plant and animal life;
>   iii. any part or combination of (i) and (ii) and the interrelationships among and between them; and
>   iv. the physical, chemical, aesthetic and cultural properties and conditions of the foregoing that influence human health and well-being.[21]

It seems clear from this definition that *environment* includes the cultural properties of the surroundings within which humans exist; therefore, it suggests that the cultural heritage should be considered in the EIA process as it is part of the environment. Its specific mention in section 24 would seem superfluous. As for socioeconomic aspects, the High Court has held that it is "abundantly clear that the [mandate of a government department carrying out environmental authorization] includes the consideration of socio-economic factors as an integral part of its environmental responsibility."[22] This conclusion was based on the consideration of the environmental right in section 24 of the Constitution, as well as several other statutory requirements, including section 24 of NEMA, but even without that section, there are several other provisions, such as the national environmental management principles in section 2 of NEMA, which amply support the Court's conclusion.

It is unlikely that the thinking behind the amendment to NEMA was to remove redundant provisions. It is apparent that the objective is to reduce the scope of EIA, which is, in my opinion, a retrogressive step. The removal of express reference to socio-economic conditions may well lead to reinforcement of the view that environmental law is concerned solely with "green" issues and not with environmental justice. While the definition of *environment* would extend to consideration of the impacts of activities on human health, it is submitted that this is not sufficient. As pointed out, however, this aspect of the amendment is unlikely to have any effect.

As far as the reach of the regulatory framework is concerned, the list of identified activities seems to be comprehensive enough, but there are some important omissions. Probably the most important omission from the list is that of mining activities. Such activities, however, are subject to environmental impact assessment in terms of legislation relating to mining and exploitation of minerals. EIA is part of a more holistic environmental planning framework, the environmental management project report (EMPR), which is a prerequisite for a mining license and includes such aspects as planning for rehabilitation of the mine works, which is not part of conventional EIA.[23] The problem with the environmental assessment procedure required by the minerals legislation is that the decision maker is the official who is responsible for the promotion

---

[20] Section 24(1).   [21] Section 1.

[22] *BP Southern Africa (Pty) Ltd v. MEC for Agriculture, Conservation, Environment and Land Affairs* [2004] (5) SA 124 (W) at 151E.

[23] Ch 4 of the Mineral and Petroleum Resources Development Act 28 of 2002.

of mining and, consequently, the EIA process suffers from the problem of the referee's simultaneously being a player.

A further noteworthy omission relates to one of the most controversial of current internationally controversial issues: genetically modified organisms. While "the genetic modification of any organism with the purpose of fundamentally changing the inherent characteristics of that organism" is an identified activity, the *release* of such organism into the environment is not. The latter activity is arguably far more potentially harmful to the environment than the former, so its omission is cause for concern.

There are clearly gaps in the list of the activities for which EIA must be required. This is exacerbated by the difficulty in some instances of ascertaining whether an activity is one of those on the list of identified activities or not.

4.2 Ease of Application

If we accept that one of the main objectives of law is to guide people's behavior, the law relating to EIA ought not to be difficult for people, developers and the deciding authorities in particular, to understand. It is especially important that developers and authorities know precisely which activities require EIAs and which are not covered by the legislation. The potential for confusion caused by unclear legislative provisions is well illustrated by *Silvermine Valley Coalition v. Sybrand van der Spuy Boerderye and Others.*[24]

In this case, the respondent had established a vineyard on land that had apparently previously been quarried and was in a somewhat degraded condition but was also part of a protected natural environment. The case involved several issues; the one relevant to this discussion is whether the activity in question qualified as one of the activities requiring authorization in terms of the ECA. Both the respondent and the competent authority, the Minister of Environmental and Cultural Affairs of the Western Cape, had received seemingly separate Senior Counsel's opinion to the effect that the activity was not one of those contemplated by the relevant provisions and, consequently, did not require authorization.

The applicant, on the other hand, alleged that the respondent's activities qualified under one or all of three activities identified in the relevant regulations: the construction or upgrading of a dam affecting the flow of a river, the change of land use from undetermined use to any other land use, and the change of land use from use of nature conservation to any other land use. While the Court decided in favor of the respondent on other grounds, in determining whether the activity was one that required authorization, it interpreted the "shoddily drafted"[25] regulations so that the activity was one that *was* contemplated by the regulations – the change of land use from undetermined use to any other land use. The provision under scrutiny in this case was drafted in such a way that two Senior Counsels and a Judge could not reach consensus as to its meaning, raising the issue of how easy it would be for developers and authorities to interpret these provisions correctly without the same skills in legal interpretation as judges and advocates.

This is not to suggest that it is possible to draft legislation that has only one agreed meaning. However, particular care should be taken in identifying activities requiring

---

[24] [2002] (1) SA 478 (C).   [25] Ibid. at 492F.

EIAs in an understandable way. The provision in dispute in *Silvermine* could have been drafted more clearly, without much difficulty.

Coordination with Other Legislation

There are several activities in the existing list of identified activities that require authorization under other legislation as well. This provides considerable scope for confusion among authorities on which organ must authorize which aspect of the activity. For example, "structures causing disturbances to the flow of water in a river bed" are on the list of identified activities, whereas "impeding or diverting the flow of water in a watercourse" is a "water use" in terms of the National Water Act 36 of 1998, requiring a license in terms of that Act.[26] In a recent case, the development of a shopping mall in Pietermaritzburg envisaged the diversion of a stream. The developers sought the necessary permission from the Department of Water Affairs under the National Water Act and applied for authorization in terms of the ECA. The provincial authorities, required to make a decision in terms of the ECA, when faced with a decision from the Department of Water Affairs, neglected to make a decision themselves since they regarded the Water Affairs decision as settling the matter.[27] This was clearly wrong, since decisions by both organs of state were required.

To prevent such confusion, the legislature needs first to consider whether it is necessary for two organs of state, which sometimes constitute two subdirectorates in the same government department, both to authorize the project from different viewpoints or different aspects of the same project. If not, then one authorization process, entailing an EIA procedure, should be provided for. For example, one of the listed activities is a "scheduled process" which requires authorization under the Atmospheric Pollution Prevention Act 35 of 1965. As the law stands, an applicant would need simultaneously to apply for what is known as a registration certificate from the Chief Air Pollution Control Officer, an official in the national Department (DEAT), and for authorization in terms of the ECA to the provincial environment department. It would be much better to provide for a procedure whereby authorization is required only once, after a procedure that includes an EIA process. In cases in which this is not feasible and different departments need to approve different aspects of the same project, guidelines should be drawn up to articulate clearly each body's responsibilities and delineate the boundaries where each body's responsibility ends.

5 THE PROCESS/PROCEDURE

5.1 The Procedure

Upon first observation of the South African legislation, the procedure provided for appears to conform to international practice. It incorporates three stages – screening, scoping, and assessment. It has been noted, however, that the procedure is overregulated, probably because there is concern that environmental impact practitioners are not

---

[26] Section 21 read with 22, subject to certain exceptions.

[27] This was not a "case" in the legal sense, but in a "case study" sense, so there is no documentary reference. Information obtained from personal communication with N. Quinn, who was involved in monitoring the project's impact on the stream (2003).

regulated as a profession.[28] Rigid regulatory requirements are presumably intended to ensure that the practitioners remain within acceptable boundaries. Overly rigid procedures are not, however, helpful in an environment of government resource constraints since they hinder decision making. This is exacerbated by the lack of time limits in the legislation with the result that the process of making decisions on applications takes an inordinately long time.

5.2 Public Participation and *Audi Alteram Partem*

Integral to EIA are consultation and participation, and NEMA contains a list of "national environmental management principles," which are binding on the actions of all organs of state that may significantly affect the environment.[29] These principles underscore the importance of the public in environmental decision making. For instance, the first principle provides that "environmental management must place people and their needs at the forefront of its concern, and serve their physical, psychological, developmental, cultural and social interests equitably." There are several other principles[30] relating to the interests of the public and their participation in environmental decision making:

- Environmental management must be integrated, acknowledging that all elements of the environment are linked and interrelated, and it must take into account the effects of decisions on all aspects of the environment and all people in the environment by pursuing the selection of the best practicable environmental option.
- The participation of all interested and affected parties in environmental governance must be promoted; all people must have the opportunity to develop the understanding, skills, and capacity necessary for achieving equitable and effective participation; and participation by vulnerable and disadvantaged persons must be ensured.
- Decisions must take into account the interests, needs, and values of all interested and affected parties, and this includes recognizing all forms of knowledge, including traditional and ordinary knowledge.
- Community well-being and empowerment must be promoted through environmental education, raising of environmental awareness, sharing of knowledge and experience, and other appropriate means.
- The social, economic, and environmental impacts of activities, including disadvantages and benefits, must be considered, assessed, and evaluated, and decisions must be appropriate in the light of such consideration and assessment.
- Decisions must be taken in an open and transparent manner, and access to information must be provided in accordance with the law.
- The environment is held in public trust for the people, the beneficial use of environmental resources must serve the public interest, and the environment must be protected as the people's common heritage.

The regulations emphasize the need for public participation, and experience suggests that this is the practice. Certain problems do, however, exist. First, it seems often that the environmental practitioners driving the process and the officials define no demarcation between adequate opportunity for participation and unnecessary obstacles to the

---

[28] Glazewski, *supra* note 2 at 287ff.   [29] Section 2.
[30] Section 2(*b*), (*f*), (*g*), (*h*), (*i*), (*k*), and (*o*).

process. Important contribution to this problem are often the affected communities, who often cannot delegate spokes people, with the result that some of their members sometimes present themselves in the course of the procedure and claim not to have been consulted. This is not a problem that can be legislated away, but one would hope that increased experience of all involved in these processes would help to smooth out the flaws.

The second problem is the failure by the authorities to observe *audi alteram partem* (hearing the other side). As pointed out, the regulations are comprehensive when it comes to the process to be followed, probably to the extent of being overly prescriptive. Nevertheless, situations do arise in which the process does not reflect the spirit of the regulations with regard to *audi alteram partem*. The impression created is that procedural fairness is simply a technical requirement to tick off a list of requirements, whereas it is far more than that. Indeed public participation should be at the heart of the process. There are several examples of failure to observe procedural fairness, most of which have not resulted in litigation and therefore have not been reported. Two illustrative examples illustrate this point.

In the reported case of *South Durban Community Environmental Alliance v. Head of Department: Department of Agriculture & Environmental Affairs*,[31] the departmental officials concerned purported to grant an exemption from certain procedural requirements of the EIA regulations in terms of s 28A of the ECA. The ECA requires that an exemption be in written form; this exemption initially was not, and the Court found that the exemption was invalid for this reason. Even had it been in writing, however, one of the flaws in the exemption decision was that the department had not consulted the public before granting the exemption, and that would have been a failure of procedural fairness probably sufficient to render the decision invalid for that reason as well.

In a second case, an appeal had been dismissed by the MEC of Agriculture and Environmental Affairs in KwaZulu-Natal. This decision was taken on review because the MEC did not give the appellant (a committee established in opposition to the development) access to, and the opportunity to respond to, responses from other interested parties to the appellant's notice of appeal that were submitted to the MEC.[32]

As pointed out previously, these problems cannot be easily removed by legislation. Part of the problem is clearly due to capacity constraints within the organs of state required to make EIA decisions, which are discussed later. Overall, however, failures in *audi alteram partem* may be reduced by increased awareness among the officials concerned and enlargement of the body of precedents.

5.3 Appeal

The ECA provides for an appeal against decisions relating to environmental authorizations. Such appeals must be made within 30 days of the initial decision.[33] According to the Act, appeals may be made only against decisions by officials exercising power

---

[31] [2003] (6) SA 631 (D).

[32] *Merebank Environmental Action Committee v. Member of the Executive Council for Agriculture and Environmental Affairs (Province of KwaZulu-Natal)*, unreported decision of the Natal Provincial Decision, delivered 14 January 2002.

[33] Regulation 11 in GN R1183 *GG* 18261 of 5 September 1997.

delegated to them in terms of the Act or conferred by regulation, and the appeal is directed to the Minister or competent authority in question.[34] The main problem here is that the appeal stands to be decided by the official heading the organ of state whose officials made the initial decision. Given that the provincial Minister (the MEC) is appointed for political and not vocational reasons, he/she relies on the officials who decided the matter in the first place for advice in deciding the appeal. This is not a problem germane to the sphere of EIAs. South African legislation typically contains such administrative appeal processes and has no general administrative appeals tribunal.

A further problem is that there is no deadline within which appeals must be decided. This lack leads to more costs and delays for the developer. This can, however, be remedied by providing for a time limit, although it is difficult to see this policy's being accepted by the Minister, through whom most legislative amendments would pass.

The possible suspension of the authorization pending finalization of the appeal is another bugbear. It is submitted that the authorization should be suspended while the appeal is finalized, and this is what happens with most other appeals. Developers often see appeals as a delaying tactic of opponents to the project and have been known to commence operations while the appeal is still outstanding since the current legislation is silent on this matter.

Significantly, the NEMA Amendment provides that the operation of the authorization is *not* suspended pending finalization of the appeal.[35] This is probably a reflection of the fact that appeals are not infrequent and that officials are often very tardy in deciding them. It is an unfortunate way of addressing the problem, however, since it suggests that an appeal against an authorization is likely to be rejected. This is because it is difficult to order a developer to dismantle what has already been carried out, were the appeal to be upheld.

The problems of delays and suspension of appeals are both related to the overall time that the EIA process, including appeal, takes, and this is a shortcoming that should be addressed, probably by providing for time limits. The capacity of the relevant departments to handle their load would probably militate strongly against this, however. The upshot is that the problem is difficult to address without the political will to provide more resources.

5.4 Postauthorization Monitoring

Most applications under the EIA regulatory regime are approved, but developers are seldom given carte blanche to proceed as they like. Typically, the authorization would contain conditions aimed at mitigating environmental damage identified in the EIA report. The enforcement of these conditions once set, however, is frequently not carried out effectively.[36] As Wood says, "The problem of crippling under-funding and under-staffing of provincial and local authorities means that they must rely on the complaints of neighbors and the integrity of developers and their consultants for

---

[34] Section 35(3).

[35] Section 43(7) of Act 8 of 2004, which reads, "An appeal under this section does not suspend an environmental authorisation or exemption, or any provisions or conditions attached thereto, or any directive, unless the Minister or MEC directs otherwise."

[36] See C. Wood, "Pastiche or Postiche? Environmental Impact Assessment in South Africa" (1999), *South African Geographical Journal,* 52 at 56.

information about non-compliance."[37] This still holds true today, and experience suggests that even where there are complaints, authorities are sometimes reluctant to take steps to address such problems because of lack of capacity or for other reasons that are less clear.

The setting of conditions presupposes the enforcement of such conditions, and the absence of monitoring seriously undermines the entire system. The NEMA Amendment addresses this problem, at least on paper, by providing that adequate capacity be established for the ongoing management and monitoring of the impacts of the activity on the environment throughout the life cycle of the activity.[38] The effectiveness of this measure is, however, dependent on availability of adequate human resources, which, as observed earlier, is predicated on political will.

5.5 Remedies

According to the ECA, any person who undertakes an identified activity without complying with the relevant requirements in terms of section 22 and the regulations is guilty of an offense and liable to a fine not exceeding R100,000 or not more than 10 years' imprisonment, or both.[39] This would appear to be the "default" enforcement mechanism, since other possible ways of addressing noncompliance are not ideal. Criminal prosecution, however, is not an ideal way to address a development that has commenced without authority, since it is not aimed at remediation of any damage done or at assessment of the project subsequent to its commencement.

From my experience as an occasional adviser to the KwaZulu-Natal Department of Agriculture and Environmental Affairs, the commencement of an identified activity without authorization is a frequent occurrence. This in itself is worrying, but a greater cause for concern is the fact that the authorities are not sure as to how to respond to this. They are not clear on how to ensure that such developments are assessed to enable them to make informed decisions on whether to allow the developments to continue or order them to cease and the land in question be remediated.

It would seem that the requiring of an ex post facto EIA in terms of the ECA is not an option. In the *Silvermine* case,[40] the applicant nongovernmental organization (NGO) asked for a retrospective EIA as a remedy when the development described earlier had already commenced. The Court refused to grant the application. On its interpretation of both the ECA requirements and s 24 of NEMA, it essentially held that requiring that an EIA be carried out once the development had commenced was inappropriate, as the purpose of an EIA is to consider the impact of the development and means to address this impact, *before* it takes place.[41] In a subsequent decision in another provincial jurisdiction,[42] the Court held that an EIA could be called for once the project had commenced provided that the activity had not yet been completed.

I have my doubts as to the correctness of the *Silvermine* decision. It will be somewhat academic to debate the merits of the decision here, however, since a provision in the NEMA Amendment serves to change significantly the legal landscape within which

---

[37] Ibid.
[39] Section 29(4).
[41] Ibid. at 488B–489C.
[38] Section 24E(a) of Act 8 of 2004.
[40] *Supra* note 23.
[42] *Eagles Landing Body Corporate v. Molewa NO and Others* [2003] (1) SA 412 (T).

Silvermine was decided. I would argue that the Court in *Silvermine* ignored one of the fundamental purposes of EIA, namely, to provide for measures of mitigation of environmental damage caused by the activity, where necessary. Far from being a pointless exercise to require an EIA after the development has commenced, an EIA could identify mitigation measures that ought to be taken prospectively. Be that as it may, there is now in the Amendment Act a remedy designed specifically for noncompliance with the environmental authorization process.

If a person commences an activity without authorization, that person may apply to the relevant authority for authorization and the authority may then direct the applicant to

(a) compile a report containing –
  (i) an assessment of the nature, extent, duration and significance of the impacts of the activity on the environment, including the cumulative effects;
  (ii) a description of mitigation measures undertaken or to be undertaken in respect of the impacts of the activity on the environment;
  (iii) a description of the public participation process followed during the course of compiling the report, including all comments received from interested and affected parties and an indication of how issues raised have been addressed;
  (iv) an environmental management plan; and
(b) provide such other information or undertake such further studies as the Minister or MEC may deem necessary.
(2) Upon the payment by the person of an administration fine not exceeding R1 million as determined by the competent authority, the Minister or MEC concerned must consider the report contemplated in subsection (1) and thereafter may –
(a) direct the person to cease the activity, either wholly or in part, and to rehabilitate the environment within such time and subject to such conditions as the Minister or MEC may deem necessary; or
(b) issue an environmental authorization to such person subject to such conditions as the Minister or MEC may deem necessary.[43]

This provides a remedy that is tailor-made for the situation in which a person commences an activity without the necessary authorization and empowers the relevant authority, in effect, to require the party to submit an EIA report, albeit after commencement of the project, and maybe even after its completion.

The preceding analysis shows that although there is a largely solid procedural framework provided by the legislation, defects often result from the implementation of the law, suggesting that the fault lies not with the legislature, but with the implementing officials. The officials are an important component of the third *P* – the people – to whom our attention now turns.

6 THE PEOPLE

It goes without saying that the people involved in the EIA process are a fundamental component of the process. These people are the public, the officials, and the environmental practitioners who carry out the process.

---

[43] Section 24G of Act 8 of 2004.

6.1 The Public

As pointed out previously, South African environmental legislation and NEMA in particular through its environmental management principle, value highly the interests of the public in environmental decision making. This attitude is coupled with a heightened awareness among people of developments taking place around them, often stimulated by NGOs, who play an important role in informing people of their rights and mobilizing them.

The most frequent role played by the public in the EIA process in South Africa is as "interested and affected parties" who are opposed to the whole or components of the developments. If the EIA process is to operate effectively, the affected public must appreciate that they not only have rights that must be respected but responsibilities as well. Often public participation processes are impeded because of dynamics within communities, as intimated previously. Some groups also resist developments because of the not-in-my-backyard (NIMBY) syndrome, rather than because of legitimate concerns for the environment. These and similar problems are unlikely to be easily solved. Moreover, it is difficult to persuade the public to follow the rules when others involved in the process, such as the officials, are not themselves doing so.

6.2 The Officials

Officials generally are faced with a mounting workload and the lack of both the necessary human resources to carry out the task effectively and the skills to make acceptable decisions. These explain conditions several defects identified earlier in this chapter, such as long delays in decisions and lack of postauthorization enforcement. The lack of appropriate skills contributes to problems such as procedural fairness flaws and decisions that do not adequately evaluate all aspects of the activity. A few years ago, it was observed that

> it is apparent that the decision to grant authorisation is sometimes being made by overwhelmed provincial staff on narrow nature conservation or other grounds, rather than on the full range of factors normally considered in internationally recognised good EIA practice. As a consequence of this (and the overwhelming pressure for development), the number of refusals is very small (probably less than 2% of applications).[44]

In the years since this observation, there is nothing to suggest that matters have changed. Indeed, evidence does not suggest that these observations apply only to provincial decision makers – decisions made by the national department are no better.

Ultimately, there is only one acceptable way in which the performance of officials will improve. This is to increase resources, by providing more officials and training them properly. This change, however, seems unlikely, and another way of addressing the problem of an overwhelmed administration is to reduce the workload. This can be achieved by reducing the number of activities for which EIAs are legally required, and this seems to be the direction taken by the NEMA Amendment Act and the new draft regulations. This direction, it is submitted, is unacceptable for the reason that diluting

---

[44] Wood (*supra* note 35) at 55, references omitted.

the EIA requirements does not adequately realize South Africans' environmental right in terms of section 24 of the Constitution[45] and does not adequately meet the objective of NEMA to "prohibit, restrict or control activities which are likely to have a detrimental effect on the environment."[46]

6.3 The Environmental Practitioners

It has been a concern, particularly among the ranks of environmental impact practitioners, that there is no accreditation system for such practitioners, with the result that there are some charlatans putting themselves out to be EIA experts with no appropriate training or experience. It can only be good for the system if practitioners are appropriately qualified and practice with integrity. To this end, accreditation is necessary. The NEMA Amendment provides for an "association proposing to register its members as environmental assessment practitioners" to apply to the Minister to be appointed as a registration authority and sets out the procedural requirements for doing so.[47] Thus the practitioners themselves will not be registered by the state, but by registration authorities. This may prove to be crucial if the Minister decides to regulate the "industry," as he or she will be entitled to do in terms of the Bill, which empowers the Minister to specify that environmental impact assessments, or other specific tasks performed in connection with an application for an environmental authorization, may only be carried out by an environmental assessment practitioner registered in accordance with the prescribed procedures.[48] How effective this will be at regulating the profession remains to be seen.

The main problem area as far as people are concerned are capacity constraints within the organs of state responsible for decision making in the EIA process. It would seem that the only way of addressing this is to provide for more resources, and that depends on political will. This brings us to the last of the four Ps – the politics.

7 THE POLITICS

Nobody ought to be surprised today if it is asserted that the law is heavily influenced by politics, and this is certainly true in the sphere of EIA. Politics operate at several levels and in different ways; the three interrelated aspects that will be examined here, all crucially important, are the politics of legislation, the politics of resource allocation, and the politics of decision making.

7.1 The Politics of Legislation

A country's legislation is determined by politics – the ruling government's policies are translated into legislation by the legislature. On paper, South Africa's legislation is

---

[45] Section 24 of the Constitution of the Republic of South Africa, Act 108 of 1996, provides that "Everyone has the right"
    (a) to an environment that is not harmful to their health or well-being; and
    (b) to have the environment protected, for the benefit of present and future generations, through reasonable legislative and other measures that –
        (i) prevent pollution and ecological degradation;
        (ii) promote conservation; and
        (iii) secure ecologically sustainable development and use of natural resources while promoting justifiable economic and social development.
[46] NEMA, Act 107 of 1998, Long Title.   [47] Section 24H of Bill 56 of 2003.
[48] Section 24(5)(e).

strong on the environment. There is an environmental clause in the Constitution,[49] and a number of environmental Acts have been promulgated by the government since 1994. This is still happening: A number of Acts have recently been enacted and several more are in the pipeline, including several amending and augmenting NEMA, South Africa's principal environmental Act.

As far as EIA is concerned, there is no obvious political reason why the powers to make regulations providing for the EIA process under the 1989 ECA were not exercised until 1997, but their exercise in that year was one example of new and progressive environmental legislation established by the new government. It would seem that the process provided by the ECA and its regulations was intended to be temporary, judging by the relevant sections' repeal by NEMA, which took effect a little over a year after the making of the regulations establishing the compulsory EIA process in South Africa. This process has, however, not yet been replaced, because the relevant regulations under NEMA have not yet been made. As far as the NEMA amendment is concerned, many of the new provisions are welcome, but the provisions amending existing provisions in NEMA have the effect of reducing the scope of compulsory EIAs in the country.[50] The original NEMA required the carrying out of EIAs for any activity requiring authorization under any law, but this provision has been changed to a process requiring EIAs only for "listed" activities. Draft regulations released just before the writing of this paper seem to have the probable effect of further diluting the strength of the EIA process and certainly its scope of operation.

Is this surprising given the positive legislative movements in the environmental management sphere in the last decade? Perhaps it is surprising from a view of the decade as a whole, but there have been several recent trends suggesting that the government is perhaps less committed to sustainable development and environmental conservation in reality than it is on paper. In the field of biodiversity conservation and, in particular, in protected areas, there appears to be a trend toward conservation's paying for itself, which will reduce the financial commitment of the government to conservation.

If the EIA process is to operate effectively, it needs resources. It would appear that these resources are not readily forthcoming from the government, with the result that there are numerous flaws in the EIA system at present. The obvious way of addressing this, if there is political commitment to the EIA process, is to provide more resources. The proposed amendments to NEMA and the draft regulations, however, suggest that the political will is absent since the apparent response to the problems is to amend the legislative requirements so as to make EIAs compulsory in far fewer instances. The intended result, presumably, is that EIA will run smoothly with the existing human resources, thus obviating the need to provide more money to the departments concerned, allowing the resources to be channeled to what the government regards as more pressing concerns. My argument is that the EIA process will work better if more resources are provided, an option that the government does not see as feasible.

7.2 The Politics of Decision Making

Authorizations that follow the EIA process are made by government officials, who are members of government Departments, either national or provincial, headed by

---

[49] Section 24, Constitution of the Republic of South Africa, 1996.
[50] See s 24 of the Amendment Act 8 of 2004.

members of the national or provincial Cabinets. It would be naïve to expect decisions made in these departments to be immune from the general policy directions taken in the executive as a whole. Development is clearly an important direction for government, not only in the narrow sense of economic development but of infrastructural development to provide services to citizens such as water, electricity, housing, and health care facilities. For example, in President Mbeki's State of the Nation Address to a Joint Sitting of the Houses of Parliament in May 2004,[51] the themes of growth and development permeate the document. This is as it should be in a developing country ravaged by poverty, unemployment, and inequality. On the other hand, there is not one reference to the environment.

Several recent EIA authorizations, some of which are currently on appeal, seem to have been made in a manner that gives far more weight to development imperatives, some of which are somewhat questionable, than to questions of sustainability and adverse impact on the environment.[52] If the government is committed to sustainable development, however, it should ensure that such decisions are, as far as possible, free of controversy and above suspicion. This may be easier said than done, and it would be almost impossible to remove all controversy, but due and proper consideration of alternatives to proposed developments and the environmental impacts of those developments will go a long way to reducing dissatisfaction with decisions.

8 CONCLUSION

EIA, as required by legislation and not merely as a voluntary exercise, is well established in South Africa. This chapter suggests that the practice of EIA, however, leaves much to be desired, particularly because of capacity constraints within government. Sadly, proposed new legislation offers no evidence that the political will to address this is present. Instead, it seems that EIA is to be reduced in its sphere of application, and that is not good news for the environment in South Africa.

---

[51] The address can be accessed at http://www.info.gov.za/speeches/2004/04052111151001.htm.

[52] The decisions in question are the decisions approving the Coega Port development (which received a positive mention in the President's State of the Nation address mentioned earlier); the Eskom Pebble Bed Reactor; and the N2 development in Pondoland.

11 From Bureaucracy-Controlled to Stakeholder-Driven Urban Planning and Management: Experiences and Challenges of Environmental Planning and Management in Tanzania

W. J. Kombe

1 INTRODUCTION

For decades, Tanzania has been experiencing a phenomenal urbanization, which is characterized by exploding population growth amid declining public capacities to plan and manage urban growth. The negative consequences of rapid growth include acute community infrastructure deficiencies, urban sprawl, depletion of natural resources, and aggravated environmental degradation including pollution. While the rapid urban growth trend in Tanzania, just as many other countries in sub-Saharan Africa, is largely attributed to the socioeconomic and political changes in the country, the major driving forces of urbanization have been high birth rates, wide disparities in basic services between rural and urban areas, and increasing rural poverty. According to the 2002 National Population Census, the country's urban population grew from 2.1 million (12.7 percent) in 1978 to about 10.0 million in 2002, representing about 29 percent of the total population. Dar es Salaam's primacy is more striking than that in other urban centers; since 1968 the city population has grown threefold, but more or less doubled between 1988 and 2002.

Even though urbanization is inevitable and a necessary condition for diversifying national economies and boosting productivity,[1] the public capacity deficits in urban planning and management have given rise to severe environmental, social, and economic problems, which are often interlinked in a complex manner and cut across many sectors. The traditional instruments established since the colonial days, such as master plans and structure plans, are unable to cope with the increasing demands and challenges in urban development.[2] The failure of the conventional tools is attributed to several factors. However, the single most important factor, which has persistently limited their usefulness over the last three decades, is the inadequate inclusion – and, at times, exclusion – of other stakeholders in urban planning and management activities. In most cases, postindependent African governments, that of Tanzania included, assigned themselves a lead role in urban development. As a result, the conception and execution of

---

[1] UNCHS/UNEP (1998), Sustainable Cities Programme (SCP), *Programme Approach and Implementation* UN-Habitat, Nairobi.

[2] Ibid., footnote 1.

The author wishes to acknowledge with thanks the generous support he received from the Urban Authorities Support Programme (UASU) Coordinator, Marthin Kittila.

urban planning and management activities have been largely a reserve of professionals, primarily the staff of local and central governments.

In Tanzania, as in many other countries in sub-Saharan Africa, the ineffectiveness of the bureaucracy-led approaches to promote social, economic, and physical development and deliver an improved living and working environment was already apparent during the 1970s. Accentuated environmental conflicts, widespread informal urbanization, and deterioration of basic community infrastructure services and facilities were among the manifestations of the inefficiencies. Already in the 1960s, initiatives had started to improve urban planning and management by adopting other types of plans.[3]

In the United Kingdom, attempts were, for instance, made to replace master plans with structure plans so as to provide a more adaptable instrument for urban planning and management. There was also increased preference for action plans based on the appraisal of the social and economic sectors. The action planning was, however, largely a result of the desire of international development agencies for immediate results, that is, an action-oriented approach to urban development problems. On the other hand, over the period, theory and practice tended to focus on improvement of organizational skills of pursuing goals and objectives in conditions of uncertainty and accelerating change.[4] Concurrent with this was the increased adoption of new concepts of public sector management that envisage integration of urban planning and management and tapping of public and private sector investment potentials so as to achieve the desired socioeconomic development objectives at both city and national levels.[5]

As environmental problems became a major threat to the livability of cities of poor countries, the call and search for alternative urban planning and management instruments and strategies increased, making scholars and international institutions increasingly concerned about and skeptical of the appropriateness and relevance of conventional approaches to urban planning and management.

In 1990, alarmed by the pathetic environmental conditions in Dar es Salaam, the Government of Tanzania (GoT), through the Ministry of Lands and Human Settlements Development (MLHSD), which is the institution responsible for urban and regional planning, requested United Nations Development Program (UNDP) technical support to review the 1979 Dar es Salaam Master Plan. The review of the 1979 City Master Plan was seen as, and understood to be, the solution to the physical, social, and economic decay, especially the persistent deterioration of basic public infrastructure services in the city of Dar es Salaam. Indeed the living and working conditions in the city then not only were pathetic but constituted an eyesore.[6] The UNDP responded affirmatively to the government request but referred the matter to the UN-Habitat for action.

---

[3] Rakodi, C., and Devas, N. (eds.), 1993, *Managing Fast Growing Cities: New Approaches to Urban Planning and Management in the Development of the World*, Longman Scientific Technical, John Wiley & Sons Inc., New York.

[4] Ibid.

[5] Ibid., footnote 4; Clarke, G. (1989), "New Approaches to Urban Planning and Management in the 1990s: The Role of UNCHS," paper presented to the *Workshop on Planning and Management of Urban Development in the 1990s*, Birmingham, September 1989.

[6] For instance, before the adoption of EPM in 1992, less than 3 percent of the over 1,400 tons/per day of the city's solid waste was being collected; dumping of toxic chemicals and heavy metals directly into the city's river system was rampant; urban agriculture was unregulated or had no any extension support services. Water supply was erratic and the quality poor (DCC/UNCHS, 1992).

Incidentally, the GoT's request to UNDP coincided with initiatives that had been taken by UN-Habitat to search for a strategy that can promote sustainable urban development especially in cities and towns experiencing environmental problems. Drawing on its vast experience in urban development and management and in collaboration with UNEP, UNCHS in 1990 launched the Sustainable Cities Programme (SCP) as a strategy for helping municipal authorities and their public, private, and community sector actors to improve their capacities to plan and manage urban developments. Environmental Planning and Management (EPM) became the operational tool of the SCP and an instrument for implementing Agenda 21 at the city and municipal levels.[7]

It envisages a cross-sectoral collaboration with other stakeholders in urban development processes. Unlike the structure or master planning approach, the EPM approach is a process-oriented, interorganizational, and multidimensional strategy that integrates spatial, social, economic, and environmental facets in addressing problems and conflicts that ensue from environment–development interactions. It also recognizes the negative and positive impacts that urban development may have on the environment.

This chapter focuses on EPM operationalization and institutionalization in Tanzania. It pulls together lessons from several municipalities where stakeholder-driven (participatory) environmental planning and management have been adopted. Data and information from the upcountry municipalities are, however, mainly used to complement observations in Dar es Salaam.

It has drawn information and data from the following sources:

- Interviews with heads of city council departments and coordinators of EPM in the city and upcountry municipalities
- Interviews with the head, Strategic Planning Unit of the Urban Planning Division of the Ministry of Lands and Human Settlement Development
- Discussions with selected former working group members
- Discussions with some of the colleagues at University College of Lands and Architectural Studies (UCLAS) who were involved in SDP activities
- Review of various reports and papers on EPM operationalization and institutionalization in Tanzania

2 THE ADVENT OF THE EPM IN DAR ES SALAAM

The Environmental Planning and Management (EPM) approach was officially launched in Dar es Salaam in 1992 but became fully operational in 1993. Commensurate with the Sustainable Cities Programme (SCP) principles, the overall goal was to establish mechanisms through which the Dar es Salaam City Council (DCC) can improve its capacity to plan and manage the growth of the city and particularly address the burning environmental problems through partnership arrangements with other stakeholders. The specific objectives were to

- Forge and build capacity of the local partners to plan and manage urban development activities collaboratively

[7] UNCHS (2003), *Sustainable Cities Programme 1990–2000: A Decade of United Nations Support for Broad-based Participatory Management of Urban Development*, UN-Habitat, Nairobi.

- Coordinate and manage environment–development interactions
- Enable partners in urban development in the city of Dar es Salaam to prepare a long-term dynamic and integrated development plan and investment strategy.

Through a citywide consultative workshop that was conducted in August 1992, the stakeholders of the city of Dar es Salaam identified and prioritized nine environmental issues of concern. Also during the workshop, a consensus on mechanisms and mandate for addressing the same through "Working Groups" representing the stakeholders was reached. The stakeholders' commitment to support and collaborate with the Dar es Salaam City Council (DCC) in addressing the pertinent environmental issues identified was forged. Most importantly, a task-specific working group for each of the nine environmental issues was established, with a mandate to analyze and prioritize issues, negotiate strategies, and formulate action plans and projects.[8] At the same time, bottom-up, demand-led interventions were acknowledged as a fundamental feature of the SCP operationalization process.

To ensure systematic operationalization and eventual institutionalization of the EPM approach in the routine functions of the city council, the Sustainable Dar es Salaam Project (SDP) was established, as a semiautonomous unit, fully furnished with both technical and support staff. Habitat appointed the Chief Technical Adviser (CTA) as the leading EPM expert.

The institutional, socioeconomic, and political environment prevailing in the country prior to the adoption of EPM is outlined so as to underscore and take account of the conditions under which EPM was translated into action: sown, grew, and propagated. The key features that characterized existing urban planning and environmental management were the following:

- The urban planning and management system, directed by a blueprint, "top-down" master planning paradigm, was spatial in focus.
- Urban authorities were bureaucrats who were preoccupied with routine operations and had few strategic planning skills.
- Urban planning and management institutions including legal frameworks, regulations, and procedures were strongly control-based and largely dependent on public (state) sector resource capacities.
- Sector agencies including public utility agencies had little experience and interest in intersectoral collaboration.

These were some of the key factors that engendered degraded urban habitats that were conflict-ridden as manifested in the escalation of social, environmental, and economic problems.[9] These were also the silent features that characterized the bureaucratically controlled urban planning and management practice.

---

[8] Nnkya, T. J. (2004), "The Sustainable Cities Program in Tanzania, 1993–2003: From Demonstration Project to Natural Programme for Sustainable Cities," unpublished report prepared for UN-Habitat.

[9] Mateso, P. E. E. (2002), "Deficiencies of the Urban Planning Institution in Tanzania," in Kreibich, V. B., and Olima, W. (eds.), *Urban Land Management in Africa*. SPRING series No. 40, Dortmund, pp. 177–199, and Kombe, W. J., and Kreibich, V. (2000), *Informed Land Management in Tanzania*. SPRING series, No. 29, Dortmund.

2.1 Chronology: EPM Operationalization

The key actors, processes, and activities undertaken in chronological order, are outlined here

1990 Government of Tanzania submits a request to UNDP to review the 1979 Dar es Salaam Master Plan.

January 1992 The Sustainable Dar es Salaam Project (SDP) is established to operationalize Environmental Planning and Management (EPM) in the Dar es Salaam City Council (DCC).

August 1992 The first citywide stakeholders' consultation is conducted to identify and prioritize environmental issues, evolve strategies for addressing them, and secure consensus and commitments of stakeholders.

1993 The sustainable Dar es Salaam Project (SDP) becomes fully operational as a unit under the Assistant City Director, with several local technical staff as well as a Chief Technical Adviser, who was appointed by Habitat.

1994 Long-term strategies and action plans for environmental issues are prepared.

1995 Demonstration projects are implemented.

June 1996 Dar es Salaam City Council (DCC) is abolished because of its unimpressive performance; instead a City Commission is established. SDP continues under the Commission.

July 1997 Nationwide consultation on EPM replication is launched. Experiences of the Sustainable Dar es Salaam Project are disseminated and deliberated upon. Twelve local authorities adopt EPM. Phase III SDP starts.

September 1997 DCC is entrusted to oversee EPM replication on behalf of the Prime Minister's Office (PMO). Meanwhile initiatives are taken to establish a national organ to coordinate EPM replication.

October 1997 The preparation of Strategic Urban Development Planning (SUDP) for the Dar es Salaam City is launched.

1998 Inception training for EPM coordinators of the nine municipalities, which had joined the SCP network, begins. Mayors and Municipal Directors from the new municipalities also have one-day inception training. Commitment by the municipalities to support and contribute funds for EPM replication is secured.

May 1998 A national coordinating body (UASU) is established under the Prime Minister's Office, Ministry of Regional Administration and Local Government (MRALG).

January–November 1998 The government declares that all urban development plans must be done through EPM approach.

1999 Moshi, Mbeya, Tanga, Morogoro, and Tabora join the SCP national network with DANIDA Support. Local Government (District Authorities Act) No. 8 of 1982 is amended.

January 2000 Arusha joins SCP network with DANIDA Support.

July 2000 Municipalization of Dar es Salaam City Council into Ilala, Temeke, and Kinondoni Municipalities occurs.

August 2001 A consultative meeting to examine and endorse SUDP for Dar es Salaam City is held. Amendment of the National Human Settlement Policy Review of the Town and Country Planning Ordinance Cap 378 occurs.

August – November 2001 Municipal consultations take place in Ilala, Kinondoni, and Temeke

January 2002–2004 Backstopping by UASU and initiatives to mobilize resources occur. EPM replication activities are held by the Ministry of Lands. Implementation of action plans occurs in DANIDA-supported municipalities.

Through sensitization, public awareness creation, and city and municipal consultations, adoption of EPM in the routine operations in the municipalities was ratified and institutionalized. Besides the consultations, the municipal and city councils kept their inhabitants informed of their limited capacities and the ways they can support one another in addressing burning urban development problems. In addition, they were able to attract and build linkages with local institutions and organizations dealing with environmental issues.

3 OUTCOMES OF THE EPM OPERATIONALIZATION

In order to exhibit the impacts the EPM approach has had on improving urban planning and management in Tanzania, the main outcomes achieved so far are discussed. While tangible outcomes show the qualitative results of EPM, intangible outputs, particularly those that relate to the changes of attitudes of people or stakeholders, as well as institutional reforms, are also examined.

3.1 Institutionalization of Stakeholders' Participation in Urban Development Activities

The adoption of EPM in urban planning and management activities by the Dar es Salaam City Council facilitated adoption of a participatory approach across sectoral actors within and without the council. Both mini- and citywide consultations and working groups sessions that were conducted under the EPM, especially over the 1992–1995 period, drew together sectoral actors to create awareness and recognition of abundant resources (skills and expertise) as well as other potentials that can be tapped to boost their sectoral capacities and that of the local authority (DCC) to address burning environmental issues regarding urban planning and management. It is also through the operationalization of the EPM protocol that partners in urban development in Dar es Salaam city were drawn together to realize and acknowledge the interconnectedness of their sectoral issues and how they could be better addressed through cross-sectoral collaborative initiatives. In so doing, the EPM approach seems to have created an environment where partners in urban development saw the need for, and the importance of, providing a room for accommodating one another in the course of discharging their routine responsibilities and addressing challenges arising from rapid urban growth.

In this regard, EPM has been a software that initiated a change of the mindset among the key stakeholders in urban development, particularly local government bureaucrats. Today it is a "norm" to involve and tap stakeholders' potentials irrespective of whether an activity or project is to be implemented at community or city level. Some of the institutions that were partners in the EPM operationalization in Dar es

Salaam City, such as Tanzania Electricity Supply Company (TANESCO) and Dar es Salaam Water and Sanitation Authority (DAWASA), have adopted the participatory approach in addressing their sectoral responsibilities.[10] Others, such as the Ministry of Works, have not emulated this approach in addressing pertinent sectoral issues and problems.[11]

Indeed, in the Dar es Salaam City Council, one can confidently say that gone are the days when a public institution or an individual would initiate an activity or a project in a community and get on with business – that is, plan, solicit funds, and implement it – without the involvement of other stakeholders. This is vividly manifested in recently initiated projects such as the Bus Rapid Transport (BRT), Lighting of the Streets (under the Safer Cities Project), and Modern Abattoir Project; all have been conceived and executed through a participatory approach, using the EPM protocol.

Adoption of the EPM approach has also been a breakthrough and a catalyst for promoting good governance as it has induced key partners not only to contribute to addressing pertinent environmental management problems, but to engage actively and dialogue with their local government, thus enhancing transparency in decision making.

Among the living legacies of the EPM, which seems to have been internalized across the municipalities that have adopted EPM, are the debriefing meetings locally referred to as "morning prayers" that are held daily by heads of council departments under the chairmanship of city and municipal directors. These meetings facilitate cross-sectoral sharing of information, prioritizing, and strategizing on issues that require swift action. In this regard, heads of council departments convene in the spirit of a "working group" to receive information from one another, deliberate upon it, and agree on the way forward. This practice has, in a way, expedited council interventions in problems facing urban development.[12]

Analysis of the decision-making process in Dar es Salaam City Council and other municipalities prior to the adoption of the EPM approach shows that the absence of stakeholder involvement was the major shortcoming that undermined the capacity of local authorities to guide urban development effectively. One of the heads of a department at the DCC interviewed asserts: "In the past, many a time an individual head of a department would receive a report about problems from affected persons or local leaders but would mainly discuss with colleagues in the department or bring the matter for the attention of the Municipal Director without cross-sectoral consultations and deliberations. Problems were handled without seeking inputs from other departments, let alone stakeholders outside the local government system."

In other institutions outside the local council in Dar es Salaam City, especially the utility agencies, the EPM process has taken root. Unlike in the past, these institutions now consult the relevant stakeholders before providing new services such as laying new pipes or erecting electric poles.

---

[10] Even though it could not be confirmed whether or not the adoption of the participatory approach by these institutions is an outcome of SDP initiatives, it is undisputable that prior to the adoption of the EPM approach in Dar es Salaam City Council, these institutions, like other stakeholders, were acting on their own.

[11] The latter refers to, for instance, the case of the Morogoro road expansion.

[12] Discussion with EPM coordinators in Iringa and Arusha, the UASU Coordinator, and some heads of departments at the DCC, August 2004.

3.2 Facilitation of "Unofficial" Land Use Development

The municipal city council and the Ministry of Lands and Human Settlement officials observed that the 1999 SUDP for the Dar es Salaam City has not been "officially" implemented. However, a number of activities and proposals outlined in the city SUDP document have been implemented, albeit "unofficially." These include the following:

- Expansion of the city (residential development) plots in Kitunda and Mbuyuni areas in Ilala Municipality, which has been implemented under the "20,000 Plots Programme"
- The designation of Kinyamwezi area in Ilala Municipality, a prime source of sand for the construction activities in the city
- Development of a waste collection dump at Kinyamwezi, with preparations to develop the site initiated by Ilala Municipality, awaiting completion of the ongoing environmental impact assessment exercise
- Designation of the land for quarry activities in Bunju and Chambazi in Kinondoni and Temeke Municipal Council, respectively

When asked why the decisions and actions taken by institutions with a mandate to implement land use development activities are considered "unofficial," the city council EPM coordinator and a town planner working for the Ilala Municipality observed: "these activities have been implemented without an approved Strategic Urban Development Plan (SUDP) document. This is against the Town and Country Planning Ordinance Cap 378, sections 31–33. Worse, if a conflict or dispute arises, we cannot defend our decision or actions because the SUDP plan does not have an approval of the Ministry responsible for land use planning and development in the country. We are lucky, so far nobody has objected to or questioned our decision."[13]

Regarding the ownership and status of the SUDP particularly after the municipalization of the Dar es Salaam City Council, the two respondents noted that there are tendencies among some city municipal officials to disown the SUDP, arguing that it is a plan for the DCC and not for their municipalities. According to the respondents, these misconceptions emerge from the unofficial status of the SUDP document. On the other hand, the little consideration given to the SUDP during the city municipalization process was said to have had an adverse effect too. As long as the formal planning approval procedures and processes have not been accomplished, the municipal authorities can hardly be taken to task for not observing the SUDP consensus.

3.3 Establishment of the Department for Planning and Coordination and Ward Environmental Committees

One of the lessons that have emerged from the EPM operationalization in Dar es Salaam is that it takes time to bring together sectoral actors and to make them agree to change traditions and approaches they are used to. This is particularly so because some of the municipal council bureaucrats feel that by bringing external actors aboard, they will

---

[13] Discussions with Maira and Mbembela at DCC, September 2004.

share or lose some of their powers or mandates. In fact, during the initial stages of the EPM operationalization there were many who doubted the effectiveness of the approach and were uncooperative and apprehensive about change.[14]

Because administratively, council departments are at par, it is often difficult for any one department to call others around a round table. For this reason the new structure for the municipalized city council proposed the creation of a new Department for Planning and Coordination whose main role is to monitor and coordinate sectoral council departments. The position of the Head of the Department for Planning and Coordination was deliberately placed a step above the other council departments so that he/she is in a position to convene meetings and ensure cross-sectoral consultation. Most importantly, following the thrust put on environmental issues through adoption of the EPM approach, environmental committees have been established at Ward level to advise and assist in addressing and resolving issues related to resource management. The Environmental Management Bill (2004), Section 38(I), has provided for environmental committees and outlined their functions in subsections (1)(a)–(d).

3.4 Amendments of the Legislation and Formalization of Land Use Plan

Review of the Town and Country Planning Ordinance Cap. 378 of 1956

The Town and Country Planning Ordinance Cap. 378, a replica of the English Town and Country Planning Act of 1947, is the principal legislation that regulates urban planning practice in Tanzania. One of the major shortcomings in this legislation, which has adversely affected urban planning and management, is inadequate consideration of the substantive engagement of stakeholders' participation in urban planning activities. Section 24(1)(ii) of the ordinance provides for stakeholders' involvement in the preparation of urban development plans – an essential tool for the preparation of detailed urban land use Planning Schemes. The Planning Authority is, however, not bound to adopt schemes prepared by the local communities concerned. Since the adoption of participatory environmental planning and management and because of promising outcomes from the EPM operationalization in Dar es Salaam, Cap 378 is being reviewed to ensure substantive participation of stakeholders in the planning process. In the new Act, the Physical Planning Act (2001), which is being prepared by the Ministry of Lands, a clause providing for a change from the Master Plan to the Strategic Urban Development Plan has been incorporated so as to consolidate and expedite reforms in urban planning and management practice.

Because of the diversified nature of land and its high demand and value in most of the rapidly growing urban areas in the country, implementation of most of the SUDP strategies would require or depend on the availability of physical land. On the other hand, most environment–development conflicts and problems occur on the land. A land use plan is therefore one of the essential outputs or components of SUDP. In all municipalities and towns that have so far adopted the EPM approach, land use plans are integral parts of the strategic urban planning framework. In this regard, the guidelines prepared by the Ministry of Lands and Human Settlement Development are a step

---

[14] Kombe, W. J. (2001), "Institutionalising the Concept of Environmental Planning and Management (EPM): Successes and Challenges in Dar es Salaam," *Development in Practice*, Vol. 11, Nos. 2 and 3, pp. 190–207.

toward the formalization of the land use plan, as one of the main components of the SUDP.

Review of Local Government (District Authorities) Act, 1982 – Local Government Laws Miscellaneous Amendments of 1999 no. 6

In order to institutionalize stakeholder participation, the Local Government Act 1982[15] has been revised to provide, inter alia, for participation of stakeholders in the Ward Development Committees (WDC). Section 6, subsection 2(d), requires the Ward Development Committee to invite persons from nongovernmental organizations (NGOs) and other civic groups involved in the promotion of development in the Ward to participate in the Ward Development Committee (WDC) deliberations. Prior to this amendment, membership to the WDC was limited to elected persons. On the other hand, section 7, subsection 31 (9), categorically specifies that the Ward Development Committee shall be responsible for initiating and promoting "participatory development" in the Ward. Since these amendments, individual citizens are now free to question decisions or actions by WDC in cases in which they have not been involved. Similarly, civil groups or NGOs may contest their rights to participate in WDC deliberations in case they are bypassed.

Apart from the amendments made to the Local Government Act, there are also ongoing Local Government Reforms that aim at promoting good governance among the local authorities. They also envisage a local government system that works with its people and that implements policies and decisions that are prepared in close consultation with the people.[16] These reforms, though not directly linked with EPM operationalization; will further consolidate stakeholders' participation in urban development activities. Indeed local government reforms are reported to have substantially benefited from and built on the awareness created among Ward and Mtaa leaders during EPM sensitization workshops.

3.5 The Environmental Bill: Land Use Concerns

As in many other countries, one of the key environmental management-related challenges facing Tanzania is the existence of many sectoral laws, policies, and programs, which are not coordinated. This has, for instance, led to conflicts and contradictions among many actors and institutions involved in urban land development.

In an attempt to harmonize the various laws and set a framework for sustainable development, Tanzania prepared the Environmental Management Bill (2004). The Bill consolidates the sectoral legislation relevant to environmental management, including the following:

- Land Act No. 4 and 5 of 1999
- Town and Country Planning Cap. 378, 1956
- Local Government (Urban Authorities) Act No. 7 of 1982

---

[15] It could not be established whether or not the amendment of this Act is a result of EPM operationalization.

[16] Chaligha, A. (2004), "Local Autonomy and Citizen Participation in Tanzania," unpublished research paper presented at a workshop organized by REPOA, August 2004, and Mushi, D. P. (2004), "Tracking Impacts of the LGRP on the Performance of Local Authorities: Evidence from Local Service Provision in Tanzania," unpublished paper presented at a workshop organized by REPOA, August 2004.

- Local Government (District Authority) No. 8 of 1982
- Wildlife Conservation Act No. 12 of 1974
- National Forest Policy 1998

The new Bill, which was scheduled for a second reading during the Parliament of November 2004, is a comprehensive document prepared in collaboration with stakeholders. At least 10 consultative meetings were held.[17]

The main objective of the Bill is to provide for and promote the enhancement, protection, conservation, and management of the environment. It gives the Minister responsible for the environment the responsibility of fostering coordination among the Government, local government authorities, and other agencies and actors engaged in environmental management. It also empowers her/him to issue general guidelines to sectoral Ministries; Government Departments; City, Municipal, and District Councils; and others.

In order to enhance coordination in environmental management, the Bill also provides for the establishment of the National Environmental Advisory Committee (Sect. II), which comprises senior officials from key sectoral ministries, public agencies, as well as private sector actors. These include the Director for Human Settlement Development, the Commissioner for Lands, and Directors for Minerals, Forest, and Water Resources. Others are the Directors of Energy, Roads, and Industries as well as the Director of the National Environmental Management Council. At City, Municipal, and District levels, the Bill provides for the appointment of Environmental Management Officers, who shall be responsible for advising their respective councils on environmental management matters as well as for ensuring the enforcement of the provisions of the Bill.

Furthermore, the Bill requires sectoral government Ministries, Departments, and agencies as well as other institutions to prepare and submit to the Minister Sectoral Environmental Action Plans. These have be undertaken every five years. The plans have to identify environmental problems prevalent in the area and recommend measures to address them (section 433).

In relation to land use planning, section 33(1) stipulates that the Standing Committees on Urban Planning and Environment established under section A2(1) of the Local Government (Urban Authorities) Act, 1982, shall comprise City or Municipal Environment Management Committees. The committees shall perform several functions related to land use planning and management outlined in section 55(1) and (2) of the Local Government Act, 1982, as well as those outlined in section 41 of the Bill.

Section 50 categorically states that the management and utilization of land shall be in accordance with prevailing land laws – including Land Act 1999, Village Land Act 1999, and Town and Country Planning Ordinance Cap. 378. However, where there are conflicts on environmental aspects of land management, the provisions in the Bill shall prevail. This gives the Bill a stronger position in the promotion of good environmental management practices.

Issues pertaining to Environmental Impact Assessment and other assessment related to environmental management are covered in Part VI. Section 81 provides for the mandatory conducting of environmental impact assessment (EIA) for a number of

---

[17] Discussion with Shauri, Director, LEAT, Dar es Salaam, September 2004.

specified projects. This includes major changes in land use to include urban development activities. In addition section 89 stipulates a requirement for public participation in EIA, especially by those to be affected by development projects.

In terms of comprehensiveness, the Bill seems to provide the necessary conditions and institutional frameworks for promoting sound environmental management and enhancing sustainable development. What remains a challenge that can hardly be resolved by the Bill is the chronic problem of poor communication and weak cooperation particularly between government institutions and agencies. For instance, even though Local Government Reforms and the EPM approach are both concerned with decentralization, good governance, and stakeholder participation, the two programs are not complementary although they are under the same Ministry. In fact, even in the municipalities where both programs are in place, each is operating without regard to the other, implying that there is weak cooperation between government institutions.

3.6 Formulation of National Guidelines for Operationalizing EPM

In order to ensure coherence in operationalizing the EPM protocol in varying urban contexts, the Ministry of Lands and Human Settlement Development (MLHSD) has formulated guidelines outlining the scope, procedures, thematic areas of concern, and form of Strategic Urban Development Plans (SUDP). The guidelines outline the preparatory process, actors, tools, and outputs including the necessary illustrations. In another development, the MLHSD has effected changes in Human Settlement Policy so as to accommodate the EPM and Strategic Planning approaches in the documents.[18]

Even though it is acknowledged that the adoption of EPM in the varying urban areas ought to be flexible and subject to changes depending on the local conditions, systematization of the approach is important to prevent misconceptions. At the same time, in view of the limited capacity to support EPM replication, the guidelines constitute a manual or reference material for the various stakeholders and other staff of the local and central governments.[19] It has also been observed that notwithstanding the fact that EPM has now been in place for at least 10 years, there are still some stakeholders, including policymakers and practitioners, who do not clearly understand the EPM concept and procedures.[20]

Besides, there are also incidences in which conflicts have emerged because of misconceptions regarding the role and mandate of working groups. For instance, in Bagamoyo, a district town about 60 kilometers from Dar es Salaam, working group members ran into conflict with the council management and politicians (councilors) because they infringed upon and tried to execute management and political functions of local governments.[21] In this regard, the guidelines constitute an administrative tool that

---

[18] The EPM documents prepared by the Ministry of Land and Human Settlement Development are based on EPM guidelines issued by UN-Habitat.

[19] Discussion with Kayega, Head, Strategic Planning Section, Ministry of Lands and Human Settlements Development, September 2004.

[20] Nnkya, "Sustainable Cities Program," unpublished report.

[21] The working group members wanted to take an active part in matters such as tendering and awarding of contracts for projects evolved by working groups. There were also expectations that the council management ought to be accountable to the working groups.

defines the "rules of the games and ensures consistence and harmony" in the day-to-day operations.

3.7 From Master Planning to the Strategic Urban Planning Unit

Commensurate with the changes in the legislation, and in order to steer the reforms from Master Planning to Strategic Urban Development Planning, the Ministry of Lands and Human Settlements Development has changed the name of the former Master Planning Section to Strategic Planning Section. The unit is mainly responsible for providing technical support to the urban centers, which do not have access to financial and technical support from donors but have resolved to adopt the EPM approach in addressing urban environmental challenges. In line with EPM protocol, the support provided by the unit is demand-driven; local governments are therefore expected to initiate the process. Despite resource constraints including those related to lack of financial resources and skilled personnel, the ministry has so far supported several regional and district councils, including Shinyanga, Songea, Karatu, Makambako, Kibaha, and Vuwa. Others are Tunduma, Masasi, and Lushoto. Except for the last three, they have gone through the entire EPM operationalization cycle and have SUDP in place. It was not possible to get information on how the replication of EPM in these towns was undertaken and what local capacity was built to take over EPM operationalization at the end of the ministry's support. Other unclear issues include the extent of influence of the SUDPs prepared for the towns, that is, how useful they are.

3.8 Review of the Training Curricula

Apart from the review of the relevant policies and legislation to embrace EPM protocol and other institutional changes effected, training programs for both undergraduate and postgraduate students in University Lands and Architectural Studies have also been reviewed. Sustainable cities concepts and principles have been mainstreamed in both studio and theory courses. In addition, the Continuing Education Unit of the college is conducting tailor-made short courses focusing on the EPM approach and urban strategic planning and management. The courses are mainly for in-service staff of the local and central government. The stages of the EPM process are exemplified in Table 11.1.

4 CHALLENGES TO THE ADOPTION OF EPM IN DAR ES SALAAM

4.1 Legal Status of the SUDP for Dar es Salaam City

According to the Town and Country Planning Ordinance Cap. 378, section 33, urban plans have to be approved by the Ministry of Lands and Human Settlement, before they are gazetted or take effect. Unfortunately the 1999 SUDP for the city of Dar es Salaam is still to be approved or gazetted. The final amendments including incorporation of the inputs of utility agencies were completed way back in 2002. The DCC was expected to convene final stakeholders' consultations before onward submission of the SUDP to the Ministry of Lands and Human Settlement for approval and gazetting; this is still to be done.

Table 11.1. Replication and institutionalization of EPM – August 2004

Activity municipal	Sensitization and awareness creation	Preparation of environmental profiles	EPM implementation stages — Holding of consultations Min	Mun. (Year)	Establishing working groups	Preparation of plans	Existence of land use development plans	Implementation of demonstration projects
Mwanza	√	√	√	√ (7/1998)	√	√	√	√
Tabora	√	√	√	√ (12/1999)	√			
Arusha	√	√	√	√ (1/2000)	√	√	√	√
Moshi	√	√	√	√ (1/1999)	√	√	√	√
Tanga	√	√	√	√ (5/1999)	√			
Dodoma	√	√	√	√ (12/1998)	√			
Morogoro	√	√	√	√ (8/1999)	√			
Iringa	√	√	√	√ (10/1998)	√	√	√	√
Mbeya	√	√	√	√ (7/1999)	√		√	√
DSM municipalities	√	√	√	√	√			
Temeke	√	•						
Ilala	√	•						
Kinondoni	√	•						

√ To be implemented.
• Under preparation.

Source: Kitila, M. L. D. (2000), "Replication of Environmental Planning and Management at the National Level: The Case of Tanzania," unpublished (documentation) paper; interviews with Arusha, Iringa, and Moshi Municipality EPM Coordinators, August 2004.

According to the follow-ups by the Ministry of Lands, the DCC is mobilizing financial resources to conduct the consultation.[22] Because the SUDP document does not have the requisite legal status, the plan is not binding on stakeholders in urban development. Further delays in getting the final endorsement from stakeholders and approval and gazetting of the SUDP for Dar es Salaam City seem to undermine institutionalization of the EPM. They also make it difficult to uphold the hard-earned stakeholders consensus that culminated in the production of the SUDP document. It should be added that actions and decisions being taken by individual stakeholders without regard to SUDP provisions can hardly be questioned in the absence of a plan with legal status.

4.2 Short-Circuiting of the Participatory Process

As pointed out earlier, many of the successes of participatory environmental planning and management were, in a way, hard earned. A lot of collective initiatives by residents and stewardship by external and internal experts have gone into the operation of the EPM in Dar es Salaam and its subsequent replication in the upcountry municipalities. Forging partnerships with and coordinating activities of actors in urban development, many of whom have diverse interests and mandates, were not easy challenges to overcome and continue to be difficult. Above all, the participatory process is time consuming and costly and many development partners who work with tight input–output time schedules, or wish to have quick results from their investments may not have the interest or patience to engage in it. This has become evident during the replication process.

Some donors who are supporting the replication of the EPM approach in upcountry municipalities have short-circuited the process, and as a result some of the key tenets of the approach such as deployment of working groups as engines for EPM operationalization, cross-sectoral participation, and emphasis on demand-driven bottom-up interventions seem to have been compromised. This is, for instance, illustrated in one of the community infrastructure upgrading projects undertaken in an informal area in one of the municipalities where EPM was replicated. Discussions with some of the municipal personnel who were involved in this project revealed that the decision to engage in this project was not an outcome of stakeholder consensus or a result of initiatives from below. It was by and large motivated by donors' desire to spend funds and realize tangible outputs in compliance with their time-activity schedule. In other words, some donors still see local communities as beneficiaries, not partners.

While innovations and improvizations to improve EPM performance are expected, as more cities and municipalities adopt and adapt the EPM approach, deviations are inevitable. Furthermore, past experiences show that it is not sufficient to mobilize resources, identify projects, and implement them in a local setting and expect sustainability simply because community leaders indicated their support. Apart from sustainability questions, ownership and replication of such projects or initiatives, which are based on a "top-down" approach, become a daunting task. On the other hand, short-circuiting the process seems to undermine conceptual premises of EPM as it makes the process-oriented reforms in environmental planning and management a one-off

---

[22] Discussions with Kayega, Head, Strategic Planning Unit, Ministry of Lands and Human Settlement Development, and Maira, City EPM Coordinator, September 2004.

event. The EPM approach is about empowering stakeholders to build long-term partnerships and create conditions for ensuring mutual benefits. It is about a change of attitudes and approaches among stakeholders concerned with urban environmental issues. These attributes can hardly be achieved through a top-down approach or one-time event.

4.3 Low Regard for Local Capacity-Building Needs

The prime objective of SCP is to strengthen the capacity of local authorities and their partners to plan and manage urban development effectively. However, experience from the replication of the EPM approach in some of the municipalities indicates that inadequate attention has been paid to local capacity-building needs. For instance, in some upcountry towns, highly paid consultants were engaged to provide technical support services to the municipal councils. In some cases, outsourcing of Chief Technical Advisers (CTAs) was done even in situations when technical capacity to operationalize and backstop EPM replication existed. As a result, insufficient regard was given to local capacity building needs.

Because of resource paucity among most District towns, sensitization meetings undertaken during replication are generally few. At the same time it is mainly the middle- and higher-level stakeholders who have participated during consultations. As a result, public awareness is very low and the capacity of the grassroots stakeholders remains unbuilt or scanty.[23]

4.4 Weak Position of EPM in the Local Government Structure

Prior to the municipalization of Dar es Salaam City Council into four local authorities, the city director was the program director for the Sustainable Dar es Salaam Project (SDP). As noted earlier, under this arrangement, an assistant city director responsible for EPM was appointed among the senior staff to oversee EPM operationalization in the council departments including convening and chairing interdepartmental meetings. This arrangement provided a fairly firm structure for EPM to flourish. It also placed EPM in a vantage position from which coordination of the various council units and activities could be done. Following the municipalization of the DCC, four EPM co-coordinators were appointed – one for the DCC and three for the municipalities. Unlike in the past, EPM coordinators in the new city municipalities are fairly junior staff. Besides, EPM institutionalization activities have been relegated to a unit under the urban planning section. As a result, EPM co-coordinators in the three city municipalities seem to be too weak to coordinate other municipal departments. Interestingly, in municipalities such as Iringa and Moshi, where the EPM institutionalization units are directly under the Municipal Director's office, stakeholder participation and the cross-sectoral coordination of urban development functions were reported to be increasingly common practices. The internalization of an EPM coordinating unit within the local government structure appears to be an issue that requires policy consideration.

---

[23] Iringa Municipality is one of the exceptions; the author was involved in the sensitization meetings held at Ward level.

4.5 Inadequate Managerial Skills

Substantive involvement of stakeholders and adoption of partnership arrangements in urban planning and management activities inevitably require sound skills and competence on the part of the municipal personnel and policymakers alike. It also implies a shift in existing balance and a readiness to share power between municipal staff and their partners. Furthermore, it calls for sound managerial skills including better organizational, entrepreneurship, and coordination capacities as well as a higher degree of accountability, which the procedural master planning approach did not necessarily require.

Demand-driven and multidisciplinary cross-sectoral approaches on the other hand, engage many stakeholders, ideas, and expertise in the routine operations of local governments and thus increase the complexity of the urban management process. Inadequate EPM capacity among most municipal personnel on-post, paternalistic tendencies, and inadequate management skills are some of the handicaps that undermine institutionalization of EPM.[24] To this, we have to add the need for resources for skills upgrading and retraining of officials on-post in various local authorities both urban and district to improve their understanding so that they can appreciate their new roles and relationships in environmental planning and management.

4.6 Overdependence on External Resources

Another shortcoming in relation to the adoption and operation of the EPM approach in Tanzania is the problem of financial resources for implementing projects evolved by working groups. In the case of Dar es Salaam, even though the City Council contributed enormously in the implementation of the projects, a large proportion of the financial resources and equipment to operationalize EPM were from external sources. For instance, projects such as environmental management information system (EMIS) and community infrastructure services, improvements in informal settlements, and rehabilitation of the city's horticultural gardens were largely externally funded. As a result of large external inputs including of hardware, most of the local authorities that have resolved to adopt the EPM approach expect to attract and receive some financial and hardware support from external resources, as was reported in a study conducted in Songea.[25] Initially most of the municipalities joined the replication process in anticipation of receiving donor funds from UNDP.[26]

Although the aim of the EPM approach is not to attract external funds or support to boost the capacity of the local government to plan and manage urban development activities, the availability of financial resources and equipment are critical inputs. However, overdependence on external resources by local authorities especially in executing

---

[24] Kombe, W. J. (1997), "Participatory Environmental Planning and Management – Is SDP Making It?" in Kombe, W. J., and Kreibich, V. B. (eds.), *Decentralized Development and Prospects of Planning in Africa*, published proceedings of a workshop organized by the University College of Lands and Architectural Studies (UCLAS) and SPRING Programme of the University of Dortmund and the University of Science and Technology, Kumasi, Ghana, pp. 59–74.

[25] Stanley, M. (2004), "Replication of Environmental Planning and Management (EPM): The Case of Songea Town," unpublished postgraduate dissertation, UCLAS.

[26] Kittila, M. L. D. (2003), "Replication of Environmental Planning and Management at National Level: The Case of Tanzania," unpublished (documentation) paper.

demonstration projects and programs evolved by working groups may restrain local
initiatives to prepare implementable plans or to marshal resources to address them.

4.7 Absence of Comprehensive Monitoring and Documentation of Local EPM Experiences

At present, the national EPM coordinating unit, the Urban Authorities Support
Programme (UASU), is mainly responsible for overseeing EPM operations and institutionalization in the 12 municipalities (Table 11.1). On the other hand, the Strategic Planning Section of the Ministry of Lands and Human Settlement Development
(MLHSD) is mainly providing technical support and, at times, token financial assistance to local authorities, which do not have external or UASU support. Even though
the two institutions communicate and cooperate regularly they are essentially operating as two distinct entities. In addition, the two have different mandates and are under
separate central government ministries. UASU is answerable to the President's Office,
Ministry of Regional Cooperation and Local Governments, while the Strategic Planning
Unit is under the MLHSD.

Problems associated with follow-ups on EPM replication are compounded by the
lack of comprehensive and systematic mechanisms for monitoring and documentation
of the local EPM experiences. As a result, at present, little or nothing is known about
what is going on in the local authorities, which have espoused the EPM approach but
are not under UASU. Because of limited capacity, the support by the Ministry of Lands
and Human Settlements to the towns that have resolved to adopt the EPM approach is
mainly limited to technical personnel, with little follow-up.[27]

In order to build upon good practices (prevent replication of bad practices) consolidate national SCP networks, and improve urban governance, comprehensive documentation of local experiences is necessary. In this regard, there is a need for UASU and
Ministry of Lands and Human Settlements Development instruments and indicators
for monitoring and assessment of local experiences across the cities and towns in the
years to come. The United Nations Centre for Human Settlements (UNCHS)[28] tools for
measuring progress in environmental planning and management are yet to be deployed.
However, UASU partly addressed this shortcoming when it employed a full-time monitoring and evaluation officer. A framework for monitoring the EPM process in the
municipalities was also put in place in the municipalities supported by UASU but not
in the others.

In this regard it would be important to find out how EPM is being replicated in
the non-UASU towns – Who is participating and how? Who is implementing which
activities and what are the qualitative impacts? What are the emerging consensus and
challenges.

4.8 Theoretical Basis for the EPM Approach: A Paradigm Shift

For decades, top-down, bureaucracy-led approaches have been the modus operandi
of urban planning and management. With the adoption of the EPM approach, the old

---

[27] Discussions with Kayega, September 2004.

[28] UNCHS (2001), Sustainable Cities Programme, *Measuring Progress in Environmental Planning and Management, Participatory Decision Making Indicators*, Vol. 9, UN-Habitat, Nairobi.

tradition is dying out. In other words, there is a change from a top-down to a bottom-up approach while the once hopeless and crisis-ridden urban planning and management environment is changing as politics of engagement, dialogue and collaborative planning, and, most importantly, concern for environmental issues in urban governance gain momentum. However, so far, the thrust or major concern in the adoption and replication of EPM has been focused on addressing practical problems in real life situations. Although this is commendable, pertinent questions relating to the how and why of the empirical world have not received much attention. As a result, a theory on the basis of which issues of the real world can be abstracted is needed.

Yet, despite more than 10 years of practical work and the achievements so far recorded, urban planning and management in Tanzania are still in transition. Therefore, the positive changes recorded have not yet stabilized. In order to concretize the changes there is a need to reassess the trends with a view to deriving some explanations of the outcomes, both good and bad, as well as explore their theoretical implications.[29]

5 DISCUSSION

From the foregoing discussion, it is evident that after more than 12 years of the SCP in Dar es Salaam and at least 5 years in various municipalities upcountry (Table 11.1), the transformation of urban planning and management practice in Tanzania has had positive outcomes. The EPM approach has grown in importance as more and more public and private institutions are deploying participatory approaches in their routine activities.

The experiences of EPM operationalization in Dar es Salaam City and nine other municipalities in Tanzania confirm that over the years, the SCP has had a catalyst effect on local and external resource mobilization. This is the outcome despite increasing poverty among the city inhabitants.

Another rewarding outcome has been the institutionalization of stakeholder participation in the execution of the routine functions of local authorities. In turn, the latter has given rise to strategic alliances between the local government bureaucrats and stakeholders in the private and community sectors. The approach has also facilitated consolidation of horizontal and vertical linkages within and outside the municipalities. The involvement of private and popular sector actors in the various sectors of municipal tax collection, upgrading of basic infrastructure services in informal settlements, formulation of an integrated environmental management information system (EMIS), management of parking, and, most importantly, contributions in cash and kind by stakeholders would have been inconceivable without their substantive participation in EPM. In this regard, the adoption of EPM in Dar es Salaam can be seen as a process that has enhanced the quality of urban governance, sown seeds for strategic management among municipal bureaucrats, and imparted a culture of and a space for negotiation among key stakeholders in urban development.

---

[29] Bad outcomes refer to (for instance) declining ownership (among municipal officials) of the city SUDP after the municipalization of Dar es Salaam City Council, laxity in getting the SUDP document approved, reluctance to establish and place the EPM coordination office on an appropriate position in local government structure, and short-circuiting of the EPM protocol during replication by some partners.

There are some institutions that are involving stakeholders in their routine operations even though at times, only middle and higher cadres have participated. At the
same time, "morning prayers"[30] are on going in the municipalities that have adopted
EPM. These trends show the indelible imprints the EPM approach has had and signal a gradual strategic shift in stakeholders' understanding and execution of routine
functions including those related to urban environmental planning and management.
Continued resident participation, however, requires that local governments recipro-
cate by acknowledging the roles and contributions of working groups with respect. It
also implies unreserved readiness to embrace transparency, a practice with which some
bureaucrats in the local authorities are still uncomfortable. This presents a challenge
that is still to be resolved.

Since the adoption of participatory planning and management, resource flows to the
municipal councils that have adopted EPM, both from external and local sources, have
increased considerably. This includes cash contributions, expertise, and equipment.
Implementation of most projects proposed by working groups would not have been
realized without improved resource flows.

For decades, municipal governments have suffered chronic shortage of resources,
while urban population growth rates and poverty are growing. Because local governments are unable to provide and maintain basic community services, they have lost
their integrity among their inhabitants, leading to erosion of the revenue base, since
many residents are unwilling to pay taxes as they have no basic services.[31]

Apart from widespread frustration with poor local government performance, in
particular the failure to provide and maintain basic community services and disregard for private and popular sector potentials, social, economic, and political reforms,
including introduction of a market-based economy and the influence of neoliberal economic thinking that advocates a leaner role for the state, are important factors that have
supported reforms in environmental planning and management practices in Tanzania.
Overall, the response by the central government and most municipal governments in
Tanzania in supporting reforms in urban management and planning practices through
the EPM approach has been exemplary. However, the pace of change has been generally
slow.

As a result of the strengthened municipal capacity to address chronic problems,
municipal councils are starting to regain their lost confidence. Some personnel from
municipalities that have adopted EPM can boast about the positive outcomes of the
EPM approach, which has reformed urban planning and management practice.[32]

At the same time, because stakeholders have participated in evolving strategies and
action plans, participatory planning and management have enhanced ownership by
the city residents. Commenting on this, DCC officials who were interviewed noted:
"Following the adoption of working groups in addressing urban development problems,

---

[30] "Morning prayers" are the early morning meetings that are routinely held by heads of departments of
local governments and chaired by chief executives – city, municipal, and town directors. Such meetings
are intended to brief each other on pertinent issues that require council attention. Above all they facilitate
teamwork or cross-consultation and sharing of information and resources including know-how, among
the key actors.

[31] Fjeldstad, O. (2004), "To Pay or Not to Pay? Citizens' Views of Taxation in Local Authorities in Tanzania,"
unpublished paper presented at a workshop (REPOA), August 2004.

[32] Discussion with EPM coordinator from Dar es Salaam city council and Iringa, August 2004.

many residents have had the opportunity to improve their city; there are many especially former members of the working groups who are openly talking about their roles and involvement in working groups which were dealing with various urban management problems such as solid waste management, traffic management and upgrading of informal settlements."[33]

The amendments to existing legal instruments including the Town and Country Planning Ordinance Cap. 378, the Local Governments (Urban Authorities) Act 1982, the formulation of national guidelines for EPM, and the change of the Master Planning Unit to the Strategic Planning Section by the Ministry of Lands and Human Settlements Development are steps toward consolidation of reforms in urban environmental planning and management.

Because of extended poor performance by local governments and deterioration of urban environmental conditions, the visible improvements that were realized after the application of EPM are likely to inculcate a greater sense of trust by stakeholders in their municipalities. In other words, more stakeholders will be willing and attracted to participate as basic public services continue to improve. In this regard, intervention through the EPM approach ought to be followed by visible improvements and outcomes, if stakeholder participation is to be sustained.[34]

From the EPM replication initiatives, which could be counterproductive to its institutionalization, variations have been observed. Some donors have not deployed working groups as agents of change. Some of the projects undertaken, though geared toward improvement of community welfare, have not been a result of stakeholder participation or among the identified priority issues. Worse, they do not seem to lead to or create an environment for improved working relationships between local government authorities and local stakeholders. In some cases, the decision to outsource or engage external consultants has been justified by arguments that there exists little or no capacity at the local level. This could be a genuine claim in some upcountry municipalities; however, it underscores the need for local capacity building.

The variations and, in particular, weaknesses in the EPM operationalization are exacerbated by weak coordination and absence of comprehensive monitoring and feedback mechanisms of EPM replication, especially in local authorities that do not have donor support.[35]

6 CONCLUSION

Up to the early 1990s, frustration and dissatisfaction among urban inhabitants and central government alike with the poor performance of the Dar es Salaam City and other municipal councils were widespread. The EPM approach was adopted in Dar es Salaam and later in the other upcountry municipalities, primarily as a tool for boosting the capacity of the councils and their partners to plan and manage urban development.

---

[33] Discussion with Kitilla and Anna Mtani, 23 August 2004 and Mwakalukwa 30 August 2004.

[34] Kombe, W. J. (2001), "Institutionalising the Concept of Environmental Planning and Management (EPM): Successes and Challenges in Dar es Salaam," *Development and Practice*, Vol. 11 Nos. 2 and 3, pp. 190–220.

[35] UASU is mainly overseeing EPM operationalization and performance in the nine municipalities, most of which have donor support for operationalization and institutionalization of EPM.

The Tanzanian experience suggests, through the EPM approach governance can be and has been improved. Through the approach, stakeholders in urban development have come together, identified and prioritized issues of concern, and negotiated and contributed to resolving them through cross-sectoral working groups. The capacities of the City Council of Dar es Salaam and other municipalities that adopted the EPM approach have been substantially improved. Above all, attitudes among bureaucrats and policymakers within and without the local authorities have begun to change. Municipal governments are acknowledging increased local capacities to plan and manage urban development and leveraging of resources. Significant changes have been recorded. Services that have improved include liquid and solid waste management, management of traffic in the central area, natural resource management, and basic community infrastructure services in some unplanned settlements.

The environmental planning and management process and the ongoing Local Government Reforms are not complementary. These ought to be complementary processes so as to respond more effectively to local environment challenges. Whereas the reforms are geared toward improving institutional organization, the deployment of the EPM would cultivate the routine operations in such reformed local councils. Poor cooperation and ineffective coordination of government institutions represent a chronic problem that enactment or amendment of a law such as the Environmental Bill (2004) is unlikely to resolve, as it requires a change of mindset in the management style of government bureaucrats. There is a potential trade-off between realizing long-term change, that is, a process-based outcome, and the need to realize short-term results that directly address burning environmental problems. Scarcity of finances from local sources to implement projects tends to emphasize the trade-offs. However, availability of financial resources alone is not an answer to nonimplementation of action plans.[36]

Mechanisms for systematic monitoring and documentation of the municipality's performance in operationalizing EPM protocol should be put in place. The high participation in and prevalence of stakeholders in working groups, "morning prayers," and, most importantly, institutional reforms effected are the assets for future EPM institutionalization, replication, and overall improvement of urban planning and management in Tanzania.

---

[36] Kittila, M. L. D. (2003), "Monitoring of the Sustainable Cities Programme in Tanzania," unpublished paper.

12 Strategies for Integrated Environmental Governance in South Africa: Toward a More Sustainable Environmental Governance and Land Use Regime

Louis J. Kotzé

1 INTRODUCTION

The corpus of environmental law in South Africa has developed in a rapid fashion since the inception of the new constitutional dispensation in 1994.[1] The National government, to its credit, enacted wide-ranging legislation that essentially aims to place the environmental provisions of the *Constitution of the Republic of South Africa,* 1996 (hereafter the 1996 Constitution) on statutory footing.[2] Section 24 of the 1996 Constitution states that

> Everyone has the right:
> (a) to an environment that is not harmful to their health or well-being; and
> (b) to have the environment protected, for the benefit of present and future generations, through reasonable legislative and other measures that:
>   (i) prevent pollution and ecological degradation;
>   (ii) promote conservation; and
>   (iii) secure ecologically sustainable development and use of natural resources while promoting justifiable economic and social development.

Section 24 contains, among other provisions, directive principles that impose duties on government to protect the environment for present and future generations through

---

[1] Glazewski J, *Environmental Law in South Africa* (Butterworths Durban) (2000) 3, and Centre for Environmental Management, *Report on an Environmental Management System for the North-West Province: Phase I* (Centre for Environmental Management Potchefstroom) (2004) 33. For a discussion on the pre-1994 environmental law regime as well as the rise of environmental concerns in South Africa, see Van Meurs LH, "Private Recourse for Environmental Harm – South Africa" in McCaffrey SC and Lutz RE (eds.), *Environmental Pollution and Individual Rights: An International Symposium* (Kluwer Deventer) (1978) 103–106; and Rabie MA and Fuggle RF, "The Rise of Environmental Concern" in Fuggle RF and Rabie MA (eds.), *Environmental Management in South Africa* (Juta Kenwyn) (1992) 11–25.

[2] This legislation includes, the National Environmental Management Act 107 of 1998, the National Water Act 36 of 1998, the Water Services Act 108 of 1997, the Marine Living Resources Act 18 of 1998, the National Forests Act 84 of 1998, the National Heritage Resources Act 25 of 1999, the National Nuclear Energy Regulator Act 47 of 1999, the National Veld and Forest Fire Act 101 of 1998, the Nuclear Energy Act 46 of 1999, the National Environmental Management: Biodiversity Act 10 of 2004, the National Environmental Management: Protected Areas Act 57 of 2003, and the Mineral and Petroleum Resources Development Act 28 of 2002.

My thanks to Willemien du Plessis for her helpful comments on an earlier draft of this contribution. The views expressed herein and any errors are my own.

reasonable legislative and other measures.[3] It is apparent from section 24 that these legislative and other measures should ensure environmental governance practices that are aimed at the achievement of sustainable results.[4]

The South African environmental governance regime is, however, characterized by fragmentation that may negate the achievement of sustainability.[5] Environmental governance in the context of sustainability may be defined as

> the collection of legislative, executive and administrative functions, processes and instruments used by any organ of state to ensure sustainable behaviour by all as far as governance of environmental activities, products, services, processes and tools are concerned.[6]

Fragmentation includes unaligned environmental governance processes, structures, policies, and procedures; fragmented legislation; vertical fragmentation among the different spheres of government and horizontal fragmentation among the different line functionaries in each sphere; as well as lack of cooperative governance and an integrated approach to environmental management.

Fragmentation is also evident in the current land use management framework in South Africa. Scheepers[7] observes in this regard that land degradation, land denudation, and soil erosion are matters of real concern in South Africa. In terms of a more sustainable land use strategy, it is emphasized that more effective resource-use planning, land- and resource-management strategies, and monitoring and maintenance of land use development are needed.[8] A more sustainable land use strategy may, however, not be achieved because "the responsibility for natural resource management is spread over different national and provincial ministries, each carrying out their jurisdictions as specified by the different Acts they have to implement."[9] The result is that the current legal, institutional, governance, and management frameworks, do not facilitate integrated approaches to land use. An integrated approach to environmental governance efforts and land use issues may accordingly be significant to achieving a sustainable land use strategy in South Africa.

It is argued in this chapter that fragmentation may also inhibit the achievement of sustainable environmental governance efforts in terms of land use issues. The fragmented environmental governance regime is investigated with reference to the nature of fragmentation, reasons for fragmentation, disadvantages of fragmented governance

---

[3] Glazewski, *supra* note 1 at 84–88.

[4] Sustainability is defined for the purpose of this chapter as "the ability to maintain a desired condition over time without eroding natural, social and financial resource bases, through a process of continual improvement in the form of sustainable development. Sustainability furthermore relates to the integration of various considerations, including: the environment, the economy, social factors, environmental governance and management efforts, and public and industry involvement." Adapted from Bosman C, *Waste Disposal or Discharge: A Harmonised Regulatory Framework towards Sustainable Use* (M Sc Environmental Management Dissertation Potchefstroom University for Christian Higher Education) (1999) 8–12.

[5] Centre for Environmental Management, *supra* note 1 at 35.

[6] Nel JG and Du Plessis W, "Unpacking Integrated Environmental Management – a Step Closer to Effective Co-operative Governance?" [2004], SA Public Law 181–190.

[7] Scheepers T, *A Practical Guide to Law and Development: An Introduction to the Law Applicable to Development and the Development Management Process in South Africa* (Juta and Co Ltd Cape Town Kenwyn) (2000) 240.

[8] Ibid.   [9] Ibid.

efforts, and the relevance of fragmentation in terms of land use issues. Two concepts are proposed and investigated that may be utilized to address fragmentation: integrated environmental management (IEM) and cooperative environmental governance (CEG). Four different scenarios that may be utilized to address fragmentation in practice are proposed. These scenarios are based on the concepts of IEM and CEG and are essentially aimed at assisting future efforts to enhance the achievement of integrated and sustainable environmental governance efforts in South Africa.

2 THE FUNDAMENTAL PROBLEM OF FRAGMENTATION

2.1 The Nature of Fragmentation

It has been stated that the environmental governance sphere in South Africa is fundamentally fragmented. Fragmentation entails, fragmentation among the three autonomous areas of government at national, provincial, and local spheres and fragmented and disjointed governance structures along separate, autonomous line functioning organs of state that operate at national, provincial, and local spheres of government.[10] Fragmented governance structures result in fragmented governance processes that culminate in fragmented policies. As a result, disjointed and fragmented legislation emanates from separate policy processes. The separate organs of state are furthermore organized either to focus on specific environmental media[11] or to address individually and sectorally-based issues.[12] Fragmented governance structures also result in disjointed and incremental governance processes that are inefficient, with significant duplication and overlap of both governance mandates and adoption and use of governance tools, including those employed in land use management and other environmental governance efforts.[13]

In light of the foregoing, it may be derived that fragmentation of the environmental governance regime manifests in a matrix framework of fragmented structures, institutions, legislation, policies, governance tools, processes, and procedures.

2.2 Reasons for Fragmentation

The existence of this fragmentation may be attributed to, inter alia, historical developments of the South African governmental sphere, especially in relation to South Africa's

---

[10] Apart from the three spheres of government, various autonomous environmental departments, or line functions, are established in each governmental sphere. The environmental governance mandate in South Africa is thus executed by various environmental departments that have been created along a silo-based and sectoral framework that, in turn, is based on different environmental media, including air, water, and land. These line functionaries in each sphere include the Department of Environmental Affairs and Tourism, the Department of Water Affairs and Forestry, the Department of Minerals and Energy, and the South African Heritage Resource Agency.

[11] Environmental media in this context include land, air, and water.

[12] These issues may include mining, radioactivity, water affairs, air quality control, land use and development planning, biodiversity, and heritage resources.

[13] Nel JG, Kotzé LJ, and Snyman E, "Strategies to Integrate Environmental Policy at the Operational Level: Towards an Integrated Framework for Environmental Authorisations" 2–3, unpublished paper delivered at the Berlin Conference on the Human Dimensions of Global Environmental Change: Greening of Policies – Interlinkages and Policy Integration, Berlin, December 2004.

colonial and apartheid past. Former colonies tend to replicate the judicial, executive, legislative, and administrative structures of the former motherland.[14] An imbalance is accordingly created because when these structures are imposed, they create a wide gulf between formal procedures and actual practices, yielding fragmented structures, processes, and governance.[15] Developing countries such as South Africa, furthermore, inherited fragmented and uncoordinated legislation that paid little attention to sustainability and to the need for an integrated, ecosystem-oriented legal regime that permits a holistic view of the ecosystem and of the interrelationships and interactions within it.[16] Rather than advocating sustainability and an integrated approach to environmental management, past practices, legislation, and policies were essentially concerned with the facilitation of resource allocation and resource exploitation.[17]

Furthermore, in the environmental context, South Africa does not have a centralized lead agent to control environmental matters directly in an integrated fashion.[18] This is because the Department of Environmental Affairs and Tourism (DEAT) does not assume the role of a strong, centralized lead agent that has total control and jurisdiction over all environmental matters.[19] The DEAT only has jurisdiction to execute certain environmental governance tasks, for example, environmental impact assessment, whereas sectoral issues such as water, energy, mining, and management of cultural heritage resources are under the jurisdiction of other autonomous environmental departments. The DEAT accordingly rather acts as a coordinator by providing framework guidance.[20] Hence, it may be derived that South Africa's decentralized environmental governance structure results in fragmented environmental management and governance efforts. It is emphasized in this regard that fragmentation is a direct result of South Africa's decentralized environmental governance structure, which leads to a general disregard of, and need for, integrated structures.[21]

A further reason for fragmented environmental management is possible confusion and duplication created by fragmented environmental legislation. For example, authorizations for waste disposal sites may be duplicated and overlap may occur. Section 20 of the Environment Conservation Act 73 of 1989 requires that no person shall establish, provide, or operate any waste disposal site without a permit issued by the Minister of the Department of Water Affairs and Forestry (DWAF). Sections 21(f) and 21(g) of

---

[14] Sharkansky I, *Public Administration: Policy-Making in Government Agencies*, 2nd ed. (Markham Publishing Company Chicago) (1972) 32.

[15] Ibid.

[16] Du Plessis W and Nel JG, "An Evaluation of NEMA Based on a Generic Framework for Environmental Framework Legislation" [2001], *South African Journal of Environmental Law and Policy* 2.

[17] Ibid.

[18] Centre for Environmental Management, *supra* note 1 at 64.

[19] Lawrence R, "How Manageable Is South Africa's New Framework of Environmental Management?" [1999], *South African Journal of Environmental Law and Policy* 61–65, furthermore highlights the difficulties that DEAT experiences by stating that the department "has had to jostle for attention and resources. It has not been a prestigious portfolio in Cabinet, nor has it been a department that commanded a large slice of the national budget." Ibid.

[20] Kotzé LJ, "Co-operative Environmental Governance: Towards the Establishment of an Integrated Authorisation System for the North-West Province" in "Co-operative Environmental Governance: In Search for the Holy Grail," 168, paper delivered at the Annual Conference of the International Association for Impact Assessment: South Africa, September 2003, George, South Africa. See also Du Plessis and Nel, *supra* note 16 at 26–27.

[21] Glazewski, *supra* note 1 at 129–132.

the National Water Act 36 of 1998 contain similar provisions that require a water-use license issued by DWAF for discharging waste or water containing waste into a water resource through a pipe, canal, sewer, sea outfall, or other conduit and disposing of waste in a manner that may detrimentally impact on a water resource. Two different authorizations for the same activity, based on two different administrative processes and acts, are required.

Glazewski[22] notes that a further reason for fragmentation may be the very nature of environmental management. Environmental management in the South African context seeks to encompass a vast variety of considerations, inter alia, natural resources, cultural resources, pollution control, land use planning, and waste management. It is accordingly a broadly defined concept that has to fit within the narrowly defined functional areas of government.[23] The latter may create further confusion and essentially gives rise to a real need for coordination, cooperation, and integration.

The problem of fragmentation is exacerbated by the 1996 Constitution, which established nine new provinces.[24] This led to geographical fragmentation whereby jurisdictions do not always correlate with legislative mandates. It may also lead to the encroachment of various environmental departments, or line functionaries, in the jurisdictional areas of line functionaries and departments that are not principally responsible for environmental governance, and vice versa. Glazewski[25] observes in this regard that the various provincial departments of environmental affairs that function under the coordination of DEAT "have no consistent or logical home in the new provinces and in each case environmental affairs finds itself with some odd bedfellows."[26]

2.3 Fragmentation and Land Use Issues

The land use management regime in South Africa forms an integral part of the entire environmental governance effort. Land use lies at the core of some of the most contentious issues surrounding development initiatives. This is especially true in the case of developing countries such as South Africa. During consideration of the viability of a proposed development, some pertinent issues need to be addressed, including the impact of development on the environment, job creation, economic growth, poverty alleviation, and provision of housing and physical infrastructure.[27] A central component in these considerations is administrative decision making by way of environmental governance efforts. Prior to the new constitutional dispensation in South Africa, governance in relation to land use was essentially concerned with development of the former "white" areas, whereas a "crude and rudimentary planning system" applied in the historically African areas.[28] The emphasis was on social engineering, rather than on environmental

---

[22] Glazewski, *supra* note 1 at 131.

[23] Ibid.

[24] Section 103 of the 1996 Constitution.

[25] Glazewski, *supra* note 1 at 130.

[26] Further confusion is attributed to the fact that nature conservation is in some instances located in a different department than the environmental departments that are traditionally deemed to be responsible for execution of environmental management functions. See Glazewski, *supra* note 1 at 130, and Du Plessis W, "Integration of Existing Environmental Legislation in the Provinces" (1995), *South African Journal of Environmental Law and Policy* 23–36.

[27] Glazewski, *supra* note 1 at 229–230.

[28] Ibid. at 231. Glazeski observes that "the apartheid [*sic*] city, although fragmented along racial lines, integrated an urban economic logic that systematically favoured white urban areas at the cost of black urban and peri-urban areas." Ibid. See *Fedsure Life Assurance v. Greater Johannesburg Transitional*

governance.[29] Past practices pertaining to land use were accordingly significantly influenced by the apartheid ideology with largely unsustainable consequences. It has been observed in this regard that past land use practices were essentially control oriented, rather than development oriented, reactive rather than proactive, and blueprint oriented rather than process oriented.[30] The result is that the current land use and planning framework is to a large extent fragmented, unequal, and incoherent.[31] This point has been reiterated in the High Court of South Africa:

> The present application illustrates that the statutory framework regulating town planning and building regulations in its present form is fragmented and cumbersome in the extreme. . . . It requires a vast bureaucratic machine to administer all these provisions. . . . The system also frequently . . . gives rise to conflicting and inconsistent decisions taken by different functionaries, officials and organs at different levels of local and provincial government. It would be of great assistance to everyone involved in the process . . . if the administrative machinery required to regulate these matters could be consolidated, simplified and streamlined.[32]

Land use (excluding environmental issues) is currently regulated by various separate, yet interrelated acts, including the Physical Planning Act 125 of 1991, the Conservation of Agricultural Resources Act 43 of 1983, the Mountain Catchment Areas Act 63 of 1970, the Development Facilitation Act 15 of 1994, the Local Government Transition Act 209 of 1993, the Local Government Municipal Structures Act 117 of 1998, the Communal Property Associations Act 28 of 1996, and the Restitution of Land Rights Act 22 of 1994.[33] Apart from these various national acts, land use and planning are furthermore regulated by a vast number of provincial ordinances and laws.[34] Environmental issues are referred to in only some of the post-1994 legislation.

It is clear in this instance that environmental governance efforts relating to land use in South Africa are fragmented along various acts that either directly or indirectly influence land use issues. Consequently, the administration of these acts is also fragmented along the various spheres of government and different line functionaries in each sphere that are responsible for the execution of environmental governance mandates with responsibilities of these acts.[35] It is proposed that this fragmented land use management regime may not sufficiently assist in addressing issues such as poverty

---

Metropolitan Council 1998 12 BCLR 1458 CC. See also Claassen PE and Milton JRL, "Land-Use Planning" in Fuggle and Rabie, *supra* note 1 at 718–738, for a comprehensive discussion on the pre-1994 land use dispensation.

[29] The first environmental impact assessment regulations were, for example, only introduced in 1995.

[30] Claassen and Milton, *supra* note 28 at 716.   [31] Glazewski, *supra* note 1 at 232.

[32] *Camps Bay Ratepayers and Residents Association and Others v. The Minister of Planning, Culture and Administration (Western Cape) and Others*, Unreported Case, Cape High Court, No. 6455/98 dated 4 August 1998, as quoted and discussed in Glazewski, *supra* note 1 at 233.

[33] Other acts that are applicable to land use include the Provision of Land and Assistance Act 126 of 1993, the Interim Protection of Informal Land Rights Act 31 of 1996, the Extension of Security of Tenure Act 62 of 1997, the Prevention of Illegal Eviction from an Unlawful Occupation of Land Act 19 of 1998, the NEMA, the National Water Act 36 of 1998, the Marine Living Resources Act 18 of 1998, the National Forests Act 84 of 1998, and the National Veld and Forest Fire Act 101 of 1998. For a more detailed discussion of these acts, see Scheepers, *supra* note 7 at 62–95.

[34] Glazewski, *supra* note 1 at 233.

[35] For a comprehensive discussion, see Glazewski, *supra* note 1 at 235–239.

alleviation, economic growth, environmental protection, and infrastructural development in a sustainable fashion.

2.4 Disadvantages of Fragmentation

Fragmentation poses several disadvantages, which may include duplication and overlap of the governance effort, with all organs of state focusing on environmental authorization processes without available resources to do postauthorization follow-up; costly delays in decision making; inefficient arrangements between organs of state that control similar activities or proposals; significant gaps in control arrangements, while some pertinent issues are not controlled at all; inconsistent behavior by government officials; conflicting conditions in authorizations; ineffective governance; and externalization of governmental inefficiencies to development costs, which may result in negative impacts on development in South Africa.[36] Moreover, it is evident from this exposition that the various disadvantages posed by fragmentation may ultimately inhibit the achievement of sustainability.

Subsequent sections argue that IEM and CEG may address fragmentation, as described previously.

3 INTEGRATED ENVIRONMENTAL MANAGEMENT

3.1 Environmental Management in South Africa

Environmental management may be defined as management skills and techniques implemented to achieve the principles of sustainability at all levels, including the macrolevel (government) and the microlevel (private sector).[37] The principles of sustainability include the precautionary approach, the polluter pays principle, the cradle to grave principle, the principle of an integrated and holistic approach, the principle that due consideration must be given to all alternatives, the principle of continual improvement, accountability and liability, and transparency and democracy.[38] Environmental management necessitates planned controls to achieve a desired ultimate outcome. The execution of planned controls is commonly referred to as *management* in its broadest possible form.[39] When planned controls are applied to aspects directly or indirectly relating to the environment, one arguably deals with environmental management. It is important to note that environmental management is not "management of the environment." It is rather "management of activities within tolerable constraints imposed by the environment itself, and with full consideration of ecological factors."[40] Hence, environmental management is the management of the activities of people in the environment and management of resultant effects of these activities on the environment. This view is supported by Bosman,[41] who states that "environmental management should not be confused with the management (manipulation) of the natural

---

[36] Nel, Kotzé, and Snyman, *supra* note 13 at 3.

[37] Bosman, *supra* note 4 at 123.   [38] Ibid.

[39] Fuggle RF, "Environmental Management: An Introduction" in Fuggle and Rabie, *supra* note 1 at 3.

[40] Beale JG, *The Manager and the Environment: General Theory and Practice of Environmental Management* (Pergamon Press Oxford) (1980) 20.

[41] Bosman, *supra* note 4 at 10.

environment (nature conservation and the management of plants and animals) but must be seen as the management of the activities of people within the carrying capacity of environmental systems." The latter reflects the notion that environmental management should guide the activities of people through governance, with the involvement of government, civil society, and industry, to achieve a desired outcome, namely, that of sustainability.

3.2 Integration in Terms of IEM

Environmental management, as a specific management paradigm, and specifically an integrated approach to environmental management, is one of the options that may be utilized to address fragmentation of the South African environmental governance regime. Integration is one of the fundamental aspects of IEM. The question of what should be integrated in terms of IEM warrants further exploration. It is proposed in this chapter that integration should primarily include integration of the three spheres of government, environmental media, different line functionaries of government, the Deming management approach (discussed later), the project life cycle, and different tools for environmental management.[42]

Integration of these various aspects is explained as follows: The South African government consists of national, provincial, and local spheres.[43] Each sphere, in turn, consists of various line functionaries. Environmental line functionaries include DEAT, DWAF, and DME. Some of these line functionaries are also represented at the provincial and local levels.[44] Integration of the various spheres and line functionaries of government may contribute to the alignment of environmental governance efforts. Alignment in this context arguably refers to uniform institutional policy, project and decision processes, and structures relating to environmental governance.

The traditional Deming management approach is an outcomes-based management approach that uses a process of continual improvement. It encompasses four actions that must be performed during the process of executing planned controls:[45] planning, doing, checking, and acting (PDCA), in that sequence.[46] The project life cycle is a further important element that needs to be integrated, and it strongly correlates with the Deming management approach. The project life cycle is specifically applicable to certain projects, whether initiated by government or by industry. It includes planning and design, construction and decommissioning, operations, and decommissioning.[47] The project life cycle is divided into a planning and design component and an implementation component, and each of these components has distinct phases with different implications in terms of their environmental impact.[48] For example, environmental impact assessment is only applicable to the planning and design component; IEM is

---

[42] Nel and Du Plessis, *supra* note 6 at 189–190.
[43] Section 40(1) of the 1996 Constitution.   [44] Glazewski, *supra* note 1 at 130–132.
[45] Kreitner R and Kinicki A, *Organizational Behavior* 6th ed. (McGraw-Hill New York) (2004) 16.
[46] See Later FK, "Vergunning op Hoofdzaken in de Praktijk" in Uylenburg R and Van der Wilt CJ (eds.), *De Milieuvergunning in Ontwikkeling* (Samson Alpen aan de Rijn) (1999) 29, and Global Environmental Management Initiative, *Total Quality Environmental Management: The Primer* (GEMI Washington) (1993) 7–8, for a more detailed discussion of the Deming management approach.
[47] Centre for Environmental Management, *supra* note 1 at 64–65.
[48] Ibid.

applicable to the whole of the project life cycle, including the implementation or operational component.

Various tools are available for implementing IEM, including, command and control tools, fiscally based tools, civilly based tools, and agreements.[49] For the purpose of this chapter, it is especially important that tools employed in land use management such as environmental authorizations and environmental impact assessment be integrated in environmental management and governance efforts. IEM tools (such as environmental authorizations in the form of, inter alia, water use licenses), waste disposal permits, and registration certificates are typically used during the implementation component of the project life cycle. It is specifically during the operational phase of the cycle that government, including all three spheres and all relevant line functionaries in each sphere, become involved in IEM, since environmental governance may be executed by way of, inter alia, regulation through environmental governance tools. It is accordingly necessary that aligned governance efforts through integrated processes and tools be established in order to achieve sustainable results.

The environment furthermore consists of different media, including air, land, and water. The necessity for integrating the various environmental media is evident from the holistic approach of IEM and the integrated, holistic and interrelated nature of the environment as defined by the National Environmental Management Act 107 of 1998 (NEMA). *Environment* is defined in section 1 of the NEMA as

> the surroundings within which humans exist and that are made up of –
> (i) the land, water and atmosphere of the earth;
> (ii) micro-organisms, plant and animal life;
> (iii) any part or combination of (i) and (ii) and the interrelationships among and between them; and the physical, chemical, aesthetic and cultural properties and conditions of the foregoing that influence human health and well-being.

Environment, in the context of the environmental management paradigm, is used in its broadest possible form and includes biophysical, social, economic, historical, cultural, and political aspects.[50] The emphasis is, furthermore, on the integrated nature of the environment with recognition that all elements may be combined and that there exists an interrelationship among the elements. It is thus clear that the term *environment* designates an all-encompassing and holistic concept that necessitates an integrated approach, because if one element or aspect of the environment is affected, whether positively or negatively, it may also have an effect on the other elements. It is furthermore argued that there exists a close correlation between the definition of environment and the objectives of IEM enumerated in section 23 of the NEMA. Section 23 states:

> 23 (2) The general objective of integrated environmental management is to:
> (a) promote the integration of the principles of environmental management set out in section 2 into the making of all decisions which may have a significant effect on the environment;
> (b) identify, predict and evaluate the actual and potential impact on the environment, socio-economic conditions and cultural heritage, the risks and consequences and alternatives and options for mitigation of activities, with a view

---

[49] Ibid.

[50] Bosman, *supra* note 4 at 10.

to minimising negative impacts, maximising benefits, and promoting compliance with the principles of environmental management set out in section 2;
(c) ensure that the effects of activities on the environment receive adequate
consideration before actions are taken in connection with them;
(d) ensure adequate and appropriate opportunity for public participation in
decisions that may affect the environment;
(e) ensure the consideration of environmental attributes in management and
decision-making which may have a significant effect on the environment; and
identify and employ the modes of environmental management best suited to
ensuring that a particular activity is pursued in accordance with the principles
of environmental management set out in section 2.

The objectives of IEM espoused by section 23 clearly emphasize the integrated nature
of IEM. The definition of *environment* and the objectives of IEM accordingly seem to
embrace the holistic character of a management paradigm that requires an integrated
approach to a holistic and interrelated phenomenon. This observation furthermore
correlates with section 2(b) of the NEMA, which requires environmental management
to be integrated by acknowledging that all elements of the environment are linked and
interrelated. It must also take into account the effects of decisions on all aspects of the
environment and all people in the environment by pursuing the selection of the best
practicable environmental option.[51] Hence, all aspects relevant to and falling within the
ambit of the definition of *environment* in the NEMA underpin the concept of IEM. IEM
should accordingly not be aimed at shifting pollutants from different environmental
media, but rather to addressing pollutants in an integrated way according to the tolerable
constraints of the environment and within the carrying capacity of natural systems.

It may be concluded from the foregoing that *integration* in terms of IEM includes
integration or alignment of authorization arrangements among the various spheres of
government; integration or alignment of authorization arrangements within the same
sphere of government, but between various line functions; recognition of the integrated
nature of the environmental management cycle to include all PDCA elements of the
Deming management approach; recognition of the need to address all the phases of
a project or development cycle, from planning and design through authorization, to
construction and use, including postauthorization follow-up and verification of conformance to authorization conditions by competent authorities; integrated use of various
environmental governance tools and implementation strategies, including command
and control, fiscal, and civil instruments, as well as agreements to ensure sustainable
governance efforts; recognition of the human–environment system as a closed system
that requires an integrated perspective on the various environmental media in order to
prevent intramedia transfer of impacts; alignment of governance policies and strategies
across the various spheres and autonomous line functions; alignment of administrative
practices, procedures, and instrumentation of separate, autonomous line functions of
all spheres and line functions to achieve effective and integrated service delivery efforts;
integration among the various spheres and line functionaries of government; integration of the environmental management cycle; and integration of decision-making cycles
in the environmental management process.[52]

---

[51] Section 2(b) of the NEMA.
[52] Centre for Environmental Management, *supra* note 1 at 65.

In light of the foregoing discussion, *IEM* may be defined as

The management of the activities of people at micro and macro level to ensure achievement of the principles of sustainability, notably to ensure the utilisation of natural resources provided by all environmental media within their carrying capacities, while promoting economic growth as a primary objective, by ensuring the implementation of decision-making and management tools for environmental management; based on the Deming-management approach, for the different phases of the project life-cycle through the integration of the activities between the different spheres of government; and within their various line functions.[53]

It is proposed that the integrated nature of IEM may serve as a foundation for initiatives that are aimed at addressing the fragmented environmental governance and land use regimes in South Africa, since it is specifically the fragmented structures, processes, and tools for environmental governance that IEM has as its objective to integrate.

4 COOPERATIVE ENVIRONMENTAL GOVERNANCE

4.1 Introduction

Criticism of the effectiveness of environmental law in South Africa focuses less on the content thereof than on the lack of adequate enforcement of the current environmental law regime.[54] The administration of environmental law, development of environmental law, and improvement in the quality of its enforcement by government are generally regarded as the main reasons for the ineffectiveness of the constitutionally entrenched right contained in section 24 of the 1996 Constitution and legislative provisions incidental thereto.[55] This criticism essentially refers to the existence of fragmentation and lack of cooperation, which is ubiquitous in the current fragmented environmental governance dispensation.[56]

It is proposed that cooperative governance may provide a possible solution to address fragmentation that is prevalent in the South African environmental governance and land use regimes. The emphasis of cooperative environmental governance, or *CEG*, as it is referred to for the purpose of this chapter, is on cooperation in order to address, inter alia, fragmentation in terms of the structures, procedures, processes, and governance tools that government uses to execute environmental governance mandates. Subsequent sections focus on the importance of cooperative governance for environmental matters. The nature of CEG is discussed and the integrative and cooperative elements of CEG are investigated with reference to legislative provisions thereon. This investigation aims to assist in the formulation of a plausible definition of this concept in order to indicate the relevance of CEG as a strategy to address fragmentation.

---

[53] Kotzé LJ, "A Legal Framework for Integrated Environmental Governance in South Africa and the North-West Province" (Unpublished LLD thesis, North West University) (2005), 67.

[54] De Waal J, Currie I, and Erasmus G, *The Bill of Rights Handbook*, 4th ed. (Juta Landsdowne) (2001) 402.

[55] Ibid.

[56] It should also be noted in this regard that the imperative for coordination and integration in government is not a new phenomenon. The achievement of holistic governance and coordination across the organizational instruments of government is described as the eternal problem in governance, hence rendering it not only a domestic concern, but also a global problem. See 6 P et al., *Towards Holistic Governance: The New Reform Agenda* (Palgrave Hampshire) (2002) 9.

4.2 Cooperative Governance and the Environment

The very fact that different organs of state are sometimes required to cooperate on certain matters during governance activities necessitates cooperative governance.[57] This necessarily acknowledges the existence of intergovernmental relations. These relations are manifested in a vertical and a horizontal sense. Whereas the vertical relationship mainly refers to provision of financial and other aid, the horizontal relationship may be described as a compact that permits the "joint administration of public services; agreements to share information or technical assistance; reciprocal legislation that permits the citizens of one jurisdiction to receive certain services within another jurisdiction [and legislation that permits administrative organs to render certain administrative services in another jurisdiction]; and the membership of governmental officials in organizations that seek to develop solutions for common problems."[58] This is also true for environmental governance in South Africa. Whereas the national sphere of government is responsible for the allocation of funds to the other spheres of government as well as other line functionaries, the vertical and horizontal relationships within the environmental governance structure emphasize that various organs and officials are necessarily dependent on one another.

It is further argued that because the environment is a holistic, integrated, and interrelated phenomenon unconfined by boundaries, environmental problems may require solutions, and cooperation on problem-solving strategies, from all spheres and line functionaries of government relevant to the particular environmental problem. The need for cooperative governance in environmental matters is also evident from the fact that most potential environmental impacts and pollution problems affect public goods, such as public health and resources.[59] The implication is that the control of potential impacts on humans and the environment is a regulatory function, since society must be protected from pollution by government action.[60] Because of vertical and horizontal fragmentation, as well as the necessity for cooperation among organs of state in their interrelationship with one another, cooperative governance also becomes relevant in the context of environmental governance. Emphasis should therefore be placed on environmental governance that is based on participation and cooperation in mutual

---

[57] Not all governmental functions are exercised by one single organ of state, because *environment* is specifically designated in section 104 and Schedule 4 of the 1996 Constitution as a matter of concurrent national and provincial competence. In addition, Chapter 3 of the 1996 Constitution provides for national, provincial, and local spheres of government, which are required to perform different functions unique to each sphere. It is noted in this regard that these provisions may in some way also contribute to the (existence) (problem?) of fragmentation, since they provide for environmental governance to be executed not by a single sphere, but by more than one. The latter corresponds with the existing decentralized environmental governance structure in South Africa, where the DEAT has an advisory and guiding role with regard to the various different line functionaries. This system may contribute to vertical and horizontal fragmentation in the total environmental governance structure.

[58] Sharkansky, *supra* note 14 at 292.

[59] Smith A, *Integrated Pollution Control: Change and Continuity in the UK Industrial Pollution Policy Network* (Ashgate Publishing Limited Aldershot) (1997) 6–7, and Hughes OE, *Public Management and Administration: An Introduction*, 2nd ed. (Macmillan Press Ltd London) (1998) 97–98, 103.

[60] 6 P. et al. *supra* note 56 at 26, also acknowledges the fact that government has a positive, albeit limited in some instances, role to play in addressing the interests of society at large through governance. It is specifically stated that the reason for this is that "society's problems are not simply conditions to be lived with." Society's problems and interests are rather the main impetus behind governance.

and reciprocal relationships among all government departments and spheres involved with environmental governance. Put in another way, for environmental governance to be effective, cooperative strategies must be a primary objective of environmental governance efforts.[61] The same may be said for governance efforts pertaining to land use.

The reasons for the importance of cooperative governance in the environmental context may therefore be summarized as including the desire to create an agreeable and convenient work environment for government officials, concern that programs of other administrative organs may affect in-house programs, the desire to support one's own projects that are funded by other administrative organs, the desire to protect the interests of the public from possible effects of programs initiated by other organs, and the desire to build rapport with other administrative organs.[62]

4.3 Legislative Provisions on Cooperative Governance

In South Africa, cooperative governance is an acknowledged governance model with its primary objective to align fragmented governance processes. This is evident from the provisions of the 1996 Constitution and the NEMA. Whereas the 1996 Constitution provides for the foundation and constitutional obligation to execute cooperative governance, certain principles, tools, procedures, and structures are provided for by the NEMA to facilitate CEG. The provisions on cooperative governance are significant because they arguably recognize the fragmented nature of the South African environmental governance structure. They moreover acknowledge that governance is based on intergovernmental relations that must be effected by way of vertical and horizontal cooperation.[63] The objectives of these provisions are arguably to foster consultative, cooperative, public participatory, open, administratively just, democratic, and accountable governance.

Constitutional Provisions

Chapter 3 of the 1996 Constitution, and more specifically section 41(1), provide for the principles of cooperative governance by stating, inter alia, that

> All spheres of government and all organs of state within each sphere must: . . .
> (e) respect the constitutional status, institutions, powers and functions of government in other spheres;
> (f) not assume any power or function except those conferred on them in terms of the Constitution;
> (g) exercise their powers and perform their functions in a manner that does not encroach on the geographical, functional or institutional integrity of government in another sphere;
> (h) co-operate with one another in mutual trust and good faith by –
> (i) fostering friendly relations;
> (ii) assisting and supporting one another;

---

[61] 6 P. et al., *supra* note 56 at 9.
[62] Sharkansky, *supra* note 14 at 306, and May PJ et al., *Environmental Management and Governance: Intergovernmental Approaches to Hazards and Sustainability* (Routledge London) (1996) 3–7.
[63] Sharkansky, *supra* note 14 at 273.

> (iii) informing one another of, and consulting one another on matters of common interest;
> (iv) co-ordinating their actions and legislation with one another;
> (v) adhering to agreed procedures; and
> (vi) avoiding legal proceedings against one another.

Chapter 3 of the 1996 Constitution provides for national, provincial, and local spheres of government, which are required to perform different functions unique to each sphere.[64] The execution of these distinct governmental functions should, however, be based on the constitutionally entrenched principle of cooperative governance. The principles of cooperative governance and intergovernmental relations govern the relationships among national, provincial, and local spheres of government as well as the different line functionaries. It is argued that these principles advocate a cooperative form of "federalism," which preempts sharing of the same responsibilities by different spheres and line functionaries of government.[65] Sharkansky[66] notes that federalism in this context explains the situation in which the inputs to an administrative organ are sometimes the outputs of another administrative organ in a different sphere or line functionary of government. Cooperative governance thus offers the impetus for governance based on participation and cooperation in mutual and reciprocal relationships, in order to facilitate the process whereby the activities of one administrative organ may affect those of another.[67]

The constitutional provisions relating to the South African governmental structure furthermore continually use *spheres* rather than *levels* of government. It is argued that this mainly attempts to move away from the past held notion that there exists a hierarchical order of spheres that is more or less powerful than another tier.[68] Furthermore, it moves away from the notion of "the old traditional stratified three-tier system of a central government at the top (and therefore the strongest), a second provincial tier in the middle and a local tier (the weakest) at the bottom."[69] It rather strives to describe the very nature of cooperative governance, where different spheres are individually but jointly responsible for different functions. Environmental governance is a good example of an instance in which all three spheres and line functions of government are required to establish and enforce legislative measures pertaining to a single and shared subject – namely, the environment. The competence to oversee matters that relate to the environment is thus shared by the different spheres and line functionaries on the basis that each sphere and line function is responsible for the particular governance

---

[64] Section 40(1) states that in South Africa, government is constituted as national, provincial, and local spheres that are distinctive, interdependent, and interrelated.

[65] De Waal, Currie, and Erasmus, *supra* note 54 at 23.

[66] Sharkansky, *supra* note 14 at 273.

[67] Bray E, "Focus on the National Environmental Management Act: Co-operative Governance in the Context of the National Environmental Management Act 107 of 1998" [1999], *South African Journal of Environmental Law and Policy* 3.

[68] Carpenter G, "Co-operative Government, Devolution of Powers and Subsidiarity: The South African Perspective" *Konrad Adenauer Stiftung Seminar on Sub-national Constitutional Governance* [1999] 49, Glazewski, *supra* note 1 at 128, and Bray, *supra* note 66 at 4. Sharkansky, *supra* note 14 at 305, also notes with regard to superior and inferior levels of government that it is "an oversimplification to assume that the involvement of a superior level of administration permits that organization to control its subordinate associates." Sharkansky, *supra* note 14 at 305.

[69] Carpenter, *supra* note 68 at 51.

that best suits its structure, resources, reach, dimension, and nature. The provisions of Chapter 3 of the 1996 Constitution are not aimed at diminishing the sovereignty of any organ of state at the expense of another. They rather presuppose and emphasize the willingness of all spheres of government to work together. For this to materialize, it is essential that conflict between laws and policies be prevented and the administration of the implementation of these laws be clearly defined in a matrix framework by way of coordination, cooperation, and alignment.[70]

NEMA Provisions

Apart from the concept of cooperative governance as enumerated by the constitutional provisions, certain principles, procedures, tools, and structures are furthermore established by the NEMA to give effect to cooperative governance. Chapter 1 of the NEMA contains a set of environmental management principles that constitute the foundation of all activities to be undertaken under the provisions of this framework act. These principles include the polluter pays principle, the precautionary principle, the duty-of-care principle, the principle of sustainability, the principle of environmental justice, the principle of integrated environmental management and governance, the principle of transparency and public participation, and, more importantly, the principle of intergovernmental coordination and harmonization of policies, legislation, and actions relating to the environment.[71] It is argued that these principles may serve as a useful tool to establish integration, since the principles are cross-cutting and apply to all sectoral environmental policies and legislation. In the case of actual or potential conflicts of interest between organs of state, the NEMA states that such conflicts should also be resolved through appropriate conflict resolution procedures.[72]

Chapter 2 of the NEMA provides for the establishment of the National Environmental Advisory Forum (NEAF), which is representative of all relevant stakeholders in environmental governance.[73] The NEAF has as its main objective to act as an advisory body for the Minister of DEAT on matters pertaining to environmental management and governance by setting objectives and priorities for environmental governance.[74] Although not explicitly stated, these objectives and priorities may arguably include any matter pertaining to the achievement of cooperative governance.

Section 7 establishes the Committee for Environmental Co-ordination (CEC). The CEC primarily strives to coordinate and integrate the implementation of all governmental policies pertaining to environmental management and governance. It is proposed that the establishment of the CEC is of special importance to the practical and day-to-day establishment, execution, regulation, and facilitation of cooperative governance at a policy level.

Chapter 3 of the NEMA deals with procedures for cooperative governance. Section 11 provides for the preparation of environmental implementation and management plans by national departments. In preparation of such plans, national departments must, in the spirit of cooperative governance, take into consideration all existing plans with a view to ultimately achieving consistency among such plans.[75] Environmental implementation

---

[70] De Waal, Curie, and Erasmus, *supra* note 54 at 24.
[71] Section 2.
[72] Section 2(4)(l)–Section 2(4)(m).
[73] Section 3.
[74] Section 3(1)–Section 3(2).
[75] Section 11(4).

plans and environmental management plans address core issues of cooperative governance by aiming to coordinate and harmonize environmental policies, plans, programs, and decisions of various national, provincial, and local organs of state. The coordination and harmonization responsibility specifically strives, inter alia, to minimize duplication of procedures and functions of organs of state, to promote consistency of functions, and to give effect to the provisions of cooperative governance set out in Chapter 3 of the NEMA.[76]

It is clear from the preceding discussion that cooperative governance is an established management strategy that may be employed by government to address fragmentation. It is furthermore clear that the idea is that all three spheres of government should strengthen capacity, supervised by way of supportive practices; employ assistance through legislative measures; and enable one another to facilitate governance effectively by way of cooperation.[77]

4.4 CEG Defined

CEG is a relatively novel concept in South African environmental law. Few definitions thereof, at least from an academic point of view, exist. *CEG* has been defined as meaning, inter alia, "the evolution of devolved governance, involving discussions, agreements and a combination of formal and informal regulation between industry, the public/stakeholders and government departments."[78] It is therefore aimed at the promotion of integrated service delivery and stakeholder involvement by government departments and all other interested and affected parties involved with the environment. In the preceding context, CEG arguably does not refer only to cooperation among the various spheres of government in the execution of their duties, its ambit is far greater.[79] It encompasses cooperation and coordination among the different spheres of government, at international and interregional levels as well as on an intragovernmental level.[80] It furthermore refers to the alignment of policies, plans, and programs across the different spheres of government and the different line functionaries within each sphere.[81] It also entails procedures and processes for the empowerment of civil society and industry to engage actively in environmental governance.[82] The foregoing describes an interactive and all-inclusive process that should ultimately make possible cooperation and exchange of information by stakeholders, better decision making, and the achievement of more outcomes that are acceptable for all.[83]

---

[76] Section 12(a)–(b).   [77] Bray, *supra* note 67 at 4.

[78] Boer A, O' Beirne S, and Greyling T, "The Quest for Co-operative Environmental Governance: Do Stakeholders Have a Consistent Map and Directions?" in "Co-operative Environmental Governance: In Search for the Holy Grail," 10, paper delivered at the Annual Conference of the International Association for Impact Assessment: South Africa, September 2003, George, South Africa.

[79] CEG includes more than the narrowly defined concept of governance that refers to mechanisms and relations between state departments. The concept is much broader and also includes the public sector, private sector, and all stakeholders that may be directly or indirectly involved with the environment. Boer, O' Beirne, and Greyling, *supra* note 77 at 9.

[80] Nel and Du Plessis, *supra* note 16 at 8.

[81] Ibid.   [82] Ibid.

[83] Bulman R, "Instant Governance: Just Add Civil Society – No Mess, No Fuss" in "Co-operative Environmental Governance: In Search for the Holy Grail," 36, paper delivered at the Annual Conference of the International Association for Impact Assessment: South Africa, September 2003, George, South Africa.

In that light, *CEG*, in the South African context, may be defined as

> the integration of the different spheres of government and line functionaries at inter-national, intra-regional and intra-governmental level; co-operation between indi-vidual government officials in each sphere/line functionary; co-operation between government officials in different spheres/line functionaries; integration of policy, regulation methods and tools, service provision and scrutiny; and co-operation with industry and the public in order to achieve the principles of sustainability.[84]

It is proposed that the integrated and cooperative nature of CEG may contribute significantly to enhance endeavors that are aimed at addressing fragmentation of the current South African environmental governance sphere.

5 POSSIBLE SCENARIOS TO ADDRESS FRAGMENTATION

Despite integration strategies available to address fragmentation, evidence suggests that fragmentation and uncooperative governance practices persist in South Africa.[85] This condition may be attributed to, inter alia, unwillingness of environmental departments, or line functionaries, to surrender their mandates and to cooperate with one another; protection of mandates and turf; lack of infrastructure; lack of human and financial resources; political unresponsiveness and noncommitment; and assignment of priority to the alleviation of poverty, affirmative action strategies, and reconstruction of South African society, rather than environmental governance concerns. Whereas IEM and CEG provide strategies to establish integration at the policy level, fragmentation at the operational level of government accordingly remains fragmented. It is therefore necessary to investigate possible strategies that may be utilized practically to achieve integration. Four different scenarios that map the potential journey of South Africa toward an integrated framework for environmental governance are proposed.[86] The scenarios imply a cumulative and progressive advancement of cooperation and integration arrangements from an initial informal, administrative arrangement to a penultimate strategy that requires fundamental legal and structural reform.[87] These scenarios are based on the concepts of IEM and CEG, since the integrated and cooperative nature of these concepts may greatly assist future endeavors that aim to address fragmentation.

   It is important to note that these scenarios represent a gradual transition from inception to ultimate achievement of integrated decision making, or the so-called one stop shop. It is not suggested that these scenarios, or scenario elements, despite their sequential character, are cast in stone. It is indeed feasible and recommended that

It is furthermore stated in this regard that CEG entails sharing of information and setting up of structures to coordinate initiatives when various groups are involved in the same focus area or resource. See Custers M and Custers C, "Cooperative Governance and Strategic Environmental Assessment: Rustenburg as a Case Study" in "Co-operative Environmental Governance: In Search for the Holy Grail," 54, paper delivered at the Annual Conference of the International Association for Impact Assessment: South Africa, September 2003, George, South Africa.

[84] Kotzé, *supra* note 54 at 56.

[85] Nel, Kotzé, and Snyman, *supra* note 13 at 2, 14–18.

[86] For a further discussion of these scenarios, albeit in the context of specific scenarios for the integration at the operational level of government, see ibid.

[87] Centre for Environmental Management, *Report on an Environmental Management System for the North-West Province: Phase III* (Centre for Environmental Management Potchefstroom) (2004) 8.

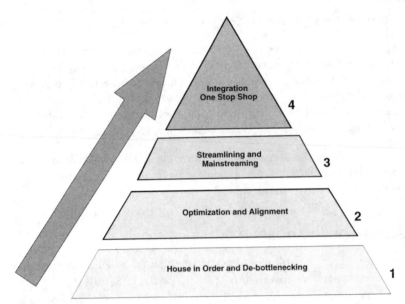

Figure 12.1. Integration scenarios.

some elements of some higher-order scenarios may be brought forward, implemented, and used should opportunities arise. Although the scenarios and/or scenario elements are not cast in stone, it is, however, strongly recommended that an overall phased, cumulative, and sequential approach to implementation of an integrated authorization framework be adopted. Higher-order scenarios are designed to increase demand on participants, while arrangements may increasingly become invasive.[88] The four scenarios identified are illustrated in Figure 12.1.[89] These scenarios are discussed in further detail in the following sections. The discussion specifically focuses on practical arrangements that need to be undertaken by environmental authorities in South Africa to address fragmentation.

5.1 Debottlenecking and House in Order

Scenario 1, debottlenecking, has two distinct elements. The first element addresses logistical, administrative, staff, and procedural issues. The second element of this scenario includes an alignment of some of the decision-making competencies vested in environmental authorities in South Africa.[90]

The proposed solutions for cooperative house in order and debottlenecking for decision-making processes by environmental authorities should begin with an informal and voluntary alignment of administrative processes only. The focus of this exercise should be to

- Establish administrative alliances between some decision-making organs of state
- Improve service delivery to would-be investors
- Improve understanding by commenting authorities of the decision processes of competent authorities

---

[88] Centre for Environmental Management, *supra* note 86 at 9–10.
[89] Ibid. at 9.   [90] Ibid. at 11.

- Improve guidance and access to information to potential investors
- Optimize governance efforts in South Africa
- Improve the consistency of governance in South Africa[91]

The process should be both informal and voluntary. It is informal in that no arrangements that would threaten the independence and decision-making mandates of the various line functions and spheres of government are proposed. No changes to existing legal provisions need to be made. Collaboration is instead focused on aligned and coordinated administrative procedures. It is voluntary insofar as line functions collaborate of their own volition. In this sense, environmental authorities are not coerced to participate. This scenario may furthermore be combined with other elements of higher-order scenarios discussed hereafter should the need arise.[92]

5.2 Increased Optimization and Improved Alignment

It is proposed that both the scope of and the process to give effect to the increased optimization and improved alignment scenario should be designed inclusively with all stakeholders. The proposals made here are therefore broad-based, conceptual probabilities. A five-pronged strategy is proposed for Scenario 2. The main purpose of the first element of this scenario is to formalize the voluntary and informal cooperation relationships established in Scenario 1. This may be done by way of memoranda of understanding among the various environmental departments or line functionaries. The second element would be to establish informal and voluntary relationships with those line functions in South Africa that have environmentally oriented mandates and that were not part of the initial Scenario 1 solution.[93] These line functions may typically include the Department of Transport, which executes environmentally-related governance tasks alongside its main mandate, which essentially concerns transport. The third element would be to establish and/or extend informal and voluntary relationships with line functions that operate at the national, provincial, and local spheres of government. It is, however, envisaged that not all such line functions would initially be willing to participate in the arrangements established in Scenario 1. The fourth element entails review and improvement of relationships established in Scenario 1. The fifth element of Scenario 2 entails improvement in postdecision phase follow-up and continual compliance monitoring and enforcement.[94] In summary, this scenario essentially aims to formalize and extend the arrangements proposed by the first scenario. Scenario 2 does not entail any significant changes to the current legal framework, structures, mandates, and resultant governance tasks. It is merely meant to provide improved, better aligned arrangements that have been established in terms of the house in order and debottlenecking arrangements proposed by Scenario 1.

5.3 Streamlining and Mainstreaming

The streamlining and mainstreaming scenario has three possible elements. The first element addresses structural and legal reform of the South African environmental authorities' decision-making mandates into a streamlined legal and structural format. It may,

[91] Ibid. at 11–12.   [92] Ibid. at 12.
[93] Ibid. at 20.   [94] Ibid.

for example, be possible to incorporate some legislative mandates of the various line functionaries into a single administrative procedure act that provides for a streamlined and integrated governance effort or administrative procedure. While legal mandates remain intact, procedural aspects are consolidated and regulated by a single procedure in terms of the act.

The second element addresses formalization of relationships with environmentally oriented decision-making structures of the national, provincial, and local spheres of government. This may be done by way of environmental management cooperation agreements (EMCAs) provided for by Chapter 8 of the NEMA. EMCAs may be concluded by various line functionaries with each other and by line functionaries and the public. It may thus specifically be utilized to facilitate more formal cooperative arrangements in order to promote compliance with the principles laid down in the NEMA, including the provisions on CEG and IEM.[95]

The third element entails formalization of governance control over the entire project life cycle, whereby government is involved from the planning and design phase of a project to the operational phase of a project through to the decommissioning and rehabilitation phase.[96] Scenario 3, in summary, essentially aims to improve on the arrangements established by Scenarios 1 and 2. This may be done by way of minor legislative amendments in terms of which the various line functionaries are legally required to integrate some of the procedural aspects of their various mandates. More formal cooperation strategies may be established in terms of this scenario by way of legislative cooperation agreements that may arguably enable various line functions to be involved on an integrated, streamlined, and aligned basis in the whole of the project life cycle.

5.4 The One-Stop Authorization Shop

Scenario 4 describes the one-stop shop scenario. It entails a fully integrated one-stop shop that is based on integrated legislative and resultant administrative arrangements. It requires a fully integrated approach based on a holistic premise. This may be facilitated by way of a single act dealing with environmental governance efforts pertaining to air, land, and water in a holistic manner. It may accordingly entail that line functionaries surrender their mandates, that the existing silo-based line functionaries are abolished, and that all, or most, environmental governance matters are regulated by a single act and administrative body. It, furthermore, may entail standardized authorization application forms and procedures as well as a centralized body that oversees and coordinates governance procedures and other matters incidental to environmental governance tasks.[97] Scenario 4 presents the most radical proposal for integration. Whereas the previous scenarios focus on more informal and less-far-reaching arrangements, this long-term scenario suggests drastic legislative reforms and integration of administrative arrangements and mandates. Although it may be the most ideal scenario as far as the achievement of optimal integration is concerned, whether the necessary political will, infrastructure, and resources exist in South Africa to facilitate such reforms is

---

[95] See Section 35 of the NEMA.
[96] Centre for Environmental Management, *supra* note 86 at 26.
[97] Ibid. at 29–30.

questionable. It is accordingly proposed that integration should be facilitated by commencing with informal arrangements that are cost-effective and less encroaching on existing mandates. As soon as reforms have been established in terms of Scenarios 1–3, government may consider implementing the arrangements proposed by Scenario 4.

6 CONCLUSION

South Africa currently has a comprehensive legal framework to facilitate environmental governance. It has been indicated that this framework is, however, fundamentally fragmented. Land use is an integral part of the environmental governance effort in South Africa. It follows that fragmentation therefore also exists in terms of the current land use management and governance framework. Fragmentation has several disadvantages. The most significant disadvantage is arguably that it may inhibit the achievement of sustainability. It is therefore pertinent that fragmentation be addressed in order to direct environmental governance efforts in general, and in particular with reference to land use issues, on a sustainable path.

It has been argued that the concepts of IEM and CEG may be utilized as strategies to facilitate integration. These concepts are well founded in South African environmental law and have as their primary objective to establish and/or enhance integration, alignment, cooperation, and coordination in terms of environmental governance efforts. Despite these initiatives, fragmentation still exists. There are various reasons for its persistence. One may be that IEM and CEG are theoretical concepts that need to be incorporated in actual day-to-day environmental governance efforts. Four possible scenarios that may be utilized to address fragmentation in actual practice have been discussed. These scenarios are based on the concepts of IEM and CEG, since the common denominator is that of integration of the various structures, processes, policies, and tools that are unique to environmental governance. It has also been argued that these scenarios be implemented in a sequential and phased approach, from less formal reforms, to the establishment of a fully integrated one-stop environmental governance shop, which arguably represents the most ideal form of integration.

In light of the foregoing, it is proposed that due recognition of the need to address fragmentation and actual unqualified reform endeavors in this regard may ultimately lead to a more integrated and sustainable governance effort in South Africa. This may assist in directing environmental governance efforts in general, and efforts relating to land use in particular, on an optimal, service-delivery-oriented, streamlined, participatory, cost-effective, cooperative, and sustainable path.

13 Environmental Law and Sustainable Land Use in Nigeria

Muhammed Tawfiq Ladan

1 INTRODUCTION

All life depends on land, for people construct homes on land, food is cultivated on land, and when people ultimately die their remains are committed to land. Usually, life's basic needs are expressed to be food, clothing, and shelter, but it is true to assert that there is only one essential or basic need of life and that is land because food, clothing, and shelter are entirely derived from land.[1]

In Nigeria, there are provisions in our Laws for the protection of the rights in property (land inclusive) and the right to use and enjoy such.[2] In recent years there have been efforts to control the use of land[3] in particular, and property in general, due to the realization of the need to protect the environment, especially land, from degradation or pollution.[4]

It is against this background that this chapter aims at realizing the objectives of providing conceptual clarification of key terms such as *environment, environmental law, land, sustainable land use,* and *land pollution* and examining the role of environmental law in regulating land use and environmental protection in Nigeria.

2 CONCEPTUAL CLARIFICATION OF KEY TERMS

2.1 Environment

The word *environment* encompasses anything from the whole biosphere to the habitat of the smallest creature or organism.[5]

In the broad sense, dictionary definitions of the term *environment* range from "the totality of physical, economic, cultural, aesthetic, and social circumstances and factors

---

[1] See Ladan, M. T., *Report on the Review of Sokoto State of Nigeria's Environmental Laws and Regulations* (All States Publishing Co., Abuja) (1997) 14–15.

[2] Sections 43–44 and 46 of the Constitution of the Federal Republic of Nigeria, 1999.

[3] The Land Use Act (of 1978) Cap. 202 Laws of the Federation of Nigeria, 1990, is the law that regulates the acquisition, use, and disposal of land.

[4] See Ladan, M. T., "Status of Environmental Law in Nigeria: Implementation, Teaching and Research," a paper presented at a Symposium for Environmental Law Senior Lecturers/Professors from African Universities. Organized by the United Nations Environmental Programme (UNEP), Nairobi, Kenya, 29 September–2 October 2004, Nakuru, Kenya, 1–30.

[5] Patricia Birnie and Allan Boyle, *International Law and the Environment* (2nd ed.) (Oxford University Press, Oxford) (2002) 3.

which surround and affect the desirability and value of property or which also affects the quality of people's lives,"[6] to "the conditions under which any person or thing lives or is developed; the subtotal of influences which modify and determine the development of life or character."[7] It embraces everything within and around humans that may have effect on or be affected by humans, namely, human environment. The broad meaning will subsume historical, cultural, technological, natural, economic, and political factors, influences, and milieus.

In ecological terms, *environment* has a more limited meaning, which is essentially physical and biological. Environment in this sense encompasses an array of ecosystems. An ecosystem consists of both living (including, humans) and nonliving components and their physical surroundings such as land, water, air. This narrower meaning restricts the environment concept to the physical or natural environment, comprising God-given natural resources, natural elements, and natural environment whether or not modified by humans. Such an approach is adopted by two principal environmental laws in Nigeria. Section 38 of the Federal Environmental Protection Agency Act[8] defines *environment* to "include water, air, land and all plants and human beings or animals living therein and the inter-relationships which exist among these or any of them." Similarly, the Environmental Impact Assessment Decree of Nigeria defines the term as including

a. land, water, and air, including all layers of the atmosphere
b. all organic and inorganic matter and living organisms
c. the interacting natural systems that include components referred to in (a) and (b)[9]

An indication of what the environment encompasses at an international level is given by the broad range of issues now addressed by international law, including conservation and sustainable use of natural resources and biodiversity; conservation of endangered and migratory species; prevention of deforestation and desertification; preservation of Antartica and areas of outstanding natural heritage; protection of oceans, international watercourses, the atmosphere, climate, and the ozone layer from the effects of pollution; and safeguarding of human health and the quality of life. Inevitably, however, any definition of the environment will have the quality of meaning we want it to have. Hence, understandably many international conventions avoid the problem of definition; however, no doubt, as Caldwell remarks, "It is a term that everyone understands and no one is able to define."[10]

2.2 Environmental Law

Environmental law in Nigeria is a body of rules and regulations that have as their object or effect the protection of the environment from pollution and the wasteful depletion of

---

[6] *Blacks Law Dictionary* (5th ed.) (1979) 479.
[7] I. A. Umezulike and C. C. Nweze (eds.), *Perspectives in Law and Justice* (Fourth Dimension Publishers, Enugu, Nigeria) (1996) 240.
[8] FEPA Act Cap. 131 Laws of the Federation of Nigeria 1990 (as amended) by Decree No. 59 of 1992.
[9] E.I.A. Decree No. 86 of 1992, Section 63(1).
[10] Victor Caldwell, *International Environmental Law and Policy* (1st ed.) (Durham, N.C.) (1980) 170.

natural resources and ensuring of sustainable development.[11] There is the proposition that environmental law has not been developed as a self-contained discipline, but has simply borrowed concepts from other areas of law such as criminal, constitutional, contract, tort, equity, and property. One result is undoubtedly a degree of incoherence; another is that the objective of the protection of the environment is not always served by the legal mechanisms available, because these other areas were not developed with the particular problems of environmental protection in mind. For example, the private law concentrates on the protection of private interests and has difficulties when it comes to protecting common or public interests in the unowned environment. No damages are payable for harm to the environment as such, and only those who have personal or property rights may bring an action (thus excluding animals, trees, rivers, etc.). No value is placed on the environment itself and environmental protection is simply an incidental by-product of the protection of other interests.[12]

Public law does recognize the public interest, but difficulties arise out of a lack of acceptance of the idea that the environment has some independent status or value, as distinct from rights conferred on individuals and communities. Even the criminal law struggles with environmental "crimes," since it has often been pointed out in the courts that many of the offences created are not criminal in the "true" sense. This is more pronounced in the acceptance by the House of Lords in *Alphacell Ltd v. Woodward*[13] that water pollution offenses are in the category of "acts which in the public interest are prohibited under a penalty."

Further, the structure of the Judicial system emphasizes adversarial and backward-looking two-party litigation and its procedural rules are not user-friendly to those wishing to bring environmental cases and fail to give the public interest a separate voice.[14] These defects notwithstanding, one would argue that environmental law has its own conceptual apparatus, in the sense that there is a set of principles and concepts that can be said to exist. Thoughtful debate about the extent to which these principles have gained universal acceptance as principles with meaningful legal effect indicates that the process of establishing environmental law as an identifiable discipline has begun. Clearly these principles provide a theoretical context in which to view the detail of environmental law, and thus it is important to stress that an environmental lawyer needs to understand the law in practice as well as the detailed rules in order to possess the tools required to carry out the task of solving particular problems properly.[15]

One of the characteristics of the law and policy of environmental protection is that it evolves, constantly reflecting the various values and priorities placed upon different aspects of the environment. This explains why environmental law has grown rapidly in recent years as environmental issues have gained in importance. In a subject area such as this in which activities have to be planned reasonably well in advance, it is always helpful to know what is likely to happen in the future as well as what the law is at the time. In this sense environmental law is forward-looking law.[16]

---

[11] See the combined effect of the inventory of relevant national legal and administrative frameworks on the environment in Nigeria, in Ladan M. T., *supra* notes 1 and 4.

[12] Ladan, *supra* note 4.   [13] (1972) AC 824.

[14] See Niki Tobi, "Judicial Enforcement of Environmental Laws in Nigeria," in Muhammed T. Ladan, *Law, Human Rights and the Administration of Justice in Nigeria* (A.B.U. Press, Zaria, Nigeria) (2001) 261–287.

[15] See generally, Struan Simpson and Lanre Fagbohun (eds.), *Environmental Law and Policy* (Law Centre, Faculty of Law, Lagos State University, Lagos, Nigeria) (1998) 86–202.

[16] Birnie and Boyle, *supra* note 5 at 5–8.

There is, perhaps, a growing realization that the different areas of law – public law, private law, and so on – merely provide, in the environmental context, a set of different tools to achieve a specified objective, in this case the protection of the environment.[17] For example, in relation to contaminated land it is clear that someone has to "pay" for the contamination, either by cleaning it up or by living with the consequences. There are essentially four possible options – the polluter could be made liable; the current owner or occupier could be liable; the state could pay (i.e., through some public cleanup mechanism), so that in effect the public world pay through some form of taxation; or finally, the loss could lie where it falls, meaning that the environment and the local community effectively "pay." For a policymaker the issue is devising a means to develop a solution that is effective, efficient, and fair; the tools that are available include, but are not limited to, legal mechanisms.[18]

2.3 Definition of *Land*

Land occupies a unique place in the development process of any individual or society. The supply of land is, however, limited.[19] No society therefore exists without a regulation of some kind peculiar to it to rationalize the mode of ownership and the use of land.[20] According to the well-established principle of law *quicquid planate solo solo cedit*, land consists of the surface of the earth, the subsoil, and the air space above it, as well as all things that are permanently attached to the soil. It also includes streams and ponds.[21]

Statutory definitions of land in Nigeria include "Land and everything attached to the earth and all chattels real"[22] and land of any tenure, buildings or parts of buildings and other corporeal hereditaments; also a rent and other incorporeal hereditaments, and an easement, right, privilege or benefit in, over or derived from land."[23]

Furthermore, the word *land*, according to Justice Andrew Obaseki (retired Justice of the Supreme Court of Nigeria), "is a specie of property. Property has been defined to mean ownership or title and sometimes the res over which ownership may be exercised. The land comprised in the territory of each state of the Federation is the res over which the governor exercised ownership in trust in accordance with section 1 of the Land Use Act of 1978. It is an immovable property"[24]

The rules relating to the distribution of land necessarily mirror the underlying current of the society's ideology. In Nigeria's traditional setting, for instance, land was not viewed as a mere economic tool; rather it had religious and other social functions.

---

[17] See generally, M. A. Ajomo and O. O. Adewale (eds.), *Environmental Law and Sustainable Development in Nigeria* (Nigerian Institute of Advanced Legal Studies, Lagos, and The British Council) (1994) 11–48 and 67–112.

[18] Muhammed T. Ladan, "Human Rights and Environmental Protection," in A. O. Obilade and C. Nwankwo (eds.), *Text for Human Rights Teaching in Schools* (Constitutional Rights Project, Lagos) (1999) 102–107.

[19] See UNEP, *Africa Environment Outlook Reporting Project, Information Brief on Land* (UNEP, Nairobi) (2002) 1–2.

[20] See, e.g., Land Use Act, *supra* note 3.

[21] C. O. Olawoye, *Title to Land in Nigeria* (University of Lagos/Evans Bros, London) 9.

[22] Section 3 of the Interpretation Act Cap. 192, Laws of the Federation of Nigeria, 1990.

[23] Section 2, Property and Conveyancing Law of Western Nigeria 1959.

[24] Quoted in Andrew Obaseki, "The Judicial Impression of the Nigerian Law of Property: Any Need for Reform?" in *Proceedings of the 26th Annual Conference of the National Association of Law Teachers* (Faculty of Law, Rivers State University of Science and Technology, Port Harcourt, Nigeria) (28 March 1988) 17–18.

Thus native rule was rightly seen to depend upon the native land system.[25] In the strict native rule and custom, land was believed to belong to the living, the dead, and the unborn.[26] Land, therefore, had metaphysical content, viewed, as it were, as an inherent part of social relations processes among people, society, and gods. The promulgation of the Land Use Decree 1978[27] was an exercise to redirect the general philosophies of preexisting land tenure systems in our society through the application of a uniform statutory regulation of ownership and control of land rights and to stimulate easier access to land for greater economic development as well as promote national social cohesion.

2.4 Sustainable Land Use

Land supports other natural resources such as forest that are vital for human survival.[28] Human survival therefore depends largely on sustainable use of existing and available renewable land resources by allowing renewal processes to occur.[29]

The development of land use systems that meet the needs of present and future generations without causing environmental degradation remains one of the major challenges we are confronted with today. For sustainable development to occur, such land use systems must have the capacity to prevent and control any form of gross abuse or unsustainable use of land resources. Hence sustainable land use implies activities that are ecologically sound, socioculturally acceptable, economically viable, as well as equitable in terms of access to land resources, benefits, and the decision-making process.[30]

2.5 Definition of *Land Pollution*

Section 38 of the Federal Environmental Protection Agency Act[31] defines *pollution* as "man-made or man-aided alteration of chemical, physical or biological quality of the environment to the extent that is detrimental to that environment or beyond acceptable limits."[32] Land is said to be polluted when any waste or noxious substance or chemical is accumulated or deposited or dumped on it in such a state or condition as to be injurious to the health of humans, animals, or vegetation or the aesthetic quality of the physical environment, or when any unlawful act or omission or thing is destructive to the surface of the land or renders the land unproductive.[33] The term also includes

---

[25] See R. L. Buell, *The Native Problem in Africa*, Vol. 1. (1928) 762.

[26] See M. G. Yakubu, *Land Law in Nigeria* (Macmillan Press, London) (1985) 6.

[27] Ch. 202 Law of the Federation of Nigeria, 1990.

[28] Forest is an important land resource that has been grossly abused and unsustainably used in poor and developing economies such as Nigeria's.

[29] People in complex and interrelated activities that have been manifested in perceptible land degradation on local, national, regional, and global scales.

[30] See National Policy on the Environment in Nigeria (revised ed.) 1999, pp. 5–11.

[31] Cap. 131 Laws of the Federation of Nigeria 1990, *supra* note 8.

[32] Environmental pollution resulting from industrialization and other activities directed at modernizing the economy has been referred to as "pollution of affluence," while that resulting from poor living conditions, unhealthy surroundings, and primitive economy and technology has been referred to as "pollution of poverty." See K. F. Castro, "Environment and Development: The Case of the Developing Countries," in R. M. Kay and K. T. Skolnikoff, *World Eco Crisis: International Organization in Response* (University of Wisconsin Press, Madison) (1972) p. 237 at 245.

[33] See Ladan, *supra* note 1 at 15–22.

anything laid in land that automatically impairs its arableness, yield, or cultivability, such as land mines, atomic bombs, and other similar devices.[34] Other forms of general land degradation include those resulting from oil spills, sludge, and the more common occasion of oil change in mechanical garages where oil use and disposal are not effectively controlled.

3 ROLE OF ENVIRONMENTAL LAW IN REGULATING LAND USE AND PROTECTION OF THE ENVIRONMENT IN NIGERIA

In order to examine the role of environmental law in regulating land-use–related environmental protection in Nigeria, this section seeks to identify land use problems in Nigeria that lead to land degradation and examines key environmental legislation that aims at regulating land use in order to protect the environment from gross abuse.

3.1 Land Use Problems and Their Impact on the Environment

In Nigeria, land use problems that result in land pollution and are accorded highest priority are related to the many causes of deforestation, soil erosion, and dumping or disposal of both industrial and domestic wastes that are hazardous or harmful and consequently render land unproductive or degraded and unsustainable.[35] Forests provide a good example of an important resource on land that has been grossly abused and unsustainably used. They provide human beings with a wealth of benefits including contribution of about 19 percent of the energy supply of lower-income countries through fuel wood resources and provision of a resource base for agriculture, tourism, recreation, religion, culture, and music.

The forests have been degraded through unsustainable logging, shifting agricultural practices, fuel wood gathering, bush burning, and overgrazing.[36] For centuries, shifting cultivation and migratory pastoral systems allowed people to derive their livelihood in a sustainable manner from nature. When soil fertility declines or pasture vegetation disappears, people move to new land and allow natural regeneration of used land to its original state. The fallow period can be 10 to 20 years. With increase in population, farming and pastoral land has become scarce and new forest lands have been opened up for both traditional and mechanized farming. An example can be found in Nigeria, where forest reserves were dereserved for palm and rubber plantation development.

Fallow periods have been shortened as in several communities ongoing farming on the same piece of land is carried out by using traditional systems that are suitable for only shifting cultivation. The effects are nonrestorable soil fertility, low crop yield, and farmers' migration from marginal land into forests. Similarly, with diminishing pasture, livestock move to tropical forest areas considered unsuitable land for such use.[37]

---

[34] See Simpson and Fagbohun, *supra* note 15 at 79 and 313.
[35] See Ajomo and Adewale, *supra* note 17 at 11–26.   [36] Ladan, *supra* note 1 at 15–22.
[37] See Federal Environmental Protection Agency Abuja, *Proceedings of the National Train the Trainer Workshop on Environmental Management in Nigeria* (1998) 179.

Further, increasing dependence on wood for fuel and building materials when combined with population growth contributes to the increasing rate of forest and woodland destruction. In the 1980s, deforestation in Nigeria was estimated at 400,000 hectares per annum. In 1998 a federal study showed that fuel wood is the source of energy for 80 percent of the rural population. With increasing cost of fossil fuel energy, it is likely that there will be increased dependence on fuel wood as an energy supply. The increasing demand for fuel wood accelerated the rates of woodland destruction, soil degradation, river siltation, desertification, and general environmental degradation.[38]

Logging is another important cause of forest loss. Farmers often engage in bush burning in logged areas, thereby making sustained-yield forest management systems difficult. Loggers themselves do not carry out afforestation activities as required by law.[39] In Nigeria, bush burning is done for a number of reasons, which include game hunting, land clearing for agriculture, and promotion of pasture for grazing. Often the fire gets out of control destroying large areas of vegetation. The hazards of bush burning, which include soil erosion and desertification, are of concern to agriculture particularly in the arid and semiarid areas. The organic matter content of the soil is depleted and volatilization of nitrogen is enhanced.[40] Overgrazing of land is a result of cattle rearing, practiced mainly by the nomadic Fulani in Nigeria. This activity leads to soil exposure, soil water loss, and ultimately erosion and desertification.[41]

Furthermore, the acquisition of operational land area is usually the very first disruption that visits an oil community. The discovery of oil in an area inevitably means the destruction of the vegetal life of the area to enable the company to set up its equipment and embark on the harvesting of the oil resource. In fact once land is occupied for oil installations or operations, unintended changes occur in the environment. These include the loss of economic and forest trees, loss of farmland and topsoil, loss of flora and fauna, habitat destruction, and loss of fishery and crop cultivation.[42]

Other effects of mining activities are general pollution and other deleterious effects on both organic and inorganic matter including living organisms. Many health problems are associated with mining, ranging from injuries, exposure to radiation, and auditory and respiratory disorders to death. The problem is rendered more intractable because several diseases are not manifested for long time.[43] When mining activities commence on land, its existing condition and use are changed by excavations and the operation of earth moving machinery. The green vegetation either disappears or is covered in a crust of dust. The absence of trees and other vegetation renders the soil vulnerable to erosion. Sometimes it may be necessary for mining purposes to divert the course of a stream or river, and this may result in its drying up. Some of the worst cases of damage to the landscape in this country are to be found in parts of the Jos Plateau, Plateau State of Nigeria, which, from an aerial view, look like a lunar landscape with pits, gullies, and ravines. The landscape can also be damaged by tailing and dumping of waste from excavations.[44]

---

[38] Ibid. at 179–180.

[39] Ibid. at 180.

[40] *Supra* note 17 at 162–164.

[41] Ladan, *supra* note 1 at 15–22.

[42] See J. A. Omotola (ed.), *Environmental Laws in Nigeria, Including Compensation* (Faculty of Law, University of Lagos) (1990) 231–285.

[43] See Simpson and Fagbohun, *supra* note 15 at 398.

[44] Ibid at 398.

Finally, every industrial activity from the thousands of industries in Nigeria involves the input of raw materials through some mechanical processes and the result is waste by-products. These may be harmful, toxic, hazardous, or radioactive. If they are dumped in surface dump sites or in gulleys, valleys, or drainage basins, leacheates from them percolate freely and are swept by rain and flooding into the surface water system. The result is extensive chemical pollution of water. Moreover, industrial effluents may flow directly into surface water and groundwater, thereby again polluting the water. The ultimate victims of environmental pollution are human beings and animals.[45]

3.2 Key Environmental Legislation on Land Use Regulation and Environmental Protection

The freedom to use and enjoy land in particular, and private property in general, is guaranteed by our laws in Nigeria,[46] but it is trite to state that the rights cannot be absolute. They have to be regulated in the interest of the generality of the populace and in the protection of the rights of all in society.[47] To minimize and control the problems of land use discussed and their negative impact on land resources, the Nigerian government has established a number of local legislative measures.

The Land Use Act

The objectives of the Land Use Act are, among others, to ensure that there is sound land and environmental development and that the ecological and aesthetic values of the nation are preserved and enhanced.[48] The Act[49] deals primarily with the acquisition, use, and enjoyment of land in accomplishing these objectives; therefore, the activities of an individual, government, or organization either private or public are likely to create environmental problems. For example, where permission is given for land to be used for mining or industrial purposes, for a town or country planning purpose, or for any other commercial or public work or convenience, environmental issues are surely going to crop up in the use and enjoyment of any of these services or purposes.

The Land Use Act is not strictly an Act for environmental protection.[50] However, environmental protection is one of those considerations that a holder of a certificate of occupancy has to observe even though it is not explicitly provided for in any of the provisions of the Act. It is my view that if the Act is read without such considerations, the result is bound to be absurd and environmentally unsound.[51]

[45] See Omotola, *supra* note at 65–86.
[46] For detailed analysis of the Status of Environmental Law in Nigeria, see Ladan, *supra* note 4.
[47] See Omotola (1990), *supra* note 42 at 51–64.
[48] See Y. Aboki, "The Land Use Act and Environmental Protection in Nigeria," in Muhammed T. Ladan (ed.), *Law, Human Rights and the Administration of Justice in Nigeria* (A.B.U. Press, Zaria, Nigeria) (2001) 288–299.
[49] *Supra* note 3.
[50] Ignatius Ayu and Olawale Ajai (eds.), *Implementing the Biodiversity Convention: Nigerian and African Perspectives* (Nigerian Institute of Advanced Legal Studies, Lagos) (1997) 130.
[51] See Aboki, *supra* note 48.

The Urban and Regional Planning Act

The Urban and Regional Planning Act[52] has some feeble provisions on environmental impact assessment that are in fact not integrated with the Environmental Impact Assessment Act. Other than that, the Planning Act does not explicitly require or articulate criteria for integrating environmental conservation into the planning process. Yet, planning law ought to be able to establish regional land use frameworks geared toward total and holistic environmental conservation. Suffice it to say, therefore, that existing legislation will not assure adequate management and conservation of biodiversity in Nigeria. However, the planning law has a firm hold on the environment through the issuance of development permits for any development that has to take place in the environment. It also has the powers to prepare physical development plans showing how every square inch of land in the country will be used.[53]

Mining Law

Mining activities in Nigeria today are governed by the Minerals Act,[54] the Minerals Regulation and Minerals (Safe Mining) Regulations made under it, as well as by amendments and modifications such as the Minerals Act (Amendment) Decree 29 of 1984. Sections 46–47 of the Act dwell on the problems of pollution associated with mining activities. They make provisions for the safe disposal of overburden and excessive tailing from mining operations, with a primary focus on the protection of water and water sources. Sections 52–63, in particular, set out the procedure for obtaining a water license and the obligations of a holder of a water licence. Likewise, the Safe Mining Regulations prescribe the obligations of a prospective holder of a license, mining right, or mining lease with regard to the protection of the landscape, while Regulation 131 sets out the requirements for handling water that contains toxic or injurious chemicals discharged from the treatment of minerals.

The poor level of enforcement of the law and safety regulations, the increasing sophistication in the mining industry the world over, and the increased level of environmental awareness have all combined to render the safety requirements in the existing laws rather obsolete and inadequate. The modern concept of the environment has now been expanded by the Federal Environmental Protection Agency Act[55] beyond water quality and landscape as envisaged under the Minerals Act to include air quality and atmospheric protection, noise control or abatement, and discharge of hazardous substances into the environment. Consequently, persons engaged in solid minerals exploration and exploitation are now compelled to conform to a higher standard of environmental protection than that prescribed by the Minerals Act. In order to attain fully the objectives of the Federal Environmental Protection Agency Act, the Environmental Impact Assessment Decree[56] confers specific powers on the Agency, now the Ministry of Environment, to facilitate its environmental assessment of projects and sets out the procedures and methods for conducting environmental impact assessment of projects for which they are statutorily required.

---

[52] Decree No. 88 (1992).

[54] Ch. 226, Laws of the Federation of Nigeria (1990).

[55] *Supra* note 8.

[53] Ibid., section 1, 13, 28–31, and 47.

[56] *Supra* note 9.

Other Laws

The Nigerian Forestry Act[57] governs the forestry sector in the country. There are extensive powers under it and under some state laws to deal with indiscriminate deforestation for timber and other uses. Certain specific land areas are designated as forest reserves, activities within which are permissible only with a license. Penalties for violation include both fines and imprisonment.

There are no direct Federal provisions as such in respect of soil conservation. The Imo State Land and Water Resources Conservation (Erosion Prevention) Edict of 1986 addresses such problems as gully erosion, sheet erosion, quarrying, farming, bush burning, road design, and construction procedures. It appears to be a solitary effort in the federation. Considering the very grave problems of land and coastal erosion, comprehensive national legislation to address the problem of soil conservation is quite clearly overdue.[58]

In an attempt to sanitize the environment and to protect public health, the Sokoto State Public Health Edict No. 5 of 1985 indicates and prohibits the following instances of land pollution: any accumulation or deposit of rubbish of any kind, any overcrowded premises dangerous to the health of the occupants, any dumping of industrial waste or building materials on a building site that may be injurious to health, any littered and neglected frontage or backyard of any building, and any carriage of refuse, sand gravel, or noxious substance without covering such substance properly on the highway.[59]

Further, Section 17 of the Edict imposes a duty on every occupier or owner of any premises to keep free and clear drains, gutters, or channels on the streets of all filth, rubbish, and refuse of any description. Section 18 generally prohibits indiscriminate disposal of refuse into gutters, other such channels, and streets. The penalties provided for contravening these provisions are a fine of ₦100 or three months imprisonment.

The obvious shortcoming of this Edict is that it did not set up any body to designate proper refuse or waste disposal sites or treatment. The penalty or fine provided here is also very paltry for any effective enforcement, at least against corporate polluters. Further, the provisions of Section 7 of the Edict did not clearly prohibit the depositing, storage, or dumping of industrial, harmful, or human wastes or feces on land. It, however, clearly covered domestic and commercial wastes.

Furthermore, the provisions of the Edict of 1985 did not cover an important instance of land pollution, namely, damaging the aesthetic quality of land. In fact, the indiscriminate use of billboards and posters everywhere there is space in our urban centers, advertising this product or that service, has defaced buildings that should be monuments and even educational institutions. This has rendered the skyline of our major cities and towns aesthetically poor.

The Town and Country Planning Law[60] makes provisions for planning schemes with respect to lands, whether or not there are buildings thereon, with the general object of controlling the development and use of land in the area to which the scheme applies; of

---

[57] It has been reported that by 1990 the country had lost about 25,000 hectares of land to water erosion in Anambra, Imo, and Cross River States, and 12.5 million hectares of land to wind erosion in the arid and semiarid zones of the Northern States of Nigeria, quoted in Ajai and Ayua, *supra* note 54 at p. 129.

[58] See, however, the National Policy on the Environment in Nigeria (revised ed.) (1999) at pp. 10–37.

[59] Section 7 (f), i, k, o, p, q, and t.   [60] Ch. 130, Laws of Northern Nigeria, Vol. III (1963).

securing proper sanitary conditions, amenities, and convenience; of preserving buildings or other objects of architectural, historic; or artistic interest and places of natural interest or beauty; of protecting and extending the amenities and of conserving and developing of the resources of such areas; and of coordinating roads and public services. This law has now been repealed by Section 79 (1) of the Sokoto State Edict No. 7 of 1995.

The Edict aims at controlling the carrying out of any building, engineering construction, or other operations in, on, over, or under any state land, or the making of any environmentally significant change in the use of any land or demolition of buildings. It made some improvements on the repealed law in terms of content and provisions for penalties for effective enforcement. For instance, under Section 2, the meaning of *development* has been broadened slightly to cover engineering and mining operations specifically; development has also been categorized as commercial, industrial, and institutional and each clearly defined in order to cope with modern needs and challenges. Under Section 3, the composition of the Board has been broadened to accommodate relevant professionals for efficient performance. Under Section 58 the penalty for violating the Edict should not exceed a fine of ₦10,000 in the case of individuals and of ₦50,000 in case of a corporate body. The control department is empowered to regulate the dimensions, appearance, display, and siting of advertising billboards and the manner in which they shall are attached to land.

In Section 69(1), however, the amended Planning Law contains more elaborate provisions or approaches for the distribution of human pressure on the physical environment to improve the aesthetic quality of the environmental standard for buildings.[61]

One obvious shortcoming of all the laws on land pollution is the apparent omission of control of soil erosion and desertification, which are among issues accorded highest priority in Nigeria, especially in the north.

Apart from overgrazing, which promotes erosion and desertification, lack of tree-planting culture coupled with deforestation due to uncontrolled timber lumbering lead to the rapid southward advance of the Sahara. Most soils have been rendered infertile by overcultivation and bush burning, and replacement of the essential minerals of topsoil takes place over very long periods.

Nigeria's coastal resources have been greatly damaged by erosion, and this has had severe financial consequences. Erosion, like flooding, sometimes affects property and means of livelihood, especially where most people in the area are farmers. About 351,000 square kilometers of Nigeria's land is desert land, and the desert continues to advance at yearly rate of 0.6 kilometer.

4 DEFORESTATION

Land degradation also results from the many causes of deforestation. The Forestry Law (Cap. 44) provides for the preservation and control of forest in Sokoto State. The Law makes special provisions for the creation of forest reserves and protected forest sets forth the procedure for constituting forest reserve. It also prohibits the illegal felling of timber and illegal installation or operation of sawmills. The offenses and penalties provided range from a fine of 50 pounds or six months imprisonment for offenses

---

[61] Pt. 2 and Pt. 3 of the repealed planning Act, regulations made thereunder and the first schedule.

in protected forests and for contravention of any regulation made under this law or the conditions of any license or permit issued thereunder, to a fine of 100 pounds or one year imprisonment or both for acts prohibited in a forest reserve. Additional penalties include forfeiture of any forest produce, destruction of any farm or plantation, confiscation of any farm, or cancellation of any license or permit held under this Law.

This Regulation further makes provisions for the protection and conservation of timber and protected trees. It grants privileges to owners of protected trees, persons making canoes, and the postal authority. The procedure for the issuance of permits is specified in the Regulation.

All in all, the Law is antiquated in that it basically came into existence in 1933 under colonial rule. Although there might have been a few amendments to the law, the main provisions have not been essentially altered. Second, because the law is ineffectively enforced as a result of its very paltry penalties and fines, large-scale deforestation activities such as bush burning, overgrazing of land, logging or timber exploitation, infrastructural developments, farming, population growth, urbanization, and the conversion of forest land to agricultural and other government uses have occurred. Third, the law is narrow in scope, lacking provisions for grazing reserves and demarcation of grazing reserve areas and for licenses or special permits to graze on forest reserves or protected forests. There is no provision prohibiting overgrazing of land in order to assess and control the environmental impact of nomadic pastoralism. Fourth, the law does not balance forest conservation and institutional, industrial, or agricultural developments that cause deforestation.

A further obvious shortcoming is lack of provisions for the establishment of any organ or body to formulate both short- and long-term policies on planned forestry protection, control, and management that cover the whole range of forestry activities.

By virtue of the power of the Governor to make regulations under Section 46 of the Forestry Law, Sokoto State Legal Notice No. 7 of 1996 provides for the prohibition of willful felling, trimming, or lopping of trees without permission. The penalties prescribed for contravening the regulations are for the first offense, a maximal fine of 1,000 naira and an order to plant three replacement treas for every tree felled, to be nurtured to maturity, and for each subsequent offense, a maximal fine of 3,000 naira and an order to plant three replacements for every tree felled to be nurtured to maturity. This regulation is an improvement on the existing law in terms of penalties for noncompliance.

In 1965, the Grazing Reserves Law came into effect with provisions for the establishment and control of grazing reserves. The Law requires the Government to publish a notice of intention to create a grazing reserve in the state *Gazette* together with details of such reserve and to appoint a reserve settlement officer. It empowers the Governor to constitute lands for which reserve status has been requested as Government grazing reserves. The Governor is empowered to dereserve any grazing reserve by order and to make regulations for Government grazing reserves. It further deals with the power of Local Government Councils to constitute and manage grazing reserves.

It is sad to note that in the three decades since it was formulated, no attempt has been made to update it in the light of today's challenges. One such challenge is that the environmental impact of nomadic pastoralism does not augur well for conservation practices. There are also frequent clashes between cattle herders and crop farmers over scarce resources, including land.

It is noteworthy that 27 years after the coming into effect of the Grazing Reserves Law the Sokoto State Government enacted a regulation demarcating some areas in the state as grazing land. The Sokoto State Legal Notice No. 14 of 1992 empowers the Commissioner for Agriculture and Natural Resources to take control of and manage the 13 grazing reserve areas created out of nine local governments accommodating about five such reserves.

The need for amendments of this latest Regulation passed by the Sokoto State Government to ensure proper redemarcation of such reserves for the present Sokoto State cannot be overemphasized because of the recent creation of Kebbi and Zamfara States as well as some local governments from Sokoto State. The effort of the Sokoto State Government in promulgating the Agricultural and Rural Development Authority Edict, 1985, is commendable. More specifically, the establishment of the Authority to carry out forestry development; to collect and process data for long- and short-term land use planning; and to secure disease-free stock for breeding is commendable.

However, it did not provide for a unit to collect and process data for both short- and long-term forestry protection, control, and management planning. The Sokoto State Forestry II Project Unit Edict No. 2 of 1987 established a unit to administer comprehensive farm forestry extension services in the state; applied research in afforestation in nurseries, shelter belts, and agroforestry; sand-dune fixation; and soil conservation. This effort is also commendable since it begins to address the problem of deforestation.

5 CONCLUSION

In conclusion, it is worth nothing that environmental law must be seen as forward-looking law not necessarily because it is future-oriented but also because it has the necessary tools and principles to promote sustainable land use for sustainable development. This must, however, be complemented by the necessary political will of governments to ensure that reforms relevant to land use activities that are ecologically sound, socioculturally acceptable, economically viable, as well as equitable in terms of access to land resources, benefits, and decision making, are promoted. It is evident from the discussion in this chapter that concerted efforts need to be made in terms of afforestation and reforestation programs to combat land degradation.

There is also a need for an effective system of forest extension and public education, to ensure better awareness, appreciation; and management of forests with regard to the multiple roles and values of trees, forest, forest land, and wildlife. It is here recommended that the education of pastoralists should be strengthened and efforts made to encourage them to settle in specified grazing reserve areas within a given state and to adopt modern animal husbandry practices. Finally, there is a need for proper management of industrial waste that results from such management, but mainly from the many harmful effects of poorly managed industrial and domestic wastes.

14 The Role of Administrative Dispute Resolution Institutions and Processes in Sustainable Land Use Management: The Case of the National Environment Tribunal and the Public Complaints Committee of Kenya

Albert Mumma

1 INTRODUCTION

The development of laws relating to sustainable environmental management is relatively recent. Consequently, the courts, as the principal avenues for resolving disputes, are not quite prepared to deal with the issues arising from them. Additionally, the court processes tend, typically, to be slow, costly, and complex.

Administrative tribunals, on the other hand, are often deliberately designed to be more accessible to the public and are therefore less expensive, less complex, and speedier, because the rules allow them a measure of discretion and flexibility in due process. Administrative tribunals do not comprise only lawyers. Typically, the bench comprises a mix of lawyers and specialists in the subject matter of the tribunal. Additionally, they are often empowered to introduce specialist technical knowledge in the form of assessors who can help to clarify technical and factual issues. These factors facilitate resolution of disputes over technical and factual matters with greater accuracy and confidence.

In December 1999, the Kenya Parliament enacted the Environmental Management and Coordination Act[1] (EMCA or "the Act"). The Act went into effect and became law shortly thereafter, on 14 January 2000. But, as events were subsequently to demonstrate, this commencement date was premature, and almost two years elapsed before the process of setting up the institutions established under the Act began in earnest.

EMCA's principal object is to guide and regulate environmental management in Kenya. To this end, it establishes an institutional framework consisting of three key institutions: the National Environment Council (the Council), the National Environment Management Authority (NEMA), and the National Environment Tribunal (the Tribunal). The Act also establishes a number of committees, described as Committees of NEMA, even though administratively they are not an integral part of NEMA. These committees include the Standards and Enforcement Review Committee, the Provincial and District Environmental Committees, and the Public Complaints Committee.

The Council is primarily a policy-setting organ, charged with the task of setting national environmental policy. NEMA is an administrative and regulatory body. Its task involves making both administrative and technical decisions. Appeals from NEMA's decisions are to be dealt with by the National Environment Tribunal. As is often the

---

[1] Act No. 8 of 1999.

case with administrative tribunals, the decisions, orders, or awards of the Tribunal are appealable to the High Court of Kenya.

This chapter analyzes the role of administrative tribunals in the sustainable management of land use, taking the case of the Environment Tribunal of Kenya. It argues that there is great potential in such arrangements for facilitating sustainable land use, even though this potential has yet to be realized in the Kenya case. It explores some of the reasons that the effectiveness of the National Environment Tribunal has been hampered and offers some proposals for a way forward.

2 KENYA'S INSTITUTIONAL AND LEGAL FRAMEWORK ON LAND USE AND ENVIRONMENTAL MANAGEMENT

2.1 The Institutions

The first institution established in Kenya with an express mandate over environmental matters was the National Environment Secretariat (NES). NES was established in 1972 to perform a coordinative and catalytic role in the protection and enhancement of the environment for the improvement of the quality of life of all peoples of Kenya. Subsequently, posts of District Environment and Conservation Officers were created, and officers were posted to at least 48 districts all over the country.

In 1975, the Government established the Department of Resource Surveys and Remote Sensing (DRSRS), whose task was to collect data and information on land and natural resources for use in planning, management, and policy formulation at district, national, and regional levels. The DRSRS not only collects land use information but also carries out aerial census of animals, especially in semiarid areas; forest cover mapping; and crop forecasting.

In 1981, the Permanent Presidential Commission on Soil Conservation and Afforestation (PPCSCA) was created through a presidential decree. The mandate of this institution had direct relevance to land use, as its task was to spearhead national efforts to reverse land degradation, and soil erosion in particular. Its creation arose from the perception that the country needed an institution dedicated to tackling the increasingly alarming degradation of land and water catchments that was undermining agricultural productivity in the country.

In all cases, these institutions were created administratively. They discharged their mandates by virtue of the administrative authority assigned to the President in the Constitution of the Republic of Kenya to create institutions in the civil service and vest powers and functions in them. As long as these institutions enjoyed the support of the President they operated effectively, but when they were left on their own, their effectiveness increasingly declined, with the exception perhaps of DRDS, whose mandate is primarily technical in nature.

On the whole, these institutions played a largely advisory and facilitative role. They did not have licensing functions and operated as regulators only indirectly. Consequently, their decisions, such as they were, were not viewed as appealable, and no particular appeal mechanism was established to deal with their decisions.

The enactment of the Environmental Management and Coordination Act, in 1999, changed all that. EMCA introduced a legal and institutional framework for the management of the environment in Kenya that put in place legal, rather than purely administrative, processes for decision making. As part of the process of setting up NEMA and rationalizing the institutional arrangements for the management of the environment and land use in Kenya, in July 2002 the Government decided to merge the three institutions – the National Environment Secretariat, the Department of Resource Surveys and Remote Sensing, and the Permanent Presidential Commission on Soil Conservation and Afforestation – to form NEMA. The three new institutions established under EMCA – NEMA, the Tribunal, and the Public Complaints Committee (PCC) – were housed in offices that until then had housed DRSRS. Shortly thereafter, however, in January 2003, DRSRS was delinked from NEMA and restored to its previous status. These institutions all operate under the umbrella of the ministry in charge of the environment, presently known as the Ministry of Environment and Wildlife, whose portfolio includes forests.

Despite the existence of several institutions with an environmental and land use management mandate, Kenya suffers from extremely poor implementation of policies. These institutions have lacked the statutory powers and institutional capacity to implement Government policy on the management of the environment and rational land use. Thus, despite Government policy that the country's future development depends on the sound and rational utilization of the environment and natural resources, acts of environmental degradation have continued unabated: Forests have been excised, water has been abstracted without permits, and land has been degraded through soil erosion arising from land use malpractices.

2.2 The Legal Framework

Several statutes in Kenya make reference either directly or indirectly to environmental management and sustainable land use. Each statute is separately concerned with a particular sectoral issue. Often the objective of the particular law is not connected to environmental protection per se. The Water Act of 2002, for example, deals mainly with "the conservation, control, apportionment, and use of the water resources of Kenya." It is not concerned with the larger picture of environmental protection in general. The Agriculture Act aims to "provide for the conservation of the soil and its fertility and to stimulate the development of agricultural land."

Each statute has its own management institution(s) to achieve its declared objectives, usually bolstered by penal sanctions in case of contravention. Such institutions basically pursue their own mandate, rarely taking into account the role of other sectoral players. Even where the overall aim is similar, approaches and styles tend to differ when implementing such diverse legislation.

The enactment of the framework environmental legislation, EMCA, was intended to provide an overall coordinating framework for environmental governance in Kenya. Its main object was to provide for the establishment of an appropriate legal and institutional framework for the management of the environment. Another object was to harmonize the various sector-specific laws touching on the environment in a manner designed to ensure greater protection of the environment. It was also the object of the Act to provide a framework for integrating environmental considerations into the country's overall economic and social development.

The framework law gives a right to every person in Kenya to a clean and healthy environment and imposes a duty on all in Kenya to safeguard and enhance the environment.

This right includes a right to access by any person in Kenya to the various public elements or segments of the environment for recreational, educational, health, spiritual, and cultural purposes.

2.3 The Interrelationships among the Environmental Management Institutions

The interplay among the various institutions set up to promote and facilitate better environmental management, including access to environmental justice, is critical for the effectiveness of these institutions. The effectiveness of the Tribunal, for example, is directly dependent on the quality of decisions made by NEMA and its committees.

The institutions set up under EMCA have already been mentioned. They include the Council, NEMA, its various Committees, the Public Complaints Committee, and the National Environment Tribunal. The first three institutions are designed to be instruments for achieving effective and efficient management of the environment. The latter two, apart from the courts of law, have the role of providing access to environmental justice.

The Council

The Council is a high-profile interministerial institution made up of eminent public administrators, scholars, business people, and representatives of nongovernmental organizations. Specifically, its membership comprises the Minister in charge of environmental matters as the chairperson; 18 Permanent Secretaries; two representatives each of public universities, research institutions, the business community, nongovernmental organizations; and co-opted members. The Director General of NEMA is the Secretary to the Council. The law does not allow the Permanent Secretaries to designate representatives. They are supposed to attend personally in order to enhance their participation.

This composition of the Council is designed to ensure the participation of all the major interests on environmental management in policymaking at the highest level. Its functions include policy formulation and direction, setting of national goals and objectives, determination of policy and priorities for the protection of the environment, and promotion of cooperation among public and private bodies engaged in environmental protection programs.

The Council has additional functions, some of which have relevance for the work of the Tribunal, particularly with respect to the Public Complaints Committee. The PCC is responsible and accountable to the Council, to which it must submit all its reports and findings. The Council also determines the remuneration, fees, and allowances payable to the chair and members of the PCC. The PCC's recommendations are in turn appealable to the Tribunal, whose jurisdiction extends to all committees of NEMA, of which the PCC is one. Therefore, should the action taken by the Council on the PCC's recommendations prove unsatisfactory, the complainant would be entitled to make a complaint to the Tribunal.

The Council is empowered to regulate its own procedure. It must meet four times every financial year with the Minister presiding at the meetings himself or herself or by appointee. The Secretary, who is the Director General of NEMA, must prepare and keep records of business at such meetings. So far the Council has merely been noting the recommendations of the PCC, and no concrete action has been taken by it. Action, if any, would have to be taken by the Director General of NEMA. Therefore, strictly speaking, failure by the Council to take action can be construed as failure by NEMA to take action and should be appealable to the Tribunal.

The National Environment Management Authority

NEMA's key functions are to

- Exercise general supervision and coordination over the matters relating to the environment
- Be the principal instrument of Government in the implementation of all policies relating to the environment
- Consider and determine applications for environmental impact assessment licenses

In view of the numerous sectoral laws and agencies that are currently charged with various functions in relation to the management of natural resources and the environment in Kenya, NEMA is given quite a wide and challenging mandate. Because of the extensive authority that it wields, inevitably some of its decisions will cause grievances, and there must be institutions that provide avenues for the redress of grievances arising from NEMA's decisions.

Among NEMA's powers relevant for land use that are appealable are the power to

- Direct any lead agency – including agencies dealing with land use management – to perform any of the duties imposed upon that lead agency in the field of environment by or under the Act or any other written law
- Issue guidelines for the management of the environment of lakes and rivers
- Develop, issue, and implement regulations, procedures, guidelines, and measures for the sustainable use of hillsides, hilltops, mountain areas, and forests
- Issue guidelines and prescribe measures for the management and protection of any areas of environmental significance declared to be protected natural environment areas
- Issue guidelines and prescribe measures for the sustainable management and utilization of genetic resources of Kenya for the benefit of its people
- Require any proponent of a project to carry out at his or her own expense further evaluation or environmental impact assessment study
- Issue an environmental impact assessment license
- Issue a waste disposal license to any person who intends to transport wastes or to operate a waste disposal site or plant or to generate hazardous waste
- Grant a temporary permit allowing emission of noise in excess of established standards for certain activities

After the establishment of NEMA, almost a whole year passed before it commenced the exercise of recruiting its own staff, with the result that applications were rarely processed. This position is now being redressed, with appointments to all key positions being undertaken.

Provincial and District Committees

In addition to the national bodies discussed previously, there are a number of province- and district-based committees. These committees are specifically provided for in the Act as Committees of the Authority, to be chaired by the respective Provincial Commissioners and District Commissioners. The committees comprise various provincial and district representatives of Government and nongovernmental organizations, regional development authorities, business communities, farmers, or pastoralists, where applicable.

Institutionally, it is not clear in what way these are "Committees of the Authority." They do not function under the direction of or report to the Authority but, rather, report to the Minister, who may, from time to time, assign to them additional functions by notice in the *Kenya Gazette*. Thus, no functional link with the Authority is discernible, apart from the fact the District (and, in the province, the Provincial) Environment Officer, who is an employee of the Authority, is the Secretary to the Committee.

However, as Committees of the Authority, these Committees take actions and decisions that are also appealable to the Tribunal.

Other Committees of the Authority

The Act also provides that the Authority may set up other committees. Under the Tribunal's mandate, the decisions of all the Committees of the Authority are appealable to the Tribunal.

Among the committees is the Technical Advisory Committee, to advise the Authority on environmental impact assessment reports. Section 58 of the Act requires that certain projects, which are listed in Schedule II to the Act, must undergo environmental impact assessment and submit project reports to the Authority. Such projects include any activity out of character with its surrounding, major changes in land use, urban developments, transportation, dams, aerial spraying, mining, forestry-related activities, agriculture, processing and manufacturing industries, electrical infrastructure, management of hydrocarbons, and natural conservation areas. All of these activities have relevance for land use.

Another Committee of the Authority is the National Environment Action Plan Committee, which is chaired by the Permanent Secretary in the Ministry responsible for national economic planning and development. A Director of the Authority is its member and Secretary. This Committee's role is to prepare five-year national environment action plans for consideration and adoption by the National Assembly. Such plans shall, among other requirements, contain an analysis of natural resources of Kenya, an analytical profile of their uses and value, and recommendations for appropriate legal and fiscal incentives for the business community to incorporate environmental requirements into its planning and operational processes and for building national awareness.

Third is the Standards and Enforcement Review Committee. It is chaired by the Permanent Secretary in the Ministry responsible for the environment, with a Director of the Authority as its member and Secretary. In consultation with relevant lead agencies, this Committee is expected primarily to make recommendations with regard to environmental quality standards.

The National Environment Restoration Fund

The National Environment Restoration Fund was established as supplementary insurance for the mitigation of environmental degradation where the perpetrator is not identifiable. It may also be resorted to where the Authority, in exceptional circumstances, must intervene for the control or mitigation of environmental degradation. A fund of this kind is of great significance for land use. Monies to be paid into the fund include levies and fees imposed on those who have applied for an environmental inpact assessment (EIA) license. One of the decisions that may be appealed to the Tribunal is a decision by the Authority on the amount of fees to be imposed on an applicant for a license. Consequently, fees to be placed in the National Environment Restoration Fund may be appealed to the Tribunal.

NEMA's Licensing Function

The Tribunal is empowered to deal with the grant or transfer or imposition of conditions on and revocation or variation of licenses, the fees payable, and imposition of restoration or improvement orders.

As has been stated, NEMA is empowered to issue an environmental impact assessment license on such terms and conditions as may be appropriate and necessary to facilitate sustainable development and sound environmental management. Before doing so, it must be satisfied as to the adequacy of an environmental impact assessment study, evaluation, or review report. However, on the advice of the Standards and Enforcement Review Committee, the Authority must cancel, revoke, or suspend such a license for a period not exceeding 24 months when the licensee contravenes the provisions of the license. In that event, the holder of the license cannot proceed with the project that is subject of the license until a new one shall have been issued by the Authority.

Second, an effluent discharge as well as a waste disposal license must be obtained from the Authority by a local authority operating a sewerage system and an owner or operator of any trade or industrial undertaking who discharges any effluents or other pollutants into the environment. The application for such a license must be in prescribed form and be accompanied by a prescribed fee. The license, if granted, must be in prescribed form, subject to prescribed or specified conditions. Should the Authority reject an application for the grant of an effluent discharge license, it must notify the applicant within 21 days, stating reasons for the rejection. An applicant who is aggrieved may appeal to the Tribunal.

The Authority may in writing cancel the license when the holder contravenes the Act or regulations made thereunder or fails to comply with any condition specified in the license. The license may also be cancelled in the interest of the environment or the public. Again, the licensee, if aggrieved, may appeal to the Tribunal within 60 days of such cancellation.

Under the Act, there is no express provision that an omission or failure to observe requirements by NEMA is itself appealable to the Tribunal. But under the Tribunal's rules, a provision that would allow a person who might be aggrieved by an omission or failure to appeal to the Tribunal has been included. This was included in the National Environment Tribunal Procedure Rules, LN 191, of 2003. It is also possible that the actions or omissions of the Authority could be the subject of investigations by the Public Complaints Committee under section 32, in which case the recommendations of the PCC could also be appealed to the Tribunal.

NEMA is required to give reasons for its decisions and to advise the applicant within 21 days of its decision. It should also advise the applicant of his or her right to appeal to the Tribunal.

3 DISPUTE RESOLUTION MECHANISMS UNDER EMCA

EMCA provides for two kinds of dispute resolution mechanisms: the Public Complaints Commission, which is in the nature of an environmental ombudsman, whose function is to receive complaints and petitions of a technical or nontechnical character, and the National Environmental Tribunal, whose function is to review administrative decisions.

3.1 The Public Complaints Commission

The PCC receives complaints directly from members of the public. It is not bound by any technical legal procedures in receiving or hearing complaints and petitions. The Tribunal comprises technically qualified persons. It receives and handles matters referred to it by the Director General, the PCC, or proponents of the various projects.

The Public Complaints Committee is placed alongside the Provincial and District Environment Committees under the part of the Act dealing with "Administration." This is inappropriate, as it conveys the impression that the PCC is directly under or subordinate to the administrative structures of the NEMA. Indeed the NEMA Board and management argued for some time that the PCC was an integral part of NEMA.

Matters were compounded when the Government opted to fund the PCC (as well as the Tribunal) through the Parliamentary allocation given to NEMA. NEMA was thus in a position to control the purse strings of the two institutions charged with resolving disputes and dealing with complaints against NEMA. The staff assigned to the two institutions were also employed by NEMA and merely seconded to the two institutions. It took more than a year of presentations before this issue could be resolved in favor of funding the two institutions directly. The staffing situation is yet to be rectified.

The nature of an ombudsman institution is that its proceedings are designed to allow members of the public easy access to a remedial system. For this reason, all that the complainant need do is lodge the complaint. The institution itself conducts the investigation. As one commentary described it:

> A common factor is that Ombudsman procedure is invariably inquisitorial. All the complainant has to do is complain; no expensive lawyers are necessary, no evidence has to be amassed and no case has to be proved. The Ombudsman takes over control of investigation, typically possessing powers to trawl through government documents and offices and question officials informally in their offices.[2]

The Public Complaints Committee has been designed along these lines. Its principal function is to investigate any allegations or complaints against any person or against the Authority and to make a report of its findings and recommendations to the National Environment Council. The Act provides also that the PCC may perform such other functions and exercise such powers as may be assigned to it by the Council. The Act empowers the Committee additionally to initiate investigations on its own motion when environmental degradation is suspected. The Committee's powers are therefore quite wide.

In the conduct of its investigations, the PCC may seek all reasonable assistance in connection with the investigation of any complaint or the attendance of persons for

---

[2] Cesare P. R. Romano, "A Proposal to Enhance the Effectiveness of International Environmental Law: The 'International Environmental Ombudsman,'" Earth Summit Watch Programs, New York University Law School, Clinic on International Environmental Law, spring 1997.

examination before it. These powers are enforced by way of a fine of up to 50,000 Kenya shillings (Ksh) for failure to comply with requirements of the Committee, or of obstruction or hindrance of the PCC in the exercise of its powers.

The PCC has seven members. Its chair must be a person qualified to be a judge of the High Court. Other members are representatives of the Attorney General, the Law Society of Kenya, nongovernmental organizations, the business community, and two members active in environmental management. They can hold office for up to two three-year terms, except the representative of the Attorney General, who holds office ex officio.

It stands to reason that the PCC is not meant to be subordinate to NEMA. It reports to and is subject to the direction of the NEC only. If NEC were to take prompt steps to act on the Committee's recommendations, the Committee could easily turn out to be one of the most important dispute resolution institutions in environmental and land use management in Kenya. For this potential to be realized, the PCC must not, through administrative devices such as the channeling of its funds through NEMA or the secondment of NEMA employees to it, be subordinated to NEMA. If that were to happen, public confidence in the PCC would be undermined completely.

The Act does not provide for recommendations of the PCC to be made public, but there is no bar to making them public contemporaneously with their submission to the NEC. The PCC is required to prepare and submit to NEC periodic reports of its activities, which shall form part of the annual report on the state of the environment. The Minister is then expected to lay this annual report before the National Assembly as soon as reasonably practicable after its publication when the National Assembly is in session. When the National Assembly is not in session, the report should be tabled within 21 days of the day of its next sitting. The PCC's periodic reports should be published as and when they are prepared, at least in summary, since wide and regular publicity is likely to provide a more effective weapon than prosecution.

The experience of the PCC so far bears out its potential as an effective mechanism for the resolution of environmental land use–related disputes. Its investigations have concerned issues such as deforestation, changes in land use without environmental impact assessment or mitigation measures, quarrying activities, industrial pollution, and poor solid waste management practices. In several cases, the respondents have taken remedial action without the need for any enforcement action. This demonstrates that in itself an investigation of a complaint can be effective in resolving disputes in certain cases.

The PCC will be a key partner of the National Environment Tribunal in the process of dispute settlement. Even though it does not have the power to determine disputes, it clearly serves a valuable role in providing individual complainants with an avenue for dispute resolution that enables them to avoid costs and expenses.

3.2 The Tribunal

Tribunals are diverse in their nature and in what they do. The word *tribunal* is not a technical term, and dictionaries attach various meanings to it, such as "a court of justice or arbitration," "a body appointed to adjudicate in some matter or to inquire into some disputed question," "a confessional," and "a special court convened by the government to inquire into a specific matter."

The popularity of tribunals emanates from the fact that courts of law are not able to dispense justice expeditiously and the process of litigation is too expensive and slow. Often, governments seek to install systems of administration that safeguard the interests of citizens in their dealings with authority while aiming to preserve the efficiency of government. The advantages that tribunals enjoy over courts of law are seen to be cheapness, accessibility, freedom from technicality, expeditiousness, and expert knowledge of their particular subject.

Tribunals are commonly referred to as "administrative tribunals." This simply connotes that the reason for the establishment of the tribunal is administrative; that is, that the reasons for preferring it to an ordinary court are administrative reasons. The term *administrative tribunals* may sometimes be used to distinguish such bodies from the courts of law or to denote that they form part of an administrative arrangement of Government.

Tribunals can be ad hoc or standing. Ad hoc tribunals are set up for specific if not intermittent purposes only. This happens when the applications, appeals, or other tasks involved are unlikely to be frequent or continuous. This usually occurs when appeals are made to an administrative authority, and that authority, in turn, seeks the appointment of a suitably qualified individual or a panel of persons to serve as a tribunal. As is often the case, an ad hoc tribunal usually addresses a specific area of activity, and relevant qualification and experience are the guiding factors to nomination or appointment. Very frequently, too, the chairperson is picked from persons with legal background if the tribunal has adjudicative functions. A standing tribunal, such as the National Environment Tribunal, is established to deal with dispute resolution on a routine basis.

The primary role of a tribunal is to hear appeals, usually from a decision taken initially by a department of government or other public body. The perceived advantages of courts of law over tribunals have been adverted to. Courts of law are often presided over by lawyers. Very rarely will one find a member of the bench with extra expertise in other technical fields. This means that when a technical matter is referred to a court, the first thing to do is to take time to explain the technical details to the judge or magistrate presiding over that particular matter. The time taken – as compared to that which would be taken before a specialized tribunal – can be, and is often, considerable. Second, there is no guarantee, even within the same jurisdiction, that a technical matter will end up before the same judge who had handled similar matters before. This often means that each time the same process of explaining technicalities must occur.

Another reason for preferring a tribunal to settle environmental disputes is that tribunals are designed to be free of legal and procedural technicalities. In this respect the law often provides that the tribunal need not be bound by the legal rules of evidence. As is the case with courts of law, a tribunal must make its decisions only according to law and without any influence whatsoever from any person or body whose decision is appealed before it or from any other quarter. The tribunal should reach its decision independently. This means, too, that its procedures are clearly understood and that its proceedings are reasonably predictable.

The National Environment Tribunal is empowered to inquire into matters arising from

- The refusal to grant or transfer a license
- The imposition of any condition, limitation, or restriction on a license

- The revocation, suspension, or variation of a licence
- The amount of money required to be paid as fee
- The imposition of an environmental restoration order or environmental improvement order by the Authority

Such appeals must be lodged within 60 days after the occurrence of the event in accordance with such procedures as may be established by the Tribunal itself for the purpose. The Tribunal has made rules known as The National Environment Tribunal Procedure Rules, LN 191, of 2003 (*Kenya Gazette Supplement* No. 92 of 21 November 2003). The Rules have taken account of certain basic principles included in the Act, such as the following:

- The Tribunal is not to be bound by rules of evidence as contained in the Evidence Act.
- Appeal to the Tribunal must be written.
- The Tribunal must choose times and places it will sit.
- Proceedings of the Tribunal are open to the public. However, if there is good cause, it may direct otherwise.
- The quorum of the Tribunal while hearing and determining any cause or matter must be three, the Chair and two other members.
- When a member has direct interest in any matter before the Tribunal he or she must not participate in the relevant proceedings.
- Appeals to the Tribunal must be preferred within 60 days after the occurrence of the event.

The Tribunal may make an award, give directions, make orders, or make decisions thereon without reference to any other party. In this respect, it has the following powers:

- To confirm, set aside, or vary the order or decision in question
- To exercise any of the powers that could have been exercised by the Authority
- To make such other orders, including an order for costs, as it may deem just
- To make orders for compelling attendance of any person
- To make orders for the discovery or production of any relevant document
- To order the investigation of any contravention of the Act
- To take evidence on oath and administer oaths
- To hear, on its own motion, any person as a witness
- To appoint, through its Chair, persons to act as assessors in any advisory capacity

In turn, its decisions and orders are appealable to the High Court of Kenya. The decision of the High Court on any appeal from the Tribunal shall be final.

In the course of its deliberations, the Tribunal may compel attendance of any person and issue orders for discovery, or production of documents, or investigation of any suspected contravention of the Act, much in the same way as courts of law do. Similarly, it may take evidence on oath and, for that purpose, administer oaths. And to secure obedience to the Tribunal's orders and decisions and respect for its proceedings, the Act makes failure to attend Tribunal proceedings or refusal to take an oath or affirmation before the Tribunal or knowingly giving false statement before the Tribunal, among others, an offense.

In order to guarantee the independence of the Tribunal, it is important that its administrative staff must not be seconded from NEMA, as has happened. The Act empowers the Minister responsible for environmental matters to appoint a public officer to be the Secretary to the Tribunal. Therefore, the staff should be persons who are employed by the Ministry, and not by NEMA.

Second, as has been adverted to with respect to the PCC, the funds of the Tribunal must be voted directly for the Tribunal, and not channeled through NEMA. This has now been achieved, but only after effort. Additionally, the Tribunal should operate at arm's length from the sponsoring ministry as well as from NEMA. This includes the physical location of the Tribunal. Presently, the Tribunal operates from the same premises as NEMA, a location that might create the impression that it is an organ of NEMA. The danger in keeping the Tribunal in close proximity to NEMA, whose decisions it has to review or consider, is that the public will always tend to see it as an appendage of NEMA. This can lead to claims of bias or lack of independence or outright complicity against appellants.

Another factor to be taken into account relates to membership on the Tribunal. The Tribunal consists of five persons. Its chair is nominated by the Judicial Service Commission and must be a person qualified for appointment as a judge of the High Court of Kenya. Other members include

- An advocate nominated by the Law Society of Kenya
- A lawyer who has professional qualifications in environmental law, appointed by the Minister
- Two persons who have demonstrated exemplary academic competence in the field of environmental management appointed by the Minister

The appointments of members of the NET must be made by name and notified or published in the *Kenya Gazette* by the Minister. They are appointed at different times for periods of three years only. Even though there is no express provision permitting their reappointment, there is no bar to reappointment.

To be credible, the appointment procedures must be fair and independent of the administrative authorities of government that have a direct interest in the Tribunal's decisions. Additionally, the appointees must also enjoy security of tenure, subject, of course, to clearly established rules for removal from office in case of poor performance, misbehavior, or incapacity. In this respect, the National Environment Tribunal has a shortcoming: Its members can be removed merely for misbehavior. The term is not defined, and the Minister does not have to give reasons. This potentially could be abused. The reasons for removal must be clearly indicated in order to remove the risk of abuse.

Remarkably enough, the Act provides that the Minister may be empowered to establish such other Tribunals in any part of Kenya as he or she deems appropriate. In other words, the Minister can establish other *National* Environment Tribunals. Whether they would each have similar and coextensive jurisdictions is not clear, but there is nothing that suggests that any Tribunal so established will be subordinate to the first one already established. If this occurs, the present and other national Tribunals will presumably have jurisdictions like those of the High Courts established under the Constitution. As we point out later, existence of multiple Tribunals with concurrent powers could lead to many contradictory rulings. Only one Tribunal should have been provided for, which may sit in various provincial or other towns or places alternately.

Although the main function of the Tribunal is to hear appeals from the decisions of the Director General, the Authority, and committees of the Authority, the Tribunal may also act when the Authority or any of its committees makes a referral to it regarding any matter. The Act provides that the Authority may refer to the Tribunal a matter that appears to the Authority to involve a point of law or that appears to be of unusual importance or complexity. The Authority and the parties thereto shall be entitled to be heard before any decision is made in respect of such matter.

The establishment of the Tribunal holds great potential for the resolution of land use and environmental disputes in Kenya, even though this potential has yet to be realized, as no appeal has been lodged with the Tribunal. The Tribunal represents a middle way between leaving appellants to go directly to the ordinary courts of law and setting up an Environmental Court, as a division of the High Court of Kenya, as has at times been proposed. The latter option will take some time to realize.

If established, an environmental court would deal specifically with special interests and issues related to the environment. The judges serving on such a court would be specialists in environmental matters, and, because it would be a court of law, all its members would need legal qualification.

4 CONCLUSIONS

This review has indicated that Kenya possesses institutional arrangements for the resolution of environmental and land-use–related disputes. The experience so far has been limited, however. The PCC has been able to resolve a number of complaints, but the Tribunal has yet to determine any appeal, as no appeal has been lodged with it so far.

On the whole, the Tribunal has the requisite powers to play a decisive role in environmental and land use management in Kenya. The present obstacles are largely administrative in nature and can be overcome through the development of appropriate administrative practices and arrangements.

15 Managing the Environmental Impact of Refugees in Kenya: The Role of National Accountability and Environmental Law

George Okoth-Obbo

> Safeguarding the environment is one of the foundations of peace and security.
> Kofi Annan, Secretary-General of the United Nations

> Caring for the environment is not an option. As a direct part of its mandate, it is something that UNHCR cannot afford to ignore. To do so would be to jeopardise the basic rights and needs of refugees – the institution of asylum. That is why we have made environmental issues a policy priority in our work.
> Ruud Lubbers, Former United Nations High Commissioner for Refugees

1 INTRODUCTION

In the popular imagination, refugees and sustainable environmental outcomes are not easily twinned. More typical is the image of masses precipitously pouring across borders with the same danger to local natural resources as might be associated with "a swarm of locusts."[1] Although it is well established that refugees can have profound multiple effects on their host environments,[2] this ravaging image of refugees is clearly an exaggeration. Nevertheless, in many an asylum country today, the relationship between refugees and ecology has become a "hot potato" in both community and State responses to cross-border forced displacement.

The outcry by the Garissa Town Council in Kenya against refugees in Dadaab Camp is illustrative of complaints routinely leveled against refugees; its litany of environmental woes includes:

---

[1] Ray Wilkinson, writing about the refugee exodus triggered into the Great Lakes region by the Rwanda genocide of 1994, talks of the eastern towns of Zaire (as it was then known) and northwest Tanzania as "being overwhelmed by frenzied and then exhausted hordes of frightened exiles." The refugees, he continues, went ahead to "consume more than 1,200 tons of wood per day. Local gunmen, poachers and refugees trapped or shot wildlife, including the gorillas." See his "Living on the Edge," *Refugees Magazine* No. 127 (July 2002). See also, Craig Sanders, "Environment: Where Have All the Flowers Gone . . . and the Trees . . . and the Gorillas?" *Refugees Magazine* Vol. 110 (1994).

[2] See B. E. Whitaker, "Changing Opportunities: Refugees and Host Communities in Western Tanzania," *New Issues in Refugee Research, Working Paper No. 11* (1999), and C. L. Chisolm, "Refugee Settlements Are an Economic Magnet for Host Populations: A Case Study of Meheba Refugee Settlement, Northwest Province, Zambia" (unpublished monograph) (1966).

The views expressed in this chapter are, however, personal and do not necessarily reflect the official position of the United Nations High Commissioner for Refugees (UNHCR) or the United Nations.

indiscriminate clearing of vegetation, harvesting of fuel wood for both domestic and commercial purposes, harvesting of building and fencing materials, wildlife hunting and poaching, harvesting of sand and gravel, insecurity, social disruptions, damage to infrastructures, uncontrolled grazing of pastures and fodder, uncontrolled over-exploitation of underground water among others.[3]

At the State level, in Tanzania – one of the few countries to have formally issued a comprehensive national policy on refugee asylum[4] – environmental security has been officially and explicitly set as a threshold line along which the country's asylum policy is to be defined. Although other asylum States have not formally gone this far, many are insisting that the asylum obligations that they can or should bear must be measured against the security and sustainability of their natural resources.[5] In addition, the international community is increasingly being "called upon to foot the bill for cleaning up" environmental damage, even if "it is often not clear if refugees were the cause of the degradation in the first place."[6]

Focusing on the case of Kenya, this chapter examines the refugee–ecology relationship with particular emphasis on ways that measures to stem deleterious impacts are or should be established. After this introduction, the refugee–environment state of affairs is described, highlighting the impacts that have occurred. Next follows an explanation of the way the country structured the refugee program to mitigate these impacts. It emerges that the programmatic, implementation, and regulatory system currently in place is less than what is required to assure environmental balance and to prevent conflict over resource issues in a refugee setting. In Kenya, as in other countries in Africa, the Government does not exercise telling national policy, legal, and management oversight over refugee operations in general and over environmental imperatives in particular, even if the legal machinery for this is in place. Rather, international humanitarian organizations – most notably, the United Nations High Commissioner for Refugees (UNHCR) – are relied upon as the pivotal fulcrums for regulation, management, and, ultimately, accountability for the environmental priorities at stake.

The international refugee regime and the UNHCR institutional, policy, and operational apparatus, which thus make up the quintessential regulatory framework for refugee operations, are inadequate by themselves to guarantee implicitly that critical objectives will be realized. Thus, if baseline environmental goals are to be assured in the refugee context, they must be anchored firmly as both a jural postulate[7] and a priority of State accountability and must not be left to the vicissitudes of international humanitarian imperatives. The chapter outlines the key elements of this corrective program, underscoring the pivotal role that should be assigned to environmental law because of its action-forcing, precautionary, and reparatory character.

---

[3] Garissa Town Council, *Preliminary Environmental Impact Assessment of Refugees on Garissa County Council Trustland of Dadaab, Liboi and Jarajilla Divisions*, 25 January 2002.

[4] See United Republic of Tanzania, *The National Refugee Policy*, Ministry of Home Affairs, Dar es Salaam.

[5] See overview contained in UNHCR Executive Committee, "Economic and Social Impacts of Massive Refugee Populations on Host Developing Countries as Well as Other Countries: A Quantitative Assessment on the Basis of Special Case Studies," EC/48/SC/CRP.40.

[6] Ray Wilkinson, *supra* note 1.

[7] That is to say, the goals and objectives under which a legal order functions. See R. W. Dias, *Jurisprudence*, 4th ed. (Butterworths) (1976) 579–600.

2 THE ENVIRONMENTAL IMPACTS OF REFUGEES IN KENYA

The environmental question arises in two somewhat different debates over forced migration. The first debate is over whether involuntary displacement can be triggered by environmental factors. One school of thought considers this a misleading, highly politicized, and potentially dangerous notion.[8] The opposing school of thought argues that "environmental refugees" make up an important yet unrecognized category of forced migration, which, it is claimed, already in the 1990s exceeded 25 million people. This school projects that "environmental refugees" are set to double in number by 2010, and possibly even climb to over 200 million because of the effects of global warming,[9] setting the stage for the single greatest environmental disaster of this millennium.

This is clearly a crucial theoretical and concrete issue in any discussion of the refugee–ecology problem. The concern of this chapter is, however, with the second – and no less important – debate: over the impact that large numbers of people displaced into another territory under emergency conditions can have on the environment.[10]

In Kenya, since the country started to be faced with massive outflows of refugees from Somalia and the Sudan in the early 1990s, refugee numbers have remained compelling not only in absolute terms but also in relation to the carrying capacity of the locations into which the refugees are displaced.[11] The country presently hosts some 240,000 refugees: approximately 15,000 so-called urban cases; 135,000 refugees in Dadaab Camp, in Garissa District, in the eastern part of the country; and 88,000 in Kakuma Camp, in Turkana District, in the northwest. Most of the refugees in Dadaab (133,000) are from Somalia, while 60,000 of those in Kakuma are from the Sudan. Others are from Burundi, the Democratic Republic of Congo, Ethiopia, Rwanda, and Uganda.

The Dadaab and Kakuma refugee camps are located in arid and semiarid areas characterized by poor and unreliable rainfall (300–350 millimeters annually) and soils with limited productivity. The areas are generally ecologically fragile and are especially prone to disturbances arising from overconcentration of human beings and livestock and from inappropriate land uses. Dadaab Camp, covering a total area of 50 square kilometers, is located in the Lag Dera floodplain, which has hitherto served as dry-season grazing lands for the local community. It would be simplistic to assert that these locations experienced no environmental stresses before the arrival of refugees. And it must be stressed that some positive outcomes have flowed to the local communities from the presence of refugees, in that the communities can access social, economic, and other services either directly or collaterally under the organized refugee programs. That

---

[8] R. Black, "Environmental Refugees: Myth or Reality," *UNHCR Working Papers* No. 34 (2001). See also R. Black, *Refugees, Environment and Development* (Longmans) (1988).

[9] N. Myers, "Environmental Refugees," *Population and Environment* Vol. 19 (2) (1997) 167. See also N. Myers and J. Kent, *Environmental Exodus: An Emerging Crisis* (Climate Institute) (1995); Stephen Castles, "Environmental Change and Forced Migration: Making Sense of the Debate," *New Issues in Refugee Research Series, Working Paper No. 70* (October 2002), reviews and explains these different outlooks.

[10] The various typologies of the exacerbation of environmental damage in situations of displacement are described in UNHCR, "Refugees and the Environment," at http:/www.unhcr.ch/cgi-bin

[11] Kenya's total population is about 31 million. Its total area is about 225,000 square miles, or about 583,000 square kilometers.

having been said, the negative environmental impacts of this presence, with which this chapter is particularly concerned, are also clearly demonstrated.

2.1 Alienation of Land

One of the most socially and politically explosive of these impacts is rooted in the actual or perceived alienation of land. Kakuma Camp, covering an area of 24 square kilometers, is located at the confluence of the Tarach and Lodoket seasonal rivers. This area, hitherto characterized by a riverine forest, also served as dry-season grazing land for the local Turkana pastoralists. The establishment of the camp there required about 400 hectares in Kakuma. In Dadaab, which at this time was inhabited by about 5,000 Somali pastoralists, 1,230 hectares were appropriated.

Under international refugee law, States bear the obligation to provide lands upon which refugee camps, settlements, and programs are to be established. In Africa, they have done so with what has been hailed as traditional African selflessness and hospitality. Today, however, even where local community response to refugees otherwise remains essentially positive, attitudes are at best contradictory where land is concerned. Thus, in both Kakuma and Dadaab, there has been no more significant source of tensions – and indeed of frequent fatal conflicts between refugees and local communities – than the perception that communal lands have been unjustly alienated. Even allowing for its evident hyperbole, the following statement by the Garissa Town Council illustrates this problem:

> Refugees have vehemently reduced the land space previously available to the local community to support their livelihood.... [T]he actual land area surrounding refugee camps that has been rendered valueless and unavailable for the utilisation of the local pastoralists is 50 km sq and is soon spreading to 100 km sq.... [T]he concern of the local Council is: with so much land space being occupied by UNHCR and supporting agencies offices, refugee camps and other infrastructures coupled with complete destruction of 50 km sq land area radius around these camps, what is fate of the innocent local pastoralist to sustain his livelihood?[12]

2.2 Deforestation and Soil Erosion

There have been devegetation and deforestation in both Kakuma and Dadaab. In the period between the establishment of Dadaab Camp in 1991 and the introduction in 1994 of the main environmental project there, Rational Energy Supply, Conservation, Utilisation, and Education (RESCUE),[13] refugees ranged freely as they sought firewood and shelter construction materials. This resulted in extensive land degradation through devegetation, which extended some 7 to 10 kilometers beyond the camps. In Kakuma Camp, on the other hand, refugees were forbidden to harvest natural resources. However, they provided a ready market for woody biomass such as charcoal, firewood, and fencing materials. As a result, the riverine forest spanning the banks of the Tarach and Lodoket Rivers has experienced severe destruction not only by refugees, who nevertheless foraged

---

[12] Garissa Town Council, *supra* note 3.
[13] *See* discussion of this project, *infra* note 28 and accompanying text.

for firewood and other needs, but by the host communities themselves, for whom the refugee presence has provided an opportunity for commercialization of those products. This polarized situation was evoked in the following statement by the Garissa Town Council:

> 90% of the local community in the refugee settlement area of Garissa District trust land are nomadic pastoralists rearing livestock as their basic livelihood. . . . Before the refugees came the land carrying capacity was 26 ha/year/animal. This was reduced to 50 ha/yr/animal in 1995 and is now estimated at 100 ha/yr/animal. Reduced land carrying capacity coupled with theft of animals by refugees, disease outbreaks, disruption of traditional and organised grazing patterns has reduced local herds to be below sustainable levels rendering the local pastoralists become impoverished and displaced. . . . They are in a situation worse than alien refugee as no one cares about them.[14]

The related problem of soil erosion is more pronounced in Kakuma than in Dadaab. Devegetation coupled with deforestation has led to exposure of the soils to both wind and water erosion as characterized by frequent dust storms in the dry season and extensive gully and sheet erosion during the wet season.

2.3 Pollution and Urbanization

Pollution has also been a problem. Within the refugee camps, there is the problem of solid waste disposal, including food waste, sewage, medical waste, and recyclable materials.[15] Discarded plastic bags pose a health hazard for the free-ranging livestock owned by the local community, especially in Kakuma.[16] Here, too, the prevailing cultural practice among some communities of open field human waste disposal poses a health hazard.[17]

Along with these problems has also come what may be referred to as spontaneous, unplanned urbanization, as the two camps have acted as pull factors for outlying local populations, resulting in all manner of social problems. For instance, before the establishment of Kakuma Camp in 1991 and 1992, the area consisted of a very small town, the remnant of a staging post for the company that had constructed the highway to Lokichoggio, with no more than 2,000 local Turkanas.[18] In less than 10 years, the local population had grown to some 9,000 Turkanas.[19] The drought that ravaged the District between 1998 and 2000 swelled numbers even more exponentially, raising the total to

---

[14] Garissa Town Council, *supra* note 3.

[15] A study commissioned by UNHCR established baseline data on the environmental impacts in Kakuma Camp in five main areas: (1) surface water and the environment, (2) waste management and the environment, (3) resource-related violence, (4) gender concerns and environmental management, and (5) income-generating activities and the environment and domestic energy market in Kakuma. See Moi University Centre for Refugee Studies, *Executive Summary of Kakuma Environmental Baseline Surveys Submitted to UNHCR's Nairobi Office*, July 1998.

[16] Ibid.   [17] Ibid.

[18] Government of Kenya Central Statistics Bureau, *Kenya Population Census 1989*, Vol. 2, Government Printer, Nairobi.

[19] Government of Kenya Central Statistics Bureau, *1999 Population and Housing Census*, Vol. 1, Government Printer, Nairobi.

an estimated 35,000.[20] Today, UNHCR estimates that this figure has grown to 45,000, with large numbers of local people living within the camp itself.[21]

In effect, what was a traditional, pastoral society has increasingly become resocialized from communalist relationships to those defined by monetary exchange, trade, commerce, and apparent dependence on the refugee relief program. Itaru Ohta, who has lived among and studied the Turkana for nearly three decades, argues that although aid agencies may see them as failures, they have taken "full advantage of the resources and opportunities that have been brought from the outside."[22]

Whether the transformations are bad or good is, however, not the key question that this chapter concerns. The point is that the changes indisputably are quite profound and far-reaching. For our purposes, attention is thus drawn to the accountability structure under which these changes are occurring, a point to which we shall return shortly.

3 THE RESPONSE

What is the operational and decision-making structure that ensures that the environmental problematic sketched is properly addressed? Who is the primary actor? What are the programs?

UNHCR programs are at the very frontier of the response to the problem, often exclusively. They are designed to meet, above all, the basic protection, survival, and sustainability needs of refugees in the most critical sectors, including those that have a direct bearing on the physical and human environment of the camps and settlements: nutrition, shelter, water, sanitation, health care, and social and community services. Service delivery is also established in such a way that the pressure on the host ecology will be minimized. Baseline standards and indicators have been established to govern the construction and implementation of service delivery in protection, care, and maintenance[23] as well as for specific or priority sectors.[24]

As far as the environment is concerned, refugee operations under the aegis of UNHCR are not simply left to the vagaries of good or bad fortune. They are governed by the organization's guidelines on refugees and the environment, adopted by its Executive Committee in October 1995.[25] Elaborated in the watershed of the Rwanda refugee crisis of 1994, which acutely heightened attention on the refugee–ecology relationship, the

---

[20] Maria de Conceicao das Neves Silva, "Impact of Kakuma Refugee Camp on Turkana Women and Girls" (unpublished mimeograph) (2002).

[21] Periodic surveys carried out by UNHCR. See also National Environment Management Authority, *Report on Fact-Finding Missions to Kakuma and Dadaab Refugee Camps* (May 2003) 5.

[22] Itaru Ohta, "Multiple Socio-Economic Relationships Improvised between the Turkana and Refugees in Kakuma Area, Northwestern Kenya" (research paper submitted to the UNHCR Nairobi Office) (25 January 2003).

[23] See *Practical Guide to the Systematic Use of Standards and Indicators in UNHCR Operations*, 1st ed. (January 2004).

[24] Guidelines have been elaborated for, among the more important topics, education assistance, the protection of refugee women, the protection of refugee children, service delivery in refugee emergencies, human immunodeficiency virus and acquired immunodeficiency syndrome (HIV/AIDS) and reproductive health, and, of course, the environment, discussed in this chapter. They can all be found at the UNHCR Web site: http://www.unhcr.ch/cgi-bin/texis/vtx/home.

[25] UNHCR Executive Committee, "Progress Report on the Guidelines on Refugees and the Environment," Doc. EC/SC.2/79, 1995. See also "UNHCR's Environmental Policy," in *UNHCR Environmental News*, Vol. 1, Issue 1 (June 1996).

policy acknowledges that the sudden influx of large numbers of refugees into what are often remote, fragile locations in countries of asylum can have, and indeed usually does have, significant environmental consequences. The Rwanda refugee crisis resulted in the destruction of entire ecosystems and economic infrastructures and had a burgeoning ripple effect on the social, economic, and political life of the two main asylum nations, Tanzania and Zaire (as it was then known). The guidelines were thus designed to prevent or mitigate ensuing environmental degradation, protect the welfare of refugees and host communities, and, of course, thereby buttress and secure the institution of asylum.

The key principles on which the guidelines are elaborated are the following:

a. An integrated approach, namely, that environmental baselines should be considered at all levels and in all sectors of UNHCR's activities
b. Prevention before cure
c. Cost-effectiveness and maximization of benefits and
d. Both refugee and local host and community participation

The organization's institutional resources, including budgets, organizational capacities, roles, coordination, and operational policies, are projected as important instruments in giving effect to these principles. Environmental assessment, planning, and monitoring are underlined as key methodological instruments. The principal areas underscored for environmentally specific interventions in all operations include the siting and physical planning of camps and settlements, the provision of domestic energy and household needs for refugees, forestry and natural resources management, and environmental education and awareness.[26]

These are the policy platforms upon which UNHCR's refugee operations in Kenya are planned and implemented as far as the prevention and mitigation of environmental impacts are concerned. In all the other sectors, environmental thresholds are also secured either directly or discretely through sector- or issue-specific guidelines.[27]

The Rational Energy Supply, Conservation, Utilisation, and Education (RESCUE) project that has been in operation since 1994 in Dadaab and since 1999 in Kakuma is an example of a program that has been designed specifically to address environmental management, rehabilitation, and renewal. Under the project, a wide range of activities is undertaken: first, to mitigate the negative impacts on the environment incidental to refugee presence and then to rehabilitate already degraded areas. Accordingly, through selected protection areas (greenbelts), a total of 482 hectares have been rehabilitated in Dadaab (456) and Kakuma (26). There are also reforestation activities, which include a total of seven tree nurseries maintained in both camps as of today, four in Dadaab and three in Kakuma. Over the years, some 2.4 million tree seedlings have been planted in Dadaab (1.6 million) and Kakuma (800,000) with a survival rate of 60 percent and 40 percent respectively.[28]

---

[26] See UNHCR, *Refugee Operations and Environmental Management: A Handbook of Selected Lessons Learned from the Field* (2002). See also Christopher Talbot, "Refugee Environmental Education: A Concept Paper," UNHCR Mimeograph (1995).

[27] See *Practical Guide to the Systematic Use of Standards and Indicators in UNHCR Operations, supra* note 23.

[28] For information on and review of the project, see Nicolas Blondel, *Firewood Survey around Dadaab Refugee Camps*, EESS Mission Report No. 00/13, UNHCR Geneva (September 2000); and by the same

Related to this, special programs are implemented to meet domestic energy require-ments, perhaps the single most important threat to the physical environment in both camp locations as refugees forage for firewood in what is already a fragile and denuded environment. Thus, firewood has been provided to refugees as part of the program in Dadaab since 1998 and in Kakuma since the inception of the camp. Although this intervention caters for only a fraction of the domestic energy requirements (between 30 percent and 40 percent), it nevertheless eases pressure on vegetation in the vicinity of refugee camps. Under a complementary program, over 64,000 improved energy-saving stoves have been distributed to refugees in Dadaab and 19,000 in Kakuma. Solar cookers have also been introduced in the camps since 1995. A pilot project is now under way to test and promote the use of a special product called *Ilanga* – Zulu for "sunshine" – but the project is thus far producing mixed results.[29]

Participatory environmental management is fostered, with a number of activities undertaken routinely to empower the stakeholders and beneficiaries, both refugees and local Kenyans alike. There are thus five standing Environment Working Groups (EWGs) that have been established, in Dadaab (four) and Kakuma (one).[30] Environmental education and awareness form part of these objectives and activities. Environmental clubs are operational in all the primary and secondary schools in each camp. In addition, environmental resource books and materials for primary school teachers and pupils have been developed by UNHCR in collaboration with UNESCO-PEER.[31]

4 CRITICAL REVIEW: NATIONAL STATE VERSUS INTERNATIONAL AGENCY ACCOUNTABILITY

These responses are impressive in their own right, but a critical review will reveal the challenges. First of all, even though the environmental issues that have been summarized in the preceding paragraphs occur within a refugee setting, in reality they are national in character and touch on fundamental and undifferentiated interests of sustainable natural resource use and exploitation. Yet, as is the tendency in many other countries in Africa, the Government does not exert a palpable influence in policy setting, planning, organization, implementation, and oversight of refugee operations, including thereby the environmental priorities.

In fact, for most of the period from the early 1990s, when the country started to be faced with large-scale influxes, the outlook and approach of the Government on refugee management were primarily externalist and nonintegrative from the point of view of the national planning and governance framework. The refugees were viewed first as only a problem and, second, one for which UNHCR and the international community, not the asylum state, were responsible. To the extent that the Government did concern

---

author, *Action Plan for the Sustainable Collection of Firewood and Management of Natural Resources around Dadaab Refugee Camps*, EESS Mission Report No. 00/14, UNHCR Geneva (October 2000).

[29] See Matthew Owen, *Pilot Promotion of Parabolic Solar Cookers – Monitoring Inception Report*, UNHCR, Geneva (December 2003); and Anna Ingwe-Musungu, *Promotion of Parabolic Solar Cookers in the Kenyan Refugee Camps (Dadaab and Kakuma)*, Interim Consultant's Report, GTZ, Nairobi (November 2003).

[30] The EWGs are reviewed in UNHCR, *A Handbook of Selected Lessons Learned from the Field*, UNHCR, Geneva, at 15.

[31] See Lindsay Bird, *Environmental Education Review*, EESS Mission Report, 03/07, UNHCR Geneva (June 2003).

itself with refugees from a policymaking and decision-making point of view, it did so because its attention was triggered by security or political imperatives. However, even in this case, the outlook was still mainly defensive, not oriented to the positive and deliberative attainment of goals. This is in fact the reason the refugee camps came to be sited in topographically difficult and environmentally fragile settings, as explained earlier.[32] This also explains the otherwise curious fact that the development plans for both Garissa and Turkana Districts typically do not refer to refugees or the refugee locations or issues in their very midst in any particular context.[33]

Thus, in real terms, the impetus and structures for refugee governance generally – and, for purposes of the present discussion, environmental response and management in a refugee setting – remain centered principally in international institutions, above all UNHCR and its nongovernmental organization (NGO) partners, which are also mainly international. Outside this framework, there are no really effective institutional systems through which policy setting, regulation, planning, and oversight of environmental management in a refugee setting are exercised and driven by the Government in a decisive manner.

UNHCR and other international or national humanitarian agencies indeed do bear mandated monitoring and operational responsibilities. They are aware that the refugee problem calls for deepening and widening, not diminishing, their mandated responsibilities so that they can plan and implement their responses within a more comprehensive and integrated national optic. Environmental activities in the refugee camps take into account the broad national legal requirements discussed in detail later. To facilitate even further this interplay on other levels, including coordination, a National Committee on the Impact of Refugee Settlements in Kenya was established, chaired by the Ministry of Environment and Natural Resources. Furthermore, at the global level, UNHCR recognizes the importance of addressing the needs of the local host populations and the necessity of bridging humanitarian action to national development platforms. UNHCR is thus developing deeper partnerships and synergies to this end, with environmental protection in refugee operations a key objective.[34]

---

[32] According to Itaru Ohta, *supra* note 22, "The Kenya Government selected these areas because, for one thing, it becomes easy to control the movement of refugees and, for the other, it becomes possible to isolate problematic refugee camps away from densely populated areas."

[33] See, e.g., Republic of Kenya, *Turkana District Development Plan 1999–2001*, Office of the Vice President and Ministry of Planning and National Development, Government Printer, Nairobi; and Republic of Kenya, *Garissa District Development Plan, 1997–2001*, Government Printer, Nairobi. Although the two Districts concerned are the homes of the two major camps in Kenya, neither document mentions refugees in any context whatsoever.

[34] These policy orientations received particular emphasis under the recent High Commissioner for Refugees, Ruud Lubbers, who strongly advocated the reconfiguration of refugee programs so that they are anchored on self-reliance and self-sustaining strategies and secure medium- to longer-term development-related goals for refugee programs. Initiatives to this effect are being elaborated within the Organization under a concept referred to as Development Assistance for Refugees (DAR), which involves obtaining additional development assistance to mitigate the burden of countries hosting large numbers of refugees, and to promote better quality of life and self-reliance for refugees pending durable solutions, and better quality of life for host communities. Another initiative, referred to as the "4 Rs," addresses repatriation-related situations and emphasizes the nexus of Repatriation, Reintegration, Rehabilitation, and Reconstruction. Under this approach, UNHCR organizes voluntary repatriation and provides protection and assistance for the initial reinsertion of refugees into their homes, whereas development actors address longer-term reintegration needs.

However, as UNHCR and its partner agencies continue to engineer new policy and operational constructs and collateralize existing ones, for legal reasons, on one hand, and accountability reasons, on the other, their role, management, and regulatory frameworks cannot be the preeminent ones for securing the environmental priorities at stake.

Starting with the legal consideration, UNHCR's mandate and its operations as a whole are based on international refugee law. The specific rights, obligations, and principles elaborated within this system are directed to securing the protection of refugees. This system does not establish rights, standards, and obligations directed to the environmental aspects of a refugee situation. Nor does the Statute of UNHCR directly mention obligations directed to the environment as such. Of course, as explained already, UNHCR has elaborated quite a forward-looking and broad-ranging policy on the environment. Moreover, both UNHCR's Executive Committee and the United Nations General Assembly have passed several resolutions that call attention to the need to address the refugee–ecology relationship within the refugee operational framework.[35]

Evidently, these are all part of the "soft law" of the international operational and regulatory regime on this question. They do not, however, represent hard law, equipped with action-forcing effect, obligations, and principles for environmental regulation, damage mitigation, or securing of stipulated environmental goals.

The limitations of international organizations as the preeminent entities to manage environmental issues in a refugee context are even more starkly highlighted when the political dimension of those problems is taken into account. When the Government is not present as the principal regulatory agency, the politicization of the refugee presence can reach dangerous levels, especially as unscrupulous politicians and local opinion movers opportunistically manipulate the subject. Although in Kenya this process has not risen to the xenophobic levels and the irrational hatred of refugees and foreigners seen in other parts of Africa, the perception of competition between refugees and their host communities over resource access and allocation has been real and critical in both Garissa and Turkana Districts. Regrettably, both conflict and loss of lives have resulted.

These deficits at the legal level in the reliance on an international organization as the critical regulatory force for environmental management in a refugee setting highlight the imperative to anchor that question firmly within the arena of national state responsibility and accountability. Environmental security in the refugee camps and settlements is thus not a foreign or externalist challenge to be left solely to international organizations. It is no less a national priority than are environmental problems elsewhere and calls into

---

[35] For instance, UNGA Resolution 44/139 of 15 December 1989 "calls upon the cooperating countries and the relevant agencies of the United Nations system to assist in restoring the ecological balance of the areas in the countries of asylum affected by the massive presence of refugees in order to provide the populations of those areas with the conditions conducive to development." In a series of other resolutions, the General Assembly has expressed "deep concern at the serious and far-reaching consequences of the presence of large numbers of refugees and displaced persons in the countries concerned and the implications for their security, environment and their long-term socioeconomic development" and "reaffirmed the importance of incorporating environmental considerations into the programme of the Office of the United Nations High Commissioner for Refugees, especially in the least developed countries, in view of the impact on the environment of the large numbers of refugees and displaced persons of concern to the High Commissioner." See UNGA Resolutions 48/116 of 20 December 1993; 48/118 of 20 December 1993; 50/152 of 20 December 1995; 52/101 of 12 December 1997; 53/126 of 9 December 1998; 54/147 of December 1999; 55/77 of 4 December 2000; 56/135 of 19 December 2001; and 57/183 of 18 December 2002.

play the same duty of accountability that the State bears for all environmental regulation and management in Kenya. That the Government is not the critical policy setter, driver of planning, overseer of implementation, and evaluator of both outcomes and outputs of refugee operations in terms of baseline national environmental goals means that it is not fully accountable for those priorities.

The situation whereby the Government's principal point of engagement with the refugee situation is limited to security not only is inadequate but can itself lead to serious environmental consequences. That is how the decision on the location of the present camps was made. As refugees poured into Kenya in their thousands from the collapse of the Siad Barre regime early in 1991, and with the arrival from the Sudan of the so-called Lost Boys later in the same year, a total of 14 refugee camps were established across the country. Driven by security concerns, the Government was determined not to admit the refugees farther inland into the country and restricted them to camps in the most marginal, topographically difficult, and environmentally fragile settings of the country in Mandera and Garissa Districts in eastern and northeastern Kenya and the similarly semiarid Turkana District in the northwest.[36] That these already fragile and limited ecological locations now had to provide for thousands of more claimants simply added greater stress to an already very stressed natural resource setting.

How then are the necessary legal, policy, and institutional reforms to change this situation to be engineered? We now turn to this question, focusing our attention on the action-forcing role of environmental law.

5 THE ROLE OF ENVIRONMENTAL LAW

Clearly, law is not the only means by which environmental goals, standards, and sustainability can be assured. It is, however, uniquely pivotal in that it alone among the other interventions can specify obligations and responsibilities in an action-forcing manner. It is for this reason that this part of the chapter examines the instrumental effect of law in bridging both the legal and the accountability chasms demonstrated thus far. Our argument is that environmental regulation within the refugee settings in Kenya should be articulated squarely within the national regulatory framework that addresses environmental protection and management as such.

Kenya in fact has a legislative regime that mandates environmental management and protection priorities at the national level. This regime comprises two clusters of interrelated legislative typologies. On one hand is legislation that caters to the regulation and management of particular sectors of the nation's natural resources and mandates the attainment of stipulated goals and thresholds.[37] On the other hand Kenya has promulgated overarching legislation for the protection of the environment: the Environmental Management and Co-ordination Act.[38] In this chapter, we concentrate our discussion on the latter legislation.

---

[36] See *supra* note 32.

[37] For a typological study of the environmental law of Kenya, see George Okoth-Obbo, "A Conceptual Analysis of Environmental Impact Assessment as a Legal Mechanism for the Protection and Management of the Environment: The Case of Kenya" (unpublished LLM thesis, University of Nairobi, 1995), especially 64 to126.

[38] The Environmental Management and Co-ordination Act, Act No. 8 of 1999.

The objective of the Act is the "the establishment of an appropriate legal and institutional framework for the management of the environment and for matters connected therewith and incidental thereto." It declares that "every person is entitled to a clean and healthy environment and has the duty to guard and enhance the environment."[39] It proceeds to establish a cascade of management structures at the National, Provincial, and District levels. This last point is particularly important in the refugee context, as it means that there are structures for refugee–environment management on the ground at the refugee locations.

All these bodies are differentially charged with the protection and conservation of the environment, which the Act breaks down into the protection of rivers, lakes, and wetlands; traditional interests; hilltops, hillsides, mountain areas, and forests, trees, and woodlots; conservation of energy; conservation of biological diversity; access to genetic resources; protection of environmentally significant areas; protection of the coastal zone; and protection of the ozone layer. So as to secure these protection and conservation goals, the Act first requires the implementation of environmental impact assessments before the implementation of projects in the sectors specified in the Act.[40] Second, the management structures referred to earlier are required to assess and analyze the natural resources of the country and to develop National, Provincial, and District Environmental Plans, as the case may be, recommending measures to be taken to protect, conserve, manage, or utilize them in a sustainable way. Third, incentives, disincentives, or fees may be instituted so as "to induce or promote the proper management of the environment and natural resources or the prevention or abatement of environmental degradation."[41] Fourth, a National Environment Restoration Fund is established for the mitigation of environmental damage "where the perpetrator is not identifiable" or where exceptional circumstances require "intervention towards the control and mitigation of environmental degradation."

There are two even more pivotal legal mechanisms established in the Act for fostering environmental protection. The first is the precautionary principle, meaning that the absence of actueric or scientific proof of environmental harm shall not forestall the taking of preventive or mitigation measures. Second, and more tellingly, the Act highlights the "polluter-pays principle," which is defined to mean

> that the cost of cleaning up any element of the environment damaged by pollution, compensating victims of pollution, cost of beneficial uses lost as a result of an act of pollution and other costs that are connected with or incidental to the foregoing is to be paid or borne by the person convicted of pollution under this Act or any other applicable law.[42]

These and other cornerstones of the Act could attract critical examination. It may be pointed out, for instance, that although *pollution* is defined in the Act in general terms and in that other forms of effluents and waste are indicated in some detail, the Act contains no definition of *environmental damage*. Also, while the polluter-pays principle

---

[39] *Id.* § 3 (1).

[40] *Id.* § 58. The projects themselves are specified in the Second Schedule to the Act.

[41] *Id.* § 57.

[42] *Id.* § 2. *Beneficial use* is defined in this same section as "use of the environment or any element or segment of the environment that is conducive to public health, welfare or safety and which requires protection from the effects of wastes, discharges, emissions and deposits."

is in essence the bedrock for the whole body of tortious liability in common law, ranging from negligence, trespass, and nuisance to absolute liability – which in themselves are important foundations of environmental law[43] – it may be said to be mainly reactionary and not proactive as a way of ensuring precautionary measures of enforcement or goals attainment. As major environmental degraders tend to be economic concerns, financial constraints are likely to be treated by them in terms of purely economic costs rather than of environmental and social considerations. From this point of view, a fine may even be preferred by the entrepreneur, as opposed, for instance, to in-plant modifications for pollution abatement, because the fine can be passed on to the consumer. Here, instead of motivating environmental compliance, the polluter-pays principle is appropriated as the polluter's business partner![44]

Specifically in a refugee context, the strongest criticism of the Act has to be that its schedule does not include refugee operations among the "projects" for which environmental impact assessments are required. While, of course, the environmental plans provided for in the Act could yield information on the state of the environment in the locations in question, only impact assessment can specifically identify and predict the impacts of a planned activity on the biogeophysical environment and interpret and communicate information about those impacts in a way that both allows and calls for preimplementation corrective measures.[45]

Still, there is no denying the beneficial norm-creating and action-forcing importance of the provisions of the Act and the environmental management architecture it establishes. For all the criticism that might be leveled against particular instruments of the Act, it actually establishes an impressive catalogue of varied interventions that range from forcing compliance through criminal sanctions – the law-and-order approach – to public responsibility, facilitation, and managerial, nonmarket interventions. This choice provides critical flexibility in an operation driven by humanitarian, not commercial, goal, and in which, therefore, collaborative, synergetic, and not adversarial efforts are likely to be more effective in yielding the desired results.

To the extent to which the force of law remains an undeniable decisive factor in engendering compliance, the application of the Act would most certainly create a predictable policy and legal basis for compelling environmental priorities as an issue of legal compliance. Most crucially, the Government would now be in the driver's seat in both articulating and being accountable for these goals, along with a nationally coherent structure for bringing its role to bear in planning, implementation, and oversight over environmental priorities in that context according to established legal and policy platforms. The exercise of State accountability as argued in this chapter, and the instrumentalization of that function through the country's environmental law, would

---

[43] For a good introductory review of these common law principles as the foundation of environmental law, see the "Background to Environmental Litigation" in the 3-volume series by UNEP/UNDP/Dutch Government Joint Project on Environmental Law and Institutions in Africa, *Compendium of Judicial Decisions on Matters Related to Environment*, UNEP, Nairobi (December 1998, July 2001, and October 2001). For a review of international treaties, see Elizabeth Maruma Mrema, *Liability and Compensation Regimes Related to Environmental Damage: A Review* (UNEP) (August 2003).

[44] See George Okoth-Obbo, *supra* note 37 at 110. See also K. H. Hansmeyer, "Polluter-Pays versus Public Responsibility," *Environmental Policy and Law*, Vol. 6, No. 1, 23 (15 February 1980).

[45] See George Okoth-Obbo, *supra* note 37; and also see R. E. Munn, *Environmental Impact Assessment*, 2nd ed., Scope 5 (John Wiley & Sons) (1977) 1.

include, through an amendment that should be easy to engineer, environmental impact assessment as a threshold application to refugee operations, allow for State oversight, enable environmental audits to be performed periodically, and allow for decisions to be made in favor of environmental sustainability, all as provided for in the Act.

None of this is intended to suggest that UNHCR or the international community would be abdicating its responsibility. The argument of this chapter is not about increasing the burdens of the Government or shifting to it those that lie elsewhere. On the contrary, Government accountability and the instrumentalization of its environmental law will provide a stronger foothold for pursuing an even more robust system of international solidarity and burden sharing in favor of environmental security. Dialogue with international donors on resource support can now be situated within the framework of national developmental and environmental priorities and not be projected only as the province of relief efforts by international humanitarian organizations. This is exactly what Malawi was able to achieve when, confronted with a situation in which 10 percent of the people on its territory were refugees, it projected itself actively in the problem of impact management and was assisted by the international community in elaborating an emergency program to offset the diversion of funds toward the refugee hosting areas.[46] Sovereign State leadership in policy setting, planning, and driving forward of the priorities in this case proved critical to the ultimate scope of the initiative.

There is no reason that readily explains the nonapplication of Kenya's environmental regime to the refugee situations in Kenya thus far. The externalist mentality mentioned earlier that made the Government generally absent from refugee governance may be a crucial reason. Focused attention within the Government machinery on refugee issues also disappeared, as such refugee management structures as were previously in operation in effect dissipated. Conditions are evidently changing now since the new administration came into power. For instance, a bill for refugee legislation for the country was presented before Parliament within the first few months of its assumption of power. The bill intends to put the Government back at the center of refugee governance in Kenya. Whereas, strictly speaking, that legislation is not necessary for the anchorage argued in this chapter as far as the environment is concerned, it will certainly prove helpful if, within its four corners, the environmental question is dealt with in the manner argued here.

6 CONCLUSION

The argument of this chapter has been that large-scale refugee presence of the kind with which Kenya is faced and to which it remains vulnerable in view of the strife and instability that surround it, is liable by definition to cause serious environmental impacts. To ensure that these impacts are prevented, it is necessary to have, in addition to the role played by international humanitarian organizations such as UNHCR, a refugee governance structure for policy setting, planning, implementation, and oversight anchored in the authority of a national state machinery. The tendency to view

---

[46] See Government of Malawi, World Bank, UNDP, and UNHCR, *Report to the Consultative Group for Malawi on the Impact of Refugees on the Government Expenditure Programme* (April 1990). When Tanzania was faced with a massive influx of new refugees from Burundi and Rwanda in 1993 and 1994, it also established a multiparticipant Task Force to assess the negative impact of refugees on national resources. See United Republic of Tanzania, *Assessment Report on the Impact of Refugees on the Local Communities in Kagera and Kigoma Regions* (September 1994).

refugees principally as an international problem for which UNHCR and other actors in the international community are responsible cannot be sustained within the optic of national accountability. Nor can that accountability be limited to State security and political priorities. Environmental priorities in refugee settings must be mainstreamed and anchored within national policy and planning because the imperatives and interests at stake are national and therefore fall within a national structure of policy direction, governance, and accountability. No matter that international humanitarian organizations may discharge their roles and responsibilities in the most effective way possible; they cannot be the only bearers of accountability to ensure that these interests are secured.

16 Environmental Impact Assessment Law and Land Use: A Comparative Analysis of Recent Trends in the Nigerian and U.S. Oil and Gas Industry

Bibobra Bello Orubebe

1 INTRODUCTION

The topic of environmental impact assessment (EIA) has generated a lot of interest among scholars, researchers, policymakers, politicians, advocates, and citizens. This perhaps accounts for the concern governments now attach to the topic. Most governments have reacted to this growing environmental concern by enacting statutory legislation regulating the environment, particularly on the subject of EIA and sustainable land use. In the United States, the main environmental statute is the National Environmental Policy Act (NEPA) of 1969.[1] The general principles, regulations, practice, and procedures for EIA are contained in the Council on Environmental Quality (CEQ), NEPA regulations, and Environmental Protection Agency (EPA) guidelines. In Nigeria, the main environmental statute is the Federal Environmental Protection Agency Act (FEPAA).[2] The rules, practices, and procedures for the EIA process are governed by FEPA and the object-specific legislation – the Environmental Impact Assessment Act.[3]

Whereas NEPA sets forth significant substantive national environmental goals, its mandate provides for procedural action forcing national environmental policy–based general principles for EIA in the United States to ensure a fully informed and well-considered decision. Such a decision is not necessarily a decision the judges of the Courts of Appeal or of other courts would have reached had they been members of the decision-making unit of the agency.[4] In the case of Nigeria, FEPAA took a "command and control" approach providing excruciating details of a national adjectival environmental protection objective. This is in spite of the lack of a coordinated three-tiered federal environmental decision-making-cum-legal framework and low-level interdisciplinary capacity in both the public and private sectors.

2 THE PROBLEM OF DEFINITION WITH THE TERMS *ENVIRONMENTAL IMPACT ASSESSMENT* AND *SUSTAINABLE DEVELOPMENT*

The United States' and Nigerian statutes do not provide conclusive statutory definitions of the term *environmental impact assessment*. However, definitions, albeit important,

---

[1] (Pub. L. 91–190, 42 U.S.C. 4321–4347, January 1, 1970, as amended by Pub. L. 94–52, July 3, 1975, Pub. L. 94–83, August 9, 1975, and Pub. L. 97–258, & 4(b), Sept. 13 (1982).

[2] Federal Environmental Protection Agency Act, Cap. F10 LFN (2004).

[3] Environmental Impact Assessment Act Cap. E12 LFN (2004).

[4] *Vermont Yankee Nuclear Power Corp v. NRDC* 435 U.S. 519 [1978] at 558.

are translations of thoughts into words that usually create a problem for the lawyer. Law itself is mainly an exercise in controversy, and so the actual scope and intent of the legislature, with regard to the true meaning of the term *environmental impact assessment*, remain illusory. Therefore, every scholar or judge ascribes to the term his or her own ideological or prejudicial slant.[5] In other words, depending on the scholar's or judge's abstraction, the term *environmental impact assessment* is no more than a verbal recommendation within the context used. Although imperfect, definitions are necessary as a working premise and, if only for the sake of clarity and the prevention of futile disputes, ought to be encouraged in environmental law.

With this as a background, one may then ask what the term connotes. What do we mean by the words *environment, impact assessment*, and *sustainable development*? Essentially, and in its broadest sense, the word *environment* embraces the conditions or influences under which any individual thing exists, grows, or develops. Thus, it consists of land, water, plants, biota, atmosphere, human beings, animals, aesthetics, and other entities, and the interrelationships that exist among these.[6] The United States, as was Nigeria, was once ruled by Britain and accordingly they both still have Anglo-Saxon vestiges within their jurisprudence. In Great Britain, the term *environmental assessment* is often used instead of *environmental impact assessment*, just as *environmental statement* is often used instead of *environmental impact statement*. In both cases the word *impact* is removed and in this context, it is the effect of one thing upon another.[7] As such, an impact can range from the "effects of mine blasting" or the "striking of a hammer" to the insidious effects of radiation or ozone destruction. In other words, it is more apparent than real to think of an impact as being anything but a sharp blow. Hence, within this normative paradigm or context, the description and/or term *environmental impact assessment* is a misnomer or perhaps not the preferred description.[8]

In the 21st century, all emerging and novel fields of human study/specialization draw from the peculiar experiences of their pioneers as depicted in their acknowledged works of scholarly value. Thus, the beauty and symbolism of words, phrases, and definitions, howsoever described, appear to be tied to the way society links the new concept to its existence or value system. To this extent, the word *impact* is inextricably interwoven with the efficacy, or better still, the need for environmental sustainability in the oil and gas industries.

To most scholars of modernization, EIA is the process by which humans in their search for a rational system or method – procedural or substantive – attempt to inquire about, evaluate, and address the critical environmental consequences or concerns of a proposed activity in relation to the effect of action or inaction.[9] To others, EIA is the prior environmental assessment of proposed activities that may affect the environment,

[5] M. A. Ajomo, *Of Order and Disorder: The Relevance of International Law* (Lagos University Press-Inaugural Lecture Series) (1984) 5.

[6] B. B. Orubebe, *Environmental Impact Assessment Act Law and Policy in Nigeria (2004)*, NigerDelta Public Lecture Vol. 8 P. 3.C/F with S. 38 supra, note 3 at F10–16.

[7] Alan Gilpin, *Environmental Impact Assessment* (1993) 5.

[8] *Id.* at p. 5.

[9] B. B. Orubebe, "EIA Laws in Nigeria and the US" (2001) LL.M Seminar at American University Washington College of Law p. 2.

amenity, and land use.[10] These definitions, as do many others too numerous to list in this chapter, raise serious philosophical and analytical and a host of other intellectual questions such as the following:

- What clear discernible variables, that is, social, economic, psychological, physical, political, cultural, or other measurable variants, ought to be considered when conducting an EIA?
- What is the threshold or standard by which an impact can be adjudged as negative or positive?
- What institutional framework or interdisciplinary balance can produce the required functional EIA and to what extent should findings be subject to unfettered review by quasi-judicial (administrative) and/or rights-based judicial adjudication by special or general national courts?
- What are the power dynamics and relationships inherent in determinations made in EIA(s) and to what extent should decisions reached affect future policy or other interventions?

Notwithstanding these questions, it is instructive to note that in the 21st century and beyond, the importance that society attaches to the environment, and by necessary implication environmental law and related concepts, will increase so much that definitions or conceptualizations by environmental scholars need to be inclusive and above all emphasize the inter- or multidisciplinary approach in the EIA process.

The definition of *sustainable development* – "development that meets the needs of the present generation without compromising the ability and rights of future generations to meet their own needs" – was to an extent popularized by the World Commission on Environment and Development (WCED), headed by Gro Harlem Brundtland in its report *Our Common Future*, 1987.[11] However, it is a truism that most of the central ideas of sustainable development were already central provisions in African regional environmental treaties as far back as 1968. For instance, such treaties included provisions requiring the adoption of measures to ensure conservation, utilization, and development of soil, water, floral, and faunal resources in accordance with scientific principles and with due regard to the best interests of the people; that in the formulation of development plans, full consideration be given to ecological as well as economic and social factors; and that both individual and joint action for the conservation, utilization, and development of resources include establishing and maintaining their rational utilization for the present and future welfare of humankind.[12]

In the United States there are similar ideas with an emphasis on public concern for environmental quality: the need to regulate air, water, pollution, use of pesticides, and handling of toxic chemicals and hazardous wastes; the fundamental interdependence of human populations and their environment; the need to internalize the socioeconomic and environmental costs of development; the efficacy of industry-specific environmental standards; the desire to use the EIA as a veritable or important analytical tool in an

---

[10] Margaret T. O. Fubara, *Law of Environmental Protection* (1998) p. 189.

[11] World Commission on Environment and Development (WCED), 1987, *Our Common Future*, Oxford University Press, 43.

[12] African Convention for the Conservation of Nature and Natural Resources (1968). Article 11, XIV and Para. 6 of the Preamble (signed September 15, 1968).

integrated multidisciplinary/coordinated decision-making and planning process. These ideas can be traced as far back as the 19th and 20th centuries in the writings and activities of conservation philosophers such as Henry David Thoreau, George Perkins Marsh, John Muir, and great governance theorists such as Theodore Roosevelt, Gifford Pinchot, Aldo Leopold, and Rachel Carson, to mention just a few. No doubt, their thoughtful, sometimes passionate, and incisive expressions (as they were often perceived then) for the preservation of natural habitats and wild creatures were to a large extent responsible for the passage of numerous laws with EIA and sustainable development undertones. Examples include the creation of the world's first national conservation park (Yellowstone in 1872), the Forest Preservation Act in 1891, the National Park Service in 1916, the Wilderness Act in 1964, the Wild Scenic Rivers Act in 1968, *NEPA* in 1969, and the Endangered Species Act in 1973.[13]

This critical history and the weight of environmental law development, among other factors, have contributed to the broadening of the meaning of the environmental law principle of sustainable development in the last three decades.[14] For example, it is now settled opinion that the concepts of "sustainability" and "sustainable yield," howsoever described, are integral parts of sustainable development. Also, the practical functional meaning of sustainable development has been extended to embrace living and nonliving resources.[15] Thus, sustainable development must have regard to the conservation of resources, the long-term character of the oil and gas market, and the advantages and disadvantages of alternative courses of action for future generations. With specific reference to the oil and gas industry, an efficient or functional EIA-based land use for sustainable development presupposes the use of nonrenewable oil and gas resources, which are decreasing, in a rational manner with a view to their ultimate substitution with other environmentally friendly energy sources that are affordable and increase human welfare. In fact, this ought to be the strategic long-term goal of national EIA processes with respect to oil and gas resources.

This is more important because we cannot pretend to know the developmental needs of future generations with the least infinitesimal accuracy, or even with approximation, but through an efficient EIA process we can ensure the maximal possible range of environmental-cum-developmental options and opportunities for generations yet unborn.

In both the United States' and Nigerian *juris corpus*, it is trite that EIA is a strategic legal and policy response mechanism for land use and sustainable development. What differs is the degree of observance or compliance.

In the United States, the EPA is charged with the congressional mandate for NEPA compliance in all federal actions that could significantly impact the human environment, including the oil and gas industry; the Federal Environmental Protection Agency (FEPA) oversees EIA in the case of Nigeria. Both agencies are federal in character, established by statute and funded by the respective federal governments. Thus, it is plausible to argue that to a large extent the EIA is a strategic legal and policy response mechanism

---

[13] Ray Clark and Larry Canter, *Environmental Policy and NEPA: Past, Present, and Future* (St. Lucie Press) (2000) 16.

[14] Professor C. O. Kiddy, "Environment, Natural Resources and Sustainable Development in Kenya's Constitution-Making" (2002), p. 4. Note that this position paper is frequently revised, e.g., on 20 February 2002.

[15] *Supra* note 15.

or, better still, an integral part of environmental compliance in both countries capable of achieving proactive environmental governance/conformance in land use and sustainable development within the oil and gas industry. The question is, Has this laudable national objective been achieved?

There could be no better time to ask this rather rhetorical question than the Second Colloquium of the International Union for Conservation of Nature (IUCN) Academy of Environmental Law, held in Nairobi in November 2004, whose theme was sustainable land use. But at a deeper level of analysis, it is also worth asking whether current bureaucrat-dominated notions of EIA and sustainable land use, currently symbolized in EPA and FEPA guidelines/practices, need to be reconceptualized. Both apostles and protagonists of EIA now agree that years of conventional exegesis-cum-analysis, including a plethora of flawed and a few impeccable court judgments, have not produced the much desired results.

It is against this backdrop that scholars of environmental law feel compelled to consider a slightly different approach, including a dynamic shift in EIA nomenclature, methodology, and contextual paradigm. This chapter proposes just that; however, for purposes of easy analysis and comprehension and in answer to the earlier expositional question, it is imperative first to attempt a concise analysis of the current EIA processes in the United States and Nigeria.

3 PREPARATION OF THE EIA

The time required to prepare an EIA is not *strictu sensu* envisaged in either the U.S. or the Nigerian legislation. In the United States, the courts have enunciated the legal principle that considering the sensitive nature of oil and gas industry operations, an Environmental Impact Statement (EIS) must be prepared before any irreversible and irretrievable commitment of resources. As a result, having a "No Surface Occupancy" (NSO) oil lease is deemed as having a right of first refusal, which is a priority legal right that does not constitute an irretrievable commitment of resources. On the other hand, a sale of a non-NSO oil and gas lease constitutes the "point of commitment because after the lease is sold the government no longer has the ability to prohibit potentially significantly inroads on the environment."[16] In practice there is real difficulty in determining the right time to commence an EIA in controversial projects, particularly in the oil and gas sector, to a large extent because the bureaucrats in charge of most countries' EIA agencies, as are their judicial counterparts, are required by the statutes establishing these bodies to be appointed the president (politicians). Top EIA agency officials, however, do not enjoy the constitutional and/or institutional independence judicial officers enjoy. This no doubt creates enormous pressure and difficulty in agency decision making in nascent democracies such as Nigeria. However, in most advanced democracies such as in the United States, the courts appear to have espoused the "rational basis test" in determining whether the time is ripe for an EIS.

In the hallmark case of *Park County Resources Council, Inc. v. United States Department of Agriculture,*[17] The court held that certainly the project must be of sufficient

---

[16] *Conner v. Burford* 836 F2d 1521 [9th CIR 1988], particularly at 1527, 1529, and 1531.
[17] *Park County Resources Council, Inc. v. United States Department of Agriculture,* 817 F.2d 609 [10th Cir. 1987].

definiteness before an evaluation of its environmental impact can be made and alternatives proposed. Thus to require a cumulative EIS at the leasing stage in this particular case would be tantamount to "demanding that the Department specify the probable route of a high way that may never be built from points yet unknown to other points as yet unknown other terrains as yet uncharted in conformity with state plans yet undrafted. A more speculative exercise can hardly be imagined."[18]

Furthermore, under the U.S. Statutes, the issue regarding who is responsible for preparing the EIA is governed by the unambiguous provisos of CEQ NEPA regulations. Under these provisions, the lead federal agency prepares the EIA, including the EIS and, if necessary, the environmental assessment (EA). The contractor selected by the lead agency cannot be responsible for preparing the EIA because doing so it is considered a conflict of interest. He or she is statutorily required to disclose any conflicts of interest in a prescribed format, namely, the disclosure statement. The lead agency's responsibilities include guiding the contractor as well as evaluating the EIS or the EA according to the situation, regardless of the project proponents. It can also be assisted by another agency that would carry out the field research, by conducting either statistical or technical analyses. In summary, the lead agency is statutorily presumed to be responsible for the preparation of the EIA both in scope and in content. It must also make sure to comply with the NEPA requirements.

It must be noted that the CEQ NEPA regulations often lack precise meaning. This often leads to otherwise preventable litigation. On a positive note, this series of litigation has provided the opportunity to add content to the CEQ regulations. For example, the courts have added the legal principle that a lead agency cannot abdicate its statutory responsibility.[19] They have also added the principle allowing applicants or participants outside the lead agency to participate in the preparation of the EIS or EA, provided that the lead agency sets out the limits and the requirements of the environmental information required. Through its independent judgment, the lead agency must also control the extent of the applicants' participation through all stages.[20]

It has also been explained by the courts that when there is more than one agency involved in the preparation of an EIS or in the assessment process of a particular project, there is no need for the cooperating agencies involved in the project to duplicate the work of the lead agency.[21]

Under sections 9(1), 14, 18, 22(2), 23, 24, 30, and 63(1) of the Nigerian Environmental Impact Assessment Act 2004,[22] the Federal Environmental Protection Agency (FEPA) prepares the EIA, which can be mandated to a screening panel under section 30.[23] The Nigerian statutes do not envisage the responsibility for information, either technical or other. They also do not envisage the scope and liability of the EIA. Under the U.S. CEQ NEPA regulations and most agency NEPA guidelines, the statutory provisions do not require that detailed, systematic, and analytical procedures be followed. The absence of

[18] *County Resources Council, Inc. v. United States Department of Agriculture, supra* note 18 at p. 624.
[19] *Green County Planning Board v. Federal Power Commission,* 455 F2d 412 [2d. Cir 1071 Cert Denied, 409 U.S. 849 1972].
[20] *Sierra Club v. Linn,* 502 F.2d 43 [5th Cir. 1974, Cert denied, 421 U.S. 994 1975] Rehg denied, 422 U.S. 1049 [1975].
[21] *LaFlamme v. FERC* 945 F. 2d 1124 [9th Cir. 1991].
[22] Environmental Impact Assessment Act Cap. E12 LFN (2004).
[23] Environmental Impact Assessment Act Cap. E12 LFN (2004). *Supra* note 3, S. 30.

action forcing interdisciplinary or tripartite procedural guidelines largely accounts for the ineffectiveness of the Nigerian EIA process. In addition, the experience and expertise required to prepare an EIA are lacking, especially in the oil and gas sector. This lack is due to the fact that there is a known tendency to rely too much on FEPA.

Although effective at the beginning, the American statute and CEQ NEPA regulations are gradually leaning toward the use of private contractors instead of experienced environmentalists to conduct the EA . This trend is mostly due to the increasing dissatisfaction of the public with regard to pro-government biases. This new tendency derogates from the initial goal of NEPA, which was to build interdisciplinary and procedural capacities with different governmental agencies in order to be in compliance with the NEPA requirements.

4 WHEN AN EIA IS EXCLUDED OR EXEMPTED

Under the CEQ NEPA regulations, there are four discernible exemptions from the EIA process.[24] For example, section 1508.4 states:

> "Categorical exclusion" means a category of actions, which do not individually or cumulatively have a significant effect on the human environment and which have been found to have no such effect in procedures adopted by a Federal agency in implementation of these regulations (Section 1507.3) and for which, therefore, neither an environmental assessment nor an environmental impact statement is required. An agency may decide in its procedures or otherwise, to prepare environmental assessments, even though it is not required to do so. Any procedures under this section shall provide for extraordinary circumstances in which a normally excluded action may have a significant environmental effect.[25]

The combined effect of the provisions conceptually implies that all activities to be carried out during an emergency, as officially declared by the U.S. government, appear to be excluded from the NEPA requirements. Also, if there is a statutory conflict between NEPA and any other federal statute or legislation, then an EIA may not be required.[26]

Furthermore, when a statute provides for a regulatory framework, which is perceived to be an orderly consideration capable of addressing the diverse environmental factors, advantages, and disadvantages of a full application of the NEPA, then the legal doctrine of "functional equivalent" applies.[27] The jurisprudential effect of this emerging trend is that the functional equivalent doctrine has been applied to too many statutory environmental programs critical to EIA and sustainable land use. For example, the courts have applied the doctrine to many U.S. EPA Programs (for instance, under the following statutes: Clean Air Act;[28] Comprehensive Environmental Response, Compensation, and Liability

---

[24] 40 CFR 1508.4, 1501.3 (b), 1508.7, and 1506.11.

[25] Sec. 1508.4 of *CEQ – Regulations for Implementing NEPA* (http://ceq.eh.doe.gov/nepa/regs/ceq/1508.htm#1508.4).

[26] *Flint Ridge Dev. Co. v. Scenic Rivers Ass'n of Oklahoma*, 426 U.S. 776 (1976).

[27] *Alabamians for Clean Environment v. Thomas*, 26 ERC 2116 (D. Ala. 1987).

[28] *Portland Cement Association v. Ruckelshaus*, 486 F.2d 375 (D.C.Cir. 1973), cert. denied, 417 U.S.921 (1974); see also 15 U.S.C. 793 (c) (1).

Act;[29] Toxic Substances Control Act;[30] Insecticide, Fungicide, and Rodenticide Act;[31] Safe Drinking Water Act,[32] and the controversial Resource Conservation and Recovery Act, or RCRA,[33] which governs the issuance of hazardous waste facility permits). It is important to note here that after the Courts determined that the Clean Air Act was functionally equivalent to NEPA, Congress in a rare show of Legislative activism subsequently and indeed unequivocally exempted it.[34] Accordingly, the U.S. courts have held repeatedly that NEPA is the general statute that forces agencies to consider the environmental consequences of their actions and that obliges them to give the public a meaningful opportunity to learn about and comment on the proposed actions.[35] In an apparent show of the lack of doctrinaire reasoning the same Court also held that "if there were no agency object-specific EIA guidelines, such as with RCRA, NEPA would seem to apply here. But RCRA is the later and more specific statute directly governing the EPA's process for issuing permits on hazardous waste facilities. As such, RCRA is an exception to NEPA's controls."[36]

There is a growing controversy because the courts' interpretation of this principle of functional equivalence, or emerging EIA-cum-legal doctrine, suggests an apparent exclusion but no implied exemption. In *Calvert Cliffs' Coordinating Committee, Inc. v. Atomic Energy Commission*,[37] the court enunciated the legal principle that there are no implied exemptions from NEPA merely because an agency's enabling legislation does not address environmental protection. The Court stated with emphasis and perhaps with impeccable adoration that NEPA does not exempt any federal agency from its requirements and provides that those agencies must comply to the fullest extent possible.[38] The court held, inter alia, that this language required compliance with NEPA unless there is a "clear conflict" of statutory purpose.[39]

Also in *Flint Ridge Dev. Co. v. Scenic Rivers Ass'n of Oklahoma*,[40] the Court, while attempting to resolve the existence and effect of an apparent functional conflict, also held that

> the question we must resolve is whether, assuming an environmental impact statement would otherwise be required in this case, requiring the secretary to prepare such a statement would create an irreconcilable and fundamental conflict with the secretary's duties under the [Interstate Land Sales Full] Disclosure Act. . . . The Secretary cannot comply with the duty under the Disclosure Act to allow statements of record to go into effect within 30 days of filing, absent inaccurate or incomplete disclosure, and simultaneously prepare impact statements on proposed developments.[41]

[29] *Schalk v. Reilly*, 900 F.2d 1091 (7th Cir. 1990), cert. denied, 498 U.S. 981 (1991).

[30] *Twitty v. State of North Carolina*, 527 F. Supp. 778 (E.D.N.C. 1981).

[31] *State of Wyoming v. Hathway*, 525 F.2d 66 (10th Cir. 1975), Cert. denied, 426 U.S. 906 (1976).

[32] *Western Nebraska Resources Council v. EPA*, 943 F.2d 867 (8th Cir. 1991).

[33] *State of Alabama ex rel. Siegelman v. EPA*, 911 F.2d 499 (11th Cir. 1990).

[34] Clean Air Act 42 U.S.C. 7401–7626, also reprinted in *Selected Environmental Law Statutes*.

[35] *Alba v. EPA*, 911 F.2d 449 11 th Cir. 1990.

[36] *Alba v. EPA*, 911 F.2d 449 11 th Cir. 1990 (D. Ala. 1987).

[37] 449 F.2d 1109 (D. C. Cir. 1971). Cert. denied, 404, U.S. 942 (1972).

[38] *Calvert Cliffs' Coordinating Committee, Inc. v. Atomic Energy Commission*, 449 F. 2d 1109 (D. C. Cir. 1971).

[39] 449 F.2d 1109 (D. C. Cir. 1971). Cert. denied, 404, U.S.942 (1972). See also Ronalds Bass, Albert Herson, and Kenneth Bogdon, *The NEPA Book* (2001) 37.

[40] *Flint Ridge Dev. Co. v. Scenic Rivers Ass'n of Oklahoma*, 426 U.S. 776 (1976).

[41] *Supra* note 41.

Here the learned judges found without equivocation that NEPA's impact statement requirement is inapplicable.[42]

Whatever can be said of the correctness or otherwise of these two landmark EIA/NEPA decisions, one enduring attribute or comment of the judges' jurisprudential reasoning is the truism, with all respect, that they appear to have preferred the most liberal interpretation one could imagine of Section 102. This Section is the most critical general proviso that reaffirms the intent, spirit, and scope of EIA, as well as sustainable development and land use, as it had been contemplated for the United States by Congress. In effect, Congress authorized and unequivocally directed that, to the fullest extent possible, the policies, regulations, and public laws of the United States of America shall be interpreted and administered in accordance with the policies set forth in NEPA.[43]

Moreover, the US statute accorded a great deal of discretion to agencies in the course of formulating their NEPA regulations. Thus, any exemption or exclusion that is categorically stated in an agency regulation is deemed to be excluded. Because there is no comprehensive or uniform list of approved exclusions by the federal agencies, there appears to be a dire need for a uniform or harmonized standard guideline for EIA/NEPA exclusions. It is further explicated that such a standard list of existing exclusions howsoever described should be readily accessible and considered among other critical concerns such as whether the activity in question usually causes "no significant environmental effects, the need for agency documentation and other permissible rational exceptions borne out of extraordinary and special circumstances,"[44] which should include the role of agencies in the fight against terrorism, particularly the environmental imperatives of counterterrorism and homeland security as dictated by post–11 September 2001 reality.

The EIA or NEPA process can also be excluded in the United States by necessary legal implication. For example, it is trite law that NEPA does not apply to the Presidency and Congress. As such, it can be argued that distinct institutionalized acts of the President or Congress are excluded *ab initio*. This is by necessary operation of the constitutionally mandated principle of the separation of the organs of government.

The author notes with impeccable curiosity that although Congress and the Presidency have this exclusion or exemption privilege, which is fast growing into the power dynamics of environmental decision making in the United States, and notwithstanding the fact that the price of oil is at its all-time-high of about 50 dollars, *the power ought to be exercised with great caution*. In fact, there could be ramifications if a Republican-controlled Congress or if Republican President George W. Bush excluded projects, such as the opening of Alaska's wildlife reserves for oil and gas exploitation. There could be far-reaching social and political implications that could further divide Americans and precipitate civil disobedience if such exclusions were made while circumventing the perceived due process of EIA/NEPA or by excluding NEPA on the ground that previously conducted EISs were adequate, or by any other waiver clause, howsoever achieved. America, as the world's sole superpower, faces deep-seated and growing

---

[42] *Id. supra* note 41.

[43] 42 U.S.C SS 4321 to 4332 also reproduced in Richard L. Revesz, *Environmental Law and Policy, Statutory and Regulatory Supplement* (2003–2004) Ed., 1–5.

[44] *Rhodes v. Johnson*, 153 F.3d 785 (7th Cir. 1988).

anti-Americanism, and, therefore, needs a Congress and a President that can unite and not divide its people and revered institutions of old.

The clearly written Nigerian EIA statute provides for substantive, widely open-ended discretion, particularly regarding the classes and circumstances for exclusion and exemption. For example, Section 2(4) states that

> [a]ll agencies, institutions (whether public or private) *except exempted* pursuant to this Decree, shall before embarking on the proposed project apply in writing to the Agency, so that subject activities can be quickly and surely identified and environmental assessment applied as the activity is being planned.[45]

In addition, the statute categorizes institutional and project exclusion or exemption. For example, Section 15(1) states that

> [a]n environmental assessment of project shall not be required where –
>
> (a) *in the opinion of the Agency the project is in the list of projects which the President, Commander-in-Chief of the Armed Forces or the Council is of the opinion that the environmental effects of the project is likely to be minimal;*
> (b) the project is to be carried out during national emergency for which temporary measures have been taken by the Government;
> (c) the project is to be carried out in response to circumstances that, in the opinion of the Agency, the project is in the interest of public health or safety.[46]

These provisions suggest that the exemption or exclusion from the EIA process or statute is a discretionary power given to the President. Also, the Agency has unfettered discretion to decide whether or not to carry out an assessment regardless of the nature of the project. It is in reference to this pathetic legislative backdrop that the few scholarly writers on the subject have talked of a lack of doctrinal refinement, legislative clarity, ideological consistency, and visionary predictability in Nigerian environmental law and environmental politics. These confusions extend to more fundamental issues, such as whose ethnic, business, or personal interest is protected by the current Nigerian federation.

It is submitted that most, if not all, presidents and top agency officials are corrupt and almost always exercise their wide discretionary powers without proper consideration of the environment and its people. This is more so because the political leadership of Nigeria is in the hands of the three main ethnic nationalities, Hausa-Fulani, Yoruba, and Ibo, all of whom occupy land that bears few or no oil and gas deposits. These groups do not suffer the immediate environmental degradation that the minorities of the Niger Delta region face. Yet, they benefit from the oil and gas revenues extracted hundreds of kilometers from the urban settlements they inhabit. Worse, the oil and gas resources are extracted from lands occupied by indigenous minority tribes who have inadequate or no representation in the Federal Government of Nigeria.

These indigenous minority tribes include the Ijaw, Ogoni, Isoko, Ikwere, Urhobo, Itsekiri, Anioma, Anans, Ibibios, Eche, and Efface of the old Calabar province (excluding the Bakassi territory). These people suffer doubly in that they do not benefit from the oil and gas revenues taken from their lands. Quite often their lands are expropriated without

---

[45] Environmental Impact Assessment Act Cap. E12 LFN (2004). Please note that the underlining is mine for emphasis.
[46] *Supra* note 47.

adequate compensation.[47] Furthermore, the land occupied by the multinational oil and gas corporations[48] is destroyed. Additionally, extraction activities result in deleterious effects on the habitat and environment of these helpless indigenous minority people, along with the debilitating environment-induced socioeconomic, cultural, medical, and political consequences attendant upon these same activities.

The lack of appropriate use of the discretionary powers accorded to the President and the Agency is opposed to the clear and unambiguous provisions of Sections 23 and 25 of the Nigerian EIA Act, and Section 12 of the Schedule to the Act, which unequivocally declared *petroleum, oil, and gas activities as requiring mandatory environmental impact assessments.*[49] Section 23 provides that

> [w]here the Agency is of the opinion that a program is described in the mandatory study list, the Agency shall –
> (a) ensure that a mandatory study is conducted, and a mandatory study report is prepared and submitted to the Agency, in accordance with the provisions of this Decree; or
> (b) refer the project to the Council for a referral to mediation or a review panel in accordance with section 25 of this Decree.

Section 12 of the Schedule to the Statute covers

> (a) Oil and gas fields' development.
> (b) Construction of off-shore pipelines in excess of 50 kilometers in length.
> (c) Construction of oil and gas separation, processing, handling, and storage facilities.
> (d) Construction of oil refineries.
> (e) Construction of product depots for the storage of petrol, gas or diesel (excluding service stations) which are located within 3 kilometers of any commercial, industrial or residential areas and which have a combined storage capacity of 60,000 barrels or more.[50]

5 EXTENT OF PUBLIC PARTICIPATION

5.1 U.S. Experience

In the United States, the CEQ's NEPA regulations explicitly provide for public participation in the EIA process. Section 1506.6 states that Agencies shall:
(a) Make diligent efforts to involve the public in preparing and implementing their NEPA procedures.
(b) Provide public notice of NEPA-related hearings, public meetings and the availability of environmental documents so as to inform those persons and agencies who may be interested or affected.

---

[47] S. I. Land Use Act LFN (2004), now part of the Nigerian Constitution by operation of law.
[48] Shell Petroleum and Development Company (SPDC), SNEPCO, ChevronTexaco, Star Deep, Exxon Mobil, Agip, Total Elf Fina, Start Oil, and their subsidiaries in collaboration with the Federal Government of Nigeria's Nigeria National Petroleum Corporation (NNPC).
[49] *Supra* note 46.   [50] Ibid.

1. In all cases the agency shall mail notice to those who have requested it on an individual action. [51]
2. In the case of an action with effects of national concern notice shall include publication in the Federal Register and notice by mail to national organizations reasonably expected to be interested in the matter and may include listing in the *102 Monitor*. An agency engaged in rulemaking may provide notice by mail to national organizations that have requested that notice regularly be provided. Agencies shall maintain a list of such organizations.[52]

The EIA process entails an environmental review of a proposal for an action that has been judged to be subject to NEPA. First, all interested agencies select a lead agency to coordinate the EIA. The lead agency normally then undertakes the optional step of preparing an environmental assessment. The environmental assessment evaluates whether the proposed action will significantly impact the environment. This assessment can then be used to determine whether a detailed EIS is required or whether a "finding of no significant impact" (FONSI) can be prepared.[53]

The CEQ's regulations at § 1508.13 define a FONSI as "a document . . . presenting the reasons why an action . . . will not have significant effect on the human environment and for which an [EIS] therefore will not be prepared." A U.S. court described the reasoning behind a FONSI as follows:

> [A]n EIS must be prepared only when significant negative environmental impacts will occur as a result of the proposed action. If, however, the proposal is modified effectively or in a functional way prior to implementation by adding specific mitigation measures which completely compensate for any adverse environmental impacts likely to stem from the original proposal, the statutory threshold of significant environmental impacts is not crossed and an EIS is not required. To require an EIS in such circumstances would trivialize NEPA and would diminish its utility in providing useful environmental analysis for federal actions that truly affect the environment[54]

If a FONSI is not declared, an EIS must be completed for the proposed action. The EIS considers the significant environmental impacts and weighs them against the positive project objectives. For this process, a notice of intent is published, a scoping process is conducted, and a draft EIS is prepared and circulated for review. A participatory public hearing is held if required or ordered. The draft EIS is then filed with the EPA. An open public hearing is held, after which the final EIS is prepared, circulated, and filed with the EPA. The final EIS is adopted, the lead agency makes a decision on it, and a record of decision is made. Essentially a Record of Decision (ROD) is a written public record explaining why the lead agency has taken a particular course of action. In practice, however, it includes an explanation of the decision of the proposed action,

---

[51] See 40 C.F.R. §§. 1501.7, 1503.1, and 1506.6 (2005). These sections outline specific stages in the EIA process at which the agencies shall mail notice to interested parties. These include the initial scoping stage (§ 1501.7), the comment period after preparing the draft EIS but before preparing the final EIS (§ 1503.1), and dates of public hearings, public meetings, and releases of relevant environmental documents (§ 1501.7).

[52] 40 C.F.R. § 1506.6 (2005) [emphasis added].

[53] 40 C.F.R. § 1508.9 (2005); see William H. Cohen, "Issues in NEPA Litigation" (2003) SH093 ALI-ABA 971.

[54] *Cabinet Mountains Wilderness/Scotchman's Peak Grizzly Bears v. Peterson*, 685 F.2d 678 (D.C. Cir 1982), particularly at 682.

factors considered in making the decision, alternatives considered and the environmentally preferred alternatives, any adopted mitigation measures or reasons why particular mitigation measures were not adopted, and a monitoring and enforcement program for those mitigation measures that were adopted.[55]

Each of these steps accords opportunities for public participation to interested groups including native Indian tribes. The public can obtain important baseline information about the proposed action. The proceedings maintain a transparent nature by making information readily available through a host of technologies, including geographical information systems (GIS) high-resolution remote sensing, satellite imagery, and Internet technology. Thus, the average citizen interested in a particular agency action can keep track of the EIA process and participate meaningfully, with or without a nongovernmental organization's (NGO's) assistance.

NEPA's procedural nature coupled with the fairly high level of public participation help to ensure that the lead agency modifies its proposals to minimize negative environmental impacts. The EIA process has forced lead agencies to abandon proposed actions that were found to have unjustifiable significant environmental impacts. Through the public participation process, citizens' groups and environmental NGOs have obtained enough information on particular projects to use as a tangential point for future judicial challenges in U.S. courts.

5.2 Nigerian Experience

In Nigeria, the EIA Act[56] provides for some degree of public participation in the EIA process. Relevant sections of the Act include ss. 7, 9(3), 11(1), 25(2), 57(1), 57(2), and 57(3).

Section 7 suggests that the agency provide the opportunity to make comments on an EIA to government agencies, members of the public, experts in any relevant discipline, and interested groups before the agency makes its final decision on an activity.

Section 9(3) provides that even if no interested person or group requests a report, the agency still has the duty to publish its decision in a manner by which members of the public or persons interested in the activity will be notified. Section 9(4) mandates the Council to make a reasoned determination on an appropriate method by which the decision of the agency shall be published so as to reach interested persons or groups, in particular, the originators or persons interested in the activity subject to the decision.

Section 11(1) states that when information provided as part of EIA indicates that the environment within another state in the federation or a local government area is likely to be significantly affected by a proposed activity, the state of the local government area in which the activity is being planned shall, to the extent possible,

(a) notify the potentially affected state or local government of the proposed activity
(b) transmit to the affected state or local government any relevant information of the environmental impact assessment
(c) enter into timely consultations with the affected state or local government

---

[55] 40 CFR, CEQ NEPA Regulations S.1505.2 at p. 20, Reprint (1992). See also Ronalds Bass, Albert Herson, and Kenneth Bogdon, *The NEPA Book* (2001) 83.
[56] *Supra* note 3.

Section 25(2) declares that "[p]rior to the deadline set out in the notice published by the agency, any person may file comments with the agency relating to the conclusions and recommendations of the mandatory study report."

Section 57(1) states that "[f]or the purpose of facilitating public access to records relating to environmental assessments, a public registry shall be established and operated in accordance with the provisions of this decree in respect of every project for which an environmental assessment is conducted."

Section 57(2) provides that "[t]he public registry in respect of a project shall be maintained (a) by the agency from the commencement of the environmental assessment, and (b) until any follow-up program in respect of the project is completed."

Section 57(3) states that "[s]ubject to subs. 4 of this section, a public registry shall maintain all records and information produced, collected or submitted with respect to the environmental assessment of the project, including (a) any report relating to the assessment, (b) any comments filed by the public in relation to the assessment; and (c) any record prepared by the agency for the purpose of Section 35 of this Act."[57]

All these sections read together affirm the view that public participation under the Nigerian EIA process, although copiously provided for in the statute, most often with flowery language, remains limited and discretionary. The implementation of a robust public participation scheme has been "bogged down" by many factors, including the endemic corruption in the country, the lack of interagency and multidisciplinary human capacity, the lack of compliance-enforcing incentives in the oil and gas industry, the nonexistence of an actual enforcement machinery supported by a coordinated legal framework for EIA and sustainable land use decision making in the three tiers of government in the federation, the lack of transparency in the industry, the failure of the judiciary and legislative arms of government to assume their expected roles, the level of poverty and diabolic ethnic ramblings among oil- and gas-producing indigenous communities, the nonexistence of credible EIA compliance NGOs, the lack of political will and vision by the leadership and so on.

In spite of the specified and other fundamental shortcomings in the Nigerian EIA process and statutes, much power is still vested in the agency bureaucrats. These bureaucrats, in most instances, exercise their discretion in a manner that undermines the public's involvement. This undermining happens when EIA reviews that concern affected stakeholders in the interior are organized in hotels in the cities, without transparency at the insistence of multinational oil and gas corporations. This tendency is further aggravated by the fact that the actual victims or the persons who are impacted by these oil and gas projects are hundreds of kilometers away from the places where the supposed notices are displayed. Furthermore, many of these people are not literate in the English language and are unaware of the notice regulations. These deficiencies in the public participation process result in the denial of any meaningful opportunity to comment to those who are most inordinately affected and whose lives will potentially experience the greatest impacts of the proposed projects.

6 SOCIOECONOMIC IMPACTS AND THE EIA PROCESS

Socioeconomic impacts are emerging trends in the EIA process. In Nigeria, the EIS has not been properly conducted in the oil and gas sector. The expected synergies critical to

---

[57] Ibid.

a robust and qualitative, or better yet, functional process thus have yet to emerge. Before April 29, 1999, the thinking of scholars and analysts was that because the military was an authoritarian regime it had no commitment to EIA because of its civil participatory process. But six years into President Olusegun Obasanjo's civilian administration, the statutes or legal, institutional, and policy framework for EIA in the oil and gas sector and Nigeria in general had not changed. This lucidly explains why Nigeria,with most African countries, cannot use the concept of EIA and sustainable development as a panacea to address socioeconomic and political problems, such as environmental pollution and degradation, poverty, lack of fresh water, general decay in basic public amenities, food insecurity, loss of biodiversity, purposeful employment, inadequate shelter and habitat, unhealthy rural to urban migration, unsustainable natural resource exploitation, intergenerational equity, bureaucratic bottlenecks, and inter- and intraethnic conflicts, including the potent threat of disintegration. All of these are, to say the least, symptoms and effects that the lack of commitment by the leadership of Nigeria to EIA and sustainable land use has imposed on the population. It is against this backdrop that this author feels compelled to advocate that future debt cancellation and international aid to Africa, particularly Nigeria, be allocated only upon verifiable implementation of coordinated environmental governance based on a functional and result-oriented EIA process.

Can the EIA process be used to identify and document the socioeconomic needs of the people while meeting the EIA's primary goals and objectives?

Some scholars believe that social and economic problems are integral parts of the environment by virtue of the fact that humans, although gregarious and highly intrusive with regard to the environment, are included in the definition of the term *environment*. Social and economic problems are thus symptoms of disorder, reasonably connected to, if not directly situated within, the environment. Therefore, the objective of the EIA in contemporary society must include socioeconomic impacts, and it would be a misnomer to consider these as a separate subhead in the EIA process.

Others are of the opinion that socioeconomic, aesthetic, psychological, and other related impacts are distinct from conventional environmental impacts and require a separate impact assessment process and consequently should be treated as distinct dominant variables in a social and economic impact assessment process.

Regardless of what is said about the EIA process, the fact remains that in both the United States and Nigeria, the process is a creature of statute. In the United States, CEQ regulation 1508.14 provides that the "human environment shall be interpreted comprehensively to include the natural and physical environment and the relationship of people with that environment."[58] CEQ regulation 1508.8's definition of *effect* states that economic or social effects are not, on their own, intended to require preparation of an EIS. However, once an EIS is prepared and economic or social effects are interrelated with natural or physical environmental effects, the EIS will discuss all of these, including their effect on the human environment.

In *Metropolitan Edison Co. v. People against Nuclear Energy*,[59] the court was faced with the issue of deciding whether the concerns of people who may suffer from psychological anxiety, tension, fear, sense of helplessness, and other accompanying physical disorders

---

[58] Council on Environmental Quality, Executive Office of the President CEQ NEPA Regulations 40 CFR Parts 1500–1508 (1992), reprint at p. 29.

[59] *Metropolitan Edison Co v. People against Nuclear Energy*, 460 U.S. 766 particularly at 773–778.

relating to the risk that their relatives may be harmed in a nuclear accident should be considered in the renewed operation of a nuclear reactor. The court held that

> [it did] not mean to denigrate the fears or to suggest that psychological health damage they fear could not, in fact, occur.... [However,] until Congress provides a more explicit statutory instruction than NEPA now contains, [the court does] not think agencies are obligated to undertake the inquiry.... If a harm does not have a sufficiently close connection to the physical environment, NEPA does not apply.[60]

The Nigerian EIA statute does not expressly provide for socioeconomic impacts. This is a fundamental problem, because oil and gas operations are typically carried out by multinational energy corporations in collaboration with the federal government through dubious legal trust–based mechanisms, such as joint ventures, leases, profit-sharing enterprises, and joint stocks. These options *create a virtual oligarchy, in which the multinationals make all the profits, leaving the Niger Delta's indigenous minority population poverty stricken and the environment ecologically devastated.*

The government responded to this situation by creating a "corruption entangled" special development agency called the Niger Delta Development Commission (NDDC). However, the government appointed its political cronies as commissioners or administrators and reduced the commission's hope of success to that of despair and "developmental destitution" by not allocating to the NDDC requisite funds to enable it to fulfill its mandate properly.

The divergence of wealth and poverty has precipitated the unending crisis in the region. Armed conflict has arisen among dissatisfied youths, multinational oil and gas corporations, and the federal government of Nigeria. The resulting socioeconomic, psychological, and political consequences include the threat of disintegration.

Could the Nigerian government and the multinational corporations (Shell [SPDC], Chevron, Texaco, Exxon-Mobil, Total Elf Fina, Agip, Start Oil, etc.) have acted more effectively? If so, how?

The answer to both of these questions is yes. This situation could have been prevented through the implementation of a functional participatory-cum-interdisciplinary EIA process, capable of producing the following outputs:

- Providing government with all conceivable data concerning sociological trends, economics, infrastructural needs/requirements, and environmental concerns: The latter category should include information regarding the ecosystem, biodiversity, wetlands, species extinction, rights issues, and other considerations. If the government would use its institutions/agencies and human resource capacity to implement a transparent, accountable, participatory action-forcing-enforcing EIA process, this would help improve its decision-making capabilities with regard to long-term planning, lawmaking, general governance, sustainable development, and land use.
- Giving the multinational corporations the opportunity to identify proactively the socioeconomic and environmental complexities/imperatives of the market, including their social-cum-corporate responsibilities: This would enable them to draft policy and undertake other interventions that would help them secure the goodwill of the host communities, achieve a sustainable operating environment, maximize

---

[60] *Supra* note 60 at 778.

economies of scale, and improve their performance from the sustainable land use perspective.

- Improving the quality of participation of host communities in the decision-making process via public forums: This will help improve their socioeconomic, cultural, psychological, and environmental well-being. As a result, they will develop a choice sense of belonging and their standard/quality of life, among other factors, will also improve.

7 CUMULATIVE IMPACTS, ECOSYSTEM ANALYSIS, AND BIODIVERSITY

In the United States, the Council on Environmental Quality (CEQ) NEPA regulation 1508.5 defines *cumulative impact* as

> the impact on the environment, which results from the incremental impact of the action when added to other past, present and reasonably foreseeable future actions regardless of what agency [federal or nonfederal] or person undertakes such other actions. Cumulative impacts can result from individually minor but collectively significant actions taking place over a period of time.

There is a growing controversy regarding the right analytical approach to assessing cumulative impacts. This problem has progressively worsened with the numerous CEQ NEPA guidelines adopted over the years, notably in 1970, 1971, 1973, and 1979.[61] These guidelines have raised questions regarding the validity of the analytical methods conceived, as they relate to direct, indirect, and cumulative impacts that most often encompass either specific local projects or multiple projects that cover a large geographical area. Ray Clark and L. W. Canter suggest that "the simplest approach for impact prediction is to utilize analogs, or comparisons to the experienced effects of existing similar projects or types of actions. This could be termed a 'look-alike' approach."[62] This conclusion simply reemphasizes the need to assess cumulative impacts, ecosystem analysis, and biodiversity in EIA.

In 1997, the CEQ published the handbook *Considering Cumulative Effects under the National Environmental Policy Act*,[63] which contains general principles and a step-by-step approach to the evaluation of cumulative impacts.[64] Although it has no legal authority, it is generally considered to be persuasive. In 1999, the Environmental Protection Agency (EPA) published a memorandum on cumulative impact analysis.[65] This document suggested that resources; ecosystem components; geographic boundaries; periods, including past, present, and reasonably foreseeable future actions; environmental conditions; and the thresholds used to assess resource degradation should all be key components used in the course of cumulative impact analysis.[66]

There is continuing controversy over what cumulative impacts can be assessed when dealing with habitat and vast geographical areas. This dilemma should be taken into

---

[61] C. Wood, *What Has NEPA Brought Abroad? In Environmental Policy and NEPA: Past, Present, and Future* 115 (Ray Clark et al., eds. 1997).

[62] *Supra* note 14 at 20.

[63] Council on Environmental Quality [CEQ], *Considering Cumulative Effects under NEPA* (1997).

[64] Ibid. at p. iii.

[65] EPA, *Memorandum on Cumulative Impact Analysis* (1999).

[66] Ibid.

consideration when conducting an assessment. Commenting on this issue, Mandelker and Cohen noted that the dispute over the northern spotted owl habitat in the old-growth federal forests of the Pacific Northwest has continued since the 1970s.[67] There have since been court injunctions that have severely restricted new timber sales programs in federal forests located within the northern spotted owl habitat. In 1993, President Clinton convened the Forest Conference, in Oregon, to address the significance of the human and environmental needs served by the federal forests.[68]

> The President directed his Cabinet to craft balanced, comprehensive and long-term policy for the management of over 24 million acres of public land. The proposal of the Departments of the Interior and Agriculture was analyzed in a draft EIS that received over 100,000 public comments during a three month public comment period. The final EIS was made available to the public in February 1994. It took an ecosystem analysis approach.[69]

Under the Nigerian statute, section 4(d):

> An environmental impact assessment should include at least the following minimum matters:
> (a) An assessment of the likely or potential environmental impacts of the proposed activity and the alternatives, including the direct and indirect, cumulative, short-term and long-term effects.[70]

The Nigerian statute mentions cumulative short-term and long-term effects only in passing. Subsequently, the statute falls short of a results-oriented cumulative impact assessment similar to the one in the United States.

8 EIA IMPERATIVES CRITICAL TO THE ASSESSMENT OF THE OIL SECTOR

In the United States, the procedural action forcing an interdisciplinary approach usually leads to a detailed EIA in the oil sector. Because of the high level of environmental concerns, the NEPA process is usually commenced very early in the decision-making process. The EIS addresses a proposed federal action that will offer for lease oil blocks either onshore or offshore, including the offshore continental shelf (OCS), and the exclusive economic zone (EEZ) that may contain economically recoverable oil and gas resources.

Analytical methods that are used to commence the environmental impact assessment process begin with the lead agency's decision to explore for, then produce, and then transport hydrocarbon resources that are eventually developed as a result of an oil company's exploitation program. This process requires a complex and interrelated series of operations. It begins with geological and geophysical exploration; continues through the leasing of the blocks, postlease seismic surveying operations, drilling of exploration wells, installation of production facilities, drilling of development wells, movement of hydrocarbons via pipeline or barges; and ends with the removal of production facilities. These diverse activities have associated and potentially cumulative impacts on both

---

[67] Daniel R. Mandelker and William M. Cohen, "Issues in NEPA Litigation 48" (Draft April 3 2001) (unpublished manuscript on file with authors).

[68] *Id.*   [69] *Id.* At 48–49.

[70] *Supra* note 46.

offshore and onshore resources. These kinds of operations and activities are generally treated under NEPA as capable of affecting both the environmental and the *socioeconomic resources of the area; in terms of both the cumulative ecosystem and biodiversity.*

For an adequate assessment of the impact of these activities, an EIS is usually produced for the area of interest. The government or regulating agency (i.e., Minerals Management Services [MMS]) develops a scenario depicting an accurate representation of the location. Each scenario represents an alternative mitigated plan, which includes a hypothetical framework of assumptions based on estimated amounts; timing; general locations of exploration, development, and production activities and facilities; either onshore or offshore, in relation to the human environment.

The major issues of concern that form the environmental analysis have been derived from both the concerns raised over years of operations and the current NEPA process. The issues of concern related to offshore exploration, development, production, and transportation activities include possible oil spills, loss of wetlands, air pollution, water quality degradation, accumulation of trash and debris, structure and pipeline placement activities, platform removal, increase in vessel and helicopter traffic, multiple-use conflicts, support services, population fluctuations, changes to demands on public services, land use planning, tourism, aesthetic interference, cultural impacts, and consistency with state coastal zone management programs.

The resources and activities considered in an environmental analysis are sensitive coastal environments, sensitive offshore resources, water and air quality, marine mammals, coastal and marine birds, commercial fisheries, recreational resources and activities, archaeological resources, and socioeconomic conditions. The potential impact of proposed activities could be detrimental effects to any and all of the specified concerns and issues. Hence, a representative simulation of the scenario is done to address the effects of future emission of pollutants into the environment.

The environmental impact statements or assessment scenarios are based on the following factors:

- Recent trends in the amount and location of leasing, exploration, and development activity
- Estimates of undiscovered, not-yet-leased, and conventionally recoverable oil and gas resources within the planning area
- Existing offshore and onshore oil and/or gas infrastructures
- Industry information
- Oil and gas technologies, economic considerations, and environmental constraints of these technologies

The conclusions and recommendations resulting from these assessments define the cumulative impacts of activities and disturbances associated with the proposed program on biological, physical, and socioeconomic resources.

This assessment is performed with active public and stakeholder participation. The decision to lease an oil block is made after the *agency decision has been recorded and, where necessary, a mitigation plan capable of implementation is put into place.*

In Nigeria, however, the President acting through a Special Adviser from the Ministry of Petroleum and Natural Resources, with or without the knowledge or participation of indigenous native tribes of the Niger Delta, the Federal Environmental Protection Agency (FEPA), the Nigerian National Petroleum Corporation (NNPC), or the Nigerian

Property Investment Services (NAPIMS), offers oil blocks for tender through supposedly public offers. Yet, these offers are better described as secret tender mechanisms. The blocks are sold, and exploration, production, and exploitation are then carried out without a comprehensive EIA process.

This reality, coupled with the Nigerian Supreme Court's decision on resource control, which removed property or ownership rights of natural resources (particularly oil and gas) from the Niger Delta indigenous minorities and their states,[71] accounts for the high level of corruption in Nigeria because the political leadership of the country treats oil and gas revenues as free.

9 COST OF PREPARING AN EIA

Given the increasing scarcity of budgetary funding allocations to environmental agencies in both the United States and Nigeria, the cost of EIA is a real issue. Two closely interwoven are trends emerging:

- The idea that since the EIA process in the oil and gas sector is triggered by a private desire for benefit, which flows primarily to the applicant, agencies should recover the EIA process costs in whole or in substantial part from the applicant.
- The broader jurisprudential thinking that the environmental impact assessment, in a highly sensitive industry such as oil and gas, is critical to the very essence of government, multinational business development, and since ultimately all of society benefits, the cost should be borne by government.

In the United States, the weight of judicial authority favors agency inquiry into whether, and to what extent, the costs of environmental impact studies are triggered by applicant applications. The focus is on the value of the service provided to the recipient, rather than on any considerations of public policy. Although some incidental benefit clearly flows to the public, the recipients' application is deemed voluntary, with an eye to a lucrative reward if the answer is in the affirmative. Therefore, the agency can reasonably pass the full cost of the EIA to the applicant.[72] But where the benefit is incurred for both the general public and an individual recipient the reasonable factors principle of shared cost applies.[73]

In Nigeria FEPA is held solely responsible for the costs by statute, but sections 10 (1) and 11 of the FEPAA provide that

> the Agency may accept gifts of land, money, books or other property upon such terms and conditions, if any, as may be specified by the person making the gift.

It is generally believed that this allowance, coupled with corruption, a lack of institutional capacity, a failing institutional legal framework, a lack of interdisciplinary and interagency cooperation, a lack of government(s) will/commitment, and the overwhelming negative influence of the multinational oil and gas corporations operating in Nigeria, accounts for the devastating environmental degradation in the Niger Delta Region of Nigeria.

---

[71] *AG-Federation v. Abia State & 35 ORS (2002)*. 6NWLR PT.764.P.542, R.33 at p. 653 Paras. B–C.
[72] *Solhio Transp. Co. v. United States*, 5 CL. Ct. 620 (1964), affd, 766 F.2d 499 at 626–628.
[73] *Nevada Power Co. v. Watt*, 711 F.2d 913 (10th Cir. 1983).

10 PROSPECT OF EIA APPLICATION ABROAD

The central theme under the subheading of the impact of the EIA application abroad is whether or not a national EIA in the oil and gas sector should be extended abroad from its exclusive economic zone. The contrast between a court case from the United States and the Nigerian EIA regime provides an example of contrasting ideologies regarding the extension of EIA abroad. Whereas the legal situation in the United States is unsettled, the case of *Natural Resources Defense Council v. U.S Department of the Navy*[74] demonstrates a restrictive approach to monitoring national environmental impact. The court held:

> It is undisputed that, with regard to natural resources conservation and management, the exclusive economic zone of the U.S. has substantial if not exclusive legislative and environmental control stemming from its sovereign rights, for the purpose of conserving and managing natural resources.

A more global approach to environmental control is demonstrated by the Nigerian EIA regime. In Nigeria, the Minister of Foreign Affairs (MFA) may create an EIA review panel to study environmental effects of an international nature. Section 50(f) of the Nigerian EIA regime states that the authority of the MFA is contingent upon the discretion and permission of the President after due consultation. The Nigerian experience demonstrates a new trend in this aspect of EIA development. Where necessary, EIA needs to be extended abroad and tied to foreign developmental aid

11 WHAT LESSONS EXIST FOR PROFESSORS OF ENVIRONMENTAL LAW AT AFRICAN UNIVERSITIES?

Increasingly, there is a need for the role of the educator to be more responsive to societal problems, including critical environmental issues.

The emergence of "democratic" or "civilian" governments on the African continent provides no guarantee of environmental governance. There is no assurance that these governments will take measures, such as improved qualitative or functional EIA processes, aimed at controlling sustainable development and land use.

Leadership and functional institutional capacity are critical to the management of Africa's resources. The central objective of the various heads of government ought to be an unabated commitment to the basic existential needs of Africa's citizens. A consensus must be found among leaders, multinational corporations, civil society groups, and other institutions to commit themselves to environmental sustainability. This commitment needs to be demonstrated through the development of law and policy. This development must encourage honest performance and conformance to environmental standards. Organizations must be held accountable for their environmental infractions. Law and policy should facilitate the enforcement of environmental infractions, through a transparent system of due process.

A change in environmental legal education is necessary to achieve functional institutional capacity and strong leadership in environmental management throughout Africa. Course curriculum, research, and teaching methodologies should be revamped. When

---

[74] (Dist. Ct., Central Dist. California, and Case No. CV-01-07781 CAS (RZX), 9/17/2002).

restructuring environmental legal education, one must consider costly experiences of other states so that they are not repeated. Regional, national, and international networking may provide tools and linkages with which legal education in Africa could improve. African universities should teach Environmental Impact Assessment Law and Practice in addition to other environmental law and policy courses. As a matter of urgency, environmental courses should be mainstreamed into regular curriculums.

Moreover, to strengthen environmental control in Africa, legal change is required. Environmental rights should be enshrined in the constitutions of various countries. This will elevate environmental rights to the same constitutional status as fundamental rights, as suggested by Professor C. O. Okidi in his memorandum to the Constitution of Kenya Review Committee, February 2002.

12 RECOMMENDATIONS AND CONCLUSION

In Nigeria, the statute that tends to represent the legal framework for EIA best is a declaration of limited concern for environmental assessment principles. A cursory perusal of the decree reveals poor legislative drafting skills under military regimes. Several section(s), although with good substantive intent, were reduced by poor grammar and language to obscurity. For example, the first section of the decree intends to require an EIA if an activity has a significant effect on the human environment. However, the language of the statute had the opposite effect. It conveyed a requirement that an assessment be made on how the environment impacts the activity.

The decree contains 64 sections arranged in three related parts followed by a schedule. Section 12 is omitted from the decree. The cross-references to other sections of the decree are incorrect, particularly the cross-references pertaining to Sections 26(a)(f), 27(f), 29(f), 47(a)(f), 53(1)(f) and (2)(f), 54(1)(f) and (b)(f), and 51(1)(f).

In the United States, the action-forcing environmental impact process needs to be more cost-effective. The current process is very expensive and time-consuming. More often than not, agencies and bureaucrats use the environmental impact process to justify decisions already taken.

There is also a need to broaden the scope of remedies, and perhaps remove the current limited administrative review process. The objective is to expand the public's capacity to bring claims before the courts. Courts could address a broad variety of remedies other than the current limited judicial review and administrative record relief.

Furthermore, there appears to be a growing difficulty in inducing upper-echelon administrative officials to be more responsive to the NEPA process. The capacity-building intent of NEPA for administrative officials is frustrated in this case. Finally, activities by the private sector that could significantly affect the environment should be within the realm of the NEPA process.

Nigeria certainly needs a better EIA statute, which is capable of addressing the overwhelming concerns of its environmental vulnerability. Such a reformed statute must be people oriented. It should be able to blend strict substantive and procedural action to execute an enforceable legal regime in the EIA process. To this extent, laws and environmental statutes need to be harmonized and reformed. They should adopt a fundamental human rights approach with particular emphasis on the rights of indigenous minorities' sensitive ecosystems such as the Niger Delta and other identifiable environmentally vulnerable groups such as women, children, and the physically challenged.

A strict liability regime with detailed self-executory clauses that will allow international environmental treaties is long overdue. Such a regime would target environmental degradation in the course of oil and gas exploration, production, and exploitation. Sound sustainable development, land use policies, and people-oriented EIA principles, practice, and procedures need to be developed. These concerns should be made part of the educational curriculum early in the educational process so as to raise the necessary environmental awareness.

17 Managing Land Use and Environmental Conflicts in Cameroon

Nchunu Sama

> One of the most widespread contemporary problems is the failure of states to recognize the existence of indigenous land use, occupancy and ownership, and the failure to accord appropriate legal status and legal rights to protect that use, occupancy or ownership.
>
> Erica-Irene Daes. 2001[1]

1 INTRODUCTION

Cameroon's historical past accounts for the unique legal culture it has today. It is the only bijural African country. This is because of the coexistence of French civil law and English Common Law in the postcolonial period.[2] However, attempts were made after the 1972 reunification to codify the laws in certain areas including land law.

Land remains a basic environmental asset in Cameroon as well as in other developing countries in the world. The rural poor who form the bulk of the Cameroonian population are principally agrarian. The government itself depends basically on the export of primary products to gain foreign currency. The growing urban areas, institutions, and other corporate bodies need land for various uses. Land is cherished as a means of production of crops, livestock, and forest yields; as a source of power; as a representation of culture; and as nature itself given its role in other life-supporting factors.

With increasing population and competing needs for land by different stakeholders, land is increasingly perceived as being under pressure. Consequently, satisfying the desire among many users to attain a clearer and assured right to control and access land resources becomes imperative.

Because of its worth, the acquisition, possession, control, management, exploitation, and disposal of land render natural resource conflicts unavoidable. Effective land use management laws, policies, and practices are therefore necessary instruments for preventing, mitigating, and resolving environmental conflicts.

Long before colonization, land use management was based on customary values inextricably linked to the culture of the people. This customary tenure has survived the

---

[1] Erica Irene Daes, "Indigenous People and Their Relationship to Land" 2001 E/CN.4/Sub.2/2001/21 para 124.

[2] While Civil Law applies in the French-speaking part of Cameroon (former East Cameroon), Common Law applies in the English-speaking part (Former West Cameroon).

colonial period and remains a tradition in a multitude of Cameroonian villages today. However, postcolonial land tenure legislation in Cameroon retained the centralized, state-owned, and private property colonial land tenure system, which failed to recognize the traditional land tenure system of communal ownership. This dichotomy between statutory land law and the indigenous system has persistently generated land-related natural resource conflicts with their concomitant effects on sustainable development.

This chapter attempts to explore the way the formal land use system in Cameroon negatively impacts on environmental conflicts. Specifically, the analysis seeks to show how managing land use in Cameroon under statutory laws while excluding the customary system of tenure, has persistently provoked environmental conflicts, contributed to immortalizing existing conflicts, and hindered access to environmental justice for victims of such conflicts. It presents one case study (judicial decisions) to illustrate the argument. The chapter also makes references to similar conflicts in order to support the arguments. The analysis highlights some recent innovative land use–related laws in Cameroon and presents conclusions and recommendations for the way forward.

2 DEFINITION OF TERMS

The following presents working definitions for some of the key words and phrases used in the chapter in order to specify the context of the discussion:

1. *Land* will mean the physical entity in terms of its topography and spatial nature as well as the natural resources land encompasses. These include the soil, water, minerals, trees, air, and other things permanently attached to land. From an environmental perspective, therefore, land entails all natural resources of the planetary system.
2. *Land use management system (land tenure)* refers to the laws and practices related to governance of land as an environmental asset. These include regulations and practices under the statutory and customary systems. The term encompasses rules relating to land acquisition, management, and disposal; resolution of land conflicts; and other fectors. It is germane to note that land tenure forms part of the corpus of Environmental Law.
3. *Environmental conflicts* are the disputes that occur between various stakeholders to land.[3] Examples of such conflicts are land boundary disputes between two individuals or between tribes, farmer–grazer disputes, land ownership disputes between two adverse contestants, compensation disputes between a natural resource exploiter and a village community, and disputes between the state and local communities over resource access and control. The Niger Delta crisis in Nigeria, the dispute between Nigeria and Cameroon over the Bakassi Peninsular, and the dispute between Hungary and Slovakia about the Gabcikovo dam project[4] are also instances of *environmental conflicts* at various levels. In the discussion, the term *environmental conflicts* is used interchangeably with *natural resources conflicts*.

---

[3] They could be physical or corporate persons.
[4] *Gabeikovo-Nagymarous Dame Case: Hungary v. Slovakia* (1997) ICJ Reports.

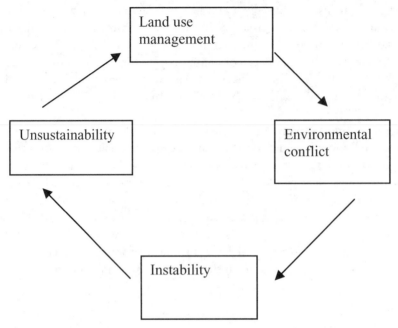

Figure 17.1.

3 VICIOUS CIRCLE OF CONFLICTS: LAND USE MANAGEMENT AND ENVIRONMENTAL CONFLICTS

Although natural resource conflicts may occur for other reasons, this author holds the view that unjust land use laws and practices will naturally provoke environmental conflicts because of the stakes and competing interests in land. Consequently the prevalence of environment conflicts will invariably perturb the implementation of sustainable land laws no matter how benign are the laws. Such conflicts may inevitably drag the entire society into a vicious circle of unending environmental problems. For instance, skewed land use regimes = environmental conflict = instability and unsustainability = worse land use practices and further conflict (see Figure 17.1). It is evident from the Figure 17.1 that the nature of land use management laws and practices directly impacts on the scale and gravity of environmental conflicts. Environmental conflicts, though unavoidable, are counterproductive and at times inherently destructive of environmental assets. In order to meet the exigencies of sustainable development as envisaged by the Bruntdland Commission,[5] therefore, the existing land use laws and practices must ensure sound management of land so as to eliminate, prevent, or promptly settle environmental conflicts justly.

---

[5] This Commission defined *sustainable development* as "development that satisfies the needs of present generation without compromising the ability of the future generation to satisfy their own needs." WCD, *Our Common Future* (Oxford, 1987) 43. This is the definition adopted in the 1996 environmental management code of Cameroon, Law No. 96/12 of 5 August 1996, "Relating to Environmental Management."

4 SOME BASIC LAND USE LAWS IN CAMEROON

Taking cognizance of the fact that readers may live in different parts of the globe with varying legal traditions, it may be helpful to highlight some of the main Cameroonian laws relating to land use management and the environment. They are as follows:

- Ordinance No. 74/1 of 6 July 1974, establishes rules governing land tenure.
- Ordinance No. 74/2 of 6 July 1974, establishes rules governing state lands.
- Ordinance No. 74/3 of 6 July 1974, on the procedure governing expropriation of land and conditions for compensation.
- Decree No. 76/165c of 27 April 1976, establishes conditions for obtaining land certificates.
- Decree No. 76/166 of 27 April 1976, establishes the terms and conditions for management of national lands.
- Decree No. 76/167 of 27 April 1976, establishes the terms and conditions of management of private property of the state.
- Decree No. 77–193 of 23 June 1977, establishes the Urban and Rural Land Development Equipment Authority.
- Decree No. 79–17 of 13 January 1979, relates to private real property transactions.
- Decree No. 79–189 of 17 May 1979, sets out rules governing delimitation of urban areas.
- Law No. 8–21 of 14 July 1980, amends certain provision of the 1974 ordinance to establish rules governing land tenure.
- Law No. 80–22 of 14 July 1980, represses infringements on landed property and state lands.
- Law No. 94/01 of 20 January 1994, sets out Forestry, Wildlife and Fisheries Regulations with the implementation decrees.
- Decree No. 95/678/PM of 18 December 1995, establishes a framework for land use in southern forested areas.
- Law No. 96/12 of 5 August 1996, relates to Environmental Management.
- Law No. 96/06 of 18 January 1996, is the Constitution of Cameroon.
- Law No. 78/263 of 3 July 1978, establishes the terms and conditions for settling farmer–grazer disputes.
- Law No. 1 of 16 April 2001, is the mining code with its implementation Decree of March 26, 2002.

It is worth noting that many new texts come into existence with contradictory provisions and without sufficient reference to existing laws and customary practices. Worse still, some of the laws described have become too remote with the passage of time[6] and fail to appreciate the evolving legal needs of the present society, thus fueling environmental conflicts.

---

[6] For instance, the Land Tenure ordinance of 1974 categorized land as State Land, National Land, and Private Land. This has been amended to incorporate the concept of community management of natural resources in recent laws such as the Community Forestry Law. There are bound to be conflicts when the community wants to consolidate their rights over such resources given that there is no provision for communal land ownership in the land tenure laws. See the case study that follows for further discussion.

5 LAND USE SYSTEM IN CAMEROON IN BRIEF

5.1 Statutory Land Use System

The rebirth of independence in Cameroon[7] necessitated administrative and legal reforms for effective functioning of the decolonized institutions. Paradoxically, postcolonial tenure reforms in Cameroon mirrored the French colonial policies of extraction and assimilation characterized by state nationalization of all lands and resources.[8] For instance, the land tenure ordinance declares in its section 1 (S 1) that "the state shall be the guardian of all lands. It may in this capacity intervene to ensure rational use of land in the imperative interest of the state or economic policies of the nation." The 1973 and 1981 forestry laws had similar provisions. Further, the 2001 Mining code in effect declares the state the owner of all mining resources.

Land under the law is categorized as state land, national land, and private property.[9]

a. *State land* comprises waterways, coastlands, subsoil and airspace, motorways (public property), and private property of the state. State land is acquired through a simple administrative declaration that the land is state property or by way of expropriation.[10] Of interest is the fact that, *concessions of traditional chiefdoms and property relating thereto* (and more particularly in the provinces where tradition considers such concessions as community property) have been referred to by the land tenure law as constituting the artificial public property of the state. Empirically, all customary communities consider concessions of traditional chiefdoms as constituting community property. This explains why it is believed that the chief never dies. But the land tenure provisions have nationalized traditional chiefdoms. This implies that the land tenure ordinance declares that traditional chiefdoms constitute state property as against communal property; this policy breeds conflict because customary law recognizes traditional chiefdoms to be community property.

b. *National land* includes "land occupied with houses, farms, plantations, grazing land manifesting human presence and developments as well as land free from effective occupation." This extended definition of national land invariably includes land held by customary communities. National land is administered by the state through the administrative authorities. It can be allocated by grant, lease, or assignment as the case may be.

Land Consultative Commissions convened and headed by administrative officers help resolve conflicts. The Commissions are charged with dispute resolution over national land and farmer–grazer disputes. The role of the Commission is limited to making recommendations while the administrators make decisions, which may differ from such recommendations. Practically, the process before the administrative conflict management bodies is not only slow but also fraught with extensive irregularities and administrative excesses.

---

[7] The term *rebirth* is used to sign that African empires and kingdoms had existed independently before imperialism.

[8] David Brown, "European Union Topical Forest" (1999), Paper 2.

[9] See the 1974 Land Tenure Laws, p. 5.

[10] *Expropriation* refers to the acquisition of the private property for public purpose. The individual is compensated for any developments on the land.

c. *Private property* is land owned by individuals and must be evidenced by a land certificate (title deed) granted by the state.[11] The land certificate is issued by the government and is proof of private ownership of land. However, the individual is obliged to pay annual taxes to the state for the land. Practically, the procedure for obtaining a land certificate is quite expensive, ridiculously cumbersome, and thus difficult to comprehend for the common man or woman. That aside, the granting and revocation of a land title occur at the discretion of the administration, and this practice is perfidious in the sense that there is tenure insecurity even with respect to private property.

5.2 Customary Land Tenure

The state patrimony and private property regimes elucidated here gloss over the generic notion of communal ownership of land that exists in the various customary communities in Cameroon. Land is central to the lives of the indigenous communities. It is the basis for their economic survival, spiritual well-being, and cultural identity. The concept of land embraces their culture and the whole territory they use, including forest, river, sea, mountain, and the surface of the land as well as the subsurface and natural resources.

It is trite law that the concept of communal ownership of land is a customary system that has survived in most African communities including in Cameroon for ages.[12] In the view of Oluyede, communal ownership of land means an unrestricted right of individual community members or families to have access to what is held to be their common asset with the tacit understanding that absolute ownership is vested in the community as a whole.[13] This notion of communal ownership was succinctly affirmed by the Judicial Committee of the Privy Council in the landmark case of *Amodu Tijani v. Secretary of Southern State Nigeria*[14]: "Land belongs to the community, the village or the family, never to the individual. All the members of the community, village or family have an equal right to the land."[15]

Annie Patricia rightly describes this long-cherished culture as "intergenerational equity" in Africa.[16] The customary system ostensibly constitutes an element of sustainable natural resource management through the belief that land is a planetary resource to be held in trusts and managed by the present generation for their interest and that of future generations. Members of the community perceive land as belonging to the entire community and accessible to all of them: the dead, the living, and the unborn. Ostensibly, such a customary land ownership concept presents a threefold perception of community property: those who went before us, those who are alive now, and those who are to come. It embodies the concept of trusteeship of land, which is now gaining prominence in the field of environmental law.

Ironically, the Cameroon statutory laws empower customary communities or individuals of Cameroonian nationality who were peacefully occupying or using "National

---

[11] Articles 2, 4, and 5 of the 1974 Ordinance, p. 5 *supra.*
[12] P. A. Oluyede, "Nigerian Law of Conveyancing" (Ibadan University Press, 1978), p. 2.
[13] Ibid., p. 13.
[14] *Amodu Tijani v. Secretary of Southern Stat Nigeria* (1921) AC 399.
[15] *Amodu Tijani v. Secretary of Southern Stat Nigeria* (1921) 2 AC 399 at 405.
[16] Annie Patricia, "Law, Colonization and Environment in Africa" (1997) RECIEL.

Land" before August 1974 to continue using or occupying the same. They can apply for land certificates for such land.[17] Stricto senso, the occupants have unsecured user rights because the land remains national land, which can be assigned for any specific purpose at any time by the state.[18] However, the communities can secure their rights to land by obtaining a land certificate. This would require the impoverished communities to engage the costly, cumbersome, and practically difficult procedure for land certificates or remain as squatters on their ancestral land.

6 CASE STUDY (THE MEJANG QUARRY CASE)

The preceding analysis portrays the wide gap between statutory land law and customary land rights in Cameroon. Such a dichotomy relating to a delicate yet indispensable environmental asset such as land has invariably generated natural resource conflicts in many parts of Cameroon. That aside, the laws practically hinder the rights of citizens (conflict victims) to have access to environmental justice even against foreign companies. The Mejang quarry exploitation case presents the ongoing scenario of land use management and environmental conflicts in Cameroon.[19]

6.1 Kimbi Moses Ndoh v. Groupemnt d'Enterprise Trapp-Strabag Belfinger & Berger (WHC/2/98) Unreported

Mejang is a village community located in the Boyo Division of the North West Province of Cameroon. The people of this agrarian community have been living and sustaining their livelihoods on their ancestral land for ages. They have carried out activities such as crop farming, hunting, grazing, and performance of spiritual rights on the land. Sometime in the 1990s, the defendants (a German road construction consortium) had a contract with the Cameroon Government to construct a road from Bambui to Foundong.[20]

> The defendant company discovered good granites in Mejang village and decided to exploit the quarries for their road construction project. Before commencing their activities in 1993, the defendant sought and obtained a licence from the government to exploit quarries at Mejang over an area of 15 hectares. The licence expressly stated that the area was national land, clearly imputing that the indigenous community had no say in the negotiations but rather should quit the land. Out of pressure, some few farmers were given meagre compensation for their crops that were destroyed by the defendants.[21]

The defendants carried out excavations, blasting operations, crushing of rocks to concretes, and other mining activities from 1993 to 1997. As a result of the heavy

---

[17] See Articles 17 and 18 of Ordinance No. 74/1 of 6 July 1974, p. 5 *supra*.

[18] For instance, PLANTECAM, a pharmaceutical company, exploited mass quantities of pygium (*Prunus africana*) on the Kilum Mountain under government license in the early 1980s to the extent that this species was almost becoming extinct. Pygium is a medicinal plant used extensively by the local people of the Kilum Mountain area.

[19] Note that the author took part in this case as co-counsel for the plaintiffs.

[20] Note that Mejang village is about eight kilometers from the said road.

[21] Prefectoral Order No 019/AP/E32/93 of 11 May 1993.

exploitation, the defendants created mammoth ditches and huge trenches on the land.[22] Consequently, the local population was deprived of their vast arable land and movement in the area was rendered very risky for both humans and animals. The quarrying activities even diverted the course of a stream that was used by the villagers for irrigation and other activities.

At the end of their exploitation the defendants simply removed their equipment from the area, leaving behind massive environmental destruction. Aggrieved by the actions of the defendants, the village chief and his people requested that the defendants return the place to its original condition or pay compensation for the destruction done to their land. Attempts to resolve the matter amicably were frustrated by the defendants, who claimed that they were authorized by state officials to exploit the quarries on national land, which belongs to the state and not the plaintiffs.

Left with no other option, the village chief (His Royal Highness Fon Ngochia) and other notables assigned a power of attorney to Kimbi Moses Ndoh (one of the victims) to file an action against the defendant. The plaintiffs introduced a civil suit before the High Court of Menchum Division claiming the sum of 1.5 trillion FCFA (1.5 million pounds) against the defendants for trespass, nuisance, and destruction. In its defense, the company brought in the state of Cameroon as a third party on the premise that they exploited a parcel of national land assigned to them *free of charge* by the state. During the hearing, the company in their defense averred inter alia:

> The land in question was a piece of national land which was exploited by the defendants with the consent of the appropriate institutions representing the State of Cameroon . . . that the Plaintiffs are not the proper persons to complain.[23]

The defendant company honestly accepted that the destruction, borrow pits, and degraded quality of the land were the natural consequences of their quarry exercise. However, they equally argued that the plaintiffs (indigenous community) had no land certificate on the land (their ancestral land) and consequently had no *locus standi*. Thus, according to their argument, the land was national land in accordance with the 1974 land tenure laws, subject to state management, and as such the plaintiffs could not claim any right to it. After hearing the case, the court decided in favor of the defendant company and dismissed the case. It held inter alia that the defendant company exploited the quarries on national land.[24]

Consequently, the indigenous community of Mejang is obliged to bear the awful environmental harm caused by the transnational road construction company, because within the purview of the land use laws, their land is national land and thus subject to state management. This is equally an apposite case of denial of access to justice by the skewed statutory land tenure laws even when the defendants accepted that damage was done to the land.

---

[22] An expert report was made at the behest of the Plaintiffs (report dated 6 June 1997, admitted as exhibit A at p. 68 of the record of Proceedings). The report stated inter alia that at the locus "there is a large excavated area on the hill about 4000 SQ M and about 180–200 m deep." It further stated that there was a large quantity of stones below the waterfall area as a result of the collapse of the walls of the excavated area and that there were "two compounds on top of the hill and farms below which from every indication will be affected in future if the walls of the excavated area continue collapsing." See *id.*

[23] See Statement of the defense filed 3 February 1998.

[24] Judgment delivered 21 August 1998.

The injustice orchestrated in the Mejang Quarry case is similar to a previous conflict in *Amidu Lukong v. Razel Construction Company Ltd.*[25] In this case, the plaintiff was a peasant farmer residing at Sob Village (his village) in the Nso Fondom in Bui Division of North West Province. The defendant was a French multinational road construction company with a branch in Cameroon. Defendant exploited quarries on land in the plaintiff's possession at Sob in the Bui Division. The plaintiff was never compensated for the exploitation or destruction. He then sued the defendants for conversion and trespass. The Bui High Court decided against the plaintiff and held that without a Land Certificate, the land was national land and subject to state management.

7 EMERGING LEGISLATION

Some innovative land use–related laws are being enacted in Cameroon. But the crucial issue is whether these emerging regulations have the potential to water down the rigors of the land tenure ordinance. Highlights of some of these laws will provide some indication of whether they can engender considerable change in the land use practices.

7.1 Constitutional Provisions

Cameroon's new Constitution came into force in February 1996. The Constitution obliges the state to "ensure the protection of minorities and preserve the rights of indigenous populations in accordance with the Law."[26] This constitutional requirement entails the preservation of the rights of indigenous people and reasonably includes the rights to management and development of their traditional lands, access rights, and control over their ancestral lands.

The Constitution further provides that the state "shall recognise and protect traditional values that conform to democratic principles, human rights and the law." Recognition and protection of traditional values certainly include recognizing and respecting the traditional land tenure system of communal ownership of land and free access to same as elucidated previously.

However, the Cameroonian position seems to provide a cosmetic change, which is at a distance from any innovative line of thought. For instance, qualifying phrases such as "in accordance with the law" or "conform to democratic principles, human rights and the law" rather retain the rigors of the land tenure ordinance and practically introduce trivial or no change, as expected. The qualifiers equally dilute the projected constitutional guarantees and provide legal opportunities for the government in effect to override these provisions at any time via the administrative hammer.

7.2 The 1994 Forestry Laws

The ongoing decentralization process in Cameroon and many parts of Africa has begun to reopen good environmental governance strategies when communities are involved in resource management. The 1994 law[27] is the first that provides for an integrated

---

[25] *Amidu Lukong v. Razel* (1999) unreported (HCK/5/95).

[26] Preamble of the 1996 Constitution (*supra*) rendered enforceable by Article 65.

[27] Law No. 94/01 of 20 January 1994 to lay down Forestry, Wildlife and Fisheries regulations.

approach to resource management, incorporating community participation in natural resource management (NRM) and decentralizing governance of environmental assets such as community forest management (CFM) and community hunting zones (CHZ).

Through CFM, resource-based village communities are empowered to manage their forests through a management agreement with the Ministry of Environment and Forestry (MINEF) and in accordance with a simple management plan. Ideally, this amounts to recognizing the customary rights of the people over their indigenous forestland. However captivating it may appear to be, the CFM law seems to complicate rather than solve the land use management problems.[28] The same law provides that

> the state, local councils, village communities and private individuals may exercise on their forest and aquacultural establishments all the rights that result from ownership, subject to restrictions laid down in the regulations governing land tenure and state lands.[29]

Further, community forest (CF) is nonpermanent forest,[30] which can be used for purposes other than forestry at any time it is limited to 5,000 hectares, it is granted for 5 years and may be renewed for a maximal period of 25 years. The forest is managed with the strict supervision of MINEF, which can revoke the license at any time. Practically, this scenario reverts to the position of nonrecognition of customary rights to, access to, and control of forestland by the resource-based communities.

The restrictions described create a fragility of tenure to the detriment of local communities and have practically plagued the community forest process in Cameroon to date and generated enormous conflict. For instance, the CF process in the Kilum Mountain Range met with much resistance from Oku grazers, who were supported by His Royal Highness the Fon of Oku. The situation degenerated into severe conflicts between the grazers and the staff of the Kilum Ijim Forest Project,[31] igniting a series of court actions. Despite the court decisions against the indigenous grazers, they have contemptuously continued to graze in their ancestral forest.[32] The conflict has completely frustrated the CFM process in this area.

7.3 Law Number 96/12 of 5 August 1996, on Environmental Management in Cameroon

Law number 96/12 is the first comprehensive law on environmental management in Cameroon and emphasizes a participatory approach. Though a framework law, it addresses various aspects of the environment, including air, water, and land; environmental impact assessment (EIA); sustainable development; marine and coastal ecosystems; the urban environment; waste management; risk and natural disasters; pollution; and environmental liability. It is incumbent on any promoter of a project that may endanger the environment to conduct an EIA in accordance with the prescriptions. It equally renders it criminal for a person not to conduct an EIA for a required

---

[28] See Article 37 of the 1994 law on Forestry, Wildlife and Fishery Resources (note 25 *supra*).

[29] See Articles 6 and 7 of the 1994 law (note 26 *supra*).

[30] See Article 20 of the 1994 law (note 26 *supra*).

[31] This project is a biodiversity project of Bird Life International for the conservation of Kilum-Ijim montane forest.

[32] *The People v. Isaiah Mangeh & 138 Ors* (2003) unreported, BCA/35/2002 delivered 16 July 2003.

project.[33] The mandatory provision for EIA is quite reflective of sustainable land use management approaches, but the provision is subject to an implementation decree, which was not yet in force after eight years.

8 CONCLUSIONS AND RECOMMENDATIONS

As indicated by the foregoing discussion, the difficulties in resolving natural resource disputes occasioned by the centralized, private property, and rather exotic land tenure regime in Cameroon cannot be overemphasized. The dissonance between the formal system and customary tenure perpetrated by the land use laws promotes the environmental conflicts. As mentioned, this skewed tenure system is a French colonial heritage even though Cameroon is theoretically bijural. The experience in Anglo-Saxon states with their support of customary land use practices[34] provides a set of lessons in which might be found a more decentralized system of land administration for Cameroon.

In conclusion, it cannot be denied that the nagging problem of managing land use and environmental conflicts in Cameroon needs an immediate solution in order to meet the exigencies of sustainable development. Considering the urgency, dispersed effects, and irreversible nature of some environmental conflicts, the existing land use laws are in need of urgent reform. To that end a number of tasks appear particularly important:

- Reform land tenure laws to recognize and give legal status to communal land rights, security, and access to land. Over time, some governments have recognized that formal legal codes do not fit the diverse settings and associated customary tenure systems in practice among the local people. There is urgent need in Cameroon to end the dichotomy between formal law and local land-holding systems. This paradigm shift will enable local communities to escape from the precarious legal situations in which they find themselves in the phase of conflicts and will help ensure sustainable development.
- Decentralize the land use management system.
- Reform land tenure policies to be in synchronization with emerging environmental laws such as the 1994 forestry law, 1996 environmental management code, 2001 mining code, and 2004 law on decentralization.
- Prevent the enactment of fragmented natural resource laws.
- Facilitate access to environmental justice and set up a potent environmental conflict resolution mechanism.
- Formulate proactive land policies that reflect practical realities.
- Promote the use of traditional authorities in settlement of natural resource conflicts.
- Combat corruption in the land tenure sector.

---

[33] Section 79 of this 1996 law provides for 6 months to 2 years of imprisonment or fine of from 2 million to 5 million FCFA.

[34] This is reflective of the British colonial approach of indirect rule.

18 Environmental Law Reform to Control Land Degradation in the People's Republic of China: A View of the Legal Framework of the PRC–GEF Partnership Program

Ian Hannam and Du Qun

1 INTRODUCTION

Land degradation in the People's Republic of China has accelerated over recent years for many reasons, including inappropriate land use practices and ineffective laws.[1] Many land use initiatives in the past have not been well supported by legislation, resulting in severe environmental impacts in the dryland agricultural area of China. Land degradation now adversely affects around 40 percent of the area of China.

1.1 Definitions

Land degradation is a broad term that includes degradation of land, water, and vegetation, as well as the processes of soil erosion and desertification; it is defined as the "overall reduction in the capability of land to produce benefits from a particular use under a specific form of land management."[2] The Convention to Combat Desertification defines land degradation as

> the reduction or loss, in arid, semi-arid and dry subhumid areas, of the biological or economic productivity and complexity of rain-fed cropland, irrigated cropland, or range, pasture, forest and woodlands resulting from land uses or from a process or combination of processes, including processes arising from human activities and habitation patterns, such as: (i) soil erosion caused by wind and/or water; (ii) deterioration of the physical, chemical and biological or economic properties of soil; and (iii) long-term loss of natural vegetation.[3]

---

[1] SMEC International, *Preparing National Strategies for Soil and Water Conservation* (2002), Report TA 3548-PRC, Ministry of Water Resources, People's Republic of China.

[2] See B. W. Boer and I. D. Hannam, "Legal Aspects of Sustainable Soils: International and National" (2003), Review of European Community and International Environmental Law, 12(2), at 151–152.

[3] UN Convention to Combat Desertification in Countries Experiencing Serious Drought and/or Desertification, Particularly in Africa, Article 1, reprinted in 33 ILM (1994), 1328 (Paris, 17 June 1994).

Acknowledgments are given to the GEF–PRC OP12 land degradation control program and the national natural science foundation of PRC (Project 40471056) and the Asian Development Bank. Special thanks go to Bruce Carrad, Principal Project Specialist, East and Central Asia Department, ADB, and Dr. Zhming Niu, Program Officer, PRC–GEF Partnership Program on Land Degradation in Dryland Ecosystems, ADB Beijing.

Desertification is defined in the Convention as "land degradation in arid, semi and dry sub-humid humid areas resulting from various factors, including climatic variations and human activities."[4]

Land degradation has been accelerated by ineffective laws and inappropriate land use practices.[5] Many agricultural, industrial, and domestic land use activities have not been properly supported by legislation, and negative environmental impacts on the dryland ecosystem agricultural areas have resulted. China's dryland agricultural region supports around 350 million people, including many of the nation's poorest. Desertification is concentrated in the northern and northwestern arid, semiarid, and dry subhumid zones. The social and economic consequences of land degradation have reduced household incomes in many rural communities and increased poverty, unemployment, and migration to other areas. These trends have led to reduced productive capacity of agricultural and pastoral lands, damage to roads and other infrastructure, and loss of watershed protection functions. Dust storms are of global significance in relation to atmospheric conditions, and their impact is also felt on the Korean Peninsula and in Japan.[6]

1.2 Environmental Law Reform: PRC–GEF Partnership Program

Recent studies show that the current environmental law framework of China varies substantially in its capability to recognize the different types of land degradation problems and to implement programs needed for effective land degradation control. A few years ago, China realized the benefit of adopting a sustainable development approach in its legal system and introduced some quite progressive land management laws and revised other of its laws.[7] At the provincial level, regulations are poorly understood or enforced, land tenure arrangements are often uncertain, and land use rights for rural communities require significant change to promote a long-term perspective on natural resource use. Significantly, the scale and impact of China's land degradation have drawn world attention and attracted international support.[8] In 2000, the People's Republic of China (PRC) government asked the Asian Development Bank to take a lead role in facilitating the preparation of a PRC–Global Environment Facility Partnership on Land Degradation in Dryland Ecosystems (the PRC–GEF Partnership Program).[9] The aim of the first phase of the PRC–GEF Partnership Program (2004–7) is to strengthen China's enabling environment and build institutional capacity to adopt an integrated approach

---

[4] *Id.* art. 1(g); the term *arid, semiarid, and dry subhumid areas* refers to areas other than polar and subpolar regions in which the ratio of annual precipitation to potential evapotranspiration falls within the range 0.05–0.65.

[5] See Asian Development Bank (ADB), *Report and Recommendations of the President to the Board of Directors on a Proposed Global Environment Facility Grant and Technical Assistance Grant to the People's Republic of China for Strengthening the Enabling Environment and Building Institutional Capacity to Combat Land Degradation Project* (March 2004) (hereafter Main Report).

[6] *Id.*

[7] E.g., introduction of the Desertification Law in 2002 and the reform of 1985 Grassland Law in 2003.

[8] China currently has to feed 22 percent of the world's population, based on 6.5 percent of the world's land area, 7.3 percent of the world's farmland, and 5.8 percent of the world's water resources; Main Report, *supra* note 5, at 5.

[9] Main Report, *supra* note 5, at 1; the total cost of the project is $150 million over 10 years.

to control land degradation. The Legal Component is a principal part of the Program, and its objective is to improve the legislative framework and associated support systems to combat land degradation. The 2004–2007 legislative reform agenda includes the following:[10]

- Improving the quality and consistency of legislation for sustainable natural resource management; strengthening linkages, including reform of existing laws;[11] and introducing new laws with the appropriate elements for land degradation control.[12]
- Developing administrative procedures to improve the effectiveness of environmental law
- Building capacity and providing education in the legislative aspects of land degradation management
- Establishing specialist legal and regulatory advice and problem-solving procedures

2 RATIONALE OF ENABLING LAW TO COMBAT LAND DEGRADATION

The environmental degradation of air, water, and land resources is threatening the quality of life of China's 1.3 billion people, and China has many of the worst land degradation problems in the world, with over 40 percent of its land area (between 3 million and 4 million square kilometers) adversely affected.[13] China's arable land per capita is only 0.11 hectare, which is very low by world standards, and water availability is only one-quarter of the world average. The shrinking arable land area and increasing demand for agricultural products cause farmers to extract higher yields from their land, at the expense of stable soil structure and adequate organic matter content, leading to increased soil erosion.[14] Annual soil loss is estimated at around 5 billion tonnes. Moreover, 90 percent of China's natural grassland area suffers from moderate to severe degradation, while demand for meat and other livestock products is rising as urbanization and standards of living increase, putting more pressure on land and water resources. In the arid areas, rapidly increasing livestock numbers have exacerbated the spread of deserts. Land degradation due to wind erosion, salinization, and desertification increased from around 1,500 square kilometers per year in the 1970s to around 3,500 square kilometers per year by the late 1990s.[15]

---

[10] *Id.*

[11] The process commenced in 1998 with the amendment of the Forestry Law and the Land Administration Law, and the reform of four other major natural resource laws, the Water Law 2002, Grassland Law 2003, Agriculture Law 2003, and Environmental Impact Assessment Law 2003.

[12] E.g., the proposal by China to formulate a law for the management of the Yellow River Basin; see ADB, *Strategic Study for the Yellow River Law* (2004), TA 3708.

[13] In this chapter, *land degradation* includes wind and water erosion, overgrazing and loss of biomass in grasslands, deforestation, and related disturbances to the hydrological balance resulting in erratic river flows, excessive crop nutrient loss, soil fertility decline, poor soil drainage, and salinization.

[14] ADB, *Technical Assistance to the People's Republic of China for Monitoring and Management of Fragile Ecosystems in Shanxi Shaanxi-Inner Mongolia* (1991) Manila.

[15] Despite inconsistent national data, provincial data show that from the 1950s to the 1990s the rate of land degradation due to wind erosion, salinization, and desertification increased from around 1,500 to almost 3,500 square kilometers per year. The root causes are primarily human induced and are not the result of natural factors.

The policies and human activities of the past 50 years have accelerated land degradation. Previous well-intentioned policies that had negative environmental impacts and poorly supported by legislation, include the following:[16]

- Relocation of people from densely populated areas to ecologically sensitive arid and semiarid areas of the north and west
- Food self-sufficiency and enforcement of grain quotas
- Conversion of grasslands for cropping and intensive grazing in climatically marginal areas
- Large-scale industrial development in remote, water-scarce parts of the country, allowing factories unlimited access to state-financed water supplies
- Expansion of irrigated agriculture into some of the driest parts of the country, with low prices for water that offer little incentive for farmers to adopt water-efficient techniques
- Inappropriate land use practices (little use of conservation farming techniques), land tenure arrangements, and restrictions of labor mobility

The social and economic consequences of land degradation are profound, notably lower household incomes and increased rural poverty, high unemployment, and migration to other areas.[17] These disturbing trends have led to reduced productive capacity of agricultural and pastoral lands, damage to roads and other infrastructure, and loss of watershed protection functions, resulting in increased sedimentation of productive lands and reservoirs.[18] Economic losses due to land degradation have been estimated at Y 6.4 billion annually (Y 176 million, equivalent to U.S. $21.2 million, per day). Dust storms originating in western China are a dramatic outcome of land degradation and increased from an average of 0.5 per year in the 1950s to 2.3 per year throughout the 1990s. They now regularly impact on Beijing and other major urban areas. These storms have been estimated to result in the loss of Y 1.3 billion annually and are a global concern.[19]

2.1 Existing Legislative Framework for Land Degradation Control

The environmental protection of China was declared an important national policy goal in the early 1980s, and a comprehensive framework of environmental legislation, policy, and institutions soon followed. Rapid growth of the economy in an environmentally unsustainable way and the transition from a centrally planned economy to the market economy have intensified the conflict between the need for economic development and sustainable land management.[20] China now has many natural resource management agencies with varying responsibilities in land degradation control, including the Ministry of Water Resources (MWR), State Forest Administration, Ministry of Agriculture,

---

[16] The World Bank, *China: Air, Land and Water, Environmental Priorities for a New Millennium* (2001).

[17] The World Bank, *China: Overcoming Rural Poverty* (2001).

[18] The Yellow River has an annual sediment load of 1.6 billion tonnes; the annual sediment load of the Changjiang River is 500 million tonnes.

[19] J. Voegele, *Combating Desertification in Western China: A Perspective* (World Bank) (2001).

[20] Wang Xi, "Environmental Protection in the People's Republic of China: Legislation and Implementation," in B. W. Boer, R. Fowler, and N. Cunningham (eds), *Environmental Outlook No 2: Law and Policy* (The Federation Press) (1996) 93–116.

Ministry of Land Resources, State Environmental Protection Agency, State Development Planning Commission, and organizations for State Flood Control and Drought Relief. The structure of China's legislative framework for land degradation control (comprising national laws and regulations, provincial laws, and supportive legislative materials) has four levels:

Level 1   China's Constitution and international conventions and agreements to which China has become a party[21]

Level 2   Laws promulgated by the National People's Congress (includes the administrative, civil, and criminal laws) and the Standing Committee of the National People's Congress

Level 3   Regulations, orders, decisions, and other documents with binding force of law promulgated by the State Council (note that those of its subordinate ministries and commissions without the power of the State Council no longer qualify as law under the 2003 Administrative Permission Law but are recognized as policy)

Level 4   Regulations, decisions, and orders promulgated by the People's Congress of provinces, autonomous regions, and municipalities directly under the Central Government, and by municipalities with local legislative power

Environmental Law for Land Degradation Control

China's legislative instruments relevant to land degradation separate into two main categories. The first category includes a group of environmental laws used directly for the management and conservation of water and land – the conservation-based law regime. The second category includes a number of related environmental laws, referred to as *natural resource utilization–based laws*.[22]

Determining the capacity of legislation to control land degradation. The capacity of a legal and institutional framework to control land degradation has been described as the ability of the legal and institutional system to achieve sustainable use of water and land.[23] "Capacity" is determined by the number and type of essential legal and institutional elements present within the relevant laws and legal instruments, in a format that enables the sustainable use of land to be identified and with the legal, administrative, and technical capability within the particular laws or instruments to take some form

---

[21] China Constitution (adopted 4 December 1982), art. 9(2): "The state ensures the rational use of natural resources and protects rare animals and plants."

[22] See I. D. Hannam, *Legal and Institutional Frameworks for Water and Land Management with Particular Reference to Marginal Areas in Selected Countries in South and South East Asia and the People's Republic of China* (International Water Management Institute) (2002); I. D. Hannam, *A Method to Identify and Evaluate the Legal and Institutional Framework for the Management of Water and Land in Asia: The Outcome of a Study in Southeast Asia and the People's Republic of China*, Research Report 73 (International Water Management Institute) (2004).

[23] See I. D. Hannam 2004, *supra* note 22, at 2. *Sustainable use* is defined as "the utilisation of water and land in a manner that preserves the balance between the processes of soil formation and soil degradation, and the maintenance or improvement of the quality of water, while maintaining the ecological functions and needs of water and land. In this context, the term 'the use of water and land' means the role of water and land in the conservation of biodiversity and the maintenance of human life."

of positive action for land degradation control.[24] In some cases, the capacity is direct and obvious; in other, it exists in a format that allows some form of indirect action. Capacity is represented in the form of legal rights, the type of legal mechanisms, and, importantly, the number and comprehensiveness of the essential elements and their functional capabilities.[25] As most land management issues are multifactorial (i.e, many include a sociological, a legal, and a technical component), generally more than one piece of environmental legislation (along with detailed regulations) will be needed to manage each type of land degradation issue effectively. A variety of legal and institutional elements and mechanisms may also be required. This structure reinforces the benefits of analyzing existing environmental legislation at each level to ascertain current management regimes.[26] Information gathered by a number of studies in China (and in other dryland regions of the world) has been used as a guide to the type of legal and institutional elements to be included within the legislative regime for land degradation control in China. In this regard, for a law to be effective in controlling land degradation it must contain specific legal and institutional elements. An *element* is defined as a principle or suggested rule or direction of conduct that may be used in its existing form or modified to perform the role of a legal mechanism,[27] or as a legal principle (a rule of conduct) in legislation. An element can also be used individually, or in combination with other legal mechanisms or principles, to allow or invoke a legally based action to achieve sustainable land use.[28] Legal and institutional elements are used in either or both of two roles:

- To assist in the evaluation of an existing legal instrument (to determine its capacity to meet certain standards of performance for the sustainable use of land).
- To guide the reform of an existing soil law or to develop new legislation for the sustainable use of land. Each legal and institutional element must have the capacity to achieve a prescribed level of land management.

Existing Legal Regime for Land Degradation Control

Conservation-based law regime. Specific laws in the conservation-based group include (in assessed order of practical contribution to land degradation control) are the following:

- The 1991 Water and Soil Conservation Law and the 1993 State Measures for Implementation of the 1991 Water and Soil Conservation Law
- The 2001 Desertification Prevention and Restoration Law
- The 1989 Environmental Protection Law

---

[24] *Id.* at 15–18. Basic elements include general intent, jurisdiction, responsibility, objectives, definitions, duty of care, hierarchy of responsibility, institutional, policy, education, research, community participation, land use planning, land management, finance, enforcement, and dispute resolution.

[25] See Boer and Hannam 2003, *supra* note 2.

[26] See I. D. Hannam, Wang Xi, Zhou Yanfang, and Hu Yuan, *Report on National and Provincial Legislation*, Strategic Planning Study for the Preparation of the Yellow River Law, Working Paper, ADB TA 3708-PRC (2004).

[27] Such as a direct statutory function or an administrative function.

[28] The *essential elements* referred to in this chapter were derived through an evaluation of legal and ecological principles where, in combination, they are aimed at achieving a desired level or standard of performance in sustainable land management.

- The 2002 Law for Appraising Environmental Impacts
- The 1996 Water Pollution Prevention and Treatment Law and the 1996 Law for the Prevention and Treatment of Solid Waste from Polluting the Environment
- Various measures for implementation of the State Council, People's Congress of provinces, and autonomous regions

Water and Soil Conservation Law. The 1991 Water and Soil Conservation Law has a wide range of legislative elements suitable for land degradation control, but there is a substantial variation in their capacity to manage water and land issues.[29] This law does not give adequate recognition to the diverse physiographical characteristics and regional ecological differences of China's dryland area. Many elements are directed toward soil-erosion control (wind and water erosion) activities, and there are basic procedures for land planning and rehabilitation activities. However, the ability of this law to address the wider, more complex issues of land degradation – in particular, soil salinity and vegetation depletion from overgrazing – is very limited. Moreover, the stated intent of this law, which includes the mandate to consider ecological aspects of the environment,[30] cannot effectively be achieved because of an absence of policymaking responsibilities, poor provision for education and capacity building, and an absence of procedures to determine the ecological condition of soil resources and to prioritize soil degradation control programs.[31]

The intent of the 1993 State Measures for Implementation of the Water and Soil Conservation Law is to guide the provinces and autonomous regions in the preparation of their specific, localized laws. Compared to the principal 1991 law, the 1993 Measures for Implementation have many weaknesses. In the first instance, it has fewer "essential elements" present than the 1991 law. There are no goals or objectives, no definitions, no policymaking direction, and no provisions for engaging community participation. The Measures for Implementation outline a number of important soil conservation problems for the provinces and autonomous regions to consider, but the law lacks the specific guidelines and land evaluation criteria considered necessary for the provinces to prepare land management standards and measures. A major weakness of the Measures for Implementation is the absence of provisions to alert the provinces and autonomous regions of the need to consider the particular environmental characteristics of the region in the preparation of their special local legal instruments, land planning, and land management procedures. The similarity in scope and content of the Water and Soil Conservation Law and the Measures for Implementation may be reasonable justification for dispensing with the Measures for Implementation altogether.

The provincial Water and Soil Conservation Laws follow a format similar to that of the Measures for Implementation, lacking in detail and scope and with little recognition of local landscape variations. Within the provincial law there is a reasonable presence

[29] I. D. Hannam, *Legal and Institutional Aspects of Soil Conservation in the People's Republic of China*, Report to TA PRC 3548 (2002).

[30] See 1991 Water and Soil Conservation Law art. 1.

[31] The Minister of Water Resources (MWR) has been planning to revise this law for many years with various representations being made to the State Council. The Asian Development Bank has provided MWR with a country-based best practice study to support the revision of the 1991 Water and Soil Conservation Law. This study is now part of the technical assistance project "Implementation of National Strategies for Water and Soil Conservation," which commenced in September 2005.

of elements for land planning, land management, and enforcement, but elements for community participation, resolution of disputes, development of policy, undertaking of research and investigation, and educational responsibilities are generally absent. A major concern with the provincial and autonomous region level of laws for water and soil conservation is that a number of the legislative elements represented in the State Water and Soil Conservation Law and the State Measures for Implementation do not appear in the provincial and autonomous region law. The result is a substantially weaker body of law at the geographic level, where it should normally be more comprehensive, with a capacity to identify and control land degradation at the level where it originates.

The 2001 Desertification Prevention and Restoration Law. The 2001 Desertification Law is a more comprehensive and complete environmental law than the 1991 Water and Soil Conservation Law. It has well-developed goals and objectives, comprehensive definitions, a clear duty of care, and reasonable responsibilities for policy development, education, research and investigation, land planning, and enforcement.[32] In its current form, this law has a greater capacity to deal with many aspects of land degradation. However, the potential of the Desertification Law to do so is hindered by the fact that the responsibility for its administration is divided among three agencies with different agendas – one with conservation interests and two with agricultural-development interests – thus presenting many conflicting interests for successful implementation.[33]

The 1989 Environmental Protection Law. The Environmental Protection Law is regarded as China's principal law for environmental management. It has played a significant role as the foundation for the development of a comprehensive set of sector environmental laws in China, especially in pollution control, urban environmental protection, and various nature conservation and nature reserve regulations. The purposes of the 1989 Environmental Protection Law are to protect the human and ecological environment of China and to prevent pollution. The definition of *environment* specifically provides for land, water, and rural area protection.[34] This law has many elements that can be used directly for land degradation control, including making national economic plans that include environmental protection procedures,[35] establishing national and local environmental protection standards,[36] and preparing systems for monitoring the protection of the environment.[37] The provision for environmental protection of important regional and local ecological systems could be used much more effectively for land degradation control as there is a specific provision for the protection of the agricultural environment by preventing and controlling soil pollution, desertification, and vegetation damage and correcting ecological imbalances.[38] The legal liability procedures

---

[32] Under the Desertification Law, *desertification* means "land degradation," so this law could be considered as a more highly specialized form of water and soil conservation law than the 1991 Water and Soil Conservation Law.

[33] For a more detailed analysis of this law, see Dr. Du Qun's paper to the second Colloquium and Collegium of the IUCN Academy of Environmental Law, *Optimising Environmental Law to Combat Desertification, A Case Study of Gansu Province, People's Republic of China.*

[34] See 1989 Environmental Protection Law, arts. 1 and 2.

[35] *Id.* art. 4.

[36] *Id.* art. 10.

[37] *Id.* art. 11.

[38] *Id.* art. 20.

for environmental protection violations, compensation, and administrative sanctions could also be more effectively applied to land degradation control.

The 2002 Law for Appraising Environmental Impacts. The 2002 Law for Appraising Environmental Impacts has many procedures that give it the potential to play a significant role in the management and protection of agricultural land and thus in land degradation control. It provides for the implementation of a strategy for sustainable development and for prevention of unfavorable impacts of programs and construction projects on the environment and promotes the development of the economy, society, and the natural environment in a harmonious way. It also provides for countermeasures to be applied to adverse impacts.[39] Importantly, this law requires many types of government programs and activities to be subjected to environmental impact appraisal (in the past, only construction projects were subject to such appraisal). As part of the government's overall plan to control land degradation, it is imperative that environmental impact procedures and reports be prepared for all major development activity relating to industry, agriculture, animal husbandry, forestry, energy, water conservancy, communications, municipal construction, tourism, and natural resources development.[40] A major limitation of this law at this point is that there are no implementation procedures and guidelines for environmental impact assessment at the central and provincial levels.[41]

The 1996 Water Pollution Prevention Control Law and the 1996 Law for the Prevention and Treatment of Solid Waste from Polluting the Environment. Various responsibilities of the 1996 Water Pollution Prevention Control Law overlap with those of the 1991 Water and Soil Conservation Law.[42] The former law could be implemented in conjunction with the water and soil conservation laws to manage sedimentation processes that lead to the degradation of regional and local watercourses and the aquatic environment. Likewise, the 1996 Law for the Prevention and Treatment of Solid Waste from Polluting the Environment can help control the degradation of land and water that is caused by poor waste management and disposal techniques.

Natural resource utilization–based law regime. The resource use–based category of laws comprises a number of primary environmental laws of China that have a substantial capacity to assist with land degradation control, including the 1998 Forestry Law, the 1998 Land Administration Law, the 2002 Water Law, the 2002 Agricultural Law, and the 2002 Grassland Law. Although the general purpose of these primary laws covers a wide range of environmental and land management responsibilities, in practical terms there are many overlapping roles, activities, and functions as well as conflicting legislative priorities and objectives. There is also an absence of cooperative, cross-linking

[39] See 2002 Law for Appraising Environmental Impacts, arts. 1 and 2.
[40] *Id.* art. 8.
[41] The State Environmental Protection Agency and the National Development and Reform Commission are currently preparing guidelines and implementation procedures in partnership with some international organizations, i.e., the World Bank and the Canadian International Development Agency.
[42] This situation arises from the definition of *pollutant* and the process associated with *water pollution* under the 1984 Water Pollution Prevention Control Law, where each creates a legal responsibility to soil degradation management.

mechanisms. In relation to effective land degradation control, specific characteristics and limitations of these laws include the following:

- Some basic responsibilities of the 2002 Water Law are similar to those of the 1991 Water and Soil Conservation Law.
- The 1998 Forestry Law has overlapping soil-conservation responsibilities with the 1991 Water and Soil Conservation Law.
- The 2002 Agriculture Law focuses on production, but its powers to make decisions on resource utilization conflict with the objectives of the 1991 Water and Soil Conservation Law and the 2002 Grassland Law.
- The 2002 Grassland Law focuses on grazing activities and animal production, but its responsibilities for planning and protecting ecological aspects of grasslands and establishment of ecological reserves overlap with similar responsibilities under the 2001 Desertification Law.
- The application of "Basic Farmland" responsibilities of the 1998 Land Administration Law is an important function in land degradation control as it determines the location and quality of land used for agriculture. In the long term, it may be prudent to place this responsibility under one of the primary natural resource laws.
- The sensitive relationship between land type and potential for land degradation suggests that there should be formal links between the 1998 Land Administration Law and many of the conservation-based laws, in particular the Water and Soil Conservation Law, to improve the coordination between land-selection and land-evaluation procedures in the interests of environmental protection.

Collectively, within the preceding two groups of legislation, all "essential legal and institutional elements" considered necessary for land degradation control are represented.[43] However, a detailed examination of the individual laws reveals a substantial variation in the way these "elements" occur within the laws, and there is also a substantial variation in the capacity of individual procedures within the specific laws to achieve effective land degradation control.[44] Overall, the inadequacies within the current environmental law system of China present a severe limitation for effective land degradation control, and despite the prominence of enforcement procedures at each legislative level,[45] the increasing scale and severity of land degradation suggest that the laws have had little effect.[46] A good knowledge of this situation played a prominent role in supporting China's case and justification for further significant legislative and institutional reform to control land degradation and to improve the effectiveness of natural resource conservation and ecological management generally.

2.2 Efforts to Improve Environmental Law

The issues of the effectiveness of Chinese environmental law discussed previously have been generally known by Chinese legislators and scholars for some time, but the process

---

[43] Eighteen individual laws are examined.

[44] See I. D. Hannam 2002, *supra* note 22, Part III – Legislation Appendices, an Assessment of the Capability of Individual Articles, and I. D. Hannam, Wang Xi, Zhou Yanfang, and Hu Yuan 2004, *supra* note 26.

[45] All laws examined have enforcement capabilities and most have dispute resolution capabilities.

[46] See I. D. Hannam 2002, *supra* note 29.

of improving the quality of environmental law, reviewing existing laws, and introducing new environmental law has been slow. The legislative agenda of the National People's Congress for 2005–2010 demonstrates an ongoing commitment to legislative reform of environmental law. For example, two new laws listed in the agenda that are significant for land degradation control are a new Renewable Energy Utilization Promotion Law and a new Nature Reserve Zones Law. Two existing laws – the 1996 Law for the Prevention and Treatment of Solid Waste from Polluting the Environment and the 1998 Land Administrative Law – are on the agenda to be revised.

3 LEGISLATIVE REFORM UNDER THE GEF–PRC PARTNERSHIP PROGRAM

China has successfully attracted international assistance and attention to improve its enabling environment of law for land degradation control.[47] In 2000, the Chinese Government began negotiations with the Asian Development Bank for it to take a lead role in facilitating the preparation of a PRC–GEF Partnership Program on land degradation control in the western dryland region. This culminated in GEF approval of a long-term country-programming framework in 2002.[48] The PRC–GEF Partnership Program seeks to strengthen China's enabling environment and build institutional capacity to adopt an integrated approach to land degradation control.[49] The principal objective of the Legal Component of the PRC–GEF Program is to improve the policy, regulatory framework, and institutional system to combat land degradation. The Legal Component recognizes that despite the substantial improvements from the legislative revision and the introduction of new legislation, considerable effort is still needed to remove current gaps and overlaps in the principal law regulatory system at the central and provincial levels and to create further substantial provincial-level law. Currently, no effective institutional coordination mechanisms exist at the central or local level, and this lack severely limits the effectiveness of the provincial land planning and land management functions. Local level regulations are not satisfactorily understood or enforced, land tenure arrangements are often uncertain, and land use rights for rural communities require further reform to promote a long-term commitment to natural resource conservation.[50]

3.1 Taking the Approach of Integrated Ecosystem Management

A significant aspect of the approval process for the PRC–GEF Partnership Program was a recognition that many new environmental benefits will eventuate from an improved understanding of the root causes of land degradation and through a better planned and coordinated approach at the ecosystem level, and that this will occur through the introduction of an integrated ecosystem management (IEM) approach. Thus IEM has

---

[47] China currently has to feed 22 percent of the world's population, based on 6.5 percent of world's land area, 7.3 percent of world's farmland, and 5.8 percent of world's water resources; Main Report, *supra* note 5 at 5.

[48] Main Report, *supra* note 5, "the Proposal," at 1. The total cost of the project is U.S. $150 million over 10 years.

[49] The long-term CPF is from 2003 to 2012; the Legal Component as described in this chapter will be undertaken in 2004–2007.

[50] Main Report, *supra* note 5.

become the fundamental concept underlying the environmental law reform program of the PRC–GEF Partnership Project, and the individual activities of the reform program have been selected and developed on this basis. Integrated ecosystem management is presented as

> a holistic approach to addressing the linkages between ecosystem functions and services (such as carbon uptake and storage, climatic stabilisation and watershed protection, and medicinal products) and human social, economic and production systems (such as crop production, nomadic and sedentary livestock raising, and provision of infrastructure). IEM also recognises that people and the natural resources they depend upon, directly or indirectly, such as land, water, and forests, are inextricably linked. Rather than treat each resource in isolation IEM offers the option of treating all elements of ecosystems together to produce multiple benefits.[51]

As a result, China's existing environmental law system is now challenged by the emergence of integrated environmental law and the increasing demands for the legal protection of natural resources and ecosystems. The existing environmental law is focused largely on pollution control and urban environmental protection, with some limited attention to natural resource conservation, and either excludes or neglects a number of important natural resource management activities, such as resource exploitation, utilization and protection of the environment, sustainable management of ecosystems, and prevention of natural resource degradation. This is a major limitation, which means that environmental protection and natural resource management are not effectively linked within the current environmental legislative system. The objective of the Legal Component of the PRC–GEF Partnership Project is to reform environmental law by integrating ecosystem management principles into natural resources utilization by taking the IEM approach. In a limited way, this process has already commenced with the reform of the Water Law 2002 and the Agriculture Law 2002 and with the introduction of the Environmental Impact Appraisal Law 2002. The major challenge becomes the effective introduction of IEM principles and procedures into the Chinese legal and institutional framework in a manner that allows successful implementation of the laws and regulations for land degradation control. In this regard, the fundamental aspects of the individual activities that have been selected under the PRC–GEF Partnership Program include the need to develop[52]

- Effective linkages between different sectoral institutions that have responsibilities in land degradation control, particularly those institutions with responsibilities for grassland management, desertification control, water and soil conservation, water resources management, agriculture, land administration, and forestry
- National and regional strategies for land degradation management, including an integrated river basin management approach
- Rural poverty reduction programs

---

[51] Id. at 11.

[52] Main Report, supra note 5. In addition to the Legal Component, other components provide for strengthening national and provincial coordination; improving operational arrangements at the provincial and county levels; developing capacity for investment projects; monitoring and evaluation systems for land degradation control; and strengthening implementation arrangements for the country programming framework.

- Programs for the sustainable use of natural resources and management of ecosystems for future generations
- Comprehensive technical programs for land management
- Effective communication, capacity building, and training programs in land degradation control techniques
- Performance reporting and monitoring programs to determine the effectiveness of legal and policy measures

Many current provincial level activities will provide valuable direction as to what specific types of legislative, regulatory, and policy tools are best suited to implement the land degradation management and decision-making systems

Method

Two key requirements have been established under the PRC–GEF Partnership Project to meet the objective of improving the policy, laws, and regulations for land degradation control. The first requirement is to investigate the existing laws to identify the legal elements, legal mechanisms, and ecological and scientific concepts, definitions, and standards for land degradation control, so as to determine their scope for modification or expansion to accommodate the IEM approach.[53] The second requirement is that current "best practice" international standards, principles, and procedures specified for national legislative systems for effective land degradation management be investigated as a guide to the selection of suitable legal, regulatory, and policy reform tools for China's legislative and policy system. This method closely follows that advocated by key international environmental law institutions as being appropriate to achieve the environmental law reform objectives set out by the United Nations Conference on Environment and Development in 1992[54] and restated by the World Summit on Sustainable Development in 2002.[55] This approach also conforms with the general requirements and obligations of the Parties to the Convention to Combat Desertification, of which China is signatory.

Activities

The three principal activities of the Legal Component were selected as a framework to ensure that the preceding two requirements will be met, and they take into account the specific legal needs and concerns advocated by the provinces and regions of the dryland area.[56]

---

[53] That is, laws covering environmental planning, pollution control, forestry, reafforestation, soil and water conservation, water management, environmental protection, mining, agriculture, agricultural reform, and land administration tenure. Component 1 was prepared in consultation with a legal and policy expert advisory group that was convened to provide external guidance. This group comprised representatives from relevant central agencies and the three provinces and three autonomous regions. The *capacity* of the legal, regulatory, and policy framework is determined by the number and type of essential legal and institutional elements present in the PRC's legislative system, in a format that allows the key issues of land degradation to be identified, and with the technical capability to take effective action.

[54] Rio Declaration on Environment and Development, U.N. doc. A/CONF.151/26(Vol. I), 13 June 1992, 31 I.L.M. 874 (1992).

[55] Johannesburg Declaration on Sustainable Development, U.N. doc. A/CONF.199/20, 4 September 2002.

[56] Many discussions and seminars were held with representatives of central and provincial agencies throughout the project development phase, including field visits, to make sure all needs, views, and requirements for legislative reform were properly understood and provided for prior to the development of the specific reform activities.

The following are the three key activity areas:

- Development of procedures and mechanisms to determine and improve the capability of China's law, regulations, and policy to control land degradation
- Building of the capacity and provision of education in legislative and policy aspects of land degradation control
- Development of a range of specialist policy, legal, and regulatory tools for problem solving and further enhancement of the effective implementation of China's law for land degradation control at the provincial and local levels

Implementation of the three key activity areas will improve the effectiveness of the China's sector laws and policies for land degradation control, particularly through the introduction of comprehensive standards and principles for IEM.[57] New procedures will be developed to create and improve linkages among the different laws, regulations, and policies and the institutions that are responsible for them. Some activities will assist the ongoing law reform process by incorporating IEM within key national and provincial laws, regulations, and policy relevant to land degradation and intensifying the enforcement of laws and policies for land degradation control. These programs are supported by the capacity-building activities, which aim to improve community awareness and understanding of the role and benefit of environmental law in land degradation control and will lead to a greater understanding of relationships between the law and land management generally.[58]

3.2 Developing Procedures and Mechanisms to Improve the Capability of Law and Policy to Control Land Degradation through IEM

An Environmental Law and Policy Information System
The aim is to prepare a computer-based legal and institutional information system as a joint central and provincial level exercise, based on current provincial-level land degradation issues and rigorously tested and implemented at the provincial level.[59] It will draw on international and overseas legislative experience of IEM and land degradation control and introduce relevant aspects to China. This system will be a compendium of existing national laws, regulations, and implementing measures with an explanation of their capacity to implement IEM. It will also include legal and institutional recommendations to deal with key issues of land degradation at the provincial level and be developed sequentially over the 2004–2007 period.

---

[57] The selection of activity areas and specific implementation actions is based on knowledge and experience of environmental law reform assembled under the IUCN Environmental Law Program, including the Commission on Environmental Law Specialist Working Group on Sustainable Soil. See Boer and Hannam 2003, *supra* note 2 at 160–161; I. D. Hannam and B. W. Boer, *Legal and Institutional Frameworks for Sustainable Soils: A Preliminary Report* (IUCN)(2002); I. D. Hannam and B. W Boer, *Drafting Legislation for Sustainable Soils: A Guide* (IUCN) (2004).

[58] See D. G. Craig, N. A. Robinson, and K. Kheng-Lian (eds); *Capacity Building for Environmental Law in the Asian and Pacific Region; Approaches and Resources*, Volumes I and II (ADB) (2002).

[59] The concept of the "environmental law and policy information system" arises from the specific national legislative needs identified in the Report of the Committee for the Review of the Implementation of the Convention to Combat Desertificatiin in its first session (ICC/CRIC (1)/10, 2002), paras. 124–128. The PRC will be the first country to follow the recommendations of the CRIC in law and policy reform for land degradation and desertification.

Provincial Procedures to Assess and Improve Capacity of the Laws, Policy, and Institutions to Implement IEM

This activity will compile and assess the legal and institutional elements for IEM, based on the most available "best practice" legislative and ecological criteria applicable to China. It will cover organizational, land management, community participation, financial, and enforcement procedures for both regulatory and nonregulatory approaches to land degradation control at the provincial level.

Assess and Harmonize Laws and Regulations Relevant to Land Degradation Management

This activity will make recommendations on specific areas of law for harmonization – including the laws and implementing measures for desertification, grassland, water and soil conservation, water, forestry, agriculture, land administration, environmental protection, and environmental impact assessment. Specific procedures and instruments will be prepared to allow the implementation of IEM within the respective laws for the equitable utilisation of natural resources at the provincial level.

Increase the Capacity for the Administration of the Laws and Policies

This activity will mainly focus on the development of a coordination mechanism for decision making applicable to China's 11th Five-Year Plan and China's Action Plan for the Convention to Combat Desertification. It will also include the preparation of a legislative procedure to integrate China's system of ecosystem function zones more effectively in the legal decision-making procedures for agriculture, forestry, and desertification control. A mechanism to monitor the effectiveness of the implementation of the laws and policies for dryland ecosystem management will be prepared.

Assess the Role of Environmental Impact Assessment in Land Degradation Control

The aim of this activity is to establish the links between China's Law for Appraising Environmental Impacts (EIA Law) and its role in land degradation management, including the legal operational procedures to implement the practical aspects of the EIA Law. Interest will focus on the improvement of farmland quality, management of natural grassland areas, maintenance and improvement of water quality, and comprehensive technical standards and indicators for sustainable land management. A mechanism to monitor the technical guidelines for the EIA Law will be based on ecological criteria and decision-support information.

Improve Legal and Policy Measures for Private Sector Involvement and Public Participation in Land Degradation Management

This activity will focus on the legal aspects of land tenure, land use rights, gender rights, and access to markets as they relate to land degradation management. It will require the preparation of provincial-level procedures to determine the circumstances for compensation after the closure of grassland areas and to decide when grazing activities will be banned from other types of protected areas. It will also develop procedures to integrate programs within the law to improve sustainable livelihoods in consideration of poverty alleviation and minority and gender rights issues. There will also be new procedures and guidelines for the provinces and regions to follow when informing the public about legislative and policy responsibilities for land degradation control, the obligations of different rural sectors, procedures for public display of legislative and policy information, and procedures for assessing responses and effective ways to communicate the law to rural people.

3.3 Building Capacity in Legislative and Policy Aspects of Land Degradation Management

Develop Capacity-Building Programs in Legislative, Policy, and Institutional Measures

A comprehensive capacity-building program[60] will cover international environmental issues relevant to land degradation control in China, as well as the national legislative principles and methods to improve institutional cooperation and communication in environmental law and policy. Specific target groups include legal officers, legislative draftsmen, judicial officials, policymakers, government officials, and the private sector, at both central and provincial levels.

Training Workshops in Environmental Law

Detailed materials will be prepared and a series of central-provincial workshops will be held to focus on the role of IEM in the law, legislative aspects of land degradation, establishment of links between policy and law, EIA, and access to judicial and administrative remedies.[61] To meet China's needs for ongoing professional training of legal personnel in legal aspects of land degradation control, a number of special workshops will be held to train selected officials to become permanent trainers in legislative and policy issues.

Study Visits and Exchanges

To help Chinese legal officials understand the latest and most innovative environmental law and policy techniques for managing land degradation, an intensive environmental law education course will be conducted at a recognized international environmental law training institute in the Asia–Pacific region, preferably in a country that has land management experience in dryland ecosystems. There will be opportunity for provincial legislative officers to visit relevant overseas government institutions and judicial institutions to improve their knowledge and skills in legislation and policy for land degradation control.

3.4 Specialist Policy, Legal, and Regulatory Advice and Problem Solving and Support

A National Legal and Policy Expert Advisory Group (LPEAG)

The LPEAG will comprise legislative representatives from central institutions who are considered to be authorities in areas of environmental law, policy, and procedures

---

[60] *Capacity building* means improving the broad base of relevant environmental law and policy knowledge and capability to improve understanding of legal and institutional issues in dryland ecosystems.

[61] Training workshops would be conducted through a PRC institution with a recognized capability in environmental law teaching, e.g., the Research Institute of Environmental Law at Wuhan University and Beijing Normal University.

relevant to the management of dryland areas. The LPEAG will guide and review the progress of implementation of the legal program and provide recommendations, reports, and expert advice and direction on specific legislative problems and issues. LPEAGs will also be formed at the provincial level.

Feasibility Study on Legal Training in Land Degradation Control

A specialized study will investigate the requirements for ongoing and future legal training in environmental law and policy aspects of dryland management. Detailed training guidelines will be prepared for government and provincial officials to undertake legal training and community education in environmental law and policy and the promotion of IEM.

Undertaking Special Legal Studies

A number of special legal studies will investigate land degradation issues common in the dryland region. The information gained from the studies will be used in the legal training programs and will provide direction for new administrative procedures to manage land degradation at the provincial level.

4 BENEFITS OF THE ENVIRONMENTAL REFORM PROGRAM

One of the main challenges for the law in land degradation control is that society in general must improve its awareness and knowledge of the critical role that the law should actually play in achieving a sustainable land use goal.[62] In this regard, for the Legal Component to be successful, the PRC–GEF Partnership Program in general will require a major change in attitude in Chinese society toward the vital importance and benefits of soil and water conservation and ecosystem protection in general. An important part of this change will be acceptance of the idea that soil resources are nonrenewable when considered over the span of two to three human generations at least. This will be a major consideration for China, given the current severe state of land degradation in the dryland regions and the significant level of impoverishment among the rural society.

Despite these great challenges ahead for China, the legislative reform program under the PRC–GEF Partnership Program is of major significance not only for China itself but also for the world. This latter aspect arises from the fact that the Legal Component of the PRC–GEF Partnership Program is considered the most comprehensive national environmental law program attempted in the world to date for land degradation control. Under the circumstances, the benefits will accrue not only to China but to the world in general as the knowledge and expertise gained from the Chinese project can be utilized to help expand the foundations of an international front against land degradation. Other nations that are considering undertaking reform in this aspect of environmental law can benefit from China's experience. In this regard, many of the legislative tools, principles, and guidelines developed under the Chinese program will be transferable to similar

---

[62] See Boer and Hannam 2003, *supra* note 2, at 158; E. M. Bridges, I. D. Hannam, L. R. Oldeman, F. Penning deVries, S. J. Scherr, and S. Sombatpanit (eds), *Response to Land Degradation* (Science Publishers) (2002) at 1; H. Hurni, H. Meyer, and K. Meyer (eds), *A World Soils Agenda: Discussing International Actions for the Sustainable Use of Soils*, prepared with the support of an international group of specialists of the IASUS Working Group of the International Union of Soil Sciences (IUSS), Centre for Development and Environment, Berne (2002).

dryland regions of the world and will help fulfill the objectives of many international environmental law reform initiatives. They will also be of considerable value to other technologically and advanced economies, as many of the outcomes could be adapted to Western environmental law and institutional systems.

Key international environmental law initiatives that would benefit from this project include the following:

- Implementation of the Montevideo Program III – the Program for the Development and Periodic Review of Environmental Law for the First Decade of the Twenty-First Century[63]
- Implementation of the World Soil Agenda[64]
- Achievement of the legislative recommendations of the Committee for the Review of the Implementation of the Convention to Combat Desertification[65]
- Achievement of various objectives of the Plan of Implementation of the World Summit on Environment and Development 2002[66]
- Fulfilment of the objectives of UNEP's Strategy on Land Use Management and Soil Conservation[67]
- Achievement of various objectives of the Resolution of the International Union for the Conservation of Nature and Natural Resources (IUCN) World Conservation Congress of 2000 on Sustainable Use of Soil, in particular the development of legal guidelines and explanatory material, and investigation into a global legal instrument for the sustainable use of soils[68]

5 CONCLUSION

The legal aspects of land degradation have in the past been generally neglected at the international level and, in many of the world's regions, at the domestic level as well. China has been one of the worst affected areas because of the natural dryland state of the country combined with the scale and intensity of human occupation and its long period of civilization and intensity of agricultural land use. Although China only began to introduce comprehensive environmental laws in the 1980s, it soon recognized that specialized forms of law were needed to control land degradation. Moreover, because of the manner in which these laws were developed, coupled with many institutional inadequacies, they soon became ineffective in reaching the goal of land degradation control. The realization of this situation, combined with growing interest and assistance from international agencies, has seen China develop under the PRC–GEF Partnership

---

[63] *Decision 21/33 of the 2001 Governing Council of UNEP*, February 2001; and http://www.unep.org/GC/GC21/Documents/gc-21-INF-03/K0000295.E.PDF.

[64] Hurni, Meyer, and Meyer, 2002, *supra* note 62.

[65] CCD Secretariat, *Report of the Committee for the Review of the Implementation of the Convention*, Report of the Committee on its First Session (ICCD/CRIC (1) /10, 2002, paras 124–128, www.unccd.int//cop/officialdocs/cric1/pdf/10eng.pdf7.

[66] *Plan of Implementation*, United Nations World Summit on Environment and Development (2002), *The Johannesburg Declaration on Sustainable Development, supra* note 54.

[67] UNEP, *Strategy on Land Use Management and Soil Conservation. A Strengthened Functional Approach*, UNEP Policy Series (2004).

[68] Boer and Hannam 2003, *supra* note 2; see Section 1, for complete wording of the 2000 Amman Resolution on Sustainable Use of Soil; a supplementary resolution to this 2000 resolution was passed at the November 2004 IUCN World Conservation Congress, Bangkok, Thailand.

Program the most comprehensive national environmental law reform project for land degradation management attempted in the world. The implementation of the Legal Component of the PRC–GEF Partnership Program provides China with an opportunity unparalleled anywhere else in the world to improve vastly the capacity of its environmental law, policies, and institutional arrangements manage land degradation to more effectively. Many of the legislative tools, guidelines, and procedures prepared under China's four-year PRC–GEF Partnership Program will be transferable to other countries with similar climatic and socioeconomic characteristics.

19 Urbanization and Environmental Challenges in Pakistan

Parvez Hassan

1 URBANIZATION IN PAKISTAN

In 2004, Pakistan continued its inexorable ascent on the world demographic charts when it overtook Russia and became the world's sixth largest nation after China, India, the United States, Brazil, and Indonesia.[1] In common with most other developing nations,[2] Pakistan is entering the high-growth phase of urban transition with most of the population increase occurring in the urban areas.[3] These demographic trends present the policymakers and citizens of the country with both a significant opportunity and a serious peril.

The outsized contribution of cities to national economies made possible by the capital investment in infrastructure and the concentration of a diversified and skilled labor pool is a well-documented phenomenon.[4] As in many other parts of the world, the

---

[1] "The Government estimates the current rate of population growth at 2.1 per cent a year. Nonetheless, demographic inertia will continue to increase the size of the population, and if present trends do not change, Pakistan could overtake Indonesia, Brazil and the United States and become the world's third largest country by the year 2050." See Shahid Javed Burki, "Demographic Convulsions" *Dawn* (Pakistan) 14 September 2004.

[2] In a major study, the World Bank's Urban Development Group has noted, "Over the next two decades more than ninety-five percent of the population growth in developing countries, even in South Asia, will occur in urban areas. The scale of this urbanization, and its implications for the ability of countries to meet the needs of their people at relatively low levels of national income, are unprecedented." World Bank, *Cities in Transition – World Bank Urban and Local Government Strategy* (The World Bank, Washington, D.C.) (2000) at 32–33.

[3] In a policy paper, the Ministry of Environment, Local Government and Rural Development of Pakistan has pointed out that "[a]ccording to the 1998 census Pakistan's urban population is 42.5 million, representing 32.5% of the total national population, and growing at a rate of 3.5% per annum. By 2015, the urban population of Pakistan is expected to exceed the rural population." The Ministry of Environment, Local Government and Rural Development of Pakistan, *National Policy on Katchi Abadi, Urban Renewal and Slum Upgradation*, Islamabad (2000). Pursuant to these trends, Pakistan will contain 2 of the world's 30 largest cities in 2015 with Karachi having a population of 20.6 million and Lahore about half that number, 10.8 million persons. See the *World Bank Urban and Local Government Strategy, supra* note 2 at 152.

[4] "Urban areas account for a disproportionate share of national economic production and are the main sources of economic growth.... According to the UNCHS Urban Indicators database, for 150 cities of all sizes the per capita output ... is more than 10 percent higher on average than their country's per capita gross national product.... The metropolitan area of Bangkok is estimated to account for 37 percent of Thailand's national income but only 19 percent of its population, while Metropolitan Manila, with

This chapter has relied extensively on the research of Azim Azfar, and the author gratefully acknowledges this support.

urban setting in Pakistan continues to be the choice of destination for both traditional manufacturing industries, which are highly sensitive to costs of labor, land, and infrastructure, and the knowledge-intensive industries and service sector firms reliant on an educated workforce and sophisticated information technology services.

In addition to the generation of national wealth and contribution to fiscal revenues, the built environments of cities are often showcases of a country's cultural heritage and the civic pride of its citizens. Because of its rich history, which has seen the ebb and flow of important civilizations, Pakistan is well endowed with cultural heritage assets. In ancient times, the Indus civilization flourished in Northern Sindh and Southern Punjab, and the ruins in the towns of Mohenjo Daro and Harappa have revealed evidence of fine craftsmanship, sophisticated drainage systems, and the first large-scale use of kiln-fired bricks for architecture. Subsequently, the Indo-Muslim Mughal culture graced the northern Indian subcontinent and the town of Lahore in present-day Punjab in Pakistan boasts magnificent monuments, mosques, and gardens. Modern colonial history has also made a distinctive imprint on the cityscapes, and Lahore and Karachi, in particular, contain many examples of Victorian architecture fused with subcontinental themes.

2 ECOLOGICAL THREAT OF URBANIZATION

The importance of well-managed cities to Pakistan's economic, social, and cultural welfare cannot therefore be overstated, but, unfortunately, orderly urban planning and development in the country remain elusive goals. Several issues such as pressures for development, poverty, and resource constraints common to developing countries are highlighted in the remarks of the author, as Chairman of the session on Comparative Law in a Colloquium on Landscape Conservation Law[5] held in Paris, France, in 1998. As a result of state failure to provide adequate housing for the poor,[6] an estimated 35–50 percent of the urban population in Pakistan is living in slums and underserviced areas known as *katchi abadis* (literally translated as impermanent abodes). Vidal notes that the escalation of slums is a global predicament that is on the mind of planners everywhere:

> What scares many governments, planners and policy makers is the very real prospect that the majority of cities in developing countries will become sprawling slums, with people living without piped water or sanitation, with poor standards of housing,

13 percent of the Philippine population, produces 24 percent total national income. The GDP of Mexico City alone equals that of Thailand, and Seoul's GDP compares with that of Argentina." See the *World Bank Urban and Local Government Strategy, supra* note 2 at 84.

[5] See IUCN, *Landscape Conservation Law – Present Trends and Perspectives in International and Comparative Law,* IUCN Environmental Policy and Law Paper No. 39 (IUCN, Gland) (2000), at 37–39.

[6] In spite of specialized public sector funding agencies, access to financing for the poor remains a major unfulfilled goal. It has been noted that "[t]he informal sector has been responsible for financing over 80% of the total housing stock. Access to formal sector housing and to improvements in non-formal sector housing is constrained by a number of factors: design of housing schemes, misuse of government subsidies, speculation, access to finance etc. Although housing construction is normally financed through multiple sources over an extended period of time, the formal financial sector (House Building Finance Corporation and First Women's Bank) has been unable to design successfully, flexible financial instruments targeted to the poor. The House Building Finance Corporation, the largest public sector institution to provide housing loans, provides house construction loans only to clients with secure and regular incomes." *National Policy on Katchi Abadis, supra* note 3 at 9.

and health and nutrition problems at par with anything found in the most poverty-stricken rural areas today. Last year the UN commissioned a 300-page report on the growth of slums. The authors found that slum dwellers account for an average 43% of the population of developing countries.[7]

In a major policy review of the housing sector, the Government of Pakistan has expressed its alarm at the rising rate of slum creation, which has not abated in spite of a decision not to regularize any settlements established after 1985:

> The mushroom growth of slums and *katchi abadis* in urban areas is the product of unprecedented population growth, rapid urbanization and large scale influx of refugees forcing unauthorized encroachments on urban spaces especially state land including strategic, hazardous areas in and around river beds, near railway tracks and the like. Poor estate management by the Land Owning Agencies (LOAs) coupled with poor development controls add to these problems.[8]

Even the nation's capital, Islamabad, which is one of four capitals planned and built in the 20th century[9] and is otherwise described as "clean, green and well-served by the municipal authorities and utilities," has not escaped the blight of squatter settlements.[10] As the World Bank Urban Strategy notes, "The environmental problems of urban areas (the 'brown' agenda) – air, soil, and water pollution, noise, and traffic congestion – have more direct and immediate implications for human health and safety, especially for the poor, and for business productivity than do 'green' environmental issues."[11] Unfortunately, this is precisely the case in Pakistan, where the urban predicament is characterized by squalid living conditions, growing income inequality, and inadequacy of services where half of a nation's population does not have adequate access to sanitation and water supply.[12] This is a serious concern for policymakers as urban poverty has been

---

[7] John Vidal, "Beyond the City Limits," *The Guardian Weekly* (UK), at 17–18 (17–23 September 2004). The author notes that "[m]assive urbanization means hundreds of already nearly bankrupt cities trying to cope in 20 years with the kind of problems that London or New York only managed to address with difficulty for 150 years. The strains are showing in a growing global freshwater and sanitation water crisis, air pollution leading to continent-wide smogs and 48-hour traffic gridlocks-and reports of dwindling food reserves in many countries. According to the UN, hundreds of cities will be in real trouble within a decade. In China, where urbanization has been extreme in the past 15 years, 400 out of the 670 biggest cities already have serious water deficits. Elsewhere many cities are depleting underground stocks and finding saltwater getting into the aquifers." Ibid.

[8] *National Housing Policy 2001*, at 10. The recurring annual backlog of unfulfilled housing needs totals about 270,000 units, ibid., at 2. For an earlier comprehensive overview by the author of the housing policies in Pakistan, see "Importance of Housing in the National Economy of Pakistan" in Parvez Hassan, *Perspectives on Pakistan*, at 145–173 (Progressive Publishers, Lahore, 1992).

[9] The others are Brasilia (Brazil), Canberra (Australia), and Astana (Kazakhstan).

[10] UNDP Pakistan, *Katchi Abadis and Some Viable Alternatives – A Case Study and Operational Guidelines* (2002), at 1. The study found no fewer than 11 slums in the Federal Capital.

[11] See *The World Bank Urban and Local Government Strategy, supra* note 2 at 39. The global impact of the "brown agenda" is described as significant: "[w]orldwide, airborne particulates pollution has been associated with at least 500,000 premature deaths and up to 5 million new cases of chronic bronchitis each year. Lead pollution from motor vehicles leads to hundreds of premature deaths, reduced intellectual capabilities in children, and other health damage in large cities. Microbial diseases due to poor sanitation and dirty water cost billions of dollars a year in lost lives and poor health, especially in the poorest cities." Ibid.

[12] "Nationally, provincially and within the city, variations in quality of service by income groups are very high, and contrary to popular perception, households rich and poor pay for the services. According to the Pakistan Integrated Housing Survey (1996–97), 19% of the people in the lowest income bracket in urban areas have no access to a sanitation system, 65% have access to open drains and 16% to underground

rightly said to go beyond material deprivation to encompass "a sense of powerlessness, and an individual and community vulnerability that undermines human potential and social capital."[13]

It would be challenging enough if urban environmental problems in Pakistan were limited to systemic weaknesses in housing supply and management in the informal sector. However, this is only the tip of the iceberg as the planned sectors in the major urban centers suffer from widespread irregularities caused by unbridled commercial development, unauthorized construction of high-rise buildings,[14] and illegal conversion of amenity plots, which have led to a massive erosion of the quality of life of the residents. De Souza notes the following developments in Karachi, which can be applied to any other major urban center in Pakistan:

> The city is being silently converted into a vast concrete slum. Overloading of electricity, water/sewerage and other utility/infrastructure systems, load-shedding, break-downs, low-voltages, garbage and sewage on the streets . . . and other familiar signs of civic collapse that we have come to silently accept in Karachi. . . . The necessary infrastructure (parking, schools, playgrounds, police stations, roads, parks, garbage collection etc.) and utilities (electricity, water, sewerage etc.) are just not available in the inner city areas, and the lives of existing residents are being made miserable by illegal densification of the residential areas with new multi-storied flats, office flats, offices and shopping centers.[15]

Tragically, it is not just quality of life that is affected by rampant commercialization and overstrained services; the lives of residents have also been imperiled by the deterioration in urban management. In 2004, over three dozen people in the second-largest city of Sindh, Hyderabad, lost their lives by drinking poisonous water supplied from the Indus River. The tragedy occurred when one of the Indus River's catchment areas, Manchar Lake (once the largest freshwater lake in Asia), which is used as a reservoir for Lower Sindh during the winter season, became excessively polluted by saline and other effluents deposited from Baluchistan, Punjab, and Upper Sindh. In a classic case of lack of coordination between government agencies, neither the irrigation department (the agency responsible for maintaining barrages and regulating water flows of rivers) nor the city's Water and Sanitation Department was able to take timely corrective measures.[16]

drains as compared to the highest income bracket where 70% have access to underground drains and 26% to open drains. Similarly for water, 28.7% of the lowest income bracket gets water through taps compared to 73.1% of the highest income bracket." *National Policy on Katchi Abadis, supra* note 3 at 8.

[13] See *The World Bank Urban and Local Government Strategy, supra* note 2 at 3.

[14] A representative of the Pakistan Engineering Council has estimated that only 30 percent of construction in the megapolis Karachi is legal. See *Shehri* (Seminar: A Citizen's Perspective on the Law Pertaining to Buildings Constructed in Karachi, 20 October 2001).

[15] Roland De Souza, "The Myths about Regularization of Illegal Buildings," *Shehri*, at 1 (May–August 2000).

[16] A journalistic account of the tragedy notes that "nobody knows the exact number of people affected by the contaminated water, which is also being used in other towns and villages while the civic authorities are busy debating which agency is to take corrective measures and how." About 600 cusec of toxic water flow into Manchar Lake every day and over time the accumulation of toxins reached dangerous proportions. Not only did the Irrigation Department fail to release adequate water from other barrages to dilute the collection of toxins, it also transpired that the chlorine plant maintained by the city's Water and Sanitation Department was out of order. Faraz Sheikh, "None Held Responsible for Hyderabad Water Casualties," *Pakistan Illustrated* (July 2004), at 96.

Disaster management remains a very weak area of Government. In August 2003, the grounding and structural collapse of the MV *Tasman Spirit* in Karachi port resulted in the greatest marine environmental disaster in the history of Pakistan when 26,000 tonnes of light crude oil flooded the coastline. The state of preparedness and response of national authorities were found to be fundamentally inadequate; operationally, there were no contingency plan, a lack of adequate stockpiles of antipollution agents, and an absence of interagency coordination, all compounded by a failure to implement the 1990 International Convention on Oil Pollution, Preparedness and Response.[17] Although the high death toll in the Hyderabad tragedy and the graphic accident of the *Tasman Spirit* caught the media attention, urban water pollution in Pakistan wreaks daily havoc on residents and is a major cause of diseases that arise from the mixing of sewerage and water lines and the lack of treatment facilities.[18]

So far, the urban blight caused by the spreading of slums, illegal construction, loss of amenity plots, and breakdown of civic services has been noticed, but the cultural heritage scene presents its own set of problems. In spite of the presence of modern laws on cultural heritage protection,[19] the conservation regime is very weak and progress is hampered by lack of qualified architects and technical assistance from the government as well as private owner apathy and desire to use the properties for their highest commercial value.[20] Even more worrying is the fact that ancient ruins are in a state of disintegration. It has been estimated that nearly 150 of Mohenjo Daro's 370 walls are about to collapse because no funds have been allocated for the upkeep and maintenance of this major center of the Indus civilization.[21]

3 FAILURE OF GOVERNMENT PLANNING AND MANAGEMENT

3.1 Myopic Vision

A major cause of the serious deterioration in Pakistan's urban environmental management is the failure of government planning, management, and prioritizing of commercial growth over ecological considerations. The World Bank Urban Strategy observes

---

[17] See Masoud Ansari, "The Untold Story" *Newsline* (September 2003).

[18] Beg notes that "water from almost 90% of the wells in the cities of Karachi, Hyderabad and Sukkur and over 90% of their suburbs is contaminated with sewage bacteria and also contains total dissolved solids beyond permissible limits. Some of the toxic materials like inorganic and organic chemicals like dyes, pesticides etc. discharged by large scale consumers, immediately outside their shops and working areas, often find their pathway into the ground water through seepage and thus contaminate it seriously." Mirza Arshad Ali Beg, "Drinking Water Pollution: A Criminal Neglect?" *Shehri* (January–June 2004).

[19] The most important provincial laws in this field are the Sindh Cultural Heritage Act, 1994, and the Punjab Special Premises (Preservation) Ordinance, 1984.

[20] A Government conservation committee members notes that "heritage is priceless and is protected by law but many important buildings have been demolished and converted into commercial plazas." Zulfiqar Shah, "Far from Protection – Unless Private Owners Are Provided with Incentives to Protect Their Buildings, the Market Is Going to Gobble Up the Rich Cultural Heritage of Karachi." *The News Special Report*, at 25 (15 September 2004).

[21] Local officials complain that the Government has "not allocated even a single penny for the current fiscal year for preserving Mohenjo Daro." See Massoud Ansari, "Monumental Disaster" *Newsline* (August 2004).

that governmental control over land use make it the most important arbiter of the development of cities:

> Although cities are largely built by private investment, they are shaped substantially by public action, through government (usually local) zoning regulations, building codes, taxation, and the nature and location of direct public investment such as transport networks.[22]

It is one thing to plan improperly, but the errors in Pakistan have largely been of omission as successive governments have failed to plan altogether; in its National Housing Policy (2001), the Government of Pakistan has itself admitted to its myopic vision:

> One of our major weaknesses reflective in the rudderless growth of our urban and rural areas is lack of planning on a long term basis. . . . With proper plans and implementation, housing moves in a systematic manner which is cost effective and provides quality environment. . . . The development of slums, *katchi abadis* and squatter settlements is also directly linked with the lack of plans and their implementation. The beneficiaries of this lack of planning and building and zoning regulations are the land and building mafias.[23]

It is incredible that the megapolis Karachi has no functioning Master Plan as neither the 1974 nor the 1992 Master Plan were notified. Ahmed notes that this lack of legal cover is a serious impediment to orderly planning but works to the advantage of authorities motivated by short-term goals or self-interest:

> Master plans cannot move by themselves. These are implemented through institutionalized arrangement, which join all concerned agencies together to honor their commitments, make their investment decisions in line with the plans/proposals, and take all possible measures to accomplish their part of the city development programme. Without a legal cover to the plan, this objective cannot be achieved. Unfortunately, some elements within the Governments do not feel comfortable in being strait jacketed by the provisions of such legal provisions and planning.[24]

The lack of proper planning is compounded by a disjointed administrative system whereby responsibility is divided into a multiplicity of agencies. Ahmed again notes in the context of Karachi that "a city which is being looked after by more than two dozen development organizations and departments and which can boast of about 15 major landholding agencies has undergone unspeakable decay of urban services and deterioration of living environment."[25] This conclusion has been reproduced at the country level by the National Housing Policy (2001):

> The present institutional set up in the housing sector is fragmented, overlapping, inconsistently funded and lacks clearly defined roles and lines of accountability. It is in dire need of professionally trained housing experts. The rationalization of the existing institutional capacity within a coherent long term strategic policy framework can significantly contribute towards initiating enhanced and sustainable housing

---

[22] See *The World Bank Urban and Local Government Strategy, supra* note 2, at 51.

[23] *National Housing Policy 2001*, at 12.

[24] Nooruddin Ahmed, *Urban Renewal – Anyone for Improving Karachi's Environment? Shehri* (September–December 2001), at 1.

[25] Ibid.

delivery at the levels required to deal with backlogs and recurring demand and to improve the quality of life in the burgeoning problems of slums and *katchi abadis*.[26]

In addition to problems of lack of planning and maladministration, a serious threat to the ecology of Pakistan has also arisen because successive governments have pursued a headlong policy of commercialization without regard to the damage to the environment.

3.2 Conflicting Priorities

In recent years, two egregious examples of commercialization in total disregard of environmental considerations have been the conversion of forest land to urban development in one of the country's premier northern hill resorts (Murree)[27] and the allotment of residential land in the mangrove forests located in Karachi.

In May 2004, the Government of Punjab advertised the sale of apartment complexes in New Murree City, overriding the serious objections raised by the Forestry Department about loss of forest cover and by engineering consultants over the threat posed by landslides due to soil erosion and degradation.[28] In 1998, a Swiss study on the project had noted the symbolic importance of governmental actions:

> In a country with a high deficiency of forested areas, the government has a special exemplary function. How can the destruction of mature state forests be justified for the development of a township, when a private individual is rarely allowed to chop a tree?[29]

A similar callous disregard for ecological degradation was shown by the decision of the Sindh Government to allot 130 acres of the Eastern Backwater region of Karachi to a residential colony, the Karachi Port Trust Co-operative Housing Society. The fact that the Indus Delta mangroves are the largest arid climate mangroves in the world and that mangrove forests are among the most productive and biologically diverse wetlands on earth were brushed side for the benefit of a few officers of a government department. A Special Report prepared by a prominent urban development nongovernmental organization (NGO) concludes ruefully that a culture of expropriating state land has taken deep root in the country:

> In Pakistan, government officials and politicians have over a period of time, created a culture whereby land belonging to the citizens of Pakistan is sold for political bribe for the benefit of a few, laws are bent and the fundamental rights of citizens are

---

[26] *National Housing Policy, 2001*, at 19–20.

[27] The site selected comprises 3,849 acres of the Murree Forest Division and 262 acres of the Rawalpindi Forest Division. The feasibility study contemplates massive development in the form of numerous hotels, holiday cottages, and plots allocated for residential and amusement activities.

[28] A recent report notes that "environment experts have warned that there is a clear and present danger of major destruction through landslides which pose a serious threat to both human life and property. Deforestation, uncontrolled drainage of rain and waste-water in built-up areas, the increase of sealed surface areas by new buildings and road construction, extraction of rock and excavation of slopes for construction, loading slopes with waste and excavated material, unsuitable sites for house construction and slope cuts for the construction and widening of roads are the major factors contributing towards the destruction of Murree. A major portion of the considerable development budget allocated to Murree is spent on equipment for the removal of landslides and the reconstruction of damaged roads." Naveed Ahmed, "Ecological Debacle" *Newsline*, at 70 (August 2004).

[29] Ibid.

trampled upon. These actions have led to economic loss, disappearance of amenity plots and open spaces and have greatly contributed in deteriorating the urban and coastal environment of the city in general, including putting Karachi Port and Port Qasim in danger of silting up and therefore checking the economic life of the country to say nothing of damaging the coastal fishing industry on which 2 million people depend for their livelihood.[30]

The Murree New City Project and the Eastern Backwaters allotment point to a dismal failure of the Federal and Provincial Environmental Protection Agencies to prevent catastrophic assaults on the country's premier ecological assets. However, putting the blame on the environmental watchdogs misses the crucial point that the fault lies in the priority and value that the Government accords to commercial growth over environmental protection. For instance, the National Housing Policy (2001) places central importance on the role of the construction sector in lifting economic growth:

> According to the accepted international standards, the construction sector is the driving force in economic development. Construction strategy is important in cre- ating the necessary physical environment for all economic and social activities and in the attainment of sustainable growth. Above all, it is labor intensive and gener- ates real employment and income. The construction sector may also be viewed as a barometer of country's economic health.[31]

As a result, the Government has declared housing to be a priority industry and intro- duced a raft of subsidies and tax relief to support the sector, but the need to balance economic growth with ecological integrity does not figure prominently in the policy instrument.[32] The primacy to commercial considerations is also evident in other sectors of national planning. Textile is the backbone of the country's industrial sector and the Government has recently announced a Textile Vision 2005 to move toward value-added activities; however, environmental considerations are not mentioned once in the docu- ment even though the textile sector with its dependence on chemicals is a major source of industrial pollution. In the banking sector, consumer finance is being given top pri- ority by the State Bank of Pakistan, and loans for automobiles are at an all-time high, but no policy has been evolved to consider the horrendous effects on air pollution that higher rates of private ownership can bring, especially in the absence of a well-developed public transport network.[33]

---

[30] "Karachi's Coastal Environment: Facing Extinction" *Shehri*, at 4 (September–December 2001).

[31] *National Housing Policy 2001*, at 8. The Report noted that movement in the construction and housing sector has a beneficial impact on more than 40 industries.

[32] Incentives include soft-term loans, reduction in levies on raw material, and an increase in the budgetary allocations for the Public Sector Development Programme (PSDP) as well as reductions in the central excise duty on cement by 25% in the 2003–2004 budget. Shujauddin Qureshi, "Concrete Profits" *Newsline*, at 71 (August 2004).

[33] *The World Bank Urban and Local Government Strategy*, supra note 2, acknowledges that "[m]otor vehicles, the number and use of which are growing much faster than urban population, contribute about a third of the air pollution from fossil fuel combustion; other energy use and waste incineration account for half of air pollution. . . . Policies to curb environmental deterioration resulting from motorization and other energy consumption will have limited effect if focused only on fuel choice or internal production efficiency. Effective solutions will require addressing broader issues, including transport demand, land use planning, industrial development and location, and household income growth and distribution – all central to the urban development agenda." Ibid., at 39.

It is all too evident that in a setting where commercial development is paramount, environmental concerns will remain on the fringe of national policymaking. Mehta's comments on the toll of ecologically insensitive growth certainly fit the pattern in which development is conceived and practiced in Pakistan:

> In its race for modernization, the third world has blindly adopted the Western model for "development" – of capital and resource intensive industrialization, urbanization and mechanization, and chemicalization of agriculture – in a false belief that this type of rapid growth will eventually trickle down and eradicate poverty. As a consequence, we have paid a heavy price. Development that does not respect nature rebounds on man. Resources are exhausted, ecosystems collapse, species disappear, and people's lives, health, livelihoods, and their very survival are threatened.[34]

4 THE WAY FORWARD

Although political will and deep commitment to ecological causes are lacking, the problem does not lie in any shortage of appropriate legislation but in its steady implementation. In fact, the Pakistan Environmental Protection Act, 1997, is a good example of a framework legislation that provides for a high-level policymaking body (Pakistan Environmental Protection Council) and an enforcement arm in the form of federal and provincial environmental protection agencies. However, Wilson and colleagues caution that unless acted upon, sophisticated legislative instruments may actually be counterproductive:

> Indeed, apart from establishing appropriate legal and institutional frameworks, the effective implementation of environmental legislation remains one of the most daunting challenges for developing countries. For in the final analysis, ineffective law may be worse than no law at all. It gives the impression that something is being done whereas the existing legal arrangements are contributing little in terms of practical environmental management.[35]

The central tool of environmental management today is the environmental impact assessment, which benefits all stakeholders:

> For the local authority and other public bodies with environmental responsibilities, environmental impact assessment provides a basis for better decision making. For developers, the process should draw their attention at an early stage to the environmental effects of their proposals so that they can incorporate remedial measures into their designs. . . . The general public's interest in proposed new development is often expressed as concerns about the possibility of unknown or unforeseen effects.[36]

---

[34] Mahesh Chander Mehta, "Making the Law Work for the Environment" (1997) *APJEL* 359, at 359.

[35] P. Wilson, B. Ogolla, R. Branes, and L. Kurukulasuriya, "Emerging Trends in National Environmental Legislation in Developing Countries," in Donna G. Craig, Nicholas A. Robinson, and Koh Kheng-Lian, *Capacity Building for Environmental Law in the Asian and Pacific Region – Approaches and Resources*, Volume 1 (ADB, 2002), at 186.

[36] John Zetter, "Policies for Creating Environmentally Sound Industries," a paper presented at the Public Symposium on Revitalization of Local Economy Using Information Technology, Ogaki, Japan, 2–4 September 1996, at 2.

Under section 12 of the 1997 Act, all developers of projects that may have adverse environmental consequences need to file an environmental impact assessment (EIA). In a move toward greater specificity, the Pakistan Environmental Protection Agency has made subsidiary legislation[37] governing the operation of initial environmental examinations (IEEs) and EIAs. According to Part I of Schedule I of the Regulations (List of Projects Requiring an IEE), "urban development and tourism" projects require an IEE; these include housing schemes and public facilities with significant off-site impacts such as hospital wastes. In Part H of Schedule II of the Regulations, an EIA has been mandated for "urban development and tourism" projects that involve "land use studies and urban plans in large cities" and large-scale tourism projects (defined as having a total cost of more than 50 million rupees). It is further clarified in Part I of Schedule II that "all projects situated in environmental sensitive areas" require an EIA.

It is encouraging to note that the emphasis on IEEs and EIAs has been concretized as now it would be more difficult for different industries to avoid their obligations in this regard. However, to make the IEE and EIA regime more robust, the enforcement agencies will have to take a more proactive and aggressive stance toward industry, and this means abandoning a tradition of "soft-pedaling" that has marked past attempts at regulation. Unfortunately, traditions are hard to break, and Pakistan's administrative culture, with its deep ties to Britain, has many of the characteristics noted by Vogel with respect to the conventional British approach, which is said to be marked by an

> absence of statutory deadlines, a reluctance to prosecute, the emphasis on cooperating with industry rather than coercing it, and a flexible and decentralized approach to the making and enforcement of rules – all have remained consistent features of the British approach to pollution control for a century.[38]

A similar focus on giving primacy to commercial growth and a reluctance to penalize industry characterize the nonfulfillment of sustainable development goals in Pakistan, and it is to be hoped that appropriate legislation will gradually create its own momentum of raising environmental consciousness and compliance among the various stakeholders.

Although similar problems of implementation mar the conservation of cultural heritage, this field has the potential to galvanize a new era of environmental consciousness in Pakistan. In a heartening recent development, the restored Baltit Fort in Karimabad in the Northern Hunza region has won the coveted United Nations Educational, Scientific, and Cultural Organization (UNESCO) 2004 Asia–Pacific Heritage Award for cultural heritage conservation:

> At the award-giving ceremony in Bangkok the Baltit Fort was praised for demonstrating that historic structures can be saved, restored and recovered for continued use in the community. The judges noted that the project exemplified excellence in conservation practice applied to large scale monuments and was a model for the

---

[37] The Pakistan Environmental Protection Agency, *Review of Initial Environmental Examination and Environmental Impact Assessment Regulations, 2000.*

[38] David Vogel, *National Styles of Regulation: Environmental Policy in Great Britain and the United States* (Cornell University Press, Ithaca, N.Y, 1986) at 102.

revitalization of historical buildings throughout the northern regions of Pakistan. The fort's restoration had fostered the local revival of traditional building trades while an associated handicraft project provided livelihood opportunities.[39]

The restoration of the Baltit Fort is a testament to the excellent work being performed by the Aga Khan Foundation in Pakistan, but there is growing evidence that restoration of cultural heritage is finally becoming a governmental priority area. The Federal Department of Archaeology has prepared a new master plan for restoring the archaeological and architectural heritage of the Buddhist Gandhara civilization from Taxila up to the Swat valley. Although the Baltit Fort and Gandhara restoration are not examples of urban environmental management, they point to an environmental ethos that is bound to have repercussions in the wider society and across all connected domains. Recently, when the Lahore High Court administration decided to take down a wing of its historic colonial era building (1887), there was a huge public outcry by concerned citizens and nongovernmental organizations, which stopped the demolition.[40]

5 THE COURTS: A VALIANT STAND AGAINST ENVIRONMENTAL DEGRADATION

In contrast to the ambivalent attitude of executive authorities toward environmental concerns, the judiciary in Pakistan has an extremely strong record of defending ecological damage from short-term gain. In an earlier article, the author has discussed the origins and development of public interest litigation in South Asia and the leadership of the judiciary in breaking the barriers of civil procedure to accomplish major social goals:

> The judiciary of South Asia leads the world as guarantors of legal protection to sustainable development. It is not just in the field of substantive rights that this leadership is evident. It is also shown in an equally robust approach to procedural constraints that may prevent access to the courts. The twin hallmarks of this judicial approach are thus an ecological sensitivity and a willingness to build bridges whereby all citizens, and not just the strong, may approach the courts for vindication of their rights.[41]

It should, therefore, come as no surprise that in the field of urban planning, the courts of Pakistan have developed a mature body of case law to protect the rights of the

---

[39] Flotsam, "Gandhara Calling – Restoring Heritage" *Dawn Gallery* (25 September 2004), at 8.

[40] The Lahore High Court is among 47 buildings protected in the city under the Punjab Special Premises (Preservation) Ordinance, 1985. See "Fresh Plea against Demolition" (*Dawn*, 15 September 2004). According to section 7 of the Ordinance, "No person shall except for the carrying out the purposes of this Ordinance destroy, break, damage, injure, deface or mutilate or scribble, write or engrave any inscription or sign on such portion of a Special Building as is mentioned in section 5 [the façade of a building]."

[41] Parvez Hassan and Azim Azfar, "Securing Environmental Rights through Public Interest Litigation in South Asia" 22–3 *VELJ* 216–217 (2004). The leadership of the judiciary presented a very strong contrast to the growth-driven priorities of the other organs of government: "[p]aucity of resources, lack of general awareness, and the larger objective of attaining self-sufficiency, growth and development have prevented the Executive and the Legislature from giving priority to this area. The South Asian countries in the region, particularly, have unleashed ambitious liberalization and industrial policies in recent years to attract foreign investment and there is almost a 'no holds barred' approach for development in these countries. The buzz words are growth, development, jobs and exports. Environmental concerns are in second place. It is against this unhappy background that there is a ray of hope in the evolving judicial activism in the region." Ibid. at 219.

community and ordinary citizens over those of powerful private developers working in connivance with governmental agencies. Time and again, the courts have refused to authorize illegal construction and unlawful conversion of amenity plots on the pretext of legal grounds such as third-party rights, and they have resolutely come down in favor of protecting environmental goals rather than commercial expediency.

In *Abdul Razak v. Karachi Building Control Authority*,[42] the Supreme Court of Pakistan was confronted with a typical situation, in which a plot marked for residential development was converted by the developer for building a high-rise apartment. In such cases, the modus operandi of developers is to "regularize" the change in land use by the payment of fines. The Court held that this was completely unacceptable as the public authorities have no discretion to waive a civil liability:

> We may also point out that there is a marked distinction between a criminal liability under Sec 19 of the Ordinance and a civil liability under the Regulations to rectify irregularity/breaches. The Authority may compound a criminal liability but it can't regularize a breach of the Regulations which is of the nature which has changed the complexion or character of the structure, which was originally intended to be erected or of the plot. In such cases, it can be said that the Authority has no discretion in fact and law.[43]

After mentioning the goals of urban planning,[44] the Court went on to emphasize that the provision of adequate utilities is an essential element of urban planning, the absence of which has brought untold misery among the residents of Karachi:

> It may be mentioned that framing of a housing scheme does not mean simpliciter, leveling of land and carving out of plots, but it also involves working out approximate requirements of water, electricity, gas, sewerages lines, streets and roads etc. . . . This is what had happened in Karachi; without any planning and without expanding the provision of the above items of public utility services, the people were allowed to erect multi-storied buildings having shops and flats. In consequence everyone living in Karachi is suffering. There is scarcity of water, some people even do not get drinking water. The other items of the public utility services are short of demand. Roads and streets are normally flooded with filthy and stinking water on account of choking and overflowing of sewerage lines.[45]

In a crucial passage, the Court held that modifications in land use must be linked to public benefit and not private gain:

> However, it may be clarified that it may be understood that once a scheme is framed, no alterations can be made. Alterations in the scheme can be made for the good of the people at large, but not for the benefit of the individual for favoring him at the cost of other people.[46]

---

[42] PLD 1994 SC 512.   [43] Ibid. at 526.
[44] The Court drew extensively from and adopted the aims of urban planning outlined in the *Encyclopedia Britannica* and stated that "it is evident that the concept of modern city planning *inter alia* envisages the orderly arrangement of parts of the city – residential, business and industrial etc. so that each part could perform its functions with minimum cost and conflict. The paramount object of modern city planning seems to be to ensure maximum comforts for the residents of the city by providing maximum facilities referred to hereinabove. It must, therefore, follow that a public functionary entrusted with the work to achieve the above objective, cannot act in a manner which may defeat the above objective. Deviation from the planned scheme will naturally result in discomfort and inconvenience to others." Ibid. at 529.
[45] Ibid. at 529–530.   [46] Ibid. at 530.

Not only has this judgment survived the test of time,[47] it has emboldened the provincial High Courts to strive for the protection of public spaces against the machinations of the powerful land developers who have the capacity to influence government agencies and engage in protracted litigation. In *Dr. Zahir Ansari v. Karachi Development Authority*,[48] the High Court of Sindh underscored the importance of maintaining parks for enhancing the beauty of cities and the health of the citizens:

> It would not be out of place to mention here that open spaces, parks and greenery are not only soothing to the eyes and the mind but also for the spirit. They are necessary ingredients of town planning as they help in maintaining the physical and mental health of the residents of the town. It is, therefore, imperative that open spaces and amenities be not reduced by converting them into residential or commercial plots. . . . No person, however high he may be, can or should, therefore, be permitted to change the use of such area without exceptional reason in the public interest and that also after strictly following the procedure required therefor.[49]

As a consequence of the entrenchment of public interest litigation in Pakistan and the expansive definition of the constitutional right to life to include the environment,[50] courts in Pakistan routinely entertain petitions from private individuals and concerned citizen groups.[51] In *Shehri v. the Province of Sindh*,[52] an activist citizens group dedicated to urban improvement proactively challenged the disposal of amenity plots by a defunct government transportation authority. In upholding the petition, the High Court of Sindh drew on a variety of sources, including Islamic traditions of environmental sanctity and the Athenian city code, to highlight the nexus between the constitutional right to life and the protection of the environment:

> It would also not be out of place to refer here to the Oath of the Athenian City State "We will ever strive for the ideals and sacred things of the city, both alone and with many, we will unceasingly seek to quicken the sense of public duty, we will revere and obey the city's laws, we will transmit this city not less, but greater, better and more beautiful than it was transmitted to us."

At this juncture, we may state that in our opinion the right to life guaranteed by the Constitution includes the right to live in a clean and healthy environment. It is, therefore, the duty of the legislature to enact laws and of the government to enforce them in a manner that promotes the achievement of high intellectual and spiritual goals and happiness in life by the citizens.[53]

A survey of the cases suggests that significant gains have been achieved, including a largely uncompromising approach toward regularization of illegal construction and unlawful conversion of amenity plots along with liberalized rules of standing that make

---

[47] The extracts and *ratio decidendi* quoted previously were relied upon and validated again in another recent case before the Supreme Court of Pakistan in *Ardeshir Cowasjee v. Karachi Building Control Authority*, 1999 SCMR 2883.

[48] PLD 2000 Karachi 168.   [49] Ibid. at 177.

[50] The seminal judgment of the Supreme Court in *Shehla Zia v. WAPDA*, PLD 1994 SC 693, in which the Supreme Court first established the linkage between the "right to life" and environmental protection has become a versatile tool to attack conceivably any form of ecological assault.

[51] See also *Citizen Advice Forum v. Hanief*, 2004 YLR 1648.

[52] 2001 YLR 1139.   [53] Ibid. at 1146.

challenges by activist citizens and groups possible.[54] It is heartening to note that the courts are continuing to be vigilant about land use violations. In a recent case a land developer had controversially obtained approval from a provincial chief minister to convert an amenity plot to commercial use, and the High Court of Sindh struck out the regularization on the grounds of public injury:

> It is not a case in which the right of one individual is involved. The amenity plot for park is a public property and involves the rights of millions of citizens. The issue is to be considered on much wider plane and in the perspective of a broader horizon, keeping in view the public interest at large, as well as environmental issues. After determination of the status of the plot the consideration would be whether the state functionaries are also bound by the law of the land or they have free license to deal with the public authorities at their whims ignoring all the norms of public administration and the rule of law.[55]

However, although the courts in Pakistan have been eloquent and staunch defenders of sustainable urban growth, they can by no means become substitutes for effective government planners and managers. It is one thing to grant an injunction against an unlawful conversion of land use and quite another to manage complex technical issues such as the selection and operation of solid waste disposal sites. Even in a supervisory capacity, the Courts here have often stepped in and established commissions to inquire into matters ranging from the pollution of coal mines,[56] to an effective clean air and solid waste disposal regime for the city of Lahore.[57] Although the commissions mentioned (all chaired by the author) have played a major role in basic data gathering and proposal formulations, it should be noted that the Courts are inherently equipped to deal with adjudication of rights. The management of complex policy issues is in the end a matter of technical analysis, political judgment, and executive execution.

6 FUTURE TRENDS IN URBAN ENVIRONMENTAL MANAGEMENT

The challenge for policymakers the world over is laid bare in a recent commentary by Vidal, who argues that we are on the cusp of a huge shift in the pattern of human settlements:

> Put the global population and poverty trends together and it is clear that the world is making a major transition at a breathtaking pace. Some time in the next two years humanity will cross, probably forever, the line from being a rural species to an urban one. It will mark a turning point, a revolution as significant as the passage from the middle ages to the modern age, which will redefine culture, politics and the way we live.[58]

As Sheehan notes, cities are voracious consumers of the world's resources, "but they also hold enormous potential for environmental and social progress. Throughout history,

---

[54] In a recent case, the Supreme Court of Pakistan refused leave to appeal to a petitioner who had challenged the right of a nongovernmental organization to file a suit against unauthorized construction (see *Ghulam Habib Jadoon v. Karachi Water and Care Society,* 2004 SCMR 911).

[55] *Funfair (Private) Limited v. Karachi Development Authority,* PLD 2004 Karachi 170, at 189.

[56] *Salt Miners Labour Union v. Ministry of Industries and Mineral Development,* 1994 SCMR 206.

[57] W. P. No. 6927 of 1997 and *City Government v. Muhammad Yousuf* I.C.A No. 798/02, respectively.

[58] Vidal, *supra* note 7, at 19.

higher levels of health and education come after periods of urbanization."[59] The central challenge for policymakers is to use the urbanization trends as a positive force for national development and renewal.

Viewed against these momentous challenges, the outlook for urban environmental management in Pakistan presents a mixed picture. The upgrading of slums remains a vexing problem for policymakers as funding constraints and shortage of land have hampered resettlement efforts. However, an innovative solution that has come to be known as the "incremental development" model has emerged. The conventional model of housing supply involves complete development of residential schemes with provision of infrastructure prior to settlement of people. Proponents of the incremental development model argue that this route is completely unsuitable for developing countries with subsistence income population and shallow financial markets.[60] The alternative strategy, which was pioneered in Pakistan in 1987 by the then head of the Hyderabad Municipal Authority, Tasneem Siddiqui, sought to study and replicate the methods adopted by the land mafias in supplying affordable housing to the poor. In the words of Arif Hassan, another distinguished architect working in this area:

> The Hyderabad Development Authority adopted the strategy of the land grabber's informal development pattern. Unserviced plots are given to the poor at a price they can afford and without any cumbersome procedures. On-site screening of the applicant makes speculation difficult, if not impossible. The owners pay for services over a 10 year period [and] secure tenure rights will only be given after all services have been developed and paid for.... [Community] organizations finance and manage the development and operate services and collect revenues. As such, the Hyderabad Development Authority has overcome most of the constraints the formal sector faces in making land, infrastructure and credit available to low and lower income groups and at almost no additional overheads and costs.[61]

Fortunately, for the sake of continuity, the experiment conducted in the Hyderabad municipality has now been taken up in the form of a public–private partnership between a nongovernmental organization (Saiban) and the Government, whereby Saiban acquires state land at submarket rates and offers it to low-income families living in informal settlements. A key feature of the project is that the infrastructure needs of the community are catered to over an extended period of time:

> Minimal infrastructure is built up-front... initially communal water supply, soak-pits for sanitation and public transport through informal private transporters is arranged. Remaining infrastructure – underground sewerage, piped water, electricity

[59] Remarks attributed to Molly Sheehan of the Washington-based Worldwatch Institute, ibid. at 18.

[60] Azfar and Rahman note: "As elsewhere in the developing world, affordable housing in Pakistan has historically been built around a site and services model. A state-owned landsite is commissioned, full complement of infrastructure (underground sewerage, piped water, electricity and roads) is developed and fully serviced individual plots are made available for purchase. This approach is inconsistent with the economics and sociology of the poor and has resulted in a massive failure to supply low-income housing." Asad Azfar and Aun Rahman, "Housing the Urban Poor" *Acumen Fund* (April 2004), at 4.

[61] Arif Hassan, "Role of Formal and Informal Sectors in Provision of Housing Services" in Anjum Nasim (ed.), *Financing Pakistan's Development in the 1990's* (Oxford University Press, Karachi) (1992).

and paved roads – is developed incrementally as installment payments are collected over time.[62]

So far, an incremental development scheme has only been operationalized in the southern province of Sindh, where it has created 6,000 housing units and reached 35,000 low-income urban residents. Although this innovative approach is a good example of the need to think out of the box to provide practical solutions, the project will have to be scaled up and reproduced in other parts of the country. Sustaining the Government's ability to make land available at submarket rates for such projects will remain a difficult challenge. Moreover, experience in other countries suggests that subsidies cannot begin to tackle the scale of the problem; Keshwani's comments in the Indian context are equally apposite for Pakistan:

> No amount of subsidies can solve the problem of housing delivery in a country where the per capita income is as low as it is in India, where almost half the population in some cities live in the slums, where the growth of the economy of the country is not going to be high enough for timely solutions to the shelter issue, where people must continue to live on the pavements because they work tirelessly through the day only to be able to afford food.[63]

To pursue additional measures, the authorities in India have focused on a strategy of "technological diffusion" by the establishment of Building Centers, which seek to lower the cost of houses to the absolute minimum by pursuing cost-effective building materials and construction practices. Keshwani explains:

> The concept of Building Centers in India is less than ten years old. These training cum production building centres are targeted to help improve the housing situation for the poor. The Building Centre in India designs building components that are cost-effective and that preferably use local materials. It undertakes the design and implementation of housing projects for the low-income groups. Innovative building materials produced at the centres are used with indigenous building technologies in the execution of these projects. On-site training programs help provide the necessary skilled labour for the projects. Thus, the building centers achieve affordable housing for the poor and at the same time, increase the income-generating capacity of the artisans.[64]

There is also an urgent need in Pakistan to conduct research in low-cost construction technology and building practices; although the deficiencies in this area are explicitly

---

[62] Ibid.

[63] Kiran Keshwani, *The Contribution of Building Centres to Low-Cost Housing* (E & F Spon, United Kingdom) (1997), at 4.

[64] Ibid. at 2. Apart from technological developments, a recent BBC Report highlights the inspiration drawn by Indian architects from traditional communities. "Correa, who is famed for design principles based on low-density, low-cost architecture at a reduced environmental cost, wants architects to examine low-rise, high-density urban areas such as Rajasthan as a way of best using natural and local resources." According to Correa, "the basic principle of housing in a country like India is that you have very limited resources. . . . Therefore you have to use great ingenuity. That's when you respect what traditionally is done. If you look at a village in Kerala, everything is re-used and recycled. Leaves which fall from palm trees are used again for the roofs. There is nothing like poverty to be the mother of invention. As an architect, looking at those solutions, I was absolutely stunned by it. BBC News, "Architects Urged to Copy India" at www.bbcnews.com (14 September 2004).

recognized in the National Housing Policy (2001), it is unfortunate that no specific recommendation for nationwide building centers has come through.[65] Although the role of the government will continue to be important, it has increasingly been felt that a huge dynamism is associated with community self-help groups. Satterthwaite notes:

> A transnational movement of the urban poor and homeless with millions of member households is growing rapidly. The evidence from many nations is that community-driven approaches are more effective and far more cost-effective than conventional government programmes.[66]

Turning to environmental management in the formal sector, much depends on the manner in which the current policy of decentralization proceeds. Consistently with global trends, the Government of Pakistan in 2000 evolved a devolution that has now been enacted into law by the provincial legislature through the Local Government Ordinances. The system is based on a three-tiered local government structure (in ascending order, union, *tehsil*, and *zila* tiers)[67] and the district bureaucracy has been made responsible to the elected representatives at all the levels. These administrative changes are welcome from the point of view of introducing democratic accountability to the conservation process. In 2004, a union council elected official (*nazim*) filed a suit against the government for allowing discharge of toxic effluents from an industrial estate into the canal supplying irrigation water to his constituency.[68] The Court took a very serious view of the damage and ordered both the industrial estate management and the provincial Environmental Protection Agency (EPA) to take penal action against defaulting industrialists.[69]

In spite of the modest gains noted previously in the informal and formal sectors, lasting beneficial changes to the urban environmental regime can only occur with prioritizing of environmental management as a national objective. This change cannot result from just passing framework legislation but from changing the fundamental orientation of policymakers to induce then to integrate ecological outcomes in their outlook. Bachner has commented that "both the United States and Europe have invested heavily in their environmental future by adopting a comprehensive, precautionary principle based strategy where government department's policies are coordinated for the

---

[65] The National Housing Policy (2001) notes: "Like building materials, there has been no advancement or improvement in our construction techniques. It would not be wrong to say that over the years, there has been deterioration in skills and quality of the end product. The world has moved ahead and has developed not only building materials which are more cost effective and cheaper but have also developed ways and means and technology of mass production which gives better quality control and is more cost effective and cheaper than conventional construction." Ibid. at 14.

[66] David Satterthwaite of the International Institute of Environment and Development quoted in Vidal, *supra* note 7, at 19.

[67] A *union* area usually denotes a group of villages, aggregates of designated union areas constitute *tehsils*, and aggregates of *tehsils* form *zilas*, which are districts. The *zila* (or district) is the primary administrative unit in Pakistan since the British colonial period and there are a total of 101 districts in the country.

[68] *Nazim U.C Allah Bachayo Shore v. the State* 2004 YLR 2077.

[69] However, political empowerment cuts both ways, and there may be instances of elected officials' manipulating their position to protect their own. Already, there is an ongoing tussle between the city government and the Karachi Building Control Authority with the latter accusing the elected municipal officials of interfering in their duties. See *Citizen Advice Forum v. Hanief* 2004 YLR 1648, and Shujaat Ali Khan, "High Court Tells AG to Help Resolve Karachi City Govt, KCBCA Rift" (*Dawn*, 17 September 2004).

conservation of nature."[70] Pakistan is still in the early stages of environmental consciousness, and although public awareness of environmental issues is improving gradually,[71] continuous efforts are needed by all stakeholders to infuse the spirit of civic pride and responsibility in public officials and the citizenry. It is only to be hoped that environmental consciousness will arise in the future out of positive feedback events such as the accolades received by cultural heritage restoration projects rather than as a reaction to the damage wrought by industrial or natural catastrophes.

[70] Bryan Bachner, "Regulating Biodiversity in the Urban Environment" (2000) *APJEL* 349, at 385. The author contrasts this holistic national commitment to environmentally sound policies with the difficulties faced in Hong Kong, where implementation of green policies has long been held hostage to a focus on maintaining commercial growth.

[71] It is encouraging to note that the Federal Environment Minister has recently announced a policy to introduce environment-related subjects in school curricula. "Environment to Be Taught in Schools" (*Dawn*, 11 September 2004). See generally, Parvez Hassan, "Environmental Consciousness in Pakistan" (1990) 28–1 *Public Administration Review*, at 23–37 (1990).

20 ASEAN Heritage Parks and Transboundary Biodiversity Conservation

Kheng-Lian Koh

1 INTRODUCTION

In the summary of the Colloquium Programme, it is stated: "Land use laws are invariably national and local, and *rarely* are examined in an *international format*." The Second Colloquium of the International Union for the Conservation of Nature and Natural Resources (IUCN) Academy of Environmental Law seeks to examine how land stewardship laws work when measured against transnational and global policies of environmental law[1] and sustainable development. This chapter examines the experience of the Association of South East Asian Nations (ASEAN), which deals with such laws both at the international (i.e., regional) as well as the national level. Established in 1967,[2] ASEAN comprises Brunei, Cambodia, Indonesia, Laos, Malaysia, Myanmar, the Philippines, Singapore, Thailand, and Vietnam. This chapter considers the role of ASEAN in developing laws relating to land stewardship that will cascade down to the national level. These laws in turn percolate up to establish a regional conservation framework, thus facilitating a coordinated implementation of regional and international instruments.

The "ASEAN Heritage Parks" (AHPs) (established under the ASEAN Declaration on Heritage Parks (ADHP) 2003[3] and adopted at the Ninth ASEAN Ministerial Meeting on the Environment in Yangon, Myanmar, on 18 December 2003) and some ASEAN transboundary conservation areas (ATCAs) that have potential for transboundary protected areas (TPAs) provide an interesting study of ASEAN cooperation in land stewardship in natural resources at a *regional* level, calling for harmonization and collaboration among member states. They also provide an interface with international biodiversity instruments. (See Appendix I, the ASEAN Declaration on Heritage Parks.)

Interest in land stewardship at the ASEAN regional level has taken a quantum leap in recent years as more ASEAN member countries have ratified international biodiversity instruments such as the Convention on Biological Diversity (CBD), the Convention on Wetlands of International Importance (Ramsar), and the World Heritage Convention.[4] A number of ASEAN countries are also in the United Nations Educational, Scientific, and Cultural Organization (UNESCO) Man and Biosphere (MAB) networks – the

---

[1] The term *law* includes soft laws such as declarations, plans of action, and management plans.
[2] The Bangkok Declaration, 8 August 1967, Bangkok: http://www.aseansec.org/1212.htm.
[3] http://www.asean.or.id/15524.htm. See Appendix I.
[4] See Appendix II.

Paper presented at the 2nd Colloquium of the IUCN Academy of Environmental Law, *Land Stewardship and the Law*, 4–7 October 2004, Nairobi.

Southeast Asian Biosphere Reserve Network (SeaBRnet) and the East Asian Biosphere Reserves Network (EABRN).[5]

The year 2003 can be regarded as the high water mark for in situ conservation of protected areas in ASEAN, as its member states declared a list of 26 ASEAN Heritage Parks under the ASEAN Declaration on Heritage Parks (ADHP). The AHPs are from 9 of the 10 ASEAN countries; the Lao People's Democratic Republic (PDR) is the exception. Lao PDR will submit its nominations at a later date. The list may be amended from time to time. The ADHP replaces the earlier ASEAN Declaration on Heritage Parks and Reserves, 1984; it has taken 20 years for this new update.

2 ASEAN DECLARATION ON HERITAGE PARKS (ADHP), 2003

The concept of ASEAN Heritage Parks (AHPs) and transboundary conservation areas[6] was first introduced by the then-ASEAN Expert Group on Environment (AEGE) in 1978. AHPs are protected areas of high conservation importance preserving in total a complete spectrum of representative ecosystems of the ASEAN region. There were various stages in its development, beginning in 1978.[7]

Following the recommendation of the AEGE, an ASEAN Workshop on Nature Conservation was held 15–17 September 1980 in Bali, in which an action plan on ASEAN Heritage Reserves was discussed. The Workshop also considered transboundary conservation. The following were some of the issues raised:

- Common criteria in establishing a reserve system of regional and national importance of benefit to the local population
- Transfrontier cooperation
- Management cooperation on shared endangered species
- Establishment of several major ecotype reserves
- Establishment of regional task force to develop an action plan

The next stage saw IUCN providing the technical assistance to develop an action plan. The focus was on those ecosystems and species that either are significant to the region as a whole or require cooperation to effect their conservation. This led to the ASEAN Declaration on Heritage Parks and Reserves 1984,[8] which was adopted by the Second ASEAN Ministerial Meeting on the Environment on 29 November 1984 in Bangkok and signed by the then-six ASEAN member states, namely, Brunei, Indonesia, Malaysia, the Philippines, Singapore, and Thailand.

The objective of the 1984 AHPs was to assist the governments toward the attainment of conservation and to protect the biodiversity heritage of the ASEAN countries through the establishment of a system of national integrated protected areas based on scientific principles.

---

[5] http://www.unesco.ru/eng/pages/bythemes/mab.php; http://www.unesco.or.id/activities/science/env_sci/sitsup_env/101.php; http://www.unesco.or.id/activities/science/env_sci/102.php.

[6] See section 3, infra p. 362.

[7] Apichai Sunchindah, "ASEAN Initiatives in Protected Areas Management," presented at the Second Regional Forum for Southeast Asia of the IUCN WCPA, December 1999, Pakse, Lao P.D.R.

[8] http://www.aseansec.org/6078.htm.

All the then-six ASEAN countries except Singapore designated some AHPs under the 1984 Declaration, which provided for a master plan to be drawn up for each park, taking into consideration the following:

- Maintenance of ecological processes and life support systems
- Preservation of genetic diversity
- Ensuring of sustainable utilization of species and ecosystems
- Maintenance of wilderness that is of scenic, cultural, educational, recreational, and tourism values

However, nothing very much, if at all, was done at the national level, and no management plans were drafted for the then-six designated AHPs.

The next stage that could have further developed the AHP concept occurred in 1985, when the ASEAN Agreement on the Conservation of Nature and Natural Resources,[9] which can be considered "back to back" with the AHPs 1984, was signed by the then-six ASEAN countries. Unfortunately, it has yet to enter into force, with only three ratifications out of the six signatories. However, there has been renewed interest in the ratification of this Agreement.[10] Article 13 of the Agreement contains very comprehensive provisions on protected areas and calls for a coordinated network of protected areas throughout the region and for development of an Appendix containing principles, objectives, criteria, and guidelines in light of the best scientific evidence. It also calls for the conservation of natural areas by private owners, communities, or local authorities.

Another stage in the process was Strategy 6 of the ASEAN Strategic Plan of Action on the Environment 1994–1998 (ASPAE), which was to "establish a regional framework on biological diversity conservation." Strategy 6 states:[11]

> The absence of a regional framework for the protection and conservation of heritage areas and endangered species, only exacerbates the situation as management efforts are left to individual member countries. There is a need to develop a framework for the protection of these areas and species so as to ensure that conservation approaches are rationalized.

The "Actions" to be undertaken to implement the Strategy were (1) to promote the development of a framework for the protection and conservation of heritage areas and endangered species and (2) to strengthen capacities for Research and Development (R&D) to enhance biodiversity conservation in the region. The protection of endangered species in the AHPs would assist in the implementation of the Convention on International Trade in Endangered Species of Wild Flora and Fauna (CITES), which has been ratified by all of the ASEAN countries.[12]

The Hanoi Plan of Action 1999–2004, a continuum of the ASPAE, provided that in order to protect the environment and promote sustainable development, "it is to

[9] Koh, K-L "ASEAN Agreement on the Conservation of Nature and Natural Resources, 1985: A Study in Environmental Governance," presented at the Vth IUCN World Parks Congress on Protected Areas, 8–17 September 2003, Durban. http://law.nus.edu.sg/apcel/publications/pub/kohkhenglian/ASEANPaper.pdf; Koh, K-L, "Conventions and Their Implications on the ASEAN States," presented at the Environmental Management Seminar for Southeast Asia," 6–17 October 1997, Philippines.
[10] Ibid.   [11] http://www.aseansec.org/8950.htm.
[12] See Table 20.2, p. 366.

promote regional coordination for the protection of the ASEAN Heritage Parks and Reserves."

In 2003 ASEAN kept its Hanoi schedule and the ASEAN Declaration of Heritage Parks (ADHP) was adopted by the current 10 ASEAN member countries. The following is a summary of the Preamble, which sets out the raison d'etre of the AHPs:[13]

- The AHPs are concerned with the necessity to conserve national protected areas of the ASEAN member countries.
- They are aware that the uniqueness, diversity, and outstanding values of certain national protected areas deserve recognition regionally and internationally.
- The AHPs encourage the establishment of protected areas under the Convention on Biodiversity (in situ conservation).
- The AHPs note the target set by the World Summit on Sustainable Development (WSSD) 2002[14] of reducing the current rate of loss of biodiversity by 2010 through promoting international support and partnership for the conservation and sustainable use of biodiversity, promoting and supporting initiatives for hot spot areas and other areas essential for biodiversity, and promoting the development of national and regional ecological networks and corridors.
- The AHPs recognize that conservation areas should be managed to maintain ecological processes and life support systems, and preserve genetic diversity, to ensure sustainable utilization of species and ecosystems, and to maintain wilderness areas that are of scenic, cultural, educational, research, recreational, and tourism value.

The Preamble to the ADHP mentions the Convention on Biological Diversity (CBD).[15] All ASEAN countries except Brunei have ratified the CBD (Thailand was the latest to do so in 2004). The Preamble supports the CBD's in situ conservation of ecosystems and natural habitats as a fundamental requirement for the conservation of biodiversity in protected areas. In the "Programme of Work on Protected Areas," the CBD at its 7th Conference of the Parties (COP7) meeting in February to March 2004 in Kuala Lumpur[16] (Decision VIII/28 – Protected Areas – Articles 8 [a] to [e], Annex) recommended that the Programme take into consideration the relationship between protected areas and landscape so that goods and services flowing from the protected areas can be valued. Such an approach was in fact recommended by the IUCN World Commission on Protected Areas (WCPA) Vth World Parks Congress, 2003, in Durban.[17] This would also be within the ambit of the ASEAN Heritage Parks. The tenor of the Preamble is also wide enough to embrace the concept of "biosphere reserve" under the UNESCO Man and Biosphere (MAB)[18] program and its Seville Strategy, including Seville + 5 on the multiple functions of biosphere reserves – conservation, sustainable development, research and monitoring, training, and education. The AHPs can also take advantage of the regional MAB and biosphere reserve networks as they deal with similar ecological systems and, hence, give added value by providing a framework of activities that can be replicated in a similar ecosystem in the region (see MAB East Asian Biosphere Reserves Network

---

[13] See Appendix I.   [14] http://www.johannesburgsummit.org/.

[15] http://www.biodiv.org/convention/articles.asp.

[16] http://www.biodiv.org/meetings/cop-07/default.asp.

[17] http://www.iucn.org/themes/wcpa/wpc2003/.   [18] http://www.unesco.org/mab/.

[EABRN]; Southeast Asia Biosphere Reserve Network [SeaBRnet]).[19] Indeed, MAB is a very useful tool for the implementation of protected areas under the CBD, Ramsar,[20] World Heritage Convention, and other biodiversity agreements.[21]

The Preamble also takes note of the role of natural World Heritage sites (under the World Heritage Convention) in reducing loss of biodiversity. Some of the AHPs may well be future World Heritage sites. The interface and synergies of these and other biodiversity instruments such as Ramsar, the ASEAN Agreement on the Conservation of Nature and Natural Resources (though not yet in force), and the ASEAN Memorandum of Understanding on Sea Turtle Conservation and Protection 1997[22] must all be taken into consideration in developing management guidelines for AHPs.

The ratification of regional and international biodiversity instruments has not been even among ASEAN countries.[23] With the AHPs, perhaps ASEAN can facilitate the ratification of these instruments in order to enhance and develop further these heritage sites and reduce biodiversity loss. For ASEAN Heritage Parks (present or future) that are also transboundary conservation areas, see section 3.[24]

2.1 Objectives and Criteria of ASEAN Heritage Parks (AHPs) 2003

The objectives[25] of AHPs are as follows:

- To generate greater awareness, pride, appreciation, enjoyment, and conservation of ASEAN's rich natural heritage through the creation and support for a regional network of representative protected areas
- To generate greater collaboration among ASEAN member countries in preserving their shared natural heritage

The following are the criteria for AHPs

- Ecological Completeness – The site must demonstrate wholesome ecological processes and must have the capability to regenerate with minimal human intervention.
- Representativeness – The site embodies the variety of ecosystems or species representing or typical of the ASEAN region.
- Naturalness – The area must be, for the most part, in a natural condition. It may be a second-growth forest or a rescued coral reef formation, but the natural processes are still going on.
- High Conservation Importance – The site is recognized as a site of global significance for the conservation of important or valuable species, ecosystems, or genetic resources. It creates or promotes awareness of the importance of nature, biodiversity, and the ecological process; it evokes respect for nature whenever people see it. There is a feeling of loss whenever the natural condition is lost.

---

[19] http://www.unescobeijing.org/projects/view.do?channelId=004002001001002; http://www.unesco.or.id/activities/science/env_sci/99.php.

[20] http://www.ramsar.org/.   [21] http://whc.unesco.org/pg.cfm?l=en.

[22] http://www.aseansec.org/6185.htm.   [23] See Appendix II.

[24] Infra p. 362.

[25] *Guidelines and Criteria in the Selection and Establishment and Management of ASEAN Heritage Parks (AHP)*, in report of the 11th Meeting of ASEAN Working Group on Nature Conservation and Biodiversity (AWGNCB), Annex 3, 2001.

- Legally Gazetted Areas – The site must be identified, defined, and designated by law or any legally accepted instrument of the AMCs. Its boundaries must be defined and its use should be primarily as a protected area.
- Approved Management Plan – The site must have a management plan duly approved by authorities of the AMC.

Additional values to be sought would include the following:

- Uniqueness – The site may possess special features that could not be seen in any other site.
- High ethnobiological significance – The site may demonstrate harmonious relationships between culture and ecology.
- Importance for endangered or precious biodiversity – The site could be the habitat of importance for endangered flora or fauna.

The sites that have been designated as AHPs include inland and coastal mangrove swamps, mountain systems, limestone systems, lowland evergreen forests, and wetlands.[26]

2.2 Governance Structure of AHPs

The Governance structure[27] established under the ADHP consists of the following:

- The ASEAN Heritage Parks Steering Committee: The function of the Steering Committee is to supervise the AHPs and it will assisted by a Task Force on AHPs.
- The AHP Secretariat: The functions include receiving and processing nominations for AHPs from national offices and carrying out independent review of the nominations; managing an information system of relevant knowledge and information concerning the sites; ensuring independent review of the nominated sites is carried out. Currently, the ASEAN Regional Centre for Biodiversity Conservation (in Los Banõs, Laguna, Philippines) is acting as the interim Secretariat.

2.3 Toward an ASEAN Convention on AHPs?

At the 11th Meeting of the ASEAN Working Group on Nature Conservation and Biodiversity (AWGNCB) held in Malacca (Malaysia), 17–18 July 2001,[28] it was proposed to develop a "convention" on AHPs to be ratified by each country.[29] Currently, the AHP only sets out a Preamble[30] and does not provide a legal framework. If subsequently a convention is to be drafted, it can provide for the rights and obligations of the parties. It could also provide for the harmonization of relevant national rules and the incorporation of Article 13 of the ASEAN Agreement on Conservation of Nature and Natural Resources – though not as yet in force.[31] The Agreement was drafted with

---

[26] See Appendix I.

[27] Report of the *12th Meeting of the ASEAN Working Group on Nature Conservation and Biodiversity (AWGNCB)*, 17–18 June 2002, Yangon.

[28] 11th Meeting of ASEAN Working Group on Nature Conservation and Biodiversity (AWGNCB), 17–18 July 2001, Melaka, Malaysia.

[29] See report of the Meeting Annex 3, p. 2.   [30] See Appendix I.

[31] *Supra.*

the technical assistance of IUCN and is considered a very forward-looking instrument. Article 13 on Protected Areas lays down a comprehensive approach to land use planning and can add value to the framework of AHPs. Thus, Article 12 of the Agreement (in Chapter 4 of the Agreement, entitled "Environmental Planning Measures") calls for an integrated approach to natural resource conservation in land use planning at all levels, taking into consideration ecological factors as well as economic and social ones. It also focuses on the importance of retention of naturally high productive areas. Moreover, where appropriate, it provides for two or more Contracting Parties to the Agreement to coordinate the land use planning for conservation of natural resources. Environmental impact assessment is recommended in Article 14. As the predecessor of the ADHP (the ASEAN Declaration of Heritage Parks and Reserves 1984, is back-to-back with the ASEAN Agreement on the Conservation and Nature and Natural Resources, 1985), ASEAN is currently considering the question of update and ratification of the ASEAN Agreement on the Conservation of Nature and Natural Resources, 1985.

A convention on AHPs can also incorporate all the relevant elements in the international instruments such as the UNESCO Biosphere Reserve Network under the Man and Biosphere Programme (MAB). It can take into consideration the recommendations of the Vth IUCN World Parks Congress 2003 (WPC Rec 5.11) and the recommendations of the CBD COP 7 on protected areas held in Kuala Lumpur, 2004.[32]

2.4 Management of ASEAN Heritage Parks – from Declaration to Action

The ADHP provides for a master plan to be drawn for each of the AHPs covering management guidelines, research on structure and function of ecosystems, and education on wilderness values. It recognizes that common cooperation is necessary to conserve and manage the AHPs for the "development and implementation of regional conservation and management action plans as well as regional mechanisms complementary to and supportive of national efforts to implement conservation measures."

Although each ASEAN country is responsible for designating its heritage sites, the environmental concerns of these sites transcend national boundaries and regional coordination.

As the AHPs are within the jurisdiction of each of the ASEAN countries, the local laws will be applied in the management of the natural AHPs. However, they should be coordinated within the ASEAN regional level framework of a conservation strategy as contemplated within the 1985 ASEAN Agreement (even though not yet in force), and the ASEAN policy guidelines on "optimal land use pattern and zoning plan" under the Bangkok Declaration on the ASEAN Environment, 1984. Also, the interface and synergies with the multilateral biodiversity instruments that the ASEAN member countries have ratified must be taken into account.[33]

A Workshop on the Management and Conservation of Heritage Parks in the ASEAN Region took place 21–23 September 2004 in Khao Yai National Park, Thailand.[34] It was sponsored by the ASEAN Regional Centre for Biodiversity Conservation (ARCBC), which is based in Los Banōs, Laguna, Philippines. ARCBC currently serves as the AHP

---

[32] http://www.biodiv.org/decisions/default.aspx?m=COP-07&id=7765&lg=0_.
[33] See Table 20.2.   [34] The programme of the Workshop.

Secretariat. The structure of the Workshop gives an indication of the crucial issues that are before ASEAN in land stewardship. The topics include the following:

- Principles and Objectives of World Heritage Sites
- Principles and Objectives of ASEAN Heritage Parks
- Conservation of Biodiversity of the ASEAN Countries: Activities of AHP in Sabah, Malaysia
- Mechanisms for Sustainable Financing of AHPs
- Country Reports
- Immediate and Long-Term Plans Responding to Challenges and Opportunities

The objectives of the workshop were to determine common cooperation to conserve and manage ASEAN Heritage Parks for the development and implementation of regional conservation and management action plans as well as regional mechanisms complementary to and supportive of national efforts to implement conservation measures. More specifically, the workshop did the following:

- Reviewed and exchanged knowledge and experience on the current status, activities, management, and conservation strategies that are being implemented in the protected areas
- Identified challenges and opportunities for collaboration of AHP
- Identified common areas of cooperation and collaboration in the management of AHPs
- Developed and established a mechanism for cooperation and collaboration for the protection as well as sustainable financing of AHP
- Developed framework plans for AHP including the short and long-term plans for the conservation and management

This Workshop was convened in response to the international call for the effective management of protected areas. Delegates examined the similarities in each ASEAN heritage site to find ways to collaborate in terms of practice, operations, skills, and knowledge on the conservation of AHPs as well as inter- and intrarelationships of Heritage Parks in the region.

In the ADHP 2003, provision is made for a master plan to be drawn for each AHP, which should include but is not limited to management guidelines, research on structure and function of ecosystems, and education on wilderness values. It was also agreed that common cooperation is necessary to conserve and manage AHPs for the development and implementation of regional conservation and management action plans as well as regional mechanisms complementary to and supportive of national efforts to implement conservation measures.

Many of the designated 26[35] AHPs are in the process of implementation. Vietnam's Ba Be National Park provides a very good example where an operational plan is in place. This Plan can serve as a model for developing other operational plans. Table 20.1 is a *report summary* of the Ba Be National Park:[36]

---

[35] See Appendix I. Lao PDR will submit its nominations at a later date. The Vientiane Action Program (VAP) 2004–2010 will promote further listing and coordinated management of ASEAN Heritage Parks as a platform for ecosystem-based protected areas management (Annex 3: 3.3.8. 2): http://www.aseansec.org/VAP-10th%20ASEAN%20Summit.pdf.

[36] http://www.undp.org.vn/projects/parc/summaries/bn8.htm.

Table 20.1. Ba Be National Plan Operational Plan, 2001–2005

A 5-year plan describing management objectives and activities of Ba Be National Park for the period 2001 to 2005, including staff responsibilities, park organization, implementation schedules, and periodical review of the plan.

Introduction

An Operational Plan for Ba Be National Park has been formulated based on the Park Management Plan (1992) and the Park Investment, Construction and Development Plan (2001–2010). It identifies management and protection responsibilities undertaken by park staff and the objectives to be achieved from 2001 to 2005. The plan also indicates why and how the activities of the park should be organized, implemented, and periodically updated.

The plan was written by the Management Board of Ba Be National Park (Protected Area for Resource Conservation). It still needs approval from the Ministry of Agriculture and Rural Development (MARD), which has agreed that the three protected areas targeted by PARC would serve as pilot areas for developing of operational plans.

PART I: Status of Ba Be National Park

- Management objectives:
  ○ To conserve the integrity of various diverse ecosystems, rare plant and animal genetic resources, and the special landscapes of Ba Be Lake
  ○ To provide for scientific research, study visits, environmental education and awareness raising, and ecotourism; and,
  ○ To assist local communities to improve their current living conditions and mitigate pressures on forests and biodiversity.
- Conservation values and threats are described.
- Ba Be National Park covers an area of 7,611 hectares divided into three functional zones based on the forest protection and development law:
  ○ Strict Protection Zone;
  ○ Ecosystem Rehabilitation Zone and
  ○ Service and Administration Zone (including Tourism & Wildlife, Administration, and Residential zones)
- The presence of 3,200 permanent, legal residents in the Strict Protection Zone creates a conflict of land use in many areas of the park. This is particularly the case on sloping land adjacent to villages, which is required by villagers for upland crops. It is proposed that these areas are recognized as multiple-use residential zones within the park, thereby acknowledging the existing situation.
- Regulations on aquatic (particularly lake) resource use, tourism, and other commercial developments must be agreed between the executive local government authorities and the national park authorities.

Part II: Ba Be National Park Management, Period of 2001–2005

1. Management program (2001–2005)
2. Management activities
3. Protection activities
4. Forestry program
5. Community development program
6. Training
7. Implementation progress and budget
   - Management objectives, 2001 onward:
     ○ Strengthen park staff capacity to conduct biodiversity conservation and forest protection;
     ○ Conduct biodiversity investigation, studies, and monitoring as a basis for improved protection;
     ○ Promote forest protection contracts in order to quickly regenerate forest lands; and

- ○ Assist in the development of infrastructure and improvement of local people's living standards, particularly inside the park.
- Forest land allocation is a legal requirement yet to be completely fulfilled; 4,000 hectares have been contracted to households for protection. Village forest protection and development regulations are being developed.
- Areas of responsibility, staffing, daily rota, priority actions, housing and site management, equipment, and reporting format are outlined for each of Ba Be National Park's 10 forest guard posts.
- Forestry objectives are outlined:
  - ○ Forest rehabilitation activities in different zones by the park, and by local communities (under Programme 661);
  - ○ Fire control mechanisms and equipment needs;
  - ○ Scientific, including animal rehabilitation areas, a specimen house, biological research;
  - ○ External habitat areas with importance for conservation in the Ba Be region; and
  - ○ Impact monitoring mechanisms.
- Community development:
  - ○ A socioeconomic program conducted with PARC Project support is detailed;
  - ○ Environmental education activities are described, which are conducted with PARC Project support; and
  - ○ Ecotourism development planning is described.
- Staff training needs and plans are described.
- The implementation schedule and budget are detailed.

Annexes

I. Functions and duties of Management Board and Forest Protection Section
II. Survey and report forms
III. Equipment for Guard Stations, including Head Office of Forest Protection and Technical Section
IV. Matrix showing the landscape elements prioritized for conservation and recommended interventions

The guidelines to the management of the Ba Be National Park take into consideration a number of the elements contained in relevant international conventions and programme that Vietnam has ratified or adopted, including the CBD, MAB, and its initiatives. For example, it adopts the ecosystem approach of the CBD as it is based on resource conservation using landscape ecology and takes into consideration the livelihoods of the local communities. It also adopts the guidelines of the MAB in integrated land management by introducing "multi-use residential zones within the park" and involves various stakeholders in the park management – villagers, local government authorities, and national park authorities.

Other ASEAN member countries are also beginning to put in place their management plans for their designated Heritage Parks, but the levels of implementation vary. The following are examples:

Brunei

Although *Tasek Merimbun Heritage Park* was designated under the old ASEAN Declaration on Heritage Parks and Reserves 1984, it was only after the new ADHP 2003, that senior government officers, including those from the Forestry, Agri-Tourism, Town and Country Planning, Environment, Recreation, and Land Museums Departments, as well as officers of Culture, Youth, and Sports, met to discuss developing the park and making a plan for it.[37]

Cambodia

The World Bank and Cambodian officials have discovered rampant illegal logging in a protected Cambodian national park that the World Bank and World Wildlife Fund (WWF) have spent millions of dollars to preserve.

The World Bank and WWF gave Cambodia's Environment Ministry nearly U.S. $5 million to manage and protect *Virachey National Park* from 2000 to 2005. Specifically, the money was earmarked for preserving forest communities in the park, paying forestry guards to manage the area, planting border markers, and protecting medicinal trees.

Philippines

Mount Apo and Mount Iglit–Baco National Parks.[38] Guidelines for the buffet zone management of the heritage areas are being tested and refined.

3 ASEAN TRANSBOUNDARY CONSERVATION AREAS (ATCAs): TOWARD REGULATION AND MANAGEMENT

The terms *transboundary conservation areas* and *transboundary protected areas* (TPAs) are sometimes used interchangeably. The former, however, has a wider scope and may not be as yet subject to regulations. For the purpose of this chapter, we shall use the term ATCAs and confine TPAs to those areas that are subject to regulations.[39]

IUCN WCPA points out the benefits beyond conservation in transboundary protected areas and "Peace Parks" under an ecosystem management approach:[40]

> There is . . . growing recognition that effective biodiversity conservation depends on an ecosystem management approach that integrates protected area management into wider land- and water-use planning. Ecosystems and species do not recognise political borders, which were usually defined for historical and geo-political reasons, without reference to ecological functions or processes. Protected areas that are established and managed across borders – Transboundary Protected Areas – can therefore provide an important tool for coordinated conservation of ecological units and corridors.
>
> The benefits of transboundary protected areas can go well beyond biodiversity conservation. Such areas can also play a major role in promoting cooperation and confidence building between countries and within regions. Also Peace Parks play an

---

[37] http://www.travellersworldwide.com/14-brunei/14-brunei-rainforest.htm.

[38] http://www.iapad.org/database/modeldetails.asp?id=31.

[39] Clare Shine, "Legal Mechanisms to Strengthen and Safeguard Transboundary Protected Areas" in *Parks for Peace International Conference on Transboundary Protected Areas as a Vehicle for International Cooperation*, 16–18 September 1997, Cape Town, South Africa, Conference Proceedings, Draft of 30 January 1998; Han Qunli and Kazukiro Nitta, "Transboundary Conservation Cooperation through UNESCO World Heritage and Biosphere Reserves: An Update in East and Southeast Asia," in ASEAN Biodiversity, January–June 2003; Thomas C. Dillon and Eric D. Wikramanayake, "Parks, Peace and Progress: A Forum for Transboundary Conservation in Indochina," in *Parks for Peace International Conference on Transboundary Protected Areas as a Vehicle for International Cooperation*, 16–18 September 1997, Cape Town, South Africa, Conference Proceedings, Draft of 30 January 1998.

[40] http://wcpa.iucn.org/theme/parks/parks.html.

important role in fostering better cooperation and understanding between countries. They also help to catalyst the peaceful resolution of disputes. They also help to build bridges between nations and peoples.

Peace Parks are defined as

> transboundary protected areas managed through legal or other effective means, which are dedicated both to the conservation of biological and cultural diversity and the promotion of peace and cooperation. Peace and cooperation encompass building trust, understanding and reconciliation between nations, the prevention of conflict, and the fostering of cooperation between and among countries, communities, agencies and other stakeholders.[41]

3.1 Some Potential Transboundary Conservation Areas and Peace Parks in the ASEAN Region

Some of the challenges of transboundary management include connecting separate conservation units, often with different management systems. These areas may provide more benefits to conservation by accommodating social, political, and economic interests by coordinating cooperation among different agencies and stakeholders by promoting joint data collection. In the case of Peace Parks, they can help to promote peace and resolve conflicts through transboundary cooperation.[42]

At the First Meeting of the ASEAN Working Group on Nature Conservation (AWGNC) in Kuala Lumpur, 6–7 November 1990, it was proposed that the following transboundary conservation areas be established as transfrontier parks:

- Lanjak-Entimau/Gunung Betung-Kerihun in Sarawak, Malaysia, and Kalimantan, Indonesia[43]
- Wang Kelian-Thaleban/Belum-Helabala between Malaysia and Thailand

The Indonesia–Malaysia Lanjak project is supported by the International Tropical Timber Organisation. Inventories on flora and fauna are in the process of being created in the Malaysia–Thailand Wang project.

Apart from these two transboundary projects, which are still in their preliminary stages, nothing much was done, and it is only in more recent years that ASEAN has focused attention on transboundary conservation and has cooperated with organizations such as the Secretariat of the World Heritage Convention, UNESCO East Asian Biosphere Reserves Network (EABRN),[44] UNESCO Southeast Asia Biosphere Reserve Network (SeaBRnet),[45] ASEAN Regional Centre for Biological Diversity (ARCBC), IUCN WCPA East Asia, and WWF to consider transboundary conservation. It has, for example, participated in the Technical Workshop on the Preparation of Cluster and Transborder Natural World Heritage Nomination in the ASEAN Region, held 19–21 April 2001 in Bogor, Indonesia, to prepare and identify sites within the ASEAN region that are ready to be proposed as "cluster" and transborder Natural World Heritage sites

---

[41] http://wcpa.iucn.org/theme/parks/parks.html.   [42] See infra.
[43] http://www.ecologyasia.com/NewsArchives/Dec_2000/brunet.bn_news_bb_thu_dec28b6.htm.
[44] http://www.unesco.or.id/activities/science/env_sci/regnet_env/102.php.
[45] http://www.unesco.or.id/activities/science/env_sci/99.php.

and prepare necessary follow-up actions.[46] A "cluster" does not necessarily possess a similar ecosystem but is established to connect separate conservation units often with different management systems, which may cross national boundaries.

The participants at this Workshop noted the advantages and disadvantages of cluster World Heritage sites. The inscription and regrouping of a number of small sites to a cluster will be more beneficial to conservation by accommodating social, political, and economic interests; by coordinating cooperation among different agencies and stakeholders; and by promoting joint data collection. At the same time, however, it may not function well if ecosystems are disconnected and/or management concepts, criteria, and definitions of the areas are not consistent.

There have also been a number of other recent developments on transboundary conservation such as the one organized by ARCBC in Hanoi, Vietnam, in 2000 to consider recommendations on "Towards Harmonising the Management and Action Plans for Transboundary Reserves in ASEAN." ASEAN views ATCAs as tools to promote greater regional integration, peace, cultural heritage, and effective transboundary management of conservation areas. Interest in ATCAs was heightened particularly after the admission of Vietnam (1995), Cambodia (1997), and Laos (1998) into ASEAN. Part of the North Annamite mountains cross the three countries of Indochina, namely, Laos, Cambodia, and Vietnam. These countries have demonstrated a willingness to extend their protected areas to link the hitherto disjointed areas with the neighboring ASEAN countries, Vietnam with Cambodia, Laos with Vietnam. In these countries, the establishment of protected areas in the ATCAs is beginning to be incorporated into development plans. Other transboundary Peace Parks include Lanjak Entimau/Bentuang (Indonesia and Malaysia) and Tristane Park (Laos, Cambodia, and Vietnam).

3.2 Advantages of Transboundary Cooperation Highlighted by UNESCO East Asian Biosphere Reserves Network (EABRN)[47]

Conservation
- Better knowledge and coherent data on protected species, especially migratory species
- Conservation based on the ecosystem approach taking biodiversity as a whole
- Potential to support in situ gene bases
- Assistance in reintroduction of species extinct on one side of the border
- Identification of gaps in establishment of protected areas
- Identification of differences in conservation policy and management strategies

Scientific Research and Education
- Reduction of research duplication
- Scientific exchange in terms of research and scientific data as well as building of common scientific databases
- Better capacity for organizing integrated scientific surveys and research projects
- Better capacity for receiving support from government and outside sources for joint research
- Potential for better support for international research and training

---

[46] See Appendix II; see Dillon and Wikramanayake, see *supra*, note 39.
[47] http://www.arcbc.org.ph/arcbcweb/pdf/vol3no1–2/19–25_sr_Trans_conservation_cooperation.pdf.

Monitoring

- Better data on migratory animals under protection categories
- Greater effectiveness in control of illegal hunting and poaching across borders
- Water and air pollution control and documentation
- Fire monitoring and observatories cooperation
- Exchange of monitoring methodologies

Management

- Better knowledge on the partners' management systems, particularly specific responsibilities
- Possibility of exchanging and comparing maps owned by reserve authorities to develop clearer, consistent maps for conservation management
- Better knowledge of the technical capacity and facilities for mapping, monitoring, and communication, which might be shared when needed
- Identification and understanding of the differences in each other's management strategies
- Better preparation to respond to emergencies such as pollution problems, disease, and forest fires
- Potential to develop joint management agreements and even management plans

Development

- Better understanding of the differences in development policies adopted by the partners across borders

3.3 Legal Framework for ASEAN Transboundary Conservation Areas

There are a number of regional and international biodiversity instruments that contain provisions governing transboundary protected areas that can form the legal basis for ATCAs. These instruments have been ratified by some ASEAN member countries (see Table 20.2) and are relevant in drafting a legal regime for ATCAs. ACTAs provide an opportunity for the coordinated implementation of treaty obligations and other negotiated instruments. Indeed, a number of these instruments require the parties to consult and cooperate with each other on the establishment of transboundary protected areas. The following are the main instruments.

(i) ASEAN Agreement on the Conservation of Nature and Natural Resources, 1985

Three ASEAN countries have ratified this Agreement[48] (see Table 20.2).

Article 19 of the Agreement provides for cooperation of Parties that *share* natural resources to:

- Endeavor to conclude bilateral or multilateral agreements in order to secure specific regulations of their conduct in respect of the resources concerned;
- Conduct environmental assessment prior to engaging in activities with respect to shared natural resources which may create a risk of significantly affecting the environment of another natural resources;

---

[48] http://sedac.ciesin.columbia.edu/entri/texts/asean.natural.resources.1985.html.

Table 20.2. Ratification (accession) / adoption of relevant regional and international biodiversity instruments

Name of conventions	Brunei	Indonesia	Laos	Malaysia	Myanmar	Philippines	Singapore	Thailand	Vietnam	Cambodia
ASEAN Agreement on the Conservation of Nature and Natural Resources		X (1985)				X (1985)		X (1985)		
MOU on ASEAN Sea Turtle Conservation and Protection	X (1997)	X (1997)	X (1997)	X (1997)	X (1997)	X (1997)	X (1997)	X (1997)	X (1997)	X (1997)
East Asian Biosphere Reserves Network (EARBN)		X							X	X
Southeast Asian Biosphere Reserve Network (SeaBRnet)		X (2003)	X (2003)	X (2003)	X (2003)	X (2003)		X (2003)	X (2003)	X (2003)
CBD		X (1994)	X (1996)	X (1994)	X (1994)	X (1993)	X (1995)	X (2004)	X (1994)	X (1995)
CITES	X (1990)	X (1978)	X (2004)	X (1977)	X (1997)	X (1981)	X (1986)	X (1983)	X (1994)	X (1997)
Ramsar		X (1992)		X (1995)		X (1994)		X (1998)	X (1998)	X (1999)
WORLD heritage		X (1989)	X (1987)	X (1988)	X (1994)	X (1985)		X (1987)	X (1987)	X (1991)
BONN						X (1994)				

1, EARBN: http://www.unesco.or.id/activities/science/env.sci/102.php; 2, SeaBRnet: http://jakarta.unesco.or.id/PROG/SCIENCE/ENVIR/mab.seabrnet-01.htm; 3, CBD: Convention on Biological Diversity, 1992 (31 ILM (1992), 882; 4, CITES: Convention on International Trade in Endangered Species of Wild Flora and Fauna, 1973 (993 UNTS 243); 5, Ramsar: Convention on Wetlands of International Importance, 1971 (996 UNTS 245); 6, PARIS: Convention Concerning the Protection of the World Cultural and Natural Heritage, 1972 (11 ILM [1972], 1358); 7, BONN: Convention on the Conservation of Migratory Species of Wild Animals, 1979 (19 ILM (1980), 15).

- Notify sharing contracting parties of pertinent details of plans to initiate, or make a change in, the Conservation or utilization of the resource which can reasonably be expected to affect significantly the environment in the territory of the other Contracting Party or Contracting Parties;
- Engage in joint scientific studies and assessments, with a view to facilitating cooperation with regard to environmental problems related to a shared resource;

In particular Contracting Parties shall endeavor to cooperate in respect of:

(a) The conservation and management of

Border or contiguous protected areas;

Shared habitats of species listed in Appendix I of the Agreement;

Shared habitats of any other species of common concern;

(b) The conservation, management and, where applicable, regulation of the harvesting of species which constitute shared resources

By virtue of their migratory character, or

Because they inhabit shared habitats

(ii) Memorandum of Understanding on ASEAN Sea Turtle Conservation and Protection

All 10 ASEAN countries have adopted this Memorandum of Understanding (MOU)[49] (see Table 20.2).

The MOU provides for joint management protection and conservation of sea turtles in the ASEAN region. Sea turtle habitats include not only aquatic but also terrestrial environments where sea turtles live at any stage of their life cycle. The objectives of the MOU are to promote the protection, conservation, replenishment, and recovery of sea turtles and of their habitats based on the best available scientific evidence, taking into account the environmental, socioeconomic, and cultural characteristics of the Parties.

(iii) Seville Strategy for Biosphere Reserves: UNESCO MAB

The Seville Strategy for Biosphere Reserves was developed in 1995 and has special provisions for guiding transboundary conservation, using the biosphere reserve as a mechanism.[50] It is an appropriate instrument for the management of transboundary reserves as it deals with the integration of conservation and development through cooperation among stakeholders. It falls under the UNESCO Man and Biosphere program launched in 1971, which establishes an international network of biosphere reserves to promote a balanced relationship between humans and the biosphere. The guidelines under the Strategy for Transboundary Conservation are as follows:

- Objective I.2: Integrate biosphere reserves into conservation planning. Recommendation at the international level: Encourage the establishment of transboundary reserves as a means of dealing with the conservation of organisms, ecosystems, and genetic resources that cross national boundaries.
- Objective IV.2: Strengthen the World Network of Biosphere Reserves.

---

[49] http://www.aseansec.org/1895.htm.   [50] http://www.unesco.org/mab/docs/stry-1.htm.

- Recommendation 6 at the international level: promote and facilitate twinning between biosphere reserve sites and foster transboundary reserves.

Under the Strategy, a task force on transboundary biosphere reserves is established. The task force developed a set of recommendations at the MAB Seville + 5 Conference 23–27 October 2000 in Pamplona, Spain. The Pamplona Recommendations for the Establishment and Functioning of Transboundary Biosphere Reserves provide a general provision and definitions on the procedure for the Establishment of Transboundary Biosphere Reserves (TBRs), functioning of the TBRs, institutional mechanisms, and responses to the Goals of the Seville Strategy.

(iv) UNESCO East Asian Biosphere Reserves Network (EABRN)

Three ASEAN countries are in the EABRN network[51] (see Table 20.2).

ASEAN is cooperating with EABRN in establishing links in biosphere reserves under the UNESCO Biosphere Networks in the East Asian region. There are currently 16 Biosphere Reserves in the ASEAN Region, situated in Cambodia, Indonesia, and Vietnam.[52]

EABRN facilitates exchange and transfer of information among countries in the region. It deals with issues of common concern such as ecotourism development and transboundary conservation cooperation. It also conducts field evaluations for the Biosphere Reserves network.[53]

(v) UNESCO Southeast Asian Biosphere Reserve Network (SeaBRnet)

Eight ASEAN countries have adopted the Statute of SeaBRnet[54] (see Table 20.2).

ASEAN is cooperating with SeaBRnet on the management of biosphere reserves. SeaBRnet is part of the UNESCO MAB program under which an international network of biosphere reserves are established to promote a balanced relationship between humans and the biosphere. SeaBRnet is one of the most relevant intergovernmental programs for transboundary conservation.

The Statutes of SeaBRnet were adopted by participants at the SeaBRnet meeting in Siem Reap, Cambodia, 27–31 October 2003. The following ASEAN countries are members: Cambodia, Indonesia, Laos, Malaysia, Myanmar, Philippines, Thailand, and Vietnam.

The objectives include the following:

- Providing institutional mechanisms to exchange information, knowledge, and experience on the management of biosphere reserves
- Providing support to biosphere reserves in order to serve as models for sustainable development and conservation, applying the ecosystem approach
- Providing capacity building
- Providing and facilitating interregional cooperation with similar networks such as the East Asian Biosphere Reserves (EABRN), partnership and synergy with regional and international organizations, and programs such as IUCN

---

[51] http://www.unesco.or.id/activities/science/env_sci/102.php.

[52] http://www.unesco.or.id/activities/science/env_sci/sitsup_env/101.php.

[53] See http://www.unesco.or.id/activities/science/env_sci/102.php; Han Qunli and Kazukiro Nitta, *supra*, note 39.

[54] http://jakarta.unesco.or.id/PROG/SCIENCE/ENVIR/mab_seabrnet-01.htm.

SeaBRnet functions as a regional network of biosphere reserves in the Southeast and East Asian countries to promote biodiversity conservation, particularly at the ecosystem and landscape levels. It also promotes sustainable socioeconomic development through the biosphere reserves and comparative analysis and synthesis of SeaBRnet sites.

The activities of SeaBRnet are to be developed with the guidance of the Seville Strategy for Biosphere Reserves, the Statutory Framework of the World Network of Biosphere Reserves of UNESCO, and interaction with the implementation of the Ecosystem Approach of the Convention on Biological Diversity.

All the biosphere reserves and proposed sites located in Southeast Asia and the Member States shall be involved in SeasBRnet and given opportunities to explore the application of the ecosystem approach for biodiversity conservation, integrated landscape management, and sustainable socioeconomic development.

The main themes and focus of SeaBRnet relate to biodiversity conservation and sustainable socioeconomic development and may include, for instance, quality economy, ecotourism planning and management, rehabilitation of degraded ecosystems, integrated environmental assessment and monitoring, transboundary conservation cooperation, community-based resource management, traditional knowledge, and cultural diversity.[55]

(vi) Convention on Biological Diversity (CBD)

Nine ASEAN countries have ratified the CBD[56] (see Table 20.2).

We have earlier noted the ecosystem approach. This applies to transboundary protected areas. One of the aims of the CBD program of work on protected areas decided in its recent COP 7 meeting is to establish and strengthen regional systems of protected areas integrated into a global network as a contribution to globally agreed goals.[57] As all but Brunei have ratified the CBD, it is hoped that over time the ASEAN transboundary areas will become protected areas and become part of the global network.

(vii) Convention on Wetlands of International Importance (Ramsar)

Six ASEAN countries have ratified the Ramsar Convention.[58]

Ramsar has adopted a proactive role in encouraging Parties to take joint conservation measures in respect of transboundary wetlands. The Ramsar Strategic Plan 1997–2000 provides for the following:

- Calls for the designation of transfrontier wetlands and the improvement of international cooperation pursuant to Article 5 of the Convention (Objectives 6 and 7)
- Urges Parties to identify transfrontier wetlands of international importance, for example, in shared catchment/river basins, and to encourage the preparation and implementation of joint plans for such sites using a "catchment" approach (Res. 5.30)
- Supports twinning of transfrontier wetlands and use of successful cases to illustrate the benefits of international cooperation (Action 7.12)

[55] http://www.unesco.or.id/activities/science/env_sci/99.php#IV.
[56] http://www.biodiv.org/convention/articles.asp.   [57] See Decision VII/28, COP 7.
[58] http://www.ramsar.org/.

(viii) World Heritage Convention

Eight ASEAN countries have ratified the Convention[59] (see Table 20.2).

Transboundary conservation of natural heritage with outstanding value can be inscribed in the World Heritage List. This would ensure protection and would also call for cooperation by parties to the Convention. Some sites in ASEAN, such as the Borneo Montane Rain Forests, located among Indonesia, Malaysia, and Brunei, have been selected as a pilot project site for transboundary World Heritage nomination.

4 CONCLUSION

ASEAN has taken significant steps in developing legal frameworks in land stewardship in the context of heritage parks. It is beginning to consider potential transboundary conservation areas that could lead to the establishment of transboundary protected areas within the CBD or other international conventions and programmes.

ASEAN land stewardship is timely as the international community has also been working toward the establishment and strengthening of national and regional systems of protected areas to be integrated into a global network that would contribute to globally agreed goals. However, much work still needs to be done in ASEAN (as in other countries), and much can be gained by sharing experiences with other countries.

Regional organizations such as ASEAN can facilitate the development and implementation of regional biodiversity conservation and in the process assist in the implementation of international biodiversity conventions.

APPENDIX I: ASEAN DECLARATION ON HERITAGE PARKS, 2003

The Governments of the Member States of the Association of the Southeast Asian Nations (ASEAN):

RECALLING the ASEAN Declaration on Heritage Parks and Reserves signed by Brunei Darussalam, Indonesia, Malaysia, Philippines, Singapore, and Thailand on 29 November 1984;

RECOGNIZING that Cambodia, Lao PDR, Myanmar and Viet Nam have since joined the Association of Southeast Asian Nations;

CONCERNED with the necessity to conserve national protected areas of the ASEAN member countries;

AWARE of the uniqueness, diversity and outstanding values of certain national protected areas of ASEAN member countries, that deserve the highest recognition so that their importance as conservation areas could be appreciated regionally and internationally;

NOTING that the Convention on Biological Diversity provides for in-situ conservation of ecosystems and natural habitats as a fundamental requirement for the conservation of biological diversity and thereby encourages the establishment of a system of protected areas to achieve this end;

---

[59] http://whc.unesco.org/pg.cfm?l=en.

FURTHER NOTING that the World Summit on Sustainable Development 2002 has, among others, set a target of reducing the current rate of loss of biological diversity by 2010 through, among others, promoting concrete international support and partnership for the conservation and sustainable use of biodiversity, including ecosystems, at World Heritage sites; and effective conservation and sustainable use of biodiversity, promoting and supporting initiatives for hot spot areas and other areas essential for biodiversity and promoting the development of national and regional ecological networks and corridors;

RECOGNIZING that conservation areas should be managed to maintain ecological processes and life support systems, preserve genetic diversity; ensure sustainable utilization of species and ecosystems; and maintain wilderness that are of scenic, cultural, educational, research, recreational, and tourism values;

CONSIDERING that to achieve the aims, purpose and objectives of the national protected areas of the ASEAN member countries, a master plan should be drawn for each heritage park which shall include but not be limited to management guidelines, research on structure and function of ecosystems and education on wilderness values;

FURTHER CONSIDERING that environmental concerns transcend national boundaries and that individual states are primarily responsible for their respective identified heritage sites;

DO HEREBY DECLARE the national protected areas listed in Appendix I as ASEAN Heritage Parks. The list of ASEAN Heritage Parks may be amended from time to time by written notification from the member country concerned to the ASEAN Secretariat based on a set of criteria developed by the ASEAN Senior Officials on the Environment; and

AGREE that common cooperation is necessary to conserve and manage ASEAN Heritage Parks for the development and implementation of regional conservation and management action plans as well as regional mechanisms complementary to and supportive of national efforts to implement conservation measures.

The 1984 ASEAN Declaration on Heritage Parks and Reserves is hereby terminated.

DONE in Yangon, Myanmar, this eighteenth day of December in the year two thousand and three.

ASEAN Heritage Parks

Brunei Darussalam

a. Tasek Merimbun

Cambodia

a. Virachey National Park
b. Preah Monivong National Park (Bokor)

Indonesia

a. Leuser National Park
b. Kerinci Seblat National Park
c. Lorentz National Park

Malaysia

a. Kinabalu National Park

b. Mulu National Park

c. Taman Negara National Park

Myanmar

a. Alaungdaw Kathapa National Park

b. Meinmahla Kyun Wildlife Sanctuary

c. Indawgyi Lake Wildlife Sanctuary

d. Inlay Lake Wildlife Sanctuary

e. Khakaborazi National Park

f. Lampi Marine National Park

Philippines

a. Mt. Apo National Park

b. Iglit-Baco National Park

Singapore

a. Sungei Buloh Wetland Reserve

Thailand

a. Khao Yai National Park

b. Kor Tarutao National Park

c. Ao Phangnga – Mu Koh Surin – Mu Koh Similan Marine National Park

d. Kaengkrachan Forest Complex

Viet Nam

a. Hoang Lien Sa Pa National Park

b. Ba Be National Park

c. Kon Ka Kinh National Park

d. Chu Mom Ray National Park

Note: Lao PDR will submit their nominations for ASEAN Heritage Parks at a later date.

APPENDIX II: POTENTIAL SITES IDENTIFIED FOR CLUSTER AND TRANSBOUNDARY WORLD HERITAGE NOMINATIONS BY TECHNICAL WORKSHOP ON THE PREPARATION OF CLUSTER AND TRANS-BORDER NATURAL WORLD HERITAGE NOMINATIONS IN ASEAN REGION, 19–21 APRIL 2001, LIDO LAKES, BOGOR, INDONESIA

Possible Cluster under World Heritage Convention

• Sumatran Montane and Lowland Forests (Indonesia): Leuser, Kerinci Seblat and Bukit Barisan Selatan NPs;

- Sulawesi Moist Forests (Indonesia): Dumoga Bone and Lore Lindu NPs;
- Eastern Indochina Dry and Monsoon Forests (Cambodia): Cardamon Mountains;
- Philippines Moist Forests (Philippines): Cordillera Range, Mt. Guitingguiting, Mt. Itanglad and Palawan;
- Philippines Lowland Forests (Philippines): Panay Island;
- Thailand: Dry and Monsoon Forests of Khao-Yai

Possible Transboundary World Heritage Convention

- Central Borneo Montane Forests (Indonesia and Malaysis): Betung Kerihun NP and Lanjak Entimau;
- Peninsular Malaysian Lowland Forests (Thailand and Malaysai): Halabala and Belum;
- Northern Borneo Moist Forests (Malaysia and Brunei): Labi Forest Reserve and Gunung Mulu NP.

The participants noted that some of these possibilities could be in both cluster and transborder World Heritage (WH), if additional sites were considered for inclusion. Such possibilities should be further studied in the course of the project implementation:

- Central Borneo Montane Forests (Indonesia, Malaysia and Brunei): Sebuku Sembakung NP, Kayan Mentarang NP, Bulungan Research Forest, Batang Ai and Pulong Tau;
- Kaya-Karen Tenasserim Forests (Thailand, Myanmar and Malaysia): Andaman Coast;
- Peninsular Malaysian Lowland Forests (Thailand and Malaysia): Andaman Coast;
- Peninsular Malaysian Lowland Forests (Thailand and Malaysia): Taman Negara and Khao Sok/Khong Lan;
- Annamite Range Moist Forests (Vietnam, Laos and Thailand): Phong Nha, Vu Quang, Pu Mat and Kebang.

Source. Eleventh Meeting of ASEAN Working Group on Nature Conservation and Biodiversity (AWGNCB), 17–18 July 2001, Melaka, Malaysia, Annex 9, Summary Report, page 3.

21 Land Use Planning, Environmental Management, and the Garden City as an Urban Development Approach in Singapore

Lin Heng Lye

1 INTRODUCTION

The tiny city-state of Singapore is one of the most densely populated in the world, with a population of 4.2 million in 2003,[1] occupying a land area of 697.1 square kilometers (a population density of 6,004 per square kilometer).[2] It is also one of the most remarkable success stories in the annals of developing nations, moving from a per capita gross domestic product (GDP) of U.S. $512 in 1965, when it left Malaysia to become a republic, to a per capita GDP of U.S. $21,825 in 2003.[3] Indeed, it is no exaggeration to state that its leaders, particularly its dynamic first Prime Minister, Lee Kuan Yew, have taken the city "From Third World to First" – in the space of a few decades.[4]

Ranked the world's second most competitive state in the 2004 International Institute for Management Development (IMD) World Competitiveness Index,[5] Singapore has a strong industrial base for electronics and precision engineering, chemicals and petrochemicals, pharmaceuticals, and biosciences. It has the world's busiest port since 1986.[6] It is also the world's top bunkering port and third largest oil refining center, the location of four major oil companies (Shell, Caltex, BP, and ExxonMobil)[7] as well as others. These companies have a combined refining capacity of over 1 million barrels a day.[8]

Singapore has excellent transportation networks, with an efficient Mass Rapid Transit (MRT) system complemented by a Light Rail System (LRT), as well as an excellent network of roads and expressways. It has superb telecommunication facilities and was the first in the world to have a nationwide broadband network. This network covers

---

[1] *Statistics Singapore* at http://www.singstat.gov.sg/keystats/hist/population.html, accessed on 18 September 2004.

[2] *Statistics Singapore* at http://www.singstat.gov.sg/keystats/annual/yos/yos18.pdf, accessed on 18 September 2004.

[3] *Statistics Singapore* at http://www.singstat.gov.sg/keystats/hist/gdp.html, last updated 26 February 2004, accessed on 18 September 2004.

[4] Lee Kuan Yew, *From Third World to First – The Singapore Story: 1965–2000 – Singapore and the Asian Economic Boom* (New York: Harper Collins Publishers, 2000).

[5] http://www01.imd.ch/documents/wcy/content/ranking.pdf, accessed on 18 September 2004.

[6] See Maritime and Port Authority at http://www.mpa.gov.sg/homepage/achieve.html.

[7] The major oil refineries have the following capacities: Esso (265,000 billion barrels per day [bbl/d]), Mobil Oil Singapore Pty Ltd (300,000 bbl/d), Shell Eastern Petroleum (405,000) bbl/d), and Singapore Refining Co Ltd (285,000 bbl/d).

[8] http://www.mpa.gov.sg/homepage/achieve.html, accessed on 18 September 2004.

99 percent of Singapore and is readily accessible in schools, offices, homes, and public libraries.[9]

Ninety-three percent of Singapore's residents own their own home, and of these, 85 percent live in high-rise apartments built by the country's public housing authority, the Housing and Development Board (HDB).

Despite intensive industrial development, Singapore's air and water quality remains well within the U.S. Environmental Protection Agency (EPA) and World Health Organization (WHO) standards.[10] Water is clean and safe to drink from the tap. Refuse is collected daily by licensed contractors and incinerated; the ash is sent to an off-shore landfill site. The handling and transportation of hazardous substances and toxic wastes are subject to a strict legal regime. All inland waters support aquatic life and the coastal waters generally meet recreational water standards. The Pollution Control Department (PCD) of the Ministry of Environment and Water Resources (MEWR)[11] is responsible for ensuring that environmental factors are incorporated in land use planning, development, and building control of new developments. The PCD looks into air and water pollution control, as well as the management of wastes and hazardous substances. MEWR adopts three key strategies in managing the environment: prevention, enforcement, and monitoring. Land use planning is at the forefront of the strategy of prevention, as industries are carefully sited away from residential and commercial areas.

Apart from the efforts at pollution prevention and control, robust measures have been undertaken to enhance the living environment. Singapore has, from the time of its independence, strived to be a "Garden City" that is "Clean and Green." The island lives up to its reputation as a Garden City – trees and flowering plants line the roads, open spaces, expressways, overhead pedestrian walkways, and even the rooftops of high-rise buildings. Car parks are well shaded by trees and there are parks and gardens in every neighborhood. The National Parks Board of the Ministry of National Development ensures that plants are watered, weeded, and infused with fertilizers or pesticides at regular intervals.

The work of these two ministries has provided a clean, healthy, and pleasant environment for all residents in Singapore. This has helped Singaporeans attain an average life expectancy of 78.9 years.[12]

This chapter examines the role of land use planning and environmental laws in the transformation of postcolonial Singapore, from a poor Crown colony with overcrowded, dilapidated urban settlements and polluted river basins to a thriving "Clean and Green Garden City" with a First World economy and environment. In particular, it examines the use of land use planning in the regulation of pollution control, and in the preservation of nature areas, parks, and greenery. It begins with an overview of land use planning in Singapore and examines the planning of industrial estates in Singapore and the implementation of pollution control measures by the then Ministry of the Environment. The chapter next reviews the strategies applied in the greening of Singapore, and the role

[9] "Singapore ONE – Singapore's Broadband Initiative," 6 August 2003, at http://www.ida.gov.sg/idaweb/factfigure/infopage.jsp?infopagecategory=factsheet:marketing&versionid=7&infopageid=I776.

[10] Annual Report 2002–03, National Environment Agency at http://www.nea.gov.sg/cms/ccird/ar2002–2003/nea-ar-02.pdf, p. 24.

[11] Formerly the Minister of Environment (ENV), it was renamed MEWR with effect from 1 September 2004; see http://app.mewr.gov.sg/home.asp?id=M1.

[12] *Statistics Singapore* at http://www.singstat.gov.sg/keystats/annual/yos/yos111.pdf.

of the law in protecting natural sites. It discusses the tensions between development and nature conservation, the lack of laws mandating environmental impact assessments (EIAs), and the level of public involvement in environmental issues. It ends with a positive evaluation of the environmental management system that has developed, but also with calls for improvements in this system, particularly in the facilitation of greater participation by civil society and the passage of legislation that mandates environmental impact assessments.

2 LAND USE PLANNING

2.1 History

Land use planning started soon after Singapore was founded by Sir Stamford Raffles of the East India Company in 1819, when he realized its potential as a trading port for England.[13] The population then was about 150 residents. By 1824, the population had risen to 10,000 as immigrants flocked to the new trading port. Raffles visited Singapore only thrice, and on his third visit, the first town plan was prepared in 1822, reserving the central plain and hill (the Padang and Fort Canning Hill) for the colonial government, and a commercial area for European civilians and merchants. The areas beyond the town were zoned for the various ethnic communities. Thus, the European, Arab, Chinese, Malay, and Indian communities were physically separated at the outset, and even Chinatown itself was subdivided for the different Chinese dialect groups.[14]

In 1856, a law was passed requiring that prior notice be given to Municipal Commissioners before a building can be erected.[15] The early laws focused on ensuring public health, as many problems were starting to emerge.[16] In 1887 the Municipality was authorized to make building by-laws to provide for better ventilation around buildings and for the disposal of garbage;[17] in 1886, the law required that every new building erected upon a site not previously built upon must have an open space.[18] Overcrowding and unsanitary living conditions led to the passing of laws in 1913 providing for minimal street widths (36 feet), maximal height of buildings, and the need for alleys.[19] However, there was still no comprehensive planning legislation until 1927, with the establishment

---

[13] Singapore was founded on 30 January 1819, when Sir Stamford Raffles made an agreement with the Temenggong of Johore for the establishment of a British outpost in Singapore and for exclusive jurisdiction over it.

[14] Ilsa Sharp's Introduction to Ray Tyers, *Singapore Then and Now* (Singapore, 1993), quoted by Malcolm Grant in *Singapore Planning Law – Commentary on the Planning Act 1989*, p. 2; see also N. Khublall and Belinda Yuen, *Development Control and Planning Law in Singapore, 1999* (Singapore: Singapore Coordinating Commitee, 1999), chapter 1; Tan Sook Yee, *Principles of Singapore Land Law*, Chapter 23 "Planning and Development," (Singapore: Butterworths Asia, 2001).

[15] Indian Act XIV of 1856.

[16] Municipal Ordinances Nos. XIV of 1879, IX of 1887, and XV of 1896. "Floods were frequent in the swampy lowlands, and fires were a constant menace. Polluted water and open drains caused several cholera and smallpox epidemics, while stray dogs and dead ponies were left to rot on the beach. The roads were littered with garbage and the city's refuse thrown into swamps. . . . Pollution and stench were major blights." Gretchen Liu, *Pastel Portraits* (Singapore: Singapore Coordinating Committee, 1984) at p. 17.

[17] The Municipal Ordinance, 1887. This Ordinance separated the town from the rural areas and led to the systematic naming of roads.

[18] The Municipal Ordinance 1896.   [19] The Municipal Ordinance 1913.

of the Singapore Improvement Trust (SIT). One of its objectives was to propose a General Improvement Plan, which disallowed the erection of any building or the laying out of land for development other than in conformity with this Plan. However, these controls were very limited as development proposals had to fall within particular areas.

The Japanese invasion during the Second World War created serious housing shortages. After the war, the city had to be rebuilt and housing needs were very severe. In 1947, the Singapore Housing Committee recommended that a master development plan be created for the whole island. After four years of preparation involving extensive surveys into land and building use, traffic, population trends, and industrial needs, the Master Plan was completed in 1955 and introduced to the government in 1958 in the Planning Bill. It was based closely on the United Kingdom (UK) Town and Country Planning Act, 1947; however, its relation to the General Improvement Plan was not clear.

This was a period of rapid political change and institutional and administrative reorganization. Preparations were made for self-government and the first elections were held in 1955. Self-government followed in 1959. The 1958 Planning Bill was passed as the Planning Ordinance in 1959.[20] In 1963, Singapore joined Malaya, Sarawak, and Sabah to create the federation of Malaysia, but it was a short-lived liaison. Singapore separated from Malaysia on 9 August 1965 and became a Republic.

This was the start of a period of remarkable growth and development, transforming Singapore into "one of the most intensively – and successfully – planned cities in the world."[21] The new government was faced with the urgent task of creating economic opportunities and employment, as well as the need to build housing for the masses. Land use planning was especially important as land was very limited and the population was fast expanding. It was essential that the utilization of land resources be carefully planned and executed. A Master Plan was needed for the charting of Singapore's physical development.

2.2 The Master Plan

The 1958 Master Plan was a statutory master plan, established by the Planning Ordinance of 1959.[22] It emphasized comprehensive development through physical planning. Land use was controlled by zoning and density/plot ratios. All land was zoned for a particular use. Land owners who wish to change the use of their land or to develop their land had to comply with the requirements of the Master Plan.[23] The planning authority was given extensive powers to control all developments and subdivisions of land. Written permission from the authority had to be obtained before any land could be developed or subdivided. The Ordinance provided the machinery for the Planning Authority to plan, prepare, and review the Master Plan every five years. It also allowed the Plan to be

---

[20] No. 12 of 1959.   [21] Grant, *supra* note 14 at p. 7.

[22] The Master Plan as originally conceived, comprised four component maps, namely, the Central Area Map, Town Map, Island Map, and Additional Planning Area Map, accompanied by a Written Statement and a Report of Survey. The maps show the various zones for particular or intended use, while the Written Statement gave guidance by describing the zoning categories and the maximal intensities of development. It was the first comprehensive development plan for Singapore.

[23] The Ordinance was soon amended to allow the imposition of a development charge in 1964, and to impose a two-year time limit for the carrying out of any development.

amended at any time, but each proposal to amend or review must be publicly exhibited and a public inquiry held to consider objections and representations before the proposal can be approved by the Minister.[24] The Planning (Master Plan) Rules contain detailed provisions on the procedure for the submission and approval of amendments to the Master Plan.[25]

The Master Plan, drawn up during the early transition years, when Singapore was just emerging from colonial rule, was soon found wanting. Based on traditional planning, it was static and inadequate for a city embarking on dynamic growth through industrial development. The five-year reviews merely served to update the Plan by incorporating all ad hoc alterations in the interim.[26] A new form of planning was needed – the Concept Plan.

2.3 The Concept Plans

The 1971 Concept Plan

Singapore's rapid economic, environmental, and social developments required a long-range plan that was able to guide and coordinate the future physical development of the Republic. In 1967, a State and City Planning Project was initiated with the assistance of the United Nations Development Programme (UNDP). The following were the main terms of reference:[27]

a. To collect data for both comprehensive and project planning
b. To prepare a long-range, comprehensive physical development plan for Singapore
c. To prepare a policy sketch plan for urban renewal of the Central Area
d. To prepare a general traffic and transportation plan
e. To assist in developing the resources of the Planning Department to enable it to undertake comprehensive planning on a continuing basis

After four years, the Concept Plan emerged in 1971. It was projected to the year 1991 (20 years ahead) and envisaged urban growth in a ring of new towns surrounding the central water catchment area, served by a network of transport routes, expressways, and a mass rapid transit system. It laid the broad guidelines for long-range physical development including the building of a new international airport, as well as environmental infrastructure for waste management and pollution control. The Concept Plan took into account factors such as the following:

- Identification of development constraints and major land uses that affect the environment, such as areas for highly pollutive and hazardous industries, airport zones, and live-firing areas for military training
- Projection of land needs for environmental infrastructure such as sewage treatment plants and refuse disposal facilities (dump sites and incinerators)

---

[24] Section 10, Planning Act, Cap 232, 1998 Rev. Ed.   [25] S.245/99, Cap 232, Rule 1, 1998 Rev. Ed.

[26] Reviews were conducted in 1965, 1970, 1975, 1980, 1985, 1991, and 1997. A thorough review was made in 1997, culminating in the passing of the new Planning Act in 1998 (Act 3 of 1998). It preserved the old provisions that require the Master Plan to be reviewed "at least once in every five years," See Malcolm Grant's Commentary on this New Act, *supra* note 14.

[27] A. Doudai, "Singapore's United Nations Assisted State and City Planning Project," Singapore Institute of Planners Journal, Vol. 1 No. 1 September 1971, p. 5.

- Projection of land needs for transportation and communication (such as for future airport expansions, new railway lines, mass rapid transport systems, expressways, satellite receiving and transmitting stations)
- Identification of possible areas for major utility installations and infrastructural needs that are potentially hazardous or pollution-prone, such as power stations, gasworks, storage facilities for explosives and other hazardous materials
- Identification of ecologically sensitive areas for nature conservation
- Protection of water catchment areas
- Identification of new areas to be opened up for major developments such as new industrial estates, business or science parks, and new housing estates or new towns

The 1991 Revised Concept Plan – "A Tropical City of Excellence"

The 1971 Concept Plan was revised 20 years later. The Revised Concept Plan 1991 focused on sustaining economic growth and providing a good quality of life, with Singapore as a "Tropical City of Excellence, an exotic island and an international investment hub."[28] It was based on a time frame projected to the Year X, an unspecified year beyond 2010, when the population is anticipated to reach 4 million. This day occurred sooner than expected, at the turn of the new millennium, necessitating a review of the 1991 Concept Plan.

The review of the Concept Plan 2001 began in 1998 with a strategic assessment to identify the development directions and land requirements for various uses. Consultations were first made with the various government agencies to project the future demands on land. Eight subcommittees were formed to consider factors such as population and housing, industries, commerce, transport, recreational and community needs, as well as the future demands of the central business district.

An extensive public consultation program was drawn up, and two focus groups were established to reach out to a wide spectrum of Singaporeans. They comprised professionals, interest groups, industrialists, business people, academics, grassroots organizations, and students. The focus groups convened between August and November 2000. They were briefed by various government agencies and had on-site visits to increase their understanding of the dilemmas. The focus groups in turn consulted many members of the public. Much public feedback was also received via the Internet and other feedback channels.

A public forum was held on 8 December 2000 for the public to discuss the focus groups' interim proposals before the final recommendations were made. The focus groups submitted their final report in December 2000. After much study and consideration, many of their proposals were accepted and incorporated into the Draft Concept Plan 2001. The Draft Plan was publicly exhibited from 28 April to 11 May 2001. A public dialogue chaired by the Minister of National Development was held on 11 May 2001 to discuss views on the Draft Concept Plan for 2001. The public approved of more intensive building but wanted greenery and nature areas to be preserved and a sense of identity preserved.

---

[28] Government of Singapore, *Living the Next Lap* (Singapore: Urban Redevelopment Authority, 1991), see also Martin Perry, Lily Kong, Brenda Yeoh, *Singapore: A Developmental City-State* (New York: Wiley, 1997).

Concept Plan 2001 – "Towards a Thriving World-Class City in 2001"

Concept Plan 2001, entitled "Towards a Thriving World Class City in 2001," was drafted after taking into account public feedback.[29] It emphasized a "live–work–play environment, a dynamic city for business, leisure and entertainment," and "the cultivation of a deep sense of identity by creating a distinctive and delightful city where people can fondly call home."[30] It looked at creating a thriving world-class city for the next 40 to 50 years in the 21st century, for a projected population of 5.5 million. It promised new homes in familiar places, high-rise city living, more choices for recreation, greater flexibility for businesses, a global business center, an extensive rail network, and a focus on identity, retaining the essence of a particular area.[31] A Parks and Waterbodies Plan was drawn up by URA and NParks to guide the development of parks and water bodies for the next 15 years.[32] The plan called for

- The enlargement of existing parks and the improvement of access
- The development of new parks closer to homes and even distribution of parks throughout the island
- Greater access to nature areas and the building of four new waterfront parks
- The expansion of the park connector network, which joins parks through a comprehensive green network that links parks with town centers, sports complexes, and homes[33]
- An increase of the existing park connector system from 40 kilometers to 160 kilometers by 2015
- The linking of the Southern Ridges as nature areas

Concept Plan 2001 had taken into account the extensive public feedback received as part of the review. It provides a guide for the preparation of the development guide plans for the 55 planning areas in the Master Plan.[34]

In the future, the Concept Plan will be reviewed every 10 years. It is a strategic plan to guide the long-term physical development of Singapore, to ensure sufficiency of land as well as allow for flexibility and contingency needs.

2.4 Development Guide Plans

As the Concept Plans are only strategic plans, serving to guide and coordinate long-term public investments, providing the physical framework for the preparation of more detailed action plans for the building of industrial estates, new towns, and for the redevelopment of the central areas, more detailed plans are required. These take the

---

[29] "URA Releases Concept Plan 2001 after Extensive Consultations," 20 July 2001, at http://www.ura.gov.sg/pr/text/pr01–34.html.

[30] http://www.ura.gov.sg/conceptplan2001/index.html.

[31] See speech by Bobby Chin, Chairman of the Urban Redevelopment Authority, 8 January 2002, http://www.bca.gov.sg/newsroom/speech_080102.html; see also, http://www.ura.gov.sg/conceptplan2001/process.html.

[32] Carol Lim, "Ideas for Parks and Identity Come Full Circle," *Skyline*, January/February 2003, 7.

[33] See Clive Briffett, Belinda Yuen, Cynthia Barlow Marrs, "Multiple-Use Green Corridors in the City: Guidelines for Implementation," Environmental Planning and Management Series No. 1 (undated).

[34] http://www.ura.gov.sg/ppd/gazettedmp2003/index.htm.

form of Development Guide Plans (DGPs), which detail planning and development at the local level. DGPs are defined in the Written Statement as plans or sets of plans proposed by the competent authority to guide development with regard to land use and intensity in relation to the land demarcated in the plan.[35]

DGPs, as earlier mentioned, set out land use details, development control parameters, and urban design guidelines. They aim to optimize land use development potential at the local level and to guide both public and private sector development.[36] DGPs show the permissible land use and density for every parcel of land in Singapore. They contain detailed development guidelines on land use, including plot ratios, building height, urban design, urban conservation, and road networks. Each DGP is envisaged to have a population of 150,000, served by a town center. Each DGP area is, in turn, subdivided into planning subzones, each served by a neighborhood commercial center. The size of the DGP areas and the subzones varies, depending on the land uses, proximity to the Central Area, and existing physical separators such as expressways, rivers/canals, and major open spaces.[37] Presently, there are 55 DGPs for the entire Republic, including 11 in the Central Area. Each DGP that is completed is gazetted and replaces the corresponding part of the Master Plan.

2.5 The Current Master Plan

The current Master Plan was approved on 1 December 2003. It now comprises one Written Statement and 55 Development Guide Plans. While it is reviewed every five years, it guides Singapore's development in the medium term, over the next 10 to 15 years, translating the broad long-term strategies as set out in the Concept Plan into detailed implementable plans for Singapore. It shows the permissible land use and density for every parcel of land in Singapore.

Two new islandwide plans were introduced to guide the planning of greenery and identity for the Master Plan 2003 – the Parks and Waterbodies Plan and the Identity Plan. The two plans presented ideas on how to enhance greenery and maintain the integrity, essence, and identity, so as to improve the living environment. They were drawn up incorporating earlier public feedback from the Concept Plan 2001 that the public values identity and greenery.

All major development projects are subject to the deliberation of a Development Control Committee, which is also chaired by the Chief Planner.

3 PLANNING FOR THE ENVIRONMENT

3.1 The Singapore Green Plan 1992

In June 1992, Singapore's Green Plan was presented at the Earth Summit in Rio de Janeiro, Brazil. Prepared by the Ministry of the Environment (ENV), with the

---

[35] Para. 1, Written Statement.

[36] See Prasad Shekhu, "The Making of the New Singapore Master Plan," in *Planning Singapore: From Plan to Implementation,* Belinda Yuen, Ed. Singapore Institute of Planners (August 1998).

[37] John Keung, "Planning for Sustainable Urban Development: The Singapore Approach," in Yuen, n. 36, op. cit. p. 17.

recommendations of six Workgroups (on Environmental Education, Environmental Technology, Resource Conservation, Clean Technologies, Nature Conservation, and Environmental Noise), it envisaged Singapore as a Model Green City and a regional center for environmental technology by the year 2000.

3.2 The Revised Singapore Green Plan 2012

The Green Plan was revised in 2001–2002, under four new Workgroups (Environmental Education, Nature Conservation, Resource Conservation and Waste Minimization, and Clean Technologies),[38] and presented at the World Summit on the Environment in Johannesburg as the Revised Singapore Green Plan 2012. It is "a national blueprint to help Singapore achieve environmental sustainability over the next ten years."[39] The Plan placed strong emphasis on waste minimization and management, mindful of the fact that the new offshore landfill site at Pulau Semakau would not last beyond 30 years at current rates of waste deposits.

The Revised Green Plan 2012 served to guide planners in developing the directions for new Development Guide Plans that are to form part of the Master Plan.

4 POLLUTION PREVENTION IN AN ENVIRONMENTAL MANAGEMENT SYSTEM – THE PLANNING OF INDUSTRIAL ESTATES

4.1 Institutions, Agencies, and Strategies

The Economic Development Board (EDB) was established in 1961 to spearhead Singapore's industrialization. Initially its function was to promote industrial investment, develop and manage industrial estates, and provide medium- and long-term industrial financing. It was charged with the development of Singapore's first industrial estate, in Jurong; only in 1968 was a separate authority, the Jurong Town Corporation (JTC), set up to take charge of industrial estates.[40]

The EDB translated the economic aspirations of Singapore's leaders into concrete plans and strategies. It continues to play a leading role today in attracting investments in manufacturing and other high-value-added services, which meet the technological skills and employment needs of Singapore's future economic development.[41]

It may be said that Singapore's environmental management system (EMS) starts with land use planning and the identification of the types of industries that can be allowed in the city-state. The EDB works closely with the Ministry of Trade and Industry (MTI) to decide what kinds of industries are needed for Singapore's economic development. While these industries are identified, discussions are held with various other ministries

---

[38] The writer was a member of two of the four Worksgroups: on Environmental Education and on Resource Conservation and Waste Minimization.

[39] Environmental Protection Division Annual Report 2002, National Environment Agency Singapore, p. 6.

[40] See http://www.jtc.gov.sg/; today, JTC has become the largest landlord of industrial premises, having developed some 7,000 hectares of industrial land and 4 million square meters of ready-built factories, including specialized parts for high-technology and biomedical industries.

[41] See *Heart Work – Stories of How EDB Steered the Singapore Economy from 1961 into the 21st Century*, (Singapore: EDB and EDB Society, 2002).

and organizations to ascertain whether there are problems in accommodating them. In particular, discussions are held with the Ministry of Environment and Water Resources (MEWR) to see whether there are health and safety hazards or problems relating to pollution.

It must be emphasized that at the very start of the industrialization of Singapore, pollution control was a prime concern of its leaders. An Anti-Pollution Unit was established by the first Prime Minister, Lee Kuan Yew, in 1970, and placed under the control of his office.[42] Not until 1986 was it transferred to the former Ministry of the Environment (now MEWR) as the Pollution Control Department (PCD), even though the Ministry was established in 1972.

MEWR's statutory board, the National Environment Agency (NEA),[43] adopts an integrated approach in the planning control of new developments, to ensure that environmental considerations are incorporated at the land use planning, development control, and building control stages. This system minimizes pollution and mitigates the impact of pollution on the surrounding land use. Its PCD is consulted by the Urban Redevelopment Authority (URA) of the Ministry of National Development on the possible sites for potentially pollutive industries. Consultations are also held with the PCD by the JTC (Singapore's largest landlord of industrial premises), the Housing and Development Board (HDB), and private sector developers about the allocation of industrial premises.

The PCD assesses and evaluates the hazards and pollution impacts of the proposed industries to ensure that they will not pose unmanageable health and safety hazards and pollution. A proposed industry will only be allowed to set up if it is sited in an appropriate industrial estate and can comply with pollution control requirements. An industry that is potentially hazardous is required by law to undertake an impact analysis study.[44] Industries that are potentially pollutive must do a study on pollution control.[45]

Consultations are also held at the building development stage. Technical requirements are imposed at the Building Plan stage to ensure that the necessary pollution control equipment and facilities are incorporated in the design and comply with the NEA's requirements. Upon completion of a project, an application must be made to PCD for clearance of either the Temporary Occupation Permit (TOP) or the Certificate of Statutory Completion (CSC). PCD will issue such clearance on behalf of the Sewerage, Drainage, and Environmental Health Department and the Pollution Control Department only when satisfied that all the technical requirements imposed have been complied with. Only then will the factory be given a license to operate.

---

[42] "I decided to set up an Anti-Pollution Unit as part of my office. We had monitoring instruments placed along busy roads to measure dust particles and smoke density and the concentration of sulphur dioxide emitted by motor vehicles. Other cities had clean and green suburbs that gave their residents respite from city centres. Singapore's size forced us to work, play and reside in the same small place, and this made it necessary to preserve a clean and gracious environment for rich and poor alike." Lee Kuan Yew, *From Third World to First –The Singapore Story 1965–2000*, at p. 181 (Singapore, 2000).

[43] The NEA was established under the Ministry of the Environment and Water Resources (MEWR) on 1 July 2002 to focus on the implementation of environmental policies. It has three divisions: Environmental Protection, Environmental Public Health, and Meteorological Services. See www.nea.gov.sg.

[44] Section 26, Environmental Pollution Control Act, *infra* note 61.

[45] Section 36, Environmental Pollution Control Act, *infra* note 62.

4.2 The Development of Industrial Estates

Singapore's industrialization may be analyzed in five phases.[46]

a. The first phase was in the 1960s, when labor-intensive industries were encouraged, as the population was unskilled and the priority was job creation. Industries largely took two forms – they were either well-planned, large industrial estates in the rural/suburban part of the island (particularly in Jurong, formerly a vast expanse of swampland in the west) or planned, light industrial estates located close to housing estates or at the fringe of the central area.

b. By the early 1970s, full employment had been achieved; the emphasis shifted to the generation of higher-skill jobs and the production of high-quality goods. Industrial estates were more specialized now, with specialty clusters (such as woodworking and rattan, vehicle repairs and maintenance), some of which were pollutive backyard industries relocated from the water catchment areas. As these industries were relocated, it was necessary to build supportive premises to house them.

c. The 1980s was a period of industrial restructuring, to build Singapore into a modern industrial economy based on sound science and technology. By then, Singapore had managed to attract some high-technology industries, and the workforce was much better educated. Existing industrial parks had to be upgraded and improved to meet these needs. The construction of sophisticated science parks commenced.

d. The advent of the 1990s saw the birth of the new Concept Plan 1991. There was a need to intensify land use through increased use of existing industrial land, redevelopment of older industrial estates to higher plot ratios, and reclamation of land from the sea. Industrial estates with low value were redeveloped for high-value industries such as the electronics industry and petrochemical and chemical works. Several offshore islands were reclaimed to build Jurong Island, which houses a large petroleum and petrochemical complex.[47] At the same time, more industrial estates were built in close proximity to new housing townships. These are for clean or light industries that cause little or no pollution. They benefit from accessibility to the labor market of homemakers living close by. This was carefully planned, so that 10 to 20 percent of the total land area within each New Town had to be deliberately set aside for such clean and light industries. With increased sophistication, industries moved toward more parklike environments to facilitate research and development.

e. The 21st century saw the advent of the science and biotech parks, which are located near the universities and polytechnics, to facilitate synergies in engineering, design, and research. Biotech parks serve to springboard research and development in

---

[46] See-Toh Kum Chin, "Planning Industrial Estates in Singapore," in Briffett, Yuen, and Marrs, *supra* note 36, p. 54.

[47] Jurong Island today is home to many leading petrochemical companies, including BP, ExxonMobil, Dupont, Mitsui Chemicals, Chevron Oronite, Shell, and Sumitomo Chemical. They have taken advantage of the comprehensive infrastructure and third-party service providers of utilities, tankages and terminal facilities, warehouses, and maintenance and repair centers, such as SUT, Vopak, Oiltanking, Odfjell, Rotary IMC, and Poh Tiong Choon. The seafront at Jurong Island is particularly valued for its deep port facilities, which also facilitate marine-based industries; see http://www.jurongisland.com/history.asp; see also Goh Wee Lik and Tan Suan Swee, "Vision and Guts: The Story of Jurong Island," in *Heart Work: Stories of How EDB Steered the Singapore Economy from 1961 into the 21st Century, supra* note 41, n. 43 at p. 251.

biotechnology, which is the new emphasis for Singapore. Again, they are located near the tertiary institutions. The new Biopolis, located near the National University of Singapore, aims to be "a world-class biomedical sciences research and development hub in Asia . . . dedicated to providing space for biomedical R & D activities."[48] It includes the Bioinformatics Institute, the Bioprocessing Technology Institute, and the Genome Institute of Singapore.

4.3 Planning Guidelines for Industries

Seven planning guidelines govern the location of industries in Singapore:[49]

1. Regional balance of jobs and homes – there is a need to balance the distribution of jobs and residences to ensure that the central area is not overloaded.
2. Relocation strategies for pollutive uses – pollutive uses must be relocated, and, if possible, clustered together to derive synergies in waste management and remediation.
3. Transportation – decentralization of jobs can reduce commuting. It is essential to reduce the pressures on the Central Business District by decentralization of industries to the outlying industrial areas.
4. Preservation of water supplies – as both water and land are in short supply in Singapore, it is essential that potable water resources are protected. Very stringent controls are imposed on all developments within the water catchment areas so as to minimize the risk of pollution. The transportation of toxic waste or hazardous substances must follow specific routes that avoid the water catchment areas; warehouses near water catchments are not allowed to store hazardous or pollutive substances.
5. Moving industries to the labor source – this policy again reduces the pressure on the Central Business District. By providing jobs in the neighborhoods, it reduces transport time, facilitates efficiency, and improves the quality of life as residents save time.
6. Planning for the needs of industries – this requires an understanding of the needs of each group of industries.
7. Pollution prevention – at the macrolevel, the planning strategy is to segregate pollutive industries from residential and commercial areas, and to categorize pollutive industries according to their pollutive capacity, and to provide for buffer zones.

4.4 Types of Industrial Premises

Some 90 percent of industrial land in Singapore is owned by the government and statutory boards such as the Housing and Development Board (HDB) and the Jurong Town Corporation (JTC). JTC is the largest industrial landlord in Singapore. It offers a variety of options to potential investors, including the following:

- Ready-prepared land on which to build their own factories – these can be held on short-term temporary occupation licenses ranging from one to three years with an option for renewal. Developers need not fulfill any conditions required as investment criteria here, making it very easy to acquire such land.

---

[48] http://www.one-north.com/pages/lifeXchange/bio_intro.asp.
[49] See-Toh Kum Chun, *supra* note 46 at pp. 60–62.

- Land on short tenure of less than 20 years under the JTC Short Tenure Land Launch Scheme (STELL).[50]
- Government land sales sites – these are released from time to time and are open to be leased for use. They include land parcels released by JTC and usually have 30- or 60-year leases.[51]
- Prefabricated factories – these can be low-rise, high-rise, or stackups and are located in various areas.[52]
- Factories for start-up companies in Technopreneur Parks.[53]
- Premises in Science Parks or Business Parks for companies focusing on technology and know-how[54]

These premises may be sited in cluster developments, designed for specific industries such as for chemical and petrochemical industries (Jurong Island), water fabrication, biomedical, logistics, and food. These clusters are prime examples of sound industrial ecology, as they derive considerable synergies from their location. They may also be premises in mixed-use development, such as for electronics and electrical, communications and media, and high-tech engineering industries. JTC recently developed the Industrial Park of the 21st Century or iPark 21, in Paya Lebar iPark.[55]

The HDB also owns and manages industrial estates. These are mostly for light industries, sited near HDB housing estates, to capture the ready pool of workers living in the vicinity. A small percentage of industrial land is in private ownership. Such land is held on long leases or is freehold. However, much is being converted to nonindustrial use, as in the Hillview and Bukit Timah area.

4.5 Location, Classification, and Siting of Industries

In the early days, highly pollutive low-technology and "sweatshop" industries were allowed, but today the emphasis is on "high-tech" industries such as chemicals and petrochemicals, electronics, pharmaceuticals, and biotechnology. Many of these are highly pollutive; however, as mentioned, planners from the Ministry of National Development's Urban Redevelopment Authority check with the Pollution Control Department (PCD) of MEWR on the siting requirements for these new development projects and their compatibility with the surrounding land use.[56] This is part of the planning process, to ensure that industries are located in specially designated areas such as "ecoindustrial parks" with infrastructural measures to control, manage, and minimize pollution

---

[50] http://www.jtc.gov.sg/products/land/short+tenure.asp.
[51] http://www.jtc.gov.sg/products/land/gls.asp; see also Ministry of Trade and Industry (MITI) at http://www.mti.gov.sg/public/NWS/frm_NWS_Default.asp?sid=38&cid=1905.
[52] http://www.jtc.gov.sg/products/ready+built/index.asp.
[53] http://www.jtc.gov.sg/products/start-ups/index.asp.
[54] There are two business parks to date – the International Business Park in the west and Changi Business Park in the east: http://www.jtc.gov.sg/products/business+park/index.asp.
[55] http://www.jtc.gov.sg/products/ipark/index.asp.
[56] Today, these industries are located in Jurong Island, an amalgamation of several smaller islands just off the main island, forming a petrochemical complex with a well-planned emergency system involving the participation of all parties. See http://www.jurongisland.com/.

as well as to maximize industrial and technological synergies.[57] In particular, the PCD will examine measures to control air, water, and noise pollution; management of hazardous substances; and treatment and disposal of toxic wastes.

To guide land use planning and help industrialists in the selection of suitable industrial premises, industries are classified into four categories, namely, clean, light, general, and special industries, based on the impact of residual emissions of fumes, dust, and noise on surrounding land use.[58] Industrial premises that are located close to residential areas and within the water catchment areas may be occupied by only clean or light industries. The buffer distances to the nearest residential building vary. No buffer is required between a clean industry and the nearest residential building, but a buffer of at least 50 meters is required for light industries, at least 100 meters for general industries, and at least 500 meters for special industries. For industries that can cause extensive pollution, the buffer must be at least one kilometer from the nearest residential building.[59] No buffer is required for a Business Park.

Before a proposed development can be constructed under the Building Control Act,[60] the developer is required to submit Building Plans of the proposed works to the Building Plan and Management Division of the Building and Construction Authority (BCA) for approval. These Building Plans must also be submitted to and approved by various authorities, including the Fire Safety Bureau, the National Parks Board, and MEWR. Within MEWR, the Central Building Plan Unit (CBPU) of the PCD examines all building plans to ensure they comply with sewerage, drainage, environmental health, and pollution control requirements. In particular, CBPU screens prospective industries to ensure that they

- Are sited in designated industrial estates and compatible with the surrounding land use (industries are classified into four categories depending on their capacity to pollute)
- Adopt clean technology to minimize the use of hazardous chemicals and the generation of wastes
- Adopt processes that facilitate the recycling, reuse, and recovery of wastes
- Do not pose unmanageable health and safety hazards and pollution problems
- Install pollution control equipment to comply with effluent discharge and air emission standards
- Can safely manage and dispose of wastes

4.6 Pollution Studies Required

Developers of special industries that use or store large quantities of hazardous chemicals may be required to do a Quantitive Risk Assessment (QRA) Study to identify and quantify the hazards and risks; determine the impact zones of an accident that will lead to

---

[57] Lye Lin Heng, "Singapore: Long Term Environmental Policies" in *Cities of the Pacific Rim – Diversity and Sustainability*, PECC Sustainable Cities Taskforce, Genevieve Dubois-Taine, Christian Henriot, Eds. (Singapore: Pacific Economic Cooperation Council, 2001), pp. 155–168.

[58] See National Environment Agency, *Code of Practice on Pollution Control* (amended 2004), at pp. 24–32.

[59] Ibid. at pp. 9, 10.

[60] Cap 29, Act 9 of 1989 at http://statutes.agc.gov.sg/.

fire, explosion, or release of toxic gas and recommend measures to be incorporated into the design; as well as develop emergency response plans.[61] They may also be asked to do a Pollution Control Study[62] to identify the sources of emissions of air pollutants, discharge of trade effluent, generation of wastes, and emission of noise and propose measures to reduce pollution and to mitigate adverse pollution impacts on the surrounding land use.

Both these studies, however, fall short of an environmental impact assessment (EIA) as the parameters are confined only to pollution impacts.

4.7 Environmental Impact Assessments

Singapore has no law mandating EIAs, although these are conducted on an ad hoc basis by the government when necessitated. However, their contents remain confidential. The lack of EIA laws in Singapore has frequently been criticized[63] and has also caused considerable friction between the authorities and nongovernment organizations, when ecologically sensitive land is required for other uses. As a city-state with very limited land resources, Singapore faces constant tensions between the need to develop and the need to conserve its natural areas. These issues are discussed later in this chapter.

4.8 Cleanups

The improvement of the environment and the cleanup of polluted sites are ongoing processes. While laws providing for stricter standards to regulate industries as well as human behavior continue to be passed, at the same time, steps are taken to clean up the main sources of pollution. Specific problem areas were addressed head-on, such as the cleanup of the highly polluted Singapore and Kallang River basins. This took 10 years and a vast sum of money, but it worked.[64] Today, the rivers sustain aquatic life and are popular venues for water sports.

5 THE GARDEN CITY AND NATURE CONSERVATION

5.1 Introduction

The Garden City was conceptualized by Singapore's first Prime Minister, Lee Kuan Yew, as a strategy to woo foreign investors as well as to make the environment more pleasant, particularly to reduce the heat of the Tropics.[65] Inspired by the gardens of Cambridge,

---

[61] Ibid. at p. 11; see also S. 26 Environmental Pollution Control Act (EPCA) on impact analysis study.

[62] S. 36 EPCA.

[63] See Foo, Lye, and Koh, "Environmental Protection: The Legal Framework," in *Environment and the City*, Institute of Policy Studies (Singapore, 1995), at 86–87; Lye Lin Heng, "Legal Protection of the Natural Environment," *State of the Natural Environment in Singapore*, Clive Briffett and Ho Hua Chew, Eds., Nature Society Singapore (June 1999); Lye Lin Heng, "Singapore's New Environmental Law: The Environmental Pollution Control Act, 1999" [2000] SJLS 1 at pp. 29–32.

[64] L. M. Chou, " Restoration of the Singapore River and the Kallang Basin," *Intercoast,* Fall 2001, pp. 1–3.

[65] "To achieve First World standards in a Third World region, we set out to transform Singapore into a tropical garden city. . . . We planted millions of trees, palms and shrubs. Greening raised the morale of people and gave them pride in their surroundings. We taught them to care for and not vandalize the area. We did not differentiate between middle-class and working class areas. The British had superior

England, where he studied Law, and by the cleanliness of Switzerland and the discipline of its people, Lee modeled Singapore on Switzerland. He used the concept of a well-manicured garden to demonstrate that the people of Singapore had the necessary discipline to make things work. He recognized that it took care and discipline to maintain a garden. This, he hoped, would impress investors sufficiently to encourage then to invest in Singapore. These policies were implemented by the Parks and Recreation Department of the Ministry of National Development.[66]

Said Lee:

> I sent them (government officers) on missions all along the Equator and the tropical, subtropical zones, looking for new types of trees, plants, creepers and so on. From Africa, the Caribbean, Latin, Middle, Central America, we've come back with new plants. It's a very small sum. But if you get the place greened up, if you get all those creepers up, you take away the heat, you'll have a different city.[67]

Lee started the first Tree Planting Day in 1967 even before it became fashionable in the developed world. An Annual Tree Planting Day was launched on the first Sunday of November 1971. "In wooing investors, even trees matter," said Lee on 1 August 1996, when the Economic Development Board celebrated its 35th Anniversary.[68]

The greening of Singapore as a government policy was declared in Parliament in 1968 when, during the second reading of the Environmental Public Health Bill, the Minister stated, "The improvement in the quality of our urban environment and the transformation of Singapore into a garden city – a clean and green city – is the declared objective of the government."[69]

5.2 The Greening of Singapore

A fascinating picture emerges of Singapore's efforts to green the city in rapid time. A comprehensive strategy was devised at the start. Fast-growing, indigenous trees were nurtured and transplanted along the roads, leading to the term *instant trees*. They were selected for their color, ability to provide shade, fast growth, and ease of maintenance.[70] At the same time, road codes were developed to ensure that adequate planting areas were provided along new roads. Car parks had to be planted with trees to reduce the heat of the tropical sun. Even the grounds of car park lots had to be planted with grass, to reduce heat from the asphalt. Concrete structures such as flyovers (highways that pass over other

---

white enclaves . . . that were cleaner and greener than the 'native' areas. That would have been politically disastrous for an elected government. We kept down flies and mosquitoes and cleaned up smelly drains and canals. Within a year, there was a distinct spruceness of public spaces." Lee Kuan Yew, *supra* note 4 at p. 176.

[66] http://www.nparks.gov.sg/gardencity/gardencity.shtml.

[67] "The grass has got to be mown every other day, the trees have to be tended, the flowers in the gardens have to be looked after so they know this place gives attention to detail." Per Lee Kuan Yew, in Han Fook Kwong, Warren Fernandez, and Sumiko Tan, *Lee Kuan Yew – The Man and His Ideas* (Singapore: Times Editions, 1998), p. 12.

[68] Koh Kheng Lian, "Singapore: Fashioning Landscape for the 'Garden City,'" in *Landscape Conservation Law – Present Trends and Perspectives in International and Comparative Law*, IUCN Environmental Policy and Law Paper No. 39 (2000) at p. 40. See also Koh Kheng Lian, Chapter 9 – "Singapore," in *Biodiversity Planning in Asia*, Jeremy Carew-Reid, Ed. (Paris: IUCN, 2002).

[69] Per Chua Sian Chin, Minister for the Environment, 16 December 1968, Hansard Col. 369.

[70] "The Initial Years" at http://www.nparks.gov.sg/gardencity/initial_years.shtml.

highways) and retaining walls were to be covered with creepers. Overhead bridges were provided with planter boxes for flowering shrubs (the bougainvillea remains a popular choice today). Parks were developed in the Central Business District as well as in outer suburbs, to provide "green lungs" for the people. Developers of residential areas were required to plant roadside trees and set aside land for open space. Existing parks were improved and many new parks were developed. The emphasis was on the provision of shade in the ambiance of a garden. Thus, the planting extended beyond trees, to flowering and fragrant plants as well as to fruit trees. These were planted all over the island, in parks and residential suburbs and at schools, hospitals, police stations, and community centers.

Even industrial sites had to be greened. All factories had to landscape their grounds and plant trees before they could commence operations.[71]

5.3 The Agencies in Nature Conservation

The greening of modern Singapore was the responsibility of the Parks and Trees Unit of the Public Works Department (PWD) in June 1967.[72] This became the Parks and Trees Division in the PWD in 1970. The thrust then was to plant trees extensively along the sides of roads. In 1973, the Botanic Gardens merged with the Parks and Trees Division to form the Parks and Recreation Division under the PWD. Work commenced on East Coast Park and Fort Canning Park. In 1976, the Division became an independent department under the Ministry of National Development, and a new phase began. More trees and shrubs were introduced from other tropical countries, and scores of horticulturists and landscape architects were engaged. Planting was done in new housing estates, along highways, and even within new industrial and commercial sites. Even walls and overhead bridges were adorned with creepers and climbers, and flowering shrubs were added for color. New parks were added, and the landscaping of Changi International Airport was tended to carefully. A National Parks Board was formed in 1990 to take charge of the Botanic Gardens, Fort Canning Park, and the nature reserves. It was reconstituted on 1 July 1996, after the merger of the Parks and Recreation Department (PRD) and the former National Parks Board.

Today, the National Parks Board (NParks) is the agency responsible for the maintenance of these green expanses. Its mission is "Let's Make Singapore Our Garden." NParks is also Singapore's scientific authority on nature conservation and monitors and coordinates measures to ensure the health of designated nature areas.

5.4 Land Use Planning and Nature Conservation Laws

Tying greening in with land use planning, it should be remembered that the Master Plan was being reviewed every five years, and the Concept Plan was initiated in 1971. In 1987, the Recreation Sub-Committee of the Concept Plan Review Committee was

---

[71] Lee Kuan Yew, speech on 35th Anniversary of the Economic Development Board, 1 August 1996, at p. 181.

[72] Ling Sing Kong and Chua Sian Eng, *More Than a Garden City*, Parks and Recreation Department, Ministry of National Development, November 1992, p. 126; see also Tan Wee Kiat, *Naturally Yours*, 1992, National Parks Singapore; Shawn Lum and Ilsa Sharp, Eds., *A View from the Summit – The Story of Bukit Timah Nature Reserve* (Singapore, 1996).

chaired by the Deputy Commissioner of Parks and Recreation, Lee Sing Kong. Under his leadership, guidelines were drawn for park development over the next decade and a park connector system was suggested. Today, a comprehensive network linking major parks and nature areas is being developed. Under the Parks and Waterbodies Plan, this network of parks and park connectors will span some 360 kilometers and will facilitate the enjoyment of the island's nature through a continuous green network.

As Singapore developed, laws were passed to protect its natural heritage.[73] The Wild Animals and Birds Act was passed in 1965,[74] making it an offense for anyone to "kill, take or keep" wild animals, including birds, without a license. The Parks and Trees Act was passed in 1975 "to provide for the development, protection and regulation of public parks and gardens and for the preservation and growing of trees and plants and for matters connected therewith."[75] It is an offense to cut down a tree with a girth that exceeds one meter, measured a half-meter from the ground, if it is growing on vacant land or in a conservation area. The offense carries a maximum fine of $10,000 for each tree.[76] Such trees can only be felled with the permission of the Commissioner of Parks and Recreation. The Parks and Trees (Preservation of Trees) Order, 1991, designated two parts of Singapore as tree conservation areas. The Act also empowered the Commissioner to order any person to maintain or preserve a tree in a tree conservation area. Again the penalty for noncompliance is a fine of up to $10,000. The Parks and Trees Rules regulate the use of parks and provide for the planting and care of trees. It prohibits persons from excavating, cementing, or sealing up any ground within a radius of two meters from the collar of a tree planted on vacant land on which a street or car park is to be made, or near a public street.[77]

The National Parks Act was passed in 1990, raising the status of the Botanic Gardens and Fort Canning Park to National Parks and instituting the National Parks Board. Together, the Board and the Parks and Recreation Department further developed the greening of Singapore. Six years later, a new National Parks Act was passed to provide for the merger of the two bodies into one, the National Parks Board. The new Act provided for the transfer of the property, rights, and liabilities of the Parks and Recreation Department to the National Parks Board. It established four nature reserves (including two that were given legal protection for the first time)[78] and the two national parks.[79] The functions of the Board are many; particular, they include the following (section 6):

(a) to control and administer the national parks and nature reserves;
(b) to be an agent of the Government in the management and maintenance of the green areas;
(c) to propagate, protect and preserve the plants and animals of Singapore and, within the national parks, nature reserves and parklands, to preserve objects and places of aesthetic, historical or scientific interest;
(d) to provide and control facilities for the study of and research into matters relating to animals and plants in Singapore and the physical conditions in which they live;

---

[73] Lye Lin Heng, "Wildlife Protection Laws in Singapore" [1991] SJLS 287–319.
[74] Ordinance 5 of 1965.   [75] Act 14 of 1975.
[76] Section 5.   [77] Paragraph 11, Parks and Trees Rules.
[78] These are the Bukit Timah Nature Reserve, Central Catchment Nature Reserve, Labrador Nature Reserve, and Sungei Buloh Wetland Reserve.
[79] These are the Botanic Gardens and Fort Canning Park.

(e) to exhibit objects illustrative of the life sciences, applied sciences, history, technology and industry;

(f) to promote the study, research and dissemination of knowledge in botany, hor-
ticulture, biotechnology, arboriculture, landscape architecture, parks and recreation management and natural and local history;

(g) to provide, manage and promote recreational, cultural, historical, research
and educational facilities and resources in national parks, nature reserves
and parklands and encourage their full and proper use by members of the
public;

(h) to advise the Government on all matters relating to nature conservation and the
planning, development and management of the green areas; and

(i) to carry out such other functions and duties as are imposed upon the Board by
or under this Act or any other written law.

Section 24 regulates the conduct of visitors to the park, listing various prohibited activities. Through the years, NParks and its predecessors have developed a highly efficient
system of maintenance and management for some 1,763 hectares of parks, connectors,
and open spaces, including some 300 parks and playgrounds. NParks also manages
3,326 hectares of nature reserves and 4,278 hectares of roadside greenery and vacant
state land. Despite competing land needs, space has been set aside for parks, trees, and
greenery. Under the Concept Plan 2001, 4400 hectares of parkland will be set aside when
Singapore's population reaches 5.5 million.

Within NParks, the Parks and Trees Regulatory Section (PTRS) is responsible for
the following:

- Securing roadside greenery for all types of development projects
- Securing public open spaces in new housing developments and ensuring that parks,
  amenities, and landscaping are provided within these open spaces
- Securing greenery within the compounds of public development projects and ensur-
  ing ensure the landscaping of these compounds
- Enforcing the Parks and Trees Act

Mindful that large trees and tree-lined roads are a part of our heritage, NParks has
designated some 56 tree-lined roads as "Heritage Roads," fully appreciating that "the
preservation of Heritage Roads will add an element of permanence to the landscape
which will contribute to Singapore's sense of identity, history and continuity."[80] This
is complemented by the Heritage Tree Scheme, announced on 17 August 2001, under
which certain majestic trees can be designated "Heritage Trees" upon recommendation by a Panel.[81] A Heritage Trees Fund has been established with a grant from the
Hongkong and Shanghai Bank. However, the scheme does not have any legal status.
This will soon be resolved with the passing of the new Parks and Trees Bill,[82] which will,
inter alia, legalize the status of Heritage Roads and Heritage Trees when it comes into
effect.

---

[80] See "Heritage Roads," at http://www.nparks.gov.sg/nat_conv/nat_con-her_rd.shtml.

[81] See "Heritage Trees," at http://www.nparks.gov.sg/nat_conv/nat_con-her_tre.shtml.

[82] Bill 55/2004, read for the first time on 19 October 2004, at http://www.parliament.gov.sg/Legislation/
Htdocs/Bills/0400055.pdf.

NParks is now encouraging "sky-rise gardens" on rooftops, balconies, and the sides of high-rise buildings. This will, again, help reduce the heat plus beautify the environment for residents. NParks has even set up a Web site with tips on how this can be done.[83]

5.5 The Development versus Conservation Dilemma

While Singapore continues to ensure that it will remain "Clean and Green," there are considerable tensions between the need to develop and the need to conserve nature. For the common person, the links to nature have become more and more tenuous as Singapore's landscape has moved toward rapid urbanization. This prompted a leading botanist to write a paper, "Coping with Nature and Nature Conservation in Singapore," observing that for many Singaporeans, nature had become somewhat of a nuisance with which they had to cope.[84] But while the urban population is losing touch with nature, nature lovers are concerned that "green" Singapore is largely manicured, that too much of the "real" nature has already been lost, and that whatever remains is in dire danger.[85] Tensions have also been raised over a few development projects that were announced without discussions with the public or concerned NGOs.

One such incident arose shortly after the presentation of the Singapore Green Plan 1992 at Rio, which pledged to set aside 5 percent of the land for nature conservation. This was closely followed by its Action Programmes, which identified 19 nature sites and four coral reefs as worthy of conservation. But shortly after its presentation at Rio, there was a proposal to build a public golf course on part of the Lower Peirce Reservoir, a legally protected nature reserve. Considerable efforts were made by the Nature Society (the oldest nongovernment organization for the environment),[86] to save the reserve, including the publication of an EIA Report.[87] Fortunately, the authorities decided not to proceed with the plans, "for the time being."

There were other projects that were less fortunate. Ten years later in 2002 another major incident required strenuous efforts by the Nature Society, as well as the National Institute of Education, the Raffles Museum of Biodiversity Research, NParks, and many other nature lovers. This was to save Chek Jawa, a pristine marine habitat with six ecosystems on a short stretch of shoreline in the island of Pulau Ubin. Chek Jawa had been slated for reclamation.[88] As with the case of the Lower Peirce Reservoir, the proposal was halted at the very last moment. In both cases, the projects were halted "for the time

---

[83] See http://www.nparks.gov.sg/gardencity/start_skyrise.shtml.

[84] Wee Yeow Chin, "Coping with Nature and Nature Conservation in Singapore," Proceedings: *Environmental Issues, Development and Conservation, 1993*. Wee was a past President of the Nature Society and an associate professor of botany at the National University of Singapore.

[85] Ho Hua Chew, "Nature Areas Face Great Uncertainty in Future," *Nature Watch*, July–September 2003, pp. 16–19.

[86] The Nature Society of Singapore (NSS) is one of the oldest NGOs in Singapore. Dedicated to the study, conservation, and enjoyment of the natural heritage in Singapore, Malaysia, and the surrounding regions, it has roots that can be traced to 1940, when it began as the Malayan Nature Society (MNS). The Singapore Branch of the MNS was established in 1954 and it separated from MNS in 1992 to form the NSS. See http://www.post1.com/home/naturesingapore.

[87] Proposed Golf Course at Lower Peirce Reservoir – an Environmental Impact Assessment, 1992, Nature Society of Singapore.

[88] See http://habitatnews.nus.edu.sg/news/chekjawa/defer.htm.
http://habitatnews.nus.edu.sg/news/chekjawa/ria.

being," leaving open the possibility that these areas may be developed sometime in the future.

To date, only a handful of the 19 sites listed under the 1992 Green Plan have legal protection under the National Parks Act, and none of the marine areas is legally protected as an ecosystem.[89] After the release of the Master Plan 2003, several nature areas, including the four marine sites identified in the 1992 Green Plan, were not included in the URA's "Special and Detailed Control Plan," which lists nature sites for protection. The Nature Society has counterproposed that the areas that have been omitted should also appear as Nature Areas in the Control Plan, but with the caveat that plans that will affect their long-term survival may be formulated for their future development. The Society has renewed its call for environmental impact assessments.[90]

6 EVALUATION

While the tensions regarding conservation of natural areas and the prerogative of the government to plan for future developments remain, it cannot be denied that valiant efforts have been made to reduce pollution, clean up the environment, and improve the living environment of the people of Singapore and that these efforts have, by and large, been very successful.

It is clear that Singapore's success in managing its environment is due to the foresight and leadership of its political leaders, particularly the first Prime Minister, Lee Kuan Yew (now designated Minister Mentor), and the competence of its civil servants. Together they have devised a system of environmental governance and management that is sound and workable. The system has, by and large, worked extremely well, particularly in the management of the "brown" issues relating to pollution. While the government has made considerable efforts to involve members of the public, particularly in the deliberations on the Green Plan and the discussions on the Concept Plan and the revisions of the Master Plan, it is submitted that despite these efforts, the involvement of the public is still inadequate, as the final product of these deliberations is crafted by the authorities without further input from members of the various committees.

Agenda 21 calls for a true "partnership" between the government and its people. Chapter 27 of Agenda 21 reads as follows:

> 27.3. Non-governmental organizations, including those non-profit organizations representing groups addressed in the present section of Agenda 21, possess well-established and diverse experience, expertise and capacity in fields which will be of particular importance to the implementation and review of environmentally sound and socially responsible sustainable development, as envisaged throughout Agenda 21. The community of non-governmental organizations, therefore, offers a global network that should be tapped, enabled and strengthened in support of efforts to achieve these common goals.
>
> 27.4. To ensure that the full potential contribution of non-governmental organizations is realized, the fullest possible communication and cooperation between

---

[89] Lye Lin Heng, "Legal Protection of the Natural Environment," *State of the Natural Environment in Singapore*, Clive Briffett and Ho Hua Chew, Eds., Nature Society Singapore, June 1999.

[90] Ho Hua Chew, *supra* note 85. See a list of all the publications and reports prepared by the Nature Society's Conservation Group, at http://www.nss.org.sg/conservationsingapore/page9.html.

international organizations, national and local governments and non-governmental organizations should be promoted in institutions mandated, and programmes designed to carry out Agenda 21. Non-governmental organizations will also need to foster cooperation and communication among themselves to reinforce their effectiveness as actors in the implementation of sustainable development.

Agenda 21 goes on to provide the following:

27.5. Society, Governments and international bodies should develop mechanisms to allow non-governmental organizations to play their partnership role responsibly and effectively in the process of environmentally sound and sustainable development.

27.6. With a view to strengthening the role of non-governmental organizations as social partners, the United Nations system and Governments should initiate a process, in consultation with non-governmental organizations, to review formal procedures and mechanisms for the involvement of these organizations at all levels from policy-making and decision-making to implementation.

27.7. By 1995, a mutually productive dialogue should be established at the national level between all Governments and non-governmental organizations and their self-organized networks to recognize and strengthen their respective roles in implementing environmentally sound and sustainable development.

27.8. Governments and international bodies should promote and allow the participation of non-governmental organizations in the conception, establishment and evaluation of official mechanisms and formal procedures designed to review the implementation of Agenda 21 at all levels.

In the light of Agenda 21, a greater role should be accorded to members of the public, particularly civil societies and institutions with special expertise such as the Nature Society (particularly its Conservation Group, Bird Group, and Marine Conservation Group), the Singapore Biological Society, the Singapore Environment Council, and the Asia–Pacific Centre for Environmental Law. These groups should be seen as true partners with the government in their efforts at protecting and preserving the environment, involved not just in policymaking, but also in decision making and implementation, as stated in Chapter 27.6 of Agenda 21.

It is also time to have a law mandating environmental impact assessments (EIAs). First, such a law, if properly drafted, will not slow the decision-making process, as is feared by the authorities. Strict time limits can and should be set for the public to give their comments. Second, it can be argued that applying the concept of the public trust, the authorities are in the position of Public Trustees of the land in Singapore, for present and future generations of Singaporeans. As trustees, the authorities should therefore be given the fullest assistance possible, to enable them to make fully informed decisions on the impact of any proposed development project on the environment. Properly prepared EIAs can provide them with the fullest information possible, from all dimensions and perspectives, and should therefore be viewed positively, as assisting them in making the right decisions. The controversies over the proposed reclamation of Chek Jawa would not have arisen had a proper EIA law had been in place. Indeed, considerable damage had been done to the site by hosts of visitors taking souvenirs, before the proposed reclamation was halted at the very last minute.

Singapore today has a new Prime Minister. Lee Hsien Loong, son of the first Prime Minister Lee, became the new leader of the government on 12 August 2004, taking over from the former Prime Minister, Goh Chok Tong. The new PM Lee has called for a change, a "fresh new bold approach" that will "take Singapore another step forward, another level higher":

> [We] can't stand still because the world is changing, our people are changing and so must Singapore and so must the way we govern Singapore. To succeed, we have to balance between continuity and change, keeping what is still working and good and strong in our system, which is a lot, and changing the part which is obsolete, discarding the part which is no longer relevant, inventing new pieces, new ideas to deal with new problems and to take advantage of new opportunities and to develop new strengths and strategies to thrive in a different world. We can never afford to be satisfied with the status quo, even if we are still okay, even if our policies are still working. People say, "If it ain't broke, don't fix it." I say, if it ain't broke, better maintain it, lubricate it, inspect it, replace it, upgrade it, try something better and make it work better than before.
>
> We also need, as a government, to encourage participation and debate. We have opened up over the years. We've got the Speakers' Corner. We've allowed a lot more discussion. If you read the newspapers, what the newspapers write, the columnists, the Forum Page writers, the degree of debate is much more than we used to have, or in Parliament. But I think we can go further.[91]

Will this approach give a greater voice to the community in environmental matters? It remains to be seen, but the road ahead holds considerable promise.

---

[91] National Day Speech by Prime Minister Lee Hsien Loong, 22 August 2004, http://www.gov.sg/nd/ND04.htm.

22 The Law and Preparation of Environmental Management Plans for Sustainable Development in Thailand

Sunee Mallikamarl and Nuntapol Karnchanawat

1 ENVIRONMENTAL MANAGEMENT PLANS AT THE INTERNATIONAL LEVEL

The environment has recently become an important agenda to the world community, so much so that the first United Nations (UN) Conference on Human Environment held at Stockholm, Sweden, in June 1972, was participated in by many countries worldwide. The Stockholm Conference produced 106 recommendations and 26 Principles under the Stockholm Declaration (1972), which led to the establishment of the United Nations Environment Program (UNEP) and the Environment Fund. It should be noted that in the said Conference, no agenda on international environmental management had been included, although its mechanisms could help prevent, rectify, and alleviate environmental problems.

In 1992, the United Nations convened the United Nations Conference on Environment and Development (UNCED, or the Earth Summit), at Rio de Janeiro, Brazil, 3–14 June 1992. It was the largest environmental conference ever organized by the UN with over 30,000 participants, 103 of whom were at the level of Heads of State or Government and high-ranking officials representing 176 countries.[1]

The Conference produced the Rio Declaration on Environment and Development and Agenda 21, which is the first international environmental management plan widely adopted by countries around the globe. Under Agenda 21, a country's development will proceed jointly with proper environmental management under the concept of sustainable development. In its large part, Agenda 21 proposes concrete implementation of sustainable environmental management in harmony with the 27 Principles of the Rio Declaration. Agenda 21 consists of four major parts[2] as follows:

> Part 1: *Social and Economic Dimension*: International Cooperation, Combating Poverty, Changing Consumption Patterns, Population and Sustainability, Protecting and Promoting Human Health, Sustainable Human Settlements, and Making Decisions for Sustainable Development

---

[1] Peter H. Sand, "UNCED and the Development of International Law," *Yearbook of International Law* (1992), p. 3.

[2] Nicholas A. Robinson, editor, *Agenda 21: Earth's Action Plan*. In *IUCN Environmental Policy & Law Paper No. 27*, New York: Oceana Publications, Inc. 1993.

This chapter is part of a research project entitled "*Changwat* Action Plans for Environmental Quality Management: *Changwat* Khon Kaen," Ministry of Natural Resources and Environment, Thailand, with support from the Danish International Development Agency.

Part 2: *Conservation and Management of Resources*: Protection of Atmosphere, Managing Land Sustainably, Combating Deforestation, Combating Desertification and Drought, Sustainable Mountain Development, Sustainable Agriculture and Rural Development, Conservation of Biological Diversity, Management of Biotechnology, Protecting and Managing Oceans, Protecting and Managing Fresh Water, Safer Use of Toxic Chemicals, Managing Hazardous Wastes, Managing Solid Waste and Sewage, Managing Radioactive Wastes

Part 3: *Strengthening the Role of Major Groups*: Women, Children and Youth, Indigenous People, NGOs [nongovernmental organizations] such as workers and their trade unions, Business and Industry, Scientific and Technological Communities, Farmers, and Local Authorities

Part 4: *Means of Implementation*: Financing Sustainable Development, Technology Transfer, Science for Sustainable Development, Education, Training and Public Awareness, Creating Capacity for Sustainable Development, Organizing for Sustainable Development, International Law, and Information for Decision-making. Although not effectively binding under international law, Agenda 21 and the Rio Declaration play important roles in the present development of international environmental law. Being the principles and implementations arising from the consensus of the worldwide majority of States and international organizations, Agenda 21 is "soft law" ready to be developed into "hard law" at the international and at the national levels.[3]

2 ENVIRONMENTAL MANAGEMENT PLANS AT THE NATIONAL LEVEL

A national level environmental management plan is a plan prepared under the sovereign power of a country to be implemented in the country in which it is prepared. The plan will usually contain more details than its international counterpart, as it will be influenced by international commitments that could be in the form of the international environmental management plan mentioned earlier or by international environmental agreements (treaties/conventions) entered into by the member country preparing such national plan. Thailand's 20-year plan and policy for the enhancement and conservation of national environmental quality, in its preamble, also adopted the concept of sustainable development.

The following discussion focuses particularly on Thai and Danish environmental management plans, as the author and coauthor were researchers responsible for the complete study of the legal aspects of the *Changwat* (Provincial) Action Plans for an Environmental Quality Management Project at the province of Khon Kaen. Based on the principles applicable to Danish Spatial Planning, this Project aimed to develop integrated development tools for environmental quality management plans as well as development plans at *Changwat* or provincial levels.

2.1 Thailand's Environmental Management Plan

Section 4 of the Government Administration Act, B.E. 2534 (A.D. 1991), divides Thailand's government administration into three segments: (1) Central Administration:

---

[3] Nuntapol Karnchanawat, "Concept of Sustainable Development in International Environmental Law: Case Study of the Convention on Biological Diversity 1992" (Master's Degree Dissertation in Law, Chulalongkorn University Graduate School, 1999), pp. 71–76.

Ministries and Departments; (2) Regional Administration: *Changwat* (province) and *Amphoe* (district); and (3) Local Administration: *Changwat* Administration Organization, Municipality, *Tambol* (subdistrict) Administration Organization, Bangkok Metropolis, and Pattaya City. Most plans, including environmental management plans, are initiated in the form of master plans by the Central Administration so as to formulate frameworks on which the Regional Administration as well as the Local Administration may base their plans.

Presently, Thailand has two types of master plans dealing with natural resources and environmental management: country development plans and environmental management plans.

Country Development Plans

National Economic and Social Development Plan. The development of Thailand follows the National Economic and Social Development Plan (NESDP), a five-year plan that provides optimal facilities for the country's development. The first NESDP was formulated in B.E. 2504 (A.D. 1961) under the supervision of the World Bank. The Plan covers the country's development in various fields, including the management of natural resources and the environment. From 1961 to 2001, Thailand implemented eight NESDPs. Thailand is currently implementing its Ninth NESDP (B.E. 2545–2549/A.D. 2002–2006). This Plan clearly expressed the necessity for the implementation of the concept of sustainable development and self-sufficiency – these appear in every part of the Plan – in its Preamble, vision of development, objectives, and goals, as well as in the strategies for the economic and social development of the country.

Five-Year *Changwat* Development Plan, Five-Year *Amphoe* Development Plan, and *Tambol*/Locality Development Plans. These are plans prepared "side-by-side" with the National Economic and Social Development Plan.

The five-year *Changwat* Development Plan, the five-year *Amphoe* Development Plan, and the *Tambol*/Locality Development Plan are plans formulated under several major pieces of legislation, namely, the Government Administration Act, B.E. 2534 (A.D. 1991); the Regulations of the Office of the Prime Minister on Administration of Development for Growth Distribution to Regions and Localities, B.E. 2539 (A.D. 1996) (as amended by the Regulations of the Office of the Prime Minister on Administration of Development for Growth Distribution to Regions and Localities, No. 2, B.E. 2543 ([A.D. 2000]); and the Regulations of the Ministry of Interior on Development Planning of Local Administration Organization, B.E. 2541 (A.D. 1998).

The preparation of the *Changwat* Development Plan, *Amphoe* Development Plan, and *Tambol*/Locality Development Plan is presently carried out in an integrated[4] manner. For instance, all *Tambol*/Locality Development Plans within the same *Amphoe* are integrated to become an *Amphoe* Development Plan. All *Amphoe* Development Plans within the same *Changwat* are integrated to become a *Changwat* Development Plan, which shall be used as a master plan directing the development of each *Changwat*, *Amphoe*, and *Tambol*/Locality for a five-year period. It shall also be used for the preparation of the Annual Development Plan for each *Changwat*, *Amphoe*, and *Tambol*/Locality.

---

[4] *Integration* in the sense of planning means a planning procedure employing systematic brainstorming from all concerned to ensure coordination of planning at branch levels that would jointly achieve the main objectives or goals of the plan.

At present, every *Changwat, Amphoe,* and *Tambol*/Locality is under the five-year Development Plan (B.E. 2545–B.E. 2549) (A.D. 2002–A.D. 2006).

In perspective, this *Changwat, Amphoe,* and *Tambol*/Locality Development Plan consists of five major parts:[5]

> Part 1 – General Conditions and Basic Information of *Changwat, Amphoe,* and *Tambol*/Locality comprising physical, government and political, infrastructural, economic, social, natural resources, and environmental aspects
>
> Part 2 – Potential, Requirements, and Outcome of *Changwat* development during the latter half of the past five years.
>
> Part 3 – Vision and Strategies of *Changwat, Amphoe,* and *Tambol*/Locality development
>
> Part 4 – Nature of five-year Development Plans(Projects and Objectives comprising economic and infrastructural, social/quality of life, natural resources, and environmental aspects)
>
> Part 5 – Management and Administration to transform plans into implementation and assessment

Environmental Management Plan

Thailand's environmental management plan is provided in the Enhancement and Conservation of National Environmental Quality Act, B.E. 2535 (A.D. 1992), comprising three sets of policy and plans: Policy and Plan for (1) Enhancement and Conservation of National Environmental Quality; (2) Environmental Quality Management Plan, and (3) Action Plan for Environmental Quality Management at *Changwat* Level. It took four years before various plans under the Act came into force as the three plans are interrelated. According to the mechanism of the Act, the three plans are master plans establishing frameworks for other plans. One such plan is the Policy and Plan for Enhancement and Conservation of National Environmental Quality, B.E. 2540–2549 (A.D. 1997–2006). This law requires the National Environment Board to submit the said policy and plan to the Council of Ministers for approval. It was approved by the National Environment Board on 24 July B.E. 2539 (A.D. 1996), and by the Council of Ministers on 26 July B.E. 2539 (A.D. 1996).

For implementation, after the said policy and plan are given approval by the Council of Ministers, the law requires the Ministry of Science, Technology, and Environment (presently the Ministry of Natural Resources and Environment), upon approval of the National Environment Board, to prepare an action plan entitled "Environmental Quality Management Plan." The said plan may be a short-, medium-, or long-term plan, as appropriate. However, it shall include work plans and directions in the following matters:

1. Management of air, water, and environmental quality in any other areas of concern
2. Pollution control from point sources
3. Conservation of natural environment, natural resources, or cultural environment pertaining to aesthetic values

---

[5] The Sub Committee Coordinating *Changwat* Development Plan (SCCD), *Handbook for the Formulation of Changwat and Amphoe Development Plan during the 9th National Economic and Social Development Plan* (2002–2006), pp. 2–41.

4. Estimation of financing to be appropriated from the government budget and allocated from the Fund that is necessary for implementation of the Plan
5. Scheme for institutional arrangements and administrative orders by which cooperation and coordination among government agencies concerned and between the public service and private sectors could be further promoted and strengthened, including the determination of a personnel allocation scheme, that is required for implementation of the Plan
6. Enactment of laws and issuance of regulations, local ordinances, rules, orders, and notifications necessary for implementation of the Plan
7. Scheme for inspection, monitoring, and assessment of environmental quality by which the results of implementations to the Plan and enforcement of laws related thereto can be evaluated objectively

It should be noted that although the law authorizes the Minister of Natural Resources and Environment, by approval of the National Environment Board, to prepare short-, medium-, or long-term environmental quality management plans at his or her discretion, in practice, each environmental quality management plan in force has the same effective duration of five years. This is because four 5-year plans would fit into the 20-year Policy and Plan for Enhancement and Conservation of National Environmental Quality, and it may be for them to synchronize with the 5-year duration of each of the National Economic and Social Development Plans. No other reasons can be found for the five-year interval of the environmental quality management plan in effect.

Thailand is, therefore, presently under the second environmental quality management plan, that is, the Environmental Quality Management Plan, B.E. 2545–B.E. 2549 (A.D. 2002–A.D. 2006), comprising four major parts[6] as follows:

Part 1: Principle and Rationale, Present Situation, and Past Performance
Part 2: Vision, Main Objectives, and Goals
Part 3: Main Strategies Comprising Management and Administration Strategy, Natural Resources Conservation Strategy, Human Environment Conservation Strategy, and Pollution Prevention and Rectification Strategy
Part 4: Conclusion of Recommendations and Commitments

As a result, the implementation of the environmental quality management plan requires that it is the duty of the *Changwat* Governor to prepare an action plan/s for environmental quality management at the *Changwat* level. This can be considered in two cases:

Case I. A *Changwat* in which there is a locality designated as an environmentally protected area or as a pollution control area.

It shall be the duty of the Governor of such *Changwat* to formulate an action plan for environmental quality management at *Changwat* level, and submit it to the National Environment Board for approval, within 120 days from the date on which the Governor of that *Changwat* is directed by the National Environmental Board to prepare the *Changwat* level action plan for environmental quality management.

---

[6] Notification of Ministry of Science, Technology, and Environment re Framework of Environmental Quality Management Plan, B.E. 2545–B.E. 2549 (A.D. 2002–A.D. 2006), *Government Gazette* Vol. 119, Special Part No. 45 Ngor, dated 24 May B.E. 2545 (A.D. 2002).

In addition, in preparing a *Changwat* action plan for the pollution control area, the Governor shall incorporate into it the action plan for mitigation and elimination of pollution prepared by the local authority, and the local action plan shall form an integral part of the *Changwat* Action Plan.

Case II. A *Changwat* in which there is no locality designated as an environmentally protected area or as pollution control area.

The *Changwat* Governor may prepare a *Changwat* Action Plan, within the framework of and in conformity with the requirements of the Environmental Quality Management Plan, and submit it to the National Environment Board for approval.

As the *Changwat* Action Plan under this Act is an annual plan under the fiscal year and is prepared within the framework and directions of the Environmental Quality Management Plan, it therefore incorporates plans or groups of projects that are in conformity with the five major strategies of the Environmental Quality Management Plan, which consists of a group of management and administration projects, a group of natural resources conservation projects, a group of human environment conservation projects, and a group of pollution prevention and rectification projects.

Major essentials or elements of an action plan for environmental quality management at *Changwat* level are as follows:

1. The environmental situation of the *Changwat*: *Changwat* basic information, general situation of environmental quality (natural resources status, pollution condition, natural environment, cultural environment pertaining to aesthetic values), and major environmental problem(s) of the *Changwat*
2. Objectives of the Plan
3. Goals of the Plan
4. Directions or strategies in solving environmental problems of *Changwat* should be as follows:
   a. Efficiently and effectively prevent and rectify the incident
   b. Concretely practical and immediately implementable
   c. Acceptable to the general public and workable in practice
5. Plans and projects in accordance with the four groups of projects mentioned earlier

It should be noted that a project enhancing the capability of local administrations in environmental quality management has been implemented by the Office of the Natural Resources and Environmental Policy and Planning, Ministry of Natural Resources and Environment, to strengthen the capability of local administrations in managing environmental quality at *Changwat* level. The project is aimed at participation by local administrations in the preparation of the "Action Plan for Environmental Quality Management at *Changwat* Level,"[7] a five-year plan (B.E. 2544–B.E. 2549) (A.D. 2001–A.D. 2006), which is used as guidance for a five-year *Changwat* environmental quality management plan. The said project has been implemented in the area of 12 pilot *Changwat*. The said action plans for environmental quality management are not those

---

[7] Office of Environmental Policy and Planning, *Framework for Action Plan for Environmental Quality Management at Changwat Level* (Bangkok: Ministry of Science, Technology, and Environment), pp. 1–38.

required by law but are pilot plans initiated by the Ministry of Natural Resources and Environment.

What is interesting is the procedure by which the preparation of action plans for environmental quality management at *Changwat* level was done, in two major stages:

1. Transformation of policy and plan for national environmental quality management into implementation at *Changwat* level
2. The five-year environmental quality management plan at *Changwat* level, with emphasis on providing knowledge in two areas:
   a. Basic knowledge concerning roles or authority of local administration in the management of environmental quality
   b. Basic knowledge in the management and administration of environmental quality

Additionally, there are two approaches in the preparation of the environmental quality management plan at the *Changwat* level. Both are integrated approaches in which local people are given the opportunity to participate in the preparation of the plan with government agencies. The plans prepared by local administrations are also incorporated as part of the environmental quality management plan at *Changwat* level, in conformity with the decentralization of power under the Constitution of the Kingdom of Thailand, B.E. 2540 (A.D. 1997), with a mechanism for preparation of a plan closely resembling the five-year *Changwat* development plan now in effect.

In brief, Thailand presently has five plans related to environmental management as required by law, as follows:

1. The National Economic and Social Development Plan under the National Economic and Social Development Act, B.E. 2521 (A.D. 1978)
2. The five-year *Changwat* Development Plan, the five-year *Amphoe/Ging Amphoe*[8] Development Plan, and the *Tambol*/Locality Development Plan, under the Government Administration Act, B.E. 2534 (A.D. 1991); the Regulations of the Office of the Prime Minister on Administration of Development for Growth Distribution to Regions and Localities, B.E. 2539 (A.D. 1996) (as amended by the Regulations of the Office of the Prime Minister on Administration of Development for Growth Distribution to Regions and Localities, No. 2, B.E. 2543 (A.D. 2000)); and the Regulations of the Ministry of Interior on Development Planning of Local Administration Organization, B.E. 2541 (A.D. 1998)
3. Policy and Plan for the Enhancement and Conservation of National Environmental Quality, B.E.2540–B.E. 2559 (A.D.1997–A.D. 2016) (20-year plan), under the Enhancement and Conservation of National Environmental Quality Act, B.E. 2535 (A.D. 1992)
4. Environmental Quality Management Plans (five-year plan) under the Enhancement and Conservation of National Environmental Quality Act, B.E. 2535 (A.D. 1992)
5. Environmental Quality Management Plans at *Changwat* Level (one-year plan) under the Enhancement and Conservation of National Environmental Quality Act, B.E. 2535 (A.D. 1992)

---

[8] A *ging amphoe* is a district that has a smaller administrative jurisdiction than an *amphoe*, but has the potential to develop into an *amphoe* in the future.

2.2 Denmark's Environmental Quality Management Plan

Denmark's environmental quality management plans in accordance with the Planning Act, 1992,[9] provide for five objectives:

1. To provide appropriate development nationwide and in counties and municipalities, based on overall planning and economic considerations
2. To create and conserve valuable buildings, settlements, urban environment, and landscape
3. To continue keeping the open coasts as important natural and landscape resources
4. To prevent pollution of air, water, and soil, and noise nuisance
5. To involve the public in the planning process as much as possible

Planning is carried out at three levels in Denmark: at national, regional (counties and cities), and municipal levels in 275 municipalities. The planning legislation in Denmark is based on the principle of a framework of management and control; therefore, planning at any level must be in agreement with the framework established at the next level above. For instance, municipal level plans must be in conformity with regional and national level plans.

The Planning Act essentially contains provisions to ensure that the overall planning synthesizes the interests of society with respect to land use and contributes to the protection of Denmark's nature and environment, so that sustainable development of society with respect for people's living conditions and for the conservation of wildlife and vegetation is secured, thus the five aforementioned objectives.

Levels of Planning in Denmark

The three levels of planning are as follows:

National planning. National planning and legislation on major development projects establish an overall country framework for such tasks as protecting coastal areas and extending infrastructure.

The Minister of Environment and Energy is required to submit a national planning report to the Folketing (Parliament) after each national election. The national planning interests are specifically furthered through the powers of the Minister of Environment and Energy, who is empowered to issue binding regulations governing planning in accordance with the Act. This enables the Minister to establish legally binding regulations in the form of national planning directives applying to regional, municipal, and local planning and for the administration of individual cases, such as permits in the rural zones or exemptions. The national interests are also promoted through the power of the state to veto regional plans.

Regional planning. Regional planning implements common national interests, as it establishes the main guidelines for land use and infrastructure outside the urban zones in each region.

A regional plan determines for a period of 12 years the framework for the development of a region with regard to urban development, the overall structure of retail trade,

---

[9] Consolidated Act No. 551 of 28 June 1999.

the overall transport structure, protection of land and natural resources, recreation and tourism, and the location of large installations and enterprises.

In the City of Copenhagen and the City of Frederiksberg, the municipal plan also serves as a regional plan. Thus, the regional planning authorities comprise the 14 county councils and the Copenhagen City Council and Frederiksberg City Council.

Environmental impact assessment is an integrated provision of the Act that is based on European Union directives. The regional planning authorities normally carry out this assessment as part of regional planning.

Municipal planning. Municipal planning comprises structure and land use for an entire municipality with a special focus on urban zones. The municipal plans constitute the framework for the more detailed local plans for smaller parts of the municipality. A local plan must be prepared before major development projects are carried out.

A municipal plan determines the overall goals for the development of a municipality for a period of 12 years. The main themes are land use, transport, retail trade and other urban functions, recreational areas, and the protection of land and natural resources.

The municipal plan is not directly binding on the actions of property owners but can be made binding by the preparation of local plans. In some situations, the municipality can prohibit subdivision, construction, and other activities on the basis of the framework of the municipal plan for the relevant area.

Other Features of Land Use Planning in Denmark

Local plans. Local plans are for smaller parts of the municipality and are under the framework of the municipal plans that regulate the use of and development of each individual property and are legally binding on each individual person and property owner.

Production of plans. The main principles of the procedural rules on producing and amending the various types of plans are decentralization of the authority to adopt the plans in final form and ensuring of the public's right to participate in preparation of plans.

All proposed plans must be published, and the public has the right to submit objections and to propose amendments. In addition, the council responsible for the regional or municipal plan must solicit ideas and proposals before the plan proposal is drafted.

Regional and municipal plans cover a period of 12 years and must be revised every 4 years.

Plans do not need prior approval by an authority at a higher level. The regional and municipal authorities determine the validity of objections and proposed amendments. Nevertheless, when the Minister of Environment and Energy or a regional or state authority chooses to veto a plan proposal, the authorities must reach agreement before the proposed plan can be adopted. If the authorities cannot agree, the Minister of Environment and Energy shall decide.

Zoning and administration in rural zones. The national territory is divided into urban zones, summer cottage areas, and rural zones.

The main purposes of zoning and the provisions governing rural zones are to counter urban sprawl by keeping open land free of development projects and installations that are not necessary for agricultural purposes and to ensure that urban development is based on planning.

In general, subdivision, development, and other activities may not be carried out in rural zones without a special permit. The most important exceptions are the subdivision and construction necessary for agricultural purposes.

In summer cottage areas, residence (overnight stay) is prohibited from 1 October through 31 March, except for brief holidays.

Rural zones are transferred to urban zones or summer cottage areas through a local plan. The municipal council can decide to transfer land in an urban zone or summer cottage area to a rural zone, usually on the basis of the municipal plan.

Expropriation and takeover of property with compensation. The municipal council can expropriate property when this is necessary for constructing installations based on a local plan and for urban development based on the municipal plan. Property owners whose property is reserved for public purposes in a local plan have the right under certain circumstances to demand that the municipal council take over the property on pay compensation.

Appeals. Nearly all decisions made by the county councils and municipal councils pursuant to the Planning Act may be appealed to the Nature Protection Board of Appeal, which is also the appellate authority for nature conservation. Some of the decisions that are related to the plans and the administration of the plans can only be appealed on legal issues.

Spatial Planning in Denmark

Denmark utilized spatial planning in all three levels of planning: national, regional, and municipal levels including local plans. Planning is aimed at protection of the urban environment, and development is based on sustainable development under Agenda 21. Local Agenda 21 focuses on wastes, water, air, energy, transport planning, town planning, social, and occupation elements.

With regard to Environmental Impact Assessments (EIAs), the law ensures that large projects that are likely to have significant effects on the environment are subject to environmental impact assessment and a public hearing before being initiated.

Spatial planning is not only limited to Denmark but is carried out in the countries of the Baltic region. It is used for the planning of coasts, the urban environment, and the protection of the environment of Eastern and Central European countries as well as in several developing countries.

Denmark's spatial planning is its significant tool for national, regional, and municipal plans. The planning process involves analyses of geographical conditions, policy, plan objectives, and various regulations. It is necessary that geographical maps of relevant areas be produced and that analyses of plans for conformance to policy, objectives, and the law be made.

For instance, in an area where groundwater resources are to be protected from industrial pollution but the area is suitable for industrial uses, a conflict then arises. In order to prevent such problems, the planning laws should designate the area for industrial and other activities that do not cause pollution to groundwater resources. Spatial planning should therefore be considered.

Spatial planning is clearly effective in this instance. The geographical maps will display the location of the groundwater resources, which shall be designated as "ground water resource protected area," while areas for industrial works can be located elsewhere without affecting such a protected area. Spatial planning is therefore useful as planning is done according to area use. Other measures may be useful in protecting the groundwater resources such as afforestation. The essential principle of spatial planning is area analysis to determine size and location in order to determine the type of projects or activities desired therein.

Denmark's concept of spatial planning can be divided into four stages:[10]

Stage I: General policy, objectives of plan, and the law
Stage II: Spatial analyses and criteria of significance of the area (sector plan)
Stage III: Equilibrium of sector plan and the area designated for use or protection
Stage IV: Scope of law applicable to designated area(s)

The analyses require data and tools to display map information and Geographic Information System (GIS) spatial analysis, which can be detailed as follows:

Stage I – General Policy, Objectives, and Law

Normally, Danish law regarding the environment, nature, and planning, contains provisions for overall policy and detailed objectives of the law. The law empowers the Minister of Environment and Energy to make legislation within the framework of such law. In addition, the Minister is required to prepare a national plan highlighting vision and strategies, and stating the government's policies in regard to nature and spatial planning.

Stage II – Spatial Analysis

In preparing for spatial planning at the regional and municipal levels, significant elements of each aspect are taken into consideration as follows:[11]

Urban development. Urban development guidelines are as follows:

a. Urban development is effected only in special urban areas designated by the municipality.
b. The county prepares plans for future urban development (when the municipality is enabled to prescribe the urban limits).
c. Urban development should be done in the vicinity of an area where a city/town is to be built.
d. Urban expansion should be prevented.
e. Prescription of urban limits should take into consideration all factors affecting agriculture, groundwater, nature, beauty of the landscape, and cultural heritage.
f. Development of an industrial area is considered urban development. The environment should be taken into consideration when a future urban area is developed into an industrial area.

[10] Michael Kavin, County of Funen, Denmark, Seminar: *Spatial Planning as a Tool to Integrate Environmental Aspects in Development Plans*, Bangkok, 17 May 2002.
[11] Ibid.

g. All six elements shall be analyzed, leading to the preparation of a plan for the designation of areas for future urban development and eventually to legislation for such areas.

Afforestation. Elements that should be analyzed include the following:

a. Afforestation areas are designated by counties when government assistance has been granted to the projects.
b. National forest projects may be designated within the area for afforestation.
c. Designated areas should primarily be protected areas for groundwater resources.
d. A county shall designate afforestation areas only when they are not designated for other purposes, for instance, areas that are not scenic landscape, cultural heritage, or planned for other purposes.

The analysis would show whether the areas should be designated for afforestation.

Quality of surface water and wastewater treatment. Elements to be analyzed include the following:

a. The county's formulation of a plan for the use and protection of water resources, lakes, and coastal water
b. In the plan formulated, the county targets for water quality standards for water resources, lakes, and coastal water
c. Whether the municipality is going to invest in wastewater treatment system/s based on targets for water quality standards
d. Whether all wastewater from urban areas and villages will be treated by the wastewater treatment system
e. Whether the wastewater from households and out-of-village livestock farms will be cleaner than it is now

This plan will yield maps showing water quality targets and the prime areas from which household and out-of-village livestock farm wastewater will be treated. This has an impact on the investment directions and on the laws that must be passed. This information will be used by the municipality in the formulation of the investment plan for wastewater treatment systems.

2.3 Regional Planning in Denmark

Denmark's regional planning under the Planning Act contains the following elements:

1. Urban development
2. Rural area development
3. Agriculture
4. Recreation and tourism
5. Afforestation
6. New wetlands
7. Exploitation of ores and minerals (including sand, mud, gravels)
8. Public utilities and installation techniques
9. Use and protection of groundwater resources

10. Use and protection of water resources, lakes, and coastal water
11. Protection of biological diversity

As discussed, Denmark's spatial planning depends largely on geographical maps. In this regard, Denmark designates the land use activities of private and public sectors from eight maps, as follows:

Map 1 Urban Development, Tourism, Recreation, and Infrastructure
Map 2 Afforestation
Map 3 Landscape and Cultural Heritage (from the geological perspective)
Map 4 Nature (biological perspective)
Map 5 Noise, Windmills
Map 6 Groundwater
Map 7 Surface Water
Map 8 Water Treatment System (based on groundwater and water surface data)

3 THE APPLICATION OF DENMARK'S SPATIAL PLANNING PRINCIPLES IN THE PREPARATION OF THAILAND'S KHON KAEN PROVINCE ENVIRONMENTAL MANAGEMENT PLAN

For the preparation of the Khon Kaen province environmental management plan, the criteria, patterns, and procedures of Denmark's spatial planning were applied. This is because Denmark's spatial planning requires that the maps shall be in conformity with the law and shall not be in conflict with it. Khon Kaen's environmental management plan observed the same criteria, by analyzing Thai laws in the context of Denmark's eight maps. The only exception is part of Map 5, as Thailand does not have windmills. The analysis of Thai laws focused only on those related to land use and land management by private and public sectors.

3.1 Denmark's Map 1 – Urban Development, Tourism, Recreation, and Infrastructure (as applied in Khon Kaen province, Thailand)

The Thai law relevant to Denmark's Map 1 is the Town and Country Planning Act, B.E. 2518 (A.D. 1975),[12] in which various aspects of urban development are provided, covering existing zones, new urban zones, urban development directions, existing highways, reservation of highways, future highways, existing facilities, and future facilities.

The law defines "Town and Country Planning" as the laying out, formulation, and implementation of an integrated town and country plan and specific town and country plan in the urban or related area or rural area in order to construct or develop the urban area or part thereof or to replace the damaged urban area or part thereof so as to create or improve hygienic conditions, amenities, order, aesthetics, property use, public safety, and social welfare; to enhance the economy, society, and the environment; to maintain or restore places and materials with benefits or value in art, architecture, history, archaeology; and to maintain and preserve natural resources and scenic or naturally invaluable landscape.

[12] Ibid.

There are two types of urban plan formulations: the integrated town and country plan and the specific town and country plan.

Integrated Town and Country Plan

The Integrated Town and Country Plan includes the charts, policies, and projects including general controlling measures used as guidance for development and for the maintenance of urban and related areas or rural areas with respect to property use, communication and transport, public utilities, public service, and the environment, so as to achieve town and country planning objectives.

The enforcement of the integrated town and country plan requires the issuance of a Ministerial Regulation, which has an effective period of not more than five years. A Ministerial Regulation enforced in any locality shall contain the following particulars:

Objectives of laying out and formulation of integrated town and country plan

Map indicating boundaries of integrated town and country plan

Town or area chart(s) or map(s) substantially indicating some or all requirements as follows:
> Chart for land use as classified
>
> Chart showing open space
>
> Chart showing communication and transport projects
>
> Chart showing projects for public utilities

Chart description

Policies, measures, and methods for implementation under the objectives of the integrated town and country plan

The Ministerial Regulation that enters into force classifies all the land under its jurisdiction into different numbers in order to designate a color code for each area. The color code specifies the type of land and land use for such land. For instance, the Ministerial Regulation No. 432 (B.E. 2542 [A.D. 1999]) is issued under the Town and Country Planning Act B.E. 2518 (A.D. 1975), which enforces the integrated town and country plan in Tambol Ban Khaw, Tambol Samran, Tambol Sila, Tambol Daengyai, Tambol Nai Muang, Tambol Ban Ped, Tambol Bueng Niam, Tambol Phra Lub, Tambol Muang Kao, Tambol Ban Wha, and Tambol Ta Phra in Amphoe Muang Khon Kaen, Khon Kaen Province. Article 6 of the same Ministerial Regulation also, in its attachment, classifies land use and indicates communication and transport projects in different color codes as follows:

1. Land areas No. 1.1–1.15, designated as yellow, are for low-density residential type.
2. Land areas No. 2.1–2.11, designated as orange, are for medium-density residential type.
3. Land areas No. 3.1–3.12, designated as red, are for commercial and high-density residential type.
4. Land area No. 4, designated as purple, is for commercial and warehouse type.
5. Land areas No. 5.1 and 5.2, designated as light purple, are for specific industrial type.
6. Land areas No. 6.1–6.20, designated as green, are for rural and agricultural type.

7. Land areas No. 7.1–7.21, designated as light green, are for open space for recreation and environmental quality conservation type.

8. Land areas No. 8.1–8.44, designated as olive green, are for academic institutional type.

9. Land areas No. 9.1–9.18, designated as blue, are for open space for environmental quality conservation and fishery type.

10. Land areas No. 10.1–10.52, designated as light gray, are for religious institutional type.

11. Land areas No. 11.1–11.34, designated as blue, are for government institution, public utility, and infrastructure type.

12. Land area along the road in project type A and type B, designated as pink, are for communication and transport project type.

Thailand's Integrated Town and Country Plan is therefore displayed by different colors for the areas designated for different land uses. This Ministerial Regulation also prescribes in detail all 12 types of land use (which are not discussed in this chapter).

After an Integrated Town and Country Plan has been formulated by the designation of activities permitted in areas designated by colors, if it becomes necessary later to adjust or change the type of activities to comply with development plans, it can be done by amending the relevant Ministerial Regulation.

The Specific Town and Country Plan

The Specific Town and Country Plan uses the charts and projects implemented to develop or maintain specific areas or related activities in urban or urban-related or rural areas for the benefits of town and country planning.

Specific Town and Country Plans have a complex formulation process and require a greater budget than the Integrated Town and Country Plan, as a Specific Town and Country Plan deals directly with the details of land use. A Specific Town and Country Plan shall contain the following:

Objectives for the laying out and formulation of the Specific Town and Country Plan

Map indicating Specific Town and Country Plan boundaries

Town or area chart(s) or map(s) substantially indicating some or all requirements as follows:

Chart for land use classified by type, including boundaries dividing land into land use type and area

Chart showing communication and transport projects as well as showing details, paths, and dimensions of public ways

Chart showing projects for public utilities

Chart showing open space

Chart showing specification of ground levels

Chart showing location of places or materials valuable or useful for art, architecture, history, or archaeology that should be maintained or restored

Chart showing locations containing natural resources or scenic landscape or naturally valuable resources including trees or groups of trees that should be enhanced or maintained

Description and explanation of items in (c) including categories and types of buildings permitted or not permitted to be constructed

Requirements or restrictions in order to comply with some or all of the Specific Town and Country Plan objectives as follows:

Path and size of accessory parcels of land

Type, category, size, and number of buildings permitted or not permitted for construction

Type, category, size, number, and appearance of buildings that are dilapidated, unseemly, or hazardous to residents or passers-by that shall be ordered demolished or removed under the order of the local town and country planning administrative commission

Use of new building permitted to be constructed or modified not in accordance with use applied for at the time of construction permission application, which requires permission from local official

Type and plot of land upon which building(s) for various use is mentioned in Specific Town and Country Plan, as well as land area designated as open space for said use

Enhancement, maintenance, or restoration of places or materials useful or invaluable to art, architecture, history, or archaeology

Maintenance of open space

Enhancement or maintenance of trees or groups of trees

Demolition, removal, or modification of building(s)

Other things necessary to achieve the objectives of the Specific Town and Country Plan

Details specifying land or other immovable property to be expropriated as well as a list of lawful owners or persons in possession thereof, together with maps showing the boundaries of land or other property expropriated for the benefit of urban planning for use as highway(s)

Details specifying land or other immovable property to be expropriated as well as list of lawful owners or persons in possession thereof, together with maps showing boundaries of land or other property expropriated for other benefits of urban planning

Details and maps specifying land or other immovable property being public property owned or possessed or taken care of by a ministry, department, *Changwat*, local administration organization, or government organization, for use as highway(s) or for other benefits of urban planning

Maps, charts, or other details as are necessary

In addition, the enforcement of a Specific Town and Country Plan in any locality requires the passage of an Act with an enforcement period not longer than five years. The passage of an Act requires approval from the Council of Ministers prior to the process to obtain approval from the Parliament, after which the bill requires the signature of His Majesty the King, before it can be published in the *Government Gazette* and proclaimed as law. The process for the enactment of the Specific Town and Country Plan is therefore more complicated than that of the Integrated Town and Country Plan. The latter is within the power of the Minister of Interior by the issuance of a Ministerial Regulation. For these reasons, there has never been an enactment of an Act for the enforcement of a Specific Town and Country Plan in Thailand.

3.2 The Application of Denmark's Maps 2 (Afforestation) and 4 (Nature) to the Protection of Forests and Nature Areas in Khon Kaen Province, Thailand

There are four laws in Thailand for the protection of forests:

1. Forestry Act B.E. 2484 (A.D. 1941) – This is the main law controlling the activities of the private sector in regard to the logging and harvesting of forest products in forest areas. The last amendment, in 1989, saw considerable cancellation of logging concessions in national park areas and wildlife preservation areas. This has brought about positive results for the environment, reducing the rate of deforestation in Thailand.

2. National Parks Act B.E. 2504 (A.D. 1961) – This law designates certain lands as national parks, thus allowing forest lands to be used for public recreational and educational purposes. This law also protects national parks by prohibiting any person to hold or possess forest land or to construct anything therein or clear or burn such forests. It also prevents any person from doing anything that may be hazardous or detrimental to the soil, rock, gravel, or sand. No person shall close or block any watercourse or waterway. No cattle shall be let in or allowed into the forest.

3. National Forest Conservation Act B.E. 2507 (A.D. 1964) – This law designates certain forests as national conserved forests to maintain its forest conditions, forest products, or other natural resources. The law controls and conserves the forest by not allowing any person to possess, use, or live on such forest land, nor to construct, clear, burn, or carry out logging activities, harvesting of forest products, or the doing of anything that is detrimental to the condition of national conserved forests. However, this law is less restrictive than the provisions of the National Park Act, B.E. 2504 (A.D. 1961), in that a competent officer may issue a permit for logging activities or for harvesting of forest products. Besides, the Director General of the Forestry Department may issue a permit for use of conserved forests.

4. Wildlife Conservation and Protection Act, B.E. 2535 (A.D. 1992) – This law aims to conserve and protect wildlife and, at the same time, to accelerate wildlife repro-duction. Substantially, the law emphasizes the designation of wildlife sanctuaries for their safe harbor and conservation. In addition, no-hunting areas may be designated for any kind of wildlife.

3.3 Denmark's Map 3 – Landscape and Cultural Heritage (as Applied in Khon Kaen Province, Thailand)

There are two major laws that conserve and protect Thailand's cultural heritage:

1. Town and Country Planning Act B.E. 2518 (A.D. 1975) – This has been mentioned under Map 1.

2. Act on Ancient Monuments, Antiques, Objects of Art and National Museums B.E. 2504 (A.D. 1961). This law regulates the registration and notification of ancient monuments so as to keep, maintain, and control ancient monuments under the provisions of the law.

Once a land area has become designated as an ancient monument compound, the law on the control of building construction prohibits any person from constructing any building within the said compound of an ancient monument, except where a permit in writing has been obtained from the Director-General of the Department of Fine Arts.

3.4 Denmark's Map 5 – Noise Control (as Applied in Khon Kaen Province, Thailand)

There are three laws that control noise in Thailand:

1. The Enhancement and Conservation of National Environmental Quality Act, B.E. 2535 (A.D. 1992) – This empowers the National Environment Board to prescribe by notification the ambient standards for noise and vibration. At present, there are two notifications on noise: the Notification of the National Environment Board No. 15 (B.E. 2540 [A.D. 1997]) re: Prescription of Ambient Standards for Noise and the Notification of the National Environment Board No. 17 (B.E. 2543 [A.D. 2000]) re: Noise Level.
2. Public Health Act B.E. 2535 (A.D. 1992) – Chapter 4 provides that noise is a form of nuisance. The law empowers local officials to stop such nuisance taking place in a public place or on a public way as well as nuisance taking place in a private place.
3. Industrial Works Act B.E. 2535 (A.D. 1992) – The act provides that noise generated from factory operations must not exceed the standard values set by the Minister of Industry.

3.5 Denmark's Map 6 – Groundwater (as Applied in Khon Kaen Province, Thailand)

The law protecting groundwater is the Groundwater Act B.E. 2520 (A.D. 1977). Substantially, the Act deals with the designation of groundwater areas, prohibiting any person from engaging in activities that may have an adverse impact on the groundwater, whether or not such person has ownership or right of possession over the land within the groundwater area, except under a license granted by the Director General of the Department of Mineral Resources or his/her authorized representative. Another issue of importance is the designation of areas in which the pumping of groundwater is prohibited as such activity may damage or degrade the quality of groundwater, or may damage the country's natural resources, or may pollute the environment, or cause injury to the property or health of the public, or cause the land to subside.

3.6 Denmark's Map 7 – Surface Water (as Applied in Khon Kaen Province, Thailand)

The law protecting the surface waters of Thailand is the Enhancement and Conservation of National Environmental Quality B.E. 2535 (A.D. 1992), which empowers the

National Environment Board to issue notifications prescribing water-quality standards for any river, canal, swamp, marsh, lake, reservoir, and other public inland water sources according to their use classifications in each river basin or watershed.

At present, there are two notifications regarding this matter: the Notification of the National Environment Board No. 8 (B.E. 2537 [A.D. 1994]) re: Prescription of Water Quality Standards for Surface Water Sources, and the notification of the Department of Pollution Control (B.E. 2542 [A.D. 1999]) re: Prescription of Type of Water Sources in Pong River, Chi River, Mool River, and Lamtakong.

3.7 Denmark's Map 8 – Wastewater Treatment Systems (as Applied in Khon Kaen Province, Thailand)

There are two laws dealing with wastewater treatment systems.

The Town and Country Planning Act B.E. 2518 (A.D. 1975)

Here, in the context of the Integrated Town and Country Plan, different colors are designated for different land uses. Article 1 of the Ministerial Regulation No. 432 (B.E. 2542 [A.D. 1999]) provides that land areas designated as red are for commercial and high-density residential type; they shall be used mainly for commerce, residence, government institutions, public utilities, and infrastructure. Land use for other activities in this land type shall not be in excess of 10 percent of the total area of the same type. In addition, such lands shall not be used for specific activities such as for all categories of factories or industrial works, except for factories for the adjustment of the quality of a community's central waste. This means that central wastewater treatment systems and garbage disposal systems that are categorized as "factory" under the law on industrial works can be set up in any part of the red designated area. This law focuses only on land use without any provisions on the impacts on surface water and groundwater. The planners should therefore deliberately consider the appropriate location of the wastewater treatment system.

The Enhancement and Conservation of National Environmental Quality Act B.E. 2535 (A.D. 1992)

In regard to wastewater treatment systems, this law focuses mainly on the environmental impact that originates from the point source of such pollution, as follows:

- Requiring factories (for the adjustment of the quality of a community's central waste, particularly for refuse or unusable materials under the law on industrial works) to prepare reports on environmental impact assessment (EIA) according to the Factories Act
- Prescribing standards for the control of pollution from point sources for wastewater discharge, air emissions, or discharge of other wastes or pollutants from point sources into the environment
- Specifying the types of point sources of pollution that shall be controlled in regard to the discharge of wastewater or waste into public water sources or into the environment outside the limits of such point sources in conformity with the standards for the control of pollution from point sources set pursuant to Section 55, thus giving the owner or occupier of the point source of pollution the duty to construct, install, or bring into operation a facility for wastewater treatment or waste disposal system

- Controlling persons employed as Monitoring Control Operators or as Service Contractors for wastewater treatment or waste disposal by a licensing system

In addition to the various laws concerning the eight Maps as discussed earlier, in the preparation of the Khon Kaen environmental management plan on land use, the fact that a large part of its population is engaging mainly in agricultural activities should be taken into consideration. Maps prepared for planning preparations should therefore include irrigation areas and irrigation waterways, which shall also be in compliance with the Royal Irrigation Act of B.E. 2484 (A.D. 1941).

Not only must the provisions of law be taken into consideration in the formulation of the environmental management plan using the spatial planning technique, another consideration that should be taken into account is the government policy in the form of the resolution of the Council of Ministers regarding watershed quality classifications. Its objectives are to classify the quality of major watershed areas of the country and to determine the direction of land use and natural resource management for each watershed class so that they will be in line with the conservation of the environment and natural resources.

4 CONCLUSION

Denmark's spatial planning system, which has been applied to the Environmental Management Plan in Thailand's Khon Kaen Province, has helped planners to understand accurately the geographical conditions of the area and has, to a large extent, simplified the preparation of Khon Kaen's Environmental Management Plan. It has also helped the planners to determine the type of land use that would have the least deleterious impact on the environment, as well as to ascertain those areas that need protection, remediation, or rehabilitation of their environment and natural resources. For example, an area may require 20 percent of afforestation as the picture shows deterioration of its forests, or an area that is suitable for residential purposes can be so designated, and pollutive industrial activities prohibited.

Thailand's Khon Kaen Province has applied spatial planning to its Environmental Management Plan with satisfactory results, and its plan has become a model for many other provinces in the same region for the preparation of their plans. Spatial planning in the preparation of the Environmental Management Plan is well accepted by the National Economic and Social Development Board, which has granted financial aid to 20 provinces of the northeastern region, to implement this spatial planning model for its preparation of the environmental plan. However, this spatial planning model is a land use plan. Therefore, it is necessary to consider the existing laws that will support the preparation of the plan.

It can be said that this chapter presents a procedure for the preparation of Environmental Management Plans and land use to suit the geographical conditions of the area, and it can be seen as a guide for application by other countries.

23 Nepal's Legal Initiatives on Land Use for Sustainable Development

Amber Prasad Pant

1 LAND USE PROBLEMS IN THE HINDU KUSH–HIMALAYAN REGION

Nepal is one among eight countries in the Hindu Kush–Himalayan mountain region. The other countries are Afghanistan, Bangladesh, Bhutan, China, India, Myanmar, and Pakistan. The Hindu Kush–Himalayan region covers an area of 3.4 million square kilometers and extends 3,500 kilometers from Afghanistan to Myanmar.[1] It has more than 150 million people living in a geologically young and unstable topography, a fragile and deteriorating environment, in small and ever-decreasing landholdings. The population continues to grow at a considerable rate.[2] The mountain people in the region occupy 11 percent of the total area and depend upon agriculture for their livelihood. Their area is gradually shrinking because of new human settlements, urbanization, industrialization, and the building of infrastructure for new developments.[3] Thus, there is a big gap between the growing needs of the people and the land resources available for meeting these needs.

Another problem in the region is that the ecosystems are susceptible to soil erosion, landslides, and land degradation, leading to the rapid loss of habitat and genetic diversity. Mountain dwellers are facing problems of unemployment, poverty, poor health, and bad sanitation. Many areas are either seriously marginalized or turned into dry lands as a result of increasing desertification. Land degradation in the mountain region has caused many adverse impacts not only on the people at its source but also on people living downstream. Climate change has caused the melting of snow and the overflowing of lakes and frequent and intense floods. This results in sediment deposition in the plains. Because of the deposition of alluvial sediments in the lowlands of the Tarai, the tremendous variations of the river bed locations over a relatively short period of several decades illustrate the geomorphic dynamics of these alluvial plains. The increasing amount of river deposits that are observed in the flood plains of the Indus, Ganges, and

---

[1] See Executive Summary in Tang Ya and et al. (eds.), *Mountain Agriculture in the Hindu Kush–Himalayan Region: Proceedings of an International Symposium*, 21–24 May 2001 in Kathmandu, Nepal, International Centre for Integrated Mountain Development (2003).

[2] Tang Ya, "Poverty Reduction and Agriculture in the Hindu Kush–Himalayan Region: Some Emerging Issues," *id.* at 25.

[3] Tej Pratap, "Keynote Speech on Mountain Agriculture, Marginal Lands and Sustainable Livelihoods: Challenges and Opportunities," *id.* at 7.

Brahmaputra Rivers testify to the ecological vulnerability (mainly deforestation and soil erosion) of the upper regions and especially of the catchment areas.[4]

The problem becomes more serious when such depositions of soil and sediments flow into the seas or oceans. Such deposition of soils has caused rises in sea level, sinking of lowlands near coastal areas, as well as frequent tremors in the areas and created a small island in the Bay of Bengal through the deposition of soil. It has been said that frequent tremors have moved the Indian plate at the rate of about six centimeters per year.[5] Maldives, one of the members of the South Asian Association of Regional Cooperation (SAARC), has raised its voice several times at international UMS over the dangers of the sinking of low elevation areas in the Maldives because of sea level rise.

These issues show that the mountain areas of the region should also be of international concern. National and international initiatives are therefore equally important and urgent for its sustainability and should take into account the biogeophysical and human resource characteristics of the mountains and the natural and human processes affecting those mountains. The development of mountain areas without a proper understanding of these processes can lead to unsustainable development.[6] However, information and knowledge on mountain resources and the processes that affect them remain poor even today, and regional conventions dealing with mountain regions, such as the Alpine Convention (signed in 1991, entered into force in 1995) and the European Landscape Convention 2000[7] (in force 1 March 2004), have not yet been adopted in the Hindu Kush–Himalayan mountain region. Except for some studies made by the International Centre for Integrated Mountain Development (ICIMOD), the South Asian Cooperation Environment Programme (SACEP), and the South Asian Association for Regional Cooperation (SAARC), the eight regional Hindu Kush–Himalayan countries have been unable to cooperate and collaborate in adopting the Convention on Land Use for Sustainable Development. Thus, initiatives on land use for sustainable development are left to the individual nations in the Hindu Kush–Himalayan region.

2 BILATERAL ARRANGEMENTS OF NEPAL AND INDIA

Land use is intertwined and interlinked with water, forests, and other natural resources within and among nations. Any bilateral initiatives of Nepal and India on the use and sharing of water and inundation problems will directly and indirectly affect the land use systems in both countries. A permanent Standing Committee of Nepal and India on Inundation Problems was formed after the talk between the King of Nepal and the Prime Minister of India at the SAARC meeting in Dhaka in December 1985. Since 1986, the Committee has held 10 meetings to deal with cross-border problems arising from activities along the Nepal–India border. All these meetings have listed the serious

---

[4] Upendra Man Malla, "Geographical Features of Nepal and Conservation of Its Environment for Sustainable Development," *A Journal of the Environment, MoPE*, vol. 2 no. 1 (1997) at 12.

[5] *Id.* at 10.

[6] *Regional Collaborative Programme for the Sustainable Development of the Hindu Kush–Himalayas*, ICIMOD, Kathmandu, Nepal (Revised April 1995).

[7] Other mountain regions have launched initiatives, which include negotiations for the development of the conventions in the Carpathians and in the Caucasus, the Central Asian Mountain Charter, and the ICIMOD in Kathmandu. See International Center for Integrated Mountain Development, *ICIMOD Newsletter* no. 43 (Summer 2003) at 16.

problems in Nepalese land use due to the activities that have taken place on the Indian side, and vice versa. The Committee has tried to solve such problems at the local level on technicalities, without being able to establish the principles that should apply to the resolution of such problems between these two sovereign nations.

There are embankments, dams, reservoirs, barrages, and other features near the border of Nepal and India. Many such physical structures have affected land use in Nepal. Recently, Nepal has invited India to resolve the inundation problems created by physical structures in India in the Mahali Sagar and Rasiawal-khurd Lotan River channel – these have inundated large areas of Nepal including Lumbini, the birthplace of Lord Buddha. The physical structures on the Indian side of the Bajah, Sisah, and Marthi Sagar River channel near Kapilvastu in Nepal have also been discussed. It is realized, although not properly translated into action, that there should be an effective cooperative initiative between Nepal and India to resolve local inundation problems.

In the river water sector, these two countries have concluded some treaties for the use and sharing of water for consumptive and nonconsumptive use. While the Koshi River Agreement 1954, as revised in 1966, has safeguarded Nepal's rights of withdrawing water in Nepal, the Gandak River Agreement 1959 and Integrated Mahakali River Treaty 1996 are, however, not completely satisfactory to the interests of Nepal. This may create problems in the use of water for Nepal.

Thus, the bilateral problems of Nepal and India related to water inundation or any other areas that affect land use should be resolved on the basis of international norms and principles for the mutual benefit of both countries as well as for sustainable land use.

3 INTRODUCTION TO NEPAL'S LAND SYSTEM

Nepal (with a land area of 147,181 square kilometers) is a Himalayan mountainous country of natural beauty, spectacular landscape, rich biological diversity, extraordinary cultural heritage, and a mosaic of ethnic diversity. It includes two World Natural Heritage Sites, eight World Cultural Heritage Sites, and four wetlands of international importance. The country has over 5,400 species of vascular plants, including over 245 species of endemic plants and 700 species of medicinal plants, and 175 species of mammals, 850 species of birds, 170 species of fishes, 600 species of butterflies, 50 species of moths, and 180 species of dragonflies. These species are protected and conserved through nine national parks, three wildlife reserves, one hunting area, three conservation areas, and eight buffer zones covering 18.32 percent of the country's land area. Nepal's total land area accounts for 0.03 percent of the land area of the earth but accounts for 2.2 percent or more of the total biodiversity of the world.[8] This uniqueness has provided an enormous potentiality for tourism development in the country.

The physical features of landlocked Nepal are full of amazing variations, from the lowland plains to perpetual snowy ranges above 8,000 meters.[9] The Himalayan region comprises approximately 27 percent of the total area of Nepal, from 3,000 meters above

---

[8] *Supra* note 6 at 9. See, also, HMG, *Nepal Biodiversity Strategy,* Ministry of Forest and Soil Conservation (2002) at v.

[9] *Supra* note 4 at 11–12. See also Kashi Kant Mainali, *Political Dimensions of Nepal,* Radhika Mainali (April 2000) at 1–2.

sea level to up to 8,848 meters (popularly known as Mount Everest or Sagarmatha). There are altogether 13 peaks above 6,000 meters. Another area is the hilly region, which comprises 50 percent of Nepal's total area, ranging from 300 m to 3,000 meters in elevation. The hilly belt consists of rugged mountains with steep slopes, river valleys, lakes, and basins, such as Kathmandu Valley and Pokhara Valley. The Mahabharata Ranges lie in the southern region, passing east to west in the upper hilly area. Finally the Tarai region consists of the remaining 23 percent of the total land area of Nepal with extremely low elevations of 60 to 300 meters above sea level. The Siwalik land areas that are known to be synonymous with Churia land areas range from the northern border of the Tarai. The summer monsoon that lasts from May–June to September is a period of most natural hazards with frequent landslides and floods causing damage to farmlands as well as to the physical infrastructure.

The Nepalese mountains with valleys and plains provide unique habitats for the production of special medicinal and aromatic plants, fruits, and flowers. The mountain rivers provide hydropower (Nepal is second in the world after Brazil in hydropower potential).

However, the population of 23.2 million people with about a 2.27 percent growth rate and a stagnant economy has caused considerable environmental problems. Massive deforestation and shifting cultivation have had adverse affects on biodiversity, leading to the loss of plant and animal species, soil erosion,[10] and deterioration of soil fertility. In addition, the irrational use of chemical fertilizers and pesticides has poisoned and badly affected the soil quality. Some 3,912 village development committees of Nepal have found it difficult to use the rural land in an environmentally friendly manner. In the urban areas, it is observed that major environmental problems have emerged from unplanned urban development, rapid growth of settlements, slums, mismanagement of solid wastes and industrial effluents, roads, sewerage, drinking water, and pollution in almost all 58 municipalities of Nepal. In all respects, human-induced factors have definitely highly accelerated the degradation of land resources in Nepal.

Another feature of the land system in Nepal is that for subsistence living, a family requires more than one hectare of land in the mountains and about 0.5 hectare in the Tarai, depending upon the land productivity. However, the fact is that about half of the population has no more than 0.5 hectare of landholding.[11]

The latest physiographic data show that Nepal comprises around 427 million hectares (29 percent) of forest, 1.56 million hectares (10.6 percent) of scrubland and degraded forest, 1.7 million hectares (12 percent) of grassland, 3.0 million hectares (21 percent) of farmland, and about 1.0 million hectares (7 percent) of uncultivated lands. It has been reported that forest cover in the Tarai and hill areas decreased at an annual rate of 1.3 percent and 2.3 percent, respectively, between 1978–79 and 1990–91.

---

[10] The annual runoff of the Nepalese river systems is around 224 billion cubic meters of water. These waters wash away about 240 million cubic meters (or 1.63 millimeters thick) of fertile top soil annually. With the loss of soil, about 10,000 hectares of land in the mountain area have developed desertlike conditions. Land degradation in the highlands has induced sediment deposition in the Tarai plains with a rise of the river bed at 10–30 centimeters per year, causing a potential threat of shifting courses in major rivers and damage in significant areas of fertile land. See M. P. Ghimire et al. (eds.), *Combating Desertification: Report of the Seminar on Desertification and Land Improvement*, MoPE (4–5 November 1997) at 2. See also, M. P. Ghimire, "National Obligations and Initiatives in Implementing United Nations Convention to Combat Desertification," *id.* at 117. Also see *Biodiversity Strategy, supra* note 8 at vii.

[11] M. P. Ghimire, "National Obligation," *id.* at 117–118.

Table 23.1. Treaty obligations

Name of convention	Entry into force in Nepal
The Plant Protection Agreement for the South East Asia and Pacific Region 1956	12 August 1965
The Convention on International Trade in Endangered Species of Wild Fauna and Flora (CITES) 1973	16 September 1975
The Convention Concerning the Protection of the World Cultural and Natural Heritage, 1972	20 September 1978
Convention on Wetlands of International Importance Especially as Waterfowl Habitat (Ramsar Convention) 1971	17 April 1988
Agreement on the Networks of Aquaculture Center in Asia and the Pacific 1988	4 January 1990
Convention on Biological Diversity 1992	21 February 1994
International Tropical Timber Agreement (ITTA) 1994	1 January 1997
Convention to Combat Desertification in Countries Experiencing Serious Drought and/or Desertification, Particularly in Africa 1994	15 January 1997
Basel Convention on the Control of Transboundary Movements of Hazardous Wastes, 1989	18 January 1997

On average, both forested areas and scrublands have decreased at an annual rate of 1.7 percent and 0.5 percent, respectively.[12] Over the last 25 years, the crop production has increased by 79 percent, whereas population and cultivated land areas have increased by 83 percent and 62 percent, respectively. The increase in crop production is mainly due to the increment of marginal land.

In the past, Nepal has suffered from inappropriate land use practices, although some policies and laws were made to check it. Today Nepal has been unable to conduct elections of Parliament and local bodies because of problems of insurgency. The country is ruled by a government formed by His Majesty the King under Article 127 of the Constitution of the Kingdom of Nepal, 1990. Because of this situation, there is no effective local governance in land use for sustainable development in Nepal.

4 NEPAL'S TREATY OBLIGATIONS

As of today, Nepal has ratified or acceded to various environmental treaties related to land use for sustainable development. According to section 9 of the Treaty Act 1991 of Nepal, these treaties are more powerful than domestic law. Section 9(1) of the Act concerns treaties that the Nepali Parliament has ratified, acceded to, approved, or accepted. It specifies that when a matter in a treaty is inconsistent with existing domestic laws, the domestic laws shall be void to the extent of the inconsistency, and the provision of the treaty shall prevail as the law of Nepal. Hence, Nepal has an obligation to implement these treaties.

4.1 Obligations as a Party

Table 23.1 outlines Nepal's treaty obligations.

---

[12] *Biodiversity Strategy, supra* note 8 at 14.

4.2 Treaties Signed by Nepal

In addition, Nepal signed the Cartagena Protocol on Bio-safety to the Convention on Biological Diversity 2000 on 2 March 2001 and the following environmental instruments at the United Nations (UN) Conference on Environment and Development in 1992: The United Nations (UN) Agenda 21, 1992; the UN Statement of Forest Principles, 1992; and the UN Rio Declaration on Environment and Development, 1992. As a party and a signatory to the "hard law" and "soft law" instruments, Nepal has to meet its obligations for compliance. It will need financial resources and help in the building of capacity in every sector. It is hoped that many of these shortcomings will be gradually reduced with the maturity of our democracy.

5 LAND USE IN HISTORICAL PERSPECTIVE IN NEPAL

The present system is no doubt a legacy of the system that prevailed over several centuries. All types of land systems prevalent during the various historical epochs of Nepal are but a facet of feudalism because they were land-based both in the working and orientation of their economic and social structure.[13]

In the earliest Kirati period (early fifth century A.D.), a diffused structure of land-holding rights and tax raising authority was prevalent under which land was held by various clans together with tax-collecting powers on a permanent and nontransferable basis.[14]

During the Licchavi period (mid fifth century to late ninth century), rights over the land and all natural resources were vested with the king, and therefore it was the duty of the king to protect the land. It was during this period that land tenure and land were classified and different arrangements of tax, privileges, and concessions were made.[15] For the first time, the right to sell land was granted to individual land holders of all classes of people in the medieval period (879–1768). King Jayasthiti Malla (1382–1395) initiated the system of land classification into four categories based on the quality of productivity or areas.[16]

In 1768, Nepal was unified as a large country when King Gorkha Prithvi Narayan Shah conquered the Kathmandu valley. The Shah period (1768–1963) passed laws protecting the forests and land. The first Country Code of 1853 in particular was the first Codified Law that made provisions about land in detail. There were two different chapters providing rights to the owners of land in that Code. The local people were also given responsibility to protect and manage government forests. In 1934, the Forest Inspection Office was established; its operations continued until 1956. The modern period in the history of the land system was started in 1964 when the Land Reform Act was enacted. This defined the rights and obligations of landowners and States. Although the Civil Act of 1954 and the Constitution of Nepal 1961 had clearly protected the individual rights of use, purchase, or sale of land, it was the 1964 Act that made detailed provisions on rights and obligations of landowners and tenants.

---

[13] Rajendra Pradhan, " Introduction," in Rajendra Pradhan (ed.), *Law History and Culture of Water in Nepal*, FREEDEAL (2003) at 7.

[14] Prayag Raj Sharma, "The Licchhavi and Medieval Period Land Systems: A Sketch," *id.* at 64.

[15] *Id.* at 65–67.   [16] *Id.* at 72–73.

6 PLANS AND POLICIES ON LAND USE

6.1 Periodic Plans

Beginning with the First Five Year Plan (1956–1961), Nepal has so far implemented its Ninth Plan (1997–2002) and is now implementing the Tenth Plan (July 2002–July 2006). Although some sectoral aspects such as soil and water conservation, forestry, and environmental concerns were incorporated into the plan more precisely from the Sixth Five Year Plan (1980–1985) and the policy of an integrated approach was introduced by the Eighth Plan (1992–1997), specific mention of land use policy did not exist until the Ninth Plan.

The Ninth Plan for the first time emphasized the need for classification of agricultural land on the basis of land capability. The plan further stated the need to zone land for agriculture, forestry, residential, and industrial areas and nonagricultural purposes in order to maintain environmental balance and sustainable use of resources. The zoning of land, however, was not completed during this plan period, and therefore a land use project was established recently during the Tenth Plan for this purpose.

The Tenth Plan has additionally included the implementation of national land use programs, including: Updating Land Use Maps (1:50,000 scale), Preparation of District Level Digital Database, and Preparation of District Profiles. The Plan categorically emphasizes urban planning and sustainable land use in the rural areas.

6.2 National Conservation Strategy 1987

The National Conservation Strategy was submitted in 1987 and endorsed by the government as policy in 1988. It was the result of the extensive work carried out with the assistance of the International Union for the Conservation of Nature and Natural Resources (IUCN) Nepal. Since its endorsement, the environmental policy of the Government is based on this strategy, which emphasizes that sustainable development and conservation must be firmly linked with an objective to meet the needs and improve the quality of life of present and future generations. Hence water, land, and forest resources should be managed in such a way as first to enhance and then to sustain their inherent productive capabilities.

6.3 National Environmental Policy and Action Plan Integrating Environment and Development 1993

Nepal's National Environmental Policy and Action Plan analyzes the country's environmental issues in a multisectoral framework and sets forth the strategy for maintaining the country's natural environment, the health and safety of its people, and its cultural heritage. The strategy has the following main aims:

- To manage natural and physical resources efficiently and sustainably
- To balance development efforts and environmental conservation for the sustainable fulfillment of the basic needs of the people
- To safeguard the national heritage

- To mitigate the adverse environmental impacts of development projects and human actions
- To integrate environment and development through appropriate institutions, adequate legislation, economic incentives, and sufficient public resources

6.4 Agriculture Perspective Plan 1995

The government formulated the 20-year Agriculture Perspective Plan for improving the agriculture sector and accelerating the growth rate to about 5 percent per annum. The Plan aims to transform the existing subsistence-based agriculture to a commerce-based sector through crop diversification. The Plan's implementation strategy also involves streamlining agriculture research and extension in accordance with the Plan's priorities. The Plan focuses on limited inputs such as irrigation, seeds, rural roads, electricity, fertilizer, and appropriate technology. However, it does not give adequate attention to issues related to landownership, tenure arrangements, and potential impacts on soil fertility as intensive farming expands into the hilly and mountain areas.

6.5 Revised Irrigation Policy 1997

The Irrigation Policy 1993 was revised in 1997 in order to incorporate environmental considerations in the policy. The Revised Policy emphasizes the need for minimizing environmental impacts during the construction and operational stages of irrigation projects and proposes to design and implement irrigation projects and programs based on Environmental Impact Assessment (EIA) and Initial Environmental Examination (IEE) reports for sustainable irrigation.

6.6 Revised Forest Master Plan 1989

The Revised Forest Master Plan is another sectoral policy originally formulated in 1988 and revised in 1989 in order to incorporate community participation for forest conservation and for mitigation of problems related to land degradation. The Plan aims to protect land against degradation by soil erosion, floods, landslides, desertification, and other factors so as to maintain environmental balance and sustainability.

6.7 Hydropower Development Policy 2001

The Hydropower Development Policy provides that hydropower generation projects should take into account environmental considerations. It further emphasizes minimal average flow of water in rivers and rehabilitation and resettlement of people who were displaced for electricity generation, transmission, and distribution.

6.8 Water Resources Strategy 2001

While emphasizing sustainable utilization to ensure conservation of water resources and protection of the environment, the Water Resources Strategy provides that water resource projects should ensure water quantity and quality and meet appropriate standards for human consumption, recreation, and irrigation as well as for aquatic ecosystems, species, and habitats.

6.9 Industrial Policy 1992

The Industrial Policy liberalized the economic policy and prescribed strategies that minimize the adverse effect on the environment of industrial enterprises.

6.10 Wetlands Policy 2002

The Wetlands Policy categorically states that wetlands should be protected in order to provide habitation for diverse species as well as to maintain ecological balance. It aims to increase agricultural production by protecting wetlands. The Policy also encourages local communities to protect and preserve wetlands.

6.11 Biodiversity Strategy 2002

The Biodiversity Strategy aims for the protection and wise use of biological resources, ecological processes, and ecological systems. The Strategy emphasizes that all the ministries, the private sector, and the people have a role to play. It requires the creation of a National Biodiversity Unit as a secretariat, a National Biodiversity Coordination Committee, and a Thematic Committee for the effective implementation of this Strategy. It also emphasizes effective public information and education campaigns aimed at raising sensitivity to and awareness of the need for conservation of biological diversity and ecosystems.

6.12 Sustainable Development Agenda for Nepal 2003

According to the Sustainable Development Agenda, the goal of sustainable development in Nepal is to expedite a process that reduces poverty and provides to its citizens and successive generations not just the basic means of livelihood, but also the broadest of opportunities in the social, economic, political, cultural, and ecological aspects of their lives.

In order to achieve sustainable development as defined, the Agenda summarizes specific existing or new policies related to the following:

- Economic growth and poverty reduction
- Health, population, and settlements
- Forests, ecosystems, and biodiversity
- Education
- Good governance
- Infrastructure

Within the six policies, the Agenda emphasizes the devolution of authority to empower locally elected entities. In the area of land use, the policy emphasizes the taking of steps to minimize losses from soil erosion, floods, landslides, desertification, and other effects of ecological imbalance. It also requires local governments to prepare and enforce land use plans, so that integrated land use principles are followed, and encourages more effective interaction between forestry and farming practices to contribute to food production. The Agenda also emphasizes increasing the forest cover and biodiversity even outside protected areas. In addition, it recognizes the need to continue ensuring variability in crop species by traditional farming systems through participatory plant breeding, participatory variety selection, community seed banking, and indigenous knowledge systems. The implementation aspects of most of the policies related to these objectives are, however, not satisfactory.

6.13 EIA and Planning Guidelines

There are four guidelines that aim to minimize negative environmental impacts: First, National Environmental Impact Assessment (EIA) Guidelines 1992 make clear that projects illustrated in the schedules are subject to Initial Environmental Examination (IEE) or EIA. Second, the EIA Guideline for Industry Sectors 1995 requires that industries listed in the Schedules should conduct IEEs or EIAs in order to minimize adverse environmental effects. Third, EIA Guidelines for the Forestry Sector 1996 provide that any work or projects affecting forests that are stated in the Schedules are subject to IEE or EIA. Fourth, the National Environmental Planning Guideline 1998 provides that effective planning requires intersectoral collaboration, a participatory approach, decentralized decision making, and genuine devolution of authority for resource management to local bodies.

7 CONSTITUTIONAL AND LEGAL PROVISIONS ON LAND USE

7.1 The Constitution of the Kingdom of Nepal 1990

According to Art. 26(3) of the Constitution of Nepal, the State shall adopt a policy for mobilizing natural resources of the country in a manner that will be suitable, useful, and beneficial to the interests of the country. Further, Art.126 (2)(d) provides that any treaty with a foreign country with respect to natural resources and distribution in the utilization thereof has to be ratified, acceded to, or approved by a two-thirds majority of the members present in the joint session of Parliament. It can, however, be ratified, acceded to, or approved by a simple majority of the members present and voting at the House of Representatives if such treaty is of an ordinary nature that does not affect the nation extensively, seriously, or in the long term.

The important provisions in the area of environment are embodied in Art. 26(4), which reads:

> The State shall give priority to the protection of the environment and also to the prevention of its further damage due to physical development activities by increasing the awareness of the general public about environmental cleanliness and the State shall also make arrangements for the special protection of the rare wildlife, the forest and the vegetation.

Additionally, Art. 12(2) (E) (5) states that even the right to a profession, industry, or trade can be reasonably restricted by law on grounds of public health or morality. With respect to agriculture, Art. 26(5) provides:

> The State shall create conditions for economic progress of the majority of the people who are dependent on agriculture, by introducing measures which will help in raising productivity in the agriculture sector and develop the agricultural sector on the principles of industrial growth by launching land reform programmes.

The preceding provisions of Art. 26(5) are focused on land reform in general and agriculture in particular. The spirit of the Constitution reflected in Articles 26(3), 26(4), and 26(5) would be the basis for Nepal to launch land use initiatives for sustainable development.

7.2 Legislation

The Environment Protection Act 1997

The main aim of the Environment Protection Act is to achieve sustainable development in all areas. Any act or activity that is to be undertaken must ensure that such act or activity will not harm the environment or cause it to deteriorate. The Act has made detailed provisions for EIA and IEE as well as on the conservation of national heritage and control of pollution. It has also made provision for the closure of industries with punishment to the wrongdoer and compensation to the victim if the provisions are violated. Thus any work that will cause harm to land is not permitted under this Act.

Mines and Mineral Act 1985

The Mines and Mineral Act prohibits mining activities in any area of historical importance or where it is in the interest of the public welfare or national security to do so. The terms and conditions of a mining lease may include provisions of environmental protection or pollution control, including preventing soil erosion. This shows that this Act has an important link to the sustainable use of land even in relation to mining activities.

Petroleum Act 1983

The Petroleum Act emphasizes that any activities associated with the extraction, production, and distribution of petroleum and its products must be undertaken without, inter alia, causing damage to forests and other natural resources and pollution of the environment.

Electricity Act 1992

The Electricity Act states that the processes of electricity generation, transmission, or distribution must be conducted in such a manner that no substantial adverse effect is caused to the environment by way of soil erosion, flood, landslide, pollution, or other factors.

Water Resources Act 1992

The Water Resources Act categorically recognizes that the ownership of water will be vested with the state. Anyone interested in carrying out any project, other than for domestic use permitted by the Act, must obtain permission from the government before carrying out any water project for any purposes. The Act further provides that water should be used for beneficial purposes and maintained pure and clean without any deterioration or pollution.

The Local Self-Governance Act 1999

The Local Self-Governance Act emphasizes and empowers the local governments to manage natural resources and guides them in forest integration, biodiversity, soil conservation, land use, and environmental planning as integral parts of local development.

Organizationally it makes provisions for the establishment of local self-government entities at the district and subdistrict levels. The lowest level in self-governance units is a ward. The Act authorizes all the local units to formulate and implement policies, programs, and activities related to agriculture and land use, social reforms, and environmental and economic aspects.

Kathmandu Valley Development Authority Act 1988

The Kathmandu Valley Development Authority Act established the Kathmandu Valley Development Authority for planned development by providing essential services and facilities, which include water and sewerage facilities to the people. The Act also empowers the authority to launch land development programs including guided land development, land pooling, sites, and services for the betterment of towns.

Town Development Act 1988

The Town Development Act empowers the Government to establish Town Development Committees with the power to formulate town planning. The Committees are authorized to prescribe conditions for construction or any other activities in the area of forests, rivers, or watering places of the town. The Committees may also divide the town area into different land zones and may, within the policy of the government, develop various land use and land development techniques, which include guided land development, land pooling, sites, and services for the betterment of towns. These Committees have been established and operate in town areas.

Natural Calamity (Relief) Act 1982

The Government may, by a notification in the *Nepal Gazette*, declare a natural calamity-stricken area as a problem area and may give orders relating to relief activities.

Pesticides Act 1992

The Board established under the Pesticides Act has functions and responsibilities of controlling the standard of pesticides produced by private and government industries and determining the standards for pesticides. The Act provides for the issue of certificates of registration for pesticides that seem reasonably safe and for the competent, wise, and reasonable use of pesticides. The Act also prohibits the import, export, production, use, or sale of pesticides without registration and certification.

The National Parks and Wildlife Conservation Act 1973

The National Parks and Wildlife Conservation Act is the key legislation that governs the management of 17 different categories of protected areas and buffer zones covering 18.32 percent of the total land area of Nepal. It prevents activities such as hunting, mining, cutting or removal of trees, and cultivation inside the protected areas without permission of the authorities. The fourth amendment in 1994 added provisions for buffer zones and empowered local people in the conservation and management of protected area. Recently, the government has decided to hand over the management of some protected areas to nongovernmental organizations.

Forest Laws

In 1956, the Private Forest Nationalization Act was enacted for the purpose of nationalizing the private forests. The legislature thought that nationalizing private forests would conserve the forests by preventing the arbitrary cutting of trees. The Act nationalized all private forests. This policy, however, created problems for the local people because nationalization of forests that were managed by the local people under their traditional systems adversely affected the quality of these forests. First, it gave no recognition to the traditional system of forest management by local people for their own needs. This resulted in conflict between local communities and the Forest Department, causing in some places a decline in forest quality. This Act could not stop the local people from continuing to exploit forest resources as they felt no obligation to protect and control their use of forests as they had done previously. Second, the Act continued to assume that the Forest Department could take effective control over the forests.

The Forest Act 1961 was later passed, with the aim of categorization and restriction of forests, defining the responsibility of the Forest Department and laying down the offenses and penalties. The Act was amended in 1978 to allow the government to hand over degraded forest areas to local government councils. But this did not give any power to local people.

The 1967 Forest Preservation (Special Arrangements) Act further defined forestry offenses and penalties and reinforced the role of the Forest Department, empowering the District Forest Officers to shoot wrongdoers below the kneecap if they in any way imperiled the life or death of forest officials.

As discussed, contemporary Forest Policy in Nepal combines the environmental objective of guarding against land degradation and deforestation with the promotion of social and economic objectives. The present Forest Act 1993 was introduced to incorporate people's participation and community management of forest.

Soil and Watershed Conservation Act 1982

The aim of the Soil and Watershed Conservation Act is to make legal arrangements in respect of the control of such natural disasters as floods, landslides, and soil erosion. The Act empowers the government to declare any area of the Kingdom of Nepal as a protected watershed area. The Act further empowers the Government to appoint Watershed Conservation Officers. If needed, the Government may acquire privately owned land for the purpose of this Act, and may also shift industrial, commercial or resettlement colonies from protected watershed areas to other places, or acquire land covered by such colonies. Another important provision of the Act is that in case any person desires to use his or her land in accordance with this Act, the Department shall make available for that purpose all the necessary technical know-how and services as well as necessary financial compensation.

The Act allows the developing of physical structures in various forms in order to conserve the soil and watershed areas. It also provides that the Government may impose obligations on landowners to use their land for specified purposes with a view to conserving soil in the area. Because of the difficulty of redressing the rights of the owners and/or tenants of the land, the Government is to date unable to declare any area as a soil and watershed conservation area. The Department of Soil and Watershed Conservation has, however, launched several programs and projects for this purpose. They include a land use project to classify land into different zones for different uses and a community soil conservation program through films, broadcasts, publications, education, exhibitions, and training to farmers, women, and user groups.

Land Laws

Development of a comprehensive system of national, district, and local land use planning starts with the preparation of resource surveying and cartography mapping, which is provided by the Land (Survey and Measurement) Act 1961. The other laws on land use include the Land Reform Act 1964 and the Land Revenue Act 1977. These Acts prohibit registration of government lands in private names and cultivation of any public land or State Forest Area. Similarly, the Pasture Land Nationalization Act 1974 restricted private appropriation of pastureland and the government nationalized all pasturelands and reserved them for cattle grazing in pursuance of the Act.

The Land Revenue Act 1977 prohibits the registration in any private person's name of any land that is traditionally used as grazing meadow, graveyard, crematorium, water spout, or public pond and its bank and sources of water. Similarly, any land situated within the State Forest Area or undemarcated forest land or any barren or unregistered cultivated land situated within the first, should not be registered in a private name. Any such registration of land in private names shall be deemed void *ab initio.*

According to the Land Reform Act 1964, the government is empowered to issue directives and provide the necessary facilities to cultivate land in specified areas according to the prescribed manner and methodology, and to plant specified crops. This Act was the most comprehensive of all past measures. It protected the rights of the tenants and abolished the tax-free land (*Brita*) system. Another distinguishing characteristic of the Act was the compulsory scheme, which required all farmers to deposit a portion of their produce in kind with the local ward committee. Later, depositing the cash equivalent was allowed instead of payment in kind. This scheme was, however, stopped later because of its weaknesses in implementation. This Act also provides that the tenant has to use the land so that the quality of land or production may not be reduced. If the quality of land is damaged or has deteriorated, the owner may remove the tenant.

8 RECENT DEVELOPMENTS ON LAND USE FOR SUSTAINABLE DEVELOPMENT IN NEPAL

The most recent legal initiative of Nepal on land use for sustainable development is the Fifth Amendment of the Land Reform Act of 1961. This Fifth Amendment was passed in February 2002 and added new Chapter 9 A with details on land use. Section 51(f) of the Act established a Land Use Council at the central level headed by the Vice-Chairman of the National Planning Commission (NPC). The other members of the Council are the Secretary of Defense, Secretary of the Ministry of Forest and Soil Conservation, Secretary of the Ministry of Agriculture and Cooperatives, Secretary of the Ministry of Physical Planning and Works, three land use specialists nominated by the government, and the Secretary of the Ministry of Land Reform and Management as Member Secretary. The term of the nominated land use specialists will be for two years.

This Council possesses extensive powers including the formulation and implementation of policies and programs, directives, and supervision. The Council is also empowered to prepare land use maps, to recommend the forming of local and district level committees, and to control every activity that disturbs the carrying out of land use plans and policies. The Council is empowered to arrange and categorize land zoning for the settlement, city, industrial areas, and other private agriculture areas located within the present municipalities and village development committees.

The Act provides that the Government may declare, by notification in the *Nepal Gazette*, any area for the purpose of utilizing such land for specified projects suited to the nature of the plots. It is also noted in the Act that any land declared for special use cannot be changed without the permission of Council. The Government has been empowered by the Act to stop owners of land from further fragmenting the land.

In accordance with these provisions, the Council started their work and had already approved land use policies by 2002. These policies focus mainly on land use management and maximizing crop productivity with a view to increasing the income of rural households. Some highlights of the land-related policies are as follows:

- To implement land use plans with close coordination among land-related agencies at both the central and district levels
- To carry out land use programs with a view to increasing crop productivity, environmental protection, and social and economic growth
- To help increase and ease the supply of basic needs such as food, fuel, and feed to supply them easily
- To discourage haphazard settlements and to allocate appropriate land for the settlements with basic requirements
- To classify land for the appropriate land use zones for the use of agriculture, forest grazing settlements, urban development, industrial estates, wastelands, wetlands, herbal production areas, and other uses

Yet another development is the National Land Use project set up under the Ministry of Land Reform and Management with guidelines and directive policies from the Land Use Council. This project has already started preparing and analyzing the database of some districts for the implementation of district level land use zoning programs. The main goal is to develop, implement, and monitor sustainable land use planning in Nepal with appropriate land use policies and land use classification based on the capacity of the land and socioeconomic conditions.

9 CONCLUSION

The preceding analysis indicates that land is not a static resource. Instead, it is constantly evolving, from the erosion of the topsoil to the changing of the landscape over the course of history. Thus, sustainable land use requires support, collaboration, and cooperation among land users and governments not only at the local government level, but at the national, regional, and international levels. It is against this background that this chapter detailed at its beginning that the time has come for South Asia to adopt a Land Use Convention along the lines of the Alpine Convention, 1991, and the European Landscape Convention, 2000. At the bilateral level, Nepal and India need to implement international principles more effectively for mutual benefit and sustainable land use.

So far as Nepal's initiatives and position are concerned, the many policy documents and laws described have indicated that Nepal is gradually attempting to empower local governments and local communities. However, this objective has not been achieved completely, and the Nepalese government continues to exercise control over resources.

The current situation has not improved because of political unrest and problems of insurgency. Hence, there should be a strong effort to normalize the situation and to implement a balanced approach in recognizing both the government and the people as equally vital in the governance of land use systems for sustainable development.

There is also an imbalance in approaching the areas of land use. Even today, Nepal's initiatives are more sectoral, as detailed. The existing land laws are generally designed to cover land administration rather than influence land use. It is submitted that attempts should be made to integrate all uses of land and then develop integrated and comprehensive policies and laws on land use for sustainable development. It is then possible to eradicate all conflicts, overlaps, and contradictions in regard to institutions, jurisdictions, and implementation and enforcement of laws and policies. The present practice is that most of the cases related to agriculture are filed in the office of the Chief District Officer (CDO), who is essentially a general administrator responsible for maintaining law and order and the coordination of administrative functions at the district level. Most Government departments and district offices have duties under different laws, each responsible for conserving soil, forests, water, roads, and other natural resources and infrastructure. However, there is still no coordinating body that is fully informed and keeps proper records of the work of each department or office. Moreover, there is poor implementation of policies and laws. Thus, there is a need for the creation of one implementing body with full powers so that there will be no duplication of authority. Reform and effective implementation of land use planning and management are much needed for sustainable land use in Nepal.

Another matter that should be addressed is pesticides. Presently, there are gaps in the existing Pesticide Act with respect to disposal of outdated and confiscated pesticides. The existing legal provisions do not address agricultural insurance and the disposal of pesticides, including chemical fertilizers and hospital wastes. So laws should be made regulating and controlling such environmentally hazardous products, which have deleterious effects on the environment. Nepal also needs to develop laws on agricultural and intellectual property rights. All these areas demonstrate an urgent need for capacity building in the crafting of appropriate Laws.

Finally, it should be emphasized that those who are the users of land should know the value of sustainable land use. There is therefore a need for education and awareness programs for the people. Effective local governance and the people's support for government plans and programs can produce positive changes toward the achievement of sustainability in the land use system of Nepal.

24 Environmental Law and Irrigated Land in Australia

Karen Bubna-Litic

1 INTRODUCTION

Australia's waterways are at a crisis point. This is evidenced from the amount of water-related "reform" that the Australian Governments have embarked on over the past 10 years. Almost all of the country's capital cities are currently under severe water restrictions and experiencing a drought that has caused unprecedented shortages of water for irrigation.

Today, in Australia, irrigated agricultural land has a gross value of production of $8.6 billion/year.[1] This land occupies 2.5 million hectares,[2] which represents less than 0.5 percent of the country's land and yet uses 75 percent of all of the water harvested.[3] Approximately two-thirds of the total agricultural production derives from the Murray-Darling Basin, which spans four Australian states: New South Wales (NSW), Victoria (Vic), South Australia (SA), and Queensland (Qld). Clearly, irrigation is important to Australia, but past practices have resulted in severe degradation of its water resources. It has been acknowledged in Australia that water resources are being used inefficiently, and overexploitation and unsustainable practices have resulted. The relevant legal framework has been far too complex with separate legislation in each state and no legal recognition of water sources crossing boundaries. There was no legislative limit on the number of water users in the irrigation schemes, so demand inevitably outstripped supply. The legislation was fragmented, with separate laws covering groundwater versus surface water. The laws required no consideration of environmental impact. Over the past 10 years, Australia has been undergoing major water law reform, but more focus on better management of land uses that impact upon water quality and water sources with high environmental values are still required. This chapter examines how the law in Australia can go some distance toward achieving more effective land use through sustainable irrigation practices.

The chapter begins by considering the historical background of irrigation in Australia. Part 2 identifies the legal framework applicable to irrigated lands in Australia. In Part 3, the structural processes for water reform in Australia are examined. Part 4

---

[1] Australian Irrigation Water Provider Benchmarking Report 2002/2003. http://www.ancid.org.au/pdf/290604/ANCID2004Summweb.pdf.

[2] Ibid.

[3] Cullen, P., "The Journey to Sustainable Irrigation" paper presented to the Irrigation Association of Australia Annual Conference, Adelaide, May 2004.

focuses on water rights and the criteria necessary to achieve healthy rivers and sustainable irrigation practices. Parts 5, 6, and 7 critically examine the current debate in Australia, focusing on irrigated land.

2 BACKGROUND

Australians have traditionally assumed that water was a completely free resource, that we could use as much of it as we liked, that droughts were an imposition, not an inevitable, and natural, part of our continent's environment. In the past, farmers saw nothing wrong in using water inefficiently, with open ditches used to irrigate broad acres. They focused on low-profit, water-intensive crops. And state governments handed out authority to suck water out of inland rivers with no regard for the environment. Sometimes more water was notionally allocated than ever existed. The result was long-term damage to the land through salinity and the death of native vegetation.[4]

Originally, in Australia, water rights were tied to landownership under the riparian rights doctrine, which states that the owner of land bordering water has rights to use that water as long as that use does not interfere with its use by other riparian landowners. There was no property in water itself under the doctrine, but there was a right of access to it, which was linked to the ownership and occupation of land.[5] When the irrigation areas of southern Australia were developed, water use was tied to land title. As such, large tracts of land had to be bought in order to secure access to water. Statutory systems entered Australia in the late 1800s with states' determining the right to use and control water in rivers and lakes.

Despite the ability of the states to regulate water use, there was a lack of understanding of the complexities of both surface water and groundwater in Australia, and this, coupled with Australia's agricultural thirst for water, led to many mistakes. The lack of understanding led to the overallocation of water through granting of too many licenses to take water from rivers and aquifers. Another problem was that the country's priority for water use was first to towns, irrigation, and other human uses and any water left over was described as "environmental water."[6] Water was thought of as an unlimited resource.

By the 1970s there were many weaknesses in Australia's laws relating to water resource management. For example:

- There were many pieces of legislation.
- These laws were dependent on administrative discretion, but there were no prescribed criteria to ensure that this discretion was exercised consistently and therefore there was no limit on the number of water users in the irrigation schemes. The demand for water thus inevitably outstripped supply.
- Laws and management continued to be based on the European concept of rivers, which was that a watercourse was water that flowed in a defined channel.

---

[4] Editorial *The Weekend Australian* 26–27 June 2004.
[5] *Embrey v. Owen* (1851) 6 Exch 353.
[6] Wentworth Group of Concerned Scientists, "Blueprint for a National Water Plan" 31 July 2003 World Wide Fund for Nature (WWF) Australia, Sydney.

- Legislation was fragmented; that is, groundwater was subject to a different set of laws and its management was not integrated with that of surface water.
- There was no consideration of environmental impact in the laws.[7]

Although there were many reforms to water legislation from the late 1970s to the mid-1990s, among the major issues during those reforms were the opposing demands of security for consumptive users and the growing awareness that water needed to be allocated to ecosystem needs.[8] There has also been a tendency to exclude unconfined or overflow water from the regulatory control of the right to take water, which focuses only on surface water and groundwater.

3 THE LEGAL FRAMEWORK

The structure of Australia's federalist constitutional framework, which assigns powers among the federal and state governments, imposes artificial boundaries on the management of Australia's water resources.[9] There is no power under the Constitution to legislate for water reform. It is the states that have jurisdiction over water and other natural resources. The Commonwealth (or federal government) derives its powers under section 51 of the Constitution[10] and there is no specific power within section 51 to legislate for water. There is only one direct reference to water in the Constitution,[11] and the intention of this section was to prevent states from extracting unreasonable amounts of water as it flowed through their territories. The Commonwealth has used various heads of power under section 51, such as the trade and commerce power (s. 51(1)), the corporations power (s. 51(xx)), and the external affairs power (s. 51(xxix)), to legislate with respect to water-management issues.[12] That related to trade and commerce may become a more active source of power if water becomes a commodity under a tradable water rights scheme. Section 122 allows the Commonwealth to make laws for the government of any territory, and under section 96, the Commonwealth can grant financial assistance to any state on such terms and conditions as the Parliament thinks fit. Funding the states through this mechanism has been one of the most successful ways in which the Commonwealth has participated in the management of Australia's water resources. The Commonwealth has linked the funding for states to the implementation of water reform policies.

In recognition of the fact that environmental issues were matters that needed a cooperative approach of the Commonwealth and the States, in 1992, the Intergovernmental Agreement on the Environment (IGAE) was established. This was an agreement among the Commonwealth, the six states, the Australian Capital Territory (ACT), the Northern

---

[7] Tan, Poh-Ling, 2002 "Legal Issues Relating to Water Use" in *Property: Rights and Responsibilities – Current Australian Thinking.* Land & Water Australia, Canberra, 13 at 19.

[8] Ibid., at 22.

[9] Fisher, D., *Water Law* 2000 LBC Sydney, Australia p. 35.

[10] Commonwealth of Australia Constitution Act 1900.

[11] Section 100 of the Constitution states: "The Commonwealth shall not, by any law or regulation of trade or commerce, abridge the right of a state or of the residents therein to the reasonable use of the waters or rivers for conservation or irrigation."

[12] See Tasmanian Dams case: *Commonwealth v. Tasmania* (1983) 46 ALR 625, where the Commonwealth used its power to prevent the building of a dam.

Table 24.1. Legislation in Australian jurisdictions and their first priority use for water

New South Wales (NSW)	Victoria (Vic)	Queensland (Qld)	Western Australia (WA)	South Australia (SA)	Tasmania (Tas)	Australian Capital Territory (ACT)	Northern Territory (NT)
Water Management Act 2000	Water Act 1989	Water Act 2000	Rights in Water and Irrigation Act 1914[13]	Water Resources Act 1997	Water Management Act 1999	Water Resources Act 1998	Water Act 1992
Environmental water	Stock and domestic rights	Not addressed	Allocated to environment first in allocation plans	Environment	Domestic and livestock, firefighting and councils supply for a water district	Stock and domestic	Not addressed

Territory (NT), and the Australian Local Government Association. The responsibilities of the states and the Commonwealth are clearly set out in the IGAE. The guiding objective of the Agreement is that of ecologically sustainable development,[14] which encompasses the precautionary principle,[15] intergenerational equity,[16] conservation of biological diversity and ecological integrity,[17] and improved valuation, pricing, and incentive mechanisms.[18] After the IGAE, four new strategies, which all had implications for water resource management, were developed.[19] Despite all of these strategies, what really accelerated the water reform process in Australia was the policy reform process initiated through the establishment of the Council of Australian Governments (COAG) in 1992. See Section 4 for details of this policy reform process.

This chapter examines water management in all of the Australian jurisdictions. The current legislation in each of the Australian jurisdictions and their first priority use for water are listed in Table 24.1. It should be noted that not all parts of the Australian jurisdictions are governed by water rights. In Queensland, the extraction of groundwater is restricted only when a Water Resource Plan (WRP) is prepared or the subartesian basin is declared.[20] In South Australia, in nonprescribed areas, owners or occupiers of land can take an unlimited volume of water from either surface or groundwater sources.[21] However, in order to protect the water source when it is in danger of overuse and degradation, its use can be prescribed through the water rights regime, whereby its level of extraction will be regulated.[22] All other Australian jurisdictions operate under a system of water rights.

[13] As amended in 2000.

[14] Intergovernmental Agreement on the Environment (IGAE), para.3.2. http://www.deh.gov.au/esd/national/igae/.

[15] Ibid., para 3.5.1.   [16] Ibid., para 3.5.2.

[17] Ibid., para 3.5.3.   [18] Ibid., para 3.5.4.

[19] These were the National Strategy for Ecologically Sustainable Development 1992, the National Greenhouse Response Strategy 1992, the National Forest Policy Statement 1992, and the National Strategy for the Conservation of Australia's Biodiversity 1992.

[20] Section 20(6), Water Act 2000 (Qld). Under s. 1046 Water Act 2000 (Qld), a regulation may declare an area to be a subartesian area and regulate the types of works that can use this water. It will operate until a water resource plan is in place.

[21] Section 7, Water Resources Act 1997 (SA).   [22] Section 8, Water Resources Act 1997 (SA).

4 FRAMEWORK FOR REFORM

In 1992, to overcome the constitutional structure whereby the Commonwealth government has limited legislative powers, the Council of Australian Governments (COAG) was set up to reach cooperative agreements on matters of national importance. These include such issues as water, use of human embryos in medical research, national competition policy, reform of Commonwealth and State/Territory roles in environmental regulation, and counterterrorism measures. COAG comprises the Prime Minister, state Premiers, territory Chief Ministers, and the President of the Australian Local Government Association.

In 1994, the COAG embarked on a process of water reform to deal with the crisis in the country's water resources. They made the improved management of Australia's water resources a national priority. These COAG reforms[23] improved understanding of Australia's surface and groundwater systems and their management needs.[24] The 1994 framework allowed different approaches to emerge in different parts of the country in recognition of the differing circumstances and pressures throughout the country. This framework developed four major reforms:

- Establishment of water entitlements, which separate water rights from land title and provide clarity in terms of ownership, volume, reliability, transferability, and quality
- Acceptance of the environment as a legitimate user of water in terms of allocations and entitlements
- Enhancement and restoration of healthy river systems
- Implementation of water trading with trading arrangements that are consistent and facilitate cross-border sale where this is socially, physically, and ecologically sustainable[25]

Because of the recognition of the importance of these water reforms as an integral part of microeconomic reform, they were tied to a package of payments by the Federal Government under the National Competition Policy.[26] However, there were at the time a number of contentious questions: How would existing statutory entitlements to take and use water be converted to new rights? How would water be allocated to the environment? If there were not sufficient water for ecosystems, how would water be reallocated from consumptive use? Would compensation be payable if reallocation were to take place?[27]

Many of these questions have been answered in the period of reform since 1994. Ten years later, the COAG recognized that consolidation of these reforms and an alignment of agendas were needed, so in August 2003, COAG reaffirmed its commitment to implementing the 1994 National Water Reform Framework by developing a National Water Initiative.[28]

---

[23] The report is known as the National Water Reform Framework.
[24] COAG, National Water Initiative Discussion Paper.
[25] Council of Australian Governments Communiqué, 25 February 1994.
[26] Tan, Poh-Ling, *supra* note 7 at 24.   [27] Ibid.
[28] Council of Australian Governments 2003 Communiqué, 29 August 2003.

5 LEGAL ISSUES SURROUNDING WATER RIGHTS

The question of whether water rights are property rights has been extensively discussed.[29] In any case, it may not be of practical consequence in Australia.[30] The COAG reforms have encouraged the establishment of water rights separate from ownership of land and this chapter will proceed on this basis.

In order to use a water resource efficiently to achieve the best outcome for the environment and for all users of the resource, users need to have a reasonable expectation of the benefits received over time. The following seven criteria should be attached to the water rights to achieve this outcome.[31]

5.1 Universality

In recognition that water resources are often physically linked, all water resources need to be covered by the system. That is, surface water, groundwater, and overland flows need to be managed under one system. In Australia, only South Australia (SA) in nonprescribed areas[32] and Queensland (Qld) in areas not subject to a water resource plan[33] do not require users to obtain a water right before taking water located in a surface water channel or a groundwater source. In the Australian Capital Territory (ACT), surface water and groundwater are managed as though they are the same resource.[34] In the other Australian jurisdictions, surface water and groundwater are covered by water rights.

The question arises whether overland flows[35] should be covered by the water rights system. In the ACT, you need a license to harvest overland flows. In NSW, whether overland flows are included in the water rights system depends on the volume collected. Overland flows will be included if a user is harvesting more than 10 percent of the runoff.[36] In Victoria, it depends on the use to which the water is put. Unlicensed collection of overland flow is limited to stock and domestic purposes.[37] In Qld and prescribed areas of SA, there must be a governing water allocation plan that requires the licensing of overland flows. Without this plan, and in unprescribed areas in SA, overflow can be taken for any purpose.[38] In Western Australia (WA), the right to capture unconfined surface waters is subject to the qualification that there is no

---

[29] For example, see Tan, Poh-Ling. 2002 "Legal Issues Relating to Water Use" in *Property: Rights and Responsibilities – Current Australian Thinking*. Land & Water Australia, Canberra and ACIL Tasman in association with Freehills 2004. "An Effective System of Defining Water Property Titles." Research Report, Land and Water Australia, Canberra.

[30] See Fisher's discussion of recent jurisprudence in Fisher, D., "Rights of Property in Water: Confusion or Clarity" (2004) 21 *EPLJ* 200.

[31] Productivity Commission 2003 *Water Rights Arrangements in Australia and Overseas*. Commission Research Paper, Productivity Commission, Melbourne 94.

[32] Section 7, Water Resources Act 1997 (SA).

[33] Section 20(6), Water Act 2000 (Qld).

[34] Water Resources Act 1998 (ACT).

[35] *Overland flows* are rainwater that has fallen to the ground but not yet reached a surface water channel or aquifer.

[36] Section 54, Water Management Act 2000 (NSW).

[37] Section 8, Water Act 1989 (Vic).   [38] Section 7, Water Resources Act 1997 (SA).

significant adverse effect on the quality of water, or any ecosystem, in a watercourse or wetland.[39] This requirement exercises significant restraint on the irrigation farm dams.[40]

It can be argued that it is better to have a water rights system that covers overland flows, rather than leaving them out of the water rights system. One reason for this is that the volume of flow captured can be controlled and so the water available to drain into watercourses or aquifers provides a more predictable supply to other users who hold rights to surface and groundwater sources. Another reason is that when water is in short supply and rights are traded, the value of the water will rise, and, if overland flows are not regulated, this can create an incentive for users to intercept water before it reaches a surface or groundwater source. In extreme circumstances, the amount of water diverted may be enough to eliminate a surface or groundwater source.[41]

5.2 Predictability of Volume and Enforceability

Predictability is important to allow a reasonable expectation of volume of use for users. To ensure predictability, there needs to be an enforceable right to use coupled with a responsibility and liability on others not to interfere with that right.[42] An irrigator's decision about investing in irrigated farming is influenced by his or her expectations about the amount of water that his or her entitlements represent and the expected market value of the water amount.[43]

Predictability also gives value to a water right, enabling the holders to raise capital against that value. However, in any given year, the volume received under a right is determined by the total volume of water available and the way in which that water is allocated between consumptive and nonconsumptive uses. So predictability can be affected by the amount of rainfall, the need to restore environmental health to water sources, and the possible exercise of unexercised rights.[44]

Unpredictability Due to Rainfall

It is very difficult to predict the weather, but the risk involved can be better spread across the rights holders when surface water rights are expressed as a share rather than as a volume. The share will always be certain even though the amount may not be. Where it is expressed as a volume, as in some U.S. jurisdictions, the likelihood of receiving the specified volume depends on where the rights holder sits in the time-based order of priority.[45] The "later" claimants bear most of the risk. If predictability is really crucial, then one can apply the Victorian model, whereby water rights and licenses are defined for a nominal volume of water and therefore give rights holders a high degree of confidence

---

[39] Section 5B, Rights in Water and Irrigation Act 1914 (WA).

[40] Gardner, A, "Water Resources Law Reform in Western Australia – Implementing the COAG Water Reforms" (2002) 19 *EPLJ* 6 at 13.

[41] Productivity Commission 2003, *supra* note 31 at 98.

[42] Fisher, D, *Water Law* 2000 Law Book Company, Sydney, Australia.

[43] Goesch, T., and Hanna, N. 2002, "Efficient Use of Water: Role of Secure Property Rights" Vol. 9 No. 2 *Australian Commodities* 372 at 373.

[44] Productivity Commission 2003, *supra* note 31 at 98.

[45] Ibid. at 100.

of a minimal volume of supply. The rest of the water is known as *sales water*, which is specified as a share of the water right.

The Need to Restore Environmental Health to Water Sources

Many Australian jurisdictions operate under an adaptive management approach that recognizes that the volume of water set aside for the environment may have to be changed and shifted away from consumptive users toward environmental protection. Adaptive management regimes are likely to reduce the rights holders' confidence about the amount of water they will receive over time. Unless there is provision for compensation or guarantee of delivery, investment decisions may be affected. The issue of compensation raises the question as to whether, if water is taken to improve the health of the catchment, compensation should be paid. In the United States, *National Audubon Society v. Superior Court*[46] established that the public trust doctrine creates an ongoing duty on state water licensing authorities to keep water property rights that have already been granted under review. These authorities retain the power to amend those rights in order to protect public trust values in the environmental qualities of the water resource without a duty to pay compensation to the holder of the water property rights.[47] Even though Australia does not have a public trust doctrine, one can argue that the country's legislative and judicial definitions of property rights include the notion that these rights are defeasible when it comes to protecting public interest in the natural environment[48] and that if the just compensation clause in the Constitution[49] cannot be used, there may be no provision for compensation at the state level.

It is also important to look at community preferences in environmental management. For example, the community preference may lie in the reallocation of water to environmental use. This preference may not be adequately represented in a tradable rights market.[50]

In NSW, Qld, the ACT, and prescribed areas of SA, adaptive management changes are implemented administratively when the volume of water available for consumptive use is adjusted to achieve environmental objectives. However, even the exercise of water rights can be restricted in order to meet environmental flows. In contrast, in some U.S. jurisdictions, water rights can never be restricted; that means that the relevant agency must hold rights of sufficient priority and volume to meet environmental flow requirements.

Unexercised Rights

Another contributor to unpredictability are unexercised rights often referred to as "sleeper" or "dozer" licenses. In Australia, many holders have never exercised their rights and as these rights begin to attract a high value will be likely to sell them to players who need more water and will therefore add strain to the resource.

---

[46] (1983) 33 Cal 3d 419 (Supreme Court of California).
[47] Gardner, A., "Water Resources Law Reform in Western Australia – Implementing the COAG Water Reforms," *supra* note 40 at 27.
[48] Ibid.   [49] Section 51(xxxi), Constitution.
[50] Productivity Commission 2003, *supra* note 31 at 100.

5.3 Certainty of Title

The challenge with certainty of title is providing such certainty in order to facilitate investment and water trading, while allowing for adaptive resource management to ensure the environmental health of the water resource. The long-term productivity of irrigated agriculture is dependent on appropriate water titling regimes.[51] There must be certainty of title to encourage investment.

Rights holders need certainty of title. Should the title be accorded under a Torrens system, under which there is a central register that records all details attached to a water right? The advantage of the Torrens system is that it would give a high level of certainty of title to the holder, and the credibility of the information held in the register is strong. Any liability attached to a water right would be recorded. For such a system to work effectively, there would need to be a complete register of all information. Incompleteness would increase uncertainty, and where there was a water rights dispute between users, transaction costs would increase when ownership had to be demonstrated. Incompleteness can also be problematic when trading.

There also needs to be a common registry system across borders. Obtaining proof of title of a water right can be very costly where there are different registry systems. With water, the underlying right is a right to a share of a specified water resource available for approved purposes, and this right would need to be independent of whether the underlying entitlement provides a right to compensation when the water allocation is reduced.[52]

5.4 Duration

The length of time that a right holder can exercise a right – that is, the holder's security of tenure – will support economic efficiency over time. Where large investments are made with the intention of recovering costs over a long period, it is crucial that rights holders have certainty of access to water over the long term.[53]

All of this can be undermined by a system whereby the rights are of limited duration, the system of renewal or extension is vague, or the issuing authority has the power to cancel or suspend the right for reasons other than enforcement. All of these options need to be clarified carefully in order to achieve certainty of tenure so that there will still be an incentive to invest in water-use activities. In Australia there are some water rights granted in perpetuity, such as stock and domestic rights in all jurisdictions, bulk entitlement rights in Victoria, and all water licenses in SA.[54] Water allocations in Qld and ACT and environmental water rights are granted for approximately 10 years. Irrigation corporations in NSW hold access licenses for up to 20 years. In WA, licenses can be granted for either a fixed period with an expectation of renewal[55] or an indefinite tenure.[56]

[51] ACIL Tasman in association with Freehills 2004, "An Effective System of Defining Water Property Titles." Research Report, Land and Water Australia, Canberra.
[52] Ibid. at 7.   [53] Ibid. at 105.
[54] Table 5A. 7, Productivity Commission 2003, *supra* note 31 at 126.
[55] Sch 1, cl. 12, Rights in Water and Irrigation Act 1914 (WA) as amended in 2000.
[56] Sch 1, cl. 22, Rights in Water and Irrigation Act 1914 (WA) as amended in 2000.

Most of these nonperpetual rights can be amended or revoked to ensure the environmental health of the water resource and to allow governments to respond to unexpected changes. What is gained in flexibility and environmental flow objectives by compulsorily acquired water rights, however, will reduce the security of the water right. This reduction in security may need to be accompanied by compensation to the right holder.[57]

5.5 Exclusivity

Water rights would be regarded as exclusive if the benefits and costs of using the water accrued to the rights holder and no one else. But this is not what always happens. For example, with irrigation, the rights holder accrues the benefits and incurs some of the costs, such as the costs of pumping the water. However, there may be other costs borne by third parties, such as storing water in dams and extracting water, which may damage the ecological health of the rivers. These costs are borne by the community as a whole rather than the individual.[58] The true costs of the water must be included in the calculation of the price of the water. This makes it very difficult to establish an efficient price.

Dams and other storage facilities increase the benefits that accrue to a water right. For example, irrigation dams hold water until the start of the irrigation season, thereby producing higher yields for irrigators. This, practice, however, can damage the ecological health of river systems. Measures could be introduced that would result in releasing water from the dams to restore the natural flow of rivers as well as allowing for irrigation to help restore the ecological health of the rivers. This objective is achieved under the licensing for infrastructure provisions of the Water Management Act 2000 (NSW).

Despite some of the restrictions that have been placed on extracting water in Australia, one of the major problems remaining is the overallocation of water sources, resulting in significant environmental damage and a threat to future supplies. In addition to the environmental value of the declining water source, overallocation can affect tourism, increase the cost of purifying water for drinking, and cause the water to become unsuitable for agricultural and industrial processes.[59] Meeting these water demands requires management of environmental flows, that is, rules and targets to meet a set of economic, social, and environmental objectives. Environmental flow management is best dealt with at the local level through water catchment management authorities. It may involve applying adaptive management regimes that may reduce the amount of water available to rights holders. This course raises the question as to whether rights holders should be compensated when environmental allocations reduce the amount of water available. In some U.S. jurisdictions, the volume attached to these water rights is constitutionally protected and so has to be bought from the marketplace. Another question relates to water that is returned from irrigated land only to be reused by downstream irrigators or the environment. Who owns the return flows? The challenge is to define the obligations attached to these water rights. Are the users not to take more water than is authorized? Or must they take water only

---

[57] See discussion in section (5).
[58] Productivity Commission 2003, *supra* note 31 at 106.
[59] Productivity Commission 2003, *supra* note 31 at 108.

in the manner authorized? Or must they be required to meter and record extractions honestly?

In Australia, there is no general liability on water users except in the ACT, where all persons have a general duty of care to prevent harm to the environment.[60] In Victoria[61] and Qld,[62] injured parties can seek compensation for personal and other injuries from those who breach their obligations and water right conditions. In NSW, SA, and the ACT, water legislation does not explicitly provide for injured parties to seek compensation for breaches of obligations or conditions of water rights.

5.6 Detaching of Land Title and Use Restrictions

The criterion of detachment of title to land and of restrictions on use is essential for the effective trading of water rights. The 1994 COAG reforms recommended that water rights be separated from land title, and all Australian jurisdictions have moved toward this in the last 10 years, except in the case of stock, domestic use, and native title rights, which remain attached to land title. Riparian rights still exist in nonprescribed areas of SA and in Qld where a resource operations plan has not been established.

Within irrigation districts, it may be important that although water rights are traded, they are traded only within the district. Issuing water rights only to those who own or occupy land in the district restrains the extent to which water can be traded out of the district.

In some Australian jurisdictions, the purpose for which the water right will be used must be specified.

5.7 Divisibility and Transferability

Divisibility and transferability are also essential criteria for efficient trading. In some irrigation districts, the volume of water that may be traded out of the district is limited.

6 PROPOSALS FOR REFORM

In July 2003, the Wentworth Group of Concerned Scientists published a paper aimed at tackling the issues of water shortage and water quality in Australia.[63] Their proposal was to develop a national water plan with three objectives:

1. To guarantee river health
2. To deliver greater security for both water users and the environment by establishing a nationally consistent water entitlement and trading system
3. To engage the community and ensure fairness in water allocations[64]

---

[60] Section 22, Environmental Protection Act 1997 (ACT).
[61] Section 16, Water Act 1989 (Vic).   [62] Section 784, Water Act 2000 (Qld).
[63] Wentworth Group of Concerned Scientists, "Blueprint for a National Water Plan," *supra* note 6. The Wentworth Group advocates radical and fundamental reform to halt further degradation of Australia's landscapes.
[64] Ibid.

The Group set out strategies and outcomes for each of these objectives with the intention that COAG would consider them before their next meeting in June 2004. Each objective is now examined.

6.1 River Health

In terms of river health, the Group sets out five strategies to achieve this.[65] The first is to identify the environmental needs to maintain river health and assign first priority to the environment rather than to water users. It seems that regimes that have less than half of their natural flow will most likely produce a river that is incapable of maintaining long-term health.[66] The Group argued for an approach that accounts for environmental water and secures these environmental flows.

Their second strategy is to develop water management accounts to produce a snapshot of how water is currently used in a particular catchment so users can see at any time how much water remains for consumptive use. The Group argued that effective water management requires accounts to reflect the natural process of water movement across land, into dams, through aquifers, in vegetation, down rivers, through wetlands, and into estuaries. The move in Australian jurisdictions from specifying water entitlements as a volume of water to a share in the water available has the aim of improving the environmental flow of our rivers. Hydrological connections need to be considered. Controlling extraction of water from rivers simply encourages people to extract before the water gets to the rivers or to substitute groundwater for surface water. As argued earlier, entitlements to access water must therefore address overflow water, land use, surface water, and groundwater.[67] All state legislation extends to groundwater as well as surface water and, in some cases, to overflow water. However, in practice, an integrated approach for surface and groundwater is yet to be reflected in management practices.[68] The outcome from this strategy is that "a publicly available set of water accounts is created for each river valley and groundwater system across Australia so that all water users, the community and river managers can make informed decisions."[69]

The third strategy is to recover water for the environment in stressed rivers; the fourth is to protect those rivers that have not been degraded. The suggestion for achieving this is to develop a national river classification scheme to designate heritage rivers and conservation rivers for future generations. Finally there is a call to government to invest in the science required to make better decisions and to facilitate benchmarking exercises.

6.2 Delivery of Greater Security

The second objective is to deliver greater security to future investors. The strategies identified are intended to clarify entitlements and responsibilities in order to give farmers and irrigators certainty, to enable water to be recovered for the environment, and to set

---

[65] Wentworth Group of Concerned Scientists "Blueprint for a National Water Plan," *supra* note 6 at 7.
[66] Jones, G, "Setting Environmental Flows to Sustain a Healthy Working River," *Watershed* Feb 2002 CRC for Freshwater Ecology, referenced in "Blueprint for a National Water Plan," *supra* note 21 at 7.
[67] See Part 5(1) dealing with the essential criteria of universality.
[68] Tan, Poh-Ling, *supra* note 7 at 32.
[69] Wentworth Group of Concerned Scientists "Blueprint for a National Water Plan," *supra* note 6 at 8.

up a system of water trading.[70] The first strategy is difficult to achieve because there is currently no nationally consistent system specifying water access entitlements and little recognition of the reality of the highly variable water supply in Australia and the natural connections among land, surface water, and groundwater systems. The Wentworth Group advocates a nationally consistent system with three central components:

- Access to entitlements to use future water (a capital asset)
- Seasonal water allocations, based on the total amount of water available in the current season
- Locally based licenses governing water use, associated works, and impact on water quality[71]

There are a number of impediments to water trading. It requires a system of registration similar to land title to ensure certainty of title. This will encourage entitlements and allocations to be fully tradable. The entitlements must be specified as a perpetual share of the available resource, rather than a specific volume, so that the share always remains the same even though the volume attached to that share may vary.

6.3 Engaging the Community

The third objective is to engage communities and ensure fairness. There are four strategies attached to this objective. The first is to engage local communities, since land use has been identified as crucial for helping to determine the volume and quality of water in our rivers, and land use changes necessarily involve local communities. Changes in land use must be driven by the local communities, including farmers and irrigators, supported by the best available scientific information. State bodies must support local communities. The decisions that must be made to restore health to our rivers will create a lot of heated debate in local communities. The focus needs to be on the outcomes to be achieved. Irrigators are loath to give up their water, so where river systems have been overallocated, the people who are required to give up water should be informed about what environmental assets are being protected and the volumes of environmental water needed to protect them. To achieve this objective, the Wentworth Group has recommended that properly resourced, statutory, community-based catchment management authorities be established in each major water catchment in Australia.[72]

The second strategy is to establish active and accountable environmental management.[73] As previously identified, the need for changes in water use to improve the health of our water systems will involve large social adjustments, and this change will only be acceptable if the relevant communities are confident that the recovered water will be used in the best possible way. This condition must be assured; one method would be to set up environmental water trusts[74] that would hold the environmental water entitlements, acquire additional water needed for the environment, and manage the use of this water to achieve specified environmental outcomes. The trusts should not be representational.[75] Instead, they should be independent with a skills

---

[70] Ibid. at 11.
[71] Ibid. at 12.   [72] Ibid. at 14.
[73] Ibid.   [74] Ibid.
[75] The water catchment management committees would be representational.

base that includes expertise in freshwater ecology, water resource management, and markets.[76]

The third strategy is to improve water efficiency in towns and cities. A lot needs to be done to encourage the efficient use of potable water, storm water, and recycled waste water and consumers have to become more water literate. One suggestion is to benchmark the water efficiency of irrigation industries and districts and label packaging to show the water efficiency of milk, fruit, vegetables, and rice so that consumers can choose products that do not use excessive amounts of water. Labeling would reward those who became part of the solution to Australia's water problems.[77] It is also important to remove hidden environmental subsidies and properly price the agricultural products, including externalities such as the environmental costs of water guzzling produce.

This objective includes ensuring a fair transition. As everyone benefits from healthy rivers, the costs of improving and maintaining them should be shared. It should be the role of government to provide funding to ensure this objective is achieved.[78]

7 THE GOVERNMENT RESPONSE

At their meeting on 25 June 2004, the Council of Australian Governments released the National Water Initiative.[79] A discussion paper[80] leading up to the release of the National Water Initiative was released on 19 March 2004 and over 70 responses were received. There were seven submissions from irrigation corporations, cooperatives, and associations.[81] In these submissions, most of the concern was centered around the issue of sharing the risk when more water was needed to improve the health of the river systems. There was strong support for the concept that a share of the resource should be held in perpetuity by the user and that if the government wants to take water for environmental use, then compensation should be paid. The submissions suggested that in order to return overallocated systems to environmentally sustainable levels of consumptive use, the focus should extend beyond environmental flows alone. They also expressed support for using a partnership approach in establishing agreed environmental objectives and solutions to overallocation, involving communities, water users, and government. Encouraging investment was considered crucial, but the 10-year life span of water-sharing plans was considered too short. The Irrigation Association of Australia suggested capacity building in irrigation communities by way of training in irrigation scheduling, management, and monitoring as a prerequisite for allocation licensing.[82] The NSW Irrigators' Council set out a detailed proposal with respect to assignment of risk. It suggested that water users bear the risks of reduced water allocations arising

---

[76] Wentworth Group of Concerned Scientists "Blueprint for a National Water Plan," *supra* note 6 at 14.

[77] Ibid. at 15.   [78] Ibid. at 16.

[79] Council of Australian Governments Communiqué 2004.

[80] National Water Initiative, http://www.pmc.gov.au/docs/national_water_initiative_progress.cfm.

[81] The submissions were from Murray Irrigation Ltd, Murrumbidgee Irrigation Ltd, Irrigation Association of Australia, Australian National Committee on Irrigation and Drainage, NSW Irrigators' Council, Coleambally Irrigation Co-operative Ltd, Ord Irrigation Co-operative. http://www.pmc.gov.au/nwi_submissions/nwi_submissions.cfm.

[82] Submission by Irrigation Association of Australia to NWI discussion paper, dated 30 April 2004.

from the reductions to the consumptive pool as a result of either seasonal or long-term changes in climate and natural events and acts of God, and that governments bear the risk when agreed improvements in science determine a greater requirement for environmental water. They suggested that government should also bear the risk associated with correcting past policy decisions and risks associated with acts of terrorism on infrastructure that result in water supply disruption. They suggested that the environment bear the risks on the same basis as other water users and that during periods of drought, all environmental water above a minimal entitlement be made available for irrigation, urban, industrial, stock, and domestic users.[83]

The WA Environmental Defender's Office (EDO) submission took a precautionary approach to the issue of perpetual licenses on the basis that there is insufficient knowledge of the sustainable yield of a water resource and of aquifer function and so recommended that licenses should be granted for no more than 10 years' duration.[84] With respect to the issue of compensation, the NSW EDO suggested that the risk associated with changes in environmental conditions and knowledge about water resources should be borne by water users and risks associated with changes in government policy should be borne by government. They said there was a need to define responsibilities and obligations attached to water entitlements and accurate monitoring, reporting, and accounting of water use. They also recommended a strong public participation regime.[85] The Australian Bankers' Association had a number of concerns relating to security of title and access to finance. It stressed the importance of indefeasibility of title as financiers needed to be confident that the water title being acquired is a clear title, pointing out that this certainty would speed up the conveyancing process for water entitlements. With regard to assignment of risk, they supported the capping of risk to water users, ensuring that the risks were commercially manageable in order to minimize the social and economic impact of water reform. They argued that full compensation should be paid when changes impacting on the value of water entitlements occur outside a local planning process.[86]

According to the government,[87] the National Water Initiative will result in

- Expansion of permanent trade in water, yielding more profitable use of water and more cost-effective and flexible recovery of water to achieve environmental outcomes
- More confidence for those investing in the water industry through more secure water access entitlements; better and more compatible registry arrangements; better monitoring, reporting, and accounting of water use; and improved public access to information
- More sophisticated, transparent, and comprehensive water planning that deals with key issues such as the major interception of water, the interaction between surface and groundwater systems, and the provision of water to achieve specific environmental outcomes;[88]

---

[83] Submission by NSW Irrigators' Council to NWI discussion paper, dated April 2004, at 9, 10.
[84] Submission by Environmental Defender's Office (WA) to NWI discussion paper, dated 29 April 2004.
[85] Submission by Environmental Defender's Office (NSW) to NWI discussion paper, dated April 2004.
[86] Submission by Australian Bankers' Association to NWI discussion paper, dated April 2004.
[87] Council of Australian Government 2004 Communiqué, 25 June 2004.
[88] Paras. 23(ii) and 36–40, NWI Agreement.

- Commitment to addressing overallocated systems as quickly as possible, in consultation with affected stakeholders, addressing significant adjustment issues where appropriate
- Better and more efficient management of water in urban environments, for example, through the increased use of recycled water and storm water

Key elements of the NWI include the following:

- Water access entitlements to be generally defined as open-ended or perpetual access to a share of the water resource that is available for consumption as specified in a water plan (recognizing that there are cases in which other forms of entitlement are more appropriate)[89]
- Improved specification of the environmental outcomes to be achieved for particular water systems, improved accountability arrangements for environmental managers, and statutory recognition for water that is provided to ensure environmental outcomes are met
- Overallocated water systems to be returned to sustainable levels of use in order to meet environmental outcomes, with substantial progress by 2010[90]
- Creation of a framework to assign the risk of future reductions in water availability as follows:
    - Reductions arising from natural events such as climate change, drought, or bushfire to be borne by water users
    - Reductions arising from bona fide improvements in knowledge about water systems' capacity to sustain particular extraction levels to be borne by water users up to 2014; After 2014, water users to bear this risk for the first 3 percent reduction in water allocation, State/Territory and the Australian Government to share (one-third and two-thirds, respectively) the risk of reductions of between 3 percent and 6 percent; State/Territory and the Australian Government to share equally the risk of reductions above 6 percent
    - Reductions arising from changes in government policy not previously provided for to be borne by governments
    - Where there is voluntary agreement between relevant State or Territory Governments and key stakeholders, implementation of a different risk assignment model[91]
- More efficient administrative arrangements to facilitate water trade in connected systems
- Removal of institutional barriers to trade in water, including a phased removal of barriers to permanent trade out of water irrigation areas in the southern Murray-Darling Basin
- Regional assessments of the level of water intercepted by land use change activities and requiring new activities expected to intercept significant volumes of water to hold a water access entitlement if the catchment is at, or close to, its sustainable level of water allocation[92]
- Continued implementation of full-cost recovery pricing for water in both urban and rural sectors

---

[89] Paras. 28–32, NWI Agreement.   [90] Paras. 41–45, NWI Agreement.
[91] Paras. 46–51, NWI Agreement.   [92] Paras. 55–57, NWI Agreement.

- National standards for water accounting, reporting, and metering
- Actions to manage the demand for water in urban areas better, including a review of temporary water restrictions, minimal water efficiency standards and mandatory labeling of household appliances, and national guidelines for water-sensitive urban design[93]

These elements have been set out in an Intergovernmental Agreement on a National Water Initiative, signed by the Commonwealth and all States and Territories except Western Australia and Tasmania.[94]

There are some very positive aspects to the NWI. A national approach has been agreed upon and a national approach to water trading will encourage more efficient use of water.[95] For example, irrigators could halve their water use and double productivity by abandoning flood irrigation for rice and developing water plans for high-value crops. The agreement has given farmers security for their water rights, and thus security for investment, and it will provide legally secure water for the environment and set out the ways it should be recovered, managed, and reported. It has also alleviated many of the farmers' concerns about assignment of risk. It acknowledges the connection between groundwater and surface water and provides a commitment to return overallocated river and groundwater systems to sustainable levels. The plan provides for indigenous representation in water planning wherever possible and recommends that water plans incorporate indigenous social, spiritual, and customary objectives and strategies wherever they can be developed.[96] There is also provision for engaging water users and other stakeholders in achieving the agreement objectives.[97] Schedule A of the agreement includes a timetable for the implementation of key actions.

A national Water Commission has been set up to assess progress in implementing the NWI and to report to COAG and advise on progress and better ways to achieve the objectives of the agreement. The commission will also monitor the progress with implementing water reform commitments under the National Competition Policy.

8 THE WAY FORWARD

The proposed reforms in Australia have proceeded on the basis that water rights should be separated from land title and that a scheme of trading in these water rights should be established. The National Water Initiative has clarified who will bear the risks when the volume of water needs to be reduced. Investor confidence and security of tenure issues have also been clarified.

The Australian governments have now committed themselves to sound principles for future water policy. However, we still do not understand our water resources well enough. The NWI agreement does recognize the need for continuing knowledge and

---

[93] Paras. 90–92, NWI Agreement.

[94] Council of Australian Governments Meeting 25 June 2004 http://www.coag.gov.au/meetings/250604/index.htm.

[95] This has already been seen in the temporary market in Vic, SA, and NSW as water has moved from irrigators producing low-value commodities to those producing higher-value commodities. See McKay, J., and Bjornland, H., 2001, "Recent Australian Market Mechanisms as a Component of an Environmental Policy That Can Make Choices between Sustainability and Social Justice," in *Property: Rights and Responsibilities – Current Australian Thinking.* Land & Water Australia, Canberra, 137 at 143.

[96] Paras. 52–54, NWI Agreement.   [97] Paras. 93–97, NWI Agreement.

capacity building in such areas as changes to water availability from climate and land use change, interaction between surface and groundwater, demonstration of ecological outcomes from environmental flow management, and improvements in farm, irrigation system, and catchment water use efficiency.[98] No funding has been allocated toward this. Instead the agreement suggests the need for a more coordinated effort in integrating existing research in this area. Peter Cullen[99] has suggested that the governments need to provide more resources for scientific research to achieve real outcomes.

The implementation of this agreement will be effected through the Natural Resource Management Ministerial Council,[100] which will provide annual reports to COAG on the progress that the Australian jurisdictions are making in implementing the agreement. These reports will be publicly available.

9 CONCLUSION

Despite 10 years of water management reform in Australia, the country still has degraded rivers, low environmental flows, and severe water restrictions. What is needed is sustainable irrigation: irrigation that uses water efficiently and has effective drainage and salt disposal. It must extract only enough water so that the health of our rivers is sustained.

Irrigators must exercise a high level of control over the water and ensure that it is applied to crops efficiently so that losses in application and delivery are minimized. The amount applied should meet the need of the plant. Further research should focus on saline drainage water to ensure that it is isolated and reused in order to minimize its degradation of the land and rivers. It should be regarded as waste and methods should be employed to minimize this waste.

Irrigators must better understand the capacity of their soils and drainage systems to support different types of agriculture and try to produce crops that better match the water available – that is, plants that can be extracted without damaging the environment.

Some useful measures have emerged from the COAG process, such as recognizing the connection between groundwater and surface water and the separation of water rights from land title, allowing water to be traded. Water trading has allowed water to be traded out of inappropriate areas into new areas where wealth can be maximized. More knowledge is needed in this area, and it is unclear whether the government will support the necessary research.

There is much potential to the National Water Initiative. Australians now have to wait and see whether it is enough to enable sustainable irrigation and, with it, to restore the health of Australia's rivers.

---

[98] Para 98, NWI Agreement.
[99] Emeritus Professor at the University of Canberra and a member of the Wentworth Group of Concerned Scientists, writing in *The Australian*, "Trickle Should Be a Torrent" 28 June 2004.
[100] Paras. 104–108, NWI Agreement.

25 Environmental Impact Assessment: Addressing the Major Weaknesses

Michael I. Jeffery

1 INTRODUCTION

The concept of environmental impact assessment (EIA) has developed over recent decades into what has become accepted today as an essential tool in successful land use planning and regulation, as part of a wider integrated environmental management system. It has developed in response to growing concern over the impact of large-scale development projects on the surrounding ecological and cultural environment. In particular, this concern stemmed from the practical effects of damage caused by pollution that threatened human health, and the perceived intrinsic values of nature.[1]

EIA is defined as "a systematic process for the examination and evaluation of the environmental effects of proposed activities that are considered likely to significantly affect the environment."[2] It is distinct from other forms of environmental regulation, in that it approaches environmental problems from a preventative or mitigative perspective. This represents a significant change in policy from the retrospective and punitive nature of the traditional "command and control" style of regulation, which advocates the setting of standards and rules enforced by pecuniary and criminal forms of punishment. In particular, it was seen to provide a mechanism wherein projects or undertakings that would likely have a significant adverse environmental impact could be excluded from further consideration and approval denied outright, thus preventing damage to the environment, often entailing significant cleanup costs when found to exceed the current regulatory limits.

It is now widely recognized that the command and control approach, applied in isolation, does not deal effectively with many of the environmental impacts resulting from significant industrial development. EIA is therefore seen as a necessary requirement for all environmental law regimes, in attempting to achieve the goals of sustainable development. In recent years, EIA has been applied on global[3] and transnational

[1] I. Thomas, *Environmental Impact Assessment in Australia: Theory and Practice*, 2nd ed. (The Federation Press, Sydney, Australia) (hereafter Thomas) (1998) 5–6.

[2] G. Bates, *Environmental Law in Australia*, 5th ed. (Butterworths, Sydney, Australia) (hereafter Bates) (2002) 275.

[3] For example, the United Nations Convention on Biological Diversity, 2 June 1992, U.N. Doc DPI/130/7 reprinted in 31 I.L.M. 818 (1992), available at http://www.biodiv.org/convention/articles.asp (hereafter the CBD) provides, at Article 14, for EIA for protection of global biodiversity.

The author gratefully acknowledges the invaluable assistance of Elaine Johnson in the research and preparation of this chapter.

scales.[4] In particular, it is being applied in the financial aid sector by international funding agencies such as the World Bank[5] and the Asian Development Bank,[6] as a condition precedent to the provision of financial assistance in developing countries. This has been a direct response to a number of environmentally inappropriate projects funded by multilateral institutions.

Sustainable development was defined by the Brundtland Report in 1987 as "development that meets the needs of the present without compromising the ability of future generations to meet their own needs"[7] and is aimed at integrating the needs of development with those of a healthy environment. EIA contributes to this process by attempting to integrate both the economic and environmental objectives of the State at the *planning* stage of development projects, as opposed to prohibiting and punishing actions after the fact. As such, EIA is provided for in the 1992 United Nations Rio Declaration on the Environment and Development (the Rio Declaration), which states, at Principle 17, that

> environmental impact assessment, as a national instrument, shall be undertaken for proposed activities that are likely to have a *significant adverse impact* on the environment and are *subject to a decision of a competent national authority* [emphasis added].[8]

Given the requirement that EIA apply only to those activities that have a "significant adverse impact" and are subject to a decision by a public authority (whether it be national or provincial), it should be noted at the outset that references in this chapter to the process of EIA relate only to regulation of such activities and do not concern impact assessment of "minor" developments. Activities capable of having a significant adverse impact on the environment are typically publicly funded large-scale infrastructure projects, such as sewage treatment plants or transportation facilities; they also include large-scale privately funded land use projects, such as the development of mine sites or significant property development.

The purpose of this chapter is to provide a comparative analysis of the implementation of EIA in Canada (at both the federal and provincial levels) and Australia (similarly

---

[4] EIA, for developments likely to have transboundary impacts in Europe, is required by the United Nations Economic Commission for Europe (UNECE) Convention on Environmental Impact Assessment in a Transboundary Context, 1991, reprinted at 30 I.L.M. 800 (1991), available at http://www.unece.org/env/eia/eia.htm (hereafter the *Espoo Convention*).

[5] World Bank, "Environmental Assessment," *The World Bank Operational Manual: Operational Policies*, World Bank, 1999. Reprinted in D. G. Craig et al., *Capacity Building for Environmental Law in the Asian and Pacific Region: Approaches and Resource* (Asian Development Bank, Manila, Philippines) (2002) 599–603.

[6] Asian Development Bank, "Environmental Considerations in Bank Operations," *Operational Procedures*, ADB Strategy and Policy Office, January 1997. Reprinted in Craig et al., ibid. at 603–606.

[7] World Commission on Environment and Development (WCED), *Our Common Future* (Oxford University Press, Oxford) (hereafter the Brundtland Report) (1987) 43.

[8] United Nations, Rio Declaration on the Environment and Development, reprinted at 31 I.L.M. 874 (1992) (hereafter the Rio Declaration) at Principle 17. See also UNEP Governing Council Decision: Goals and Principles of Environmental Impact Assessment, UNEP/GC.14/17, Annex III (June 17 1987); EEC Council Directive: Assessment of the Effects of Certain Public and Private Projects on the Environment, Dir. No. 85/337 (27 June 1985); WCED Legal Experts Group, Article 5. These instruments cited in D. Hunter et al. (eds.), *International Environmental Law and Policy*, 2nd ed. (University Casebook Series, Foundation Press, New York) (2002) 434.

at the Commonwealth and State levels). In doing so, it will highlight the weaknesses of EIA regimes in practice and suggest appropriate remedies capable of addressing such weaknesses. Because of time and space constraints, only the Province of Ontario and the State of New South Wales are considered in this context. The crux of the argument presented is that in order to achieve effective implementation of EIA regimes, there is a need to provide not only legislation that accommodates the theory and philosophy of EIA, but also procedures that properly, and honestly, facilitate EIA in practice. Achievement of procedural fairness in environmental decision making is therefore considered to lie at the heart of effective EIA regimes and promotion of the principles of sustainable development. In order to understand how such procedural fairness might be achieved adequately, it is first necessary to outline briefly the role of public participation in environmental decision making and impact assessment.

1.1 Public Participation and Environmental Impact Assessment

Decisions concerning land use and development of natural resources are inherently public and political acts, rather than merely processes of technical evaluation,[9] because those responsible for environmental decision making are effectively allocating public resources and prioritizing value systems held by different sections of the community. Although EIA primarily seeks to protect and maintain environmental quality, it is inevitably linked to social equity and is therefore a vehicle for social, as well as environmental, change.[10] There is a need for effective public involvement in the process of EIA for two key reasons:

1. In pursuit of environmental quality, the local and traditional community should be involved in decision making as these are often the people best placed to provide decision makers with relevant information on the local environment to which proponents of development projects may not have access.
2. In pursuit of social equity, the surrounding community and the national public in general are affected by decisions involving use of public resources and should therefore be included in such decisions.

Public participation has been defined as "a process by which interested and affected individuals, organisations, and government entities are consulted and included in the decision-making process"[11] and is recognized as a requirement of EIA regimes through the 1998 United Nations Convention on Access to Information, Public Participation in Decision-Making and Access to Justice in Environmental Matters (the Åarhus Convention),[12] which provides for access to information and justice by the public in EIA processes. More generally, public participation is seen as an essential element in achieving the goals of sustainable development, as demonstrated by its inclusion in the Rio

---

[9] Thomas, *supra* note 1 at 17.

[10] R. Lang, "Environmental Impact Assessment: Reform or Rhetoric?" in W. Leiss (ed.), *Ecology vs Politics in Canada* (University of Toronto Press, Toronto) (1979). Cited in Thomas, *supra* note 1 at 16.

[11] A. Bram, "Public Participation Provisions Need Not Contribute to Environmental Injustice" 5 *Temp. Pol. & Civ. Rts. L. Rev.* (1996) 145 at 150–151.

[12] United Nations Convention on Access to Information, Public Participation in Decision-Making and Access to Justice in Environmental Matters (hereafter the Åarhus Convention), at Article 7.

Declaration, at Principle 10, which states that "[e]nvironmental issues are best handled with the participation of all concerned citizens, at the relevant level."[13]

It should be recognized, however, that public participation takes many different forms, some more effective than others in giving citizens a voice. This affects the *quality* of citizen participation, as recognized by Sherry Arnstein, who provides us with a typology of eight levels of public involvement in environmental decision making.[14] These levels are, in order from the least effective forms to the most effective, manipulation, therapy, informing, consultation, placation, partnership, delegated power, and citizen control. Arnstein's model demonstrates that these eight levels can be grouped into three distinct categories of participation, which proceed from nonparticipation, through degrees of tokenism, and ultimately to participation that provides for degrees of citizen power in public decision making. In her discussion of the progression through these levels and categories, Arnstein notes that in order for genuine bargaining power to exist at the community level, a citizen group must have the appropriate resources "to hire (and fire) its own technicians, lawyers, and community organisers."[15]

For these reasons, it should be the goals of EIA regimes to promote public participation that is effective, genuine, and meaningful and to facilitate a degree of "citizen power" as opposed to involvement that functions as mere tokenism or nonparticipation.[16] Effective public participation is facilitated in three key ways: through notice and access to information, citizen standing in public interest cases, and affordability of opposition to development proposals that require EIA.[17] Many EIA regimes, including those that are the subject of this chapter, provide in some respect for the first two methods of facilitating effective public involvement (notice and access to information and citizen standing). However, the legislation appears to be lacking in the third element (affordability of opposition). This chapter seeks to provide some ways in which this aspect of public involvement can be improved, in pursuit of more robust EIA regimes that appropriately apply systems of procedural fairness.

2 ENVIRONMENTAL IMPACT ASSESSMENT AS A LEGAL REGIME

In order for EIA to be integrated into the decision-making structures of the State, it must be included in a legal framework. This action was first taken by the United States, through the National Environmental Policy Act 1970 (NEPA).[18] The U.S. Act was introduced in response to growing criticism of the environmental effects of projects by government agencies, such as the Atomic Energy Commission and the Army Corps of Engineers, and a lack of public participation and access to information in environmental

---

[13] Rio Declaration, *supra* note 8 at Principle 10.

[14] S. Arnstein, "A Ladder of Citizen Participation," *AIP Journal* (1969) 216. Reprinted in Craig et al., *supra* note 5 at 623–630.

[15] Ibid. at 628.

[16] See M. Jeffery, "Intervenor Funding as the Key to Effective Citizen Participation in Environmental Decision-Making: Putting the People Back into the Picture" 19(2) *Arizona Journal of International and Comparative Law* (2002) 293 for a discussion of means to use funding of objectors to influence the quality of citizen participation and preclude mere "participatory tokenism."

[17] S. Casey Lefkowitz, "A Comparative Look at the Role of Citizens in Environmental Enforcement," *National Environmental Enforcement Journal* Vol. 12, No. 5(1997). Cited in Craig et al., *supra* note 5 at 654.

[18] National Environmental Policy Act *1970* (U.S.) (hereafter NEPA).

decision-making.[19] Primarily, NEPA provides for EIA only with respect to federal government projects that are likely to have significant impacts on the environment. This mandate is reflected in international law through Principle 17 of the Rio Declaration. State legislation providing for EIA was adopted by the majority of U.S. states in subsequent years.

Since its inception, EIA has developed into a multifaceted system, incorporating many different forms of assessment, at different levels of land use planning and regulation. However, at a fundamental level, EIA processes can generally be divided into three distinct parts:[20]

1. Preparation of technical documentation outlining the state of the environment, predictions of environmental impacts of a proposal, and recommendations for mitigation of such impacts. This is commonly known as the *environmental impact statement* (EIS).
2. Review and assessment of the documentation by government authorities, in the form of a report containing recommendations as to how and whether the proposal should be approved. This is known as the *assessment report* it is passed to the decision-making body for determination of conditions of approval of the proposal.
3. An opportunity for the public at large to comment on both the adequacy of the EIS and the appropriateness of the proposal.

In the final stage of the process, the proposal is subject to evaluation and adjudication, and approval is either granted or refused. Appeals against the decision of the consent authority are directed to adjudication either through the courts or through an administrative or quasi-judicial tribunal. In some jurisdictions, such as many of the Canadian Provinces, the ultimate decision maker is the government itself, through either an appropriate Minister or delegated authority. In these instances, although there may be a public hearing before an administrative or quasi-judicial tribunal, it is the Minister or government agency official who renders the decision after considering the report from the tribunal. In contrast, in the United States, challenges to the EIS under NEPA often take the form of litigious proceedings before the courts.

It should also be noted that with the advent of EIA, the definition in many jurisdictions of the term *environment* was widened not only to include impacts to the natural environment, but to entail a consideration of the natural, social, economic, and cultural environment. Within the definition of EIA, therefore, it must be acknowledged that impact assessment is now taken to encompass assessment of a wide range of likely impacts, such as economic, health, regulatory, social, species, cumulative, and integrated impact assessments, as well as energy and risk analyses and technology assessment.[21] In particular, social impact assessment (SIA) has become an integral part of project-based impact assessment.[22] This chapter, however, focuses specifically on the assessment of

---

[19] Thomas, *supra* note 1 at 77.

[20] The first two stages are set out in Thomas, ibid. at 18.

[21] Ibid. Chapter 3.

[22] See, for example, D. Craig, "Social Impact Assessment" 10 *Environmental Impact Assessment Review* (1990) 37; R. Howitt, "Social Impact Assessment as Applied to Peoples" 31 *Australian Geographical Studies* (1993); Beckwith, "Social Impact Assessment" 12 *Impact Assessment Bulletin* (1994) 199; Burdge, "Social Impact Assessment" 14(1) *Impact Assessment Bulletin* (1996) 59.

the ecological impacts of land use, and therefore any reference to EIA should be taken to include only such an assessment.

It should be further clarified that there exists a distinction between the type of EIA that is the subject of this chapter, which is project-specific, and impact assessment that occurs at the policy, planning, or program level, commonly known as *strategic environmental assessment* (SEA).[23] SEA was first recognized internationally as an environmental policy tool in 1992,[24] and while it has not yet been adequately defined in the literature, it refers in general to environmental assessment that addresses the impacts of government policy and is therefore able to deal more effectively with the cumulative effects of land use and development decisions that cannot be handled at a project-specific level by EIA.[25] Although this chapter does not address the application of SEA specifically, it should be considered as one method of addressing the failure of EIA to deal adequately with the cumulative impacts of development projects.[26]

3 COMPARATIVE ANALYSIS OF ENVIRONMENTAL IMPACT ASSESSMENT REGIMES IN AUSTRALIA AND CANADA

As signatories to the 1992 Rio Declaration, both Australia and Canada are now under an international obligation to provide for EIA, at least at a national level.[27] Their national implementation, as well as implementation at a provincial or state level, is examined here with respect to the EIS stage and the review and assessment stage.

3.1 Australian Federal Regime

Traditionally, land use planning and development of natural resources in Australia have been the responsibility of the state and local governments, rather than of the federal government, because when the Commonwealth government of Australia was given its legislative powers in 1900, through the Australian Constitution;[28] such powers did not include the power to legislate concerning environmental protection. It is likely that at that time, the drafters of the Constitution were less concerned with environmental protection than they were with development of the resources of the continent.[29] The Commonwealth has, however, passed some legislation concerning environmental protection and EIA, and this has been achieved primarily through use of other powers to legislate, for example, with respect to trade and commerce, external affairs, corporations, finance and taxation, and "people of any race."[30] In particular, the two key pieces of legislation that have provided for EIA at a national level in Australia were derived from the trade and commerce power[31] (which provided for the now repealed Environment

---

[23] For an Australian perspective on strategic environmental assessment, see S. Marsden and S. Dovers, *Strategic Environmental Assessment in Australasia* (The Federation Press, Sydney, Australia) (2002).

[24] United Nations Economic Commission for Europe (UNECE), *Application of Environmental Impact Assessment Principles to Policies, Plans and Programmes* (United Nations, New York) (1992).

[25] Marsden and Dovers, *supra* note 23 at 5–7.   [26] Ibid. Chapter 7.

[27] It should be noted that Canada introduced EIA at the federal level in 1972, shortly after the U.S. enactment of NEPA in 1970. The Commonwealth Government of Australia followed suit in 1974 with the enactment of the Environment Protection (Impact of Proposals) Act 1974 (Commonwealth) (hereafter EPIP Act).

[28] Commonwealth of Australia Constitution Act (Cth) (hereafter the Australian Constitution), section 51.

[29] Bates, *supra* note 2 at 48.

[30] The Australian Constitution, *supra* note 28, section 51.

[31] Ibid. section 51(i).

Protection [Impact of Proposals] Act 1974 [the EPIP Act])[32] and the external affairs power[33] (which provided for the Environment Protection and Biodiversity Conservation Act 1999 [the EPBC Act]).[34] The EIA provisions of the EPIP Act were replaced by the EBPC Act when it was introduced in 1999. Likewise, in Canada, there is no reference in the Canadian Constitution with respect to the protection of the environment, and under the British North America Act of 1867, the forerunner to the present Canadian Constitution, control over natural resources was within the constitutional purview of the provinces, save and except a specific heading of federal jurisdiction such as jurisdiction over seacoast and inland fisheries.[35]

The EPBC Act provides for environmental assessment and approval of projects that concern matters of national environmental significance[36] or that may affect Commonwealth land and are determined by the Minister for Environment and Heritage to be likely to have a significant impact on the environment.[37] These kinds of proposals are termed *controlled actions*. The public is invited to comment on whether the action should be classed as a controlled action by the Minister.[38]

Environmental assessment is required for controlled actions under Part 8 of the EPBC Act, which provides that the Minister choose the appropriate form of assessment[39] from either preliminary documentation,[40] a public environment report (PER),[41] an environmental impact statement (EIS),[42] a public inquiry,[43] or an "accredited assessment process."[44] In each of the first three assessment processes (preliminary

---

[32] The legitimacy of the Environment Protection (Impact of Proposals) Act 1974 (repealed by Act No. 92, 1999) was confirmed by the High Court in *ACF v. Commonwealth* (1980) 28 ALR 257.

[33] The Australian Constitution *supra* note 28, section 51(xxvi). The High Court in *Commonwealth v. Tasmania* (1983) 46 ALR 625 determined that the external affairs power could be used to give effect to international treaties concerning the environment through Commonwealth legislation, but only insofar as such legislation implements the purposes of the treaty.

[34] Environment Protection and Biodiversity Conservation Act 1999 (Cth), entered into force 16 July 2000 (hereafter the EPBC Act).

[35] British North America Act, 1867, 30 & 31, Victoria, clause 3, section 91(12).

[36] Matters of national environmental significance were negotiated with the States and declared under the agreement made between the Commonwealth and the States in 1997: Council of Australian Governments, Heads of Agreement, November 1997 (the COAG Agreement). In general, there are seven kinds of matters of national significance: world heritage properties, declared Ramsar wetlands, listed threatened species or endangered communities, listed migratory species, nuclear actions, actions in Commonwealth marine areas, and actions that are prescribed by the Environment Protection and Biodiversity Conservation Regulations 2000 (Cth) (hereafter the EPBC Regulations).

[37] These are termed *controlled actions*, which are set out in the EPBC Act, *supra* note 34 at Pt 3. The need for an EIS (determination on whether the proposed action is likely to have a significant impact on the environment) has not been defined in strict terms and has been the subject of judicial scrutiny (see Bates, 2002, *supra* note 2, at 297–299); however, it is useful to note that it is determined with reference to guidelines such as the Australian and New Zealand Environment and Conservation Council's (ANZECC) Guidelines and Criteria for Determining the Need for and Level of Environmental Impact Assessment in Australia (ANZECC Working Group on National Environmental Impact Assessment, Canberra, Australia) (1996).

[38] EPBC Act, ibid. section 74(3).   [39] EBPC Act, ibid. section 87(1).

[40] EPBC Act, ibid. Pt 8, Division 4, sections 92–95.

[41] EPBC Act, ibid. Pt 8, Division 5, sections 96–100.

[42] EPBC Act, ibid. Pt 8, Division 6, sections 101–105.

[43] EPBC Act, ibid. Pt 8, Division 7, sections 106–129.

[44] EPBC Act, ibid. section 87(4). The federal Minister may determine that the proposal should be subject to, for example, the State approval process, rather than approval under the EPBC Act.

documentation, PER, or EIS), the proponent must prepare the assessment documentation according to the published administrative guidelines and the regulations.[45] The draft documentation is then provided for public comment,[46] which must be taken into consideration by the proponent, before the final EIA documentation is presented to the Department of Environment and Heritage.[47]

At the review stage of the process, the Secretary of the Department of Environment and Heritage is required to prepare an assessment report for the Commonwealth Environment Minister, who then makes a decision on whether or not to approve the proposal.[48] The entire approvals process is conducted by the Minister, and there is no provision for appeal from the decision of the Minister. Public involvement is limited to comments on the draft assessment documentation, except in the case of a public inquiry, when citizen participation is formalized into an inquiry process, when the Minister determines such a process is necessary. An inquiry is generally considered by the Department to be appropriate when the relevant impacts are likely to be relatively high, the relevant impacts are perceived to be outside the control of a single proponent, or a public inquiry is necessary to ensure effective and efficient public involvement in the assessment process.[49] Once the inquiry has taken place, the matter is referred to the Minister for consideration of approval.

3.2 The State of New South Wales

In the Australian state of New South Wales, EIA is governed by the Environmental Planning and Assessment Act 1979 (EP&A Act)[50] and administered by the Department of Infrastructure, Planning and Natural Resources. EIA is required for certain types of development and land use activities under Part 4 and 5 of the EP&A Act.

The proponent of a development proposal is required to submit an EIS to the consent authority if the proposal is listed as "designated development" under Part 4 of the EP&A Act, which includes activities involving mine site development, extractive industries, agricultural produce industries, and electricity generation.[51] Proponents must also submit an EIS to a state government authority (the "determining authority") under Part 5 of the EP&A Act if their proposal requires a license or permit from that authority, and the authority determines that the proposal is likely to have a significant impact on the environment.[52] In both cases, the EIS is prepared, and paid for, by or on

---

[45] EPBC Regulations, *supra* note 36, Schedule 2, at clause 4.03.

[46] EPBC Act, *supra* note 34, section 93 (preliminary documentation); section 98 (PER); section 103 (EIS).

[47] The requirements for the proponent to take into consideration public comment are set out in the EPBC Act, ibid., s 94(1) (preliminary documentation); s 99 (PER); s 104 (EIS).

[48] EPBC Act, ibid., section 95 (preliminary documentation); section 100 (PER); section 105 (EIS).

[49] Commonwealth of Australia, *Fact Sheet 3: Environmental Assessment Processes*, Department of Environment and Heritage, available at http://www.deh.gov.au/epbc/publications/factsheets/assessment.html.

[50] Environmental Planning and Assessment Act 1979 (NSW) (hereafter EP&A Act).

[51] Ibid. section 77A. Designated development is listed in Schedule 3 of the Environmental Planning and Assessment Regulation 2000 (NSW) (hereafter EP&A Regulations), or alternatively may be prescribed by an environmental planning instrument: EP&A Act, ibid. section 29.

[52] Such a determination is essentially a discretionary governmental decision, made by reference to EP&A Regulations, ibid. clause 228; and NSW Government, Is an EIS Required? Best Practice Guidelines for Part 5 of the Environmental Planning and Assessment Act 1979 (Department of Urban Affairs and Planning) (now the Department of Infrastructure, Planning and Natural Resources), available at http://www.planning.nsw.gov.au/index1.html.

behalf of the developer.[53] Where the proponent of an activity for which an EIS must be submitted is also the determining authority (under Part 5 of the EP&A Act),[54] that authority must apply to the Minister for Infrastructure and Planning and the Minister for Natural Resources for approval.[55] In such cases, the responsibility for deciding whether an EIS is necessary rests with the determining authority.

Once an EIS has been prepared by the proponent, it must be publicly exhibited for a period of at least 30 days.[56] The proponent must consider any public submissions and provide a Representations Report to the Minister with the proposal, setting out how the proponent has dealt with the issues raised during public exhibition. Prior to determination of approval of a public authority activity, the Director-General of the Department is required to prepare an independent assessment report for presentation to the Minster. In cases in which Commission of Inquiry has been held, the Minister will rely on the Commissioner's report, rather than a report from the Director-General.[57]

NSW is unique in comparison to other Australian states in that its legislation provides for statutorily appointed Commissioners of Inquiry. The purpose of these inquiries is to mediate disputes under the EP&A Act and the Heritage Act 1977 (NSW). The Commissions of Inquiry, however, have been criticized as being merely a façade, primarily because the commissioners do not have the authority to do anything other than provide a report to the Minister for consideration in the determination of the development application.[58]

Once the Minister has approved a proposal that required EIA, members of the public are given certain rights to appeal that decision. Only objectors to the original proposal have a right to appeal to the Land and Environment Court of NSW on the merits of the approval.[59] This appeal must be lodged within 28 days of receiving notice of the determination by the Minister. Similarly, only original objectors may attend court hearings and make submissions during an appeal by the proponent upon rejection of a development application.[60] These appeal rights do not apply when a Commission of Inquiry has been held. The open standing provisions in the EP&A Act for public involvement in court proceedings are granted under s 123 of the Act, and apply only to appeals to the court that are aimed at remedying a breach of the Act, and do not permit review of a decision on its merits.

3.3 Canadian Federal Regime

At a federal level, EIA was introduced in Canada through the Environmental Assessment Review Process (EARP) in 1973.[61] However, this was by way of an administrative regime,

---

[53] EP&A Act, *supra* note 50, Pt 5, section 112(1) (a) (i).

[54] Ibid. section 110B.

[55] Ibid. Section 115A. Transitional provisions are set out in section 115E.

[56] Ibid. Pt 4, section 79 (designated development).

[57] Ibid, Pt 5, Division 4.   [58] Bates, *supra* note 2 at 279.

[59] EP&A Act, *supra* note 50, Pt 4, section 98; Pt 5, section 113.

[60] Ibid. Pt 4, section 97(4).

[61] EARP was not based on legislation, but rather on specific directives of the federal Cabinet dated 8 June 1972 and 20 December 1973. A further Cabinet Directive in 1977 initiated some additional improvements, and the Government Organization Act (GOA) of 1979 in effect reaffirmed the responsibility of the federal Minister of the Environment for the environmental impact assessment of federally related activities. A series of further improvements were contained in the Environmental Assessment and Review Process

rather than legislative provision, and as a result, federal EIA was conducted through the exercise of political and administrative discretion, rather than through legal procedure.[62] It was not until 1995 that EIA was effectively included in federal legislation, under the Canadian Environmental Assessment Act (CEAA),[63] and administered by the Canadian Environmental Assessment Agency (formerly the Federal Environmental Assessment Review Office). Prior to the CEAA, Canada's federal EIA regime was considered weak because of its lack of clear or strong institutional arrangements.[64] EIA was undertaken through issuance of a Cabinet Directive, and an environmental review board was established on an ad hoc basis by the Minister for Environment and the minister responsible for the proposal, only when a major controversy over the project seemed likely. The final decision was made by the Minister, and there was no provision for either judicial or administrative appeal from any Directive issued. When the CEAA entered into force in 1995, many of the features of this previous system were retained, and although the current system has been said to provide a firmer foundation for an effective EIA regime, it still contains several weaknesses, including lack of agreement with the Provinces as to the extent of federal jurisdiction in environmental assessment.[65]

The assessment process under the CEAA is required when a federal authority has decision-making responsibilities in relation to the proposed project. This can occur when the federal authority (the "responsible authority") either proposes the project, provides financial assistance to the proponent, or transfers control of federal land or provides approval that enables the project to be carried out. An EIA may also be required when members of the public have petitioned the Minister requesting the project to be referred to a mediator or review panel, and the Minister considers the project to have potential for significant harm of the national, transnational, or international environment.

When environmental assessment is required by the federal authority, it may take place in one of four forms: screening (including class screenings), comprehensive studies, mediation, and assessment by a review panel. The *screening processes* are conducted by the "responsible authority,"[66] which documents the environmental effects of a proposal and makes determinations on how it should be modified. Class screenings are used to assess certain types of projects with known effects on a class basis, rather than individually, or on a project-specific basis. *Comprehensive studies* are applied to large-scale

---

Guidelines brought in by an Order-in-Council under the GOA in June 1984. EARP was administered by the Federal Environment Assessment Review Office (FEARO), which reported directly to the federal Minister of the Environment; M. Jeffery, "Environmental Assessment Processes in Canada and Australia: A Comparative Analysis" 8 (1–2) *Impact Assessment Bulletin* (1989) 289 at 291.

[62] Thomas, *supra* note 1 at 79.

[63] Canadian Environmental Assessment Act, 1992, c 37 (assented to 23 June 1992, entered into force 19 January 1995) (hereafter the CEAA).

[64] A. Stern, "Using Environmental Impact Assessment for Dispute Management" 11(1), *Environmental Impact Assessment Review* 81 (1991). Cited in Bates, *supra* note 2 at 80.

[65] C. Wood, "Comparative Evaluation of Environmental Impact Assessment Systems" in J. Petts, *Handbook of Environmental Impact Assessment*, Vol. 2 (Oxford: Blackwell Science, 1999) at 22–23.

[66] A *responsible authority* is a federal authority whose actions or powers trigger the environmental assessment of a particular project. The responsible authority must ensure that an environmental assessment of the project is conducted as early as possible in the planning stages of the project and before irrevocable decisions are made. See sections 5 and 11(1) of the CEAA, *supra note* 63.

environmentally sensitive projects[67] and are subject to certain public participation processes. When there are issues to be resolved between interested parties, the Minister may appoint a *mediator* to assess the project, and when the environmental impacts of a project are uncertain or likely to be significant, or public concerns are high, the Minister may appoint a *review panel* to hear from the interested parties. In assessments other than screenings, consideration must be given to alternatives to the proposal, and follow-up programs are to be implemented.

Public participation in the federal EIA system is limited to access to information regarding assessments (through the Canadian Environmental Assessment Registry)[68] and the opportunity to make submissions or attend hearings in the screening, comprehensive study, mediation, and review panel processes. There are no provisions for appeal by members of the public to administrative or judicial proceedings. Participant funding is available under subsection 58(1.1) of the CEAA to assist with costs such as travel expenses and expert testimony. Under this funding program, limited funding is available for those interested parties who are either property owners in the project area, holders of relevant community or traditional knowledge, or technical experts.[69]

3.4 The Province of Ontario

Of all the Canadian Provinces, Ontario is unique in that it has provided for specific EIA legislation, rather than bundling EIA into other, more general environmental protection legislation. The Environmental Assessment Act entered into force in 1976 and simultaneously provided for the EIA process as well as an assessment tribunal. The Environmental Assessment Board of Ontario (EAB) maintained a quasi-judicial jurisdiction and as such was the only such body with a decision-making role *and* an advisory role. In all other jurisdictions, the Minister was the sole decision-making body. However, appeals on merit from the decisions of the EAB went back to the Cabinet. Once this happened, the Cabinet had the choice of either affirming the EAB's decision, varying it, or sending it back for another decision, but in practice, very few findings of the EAB were overturned by the Cabinet. Appeals to the courts took place only on questions of judicial review of the process. In such cases, the courts are only able to send the decision back to the EAB to be made again, using the proper process.

The current EIA legislation in Ontario is the 1990 Environmental Assessment Act (EAA),[70] which applies to "undertakings" by public authorities or private proponents proposing an activity that is designated by the regulations.[71] Such activities must be approved by the Minister through the EIA process proscribed in the Act. Under the EAA, the proponent is responsible for preparing the environmental assessment in accordance with terms of reference approved by the Minister, which must include alternative ways

---

[67] These kinds of proposals are listed in the Comprehensive Study List Regulations 1(994) SOR/94–638.

[68] Canadian Government, Canadian Environmental Assessment Registry, Canadian Environmental Assessment Agency, at http://www.ceaa-acee.gc.ca/050/index_e.cfm.

[69] Funding is available only to successful applicants. See Canadian Government, Canadian Environmental Assessment Act Participant Funding Program, Canadian Environmental Assessment Agency, April 2004, available at http://www.ceaa-acee.gc.ca/012/013/Participant-Funding_e.pdf.

[70] Environmental Assessment Act, R.S.O. 1990, c E.18 (entered into force 31 December 1991) (hereafter EAA [Ontario]).

[71] Environmental Assessment Act R.R.O. 1990, Regulation 334 Amended to O. Reg. 390/01 General.

of carrying out the undertaking, as well as alternatives to the undertaking.[72] The proponent is also responsible for giving public notice of submission of the assessment,[73] and members of the public are entitled to comment on the assessment. The Ministry must then review the environmental assessment, taking into consideration any public comments and giving the proponent a chance to correct any deficiencies identified in the submission.[74]

Upon completion of the review by the Minister, the review is placed on public exhibition. The public may submit comments to the Ministry or request that the Minister refer the application or matters relating to it to the Environmental Review Tribunal (formerly the Environmental Assessment Board)[75] for a hearing and decision.[76] If the Minister chooses to refer the matter to the Tribunal, the Tribunal is given the power to make any decision that is open to the Minister to make, and any such decision is deemed to be a decision of the Minister; however, such a decision may be overridden or altered by the Minister or returned to the Tribunal for rehearing.[77] The Minister may also refer a matter to the Tribunal, prior to a decision, for mediation. The Minister is then required to consider the report from the mediation proceedings but is not bound by the findings contained within it.[78]

Within a discussion of Ontario's provisions under the EAA for public participation, it is useful to note that public involvement under the EAA is strengthened by the Environmental Bill of Rights 1993 (EBR).[79] The EBR recognizes a "right to a healthful environment"[80] by providing for increased rights of public involvement, including the right of citizens with an "interest" in certain approvals to seek leave to appeal that decision from the Tribunal. Under the EBR, previous participation in the comment period is sufficient evidence of interest in the matter, and the instrument is "appealable" under the Act through which it was originally issued.

4 IDENTIFIED PROCEDURAL WEAKNESSES IN THE PRACTICE OF ENVIRONMENTAL IMPACT ASSESSMENT

EIA is a public and political process at all stages. As has been demonstrated through the comparative analysis in this chapter, EIA legislation attempts to involve the public in some way at the documentation (or EIS) level, as well as at the decision making and appeal stages. Further, legislation such as Ontario's Environmental Bill of Rights confirms that a healthful environment is now seen as a right of citizens as individuals, and not simply another responsibility of government.

As stated at the outset, the effectiveness of public involvement varies according to the procedures by which EIA is undertaken and assessed. Bearing this in mind, members of the executive government and the legislature must now decide what the

---

[72] EAA (Ontario), *supra note* 70, section 6.1.
[73] Ibid. section 6.3.   [74] Ibid. section 7.
[75] The Environmental Review Tribunal Act, S.O. 2000, c 26, Sch. F, amalgamated the Environmental Assessment Board and the Environmental Appeal Board into what is today known as the *Environmental Review Tribunal.*
[76] EAA (Ontario), *supra note* 70 section 7(3).   [77] Ibid. section 9.1(2); section 11(6); section 11.2.
[78] Ibid. section 8.
[79] Environmental Bill of Rights S.O. 1993, c 28 (enacted February 1994) (hereafter EBR).
[80] Ibid. at Preamble.

purpose of public involvement is in environmental decision making, and accordingly what level of public involvement needs to be implemented to achieve that purpose. This chapter presents the argument that the purpose of public participation in EIA must be to provide checks and balances in the context of the overall process. This is required primarily for two reasons. First, EIS and technical documentation is generated by the proponent; therefore, the independence of the technical expertise employed is open to question. Second, when the responsibility to grant approvals ultimately rests with the government, as opposed to an independent tribunal or court, there is the tendency to politicize the decision-making process. This is especially the case given that the circumstances surrounding the approval of large-scale development projects are inherently often of a public and political nature.

4.1 Proponent-Generated EIS

Proponent-generated EISs have been criticized for some time, worldwide, on the basis of their lack of independent objectivity.[81] Without completely independent technical assessment, for instance, by consultants who are not seen to be employed by and/or paid by the party for whom the studies are prepared, the outcome of the EIA analysis will remain under suspicion.

Typically, the argument advanced in support of proponent-generated EIS and technical documentation is that one of the purposes of EIA is to require developers to incorporate environmental impacts in their project specifications and design.[82] This is no doubt an important consideration; however, the primary purpose of EIA must be to ensure that the environment is protected, and harm is mitigated, before a proposed project is approved. The production of an EIS is therefore required primarily for the purpose of ensuring that an informed decision is made by the consent or determining authority. This point was emphasized by Justice Cripps of the NSW Land and Environment Court in an early EIA case heard by that court, when His Honour stated that "[a]n obvious purpose of the EIS is to bring matters to the attention of members of the public, the Department of Environment and Planning, and to the determining authority in order that the environmental consequences of the proposed activity can be properly understood."[83] A lack of independence of technical expertise, combined with a system that does not adequately provide for critical analysis of the information presented in EIA documentation, not only threatens this fundamental goal of EIA, but also is likely to result in the failure of proponents to incorporate environmental considerations in the project *genuinely* at the design stage.

One possible solution to the difficulties presented by proponent-generated documentation or EIS has been to suggest that the government authority perform that function. However, certain practical and political barriers would undoubtedly apply to such a proposal. For example, if a government department were to be set up specifically to perform the function of producing an EIS or preparing the documentation on the

---

[81] D. Farrier, *The Environmental Law Handbook* (Redfern Legal Centre Publishing, Sydney, Australia) (2000) 511.

[82] See, for example, some earlier NSW case law: *Warren v. Electricity Commission of NSW*, unreported, NSWLEC, 31 October 1990; *Liverpool City Council v. Roads and Traffic Authority* (1991) 74 LGRA 265.

[83] *Prineas v. Forestry Commission of NSW* (1983) 49 LGRA 402 at 417, per Cripps J.

potential impacts of a proposal, it would have to retain an expert in every relevant area of scientific expertise because of the range of possible developments that might take place. The expense of such a system is likely to be prohibitive in many jurisdictions. In addition, a major and systemic defect in this approach is that government authorities exist to carry out the policy of government, notwithstanding the fact that often the proponents of large infrastructure projects such as sewage treatment and transport facilities are in fact government authorities. In such cases, experts of the government department could not be said to be truly independent, as they are likely to be influenced to some extent by government policy. Alternatively, even when the government department might hire private consultants, rather than retain technical experts on its staff, the issues of lack of independence of technical expertise will inevitably still arise.

It appears then that partisan EIS and technical documentation is an unpreventable consequence of the EIA process. While it may not be possible to prevent preparation of EIS documentation by those with a potential vested interest in the outcome of the development application, it is suggested here that a more robust evaluation and adjudication system, which encourages and supports citizen participation, has the potential to provide a system of checks and balances that would better provide for an informed and impartial final decision.

4.2 Lack of Independence of Approval Bodies

Another major difficulty with many EIA regimes, including those presented here (with the exception perhaps of NSW), is that when the final determining authority is part of the administrative rather than judicial process, the independence of that approval body is put into question. As discussed, members of government departments and authorities are likely to be influenced to some extent by government policy and priorities at the time. While EIA should not be considered grounds for introducing an "environmental veto" to administrative decisions,[84] provision for appeal from such decisions is a necessary element in maintaining the integrity of EIA regimes and promoting genuine citizen involvement in significant environmental matters.

5 ADDRESSING THE PROCEDURAL WEAKNESSES IN THE CONTEXT OF THE ADJUDICATION PROCESS

Having determined that there is a need in EIA regimes for effective public involvement in order to counter some of the difficulties associated with lack of independence at both the EIS and approval stages of EIA, I submit that such effective public participation is best provided for through effective hearings before a court or tribunal that has the authority to decide the application independently of the government in power. Essentially, there are two aspects of the adjudication processes that need to be improved:

1. It is not enough for the public to be afforded standing without provision made for that public participation to be effective.
2. There must be vigorous and robust adjudication procedures, which enable the decision maker to arrive at an informed decision, while encouraging public participation.

---

[84] Bates, *supra* note 2 at 278.

The remainder of this chapter focuses on those elements that will ensure effective public involvement and in turn lead to better environmental decision making. Although the role of citizen or public participation is examined briefly in this chapter the outset, before embarking on a discussion of the procedures relevant to improving such participation in public interest environmental litigation, it is also necessary to consider the nature and definition of "public interest."

The term *public interest* cannot be given a precise definition; in general, it is taken to refer to an interest held by the community at large, in an issue that affects their legal rights or liabilities, and "does not mean anything so narrow as mere curiosity, or as the interest of the particular localities, which may be affected by the matters in question."[85] As such, the public interest is generally given careful consideration by the courts as the implications of its decision are inevitably extensive.[86] Recognized public interest litigants in proceedings concerning adjudication of EIA go to the court not in pursuit of any private or personal gain, but in protection of community values and needs, which include enforcement of environmental and EIA laws and processes. It is for this reason that such cases should be differentiated from traditional forms of private tort or contract law claims, particularly when considering the appropriateness of traditional court procedures, rules, and costs. A fresh approach to litigation in public interest EIA cases is therefore not only justified, but required.[87]

5.1 Affordability of Opposition

There are two aspects to take into consideration when looking at ways to reduce the costs to public interest litigants in enforcing EIA procedures provided by the legislature. First, the courts may order or the legislation may provide that public interest litigants shall be exempt from costs orders should they fail in their case. Such a system must, of course, include its own checks and balances, to ensure that frivolous or malicious litigation is not brought merely to frustrate a proposal. Second, the legislation may provide for funding of public interest litigants.

This issue of orders for costs in public interest cases has been acknowledged at common law as an important determinant of whether such litigation can be brought in practice. For example, the NSW Land and Environment Court (LEC) has recognized since at least 1988 that in some public interest environmental appeals cases, costs of the proponent's case should not be awarded against a public interest litigant if such a litigant is unsuccessful.[88] The policy of that court has been to avoid ordering costs in certain cases of appeals on the merits of an approval, save in exceptional

---

[85] *Black's Law Dictionary* (5th ed.) (1983) 43.

[86] See, for example, *Virginian Ry v. System Fed'n* No. 40, 300 U.S. 515, 552 (1937).

[87] See, for example, comments by Justice Douglas (dissenting) in *Sierra Club v. Morton*, 405 U.S. at 742–745.

[88] See, for example, *Campbell v. Minister*, unreported, 24 June 1988, per Cripps J; *Fuller v. Bellingen Shire Council*, unreported, 13 July 1988 per Hemmings J; *Nettheim v. Minister (No. 2)*, unreported, 24 September 1988. It should be noted that costs are not awarded only under certain circumstances: *Rundle v. Tweed Shire Council (No. 2)* (1989) 69 LGRA 21; *Liverpool City Council v. RTA (No. 2)* (1992) 75 LGRA 210; *Citizens Airport Environment Association Inc v. MSB*, unreported, Stein J, 9 June 1993. The criteria for determining when costs should not be awarded against public interest litigants are set out in *Oshlack v. Richmond River Shire Council* (1994) 82 LGERA 236, per Stein J, approved in *Friends of Hay Street Inc v. Hastings Council* (1995) 87 LGERA 44, per Pearlman J.

circumstances.[89] In support of this practice, applications for security for costs brought by a proponent in public interest cases have been carefully examined by both the NSW LEC[90] and the NSW Court of Appeal.[91] Security for costs in public interest environmental litigation is rarely ordered, in recognition of the fact that where such an order is made in public interest cases, it may defeat the litigation at the outset, as public interest litigants often lack the significant financial support required to provide for costs of the opposing party should their case prove unsuccessful.[92]

While costs and security for costs orders should be carefully considered by the courts in public interest EIA cases, the often prohibitive costs associated with actually presenting a case in court should also be addressed. With the exception of the participant funding program provided by Canada's federal CEAA (which is limited in its application) and standard legal aid services, none of the jurisdictions studied here currently provide for funding of opposition to development proposals. This represents a serious deficiency in most EIA regimes to date, although, paradoxically, one that was, for a brief time, rectified in the Province of Ontario through the enactment of the now repealed Intervenor Funding Project Act (IFPA).[93]

Appropriate funding of opposition to an EIA approval, including proponent-generated EISs, is necessary to ensure both the existence and the quality of citizen participation in EIA processes. Prior to the enactment of the IFPA, a Joint Board in the Province of Ontario (chaired by this writer) as early as 1984 sought to give effect to the novel approach of awarding "costs in advance" in public interest cases wherein a proponent was ordered to provide for the costs of objectors (or intervenors) to the proposal at the adjudication stage.[94] The IFPA enacted in 1989, although controversial at the time, represented a balanced piece of legislation and included provisions to prevent abuse of the process of intervenor funding. These included a set of eligibility criteria and measures to ensure accountability.[95] It provided for a "right" of certain intervenors to funding upon a determination by a funding panel as to whether the proponent in the case should be considered a "funding proponent."[96] This method of providing for

---

[89] Justice P. Stein, "The Role of the New South Wales Land and Environment Court in the Emergence of Public Interest Environmental Law" 13 *Environmental and Planning Law Journal* (1996) 179 at 181.

[90] See, for example, *Byron Shire Businesses for the Future Inc v. Byron Shire Council* (1994) 83 LGERA 59 per Pearlman J and, more recently, *Carriage v. Stockland (Constructors) Pty Ltd* (2003) 125 LGERA 414; [2003] NSWLEC 129, per Pain J.

[91] See, for example, *Brown v. Environment Protection Authority*, unreported, Priestley J, 1 April 1993; *Maritime Services Board v. Citizens Airport Environment Association Inc* (1993) 83 LGERA 107, at 111 per Kirby P.

[92] Stein, *supra* note 89 at 181.

[93] Intervenor Funding Project Act R.S.O. 1990, Ch I.13 (repealed 1 April 1996 by subsection 16 [1]) (hereafter IFPA [Ontario]). It is important to note that the legislation was repealed by a government formed by a political party other than the one under which the legislation was introduced. See Jeffery, *supra* note 16 for a comprehensive discussion of this topic.

[94] This approach was adopted by the Joint Board in Ontario (constituted under the Consolidated Hearings Act, S.O. 1981, c 19) in the *Redhill Creek Expressway* case concerning an application by the Regional Municipality of Hamilton-Wentworth for environmental approval of a roadway connecting two provincial highways. The Joint Board's Order was subsequently quashed on judicial review by the Divisional Court of the Supreme Court of Ontario. For an in-depth discussion of the costs–funding debate, see Jeffery, *supra* note 16.

[95] The eligibility criteria are set out in IFPA (Ontario); *supra* note 93, section 7.

[96] Ibid. section 4(1).

the costs of public interest litigants goes substantially further than the NSW legislative and common law model and, in this writer's view, constitutes an approach that should be seriously considered in the context of providing citizens the right to participate *effectively* in environmental decision making.

5.2 A More Robust Adjudication Process

Aside from issues of affordability, public interest litigants are prevented from participating effectively if the process under which they participate is unnecessarily complex in terms of the application of traditional legal rules such as the rules of evidence, qualification of expert witnesses, or discovery procedures that do not allow for thorough examination of evidence that is presented.

Most jurisdictions have progressed to the point where the formal rules of evidence have been relaxed or in many cases dispensed with altogether. Rather than inhibiting public participation and prolonging hearings with argument focussed on the inadmissibility of evidence, many adjudicative bodies now allow all relevant evidence to be admitted and simply weigh its probative value. This model facilitates the participation of members of the public in a less intimidating forum without the necessity of retaining counsel and invariably results in a less costly and more efficient use of hearing time. It is not surprising that many courts with civil jurisdiction also now dispense with the rules of evidence in the interests of reducing costs and increasing efficiency.[97]

The rules of science and law have been clearly defined over many years of practice. Each has its own set of standards as to what is an acceptable level of proof. Public interest environmental cases, as in civil litigation, require the civil burden of proof, namely, that an assertion must be proved on a balance of probabilities, as opposed to the criminal burden of proof – beyond a reasonable doubt. As Lord Denning observed, "[i]f the evidence is such that the tribunal can say: we think it more probable than not, the burden is discharged, but if the probabilities are equal it is not."[98] By contrast, proof of a particular hypothesis in science requires a much higher degree of certainty, often expressed in the range of an approximate 95 percent confidence level.[99] The adjudicator in EIA cases is faced with this apparent dilemma, which must be resolved in order to reach the most appropriate outcome, both technically and in the interests of justice and the public good.

One conclusion that might be drawn from this difficulty is that the adversarial process is not the most appropriate forum for EIA determinations. Alternative dispute resolution (ADR) is often suggested as a convenient way in which such cases can be determined. However, it is submitted here that adjudication procedures based solely on mediation and arbitration present public interest litigants with more problems than they solve.[100]

---

[97] In Australia, litigants, with leave of the Court, may opt out of the necessity of adhering to the rules of evidence in civil cases and, in some instances, criminal cases. Evidence Act 1995 (Cth), s 190. Identical provisions are included in the NSW Evidence Act 1995, s 190.

[98] *Miller v. Minister of Pensions* (1947) 2 *All England Reports* 372.

[99] See N. Ashford, "Examining the Role of Science in the Regulatory Process" 25(5) *Environment* (1983) 7.

[100] See, for example, M. Jeffery, "Accommodating Negotiation in Environmental Impact Assessment and Project Approval Processes" *Environmental and Planning Law Journal* (1987) 244.

ADR is useful in a number of ways in environmental disputes. For example, it is helpful in the process of *scoping* the relevant issues, dealing with those that are peripheral to the substance of the dispute, and referring on the issues still in dispute to the hearing stage for resolution in a judicial or quasi-judicial forum. ADR as a form of environmental decision making is however, limited in its application in several fundamental ways and should, in the view of this writer, be considered only as an adjunct to the adversarial process, rather than a replacement.

Negotiation and mediation are concerned with reaching consensus between interested parties. This has meant that ADR is primarily concerned in resolving disputes between private parties. When there are no private interests in a development proposal, or such interests are satisfied at settlement, the wider issues of the public interest, and critical evaluation of the technical information, are not included in the process. This does not sit well with the nature of many environmental disputes involving EIA, which typically involve a large number of "interested parties," including members of the public at large. According to the principle of sustainable development, *future* generations must also be taken into account in environmental decision making, further expanding the number of stakeholders. All of these considerations indicate that ADR may often be seen as an inappropriate method of reaching the best and most sustainable environmental decision and representing all concerned parties.

In addition, as ADR is negotiation between parties, rather than adjudication, when there is an imbalance of power, the weaker parties (typically those in opposition to the proposal) can emerge from the settlement with a feeling of being bullied or cornered into an unsatisfactory agreement by the stronger parties. An adjudicative procedure that is fair and balanced is more likely to leave the parties with a greater sense of justice and equity. Therefore, it is submitted here that environmental tribunals or courts should be considered as playing the primary role in resolution of environmental disputes, as such institutions are subject to the rules of natural justice and procedural fairness, while negotiation or mediation is not.

Environmental tribunals (and, in the case of NSW, environmental courts) operate in a different way than traditional courts, in that they seek not only to resolve a dispute between two parties as courts do, but also to advance the public interest with respect to a particular environmental issue raised by a development proposal. They must therefore adjudicate the matter on the basis of evaluation of fact as well as policy. A vigorous and robust adversarial process is, in this writer's view, the most advantageous forum for this evaluation process for the following reasons:[101]

1. It requires aspects of peer review of technical experts' theories and evidence, by way of examination and cross-examination of expert testimony. This requirement contributes to more informed decision making. This can include making provision for hearing evidence from a panel of experts when the most qualified witness can be heard on each particular aspect of the evidence.
2. It encourages technical experts to communicate their evidence in a way that is understandable to a generalist judiciary and, therefore, the public involved in the proceedings. This facilitates public involvement in the proceedings.

---

[101] See, for example, S. Smith, "Science in the Courtroom: The Value of an Adversarial System," 15(2) *Alternatives* (1988) 18; M. Jeffery, "Science and the Tribunal: Dealing with Scientific Evidence in the Adversarial Arena" 15(2) *Alternatives* (1988) 25.

3. An adversarial system of evaluation entails a notion of fairness and justice, which contributes to the furtherance of the public interest and allows community groups to participate legitimately in the proceedings, rather than merely being consulted by an administrative decision-making panel.

It is submitted that EIA approval processes that encourage meaningful public participation and that have appropriate intervenor funding mechanisms and procedural reforms will, in fact, improve decision making and thus better realize the potential of environmental impact assessment methodology. In addition, interested members of the public will leave the process with a greater sense of being afforded an opportunity for meaningful participation as opposed to being included in a form of *participatory tokenism* with no real chance of influencing the ultimate decision.[102]

6 CONCLUDING COMMENTS

Conceptually, EIA was a major advance in environmental law and policy when it first appeared in the 1970s through the U.S. legislation (NEPA) and soon afterward in jurisdictions such as Canada and Australia. It is now considered an essential element of any legal environmental regulatory system and has much to contribute to preventing environmental harm in large-scale projects that have the potential to harm the environment significantly.

The comparative analysis presented within this chapter demonstrates incorporation of EIA as a concept in environmental law systems in Canada and Australia. However, citizen participation in environmental decision making is now seen as a necessary part of EIA regimes to ensure that they are effective. Over the years, it has become evident that the process of EIA is threatened through the potential for EIA documentation, the EIS, to be presented in a biased, or noncomplete fashion, and the potential for government decision-making bodies to be politicized. It is submitted that these difficulties can be dealt with by providing for procedural regimes that ensure meaningful public involvement in decision making. This must be facilitated as a means of providing checks and balances within the assessment process. Two key areas in which this can be achieved are through increased funding (and removal of financial barriers) in public interest environmental litigation, as well as an EIA decision-making regime that is structured around an effective and legitimate appeals process, which allows for independent final assessment of the project.

Although it might be argued that meaningful public involvement will result in increased cost to either the taxpayer or proponents of large-scale development projects, it is important that the recommendations within this chapter are considered in context. When one considers the benefits to society and the environment as a whole of informed decision making in the light of the often substantial environmental, social, and economic costs associated with remedying instances of pollution or degradation resulting from inappropriate development, any added expense that may arise from effective public involvement in environmental assessment at the planning and project stage is certain to be justifiable.

---

[102] As recently stated by this writer, "[w]ithout adequate resources to properly prepare a case for hearing, to rein in experienced counsel and expert witnesses, and to participate fully throughout the entire proceeding, standing translates into little more than *participatory tokenism*": Jeffery, *supra* note 16 at 18.

In pursuit of environmental quality, social equity, and better quality of environmental decisions, incorporating the goals of sustainable development, legislatures, courts, and administrative agencies must improve public access to the decision-making process. As a result of pressure on governments to allow for this, we have seen some progress in terms of removal of strict standing requirements in public interest cases and increased opportunity for public comment. However, further reform should take place in order to recognize the unique role of environmental decisions in legal and administrative processes and to ensure that the final decision reached is one that is the most appropriate technically, socially, and economically, in terms of both the current generation and future generations.

26 Protection of Natural Spaces in Brazilian Environmental Law

José Rubens Morato Leite, Heline Sivini Ferreira, and Patryck de Araújo Ayala

1 THE RISK SOCIETY AND THE ENVIRONMENTAL CRISIS

Ulrich Beck[1] describes "the risk society" as being characterized by contingencies, or "risks," created by scientific, technological, and industrial progress that can no longer be controlled by the typical institutions of industrial society. In this new social pattern, abstract risks interact with the concrete risks that formerly characterized industrial society. Concrete risks can be foreseen and controlled. Abstract risks, however, are unforeseeable and uncontrollable. Abstract risks can only be managed.

While the risks described by Beck affect many distinct fields of social life, environmental problems are among the most prominent worldwide issues. Fernando dos Reis Condesso[2] presents the following data: Atmospheric pollution tripled in the last three decades; between the years 1992 and 1998, approximately 50,000 biological species became extinct; only four-thousandths of the planet's water is available for human consumption; because of human activities, about 10 percent of the earth's surface has been transformed from forest and fertile ground into desert.

Beck observes that environmental risks are limitless through time, global in extent, and potentially disastrous.[3] Because of the increasing complexity of these risks, industrial society has lost the ability to control them. In this context, the environmental crisis has reached a new dimension. It has become a global and complex crisis, an undivided and interdependent part of a larger crisis, which Edgar Morin[4] calls "poly-crisis." Within this poly-crisis, it is not possible to establish a hierarchy of concerns because there is not just one critical problem but many interlinked critical problems. It is necessary to pursue distinct efforts, which reach the political, economic, social, and judicial sectors, in order to achieve effective protection of the environment. These efforts, however, must be guided by a rationale different from the rationale of the industrial society.

Evidence of this necessity can be found in the judicial field: Despite the fact that environmental law has been considered innovative and advanced in many respects,

---

[1] Ulrich Beck, *La sociedad del riesgo: hacia una nueva modernidad* (Paidós) (1998). [Ulrich Beck, *The Risk Society, towards a New Modernity*. Trans. from the German by Mark Ritter (Sage Pub.) 1992 orig. pub 1986].

[2] Fernando dos Reis Condesso, *Direito do Ambiente* (Almedina) (2001).

[3] See also Emílio Lamo de Espinosa, "De bruces con la posmodernidad: ignorancia, poder y comunicación en la sociedad comunicación en la sociedad" (2001), *Política Exterior* 80, 11–20 (new environmental risks are ubiquitous, global, and invisible threats).

[4] Edgar Morin et al., *Terra-Pátria* (Sulina) (1995).

its limitations can be observed in the face of the new pattern of environmental crisis. These limitations extend not only to legislation, which is full of rules that are ineffective at managing abstract risk, but also to law enforcement, which faces a lack of secure references.[5] If the judicial–environmental system follows the industrial society rationale, it will not be able to protect the environment in a suitable way, and environmental law will have only a symbolic function.[6] The risk society mandates a new rationale. Only after considering that there are global and multiple crises will it be possible to adapt environmental protection to the requirements of the risk society.

2 THE RELEVANCE OF NATURAL SPACES PROTECTION IN THE RISK SOCIETY

Environmental law has been experiencing a greening process that began in the 1970s. This advance can be observed not only in the international sphere, where the main references are the United Nations Conference on Human Environment (Estocolmo, 1972) and the United Nations Conference on Environment and Development (Rio de Janeiro, 1992), but also in the sphere of many countries' internal regulations. Nevertheless, it is important to emphasize that mere legal adequacy to the necessities of the environmental crisis does not guarantee the effectiveness of the whole system. As seen before, there are several simultaneous problems and they must be considered together. In this case, in order to prevent environmental law's having only a symbolic function in the context of the risk society, it is necessary to think of law as a system that depends on other systems. The effectiveness of the judicial–environmental system will depend on the effectiveness of every other system.

The repercussions of the greening process have reached Brazilian environmental legislation. The Constitution of the Federal Republic of Brazil, for instance, established the right to an ecologically balanced environment as a fundamental right. The document, in Article 225, states:

> All have the right to an ecologically balanced environment, which is an asset of common use and essential to a healthy quality of life, and both the government and the community shall have the duty to defend and preserve it for present and future generations.[7]

Through the judicial protection of the environment, the lawmaker has attempted to watch over diffuse interests – interests that belong not to one single person but to all society.[8] It can also be noticed that the lawmaker has transcended the liberal myth that has kept government and civil society apart. The Constitution charged the duty of preserving and protecting the environment not only to the government but also to

---

[5] José Esteve Pardo, *Técnica, riesgo y derecho* (Ariel S.A.) (1999).

[6] Regarding the symbolic function of environmental law, see Wolf Paul, *A irresponsabilidade organizada?* in José Alcebíades Oliveira Junior (org.), *O novo em Direito e política* (Livraria do Advogado) (1997) 177–189.

[7] Constituição da República Federativa do Brasil in Odete Medauar (org.), *Coletânea de legislação de Direito Ambiental – Constituição Federal* (Revista dos Tribunais) (2003). An English translation of the Constitution is available at http://www.v-brazil.com/government/laws/constitution.html.

[8] José Rubens Morato Leite, *Dano ambiental: do individual ao coletivo extrapatrimonial* 2nd ed. (Revista dos Tribunais) (2003).

society. In this way, a shared liability system was established. This system is appropriate to complex environmental risk management because it is suitable to mutual inspection and control. In addition, the shared liability system foresees public discussion as a forum to plan and execute environmental policies. Through this process, both public information and public participation in decision making are enhanced.

This shared right and duty to protect the environment has yet to be recognized by many countries. In most of the African continent,[9] for example, the lawmaker establishes that all citizens have the right to a healthy environment. However, only the government has the duty to preserve it. The shared liability system, on the other hand, can change society's passive behavior concerning the current environmental crisis. The result is that all citizens become responsible not only for the maintenance of environmental balance but also for their own chance to exercise the right to a balanced environment.

It must be stressed that the right to an ecologically balanced environment is an extension of the fundamental right to life. In this case, the right to life must be considered as a right reciprocally conferred by living beings among themselves. The lawmaker's concern for equity among generations must extend to all living beings.[10] Special natural spaces – which are also addressed by the Brazilian Constitution[11] – can be understood as an essential part of the environment. The particular juridical regime conferred on these spaces is determined by the significance of their natural attributes. Hence, the definition of these areas by the government aims to protect species' evolutionary processes, the areas' natural resources, and ecological systems' diversity.[12] Once a space is defined as being of ecological interest, whether in a public or private geographic area, government and society will have the duty to protect and preserve it for present and future generations of life.

In spite of the evidences of a greening of the Brazilian judicial–environmental system, there are many obstacles to natural space protection. Some of these obstacles, which are typical problems of the risk society, will be considered in the next section in the context of specific conditions observed in emergent countries.

3 THE DIFFICULTIES OF PLANNING AND ARRANGING NATURAL SPACES IN THE EMERGENT COUNTRIES

The main problems faced by emergent countries in planning and arranging protected areas are (1) institutions unprepared to deal with environmental issues, (2) lack of

---

[9] South Africa Constitution of 1996, article 24; Congo (Brazzaville) Fundamental Act of 1997, article 21; Erythrée Constitution of 1996, article 10; Ethiopia Constitution of 1994, article 44; Gabon Constitution of 1991, article 1; Gambia Constitution of 1996, articles 216 and 220; Ghana Constitution of 1996 (revised), article 41; Guinea Fundamental Act of 1991, article 19; Madagascar Constitution of 1992, article 39; Malawi Constitution of 1994, article 13; Niger Constitution of 1996, article 27; Nigeria Constitution of 1999, articles 16 and 20; Uganda Constitution of 1995, article 39; Senegal Constitution of 2001, article 8; Seychelles Constitution of 1996 (revised), articles 38 and 40; Chad Constitution of 1996, articles 47 and 52; Togo Constitution of 1992, article 41; Zambia Constitution of 1996 (revised), article 112 (Mohamed Ali Mekouar, *Le droit a l'environnement dans la Charte africaine des droits de l'homme et des peuples* (Etude juridique de la FAO en ligne) (2001).

[10] Cristiane Derani, *Direito Ambiental econômico* (Max Limonad) (1997).

[11] C.F. art 225, III.

[12] José Afonso da Silva, *Direito ambiental constitucional* 2. ed. (Malheiros) (1997).

suitable legal systems, and (3) incompatibility between economic growth and the protection of the environment.

3.1 Institutions Unprepared to Deal with Environmental Issues

A suitable standard of protection for the environment in the risk society depends on a new institutional structure. This structure must join, on one side, qualified professionals and modern equipment at the disposal of the government and, on the other side, conscious and able citizens acting to preserve the environment. This improvement demands financial investments, however, and usually, emergent countries cannot afford this. Despite the noticeable economic growth of some countries known until recently as "underdeveloped," the world division between rich countries of the North and poor countries of the South is still a fact that interferes with environmental protection.

The lack of a suitable institutional structure interferes directly with natural space protection. The selection of a specific area, its delimitation, and, in some cases, the kind of activity allowed in it must depend on varied analyses conduced by qualified professionals. In addition, once a natural space is defined, inspection and management of the whole area are indispensable to the protection of its natural attributes. Throughout this process, the society must be actively involved.

3.2 The Legal Systems

Legal systems must also be adapted to the new environmental requirements of the risk society. In many emergent countries, lawmakers are still making rules under the old-fashioned rationale of the industrial society. The emergent countries have to replace the anthropocentric view with an enlarged outlook in order to make possible the greening of environmental law. Hence, in the environmental lawmaking process, the fact that nature and human beings are part of a joined and interdependent system has to be considered. From this perspective, new mechanisms and instruments will be created that consolidate a functional legal system and a social pattern characterized by doubts and uncertainties.

Correspondingly, the planning and arrangement of natural spaces of considerable ecological interest demands suitable legislation. In Brazil, for instance, after almost eight years of consideration by the National Congress,[13] Act n. 9.985, of 19 June 2000, was put in force. The Act of the National System of Conservation Units (SNUC),[14] as it is usually called, adopts measures to define spaces of ecological interest – conservation units. Despite criticisms – and the main one is that this statute was enacted with North American law as a pattern and thus may be inappropriate to the Brazilian context[15] – the

---

[13] Maurício Mercadante, "Uma década de debate e negociação: a história da elaboraçào da Lei do SNUC," in Antônio Herman Benjamin (coord.), *Direito Ambiental das Áreas Protegidas* (Forense Universitária) (2001) 190–231.

[14] Act n. 9.985/00 (National System of Conservation Units).

[15] Miguel Serediuk Milano, "Unidades de conservação: técnica, lei e ética para a conservação da biodiversidade," in Antônio Herman Benjamin (coord.), *Direito Ambiental das Áreas Protegidas* (Forense Universitária) (2001) 3–41.

SNUC Act has great potential to be effective. It is a result of a legislative effort to order and unify the procedure for definition of protected natural spaces.[16] However, enforcement of the SNUC Act effectively depends on an institutional structure able to deal with the environmental issue, something that Brazilian government has not yet developed.

3.3 Economic Growth and Environmental Protection

Once emergent countries become involved in the globalization process and desire greater economic competitiveness, they may enter the market without environmental restrictions. Because they are not able to assure environmental conservation – not only because of a lack of institutional structures but also because of unsuitable legal systems – the environment is usually exploited in an incorrect way.

A Brazilian example can be mentioned. Through Act n. 9.279, of 14 May 1996, and Act n. 9.456, of 26 April 1997, Brazil established rules for granting patents on living creatures. The main problem was that Brazil regulated the subject before it had either the basic instruments to compete in the international market or a suitable structure to preserve the nation's biological diversity. As a result, Brazil supported the acquisition by foreign business firms of its national genetic resources, causing damage to legally protected natural spaces in many situations. Two emblematic cases are the *fruta do bibiri* case, in which the Canadian laboratory Biolink registered a fruit that has been used by generations of native *uapixanas*, inhabitants of Rondônia State, as a contraceptive, and the *acerola* case, in which a typical Brazilian fruit was patented by a Japanese firm called Asahi Foods. Moreover, biopiracy of Brazilian resources causes a daily loss of U.S. $16 million, in addition to environmental injuries. It is important to emphasize that, along with illegal animal commerce, biopiracy is the third largest illicit activity worldwide, only behind illegal commerce in drugs and weapons. In general, biopiracy is a result of two main problems: the difficulty of inspection and control and the lack of legislation that truly protects the genetic property of native species.[17]

The desire for economic expansion usually conflicts with the need for environmental protection, particularly in emergent countries, and interferes with the process of planning and arranging natural spaces. According to Marc Dourojeanni,[18] environmental mercantilism is an economically profitable option for emergent countries. However, this option is completely at odds with the concept of sustainable development. Emergent countries now face the huge challenge of adapting institutional structures and legislation to the new environmental templates imposed by the risk society, in order to facilitate balance among environmental, social, economic, and political interests.

Once the relevance of environmental issues is acknowledged, the relationship between economic expansion and the environment will change. And so the protection of special natural spaces will be considered as necessary, and the preservation of their

---

[16] According to Cristiane Derani, this system joins two general attributes: order and unity, *order* because the system presents a rational content developed through an argumentative process, *unity* because it constitutes a cohesive Act with an adequate number of elements to make the whole text meaningful. *See* Cristiane Derani, *Direito Ambiental econômico* (Max Limonad) (1997).

[17] Darlene Menconi et al., "Riqueza ameaçada" [2003], Revista Istoé 1773, 92–98.

[18] Marc Dourojeanii, "Áreas protegidas de América Latina en los Albores del Siglo XXI," in Antônio Herman Benjamin (coord.), *Direito Ambiental das Áreas Protegidas* (Forense Universitária) (2001) 42–107.

natural attributes for present and future generations will be established as an expression of the fundamental rights to life and to an ecologically balanced environment.

4 PROTECTED AREAS AND NATURAL SPACES APPROPRIATION IN BRAZILIAN LAW: CONSTITUTIONAL AND LEGAL ASPECTS

The system of protection of natural spaces that exists in Brazilian law is, in its essence, a consequence of a complex process of transformation accomplished by the Republic Constitution of 1988, which involves the organizational structure of the relations of production in the Brazilian State, the legal condition of assets in the economic order, and, mainly, the relations of appropriation established over these assets. The new economic order is defined in terms of a social and ecological market economy.[19] The relations of production and appropriation regarding natural resources are oriented by a set of rules[20] that complement an existing system up to now based on the protection of private property over communal rights.

The system proposed by the Brazilian Constitution integrates a dimension we could call social appropriation with the economic one. From this perspective, any relation of appropriation must accomplish two different functions: an individual one (property economic dimension) and a collective one (property socioenvironmental dimension). Property fulfills its social function (1) in urban areas when it is developed according to the fundamental requirements of the city's master plan[21] and (2) in rural areas when it complies with legal requirements for the rational and adequate use of the area, adequate use of its natural resources and the preservation of the environment, labor regulations, and "exploitation that favors the well-being of owners and laborers."[22]

The principle of the social function of property trumps private autonomy in economic relations to protect the interests of the whole community around a right to an ecologically balanced environment. Only private property that accomplishes its social function has constitutional protection.[23] Failure to accomplish this function requires the imposition of a sanction – compulsory expropriation.[24] This sanction can be imposed for the irresponsible exercise of the right and for the inadequate management of natural resources.

When spaces of ecological interest are classified as conservation units, they fall under the rules of a National System.[25] The law proposes a National System that, however, does not include all protected spaces. The Brazilian Constitution itself gave express protection to five big ecosystems even before the institution of the SNUC, because of their importance to the protection of Brazil's biological diversity: the Amazon Forest, the

---

[19] See Cristiane Derani, *supra* note 16; Peter Häberle, *El Estado constitucional* (Fondo Editorial da Pontificia Universidad Católica del Perú) (2003).

[20] The general principles of economic activity, C.F. Title VII, ch. 1.

[21] C.F. art 182, § 2.   [22] C.F. art. 186.

[23] Fabio Konder Komparato, "Direitos e deveres fundamentais em matéria de propriedade," in Alberto do Amaral Júnior et al. (orgs.), *O Cinqüentenário da Declaração Universal dos Direitos do Homem* (Edusp) (1999) 377–384.

[24] Compulsory expropriation is the sanction specified by the Constitution for violation of the social function of urban property (C.F. art. 182, § 4) and rural property (C.F. art. 184).

[25] Act n. 9.985/00 (National System of Conservation Units).

Atlantic Forest, the Pantanal Mato-Grossense, the Serra do Mar, and the Coast Zone.[26] The protection of these spaces represents a true political–constitutional option of functional organization of spaces,[27] and, mainly, a functional definition of the relations that are established in these spaces.

The special status conferred on these spaces by the Brazilian Constitution is related to the juridical system of protection and enjoyment[28] (management and administration). The objective is the preservation or conservation of the ecological functions of the natural space, regardless of its particular qualities.[29] The Brazilian Constitution severely restricts access to these spaces and their natural resources. Thus, any use that could endanger the integrity of the natural attributes that are specifically being protected is prohibited.[30] The alteration of the territorial limits of protected areas is also prohibited; these boundaries may be changed only by law.

If the Constitution exercises a control function on the uses of the protected areas, it can be said that the National System emphasizes, among other aspects, a planning function for the natural spaces.[31] It defines different kinds of conservation units and specifies uses allowed in each of them. By defining rules that forbid some uses in areas defined as spaces of ecological interest, the Constitution did not immediately exclude these spaces from the possibility of appropriation, reserving the resolution of this gap to the law.[32] This is the case also with ecosystems designated as National Heritage.[33]

There are two types of conservation units: strict protection and sustainable use (see Table 26.1).[34] Strict protection has the objective of the preservation of nature and allows only the indirect use of the area's natural resources.[35] Sustainable use aims at conserving nature while allowing the sustainable use of some natural resources.[36] In the terms of the law, units of the strict protection group are regulated by a system that excludes the environmental asset from the possibility of private appropriation. This classification prohibits appropriation and economic exploitation not only of the spaces themselves but also of the existing natural resources that contribute to the scientific and aesthetic interest of these sensitive areas and to the maintenance of their biological diversity.

---

[26] C.F. art. 225, § 4.

[27] Derani argues that conservation units represent a particular form of social appropriation of the space. See Cristiane Derani, *supra* note 16.

[28] *Id.*

[29] Antônio Herman Benjamin, "Introdução à Lei do Sistema Nacional das Unidades de Conservação" in Antônio Herman Benjamin (coord.), *Direito ambiental das áreas protegidas: O regime jurídico das unidades de conservação* (Forense Universitária) (2001).

[30] C.F. art. 225, § 1.

[31] Cristiane Derani, "A estrutura do Sistema Nacional de Unidades de Conservação – Lei n. 9.985/2000" in Antônio Herman Benjamin (coord.), *Direito Ambiental das Áreas Protegidas* (Forense Universitária) (2001) 232–247.

[32] Act n. 9.985/00 (National System of Conservation Units).

[33] C.F. art. 225, § 4.

[34] The types of conservation units are enumerated in Table 26.1.

[35] Act n. 9.985/00 art. 7, § 1. The units of strict protection are Biological Station, Biological Reserve, National Park, Natural Monument, and Wild Life Refugee (art. 8, inc. I to V).

[36] *Id.*, art. 7, § 2. The units are Environmental Protection Areas (APAs), Relevant Ecological Interest Areas, National Forests, Extractive Reserve, Fauna Reserves, Sustainable Development Reserves, and Private Reserves of the Natural Heritage (RPPNs).

Table 26.1. National System of Conservation Units (Article n. 9.885/00)

SNUC conservation unit	Type	Purposes and uses
Ecological Station (art. 9)	Strict protection	Nature preservation and scientific research.
Biological Reserve (art. 10)	Strict protection	Full protection of the biota and other existing natural attributes within its boundaries, free of direct human interference or environmental modification except for restoration of their altered ecosystems and the management actions required to restore and preserve the natural balance, biological diversity and natural ecological processes.
National Park (art. 11)	Strict protection	Preservation of natural ecosystems of high ecological relevance and scenic beauty.
Natural Monument (art. 12)	Strict protection	Preservation of rare, unique natural sites, or others of great scenic beauty.
Wildlife Refuge (art. 13)	Strict protection	Protection of natural environments ensuring living or breeding conditions for local plant species or communities, or resident or migratory wildlife.
Private Natural Heritage Reserves – RPPN (art. 21)	Strict protection	Private area established at permanent cost for conservation of biological diversity.
Environmental Protection Area – APA (art. 15)	Sustainable use	Protection of biological diversity, orderly occupation, and ensuring sustainable use of natural resources.
Area of Relevant Ecological Interest – ARIE (art. 16)	Sustainable use	Maintaining regionally or locally important natural ecosystems and regulating the admissible use of the areas in a way consistent with conservation of natural surroundings.
National forest – FLONA (art. 17)	Sustainable use	Multiple sustainable use of forest resources and scientific research, with emphasis on sustainable native forest exploration methods.
Extractive reserve – RESEX (art. 18)	Sustainable use	Protecting the subsistence and culture of traditional extrativist populations, and assuring sustainable use of their natural resources. These are of public domain but open to exploitation by traditional extrativist populations.
Wildlife reserve (art. 19)	Sustainable use	Natural area with population of animals of natural, terrestral or aquatic, resident, or migratory species; appropriate to the scientific-technical studies about the sustainable economic management of fauna resources.
Sustainable development reserve (art. 20)	Sustainable use	Natural area settled by traditional populations who subsist on sustainable methods for exploitation of natural resources developed along generations and adapted to local ecological conditions, playing a key role in protecting the environment and maintaining biological diversity.
Biosphere Reserve (art. 41)	Sui generis category	Area under joint, participatory, and sustainable management of its natural resources, earmarked for preservation of biological diversity, sustainable development, and improvement of the quality of life of local populations, among other things.

These spaces are reserved to the permanent and intergenerational enjoyment of the community, approaching the condition of heritage[37] or collective trust.[38]

Even before the advent of the SNUC, some natural areas were already protected by Brazilian law from potential economic exploitation. These were classified by the Forest Code[39] as permanent preservation areas, which, as in the strict protection conservation units, do not admit the exercise of any economic activity. These preservation areas were established to protect essential ecological processes. Vegetation, for example, was considered indispensable for the protection of soil, of sensitive ecosystems such as the *manguezais*, of hydrological resources, and of other natural functions.

These preservation areas are distinguished from the conservation units model by the way in which they are placed under special protection. Under the Forest Code, for the first time, the vegetation and forests of some spaces were declared by the law itself to be not susceptible to economic appropriation and exploitation.[40] Their special protection does not derive from any initiative of the government. It comes from the law itself. The Forest Code allows a second form of protection, which, like the SNUC, requires an act of the government. But even in this form, designated areas are not susceptible to economic exploitation or private appropriation. As permanent preservation areas, the spaces are protected for the preservation of their ecological functions and development of the economic function of the property is not allowed.

In sustainable use conservation units, the law allows the partial or total private appropriation of the protected space but restricts the exercise of economic exploitation rights over the area and its resources to the permanent exercise of sustainable activities. There are specific and previously defined purposes that must be realized by the owner as a condition for the permanence of his or her property right in the space.

The ecosystems under constitutional protection are also not excluded from the exercise of economic activities. The Constitution itself expressly predicted the possibility of such use.[41] The Constitution did not propose the exclusion of the protected areas from the private appropriation power; it proposed the exclusion of the predatory and degrading use of these spaces. Under the Constitution, human activity either is excluded from protected spaces or is limited or conditioned.

The Brazilian National System contemplates both alternatives. Strict protection units do not admit the exercise of individual activity in protected spaces. In sustainable use units, private activity is admitted as long as established conditions and uses are respected. This system implies the achievement of the social function.

As the last, but not least important, characteristic of the Brazilian pattern, the democratic focus proposed by SNUC for the management of spaces of ecological interest, mainly by means of public consultation, must be emphasized. This has the objective of defining the main physical–natural space components, requiring social participation not only to hear from the local affected population but, above all, to inform it of

---

[37] The owner has limited powers over the asset and must conserve its resources for the next generation's use. *See* François Ost, "The Heritage and Future Generations," in Jerome Bindé (ed.), *Keys to the 21st Century* (Berghan Books) (2001) 152–158.

[38] See Joseph L. Sax, "Implementing the Public Trust in Paleontological Resources," in Vincent L Santucci, et al. (eds.), *Proceedings of the Sixth Fossil Resource Conference* (Geological Resources Division Technical Report) (2001) 23173–23177.

[39] Act n. 4771/65.   [40] Act n. 4771/65 art. 2 (a)–(h).

[41] C.F. art. 225, § 4.

the main effects and results of the establishment of the protected area.[42] The Brazilian pattern does not contemplate a system of direct management by the people already using the spaces and their natural resources – as is typical of indigenous populations. Management is the purview of Councils, composed of community members, who do not, however, always have decision-making power over the conservation units. In the case of the National Forests, for example, the Council has only an advisory function.[43]

5 THE GREENING OF THE PROPERTY RIGHT IN BRAZILIAN JURISPRUDENCE

The contribution of the Brazilian courts has been decisive in implementing rules derived from the constitutional right to an ecologically balanced environment. From Federal Supreme Court jurisprudence come the most important decisions about (1) the definition of the fundamental right to the environment, (2) the social function of the property and the sanctions for not accomplishing it, (3) the appropriation of ecosystems and areas under special protection, and (4) constitutional rules pertaining to protected areas. Concerning the protected areas, the recent recognition by the Supreme Court of a principle of public participation in the Brazilian pattern of management of the units stands out. In the Superior Court of Justice, the references to the social function of the property in a specially protected ecosystem (Atlantic Forest) and to the prohibition of the exercise of economic activity in the protected areas stand out.

5.1 The Fundamental Right to the Environment and the Environmental Asset

The first major contribution of the courts to the affirmation of a fundamental right to the environment recognized by the Constitution has its origin in pioneer decisions reported by Minister Celso de Mello.[44] In these decisions, for the first time, the Brazilian Supreme Court defined the fundamental right protected by the Brazilian Constitution. The court found that the environment is a public heritage, not because it belongs to the government but because its protection is in the interest of the community, on behalf of present and future generations.[45] The court also recognized the narrow relationship existing among the obligations imposed by the Constitution – especially regarding the protection of flora and natural spaces – for the effectiveness of the protected fundamental right.

5.2 The Social Function of Property and Spaces of Ecological Interest

The Brazilian Supreme Court also considered in the same decision important aspects of the social function of property, mainly regarding ecosystems expressly protected by the Constitution. In this context, it considered that the designation of National Heritage – attributed in the examined cases to the Serra do Mar[46] and to the Pantanal

---

[42] Federal Decree n. 4320/02, art. 5, § 2.   [43] Act n. 9.985/00 art. 17, § 5.

[44] Recurso Extraordinário n. 134297–8/SP, *Estado de São Paulo v. Paulo Ferreira Ramos E cônjuge* [1995] at http://www.stf.gov.br; Mandado de Segurança n. 22164–0/SP, *Antônio de Andrada Ribeiro Junqueira v. Presidente da República* [1995] at http://www.stf.gov.br.

[45] Mandado de Segurança n. 22164–0/SP, *Antônio de Andrada Ribeiro Junqueira v. Presidente da República* [1995] at http://www.stf.gov.br.

[46] Recurso Extraordinário n. 134297–8/SP, *Estado de São Paulo v. Paulo Ferreira Ramos E cônjuge* [1995].

Mato-Grossense[47] – does not forbid private use of the asset or impede the economic use of its attributes. These activities, however, must be accomplished in the terms of the law, and only if they permit the rational use of the resources, and they respect the necessary conditions for the environmental preservation of the spaces and their resources.[48]

Public intervention in private property in these spaces (although accomplished for environmental protection reasons) withdraws from the owner the power of exercising that right – as the creation of protected areas imposes on the government the duty of compensation. On the other hand, the failure of the owner to fulfill his or her obligations of environmental preservation in these spaces authorizes the government to intervene in a punitive way. The sanction for this failure is the expropriation of the private property in these spaces, always by means of indemnity. Thus the Brazilian Supreme Court confirms the possibility of economic exploitation of the constitutionally protected ecosystems, at the same time that it recognizes the obligation of the owner to preserve the space and its natural resources, on pain of expropriation.

The Superior Court has focused on another dimension of the relationship between property rights and the protection of the natural spaces. It deals with cases in which the protected areas do not admit the development of economic activities. Thus, it is important to note the recent decision in which the court upheld a prohibition on the enlargement of an industrial park of a multinational corporation in an area under special protection – a Permanent Protection Area.[49] Although these areas are not part of the SNUC, they are subject to special rules of protection. The most important of these rules expressly forbids the exercise of private appropriation and economic activity. In the case analyzed, the economic activity not only was forbidden but also had considerable polluting potential.

Finally, there is an important decision from the same court concerning the Ilhabela State Park, which was instituted in a private domain area for the protection of the remaining vegetation of the Atlantic Forest. In this case, the court found that there was no duty of compensation regarding nonexploited property that was the object of a measure of environmental protection through the creation of the state park.[50] Once it was proved that the social function of the property was not accomplished and verified that the owners had never given an economic designation to the asset, the creation of the park aiming at the protection of the remainder of the important ecosystem did not justify any right to indemnity.

The Participatory Principle in the National System of Conservation Units

The application of the constitutional rule limiting the power of physical change over protected areas has been recognized by the Supreme Court as a right.[51] Recently, another important aspect of the protection system for these spaces was considered by the court.

---

[47] Mandado de Segurança n. 22164–0/SP, *Antônio de Andrada Ribeiro Junqueira v. Presidente da República* [1995] http://www.stf.gov.br.

[48] Recurso Extraordinário n. 134297–8/SP, *Estado de São Paulo v. Paulo Ferreira Ramos e cônjuge* [1995] http://www.stf.gov.br.

[49] Medida Cautelar n. 6399/PR, *Koyo Steering Brasil LTDA v. Ministério Público do Estado do Paraná* [2003] http://www.stj.gov.br.

[50] Recurso Especial n. 468.405/SP, *Fazenda do Estado de São Paulo v. Fortaleza Empreendimentos Gerais LTDA* [2003] http://www.stj.gov.br.

[51] Ação direta de inconstitucionalidade n. 73–0/SP, *Procurador Geral da República v. Governador do Estado de São Paulo* [1989] http://www.stf.gov.br.

The court held that the Brazilian model of the National System is structured on democratic rules of public participation.[52] In the case examined by the court, a council intended to enlarge the limits of a protected area without public consultation of the affected population, which is required by SNUC. The court found this procedure inadequate and ruled that a state authority may not create or alter the boundaries of a protected area without public participation in the decision.

6 CONCLUSIONS

- The risk society can be described as a period of modern social development characterized by contingencies, or risks. As a result, a complex and global environmental crisis has arisen. This crisis can only be understood through an analysis of a complex system of problems that are linked and are mutually influential.
- The environmental legal system is undergoing a greening process that began in the 1970s. The consequences of this process have reached Brazil, a country where the Constitution establishes the right to an ecologically balanced environment as a fundamental human right.
- Natural spaces protection, which was included in the Constitution of the Federative Republic of Brazil, can be understood as an expression of this fundamental right to an ecologically balanced environment. Following this viewpoint, once an area is defined as being of ecological interest, both the government and the society have the duty to protect and preserve it. Through this process, a shared liability system is reinforced.
- The process of planning and arranging natural spaces presents difficulties for the emergent countries. The major difficulties can be summarized as (1) institutions unprepared to deal with the environmental issue, (2) lack of suitable legal systems, and (3) incompatibility between economic growth and the protection of the environment.
- The protection of natural spaces in Brazilian law is part of a greening process specifically related to the right to property. The Constitution of the Federative Republic of Brazil requires all national economic activity to submit to the principles of the social function of property and of environmental protection.
- The Constitution requires that any form of appropriation in protected areas will only be permitted if it allows the accomplishment of the social function of the property.
- The national pattern of protected areas is based on a National System of Conservation Units, which constitutes, in the terms of the Constitution, one of the instruments that the government has to protect the fundamental environmental right.
- An efficient model of management of the protected areas cannot be only the result of government's initiative. It must include stakeholder participation in the decision-making process related to the spaces and allow local populations reasonable autonomy in their management.
- The management and protection of natural spaces and ecosystems in the common interest cannot be accomplished in an efficient way through isolated initiatives of

---

[52] Mandado de Segurança n. 24.184–5/DF, *Aluisio Enéas Xavier Albuquerque e Outros v. Presidente da República, Ministério do Meio Ambiente e Instituto Brasileiro do Meio Ambiente e dos Recursos Naturais Renováveis* [2004] http://www.stf.gov.br.

each state or local power. Interaction and cooperation – such as the institution of networks – is required.

- Brazilian courts are performing an important role in the implementation of what we could call an Environmental Constitution, recognizing a set of principles fundamental to the protection of natural spaces, among which the principle of the social and environmental function of property stands out.
- The Federal Supreme Court recognizes that the exercise of property rights over natural spaces imposes environmental duties on the owner. The failure to fulfill the obligation of environmental preservation in these spaces generates, as a consequence, the authorization of its expropriation by the government, by means of indemnity.
- The Federal Supreme Court has also recognized that the national law establishes a participatory principle in procedures for creating and modifying protected areas. This requires the compulsory participation of the stakeholders, through public consultation.

27 Land Use Planning in Mexico: As Framed by Social Development and Environmental Policies

Gabriella Pavon and Jose Juan Gonzalez

1 INTRODUCTION

According to the World Bank, natural resources in Mexico are among the most bounteous in the world. With only 1.47 percent of the world's surface area, Mexico ranks fourth in biological diversity, first in number of species of pine trees, second in reptiles, and fifth in mammals and plants. Mexico is home to an estimated 10 percent of all known species, many of them found nowhere else on earth. It is the world's leader in the production of silver, celestita, honey, fruits, citrus, denim, and cement. It ranks as the 12th largest economy, second as the main destination of direct foreign investment among developing countries, third in economic growth, and seventh as a tourist destination.[1] Despite the country's natural resources and economic strengths, "the model of development that our country has followed ever since the last century has not been able to prevent the overexploitation of natural resources, nor revert the deterioration of the environment caused by production activities, growth in population, and expansion into urban areas."[2] Illegal logging in protected forests has shrunk important habitats; one-third of the rainforest was lost in the last 20 years; water, air, and land have reached shocking levels of pollution; and the loss of biodiversity is alarming.

The relationship between environmental protection and poverty is little understood in Mexico and puts at risk our economic and social potential. Constant migration from rural areas to the cities has been identified as harmful for society, the family, and the economy. Mexico's population growth and chaotic urbanization have been strong factors in the country's housing shortage, creating overcrowding and nonconforming land uses. In the last century, urban population has grown up to 60 percent and, at this pace, in the next 25 years will likely reach 80 percent. From 2001 to 2006, urban population growth will create a need to develop 95,000 acres, most of them for residential purposes. If nothing is done, our cities will continue to grow in a chaotic way, having a negative impact on society, the economy, and the environment.

On the other hand, most cities have no place to grow. Two-thirds of the cities' surrounding land is communal property.[3] Such is the case of Mexico City. During the

[1] Secreteria de Medio Ambiente y Recursos Naturales (SEMARNAT), Programa Nacional del Medio Ambiente y Recursos Naturales 2001–2006 [National Program of Environmental and Natural Resources] 25–28 (2001).

[2] See *id.* (statement of Secretary of the Environment and Natural Resources, Victor Lichtinger) available at http://www.semarnat.gob.mx/dgeia/web_ingles/program.shtml.

[3] See generally Direccion General de Suelo y Reserva Territorial – Presentacion [Land and Territorial Reserve Agency – Introduction] (constituting almost 17,000 hectares that could be used for satisfying

last century, Mexico City suffered a tremendous population and area growth. Back in the 1950s, the urban area was contained within the city's limit, but years later municipalities bordering the city received strong industrial investments that caused the expansion of urban limits. Later on, with restrictions on new developments, low-income families illegally occupied forestlands and became an obstacle to the sustainable development of the area.

"Environmental protection and sustainable use of natural resources represent a social mandate and a government commitment. Likewise, sustainable development is a task that, besides government action, requires the commitment of all sectors of society."[4] To define clearly the commitment of the new government to the sustainable development concept, sustainability was incorporated as a central criterion of the National Development Plan of 2001–2006.[5] This program requires balanced environmental development and promises Mexicans a higher standard of living. The goal is to provide for a pollution-free environment, where natural resources are used and exploited rationally within the framework of social coexistence and democratic policy, with that goal supported by an efficient government.[6]

Regional development needs to be socially inclusive, environmentally sustainable, and financially viable and has to follow an adequate land use plan.[7] The recently adopted Social Development Act[8] recognizes the citizen's right to a healthy environment[9] and provides for cooperation with the Secretariat of Environment and Natural Resources[10] for the expansion of social development and biodiversity protection programs.[11] This law is a positive step with broad goals and objectives, but lacking in specific standards and enforcement provisions.

The environmental damage occurring in Mexico is extensive and continuing. This situation questions the efficiency of Mexican environmental policy, the Constitution, federal legislation, and regulations and underlines the need for amendments to protect biodiversity. This chapter studies the impact of land use regulation and suggests some changes needed for the protection of the country's environment.

2 THE MEXICAN CONSTITUTION AS THE BASIS FOR PROPERTY RIGHTS

The framers of the Constitution of 1917 agreed on the need to redefine the concept of real property ownership and provide a foundation for future policies that would control

---

the growing needs for housing) available at http://www.sedesol.gob.mx/subsecretarias/desarrollourbano/index.htm.

[4] See National Program of Environmental and Natural Resources, *supra* note 1 (statement of President Vicente Fox).

[5] See generally Plan Nacional de Desarrollo 2001–2006 [National Development Plan of 2001–2006,] *Diario Oficial de la Federacion* [D.O.] May 30, 2001, available at http://www.pnd.presidencia.gob.mx

[6] *Id.*

[7] See National Development Plan, *supra* note 5, secs. 5.3.4–5.3.5 (promoting and developing a general policy whereby all people are included through comprehensive development and public participation) available at http://pnd.presidencia.gob.mx/index.php?idseccion=42.

[8] Ley General de Desarrollo Social [L.G.D.S.], D.O. 20 January 2004.

[9] L.G.D.S. art. 6.

[10] Secretaria de Medio Ambiente y Recursos Naturales [SEMARNAT].

[11] L.G.D.S. arts. 49 & 51.

inequities.[12] Article 27 of the Mexican Constitution is the basis for the country's property system and its environmental policy and legislation. The first paragraph establishes that original ownership of the lands and waters within the boundaries of the national territory is vested in the Nation, "that has had, and has, the right to transmit title thereof to private persons, thereby constituting private property."[13] On the basis of this interpretation of ownership, the ultimate owner of real property became the state, which conferred property rights on individual owners for a "social function," thereby justifying governmental intrusions on private ownership to promote public welfare. Individual property, both land and water, may be reacquired by the government. The state can use its power of eminent domain to compel a private property owner to relinquish ownership and dominion of any property to the state, but it only may be taken for "reasons of public use and subject to payment of compensation."[14]

Although the Nation does not have the ownership of natural resources such as flora and fauna, Article 27's third paragraph states two fundamental principles that make the protection of habitat and biodiversity possible:[15] First, the Nation has the right to impose limitations on private property[16] as the public interest may demand;[17] and second, the Nation has the right to regulate, for the public benefit, "the utilization of natural resources, that are susceptible of appropriation, in order to conserve them and to ensure a more equitable distribution of public wealth."[18] The direct ownership of all mineral natural resources from the subsoil,[19] as well as the ownership of the waters of the territorial seas and inland water,[20] is vested in the Nation. To ensure that the Mexican

[12] See also Leon Cortinas Pelez, *Fundamentos de Derecho Economico* [Basics of Economic Law] 28 (1998).

[13] Constitucion Politica de los Estados Unidos Mexicanos [Mex. Const.], art. 27, para. 1, available at Leyes Federales de Mexico http://www.funcionpublica.gob.mx/index1.html.

[14] Mex. Const. art. 27, para. 2. See also Ley de Expropiacion [Takings Act], article 2 (to further the Nation's objectives or for reasons of public interest and by Executive Order, the state can fully or partially take, occupy, or regulate private ownership rights).

[15] See *id.* art 27. para. 3 (giving the nation the right to impose on private property "limitations as the public interest may demand, as well as the right to regulate, [for the benefit of the public,] the utilization of natural resources which are susceptible of appropriation, in order to conserve them and to ensure a more equitable distribution of public wealth, [to achieve a balanced development of the country and to contribute to the social advancement of rural and urban populations]").

[16] These kinds of limitation are substantially different from the governmental intrusion referred to in Article 27, first paragraph, because according to the Mexican Supreme Court, the imposition of these limitations to private property can only be done through a legislative process and does not require payment of compensation.

[17] Mex. Const. art. 27, para. 3.   [18] *Id.*

[19] See generally Marc Becker, Mex. Const. art. 27 para. 4 (vesting in the nation the direct ownership of all natural resources of the continental shelf and the submarine shelf of the islands; of all minerals or substances, which in veins, ledges, masses or ore pockets, form deposits of a nature distinct from the components of the earth itself, such as the minerals from which industrial metals and metalloids are extracted; deposits of precious stones, rock-salt and the deposits of salt formed by sea water; products derived from the decomposition of rocks, when subterranean works are required for their extraction; mineral or organic deposits of materials susceptible of utilization as fertilizers; solid mineral fuels; petroleum and all solid, liquid, and gaseous hydrocarbons; and the space above the national territory to the extent and within the terms fixed by international). See also Barry Barton et al., "Energy Security Managing Risk in a Dynamic Legal and Regulatory Environment" in *Energy Security Sovereignty in Mexico,* 205 (2004).

[20] See *id.*, art. 27 para. 5 (granting the nation the ownership of "lagoons and estuaries permanently or intermittently connected with the sea; those of natural, inland lakes which are directly connected with streams having a constant flow; those of rivers and their direct or indirect tributaries from the point in their source where the first permanent, intermittent, or torrential waters begin, to their mouth in the sea, or a lake, lagoon, or estuary forming a part of the public domain; those of constant or intermittent

people preserve their national wealth, Congress stated that the utilization of these resources is deemed a matter of public use. Surface waters and air space cannot belong to individuals. This ownership is inalienable and may not be prescribed. The exploitation, use, or appropriation of these resources may not be undertaken by private persons or by companies except through concessions granted by the Federal Executive.[21] Under this principle, Mexico recovered oil fields and mineral resources that were once acquired by private foreign companies and nationalized this important source of national wealth.

As a result of several constitutional amendments passed between 1971 and 1999, Article 27 of the Mexican Constitution provides a legal basis for the protection of biological diversity and is the constitutional foundation for legislative action. The 1987 "environmental amendments" to the Constitution, which created a foundation for a more comprehensive environmental law and policy, included an amendment to paragraph three of Article 27 and the addition of section XXIX-G, of Article 73.[22] Paragraph three of Article 27 grants Congress the specific power to dictate the necessary measures for the development of human settlements and the establishment of adequate land, forest, and water reserves, with the purpose of carrying out public works, planning the

---

streams and their direct or indirect tributaries, whenever the bed of the stream, throughout the whole or a part of its length, serves as a boundary of the national territory or of two federal divisions, or if it flows from one federal division to another or crosses the boundary line of the Republic; those of lakes, lagoons, or estuaries whose basins, zones, or shores are crossed by the boundary lines of two or more divisions, or by the boundary line of the Republic and a neighboring country, or when the shoreline serves as the boundary between two federal divisions or of the Republic and a neighboring country; those of springs that issue from beaches, maritime areas, the beds, basins, or shores of lakes, lagoons, or estuaries in the national domain; and waters extracted from mines and the channels, beds, or shores of interior lakes and streams in an area fixed by law. Underground waters may be brought to the surface by artificial works and utilized by the surface owner, but if the public interest so requires or use by others is affected, the Federal Executive may regulate its extraction and utilization, and even establish prohibited areas, the same as may be done with other waters in the public domain. Any other waters not included in the foregoing enumeration shall be considered an integral part of the property through which they flow or in which they are deposited, but if they are located in two or more properties, their utilization shall be deemed a matter of public use, and shall be subject to laws enacted by the States") available at http://www.ilstu.edu/class/hist263/docs/1917const.html. See also Raul Brañes, Manual de Derecho Ambiental Mexicano 321–323.

[21] See generally Marc Becker, *supra* note 19, art. 27 para. 6 (describing the nation's ownership as inalienable with no end and prohibiting the "exploitation, use, or appropriation of the resources concerned, by private persons or by companies organized according to Mexican laws . . . except through concessions granted by the Federal Executive, in accordance with rules and conditions established by law. The legal rules relating to the working or exploitation of the minerals and substances referred to in the fourth paragraph shall govern the execution and proofs of what is carried out or should be carried out after they go into effect, independent of the date of granting the concessions, and their nonobservance will be grounds for cancellation thereof. The Federal Government has the power to establish national reserves and to abolish them. The declarations pertaining thereto shall be made by the Executive in those cases and conditions prescribed by law. In the case of petroleum, and solid, liquid, or gaseous [hydrocarbons or radioactive minerals], no concessions or contracts will be granted nor may those that have been granted continue, and the Nation shall carry out the exploitation of these products, in accordance with the provisions indicated in the respective regulatory law. It is exclusively a function of the general Nation to conduct, transform, distribute, and supply electric power that is to be used for public service. No concessions for this purpose will be granted to private persons and the Nation will make use of the property and natural resources, which are required for these ends").

[22] See Amendment 14, D.O. Aug 10, 1987 (amending art. 27, para. 3) available at http://www.cddhcu. gob.mx/leyinfo/refcns/pdfsrcs/27.pdf; also see Amendment 34, D.O. Aug 10, 1987 (adding art. 73, sec. XXIX-G) available at http://www.cddhcu.gob.mx/leyinfo/refcns/pdfsrcs/73.pdf.

growth of population centers, and preserving and restoring the environment. Article 73, section XXIX-G, grants concurrent jurisdiction among federal, state, and local governments over environmental protection. On the basis of these amendments, Congress passed in 1988 the Ecological Equilibrium and Environmental Protection Act.[23] More than a decade later, in 1999, the Constitution was again amended to recognize the right of all people to an adequate environment for their personal development and welfare and to indicate the State's duty to guarantee the integral and sustainable management of the National Development Policy.[24]

The original thrust of Article 27 was to regulate Land Reform. The text gathered the fundamental ideas of the Mexican Revolution of 1910 related to agricultural lands: the abolition of large landholdings and the protection of communal lands and *ejidos* (communal farms.)[25] "Lands registered as part of an *ejido* could never be alienated; they were considered to be permanent property of a local group or community: the residents of the *ejido*. Not only could *ejido* lands not be sold, they could not be pledged in guarantee of loans, since foreclosure and sale was impossible."[26] The idea was to achieve comprehensive rural development, to end the government's alienation of land, and to provide farm workers with the means to exploiting their land adequately. While this system gave farmers more control over their lives, it did not improve Mexico's productivity in the agricultural sector. It did provide a measure of stability to the countryside, but the inability to alienate property made it impossible to secure loans for farm improvements. By 1991, 27,399 *ejidos* existed in Mexico, with a population of 2.7 million *ejidatarios* that controlled 16.6 million hectares of agricultural land.[27]

Agrarian reform abruptly ended on 6 January 1992, when Article 27 of the Constitution was amended, repealing the provisions pertaining to land redistribution and removing restrictions on alienation of communal lands and on the use of corporate forms of investments. Presently, *ejidatarios* can transfer their individual land rights and are no longer required to work their parcels personally. Municipalities are now allowed to incorporate *ejidos* and communal property in their plans for urban development and for the creation of housing in those cities where there is no other place to expand because they are surrounded by *ejidal* and communal properties. The State still has the duties of contributing to the development of rural areas, guaranteeing the well-being of farm workers and their participation in the development of the Nation,[28] protecting

---

[23] Ley General del Equilibrio Ecologico y Proteccion al Ambiente, [L.G.E.E], D.O. January 28, 1988, available at Leyes Federales http://www.funcionpublica.gob.mx/index1.html.

[24] See Amendment 2, D.O. 28 June 1999 (adding paragraph 1 to art. 25 and vesting in the nation the management of the National Development Policy and establishing its duty to guarantee that this policy is comprehensive and sustainable) available at http://www.cddhcu.gob.mx/leyinfo/refcns/pdfsrcs/25.pdf; also see Amendment 6, D.O. 28 June 1999 (adding paragraph 5 to art. 4 and recognizing the right of all people to an adequate environment for their personal development and welfare), available at http://www.cddhcu.gob.mx/leyinfo/refcns/pdfsrcs/4.pdf.

[25] See Mex. Const. art. 27, para. 3 ("The Nation shall at all times have the right . . . to divide up large landed estates; to arrange, in accordance with the regulations, the organization and collective exploitation of *ejidos* and communities; for the development of small rural landed holdings; to encourage agriculture, stockbreeding, forestry and other economic activities in rural areas").

[26] See Stephen Zamora et al., "Mexican Law" in *Labor Law, Agrarian Reform, and Social Welfare* 414, 437 (2004).

[27] Instituto Nacional de Estadistica, Geografia e Informatica [National Institute of Statistics, Geography and Information], VII Censo Ejidal, 1991, available at http://www.inegi.gob.mx.

[28] Mex. Const. art. 27, sec. XX.

the integrity of their lands, and contributing to the social advancement of indigenous people.[29]

3 SOCIAL DEVELOPMENT POLICY

Article 26 of the Constitution charges the federal government with the promotion of the national development by creating a "democratic planning system,"[30] whereby the public not only has the right to be informed, but also has the duty to participate in its creation. Federal planning is carried out through the periodic issuance of the National Development Plan, which serves as the basis of more detailed social and economic programs adopted by the executive branch during the term of the plan. Usually issued in the second year, it covers the period of a presidential *sexenio* (six-year term of office) and describes, with clear objectives and concrete strategies, the government's agenda with which all other governmental programs should abide.

The National Development Plan of 2000–2006 establishes the need to introduce basic infrastructure to underdeveloped districts by considering the resources of each region and by using federal funds to create small businesses.[31] An important aspect of the Plan is the need to consider marginal groups in the economic and social development of the Nation. Poverty in Mexico is widespread among rural populations (most of Mexico's farm workers earn less than half the minimum wage and experience unhealthy work environments), indigenous people (most of whom live in marginal conditions and survive on unpredictable income based on commercial agriculture), and women (despite the fact that their number has increased in the workforce, female remuneration is still not as high as that of their male counterparts, although women have become essential in the economic support of their households). The plan names, as one of its main objectives, the achievement of social and human development in harmony with nature, through the strengthening of an environmental culture and by using natural resources in a sustainable manner. This task should start with the adoption of a national land use plan for urban, regional, and national development in accordance with sustainable land uses.[32]

In January 2004, Congress passed the Social Development Act to designate the governmental agencies responsible for guaranteeing the exercise of the social rights

---

[29] *Id.* sec. VII.

[30] See generally Mex. Const. art. 26 ("The State will establish a national development planning democratic system that will give soundness, energy, continuance, and equity to the economic growth for the independence and politic, social, and cultural democratization of the Nation. The project goals contained in this Constitution will determine the planning objectives. The planning shall be democratic. It shall gather the aspirations and demands of society by means of participation from different social sectors and shall include them into the plan's development programs. There will be a National Development Program by which all other public governmental programs shall abide. The law will entitle the Executive to establish participation and public consultation procedures in the National Democratic Planning System and the criteria for the formulation, instrumentation, control, and evaluation of the plan and development programs. It will also determine what agencies will be responsible for the planning process and the basis on which the Federal Executive will coordinate agreements with the states and lead and coordinate with individuals the actions for its implementation and execution. In the democratic planning system, Congress will intervene as determined by the law").

[31] National Development Plan, *supra* note 5, sec. 6.3.4 (creating development opportunities and using natural resources rationally).

[32] *Id.* sec. 5.3.5.

protected by the Constitution.[33] The Act also defines the principles that will guide the issuance of a national social development policy. The concept of sustainability (the preservation and protection of the ecological equilibrium and the rational use of natural resources for the improvement of quality of life and productivity of the population)[34] acquires significance when mentioned along with other important concepts such as liberty, justice, social participation, diversity, autonomy for indigenous groups, and legality.[35]

The National Social Development Policy has the following objectives:

- To guarantee the enjoyment of social, individual, or group rights and equal access to social development programs and to end discrimination and social exclusion
- To promote economic and social development that creates and preserves employment, raises income, and improves income distribution
- To balance and strengthen regional development
- To guarantee public participation in the formulation, execution, implementation, evaluation, and control of social development programs[36]

The Federal Executive, through the Secretariat of Social Development,[37] has the duty of adopting a federal social policy and is responsible for defining the current administration's social development objectives.[38] Social development programs, as matters of public interest, are guaranteed federal funding in the annual budget.[39] The municipalities are responsible for executing these programs[40] in priority areas with the highest levels of poverty and underdevelopment. The Secretariat of Social Development has set a term of 25 years for the achievement of effective social development, but first the Nation has to overcome poverty through a comprehensive method: by creating a sustainable urban system, within an environmental land use plan, managed through efficient local governments with the promotion of adequate housing, infrastructure, and services and the improvement of social, economic, and political conditions in rural and urban centers.[41]

---

[33] See L.G.D.S. art. 6; see also Zamora, *supra* note 26, 251 (In the early 1970s, under the leadership of President Luis Echeverria, new subject matters, also known as "social rights" were incorporated to the Constitution. These rights made the state responsible for providing certain benefits or entitlements, such as the right to family protection, the right to decent housing, protection of the right to health care and information, and the obligation of the State to promote an integral rural development (Article 27). They do not create an absolute obligation on the state or federal governments to guarantee them; but rather, governments can only be expected to implement programs that address these social rights if they have the economic resources available to do so.)

[34] L.G.D.S. art. 3.   [35] L.G.D.S. art. 12.

[36] L.G.D.S. art. 11.   [37] Secretaria de Desarrollo Social [SEDESOL].

[38] See generally SEDESOL – Mision y Vision, available at http://www.sedesol.gob.mx/quienessomos/main.htm.

[39] L.G.D.S. art. 18.   [40] L.G.D.S. art. 17.

[41] Compare the objectives of the National Development Plan and the Secretariat of Social Development with the National Program of Urban Development and Land Use Planning [Programa Nacional de Desarrollo Urbano y Ordenación del Territorio] (having as its vision the promotion of economic abilities, the reduction of social inequalities, the conservation of our natural resources, the management of our energy resources, and the provision of housing) available at http://www.sedesol.gob.mx/subsecretarias/desarrollourbano/subsecretaria/plannacional.htm.

In 2003, acknowledging the difficulties the municipalities may face in the creation of a sustainable urban system, the Secretariat of Social Development created the Program Habitat to assist the neediest populations in urban centers by applying both social and urban development programs.[42] Habitat suggests that efficient management of the cities may help overcome urban poverty, improve housing, and make the neighborhoods more enjoyable and secure, preserving their history and offering a promising future. In 2004, this program focused on areas in cities considered as high priority and addressed specific concerns such as

- The creation of new options in marginal urban centers to improve the population's social and economic situation
- The increase in the number of opportunities for women and the application of their capabilities to enhance their professional performance
- The development of better neighborhoods through the creation of new infrastructure in priority areas
- The establishment of land use plans and protection of the environment with the idea of reducing the risk of natural disasters in population centers through pollution prevention and environmental protection
- The support of land acquisition by states and local governments and the creation of land reserves for efficient urban development and for satisfaction of low-income housing needs

In 2003, many cities in Mexico successfully concluded different projects managed by Habitat agencies. The road ahead is long and Habitat may prove to be a powerful tool for social and environmental development. The program is very young and the results are promising but still not visible. The first step, approaching poverty as a cause for social and environmental problems, has been taken. We need to complete this task by combining national and urban planning policies with environmental policy instruments to achieve development that is truly sustainable in every sense.

4 ENVIRONMENTAL LAW AND POLICY

For most of the last century, Mexican environmental policy was subordinated to the development of economic activities that caused intensive exploitation of natural resources. Industrial urban development did not anticipate environmental effects such as failure to control the disposal of waste, the emission of pollutants into the air, or discharges into waters.[43] In 1971, Congress passed the first Mexican environmental law, the Prevention and Control of Environmental Pollution Act,[44] which was repealed 10 years later for lack of enforcement by the Mexican government. That same year, paragraph 4a was added to Article 73, section XVI, of the Constitution, which granted Congress the power to revise the measures adopted by the National Health Council that

---

[42] See Subsecretaria de Desarrollo y Ordenacion del Territorio (combining actions to improve the infrastructure and the services in the poorest areas and preventing natural disasters through community services) available at http://www.sedesol.gob.mx/subsecretarias/desarrollourbano/programahabitat.htm

[43] See generally Environmental Policy Backgrounds, available at http://www.semarnat.gob.mx/dgeia/web_ingles/policybackgrounds.shtml.

[44] Ley General de Prevension y Control de la Contaminacion Ambiental, D.O. 23 March 1971.

relate to the prevention and control of environmental pollution. However, this amendment did not confer on Congress the specific power to legislate on environmental matters[45] and failed to create an effective regulatory apparatus to implement environmental
objectives.[46]

> Prior to the late 1980s, comprehensive environmental protection had been effec-
> tively ignored in Mexico, at both the state and the federal levels. . . . While the states,
> pursuant to the savings clause of Article 124, had the legislative power to adopt laws
> to protect the local environment, none of the states undertook to regulate environ-
> mental affairs, other than adopting local legislation to protect public health. All this
> changed in the late 1980s, as Mexico's environmental problems worsened.[47]

In 1987, the Federal Congress was empowered to legislate regarding the roles of the
three government branches in the matter of environmental protection. On the basis
of this reform, the Ecological Equilibrium and Environmental Protection Act was
adopted the following year, establishing a foundation for environmental policy in the
country.[48] The Ecological Equilibrium and Environmental Protection Act is the regulatory law adopted under Article 27 of the Constitution related to the preservation
and restoration of the Nation's ecological balance and the achievement of sustainable
development.[49] It establishes the basis for concurrent federal and state jurisdiction
over environmental protection. Since the adoption of the Act, all states have passed
environmental laws that partially or wholly address environmental matters such as
ecology, urban development, subdivisions, water treatment, planning, sanitation, public administration, transportation, human settlements, and public works. Several states
have issued regulations to accompany these laws. "Regulations at the municipal level are
also plentiful in Mexico, and Mexico's major municipalities have begun to enact their
own municipal ecology regulations."[50]

---

[45] See Jose Juan Gonzalez, Nuevo Derecho Ambiental [New Environmental Law], 95 (1997).

[46] See Zamora, *supra* note 26 in *Federalism and Centralism* 102, 121.

[47] *Id.*

[48] See generally *Environmental Policy Backgrounds*, *supra* note 43.

[49] See L.G.E.E. art. 1 (being of public order and having as an objective to establish the basis to "I. – Guarantee
the right of all persons to live in an environment suitable for their development, health, and welfare;
II. – Determine the bases of the environmental policy and the means for its application; III. – Preserve,
restore, and improve the environment; IV. – Preserve and protect biodiversity, as well as to establish and
manage natural protected areas. V. – Exploit in a sustainable manner, preserve and, when applicable,
restore soil, water, and other natural resources in order to make that economic profit and the activities
of society be consistent with the preservation of ecosystems; VI. – Prevent and control pollution of air,
water and soil; VII. – Guarantee a joint responsible participation of the persons, either individually or
collectively, for preservation and restoration of the ecological balance and protection of the environment;
VIII. – Exercise the powers conferred, in environmental matters, upon the federation, the states, the
federal district, and the municipalities, under the concurrence principle provided in Article 73 Section
XXIX – G of the Constitution; IX. – Establish mechanisms for coordination, induction, and agreement
among authorities and the social and private sectors, as well as among the people and social groups, on
environmental matters, and X. – Establish control and safety measures to guarantee compliance with, and
enforcement of, this Law and the provisions arising there from, as well as to impose the corresponding
administrative and criminal penalties. Upon any fact not provided in this Law, the provisions of other
laws related to the matters ruled by this Law shall apply").

[50] See generally Framework of Mexican Environmental Law available at *Ventana Ambiental Mexico*
http://www.ventanaambientalmexico.com.

In 1996, the Ecological Equilibrium and Environmental Protection Act was amended, changing the basis for concurrent federal, state, and local jurisdiction, established in 1988, as well as the provisions related to land use planning, natural protected areas, and environmental impact assessments.[51] New mechanisms of environmental policy (such as economic instruments, environmental audits, and self-regulating agreements) and the establishment of new rules for public participation in the environmental policy were added to the Act. As a direct consequence of these changes, state and local governments have been incorporating these new environmental rules in a process that is not yet complete. In 2001 the Act was amended again to clarify some issues related to concurrent jurisdiction and to create new rules regarding environmental pollution.[52] These changes allowed the decentralization of environmental policy through the execution of agreements, whereby the federal government transferred to the municipalities the power to assess the environmental impact of some works and activities that were under federal jurisdiction. The Ecological Equilibrium and Environmental Protection Act has aimed at promoting an integral and uniform environmental policy by establishing general principles. However, the current environmental legal framework is still confusing. The Act left the protection of specific natural resources to other federal laws, such as the Wildlife Act[53] and the Sustainable Development of the Forest Act,[54] thereby causing conflicting jurisdiction among the three levels of government.

On 30 November 2000, the Federal Public Administration Law was amended, giving rise to the Secretariat of the Environment and Natural Resources. The Secretariat adopted a new institutional structure, which encourages a national policy of environmental protection that responds to the increasing national interest in natural resource protection, that is dedicated to determining the causes of pollution and the loss of ecosystems and biodiversity, and that establishes environmental protection as an essential issue in the work agendas of three government commissions: Social and Human Development, Order and Respect, and Growth with Quality.[55]

The new environmental policy aims at effective environmental management through the promotion of a new federalism that seeks to establish a dialogue among federal, state, and municipal authorities. It is based on the principle of *sustainable development*, defined as "the process assessable through environmental, economic, and social criteria and indicators, which tends to improve life quality and productivity of people based upon appropriate measures for ecological balance preservation, environmental protection, and exploitation of natural resources without endangering the satisfaction of the needs of future generations."[56] The strategy is to introduce updated regulations and incentives to

---

[51] See generally Jose Juan Gonzalez, *Nuevo Derecho Ambiental Mexicano (Instrumentos de Politica)* 46–76 (1997) (amendment resulting from increased public concern, the subscription to the North American Free Trade Agreement [NAFTA] and its Parallel Environmental Agreement, and Mexico's union to the OCDE in 1994).

[52] D.O. 31 December 2001.

[53] Ley General de la Vida Silvestre, D.O. 3 July 2000, available at Leyes Federales http://www.cddhcu.gob.mx/leyinfo/txt/146.txt.

[54] Ley General de Desarrollo Forestal Sustentable, D.O. 25 February 2003, available at Leyes Federales http://www.cddhcu.gob.mx/leyinfo/txt/259.txt.

[55] See *Environmental Policy Backgrounds*, *supra* note 43.

[56] L.G.E.E. art. 3, sec. IX.

promote efficient environmental performance.[57] The six mainstays of the environmental policy are the following:

- Joint and coordinated governmental management of natural resources
- Collaboration of several federal agencies to achieve the goal of sustainable development
- Ending, reversal, and restoration of the deterioration of the ecosystems through environmental control
- Social and economic assessment of natural resources in order to use them in a rational manner
- Prosecution of environmental crimes without exceptions
- Social participation in the preparation and execution of environmental policies and programs[58]

Environmental policy guidelines established in the National Development Plan have to be considered in the execution of activities by federal agencies and the states and in the regulation of economic and social actions of individuals.[59] Such guidelines are governed by the following principles:[60]

[57] See generally *Environmental Policy Backgrounds, supra* note 43.
[58] See generally *Sustainable Development and New Environmental Policy in Mexico,* available at http://www.semarnat.gob.mx/dgeia/web_ingles/six_mainstay.shtml.
[59] See generally L.G.E.E. art. 17 (establishing that "the planning of national development should include, the environmental policy and environmental land use plan established under this law. . . . The guidelines of the environmental policy established in the National Development Plan and the corresponding programs shall be observed in the planning and execution of the actions by agencies and entities of the federal public administration, according to their respective jurisdictions, as well as in the exercise of the powers conferred by laws to the federal government to regulate, promote, limit, prohibit, address, and in general, induce the actions of individuals in the economic and social fields").
[60] See generally L.G.E.E. art. 15 (observing the following principles: "I. – The ecosystems represent the common wealth of society, and the life and production possibilities of the country depend thereupon; II. – The ecosystems and their elements shall be used in such a manner to ensure an optimal and sustained productivity consistent with their balance and integrity; III. – The authorities and individuals shall assume a responsibility towards the ecological balance protection; IV. – Whoever carries out works or activities affecting or that may affect the environment, is obligated to prevent, minimize, or repair the damages caused, as well as to assume the cost for such damage. In like manner, whoever protects the environment and exploits the natural resources in a sustainable manner must be provided with incentives; V. – The responsibility regarding the ecological balance involves both, the present conditions and those conditions that will determine the life quality of future generations; VI. – Preventing the causes of ecological imbalances is the most effective method to avoid said imbalances; VII. – The exploitation of renewable natural resources shall be conducted in such a way to guarantee the preservation of their diversity and renewability; VIII. – The nonrenewable natural resources shall be used in such a way to prevent their exhaustion and the generation of adverse ecological effects; IX. – The coordination among agencies and entities of the public administration and among the different levels of government together with the agreement of society are essential for the effectiveness of ecological actions; X. – The principal subject in the ecological concert is not only the individuals, but also the social groups and organizations. The purpose of having joined ecological actions is reorienting the relation between society and nature; XI. – For exercising the powers conferred by the law upon the State, to regulate, promote, limit, prohibit, address and, in general, induce the actions of the individuals in the economic and social fields, the criteria related to the preservation and restoration of the ecological balance shall be taken into consideration; XII. – Any person has the right to enjoy an appropriate environment for his development, health, and welfare. The authority, in the terms set forth on this and other laws, shall take the necessary measures to guarantee that right. XIII. – To guarantee the right of communities, including indigenous peoples, to the protection, preservation, use, and sustainable exploitation of natural resources and the safeguard and

- Ecosystems are essential for the development of the country and their resources should be used in an optimal and sustained manner.
- The government has the duty of protecting the ecological balance and guaranteeing the right of every person to enjoy an adequate environment.
- Those who carry out an activity that may hurt the environment are obligated to prevent, minimize, or repair the damages caused by it.
- Those who protect the environment and exploit its natural resources in a sustainable manner may receive incentives.
- Renewable natural resources should be exploited in a way that guarantees their preservation.
- Nonrenewable natural resources should be used in such manner to prevent exhaustion.
- Individuals and organizations are encouraged to participate in the preparation and execution of the environmental policy and "to keep a watchful eye on the use of resources and on the environment."[61]
- All nations should promote the preservation and restoration of regional and global ecosystems.
- The eradication of poverty is necessary to achieve sustainable development. Women[62] and indigenous communities play an important role in the protection, preservation, use, and sustainable exploitation of natural resources. These groups should not be "excluded from the preparation and execution of public policies."[63]

---

use of biodiversity pursuant to the provisions established by this Law and other applicable regulations; XIV. – The eradication of poverty is necessary for sustainable development; XV. – Women play an important role in the protection, preservation and sustainable exploitation of natural resources and in development. The full participation of women is essential to achieve sustainable development; XVI. – The control and prevention of environmental pollution, an appropriate exploitation of natural resources, and the improvement of the natural environment in human settlements, are essential elements to increase the life quality of populations; XVII. – It is the interest of the nation that those activities carried out within Mexican territory and in those areas where Mexico exercises its sovereignty and jurisdiction, do not affect the ecological balance of other countries or areas within international jurisdiction; XVIII. – The competent authorities under similar circumstances before the other nations shall promote the preservation and restoration of the balance of regional and global ecosystems; XIX. – By means of the quantification of the cost the environmental pollution implies and the cost involving exhaustion of natural resources provoked by economic activities in a given year, the Ecological Net Domestic Product shall be estimated. The National Institute of Statistics, Geography and Informatics [Instituto Nacional de Estadística, Geografía e Informática] shall include the Ecological Net Domestic Product to the National Account System, and XX. Education is a means to appreciate life through the prevention of environmental deterioration, preservation, restoration, and sustainable exploitation of ecosystems and thereby avoiding ecological imbalances and environmental damage").

[61] See Victor Lichtinger, *supra 2*.
[62] See also Anna Tibaijuka, *Think of Women in City Slums around the World*, UN-HABITAT (constituting "70 percent of the poorest of the poor in the world, in spite of the actions undertaken by governments, non-governmental organizations, community based groups and the international community. . . . Although progress has been recorded in a number of areas the struggle for gender equality and women's empowerment continues. Local actions must and can deliver global goals. It is at [local] level that the benefits of all actions to reduce poverty will become visible"), available at http://www.unhabitat.org/women_in_city_slums.asp.
[63] See Victor Lichtinger, *supra 2* (providing priority to matters related to women and indigenous races and considering these social groups as fundamentally important for the protection of the environment and the preservation of biodiversity).

The preparation and management of the national environmental policy are carried out by the Secretariat of Environment and Natural Resources through the implementation of environmental policy instruments.[64] The Secretariat is responsible for the creation of the national environmental protection policy, aimed at responding to the increasing national expectations of protecting our natural resources. It is also responsible for reversing the tendencies of ecological deterioration and for establishing the basis of the country's sustainable development.[65] When required, it may exercise its power in coordination with other governmental agencies.

5 ENVIRONMENTAL POLICY INSTRUMENTS

The Ecological Equilibrium and Environmental Protection Act recognizes the importance of environmental policy instruments such as environmental land use planning, environmental impact assessments, and declaration of natural protected areas in the advancement of sustainable development in Mexico.

5.1 Environmental Land Use Planning

Environmental land use planning is defined as the environmental policy instrument aimed at regulating or inducing land uses and productive activities for the protection of the environment and for the sustainable exploitation of natural resources.[66] For the development of an environmental land use plan, the following concepts have to be considered:[67]

- The nature and characteristics of the ecosystem
- The ecosystem's imbalances caused by human settlements and economic, or human activities
- The region's natural resources, distribution of population, and economic activities
- The balance between human settlements and their environmental conditions
- The environmental impact of new human settlements, roads, and other works or activities

The environmental land use planning of the national territory is conducted through general, regional, and local environmental land use plans.[68] With respect to the general environmental land use plan, the federal government is responsible for its implementation and assessment.[69] The Secretariat of Environment and Natural Resources, pursuant to the provisions established in the Planning Law[70] and within the framework of the Secretariat of Social Development, should prepare, issue, execute, and assess the general

---

[64] L.G.E.E. art. 5, secs. I & II.

[65] See generally *What Is SEMARNAT?*, available at http://www.semarnat.gob.mx/dgeia/web_ingles/what_is_semarnat.shtml.

[66] See generally L.G.E.E. art. 3, sec. XXIII (meaning the "Environmental policy instrument aimed at regulating or inducing the use of land and productive activities in order to protect the environment; to preserve and exploit natural resources in a sustainable manner by taking into account an analysis of the deterioration trends and the potentialities for exploiting them").

[67] L.G.E.E. art. 19.   [68] L.G.E.E. art. 19 BIS.

[69] L.G.E.E. art. 5, secs. IX.

[70] Ley de Planeacion, D.O. 5 January 1983, available at Leyes Federales http://www.cddhcu.gob.mx/leyinfo/txt/59.txt.

environmental land use plan of the territory.[71] States and municipalities may participate in the consultations and provide the recommendations they deem necessary for its
preparation.[72] This general plan determines the ecological regionalization of the country, the strategies for the protection and sustainable exploitation of natural resources,
and the identification of productive activities in human settlements.[73] The states have
to prepare the state's environmental policy,[74] issue regional plans covering the whole or
part of their territory,[75] and implement environmental policy instruments as provided
by their local laws.[76] Local governments are responsible for the municipal environmental policy[77] and for application of environmental policy instruments at a local level.
According to local laws, the municipalities may create and manage ecological conservation areas of population centers, urban parks, public gardens, and similar areas.[78]
Municipal authorities must prepare and issue local environmental land use plans[79] for
land use control and for the purpose of[80]

- Determining the different ecological areas located in a region (describing the physical, biotic, social, and economic characteristics; environmental conditions; and
  technologies used by its inhabitants)
- Regulating land uses for the protection of the environment and natural resources
- Establishing the criteria considered in urban development plans for the protection,
  preservation, restoration, and sustainable exploitation of natural resources within
  population centers

When determining land uses, localities must seek diversity and efficiency. Local governments should prevent disorderly development, extensive suburbanization, and land
uses that risk the population's health or damage those areas with high environmental
value. Urban development and housing plans, besides complying with Article 27 of
the Constitution, have to consider the guidelines and strategies contained in the environmental land use plan of the territory and designate, as a high priority, ecological
conservation areas near human settlements.[81] Because of the need for a more effective land use policy, the Ecological Equilibrium and Environmental Protection Act was
recently amended. In February 2005, the definitions of *zoning* (used in the establishment of natural protected areas) and *subzoning* (used for managing natural protected
areas)[82] were included, by executive order, as new technical planning instruments. The
impact of this amendment, this new addition, effective 22 August 2005, is not yet
known.

---

[71] L.G.E.E. art. 20 BIS.   [72] L.G.E.E. art. 20 Bis 1.

[73] L.G.E.E. art. 20 ("Developed by the Secretariat within the framework of the National System of Democratic Planning having as its purpose to determine: I. – The ecological regionalization of national territory
and the areas over which the nation exercises its sovereignty and jurisdiction, based on the diagnosis
of the characteristics, availability and demand of natural resources, as well as the productive activities
developed therein, the location and condition of the existing human settlements, and II. – The ecological
guidelines and strategies for the preservation, protection, restoration, and sustainable exploitation of
natural resources, as well as the identification of productive activities and the human settlements").

[74] L.G.E.E. art. 7, sec. I.   [75] L.G.E.E. art. 20 Bis 2.

[76] L.G.E.E. art. 7, sec. II.   [77] L.G.E.E. art. 8, sec. I.

[78] L.G.E.E. art. 8, sec. V.   [79] L.G.E.E. art. 20 BIS 4.

[80] L.G.E.E. art. 8, sec. VIII.   [81] L.G.E.E. art. 23.

[82] L.G.E.E. art. 3, sec. XXXVII.

5.2 Environmental Impact Assessment

Environmental impact assessment is the administrative procedure through which the Secretariat of Environmental and Natural Resources establishes the conditions and limits for carrying out activities that may cause ecological disturbances, in order to prevent or to reduce negative effect on the environment.[83] Individuals and companies are required to have an authorization after an environmental impact assessment issued by the Secretariat of Environment and Natural Resources prior to conducting of any of the following activities or works:

- Hydraulic works, general means of communication, and pipelines
- Oil, petrochemical, chemical, iron and steel, paper, sugar, cement, and electrical industries
- Exploration, exploitation, and extraction of minerals and substances
- Facilities for treatment, confinement, or disposal of hazardous or radioactive waste
- Exploitation in tropical rainforest and species whose regeneration is difficult
- Land use changes in forest areas, jungles, and arid areas
- Execution of highly dangerous activities in industrial parks
- Real estate developments affecting coastal ecosystems
- Works and activities in wetlands, mangrove swamps, lakes, rivers, lagoons, littorals, or federal areas
- Works and activities in natural protected areas under federal jurisdiction
- Fishing, aquatic, or agricultural and livestock activities endangering the preservation of one or more species
- Works and activities related to federal authority matters, which may cause important and irreparable ecological imbalances

The authorization process begins with the submission to the Secretariat of an environmental impact statement describing the environmental impacts, mitigation methods, and proposed alternatives to the suggested activity. The Secretariat has to follow legal provisions such as regulations, development programs, ecological zoning plans, and declarations of natural protected areas to assess the possible effects of such activity in the ecosystem.[84] After evaluating the impact, the Secretariat issues a resolution in which it may authorize the activity, condition it (on the adoption of preventive and mitigating measures in order to prevent, decrease, or compensate the adverse environmental impacts that may be caused), or deny the requested authorization (if the activity violates a legal provision, causes one or more species to be declared as threatened or endangered by extinction, or includes false information). Environmental impact assessments are a national requirement and all the states have implemented an environmental impact assessment system as part of their decision-making process.

5.3 Natural Protected Areas

Natural protected areas are places that have not been significantly altered by human activities or that require preservation or restoration of their natural environments, biodiversity, ecosystems, surrounding areas, or those areas used for entertainment,

---

[83] L.G.E.E. art. 28.   [84] L.G.E.E. art. 35.

culture, and identity of the Nation.[85] Under federal jurisdiction, there are different kinds of natural protected areas such as biosphere reserves, national parks, natural monuments, natural resources protected areas, flora and fauna protected areas, and sanctuaries. By November 2001, 127 natural protected areas had been designated at the federal level, including a total amount of 17,056.4 hectares, representing 8.5 percent of the surface of the country and getting closer to international standards that establish a minimum of 10 percent under protected conditions.[86]

Even though natural protected areas are controlled by the federal government, we see a new trend in environmental policy in which their management has been delegated to the states and municipalities. States may create state parks and reserves in relevant areas at state level. In like manner, it is the responsibility of the municipalities to establish ecological preservation areas in population centers pursuant to the provisions established by their local legislation.[87] The Secretariat of Environment and Natural Resources is responsible for promoting the participation of citizens, landowners, holders, local governments, indigenous peoples, and social, public, and private organizations in the establishment, administration, and management of natural protected areas, in order to encourage integral development of the community and to guarantee the protection and preservation of the ecosystems and their biodiversity.[88] These natural protected areas combine different development systems with land use regulations and natural preservation strategies.[89] The Ecological Equilibrium and Environmental Protection Act considers the reacquisition and designation of private property as natural protected areas as mere limitations on property rights set by paragraph three of Article 27 of the Constitution; however, in reality, these intrusions represent the use of the government's eminent domain power established by paragraph one of the same article and should be subject to compensation.[90]

Because of administrative dispersion, many natural protected areas are failing to fulfill the objective for which they were created. The insufficiency or total absence of surveillance of these areas after being protected threatens their conservation. These areas are suffering from degradation by nonconforming uses of human settlements (in spite of the fact that Article 46 of the Ecological Equilibrium and Environmental Protection Act prohibits the establishment of new population centers within natural protected areas),[91] as well as by pollution, destruction, and inadequate use of their natural resources.

The Monarch Butterfly Biosphere Reserve (located in the forested hills of Michoacan and the State of Mexico) is a sad example, as people in need of firewood have endangered these migratory insects, which flutter thousands of miles from Southern Canada to Central Mexico. Even when the government protects the forests with armed federal agents, large logging operations have continued to eat away the trees. "Satellite photos compiled by United States scientists show that vast number of trees in the 140,000-acre

---

[85] L.G.E.E. art. 45.

[86] See National Commission of Natural Protected Areas Work Program 2001–2006, available at http://www.semarnat.gob.mx/dgeia/web_ingles/sec_conanp.shtml.

[87] L.G.E.E. art. 46.   [88] L.G.E.E. art. 47.

[89] See Raquel Gutierrez Najera, "*Introduccion al Estudio del Derecho Ambiental,*" *La Política Ambiental,* 83, 90.

[90] See also *The NAFTA Ruling on Metalclad v. Mexico – The Broader Context,* available at http://www.stopftaa.org/article.php?id=37.

[91] L.G.E.E. art. 46.

Monarch Butterfly Biosphere Reserve have been logged and carted out, often by armed gangs who pay off the authorities."[92]

Mexico City itself loses approximately 240 hectares of forest every year to fire, illegal logging, and nonconforming land uses. In the ecological preservation areas of Tlalpan and Milpa Alta there is much illegal logging. Every year, gangs with modern equipment and fleets of trucks cut down thousands of trees in the Ajusco. Homero Aridjis, the Mexican poet and naturalist, reported that "[t]hanks to corrupted authorities that are helping developers and illegal residents in the area, soon [there will be] no trees nor water left, and instead of breathing and drinking, the residents of this agonizing Valley will have to quench [their] thirst driving around in [their]cars, from one shopping mall to the other."[93]

6 INTEGRATING SOCIAL DEVELOPMENT AND ENVIRONMENTAL POLICIES IN LAND USE PLANNING

In spite of all the progress made at federal, state, and local levels by establishment of the legal framework for land use planning and natural resources management, there is little practical integration between social development and environmental legislation. The environmental principle of coordination among public agencies, among the different levels of government, together with the agreement of society, is essential for the preservation and restoration of the ecological balance and environmental protection,[94] which requires that the Nation address one of its principal causes: poverty. To improve the quality of life of the populations and the natural environments in human settlements, we need to identify the specific needs of each region and adopt necessary measures to encourage their growth and proper development. The Secretariat of Environment and Natural Resources and the Secretariat of Social Development will have to work together to achieve this goal, by creating a federal agency responsible for

- Carrying out their shared responsibilities
- Maintaining a national database system that includes all relevant information on natural and economic resources in each region
- Adopting regulations that implement environmental laws along with social development policies regarding land use planning
- Adopting social development and environmental policies that go beyond area boundaries to move from protecting self-contained units to integrating the whole landscape
- Incorporating *ejidos* and communal properties to achieve rational urban expansion, provide low-income housing, and stop illegal settlements in natural protected areas

The Federal Executive, through the Secretariat of Social Development, the Secretariat of Environment and Natural Resources, and state and municipal governments, should extend the scope of the Program Habitat to rural areas, where improvements

---

[92] See James C. McKinley Jr., *Chain Saw Thins Flocks of Migrants on Gold Wings, N.Y. Times,* 14 March 2005, at A3.

[93] See Homero Aridjis, *All That Is Green Will Die* [Todo verdor perecera,] *Periodico Reforma,* 28 February 2005 at A32.

[94] L.G.E.E. art. 15, sec. IX.

in infrastructure, establishment of new social services, and realization of activities that further the development of the community are most needed. It is in the rural context where the benefit of land use regulation is less evident. Although environmental benefits are widely recognized, if rural landowners do not see concrete economic value in them, they will be reluctant to bear the cost of land use regulations and restrictions.

To overcome the lack of funding in the execution of Habitat throughout the country, the Secretariat of Social Development should use economic instruments. The Ecological Equilibrium and Environmental Protection Act mentions creating and using mechanisms of a fiscal (tax incentives), financial (credits, bonds, civil liability insurance, funds, and trusts), and market nature (concessions, authorizations, licenses, and permits).[95] Using revenues derived from the use of these economic instruments, the federal and state governments can tax those who pollute and consume natural resources and can provide incentives for environmental protection, preservation, or restoration of the ecological balance.[96] By using these resources, the government will ensure that marginal populations, farm workers, and indigenous groups will recognize the economic benefit of taking care of the environment.

To encourage the use of these economic instruments, and to guarantee the integrity and balance of the ecosystems, as well as the health and welfare of the population, there should be established environmental education programs in the community, aimed at inhabitants, developers, merchants, government employees, investors, and others. These programs should emphasize the importance of the rational use of natural resources, methods to preserve the environment, ways to act in case of a natural disaster, and procedures to commence citizens' suits.

Finally, an environmental impact assessment should be more broadly required, not only for the protection of natural resources but also as a tool for social development. Environmental impact assessments have been widely used for the authorization of site-specific development projects; it may be time to extend their scope to those activities related to state and local land use activities, which may cause irreparable damage to rural and urban areas.

7 CONCLUSION

Today we live in a highly polluted environment, especially because of crowding in urban areas and the exploitation of natural resources in the countryside. In Mexico, cities are growing at a fast pace, having a negative impact on society and the environment. Rural populations leave their lands and migrate to the cities, lured by the promise of larger concentrations of wealth and economic activities; the results are chaotic urban expansion, nonconforming land uses, urban poverty, insecurity, and insufficient housing.

There is a need for financial, legal, and technical support to coordinate human activities with the environment. The implications of the Social Development Act and the Ecological Equilibrium and Environmental Protection Act are potentially far-reaching if fully implemented by the federal government, the states, and the municipalities. There is an evident legislative intention that environmental policy instruments (land use planning, environmental impact assessments, and the declarations of natural protected areas) should be used in an integrated and coordinated fashion to ensure the

---

[95] L.G.E.E. art. 22.   [96] L.G.E.E. art. 21.

constitutional goals of environmental protection and social development in urban and rural areas.

The Federal Executive, through the Secretariat of Social Development and the Secretariat of Environment and Natural Resources, along with state and local governments, should promote public and private investments for the establishment and management of social and land use planning. They should establish economic and tax incentives for individuals and public or private organizations to use their lands for preservation purposes. The Constitution, the Ecological Equilibrium and Environmental Protection Act, and the Social Development Act provide the legal basis upon which to develop laws and establish environmental policies that further protect the Nation's natural resources and help reduce poverty.

28 Argentina's Constitution and General Environment Law as the Framework for Comprehensive Land Use Regulation

Juan Rodrigo Walsh

1 IMPORTANCE OF LAND USE LAW AS AN INSTRUMENT FOR ENVIRONMENTAL POLICY AND SUSTAINABLE DEVELOPMENT

Land use legislation or planning law is a key component of any serious attempt to integrate environmental objectives into a comprehensive public policy aimed at achieving sustainable development. In most cases in which countries have been successful in implementing environmental policies, the effective use of planning tools and land use legislation appears as a common feature, in conjunction with a mix of traditional "command and control" pollution control legislation and incentives aimed at promoting and rewarding sustainable economic decisions.[1]

In many developing countries, however, land use legislation is not fully integrated into the context of public policies aimed at promoting environmental quality and sustainable development. In some cases, this is due to the scant attention that has been paid at a conceptual level to the importance of land use regulation as a key instrument for implementing environmental policies. In other cases, where land use and planning laws do exist in theory, poor or nonexistent enforcement makes them a weak tool for the achievement of sustainable development goals.

However, the awareness of the importance of land use regulation as an instrument for environmental policy is growing throughout Latin America in general and Argentina in particular. This is evidenced by a growing body of academic papers, public policy documents, and studies carried out by multilateral aid agencies, and by the increasing amount and quality of legislation relating to land use and planning procedures involving public participation and long-term development strategies.[2]

---

[1] Gordon Cherry, *The Politics of Town Planning* (Longman) (1982).

[2] See Ministerio de Planificaciçon Federal, Inversión Pública y Servicios, "Argentina 2016: Politica y Estrategia Nacional de Desarrollo y Ordenamiento Territorial" [November 2004]. Over the last decade, there have been several documents produced by the federal government dealing with the need for a comprehensive planning policy framework. See Subsecretaria de Accion de Gobierno – Secretaria General de la Presidencia de la Nacion, "Reflexiones y Orientaciones para la formulacion de una Politica de Ordenacion del Territorio" [1994]; Comité Federal de Ordenación Territorial, "Bases para la formulacion estrategia de Ordenación Territorial" [1995]. Recent planning legislation from some of Argentina's cities and provinces, such as Buenos Aires's "Plan Urbano Ambiental," also tends to reflect the increasing importance of land use regulation as a key instrument for sustainable development. For example, Córdoba established an environment policy instrument in Law 7343, Article 3; and Neuquén sanctioned Law 1875 (modified by Law 2267) stating that Environmental Impact Assessment constituted one of the

The increased awareness concerning the importance of land use as a tool for sustainable development has also been accompanied by an important shift in focus on land use instruments from a static perspective, mainly concerned with administrative restrictions to the enjoyment of private property, to a more dynamic concept of land use regulation as an instrument for achieving far broader public policy goals, such as balanced economic development, redistribution of income, or the promotion of regional economies traditionally bypassed by private-sector investment.

Recent land use legislation in Argentina reflects this trend in the evolution from "negative," or merely restrictive, land use regulations (such as zoning according to permitted uses) to a more proactive or "positive" concept of planning, in which legislation provides a mandatory framework for ensuring that broad policy goals are achieved by both private and public sectors.[3] Furthermore, this evolution in the objectives of land use law has also been accompanied by a shift toward a more open and participative planning process.

Historically, land use regulations in Argentina have been designed and enforced by architects, engineers, and land use professionals in a specialized and somewhat technocratic process with little or no citizen participation and only occasional judicial review. Recent land use legislation, in contrast, has placed strong emphasis on the values of broad public participation and transparency, with prospective land use plans being subjected to extensive public hearings and periodic review, or, in some cases, requiring qualified majorities and specific procedures at the legislative stage.[4]

This overall trend toward more participative and less technocratic land use regulation may be evidenced by a shift in judicial attitudes when faced with cases involving planning legislation. Over time, courts have evolved from a passive stance, focused mainly on compliance with formal administrative law requirements, to a more active role in reviewing the reasonableness of administrative decisions involving land use issues, particularly where the concerns of citizen groups and collective rights, such as the right to a healthy environment, are at stake.[5]

---

objectives of the law. See UGYCAMBA, University of Buenos Aires, School of Architecture, "Jornadas sobre Gestion del Territorio" [12, 13, and 14 July 1999].

[3] See Gordon Cherry, *supra* note 1. Cherry defined planning in a negative sense as being concerned with the control of abuse and the regulation of those things considered harmful to the community, and in a positive sense as representing social, economic, and environmental policies in order to achieve goals "*unattainable through the unfettered operation of the private sector.*" This broad definition of the scope and aims of land use planning remains valid for the current status of land use law as a policy tool in Latin America.

[4] This is the case for planning legislation in the City of Buenos Aires, where qualified majorities are required for legislative approval, or, in the case of amendments to the Urban Planning Code, bills are subject to a double-approval procedure with a public hearing between each legislative session.

[5] Judicial review of land use cases in the Province of Buenos Aires underwent a 180-degree change from an extremely restrictive view on issues such as standing and the test of reasonableness in local government decisions in the 1980s (*Thomann Federico v. Municipalidad de Almirante Brown* [7/12/84] Supreme Court of Buenos Aires, *El Derecho*, Vol. 113, p. 635) to a broad view of citizen standing to sue and the review of administrative decisions with planning or environmental implications after the 1994 constitutional reform (*Rusconi, Oscar v. Municipalidad de La Plata* [4/7/95] Supreme Court of Buenos Aires, *El Derecho*, Vol. 164, p. 501). More recent cases have shown much greater willingness of the judiciary to review and control administrative planning decisions, and even compliance with procedural requirements for public participation in the planning process (*Dodero, Marta v. Ciudad de Buenos Aires* [13/07/01] 1st. Administrative Law Court of the City of Buenos Aires, La Ley, 2001 – Vol. F, 914).

The Constitution of Argentina was reformed in 1994 to include, among other amendments, a right to a healthy environment. The constitutional amendment also triggered the need for a new generation of environmental legislation. One of the most important of these laws is the General Environment Law, which specifically requires the implementation of land use plans throughout Argentina.

In view of this legislative mandate, land use law and the regulation of development have taken on a new sense of importance and spurred a considerable amount of academic and political debate. The challenges are considerable and involve rethinking traditional planning law in order to meet the new constitutional and legislative requirements. There are also emerging attempts at placing land use regulations and development planning in a much broader context, so as to include issues such as rural conservation and the protection of natural areas, which have traditionally been absent or dealt with as separate "watertight compartments" from the more traditional field of urban planning and development control.

2 EVOLUTION OF LAND USE LAW AND PLANNING REGULATIONS IN ARGENTINA

Land use law in Argentina has evolved over time from simple restrictions on the right to develop private property to the more sophisticated urban and environmental planning procedures introduced at the end of the nineties, depending on the political agendas and priorities of each jurisdiction. In order to illustrate the evolution of land use regulation in Argentina, two key jurisdictions should be considered: the City of Buenos Aires and the Province of Buenos Aires.

2.1 City of Buenos Aires

In view of the urban context in which most land use regulations developed in Argentina, the City of Buenos Aires represents the jurisdiction with the longest track record in planning policies, building codes, and zoning regulations.

The City of Buenos Aires first attempted to develop land use plans in the late 19th and early 20th centuries in connection with a general trend toward enhancing the beauty and amenities of the urban environment. Major urban parks were designed by Charles Thays, an architect and landscape pioneer of French extraction.

In 1944, the city drafted its first Building Code, based upon national legislation that entitled the municipality to establish restrictions over private property in the public interest. This code represented a key step forward in the establishment of a framework for land use regulation. In 1962, city authorities approved a Directive Plan based upon a systematic review and assessment of urban needs and priorities by technicians working out of the planning department.[6] In 1977, after extensive consultations with the Central Architects Society, Urban Planners Association, Argentine Engineers Center, and other professional interest groups, an Urban Planning Code was enacted.[7] This legislation has substantially remained in force up to the present, with amendments in 2000.

---

[6] "Plan Director," approved by Municipal Ordinance 9.064/62

[7] Código de Planeamiento Urbano, Municipal Ordinance 33.387. This Planning Code is based to a considerable extent upon the 1962 Directive Plan. See GCBA-CoPUA, *Plan Urbano Ambiental: Modelo Territorial y Políticas Generales de Actuación* (Buenos Aires) (2000).

The City of Buenos Aires attained full autonomy after the 1994 Constitutional Amendment. In 1996, a Constitutional Assembly formally granted the city its own Charter or Constitution, placing the capital on an equal status with the rest of Argentina's provinces. The city's 1996 Constitution contains several innovative mandates regarding land use and development planning.

Chapter 4, Article 26, contains a broad definition of the right to enjoy a healthy environment, in accordance with the tone set by the national Constitution and other provincial charters. The "Right to Environment" is accompanied by a corresponding obligation to protect natural resources, a general statement regarding the duty to restore environmental degradation, and a formal recognition of the right freely to receive information on the impact that public or private activities may have on the environment.

Article 27 of the City Constitution states, among other aims, that

> [t]he City will develop policies for environmental management and planning, in conjunction with policies regarding economic, social and cultural development that take into account its metropolitan context. The City must implement a territorial and environmental planning process on an ongoing and participative basis that promotes:
>
> - Preservation and restoration of essential ecological processes and natural resources within its domain . . .
> - Preservation and restoration of natural architectural and urban heritage in addition to visual qualities and protection from noise . . .
> - Protection and enhancement of public spaces with free public access and, in particular, the recovery of coastal areas which guarantee common use . . .
> - Preservation and enhancement of green spaces, forested areas and parks, natural parks and ecological reserves, and the preservation of biological diversity . . .
> - Protection, remediation, pollution control and maintenance of the Rio de la Plata's coastal areas, the Matanza-Riachuelo Basin, lesser watercourses and aquifers . . .
> - Regulation of land uses, siting of human activities and habitation and safety conditions for every public or private urban area . . .
> - Provision of community equipment, services and infrastructure on a socially equitable basis . . .
> - Road and pedestrian safety, air quality and energy efficiency in traffic and transport . . .
> - Rational use of materials and energy in habitat development . . .
> - Minimization of volumes and risk in the generation, recovery, treatment and disposal of wastes.[8]

Article 29 states that "[t]he City will establish an Urban and Environmental Plan with the interdisciplinary participation of academic, professional and civil society organizations, in accordance with the special majority contemplated under Article 81, that shall constitute the framework to which all land use regulations and public works must conform."[9]

---

[8] Author's translation.

[9] Author's translation. The term *land use* is a broad rendering of the Spanish phrase *Normativa Urbanística*. Article 81 establishes a qualified majority (absolute majority of all legislators) for approval of key legislation such as the Urban Planning Code (Código de Planeamiento Urbano) and Building and Environmental Codes. The Urban Environment Plan must be proposed by the executive branch and is also subject to a "double-reading" as already described. Article 89 requires a double-approval process for the

Article 30 completes the conceptual framework for a land use regime with the introduction of a compulsory requirement for Environmental Impact Assessment (EIA) with a public hearing "for all private or public endeavors liable to have a relevant effect on the environment."[10]

The City Constitution is one of the nation's most wide-ranging charters in regard to environmental and land use provisions. In part, this reflects the fact that it is one of the most recent local bills of rights drafted after the 1994 constitutional reform and has therefore gone several steps ahead in stating detailed requirements for environmental protection. In part, it is also a consequence of the strong citizen and nongovernmental organization (NGO) participation that accompanied the constitutional assembly held in 1996.[11]

Between 2000 and 2004, the City of Buenos Aires has enacted several laws related to the constitutional provisions described. Law 71 was enacted in 1998 to implement the constitutional requirement for an Urban Environment Plan, involving public participation. The law established a council chaired by the City Governor and coordinated by the Planning Secretary. The council was made up of sector-specific decision makers from the city executive, members of the Urban Planning Advisory Board, and an additional group of experts nominated by the legislature. Additionally, the Urban Environment Plan provides for an NGO advisory board, in theory ensuring broad public participation during all phases of the plan's preparation.

Law 71 also established several policy guidelines as a framework under which the council has a mandate to prepare a political proposal based upon solid technical research and arguments.[12] After a considerable period of work involving professional associations, universities, NGOs, and technical research, a draft plan was submitted to the legislature for consideration in accordance with the special double-hearing procedure already described. The legislature, however, has not to date succeeded in fulfilling its constitutional duty to approve the Urban Environment Plan.

The City of Buenos Aires has enacted other regulations dealing with land use regulation as a consequence of its new constitutional status, such as an amendment to the Urban Planning Code, an Environmental Impact Assessment system, a general Freedom of Access to Information, and a specific Access to Environmental Information regime.[13]

Urban Planning Code, for the Environmental and Building Codes, and for the Urban Environment Plan, in addition to approval for disaffection of public assets. The procedure provides for initial approval of a bill, a public hearing within 30 days, finalized by a second session in which all objections and claims made during the public hearing must be given due consideration. These objections are not binding on the legislature but do require that reasons must be given for the ultimate decision.

[10] Author's translation.

[11] Daniel Sabsay and José Onaindia, *La Constitución de los Porteños* (Errepar) (1997) 87.

[12] CoPUA, *Plan Urbano Ambiental: Lineamientos Estratégicos del Plan Urbano Ambiental de la Ciudad de Buenos Aires* (Buenos Aires) (2000). Among other criteria contemplated in Law 71 are the preservation of natural and cultural heritage, improved horizontal integration between government agencies, the promotion of balanced and equitable development between districts, and promotion and improvement of the environmental, social, economic, cultural, and urban efficiency of both public and private investments.

[13] Law 449, Codigo de Planeamiento Urbano, is essentially an update of the Planning Code approved in 1977, described earlier. Law 123 (as amended by Law 452), Régimen Técnico Administrativo de Impacto Ambiental (Environmental Impact Assessment Regime), and Laws 104 and 303 on Freedom of Access to Information and Freedom of Access to Environmental Information.

Notwithstanding the difficulties in implementing the aims of the Urban Environment Plan as spelled out in the Constitution, and the complexities of integrating the
land use regulations established in the Urban Planning Code with the EIA regime and
the public participation requirements mandated by both Charter and subordinate legislation, the regulatory framework for land use in the City of Buenos Aires is currently
one of the most sophisticated legal systems in Argentina.

2.2 Province of Buenos Aires

The Province of Buenos Aires is by far the largest jurisdiction in Argentina, with a wide
range of ecosystems and a mix of urban and rural environments ranging from the Buenos
Aires metropolitan area surrounding the city itself to small communities dependent on
agriculture and livestock, with a number of medium-sized cities in between.

Land use legislation in the Province of Buenos Aires dates back to the early years of
the 20th century, when immigration, building of railways, and expansion of farming
drove a major process of settlement and land colonization throughout the vast ranching and agricultural hinterland surrounding the city and port of Buenos Aires. This
legislation essentially dealt with the requirements for the foundation of new cities and
towns and contained few detailed provisions for development planning other than the
compulsory relinquishment of certain percentages of private land for public use in cases
of subdivision for new urban areas.[14]

In 1977, and to a great extent as a consequence of uncontrolled spontaneous development in the metropolitan area, the Province of Buenos Aires enacted Law 8912 as
a framework for controlling land use throughout its jurisdiction.[15] The provisions of
this land use law are binding on all municipalities and on private developers, when
authorization is sought for extension of urban areas in existing cities, private land
development, or development for industrial uses in rural areas. The following are key
goals of this legislation:[16]

- Preservation of the environment and adequate organization of human activities
  within physical space
- Prohibition of environmentally degrading activities and correction of preexisting
  negative effects
- Creation of physical and spatial conditions that satisfy the needs of the community
  as regards housing, industry, commerce, recreation, infrastructure, environmental
  quality, and other considerations, at the least social and economic cost

---

[14] Law 3487, sanctioned in 1913, provided for the compulsory transfer of private land for public use, such
as parks, urban equipment, and access roads, upon the basis of the common benefits derived from this
"loss" to private property rights. These requirements were contested by private developers until the
Supreme Court ruling in *Rio Belen v. Provincia de Buenos Aires* [7/08/1970] (Fallos CSJN). The court
decided that such regulations were a reasonable restriction on private property rights derived from the
provinces' police powers.

[15] Law 8912 was adopted during a period of military government in Argentina. The text of the land use law
was, however, based upon a long period of preexisting technical work by provincial planners and staff
and did not suffer any overall modification due to the military authorities, other than the elimination
of provisions requiring public participation. See, generally, Edgardo Scotti, *Legislación Urbanística de la
Provincia de Buenos Aires* (La Plata) (2000).

[16] Article 2, Law 8912.

- Preservation of areas and sites of natural, aesthetic, historical, or tourist interest for their rational and educational use
- Provision for the organic participation of the community in the land use planning process
- Generation of awareness within the community regarding the importance of preserving and recovering environmental values

Law 8912 uses zoning as the basis for regulation of land use. Each municipality must develop a local plan with zoning restrictions, permitted and nonpermitted uses, infrastructure needs, roads, and access and circulation requirements, in accordance with the general framework of the law. Each municipal plan must be subject to provincial approval, prior to its enactment as a local ordinance. Municipalities are required to consider regional development in neighboring areas as part of the planning process established under Law 8912.[17]

During the 1990s, the province introduced a broad range of legislation aimed at setting up a framework for environmental management, along lines similar to those established under the national Constitution. The provincial Constitution, also amended in 1994, incorporated similar language regarding the right to enjoy a healthy environment and provisions for its protection.

In this context, the Provincial Legislature sanctioned General Environment Law 11.723, with a framework of principles for the protection of the environment, waste management, environmental impact assessment (EIA), legal actions in defense of environmental rights, protected areas, and land use.[18] Other related legislation deals with industrial permitting (Law 11.459), water resources (Law 5965 and Water Resources Code Law 12.257), air pollution control (Law 5965), "special wastes" (Law 11.720), and permitting for major commercial enterprises and trading premises (Law 12.088).

As is true of much land use legislation throughout the region, the theoretical basis for establishing an overall framework for regulating and planning development is sophisticated and well conceived. Law 8912 is a clear example of a progressive system for regulating land use at the local and provincial levels. However, although the law has been on the statute books for more than 25 years, many of its provisions either have been ignored or have been overtaken by social and economic realities. Notwithstanding the difficulties of poor enforcement, the existence of a legal framework does provide a strong basis for judicial interpretation of the existing rules, which, coupled with citizen and grassroots involvement in land use and environmental issues, contributes in some measure to shoring up its weaknesses.[19]

---

[17] Article 83, paragraph (a), as amended by Law 10.128, requires that municipal plans be compatible with those of neighboring municipalities.

[18] The provincial authorities have not yet issued detailed regulations implementing many of these legal requirements. In this regard, many of the law's provisions remain abstract, although the courts have applied its principles when interpreting environmentally related cases. Article 7 states that land use and environmental planning are key instruments for environmental management ("Planeamiento y Ordenamiento Ambiental").

[19] The provincial Supreme Court ruled in favor of a local association in a case involving the failure of municipal authorities to give due consideration to the provisions of the General Environment Law 11.723 as regards EIA for activities affecting a protected scenic area. *Sociedad de Fomento Cariló v. Municipalidad de Pinamar* [29/05/02] Province of Buenos Aires Supreme Court, La Ley Buenos Aires, 2002, at 924.

3 IDEOLOGICAL ISSUES IN LAND USE LAW

Over the years, land use regulation has raised a considerable degree of ideological debate in Argentina. Property rights were enshrined in the 1853 Constitution and defined under the Civil Code, based upon the principles of Continental law – notably the French Civil Code enacted under Napoléon. During most of the 19th century, the concept of private property reflected the liberal political context of the time, and the exercise of property rights was practically absolute, except for such restrictions as private parties might be willing to establish either under contract or under property law.[20]

This early conception of private property as an absolute right virtually excluded any attempts by the state to regulate the exercise of property rights in the collective interest, even when the Civil Code allowed for the establishment of administrative servitudes in order to further a public interest. These restrictions and limitations to property rights are set up by local or provincial administrative law and not by civil law.[21]

With the evolution of an ever more complex society during the 20th century, the clear-cut definition of private property as an absolute and individually exercised right began to erode. As already described for the Province of Buenos Aires, early legislation dealing with the setting up of new towns began to require the compulsory relinquishment of private land for public infrastructure purposes.

The initial legal basis for establishing restrictions on private property derived from the concept of the police power, as the public prerogative to regulate reasonably the use of property and other individual rights in the collective interest.[22] The existence of a private right implies its reasonable exercise in harmony with the existence of other rights and the rights and obligations of third parties.[23]

Various factors contributed to the softening of the notion of private property as an absolute right that was widely held by lawmakers and the judiciary during the latter half of the 19th and early years of the 20th centuries. The need to find a middle ground between an individualist conception of private property rights and a growing body of labor and social security law linked to social rights, for example, did much to introduce the need for a greater balance between private and public interests.

The emergence of a social doctrine within the Catholic Church also provided a strong intellectual underpinning and legal basis for regulating the use of private property in the public interest. In this regard, civil law underwent a major reform in 1968, with the introduction of Law 17.711 and several important provisions regarding the rational use of property, protection of property from an excess in the normal tolerance between neighboring activities, and the abuse of law.[24] The reform of the Civil Code also opened

---

[20] "Real" or property rights in land may only be created by law. Article 2503 lists the following property rights: dominion and condominium, usufruct, use, easement or servitude, mortgage, and surface right for forestry land.

[21] Civil Code, Article 2611.

[22] See Dromi, Roberto Dormí, *Derecho Administrativo* (Ediciones Ciudad Argentina) (1994) 435.

[23] Articles 14 and 28 of the Federal Constitution establish the grounds for reasonable exercise of individual rights and the limits to state regulation. Article 14 states: "All inhabitants hold the following rights subject to the laws that regulate their enjoyment." The limits to regulation under the police power are spelled out in Article 28: "The principles, guarantees, and rights recognized in the preceding articles may not be altered by the laws that regulate their enjoyment."

[24] Law 17.711, enacted in April 1968, was a landmark amendment to the Civil Code, adapting many of the individualistic provisions of the law to modern circumstances. Article 1071, amended by Law 17.711, for example states: "The Law does not harbor the abusive exercise of rights."

the gates to further legal justification for the regulation of private property whenever public or collective interests might be at stake.

At the same time that civil law began to reflect the need for a greater balance between individual rights and the public interest, administrative law began to reflect the influence of urban planners, with the introduction of the first comprehensive attempts to regulate land use through various restrictions on private property rights for the purposes of achieving planning goals. At this stage, however, land use regulation was almost entirely confined to urban areas, with little or no attempt made to establish similar restrictions for land use in rural areas or to integrate conservation or environmental considerations into the emerging planning system. The bias toward urban aspects of land use regulation is probably a direct influence of the planners and architects who pioneered the planning system in Argentina during the sixties and seventies. Most intellectual efforts at the time were clearly focused on regulating the use of private property within an urban context and on the need to provide infrastructure required to accommodate a growing population and increased urbanization.[25]

As a consequence of the urban context in which most of Argentina's land use regulations have developed, the concept of imposing restrictions on private property in order to further objectives in the public interest has been assimilated and accepted by both private developers and the courts. Although in past decades the issue of regulating the use of land has been ideologically charged, at present there is little or no debate or controversy regarding the power of provinces and municipalities to regulate the use of land in urban areas.[26] In rural areas, however, the "ideological battle" whereby regulation of land use in the public interest becomes a mainstream policy issue has yet to be fought and won. The concept of private property as an absolute value is strongly entrenched among farmers and rural communities, and a broad paradigm shift is clearly required in order to translate the need for spatial planning into a legitimate and accepted public policy goal.

In urban areas, planning regulations are widely accepted as a necessary restriction on private property rights, in the interest of seeking harmony with wider public interests, such as amenities, neighborhood character, or environmental quality. These restrictions on private rights play a role in safeguarding private interests from the risks posed by uncontrolled development. Land use regulations thus tend to be in step with the self-interest of the private sector and provide clear and tangible benefits that offset any potential costs or restrictions imposed by the land use system. In rural areas, however, the links between the potential benefits of land use regulation are far less obvious, when measured against the very real burden imposed by land use restrictions on agricultural land. Most of these restrictions relate to common and intangible goods, such as the preservation of biodiversity or native species, and although these benefits are recognized by almost everyone and enjoy constitutional protection, they do not translate into concrete and economically measurable benefits for the landowner. Rural landowners are therefore reluctant to accept land use regulations that impose direct costs related to

---

[25] CEPAL-UNEP, *La Sostenibilidad del desarrollo en America Latina y el Caribe* (Santiago de Chile) (2002) 65.

[26] At the time of the enactment of Law 8912 in the Province of Buenos Aires, there was a considerable degree of opposition to any kind of state planning or regulatory intervention that might affect or hinder the free operation of property markets. See Rodolfo Vinelli, *Planeamiento Urbano* (Buenos Aires) (1978).

the loss of productivity with no clear-cut benefits. On the contrary, rural landowners often feel that the urban population is a virtual free rider on the host of environmental services that, voluntarily or not, are being provided by rural communities to the urban population.

The need to integrate urban land use regulations with planning for development in rural areas has become manifest with the recent growth in export-led agriculture and the expansion of farming frontiers. Deforestation has become a major issue in many provinces of Argentina where agriculture is encroaching upon high-conservation-value forest ecosystems.

The wave of environmental legislation during the nineties, together with the 1994 constitutional reform, provides a new legal and intellectual justification upon which to base the enactment of land use laws for both urban and rural environments.[27] Whereas previously existing land use regulations required justification, as a consequence of either the police powers exercised by the state or the abuse of law theories developed as a result of civil law reform, Article 41 and the creation of a right and duty to protect the environment have paved the way for the construction of solid legal institutions aimed at regulating the exercise of property rights, not only in accordance with existing legal theories but also as a means of achieving the goals of sustainable development.

Finally, in addition to bridging the different perceptions and willingness to accept land use regulations between urban and rural contexts, there is also a clear need to integrate the existing land use planning systems with conservation-oriented laws and regulations. Conservation legislation in Argentina, at both provincial and national levels, has traditionally operated on a site-specific basis, considering each protected area as a self-contained unit with scant regard for integration with the land use regulations in force beyond the area's boundaries. Although attempts have been made to establish a network of protected areas integrated into an overarching conservation system, the practical and financial difficulties involved in creating and managing such areas have proved to be a major obstacle.[28]

In order to achieve full compliance with the objectives of creating an integrated environmental land use planning regime, there is clearly a long way to go in linking the various components – urban, rural, natural protected areas – which are currently separate and dispersed within the existing regulatory framework. The General Environment Law and the mandate for land use regulation as a "minimum standards" requirement provide an ideal opportunity to design and implement a comprehensive land use policy.

---

[27] Ribeiro Franco and Maria de Assunçâo; *Desenho Ambiental: Uma introduçâo a Arquitectura da Paisagem como Paradigma Ecologico*, FAPESP (Sâo Paulo) (1997) 97.

[28] During 1997, Argentina developed a National Biodiversity Strategy with a view to implementing the Biodiversity Convention at a national and a regional level. The National Biodiversity Strategy aimed at integrating conservation goals with the sustainable use of natural resources. One of its explicit goals was to develop land use plans as a means of implementing the strategy. Environment Secretariat Resolution 91/2003 adopted the National Biodiversity Strategy with legal force for Argentina. Federal Environment Council (COFEMA) Declaration no. 10 of March 2000 established the need for a system for integrating the management of the more than 200 protected areas under national, provincial, or local management into an integrated network of protected areas throughout the country. COFEMA Resolution 70/03 established the framework for this network, involving the participation of the Federal Environment Secretariat, the National Parks Administration, and COFEMA.

4 EVOLUTION OF ENVIRONMENTAL POLICY AND THE 1994 CONSTITUTIONAL REFORM

Environmental policy in Argentina has tended to follow in step with the overall political priorities established by successive administrations regarding social and economic
development.[29] During the 1970s, strong environmental awareness at the international
level and the introduction of landmark legislation in countries such as the United
States spurred the creation of a federal environmental agency in Argentina and the
first legislation specifically designed to protect the environment. During the eighties –
notwithstanding the resumption of democratic institutions – economic priorities, high
inflation, and regional financial crises tended to overshadow environmental issues on
the public policy agenda.

Environmental policies pursued by both national and provincial administrations
during the nineties reflect the high profile and importance that sustainable development and environmental issues achieved on the international agenda in the wake of the
1992 Rio Summit and the entry into force of various multilateral environmental agreements (MEAs) such as the Biodiversity and Climate Change Conventions and other
international agreements such as the United Nations Convention on the Law of the Sea
(UNCLOS).

Privatization and deregulation strategies actively pursued by the federal administration and some of the provinces during the last decade also played a significant part
in developing environmental regulations, given the perceived need for clear guidelines
on environmental liabilities and obligations as part of the overall economic strategy
aimed at attracting foreign direct investment.[30] This process of legislative overhaul and
the introduction of modern environmental regulations and laws also coincided with
an enhanced public awareness of environmental concerns and strong civil activism
on behalf of a broadly stated sustainable development agenda, which included public participation, free access to information, indigenous rights, cultural heritage, and
consumer protection, in addition to issues of a strictly environmental nature.

Clearly, a landmark in the evolution of environmental policy and law in Argentina
was the amendment to the Constitution carried out in 1994, and the explicit recognition
in Article 41 of a right to enjoy a healthy environment, together with a specific rule for the
distribution of powers between the nation and provinces where environmental matters
are concerned. Article 41 states:

> All inhabitants of the nation shall enjoy the right to a healthy and balanced environ-
> ment, apt for human development so that productive activities may satisfy the needs
> of present generations without compromising those of future generations; they have
> a duty to preserve the environment. Environmental harm will generate, on a priority
> basis, an obligation to restore or remediate such impairment, in accordance with the
> law.

---

[29] It should be borne in mind that Argentina's democratic institutions have been periodically interrupted
by military governments, such as the military administration between 1926 and 1983. However, for the
purposes of this survey, no assessment is made of the relative stress on environmental issues of democratic
or authoritarian regimes.

[30] Bradford Gentry, *Private Capital Flows and the Environment: Lessons from Latin America* (Edward Elgar)
(1999).

Authorities will provide for the protection of this right, the rational use of natural resources, preservation of natural and cultural heritage and biological diversity, information and environmental education.

It is the duty of the nation to establish norms that contain the minimum requirements for protection, and the duty of the provinces to state such norms as may be necessary to complement them, without such minimum standards altering local jurisdictions.

Entry of actual or potentially hazardous and radioactive waste to the national territory is forbidden.[31]

The basis for implementing environmental policies in Argentina lies in the terms of the 1994 constitutional reform, with a clear focus on Article 41. In recognizing the right to a healthy environment and formally adopting the definition for sustainable development, Argentina has established a human-rights-based justification for public-policy decisions related to environmental protection and sustainable development. This has provided the legal and intellectual arguments for much of the citizen activism and judicial decisions that have pushed environmental law forward since 1994.

As described, the second part of Article 41 attempts to clarify the rules for distribution of powers in a federal system of government, in which the relationship between the provinces and the union have often been the subject of tensions and rivalries.[32] Argentina is a federal country with a constitutional arrangement whereby power is divided among the federal state, the provinces, and, more recently, the City of Buenos Aires, after amendments to the Constitution in 1994 granted autonomy to the capital on a footing similar to that of the rest of the provinces.

Under the Constitution of Argentina, the federal state holds all powers expressly delegated by the provinces to the nation, with the provinces retaining all other powers. Federal powers thus constitute an exception to the general rule of provincial jurisdiction. In accordance with these provisions, all substantive legislation regarding civil, commercial, criminal, mining, and social security legislation has been vested in the federal Congress, while all procedural aspects related to implementation, conflict resolution, and judicial organization remain with the provinces. Provinces are also responsible for providing primary education and guaranteeing municipal autonomy within their respective jurisdictions.

Although the "division of powers" between both state levels appears to be relatively simple, there are a number of areas in which the demarcation of powers is not always so straightforward and a fair amount of overlap may occur. In areas such as promoting social and economic development or empowering indigenous communities, for example, both the federal government and the provinces are entitled to act concurrently. In environmental policy, given the horizontal nature of much legislation

---

[31] Author's translation.

[32] Horacio Rosatti has developed an original theory regarding the cultural and historical roots of the Argentine federal system, in contrast with the federal systems adopted by other countries as a mere instrument of decentralization. In the case of Argentina, as in other countries, federalism has been the solution for reconciling strong local identities and autonomous institutions with the need for a strong central authority. Tension between the two forces, however, remains a strong element in most fields of policymaking. See Horacio Rosatti, *Regulación Jurídica del Medio ambiente en un Estado Federal: El Caso Argentino* (Catholic University of Santa Fe) (2003).

designed with environmental objectives, there is always a potential for jurisdictional conflicts.[33]

Under the terms of Article 124 of the Constitution, amended in 1994, ownership of all natural resources lies with the provinces. The right to exercise authority and, in principle, to regulate the use of natural resources is a direct consequence of provincial eminent domain and constitutes the basis for most laws and regulations pertaining to forestry, water use, mineral rights, land use, and planning regulations.[34]

Notwithstanding the provisions of Article 124, the specific rules for environmental policymaking laid out in Article 41 vest the federal state with the power to establish minimal or threshold requirements for environmental protection applicable throughout the country. Provinces may establish complementary laws and regulations to the federal "minimum standards" either by setting more stringent requirements or by establishing their own regulations in areas in which the federal state has not established such environmental thresholds. In view of these constitutional provisions, primary responsibility for regulation of land use and the environment lies with the provinces, subject to any minimal standards that the nation may enact, although economic promotion and active policies aimed at economic development may be shared to a certain extent by both levels of government, in accordance with the rules outlined previously.

In addition to this general distribution of powers, the federal government holds responsibility for ensuring that international law is implemented and abided by in all provinces and municipal authorities.[35]

---

[33] The recent Minimum Standards Law on Environmental Management of Water Resources (Law 25.588) has encountered strong provincial resistance on the grounds that by mandating watershed management the federal administration is encroaching upon provincial autonomies. The Province of Mendoza has recently filed suit in the Supreme Court against the Federal Environment Secretariat seeking to declare the law unconstitutional. The court's ultimate decision will have a considerable degree of influence upon future environmental policy.

[34] Article 124 of the Constitution states: "Provinces may create regions for economic and social development and create agencies with authority for the accomplishment of such goals and may also enter into international agreements insofar as such agreements may not be incompatible with the nation's foreign policy and do not affect the powers expressly delegated to the federal government or the pubic credit of the nation, with the knowledge of the national Congress. The City of Buenos Aires will have a regime established to that effect. Provinces hold primary control over natural resources within their territories. Provinces therefore hold eminent domain over the natural resources existing within provincial territories ("Corresponde a las Provincias el dominio originario de los recursos naturales existentes en su territorio...")." The term *dominio originario* may be assimilated to the concept of eminent domain as understood in its public law interpretation, thereby granting the provinces the right to legislate and regulate over natural resources within provincial territory, whether such resources are actually owned or not by the province. Under the doctrine of eminent domain, ultimate "ownership" of assets lies with the state as a consequence of sovereignty over its territory. In its civil and administrative law, Argentina, like other countries with legal systems modeled upon Roman law, distinguishes between public ownership, or *dominus*, as public dominion, and private dominion. Where the State (whether federal, provincial, or municipal) holds land or other things in a public capacity – i.e., for the public interest – the legal relationship is that of public dominion. In this case, assets are subject to public law and may not be sold encumbered or leased as in private ownership. Where the State holds things as private dominion, the legal relationship follows the general rules of property law – i.e., the property may be sold, encumbered, or subject to acquisitive prescription. See Articles 2506, 2340,41 and 2342 of the Civil Code, and Catalano, *Codigo Minero Comentado*, art 7°, 56–72. An example of this latter is the case of fiscal lands owned by the provinces and subject to forestry law.

[35] The constitutional arrangements of Argentina have created a shared and complementary set of roles for legislating and enforcing environmental laws. The federal environmental authorities, in addition to

In accordance with the Constitution, direct responsibility for environmental management lies with the respective provincial authorities, with the exception of the federal government's powers to set minimal standards, as already described. The federal government also coordinates national environmental policymaking with provinces and the City of Buenos Aires, as well as interagency actions within the national government. In addition to the provisions of Article 41 of the Constitution, and the various provisions under existing ministerial laws, General Environment Law 25.675 consolidated a federal environmental system to coordinate environmental policy and sustainable development decisions among the different levels of government.[36]

The General Environment Law also formalized the status of the Federal Environment Council (COFEMA) as an interfederal agency with a statutory duty to ensure debate and coordination among the various provincial environmental agencies and with the federal environmental authorities. COFEMA, originally created by an interprovincial compact in 1990, has, under the organizational structure for environmental management in Argentina established pursuant to the 1994 Constitution, acquired a good measure of political importance as a key policymaking forum.[37] COFEMA, however, does not have concrete enforcement powers and must rely on implementation by the respective provincial administrations or the federal secretariat in areas under federal jurisdiction. As proof of COFEMA's enhanced legal status under the General Environment Law, nearly all subsequent minimal standards legislation enacted by the federal congress has assigned concrete duties to COFEMA regarding the enactment of delegated legislation and the regulatory implementation of national laws.[38]

---

setting the thresholds applicable to all provinces, are responsible for implementing multilateral environmental agreements (MEAs) throughout the country. Different offices within the Environment Secretariat act as focal points for the various international conventions and treaties to which Argentina is party and liaise with the respective provincial authorities. In practice, where Argentina has signed an agreement under international law, the provisions of these treaties become in fact "minimum standards," given the powers of the federal government to negotiate with the international community in representation of the union. Although the rules established by Article 41 for the establishment of minimal threshold requirements at a national level appear straightforward, their application in practical circumstances leads to constant conflict and tensions between jurisdictions. The Province of Mendoza has recently filed suit before the Federal Supreme Court seeking a declaration of unconstitutionality for the Minimum Standards Law for Water Resources Management (Law 25.688), on the grounds that the nation has encroached upon the province's right to administer its natural resources. The Federal Environment Council (COFEMA) has attempted to reach consensus on the meaning and limits of minimal standards by requesting a series of expert opinions on the definition and implications of minimal standards legislation. Ultimate agreement is elusive, however, because of the strong resistance of some provinces. See Juan Rodrigo Walsh, "Informe Especial al COFEMA," Agreement between SAyDS and Fundación para el Desarrollo Forestal Ambiental y del Ecoturismo Patagónico, Resolution 68/03.

[36] Article 23, Law 25.675.

[37] Articles 23 and 24 of Law 25.675 make explicit reference to the duties of COFEMA. Article 25 formally ratifies the creation of COFEMA by incorporating the Original Terms of Agreement as an Annex to the text of the legislation.

[38] One of the weaknesses of interfederal bodies such as COFEMA is that they lack a budget and strong administrative support. Although the Federal Secretariat currently acts as an administrative secretariat for COFEMA, it does not have its own funding or budgetary arrangements. In view of the fact that it has been entrusted with many concrete tasks in drafting and agreeing upon secondary regulations needed to make minimal standards laws operational, this lack of institutional strength may prove to be a serious weakness for environmental management in the future. Furthermore, the lack of coordination between sector-specific agencies (e.g., Agriculture and Environment, or Public Works and Environment) is an administrative phenomenon that occurs at both the federal and provincial levels of government.

The national executive is entrusted with the duty of proposing resolutions or recommendations to the provinces for the purposes of ensuring implementation and compliance with minimal standards requirements throughout the country, in addition to enforcement of complementary legislation and related regulations.[39]

5 "MINIMUM REQUIREMENTS" LEGISLATION: A THRESHOLD FOR ENVIRONMENTAL POLICYMAKING

The enactment of specific environmental threshold or minimal standards legislation pursuant to Article 41 has taken place only since 2002, nearly a decade after the 1994 constitutional amendment. Such a delay in establishing the legislative foundations for a coherent environmental framework for Argentina is in part a consequence of the scant political importance assigned to environmental issues in general, in contrast with more pressing economic priorities, and in part a reflection of the difficulties already described in reaching parliamentary agreement on thorny issues in which national and provincial rights and interests tend to overlap.[40]

The definition of minimal standards as the basis for the distribution of powers in Argentina's federal system has been the subject of considerable academic debate. Within the constitutional convention, there was a clear attempt to establish a common threshold for environmental protection for all jurisdictions, as a means for ensuring that the basic right to a healthy environment be enjoyed by all inhabitants of the country, regardless of jurisdiction or social condition. The representatives of the Constitutional Assembly, when drafting Article 41, were strongly influenced by the concept of "basic legislation" used in Spain for establishing a common threshold for environmental protection applicable to all regions.[41]

German Bidart Campos, a distinguished Argentine constitutional expert, has described minimal standards in his *Treatise on Constitutional Law* as a singular case of concurring powers.[42] In this scheme, the Federal Constitution binds the provinces, which may not diminish or weaken but may, however, improve and broaden environmental protection.[43] Bidart Campos's theory centers on the existence of an environmental "plus" whereby provincial legislation reigns supreme and the ceiling for environmental protection is set by each province, subject to meeting the requirements

---

Improving horizontal coordination between areas within the public sector is a major challenge for environmental policy in the future.

[39] Article 24, Law 25.675.

[40] The haphazard order in which these laws were debated and voted on by Congress is a clear demonstration of the political compromises involved in establishing the legislative agenda. Contrary to the logical framework of setting out a general law for establishing environmental policies and then dealing with more specific issues, the legislation on polychlorinated biphenyls (PCBs), for example, was sanctioned prior to the General Environmental Law, because of media and NGO pressure arising from high-profile incidents involving groundwater contamination with PCBs and public concern over high stocks of PCBs in transformers used by the electricity industry and power distribution companies. Similarly, legislation dealing with industrial and service waste was enacted prior to the General Environmental Law and with little or no consideration for the Domestic Waste Law enacted in late 2004.

[41] Santa Fe Constituent Assembly, Diary of Sessions for 20 July 1994, at 1604 et seq.

[42] Germán J. Bidart Campos, *Tratado Elemental de Derecho Constitucional* (Ediar) (2001) Vol. I-B, 237 et seq.

[43] Germán J. Bidart Campos, "El artículo 41 de la Constitución nacional y el Reparto de Competencias entre el estado Federal y las Provincias" [16/07/97], *Doctrina Judicial*, La Ley, Buenos Aires.

of the national minimal standards or threshold legislation. The task of interpretation, however, will always require a measure of harmonization of concurring powers, in a fashion similar to that contemplated under the Article 75, section 17, of the Federal Constitution, for the regulation of indigenous rights.[44]

Daniel Sabsay, another noted jurist, has also stated the difficulties in defining the limits to the implicit delegation of provincial powers spelled out in Article 41. The "million dollar question" in environmental policy lies in defining the precise watershed between both spheres of competence and the exact "quantum" of the powers that the provinces have given over to the nation.[45] In accordance with the general rules of the Constitution stated in Article 121, the provinces retain all powers not expressly vested in the nation.[46] This rule also strengthens the principle stated in Article 124, whereby provinces exercise primary control over the natural resources existing within their respective territories. The combination and comprehensive interpretation of Articles 41 and 124 lead to the conclusion that the delegation carried out by the provinces under the constitutional reform was subject to the condition that such a delegation should not emasculate the rights and powers of the provinces derived from dominion over their natural resources.[47] Sabsay, in another contribution to constitutional doctrine and academic analysis, goes somewhat further with these arguments and those expressed by Bidart Campos and finds a favorable solution in the inevitable consensus and process of agreement building among different levels of government in accordance with a model of "concerted federalism."[48]

In addition to the General Environment Law, Congress has sanctioned the following environmental threshold legislation:

- Law 25.612 on Industrial and Services Activities Waste
- Law 25.670 on the Management and Elimination of polychlorinated biphenyls (PCBs)
- Law 25.688 on Environmental Management of Water Resources
- Law 25.831 on Free Access to Environmental Information
- Law 25.916 on Domestic Waste Management

6 THE GENERAL ENVIRONMENT LAW AS THE BASIS FOR A COMPREHENSIVE LAND USE LAW SYSTEM

Notwithstanding the general provisions regarding constitutional powers to legislate on natural resources as stated, the federal Congress enacted Law 25.675 as a minimal

---

[44] Id.

[45] Daniel Alberto Sabsay, "El Nuevo Artículo 41 de la Constitución Nacional y la Distribución de Competencias Nación-Provincia" [23/07/97], Doctrina Judicial, La Ley, Buenos Aires, at 783 et. seq.

[46] Article 121 states, that "Provinces conserve all powers not expressly delegated by this Constitution to the federal government and such authority as may have been reserved by special covenant at the time of incorporation [to the union]."

[47] Id. at 785.

[48] Daniel Alberto Sabsay, "La Protección del Medio Ambiente en la Constitución Nacional," Suplemento de Derecho Constitucional (La Ley, Buenos Aires, April 2003) at 94. The term concerted federalism (Federalismo de Concertación) was first introduced by another constitutional expert, Pedro Frias. The expression has been widely used as a solution to the inevitable overlap in jurisdictional authority in wide-ranging areas, such as environmental or development policy, in which precise delimitation of powers tends to be ambiguous and blurred. The solution to such ambiguity will lie in consensus-based solutions between jurisdictions.

standards General Environment Law.[49] The text of this General Law lays out the principles and guidelines for implementing environmental policies. In view of the fact that it is a threshold law, its principles are binding on all provincial jurisdictions and both public and private sectors, regardless of jurisdiction.[50]

Article 2 of the General Environment Law requires that national environmental policy must comply with the following objectives:

a. Ensure the preservation, conservation, and improvement of the quality of environmental resources, both natural and cultural, when carrying out different human activities

b. Promote the improvement in the quality of life for present and future generations in a priority fashion

c. Promote social participation in the decision-making process

d. Promote the rational and sustainable use of natural resources

e. Maintain the balance and dynamics of ecological systems

f. Ensure the conservation of biological diversity

g. Prevent the negative or dangerous effects that human activities may generate in the environment to ensure ecological, economic, and social sustainability of development

h. Promote changes in social behavior and values that may lead to sustainable development, by means of formal and informal environmental education

i. Organize and integrate environmental information and ensure free access to environmental information by the population

j. Establish a federal system for interjurisdictional coordination for the implementation of environmental policies at a regional and a national scale

k. Establish procedures and adequate mechanisms for the minimization of environmental risks, and for the prevention and mitigation of environmental emergencies and the restoration of impairment and damages caused by environmental contamination[51]

In consonance with the aforementioned objectives, Article 4 states that

interpretation of the General Environment Law and of any other legislation whereby environmental policies are implemented, must be subject to compliance with the following principles:

---

[49] Law 25.675, sanctioned 6 November 2002, partially promulgated 27 November 2002, and published in the *Official Bulletin* 28 November 2002. Strictly speaking, Law 25.675 is not a framework law as is understood in legal regimes in which such laws prevail over ordinary legislation, either because of the qualified majority required for legislative approval or because of existing constitutional arrangements that provide for such legislative hierarchy. Under Argentine constitutional law, there is no distinction between legal categories below the Constitution and International Law. Law 25.675, although designed conceptually as a framework law providing general guidance for environmental policies, and more detailed, sector-specific regimes, does not legally bind the legislator when enacting new environmental laws. Given that general principles of interpretation will apply, whereby the most recent legislation will prevail over earlier texts, and specific statutes will hold precedence over more general laws, a framework text such as Law 25.675 loses a lot of its weight as an instrument for ensuring overall legislative consistency when future legislation may amend or distort the principles established under the General Law.

[50] Article 3 states that the provisions of the General Environment Law will be used for the purposes of interpreting and implementing specific environmental legislation. Such preexisting legislation may remain in force on condition that none of its provisions may contradict the principles of the General Environment Law.

[51] Author's translation.

Principle of Congruence: All provincial and municipal legislation dealing with environmental matters must be amended so as to be in accordance with the principles and rules established in the present law; in the event that such legislation does not conform, this law shall prevail over any other legislation which may contradict these minimum standards.

Principle of Prevention: Causes and sources of environmental problems shall be dealt with on a priority basis and in an integral fashion, seeking to prevent any negative environmental aspects that may occur.

Precautionary Principle: Where danger of a grave and imminent or irreversible environmental harm exists, lack of information or scientific certainty shall not be a reason to postpone the adoption of cost-effective measures to avoid environmental degradation.

Principle of Inter-generational Equity: Persons responsible for environmental protection must ensure an appropriate use and enjoyment of the environment for present and future generations.

Progressive Principle: Environmental goals must be achieved in a gradual fashion by means of intermediate and ultimate objectives projected on a temporal schedule in order to facilitate the adaptation of all activities related to such goals.

Principle of Responsibility: The generator of present or future degrading effects upon the environment is responsible for the costs of preventive and corrective remediation actions, notwithstanding the existence of corresponding environmental liability regimes.

Principle of Subsidiarity: The federal state through all competent administrative bodies is obliged to collaborate and where necessary participate on a complementary basis with the actions of private parties in the preservation and protection of the environment.

Principle of Sustainability: Economic and social development and use of natural resources must be carried out with an adequate management of the environment, without affecting the possibilities of present and future generations.

Solidarity Principle: The nation and the provinces will be responsible for the prevention and mitigation of adverse trans-boundary environmental effects caused by their own actions, as also the minimization of environmental risks for shared ecological systems.

Principle of Cooperation: Shared natural resources and ecological systems will be used in an equitable and rational fashion. Management and mitigation of trans-boundary environmental emergencies will be carried out jointly by the jurisdictions involved.

The General Environment Law has incorporated most of the more important principles developed by comparative and international environmental law, such as the Precautionary or Preventive Principle. The Subsidiarity Principle has been given a particular definition as an ultimate duty of the public sector to assist and support the private sector in its primary responsibility for compliance with environmental laws and obligations. This definition is somewhat at variance with other legal interpretations given to this principle, such as the vesting of responsibilities for environmental management with those jurisdictions "closest to the problem."[52]

---

[52] The Subsidiarity Principle in the Maastricht Treaty creating the European Union has been interpreted as a devolution and decentralization of responsibilities to lower administrative levels. When local levels are

The existence of these general principles may be considered as merely declamatory, until such a time that they are applied in concrete situations or are implemented by means of delegated legislation. As such, however, they will act as guiding principles for all future national and provincial environmental legislation and policy. Equally importantly, however, the principles stated in the General Environment Law, in accordance with Articles 3 and 4, serve as guidelines whenever the courts are called upon to interpret or apply environmental laws. Some of the recent landmark judicial decisions made since the entry into force of the General Environment Law and other minimal standards legislation have made explicit reference to these principles and have provided the grounds for proactive court interpretation of recent environmental legislation.[53]

Article 8 of the General Environment Law lists the instruments for environmental policy and management:

- Environmental Territorial Planning[54]
- Environmental Impact Assessment
- Environmental Control System for Anthropogenic Activities
- Environmental Education
- Environmental Diagnosis and Information Systems
- Economic Promotion Regime for Sustainable Development

Articles 9 and 10 of the law establish that land use planning ("Ordenamiento Ambiental") constitutes one of several key instruments for managing the environment.[55] Given

unable to manage an environmental problem, higher level jurisdictions may step in to provide support or assist a local jurisdiction. See Juan Rodrigo Walsh, "Informe Especial al COFEMA," supra note 37.

[53] *Asociación para la Protección del Medio Ambiente y la Educación Ecológica "18 de Octubre" v. Aguas Argentinas SA y otros s/ Amparo* [08/07/2003], Cámara Nacional de Apelaciones de La Plata (Buenos Aires) – Sala II; *Municipalidad de Magdalena v. Shell Compañia de Petróleo S. A. y otro* [19/11/2002], Supreme Court of Justice (CSJN); *Lubricentro Belgrano* [15/02/2000], CSJN. More recently, a group of landowners and Patagonian farmers have filed suit against oil industry players demanding the remediation of environmental damage caused by the industry over many years. *Asociación Superficiarios de la Patagonia (ASUPA) v. YPF y otros*), CSJN.

[54] The Spanish phrase is *Ordenamiento Ambiental del Territorio*. The concept can be broadly rendered as "environmental land use planning," with stress on the environmental nature of the planning process. The English term *land use and planning* is usually translated into Spanish as *Ordenamiento Territorial* and is identified with the traditional notion used in administrative law for regulations related to the restrictions or conditions applied to development in zoning laws.

[55] Article 9 states: "Environmental planning will develop the structure for global functioning of the national territory by means of inter-jurisdictional coordination between municipalities and provinces and between provinces, the City of Buenos Aires, and the nation by means of the Federal Council of the Environment (COFEMA); COFEMA shall take into account the harmonizing of the interests of different sectors within society and between these sectors and the public administration." Article 10 of the law states: "The process of environmental planning, taking into consideration political, physical, social, technological, economic, legal, and ecological aspects of local, regional, and national realities, must ensure the environmentally adequate use of environmental resources, ensure the maximum production and utilization of different ecosystems, guarantee the minimum degradation and misuse of resources, and promote social participation in all fundamental decisions related to sustainable development. . . . Likewise, when siting different human activities and development of human settlements, the following concerns should be considered as a matter of priority: (a) The characteristics of each zone or region, taking into consideration the environmental resources and the ecological, economic, and social aspects of sustainability; (b) Distribution of the population and its particular characteristics, (c) Nature and character of the different biomes, (d) Existing alterations in natural biomes due to human settlement, economic activities, and other human activities or natural phenomena, (e) Conservation and protection of significant ecosystems."

the fact that the General Environment Law is a minimal standards or environmental threshold law enacted pursuant to the provisions of Article 41 of the Constitution, the basic conditions for land use and planning policy have in fact become a common national environmental standard or requirement for all provinces. The wording of these articles is very broad. As they stand at present, they are more a general statement of policy, which may not necessarily translate into concrete obligations for the respective provincial administrations, other than to begin to draw up land use plans as part of environmental policymaking.

However, the mandate of the General Environment Law is clear and provides a strong legal justification for a future national minimal standards law on land use, pursuant to the provisions of Law 25.675. Such a law would contain detailed requirements for land use plans, and the respective provincial administrations and municipalities would then be required to prepare provincial or local plans and manage development in accordance with the national minimal standards requirement.[56]

As already stated, land use concerns have historically tended to be viewed from an urban perspective, with little attention paid to the need for the integration of both urban and rural planning, taking into account ecological, conservation, landscape, and socioeconomic factors and factors related to natural resource use. In this sense, planning law to date has been virtually limited to a chapter of administrative law dealing with regulation of development in an urban context and has been mainly concerned with zoning issues, occupation densities, and permitted uses. Furthermore, where land use and planning laws do exist, enforcement has tended to be lax, in part because the issue itself has not in the past been perceived to be of importance for policymakers.

In view of the enhanced awareness of the importance of land use planning and regulation as an instrument for setting environmental and sustainable development policy, and the stress currently placed upon public participation in the planning process, it is highly conceivable that future legislation will begin to introduce concrete and enforceable obligations upon the provinces as regards setting up land use plans with direct effect on various economic activities, including industrial activities, agriculture, and forestry.[57]

The General Environment Law has made environmental land use planning one of the key instruments of environmental policy. The second instrument listed in Article 8, and described in Articles 11 to 13, is Environmental Impact Assessment (EIA).[58]

---

[56] Many sources have indicated the importance of establishing minimal standards legislation for land use planning, but none have so far reached advanced debate in Congress (personal communication with congressional representatives and staff, NGO leaders, and SAyDS staff).

[57] This conclusion is based upon personal (off-record) communications and interviews with a number of public representatives, including decision makers in the Environment Secretariat and legislators from both chambers of the Federal Congress. This consensus is also very strong among the NGO and academic communities, including highly regarded organizations such as Fundacion Vida Silvestre Argentina (FVSA), Fundacion Ciudad, Asociacion Interamericana de Ingenieria Sanitaria (AIDIS), and Fundacion Ambiente y Recursos Naturales (FARN). See, for example, FARN-IUCN, *Presupuestos Mínimos de Protección Ambiental: Recomendaciones para su Reglamentación* (Buenos Aires) (2003).

[58] Article 11, Law 25.675, states: "Every Project or activity that, within the national territory, may be susceptible of degrading the environment or any of its components, or significantly affect the quality of life of the population, shall be subject to a procedure for assessing the environmental impact, prior to its execution."

EIA has been extensively introduced into both national and provincial legislation in Argentina over the last decade, and there is already considerable technical expertise and institutional experience with using EIA in the decision-making process for approving or licensing new development projects.[59]

Contemplated as an instrument of environmental policy in the General Environment Law, EIA has also become an institutional or "procedural" threshold requirement throughout the country.[60] Provinces that have an EIA system will therefore have to adapt existing mechanisms to the minimal standards requirement, and jurisdictions where EIA does not as yet exist within the local decision-making process will have to develop new regimes in conformity with the requirements of the General Environment Law.

There is an evident legislative intention that both instruments – land use regulation and EIA – be used in an integrated and coordinated fashion as a means of ensuring the constitutional goals of environmental protection and sustainable development. Although EIA has been widely used as a tool for approving site-specific development projects, either as a requirement for sector-specific regimes, such as mining or hydrocarbons operations, or as a more general requirement under industrial licensing systems, there has been little attempt to integrate EIA as a tool in land use regulation or broader development plans. In this sense, EIA as conceived and implemented in Argentina over the last decade has proved a highly useful technique for evaluating individual projects in themselves, but virtually powerless as an instrument for predicting cumulative effects and synergies of more general development processes not tied to an individual permitting or project-specific approval procedure.[61]

The implications of the General Environment Law are potentially far-reaching, if and when the law is fully implemented in letter and substance by both federal and provincial administrations. Land use plans will need to be integrated and linked with EIA procedures and should become mandatory for all jurisdictions, providing overall orientation and specific guidelines for public-sector infrastructure development and private-sector investment decisions.

---

[59] As examples of EIA provincial level regulation, Cordoba: Decree 2131/00 regulates the instrument according to Law 7343. Neuquén: Decree 2656/99. Jujuy: Environmental Framework Law 5063; Santa Fe: Law 11717. Buenos Aires: Law 11723 and Law 11459. Santa Cruz established an EIA regime by Law 2658. Mendoza: Law 5961 and Resolution 1218/03. Río Negro: Law 3266 established EIA general regulations and Law 3335 sets its proceedings.

[60] A distinction has been made between substantive and procedural minimal standards. Substantive threshold regulations relate directly to minimal environmental standards that must be attained in order to guarantee environmental quality. Procedural or institutional minimal standards relate to management requirements and procedures that are deemed indispensable for guaranteeing environmental quality. Access to environmental information and to environmental impact assessments is an example of minimal institutional or procedural requirements that contribute to ensuring that the goal of sustainable development is met by both public and private sectors. Access to information, although not in itself an environmental parameter, is a basic condition for ensuring that the right to a healthy environment may become a reality. See Federico Preuss and Juan Rodrigo Walsh, "Los presupuestos mínimos y las competencias ambientales" [06/08/97], Doctrina Judicial, Buenos Aires, La Ley S.A.).

[61] See Juan Rodrigo Walsh, Eduardo Ortiz, and Carlos Galperín, *Sostenibilidad Ambiental en el Comercio: Evaluación de los Impactos Potenciales del ALCA* (North South Center of University of Miami, OAS, FARN, World Resources Institute) (2003).

7 CONCLUSIONS

The importance of land use regulation as an instrument for environmental management and the use of a comprehensive planning system to achieve sustainable development is very clear at this stage. Decision makers, academics, and even the public are aware of the need to develop land use regulation systems as long-term public policies. Recent tragic events have served to highlight the risks in disregarding the importance of land use regulation or downplaying the need for strict compliance with land use plans when these have been put in place.[62]

Article 41 of the Constitution, the General Environment Law, and the many existing provincial laws dealing with land use or with the establishment of frameworks for the integration of environmental and land use plans provide a solid legal basis upon which to develop the laws and institutions for a sensible, practicable, and comprehensive land use planning system in Argentina.

Given that awareness of the importance of the issue has been raised, and that the legal framework is in place, there remains, however, a strong challenge to be met: defining the limits between property rights and the public interest. This is very much an ideological debate that has been ongoing for many years.

In the context of urban land use, planning regulations are widely accepted as a necessary restriction on unbridled private enterprise, imposed by the need to protect collective interests, such as infrastructure needs or environmental quality. Ultimately these restrictions on private rights end up providing the strongest guarantee for the protection of those same private property rights from the very obvious risks posed by uncontrolled and chaotic development. Land use regulations therefore play a very clear role in protecting the rights and self-interest of private property owners and land developers. In urban contexts, the benefits of orderly development and a rational system of land use regulation are tangible and concrete and therefore far outweigh the costs imposed by planning laws.

In rural areas, however, the link between the benefits of land use regulation are much less apparent, when contrasted with the tangible nature of restrictions imposed in an attempt to regulate the use of agricultural land. This is a direct consequence of the fact that most land use restrictions imposed in a rural context relate to the protection of common and intangible goods, such as the maintenance of biodiversity or the preservation of water quality. Although these benefits are recognized by almost everyone, they do not easily translate into a concrete economic value for the landowner bearing the burden of regulatory restriction.

By contrast, the urban property developer has a clear interest in maintaining the character of his or her neighborhood. Any negative change due to lack of enforcement of land use regulations will probably translate directly into a loss in value of the investment. The converse is also true: Planning decisions that translate into new infrastructure or

---

[62] The Province and City of Santa Fe suffered serious flooding during 2003. Poor enforcement of planning regulations banning development in low-lying areas served to aggravate the loss of lives and property in these neighborhoods. Upstream deforestation removed the natural buffers that historically have absorbed heavy rainfall, serving to illustrate the links between rural and urban planning. At the end of 2004, a fire that broke out in a Buenos Aires disco caused the death of 190 people. Lack of compliance with local planning regulations and fire control requirements is considered to be one of the main reasons for the high death toll in this tragic incident.

an improvement in the character of the area provide collective benefits that also accrue to the individual property interest. This example, however, is far less obvious in a rural context. Ecosystem values and other environmental benefits do not translate directly into tangible economic benefits, and therefore rural landowners are reluctant to bear with restrictions and land use regulations that impose direct costs related to the loss of productivity, with no direct benefits other than those related to good environmental citizenship.

There is a major challenge ahead for policymakers to bridge this gap between land use in urban and rural contexts, and to integrate both components with conservation legislation. Land use and planning policy must be conceived and implemented as a comprehensive exercise with the integration of urban, rural, and conservation-related systems of planning and land use regulation. In order to achieve this goal, as required under the provisions of the General Environment Law, there is a clear need for a broad policy debate regarding the key legal and economic instruments for the successful implementation of such a comprehensive land use system.

29 Ecological Economics, Sustainable Land Use, and Policy Choices

Nathalie J. Chalifour

1 INTRODUCTION

The notions of sustainable land management and sustainable development are inherently attractive as ways of reconciling human needs with the limits of the biosphere. Policymakers, however, struggle enormously to translate these concepts into reality. Part of the struggle results from the fact that managing for sustainability requires integrating a variety of values – from economic to ecological to cultural – that in some cases cannot be integrated without difficult trade-offs. Since economic values have traditionally dominated land use and development decisions, policymakers often feel able only to "add on" or "layer on" other values on top of economic considerations. This is why ecological, cultural, and social values are so often additional considerations tacked on at the margins of an economic land use or development plan. Sustainable land management and sustainable development require turning this model on its head. Land use decisions should begin by recognizing the limitations of the biosphere and then aim to maximize social, cultural, and economic uses on the basis of the best potential output of land and resources. While there will still inevitably be difficult trade-offs to make with this approach, it allows policymakers to make overt decisions about how to distribute the limited resources of the biosphere among members of society, aiming to minimize the trade-offs as much as possible.

In areas where there is an opportunity for new land use planning, policymakers can try to incorporate this "bottom-up" approach to sustainable land management. In areas where economic interests already predominate, however, policymakers are more constrained in their choices; most have relied mainly upon regulation to safeguard environmental values, often legislating emissions standards, mandating certain technologies, or requiring permits to take wild animals or plants from the landscape. There is a far broader range of policy options available to decision makers, however, which can offer greater flexibility and most importantly can reduce the trade-offs between economic and other values. In other words, these other policy options can help achieve environmental and other objectives at lower economic cost than traditional regulatory approaches.

This chapter focuses on economic instruments as a set of alternative policy approaches. As will be discussed later, economic instruments, which range from taxes and fees to subsidies and trading systems, are both substitutes and complements to traditional regulatory tools. The chapter attempts to lay the theoretical foundation for using economic instruments in pursuing sustainable land use or development in order to help broaden the policy tool kit available to land and resource managers struggling to reconcile economic and other values. While economic instruments can be used to help promote better integration between economic and other goals, such as cultural or social values, the chapter focuses on the use of economic instruments as a tool for reconciling economic and environmental goals.

The chapter begins with a brief introduction to the economic theory that underlies our economic system. It then discusses the concept of "environmental externalities," a problem framed in economic terms that helps explain why our economic system consistently overuses resources and pollutes the biosphere. Next, the chapter describes the range of policy options available to decision makers to correct for these externalities. Discussion then turns to ways policymakers can and should select among the various policy choices. The final section provides a detailed discussion of one economic instrument in particular, the reform of government tax and spending policies (also known as *ecological fiscal reform*), as this instrument holds a tremendous amount of potential for reconciling economic and ecological values and there has been relatively little written about it compared to other instruments such as tradable emissions permits.

2 INTRODUCTION TO ECONOMIC THEORY

The overarching priority of economic growth was easily the most important idea of the twentieth century.[1]

Current canonical assumptions of insatiable wants and infinite resources leading to growth forever are simply not founded in reality.[2]

Our modern economic system has evolved on the foundations of neoclassical economic principles.[3] Neoclassical economics is based on the premise that a system of free markets is the most efficient way to run the economy and the way that best maximizes social welfare for society. Markets are viewed as the ideal mechanisms for allocating resources among competing users.[4] The theory is that markets lead to efficient allocation of goods via price signals that work to balance supply and demand.[5]

While neoclassical economic theory works in practice to maximize social welfare under certain conditions, problems arise when goods and services lack certain characteristics (discussed later). Problems are very evident in the case of the environment, since many environmental values do not have the good market characteristics needed for the market to function to maximize social welfare. Environmental and natural resource economics has emerged as a subdiscipline of neoclassical economics to develop approaches and methodologies to improve the ability of economic policy to account for

[1] J. R. McNeill, *Something New under the Sun* (2000) 336 (originally quoted in Herman E. Daly and Joshua Farley), *Ecological Economics: Principles and Applications* (2004) xx.

[2] Herman E. Daly and Joshua Farley, *Ecological Economics: Principles and Applications* (2004) xxi.

[3] Economics is the study of the allocation of limited or scarce resources among alternative, competing ends. See Richard J. Lipsey et al., *Macroeconomics* (2d ed. 1990).

[4] See Lipsey et al., *supra* note 3; Daly and Farley, *supra* note 2 at 5.

[5] See Lipsey et al., *supra* note 3; Daly and Farley, *supra* note 2 at ch. 8.

environmental costs and benefits.[6] The "transdiscipline" of ecological economics has emerged in an attempt to fuse concepts of neoclassical economics, ecology, and other insights from social sciences, natural sciences, and humanities in an attempt to resituate economic policy in the context of a finite biosphere.[7]

A fundamental flaw in the theory of neoclassical economics identified by ecological economics is the fixation on growth as an end.[8] An objective of never-ending growth is bound to fail in a finite biosphere. An alternative paradigm is the notion of development, which is defined by the ecological economists Daly and Farley as "the increase in quality of goods and services, as defined by their ability to increase human well-being, provided by a given throughput."[9] Development is a more realistic and plausible objective for economic policy.[10]

This distinction between growth and development was the underpinning of the coining of the now ubiquitous notion of sustainable development. The most famous definition of the term is that "[s]ustainable development is development that meets the needs of the present without compromising the ability of future generations to meet their own needs."[11] Recognizing the limits of economic growth is critical to sustainability. It requires a shift in economic theory to better reflect objectives of quality and changes in ways we measure progress. Modern societies have tended to measure progress in quantitative economic terms of growth, rather than qualitative measures. There are emerging efforts to redefine progress so that it better reflects qualitative values such as efficient resource use, environmental quality, and good health care. However, these will take some time to develop, and in the meantime policymakers must continue to look for ways to implement sustainability concepts into land and resource management. The following section explains the economic concept of environmental externalities, a market failure, which provides a theoretical basis for policymakers to develop targeted policies that address environmental issues within the context of our modern economic system.

3 ENVIRONMENTAL EXTERNALITIES

> As the saying goes, a woman's work is never done – nor fairly compensated – and this is nowhere truer than in the case of Mother Nature. Much of Nature's labour has enormous and obvious value which has failed to win respect in the marketplace until recently.[12]

---

[6] See, for example, Thomas Tietenberg, *Environmental Economics and Policy* (4th ed. 2004).

[7] Neoclassical economics relies upon the market as the mechanism for allocation decisions, while ecological economics treats the market as only one potential allocation mechanism. See Daly and Farley, *supra* note 3.

[8] *Growth* is a "quantitative increase in size, or an increase in throughput" while *throughput* is "the flow of raw materials and energy from the global ecosystem, through the economy, and back to the global ecosystem as waste." Daly and Farley, *supra* note 2 at 6.

[9] See Daly and Farley, *supra* note 2 at 6.

[10] See generally Douglas E. Booth, *Hooked on Growth – Economic Addictions and the Environment* (2004), who argues that society's obsession with economic growth is in fact an addiction.

[11] World Commission on Environment and Development, Brundtland Commision, *Our Common Future* (1987).

[12] Gretchen C. Daily and Katherine Ellison, *The New Economy of Nature – the Quest to Make Conservation Profitable* (2002) 5.

Markets serve to allocate resources efficiently only with goods that have certain characteristics, namely, excludability[13] and rivalness.[14] In addition to requiring that goods have the characteristics of excludability and rivalness, efficient market function is dependent upon there being zero or low transaction costs and perfect or substantially complete information about all the costs and benefits of every good.[15] When these characteristics and conditions are not present, there is what is called a *market failure*.[16] Not surprisingly, market failures are quite common in reality.[17] This is certainly the case with environmental challenges. The goods and services provided by nature, for instance, are mostly not excludable. In addition, they have physical characteristics that make it very difficult, if not impossible, to make them excludable (i.e., to create well-defined and enforceable property rights).[18] They are also often not rival, as in the case of the ozone layer's offering protection against Ultraviolet radiation.

A typical example of markets' failing to function to maximize social welfare occurs when economic actors do not have to bear the full costs and benefits of their decisions. This situation produces what is called an *externality*.[19] When there is an externality, the actions of consumers or producers result in costs and benefits that do not show up in the market price of a good.[20] In other words, the presence of an externality means that the price of a good or service does not convey accurate information about the scarcity of that good or service, which can translate into inefficient levels of production and consumption of such goods and services, with concomitant social costs. Producers who can externalize costs tend to overproduce the goods in question, while those who are

---

[13] *Excludability* refers to the ability to own a good completely, either individually or collectively. In other words, the owner may use the good and exclude others from using it. Institutions (usually governments) are necessary to create and enforce the property rights that make a good excludable. See Daly and Farley, *supra* note 2 at 73, 157.

[14] When a good *is rival*, the use by one person of a unit of that good prohibits the use of that same unit at the same time by another person. In other words, consumption of the good by one person reduces the amount available for consumption by another. See Daly and Farley, *supra* note 2 at 73, 159.

[15] See Daly and Farley, *supra* note 2 at 182.

[16] See Daly and Farley, *supra* note 2 at 182. See also Steven C. Hackett, *Environmental and Natural Resources Economics – Theory, Policy and the Sustainable Society* (2001) 39–41. Structural problems, such as the absence of competition or a monopoly, are also a source of market failure. See Daly and Farley, *id.* at 157; Hackett, *id.* at 39–41. Note that Hackett identifies the definition and enforceability of property rights and the existence of a market institution to rule the interaction of agents in a market as two distinct features of competitive markets, whereas Daly and Farley include both of these under the concept of excludability. See also Terry L. Anderson and Donald R. Leal, *Free Market Environmentalism* (1991) 9 (describing market failure in an environmental context and noting that in addition to the problem of externalities, market failures are caused by unequal information among buyers and sellers and monopolies, which distort prices and outputs).

[17] See Hackett, *supra* note 16 at 44–48 (describing various market failures, from monopolies to public goods).

[18] See Daly and Farley, *supra* note 2 at 158.

[19] An externality may be defined as a situation in which an activity or transaction by an economic actor causes a loss or gain in welfare to another actor, and there is no compensation for the change in welfare. See Daly and Farley, *supra* note 2 at 175. See also Hackett, *supra* note 16 at 60–61.

[20] Externalities can be negative or positive, depending on whether there is a loss of welfare (negative externality) or a gain in welfare (positive externality). See Daly and Farley, *supra* note 2 at 175. The OECD defines a *negative externality* as a cost that one economic agent imposes upon another without taking such cost into account when making production or consumption decisions. See OECD, *Environmentally Related Taxes in OECD Countries: Issues and Strategies* 21 (2001).

unable to capture all of the benefits tend to underproduce.[21] The burden of this resulting inefficiency is borne by society at large, rather than the economic agent.[22]

Negative externalities are a very common problem in the context of biodiversity. Most of nature's goods and services are currently provided free to society. They are often public goods (nonexcludable and nonrival), such as ecosystem services, or open access regimes (nonexcludable and rival), such as fisheries. As a result, market actors from individuals to private sector companies can use these goods without bearing the full costs. The economic actors thus tend to overuse the free or underpriced goods and services provided by biodiversity, getting a "free ride" on nature's back. If the economic decision maker bears the full costs of decisions (such as the cost to clean up a river polluted by emissions or to replenish nutrients in soil degraded by agricultural practices), he or she will produce less of the relevant good or pass on the cost to the consumer, who will consume less. The production and consumption levels without externalities would produce more socially acceptable levels of environmental harm.

This externality problem extends to many aspects of the environment. Externalities contribute to ozone depletion, climate change, and air and water pollution. Even environmental resources that at first glance might appear to be excludable and rival and thus more likely to preclude the externality problem, such as privately owned forests, produce externalities relating to ecosystem services. For example, while a private forest owner might have the incentive to manage the timber resources in a way that maximizes their long-term viability, that landowner does not capture the benefits of ecosystem management that safeguards public goods such as flood control, support for pollinator species, and carbon sequestration.

4 POLICY RESPONSES

> Instead of spending time trying to calculate the "correct" price for nonmarket goods, ecological economics stresses that we should act on our knowledge that zero is the incorrect price, and spend our time trying to improve upon and implement policies that recognize they have significant, often infinite value, even if we cannot precisely quantify it.[23]

How can and should these externalities in private decision making, which are a root cause of environmental degradation, be addressed? When externalities exist in a market economy and they are related to important policy values, economists generally agree that governments should intervene in the market to correct the problem. This section reviews three types of government intervention available to policymakers.[24]

---

[21] See OECD, *supra* note 20 at 21.

[22] See Paul Krugman, *Earth in the Balance Sheet – Economists Go for the Green* (1997), at http://slate.msn.com/id/1919. Tietenberg characterizes the externality problem as a result of the failure of an adequate property rights structure. See Tietenberg, *supra* note 6 at 128.

[23] Daly and Farley, *supra* note 2 at 411.

[24] These three categories are not the only policy responses to environmental externalities or environmental problems more generally. Voluntary agreements, for example, can also help correct for externalities and are being increasingly used. For more on voluntary approaches, see Thomas P. Lyon L. and John W. Maxwell, "Self-Regulation, Taxation and Public Voluntary Environmental Agreements" (2003) 87 *Journal of Public Economics* 1453–1486.

4.1 Direct or Command and Control Regulation

The traditional policy response has been what is often called direct or "command and control" regulation, which prohibits certain activities or mandates a particular standard or technology be applied across an entire sector or industry.[25] In a land management context, examples of this type of regulation range from forest management standards to permit requirements for emissions into air or water. Another variation of such regulation is limiting a harvest season or the type of equipment that can be used for harvesting.[26] The consequences for failing to comply with the regulations are fines, penalties, or, in exceptional cases, imprisonment or creative sentencing options.[27] Although command and control regulation usually affects price signals of goods related to the regulated activity, it is generally not an accurate or efficient way to internalize an externality. It also generally fails to provide an incentive to progress beyond the regulatory threshold.[28]

4.2 Property Rights and Trading Systems

Another option for reducing or eliminating externalities is to assign property rights to the public or open access goods, essentially making them excludable.[29] The private decision maker who is assigned the property right will be motivated to maximize its value, which should produce more optimal resource use and recognition of scarcity.[30] In a well-known article on externalities, the economist Ronald Coase demonstrated the nonintuitive finding that an equally efficient outcome is attained whether the property right is assigned to the polluter (i.e., the right to pollute) or the person who desires clean air (i.e., the right to clean air).[31] This runs counter to the instinct that the polluter should pay. The Coase theorem is thus an important finding when trying to apply policy solutions, because making the polluter pay is not always simple from a political perspective.

Tradable permits are an emerging policy approach used thus far mainly to reduce air pollution. The system works by requiring society to set a cap or a quota on the amount of pollution or resource depletion to be allowed, assigning initial property rights to these allowable pollution or depletion levels and then allowing permit holders to trade among

---

[25] See Daly and Farley, *supra* note 2 at 374.

[26] See *id.* Regulations to establish protected areas would also fall into this category, since such regulation creates a land use that prohibits many uses.

[27] See *id.* (suggesting fines and penalties as consequences of failing to comply with regulation).

[28] See *id.*   [29] Daly and Farley, *supra* note 2 at 176.

[30] One advocate of the creation of property rights in response to environmental degradation argues that such property rights must be clear, defendable, and transferable. See Terry L. Anderson and Donald R. Leal, *Free Market Environmentalism* 20 (1991). Anderson argues that private property rights are a better solution to the externality problem than resource management at the political level on the basis of his further argument that the political sector operates by externalizing costs. See *id.* at 14–17.

[31] The Coase theorem is based on the assumption of a perfectly competitive market, with no transaction costs and perfect information, as well as the ability to pay by the right holders. See Ronald Coase, "The Problem of Social Cost" 3 *Journal of Law and Economics* 1 (1960). These conditions, of course, are rarely reflected in reality. See Herman E. Daly and Joshua Farley, *Ecological Economics: Principles and Applications* 178 (2004).

themselves in order to maximize efficiency.[32] A trading system is flexible, allowing, for instance, an economic actor who has a highly cost-effective means of abating pollution to reduce pollution beyond its allocation, selling the extra credits to an economic actor who has less cost-effective abatement techniques or wishes to pollute over its allocation. In the end, emissions do not exceed the overall cap, but the result is reached efficiently. One of the downsides to trading regimes is that caps and quotas may not create an incentive to reduce total pollution or depletion below the quota, but they provide incentives for reaching quotas as cost-effectively as possible.[33]

While trading systems have had some early successes, property rights are not always the best policy response. They are most easily applicable to cases of emissions or harvesting wildlife, which are easily quantified. However, creating property rights in environmental values can be very difficult, since most environmental rights cannot easily be partitioned, measured, defined, or valued monetarily. In addition to these practical problems, the creation of property rights in values such as ecosystem services raises challenging ethical questions about the ownership and distribution of resources essential to human survival.

4.3 Pigouvian Taxes and Subsidies

A third policy response to the externality problem is that of taxes and subsidies. In 1920, the British economist Arthur Pigou proposed taxes as a way to correct for externalities.[34] Since an externality problem is generated when marginal costs are not equal to marginal benefits, the Pigouvian solution is to impose a tax at the rate of the marginal external (environmental) cost.[35] This forces the economic agent to account for all economic costs in decision making and creates the equilibrium in which marginal social costs are equal to marginal social benefits.[36] The result is an efficient reduction of environmental costs.[37]

Pigouvian taxes often cannot be set at precisely the right rate, since it is generally impossible to measure marginal environmental costs accurately.[38] Thus, they will not necessarily fully internalize externalities. Even if marginal environmental costs could be measured, governments might not wish to set taxes at the rate needed to achieve full internalization. As noted in the opening quotation of this section, the policy objective should be to set corrective taxes in the right direction to begin implementing the "polluter or user pays" principle, rather than trying to achieve perfect internalization.

The converse of Pigouvian taxes are Pigouvian subsidies, defined by Daly and Farley as "a payment to each firm for each unit by which it reduces environmental

---

[32] See Daly and Farley, *supra* note 2 at 379. The cap or quota should be set at the amount at which the marginal benefit of one more unit of pollution or depletion is equal to the marginal social and private cost. See *id.* at 380.

[33] See Daly and Farley, *supra* note 2 at 381.

[34] See Arthur C. Pigou, *The Economics of Welfare* (1932).

[35] See OECD, *supra* note 20 at 21–22.

[36] See Daly and Farley, *supra* note 2 at 376. The tax shifts the marginal benefit curve down by the level of marginal environmental cost, the result is an optimal level of emission that incorporates the environmental cost. See also OECD, *supra* note 20 at 21–22 (2001).

[37] See Daly and Farley, *supra* note 2 at 377.   [38] *Id.*

costs."[39] In other words, these subsidies are an incentive to internalize negative environmental externalities. One of the problems with such corrective subsidies is that they could lead perversely to an increase in pollution or resource use by attracting new entrants to the market.[40] However, this risk depends upon the market conditions. If the market is saturated, subsidies will not encourage new entrants. More importantly, subsidies would likely be very small relative to other costs, thus not creating an incentive for entry into the market. Another problem is the risk that corrective subsidies could end up paying for action already undertaken; that would mean they are not having an incentive effect but rather simply offering payments for business-as-usual activities. This can be prevented through careful design of such subsidies so that they are targeted at additional, rather than existing, environmentally positive activities.

A conceptual problem with subsidies designed to encourage internalization of negative externalities is that they seem to run counter to the "polluter or user pays" principle by starting from the premise that the polluter or resource user has the privilege to pollute or use the resource, and that society must pay him, her, or it to stop. However, corrective subsidies can be appropriate in certain cases. For example, corrective subsidies do not run counter to the "polluter pays" principle when they are used strictly to compensate for the provision of positive environmental externalities (i.e., where private decision makers are providing nonmarket environmental goods without compensation) beyond what is already required by law.[41] An example would be the case of a landowner's voluntarily restoring a degraded ecosystem on her or his property. The landowner is voluntarily providing a biodiversity benefit, which is a public good. While that landowner may derive some benefit from the restored ecosystem, many of the benefits will be enjoyed externally, and she or he will not be compensated for these external benefits. Because of this, few landowners will go to the trouble of restoring an ecosystem unless required by law to do so. In economic terms, the positive externalities mean that landowners will supply less of that activity than is socially desirable. Pigouvian subsidies can provide compensation for provision of these social benefits to a more socially desirable level.[42]

4.4 A Note on Terminology

The lexicon of terminology used in discussing policy options for addressing the underlying economic causes of environmental loss and degradation is quite variable. The terminology stems from various disciplines, including economics, environmental science, law, fiscal and tax policy, and public policy. Even within disciplines, the terminology varies from author to author. While economics literature tends to focus on policy interventions to correct market failures, as highlighted previously, the broader literature discusses public and private sector approaches using terms such as *market-based approaches*, *economic instruments*, and *fiscal instruments* to describe these approaches.

---

[39] See Daly and Farley, *supra* note 2 at 378. The subsidy should be equal to the marginal benefit to society of abating pollution. As long as the abatement costs are lower than the subsidy, the firm will respond by reducing pollution. See *id*.

[40] If a polluter is paid to reduce pollution, for example, this policy may encourage more polluters. See Daly and Farley, *supra* note 2 at 414 (2004).

[41] See *id*.   [42] See *id*.

Since this can be conceptually confusing, I offer here a synthesis of terminology that attempts to offer consistency among these various disciplines. However, because much of my research in this area has been done in a Canadian context, my synthesis of termi-nology will inevitably have a Canadian bias.

When discussing policy interventions to address externality problems in an envi-ronmental context, all of the aforementioned disciplines use the term *economic instru-ments*. However, the term is not defined consistently. The National Round Table on the Environment and the Economy (NRTEE), for example, defines *economic instru-ments* as "instruments that directly affect the price of a product or service, behaviour or activity."[43] It offers *market-based instruments* as a synonym for *economic instru-ments* and explicitly includes certification and ecolabeling as examples of such instru-ments.[44] A recent report commissioned by the Canadian government defines *economic instruments* as "measures that use market-based signals to motivate desired types of decision-making."[45] This broad definition is stated to include the creation of property rights, imposition of fees, use of tradable permits, and implementation of liability and insurance regimes. It excludes, however, certification and ecolabeling systems.[46]

There is similar terminological inconsistency when referring to environmental taxes, fees, and subsidies. Some authors, including the Office of Economic Cooperation and Development (OECD), describe environmental taxes as a subset of economic instru-ments.[47] The NRTEE, on the other hand, does the opposite. It groups environmental taxes and subsidies and all other economic and market-based approaches under the banner of *Ecological Fiscal Reform* (EFR),[48] which it defines as "a strategy that redi-rects a government's taxation and expenditure programs to create an integrated set of incentives to support the shift to sustainable development."[49] While the definition focuses on government taxation and spending, the NRTEE states that EFR includes "other economic instruments, such as tradable permits, permitting charges and user fees."[50]

One of the distinguishing characteristics of these different categories of instru-ments is the agent responsible for delivering them. For example, one of the distin-guishing features of ecolabeling and certification systems is that they are most often delivered by the private sector.[51] Instruments such as taxes, fees, and subsidies, on the other hand, are policy tools delivered by governments. Governments are also normally the agents responsible for creating and enforcing property rights, such as developing trading systems, although a private sector institution can also play this

---

[43] National Round Table on the Environment and the Economy, *Towards a Canadian Agenda for Ecological Fiscal Reform: First Steps* (2002) 13.

[44] *Id.*

[45] See Stratos Inc., *Economic Instruments for Environmental Protection and Conservation: Lessons for Canada* (2003) 7.

[46] See *id.*

[47] See, for example, OECD, *supra* note 20 at 22, and Lester R. Brown, *Eco-Economy* 248 (2001).

[48] See National Round Table on the Environment and the Economy, *Towards a Canadian Agenda for Ecological Fiscal Reform: First Steps* (2002) 11.

[49] See *id.* at 5.   [50] See *id.*

[51] The Forest Stewardship Council, for example, is a global forest certification and ecolabeling system run independently of government. See The Forest Stewardship Council, at http://www.fsc.org/en/; govern-ments can be involved in certification and ecolabeling initiatives, but this is the exception rather than the norm.

role.[52] Changes to fiscal policy can only be delivered by national governments (including sublevels of government), since fiscal policy by definition is the management by government of taxation and expenditure policy.[53]

I propose the following terms and definitions because I believe them to be the most conceptually clear and accurate on the basis of the literature review I have conducted from various disciplines. However, I recognize that the categories are not clear-cut, and that there are certainly many other defensible ways to define these terms.

Market Interventions

Market-based approaches are all instruments or initiatives that use market-based signals (i.e., price) to motivate desired types of decision making. It is the broadest of the categories and includes economic instruments and fiscal instruments (as defined later), the creation of property rights, insurance and liability regimes, and government green procurement policies. It also includes decisions by private sector actors to increase ecoefficiency, to favor "green" procurement from suppliers, or to favor environmentally responsible companies in investments.

Policy Interventions

Direct or command and control regulation is an intervention by a national government to prohibit or regulate certain activities to achieve a desired outcome.

Economic instruments are policy instruments that directly affect the price of a product or service, behavior or activity, including fiscal instruments and tradable property rights, such as emissions trading systems and quotas. They are implemented by state-level governments, or multilateral institutions. They do not include instruments implemented by private actors. (These are captured by the definition of market-based instruments.)

Fiscal instruments are fiscal policy instruments, such as government taxes and expenditures, including all fees, charges, loans, and grants implemented through government-level budgetary processes. Fiscal instruments are uniquely instruments of all levels of national governments. Pigouvian taxes and subsidies fall into this category.

Ecological fiscal reform (EFR) is the process or strategy of reforming fiscal policy to achieve an environmental outcome. Fiscal policy reform can include changing existing fiscal policy as well as implementing new fiscal instruments. EFR could include, for example, the addition or removal of taxes, tax shifts, the addition or removal of subsidies, and subsidy shifts. EFR does not include all other economic instruments (such as tradable permit regimes).

5 INSTRUMENT CHOICE

In a recent report on nationwide regulatory reform, the Canadian government reflected that there is no analytical framework to assist decision makers in choosing policy instruments among various options when there is a need for a policy response.[54] Faced with

---

[52] Consider the example of an investment broker speculatively trading in carbon credits. An international institution could similarly be responsible for managing a trading system, as in the case of the greenhouse gas emissions trading regimes emerging out of the Kyoto Protocol.

[53] See Government of Canada, Economic Concepts: *Fiscal Policy*, at http://canadianeconomy.gc.ca/english/economy/fiscal.html.

[54] See Government of Canada, *Smart Regulation – a Regulatory Strategy for Canada* (2004) 38.

a problem of an industry that is causing harm to an ecosystem, should the government use command and control regulation, create tradable property rights, apply taxes, or subsidize a new technology? The report recognizes that there is "no single method for creating the optimal mix of instruments"[55] but recommends developing a framework of analysis to help policymakers identify the optimum design and mix of policy instruments.[56] The Canadian report also notes that Canada has limited experience in using economic instruments and recommends that the government examine expanding the use of such instruments to address environmental objectives.[57]

Discussing biodiversity conservation on private lands in the United States, Thompson notes that "policymakers have given little thought to whether and why the federal government should be pursuing different approaches and . . . what is the most effective mix of approaches."[58] Thompson goes on to make an observation that I think would apply equally well in a Canadian context: "The federal government's current mix of approaches seems less the result of conscious governmental choices among biodiversity tools than inadvertence, unrelated policy decisions, and political opportunism."[59]

The question of instrument choice is an important one. While the policymaker may be trying to correct for an environmental externality, the choice of which instrument to use in response could simply replace the externality with other distortions in economic decision making,[60] or have unintended consequences on other segments of society. The economist Martin Weitzman argued in 1974 that there is no theoretical basis for favoring the use of direct regulation (or quantitative restrictions, as he termed it) versus price instruments.[61] However, he notes that "in any *particular* setting there may be important *practical* reasons for favouring either prices or quantities as planning instruments," citing ideological, political, social, informational, monitoring, and enforcement considerations among others.[62] Taking into account these various considerations, "a central task in environmental policy making is to appraise the costs and benefits of alternative policy goals and instruments."[63] Particular instruments have certain characteristics and will impose different costs on the various actors involved. Factors such as administrative ease, public acceptability, compliance costs, and distributional impacts, for example, will affect the choice and design of an instrument. Often a mix of instruments will be desirable.[64]

5.1 Analytical Approaches for Selecting among Instruments

While there is no comprehensive, uniform analytical approach for selecting among policy instruments, various authors have proposed guidelines and commentary on the subject. The OECD, for instance, emphasizes the importance of defining a clear policy objective at the outset and then thoroughly evaluating the costs and benefits of the

---

[55] See *id.*   [56] See *id.*

[57] See *id.* at 41–22.

[58] See Barton H. Thompson Jr., "Providing Biodiversity through Policy Diversity" (2002) 38:2 Idaho L. Rev. 355, 356.

[59] See *id.*   [60] See Tietenberg, *supra* note 6.

[61] See Martin L. Weitzman, "Prices vs. Quantities" (1974) 41:4 *The Review of Economic Studies* 477, 477–479.

[62] See *id.*

[63] See William K. Jaeger, "Environmental Taxation Revisited" (Working Paper, Oregon State University, April 2003).

[64] See Stratos Inc., *Economic Instruments for Environmental Protection and Conservation: Lessons for Canada* 21 (2003).

range of policy measures that could be used to achieve the objective in order to evaluate the relative merits of these alternative options.[65] It also notes that an assessment of current practices should be carried out in order to set any new measures in the context of the current situation.[66] The Government of Canada's report on Smart Regulation states that the choice of instrument(s) will depend on a number of factors, such as the particular problem to be addressed, the risks involved, the existing legal framework, and the context of the rights and responsibilities of relevant stakeholders.[67] The NRTEE proposes that the criteria for evaluating all policy instruments are the same and are as follows: There should be broad societal support for action, clarity of objective, sufficient time and adequate analytical resources, and open consultations with stakeholders.[68]

Based on an evaluation of several measures that have been implemented in different jurisdictions to finance conservation efforts, the Stanford University professors Gretchen Daily and Katherine Ellison identified three steps that were common to each of the successful measures evaluated.[69] First, each initiative involved creatively identifying potential options that were outside conventional approaches. Second, for each of the initiatives, the proponents evaluated the implications of the various options, including the costs and benefits of each. Third, the proponents compared the relative merits of the potential approaches.[70] Daily and Ellison note, however, that the comparison of different approaches is difficult since the options being compared are often very different from each other.[71]

The ecological economists Daly and Farley consider the question of instrument choice through the lens of ecological economics. They propose that economic policy should pursue three fundamental goals: sustainable scale (in recognition of the biosphere's finite limits), just distribution (to pursue intra- and intergenerational equity), and efficient allocation (the classical goal of economics).[72] They also argue that every policy goal requires an independent policy instrument, since "you have to be very lucky to hit two birds with one stone – it nearly always takes two stones to hit two birds flying independently."[73] In other words, a policy designed to reflect sustainable scale, equity, and efficiency will require at least three separate policy instruments targeted at each goal.[74]

In addition to this general guidance, the literature offers suggestions for selecting between direct regulation and economic instruments. As noted earlier, the main advantage of economic instruments over direct regulation is that economic instruments are generally more economically efficient.[75] In a pollution reduction context, for instance, economic instruments are sufficiently flexible to provide incentives for efficient abatement across an entire industry, meaning that the industries with lower abatement costs will cut back on emissions relatively more and an industry with higher abatement costs

[65] See OECD, *supra* note 20 at 10.   [66] See *id.*

[67] See Government of Canada, *Smart Regulation – a Regulatory Strategy for Canada* (2004) 38.

[68] See National Round Table on the Environment and the Economy, *Economic Instruments for Promoting Sustainable Development* (2003).

[69] See Gretchen C. Daily and Katherine Ellison, *The New Economy of Nature – the Quest to Make Conservation Profitable* 226–227 (2002).

[70] See *id.*   [71] See *id.*

[72] See Daly and Farley, *supra* note 2 at 360.

[73] *Id.* (citing the Dutch economist and Nobel laureate Jan Tinbergen from *The Theory of Economic Policy,* 1952).

[74] See *id.*   [75] See OECD, *supra* note 20 at 22.

can purchase a credit or pay a tax instead.[76] Another advantage of economic instruments is that they create incentives for ongoing efforts to reduce pollution or maximize efficient use of a natural resource.[77] Producers, for instance, have an ongoing incentive to reduce pollution emissions through cost-effective abatement, innovative technologies, or restructuring of the design process.[78] In a command and control situation, a standard is set or a particular technology is mandated and an economic agent has no economic incentive to go beyond this threshold. Command and control regulation has also been criticized for being "unduly rigid, cumbersome, and costly . . . is patchwork in character . . . and lacks adequate democratic accountability."[79] According to the Canadian environmental consulting firm Stratos, economic instruments are most suitable when "fundamental, long-term behavioural change is desired . . . flexibility of response from individual actors is acceptable; an end-point is difficult to define, but the desired direction is known."[80]

There are times, however, when command and control regulation is a better approach. Regulations, for instance, can be administratively straightforward and have low monitoring costs.[81] There are also clear instances in which regulation is a superior option, such as when substances need to be banned outright or certain technologies must be imposed for environmental reasons. However, the reality is that policymakers seem to favor command and control regulation over other instruments even when these conditions are not present and they are less efficient. This may be in part due to the fact that government institutions are accustomed to such regulation and are slow to change.[82] There is also often a need for a regulatory approach to be combined with an economic instrument in order for the latter to function (i.e., in the case of a regulatory "cap" on a level of emissions that produces the incentive conditions for private entities to trade in order to capitalize on efficiency gains).

If economic instruments are identified as an appropriate policy approach, there is further guidance for selecting among various economic instruments. The environmental consulting firm Stratos, for example, offers five criteria to guide the process: effectiveness of instrument in meeting environmental objective, economic efficiency, distributional impacts, flexibility, and political acceptability.[83] They also note that alternative measures should be evaluated in order to make an informed selection.[84] The NRTEE suggests that economic instruments can be "part of the policy response to almost any issue."[85] However, the NRTEE proposes that such instruments are particularly well suited to environmental issues where:

---

[76] See id. The result is that marginal abatement costs are equalized between firms and abatement is achieved at the minimum total cost. This is known as *static efficiency*. See id.

[77] See OECD, *supra* note 20 at 23.

[78] This is known as *dynamic efficiency*. See id.

[79] See Richard B. Stewart, "A New Generation of Environmental Regulation?" (2001) 29 *Cap. U.L. Rev.* 21, 27 (surveying the various shortcomings of the command and control system in place for environmental regulation in the United States).

[80] Stratos Inc., *Economic Instruments for Environmental Protection and Conservation: Lessons for Canada* (2003) 21.

[81] See Daly and Farley, *supra* note 2 at 385.   [82] See id.

[83] See Stratos Inc., *supra* note 80 at 22.   [84] See id. at 21.

[85] National Round Table on the Environment and the Economy, *Economic Instruments for Promoting Sustainable Development* 12 (2003). Note that the NRTEE makes this reference in terms of EFR, but as noted earlier, the NRTEE's definition of EFR is synonymous with the definition of economic instruments

1. Flexibility of response from different actors is acceptable.
2. An end point is difficult to assess or define.
3. A command and control structure exists, but there is a desire to support performance beyond compliance.
4. A command and control structure exists, but it is ineffective or impractical.
5. A voluntary instrument is in place, but increased incentives for participation are needed.
6. There is a desire to support a transitional stage of performance and behavior.
7. Fundamental, longer-term behavioral change is the objective.[86]

An Australian author proposes four instances in which tax-based instruments have a comparative advantage over other economic instruments.[87] First, tax-based tools are more useful when trying to change behavior in a general direction over the long term. Second, tax-based tools are most effective in engaging unmotivated actors, in part because taxes manage to get the attention of most people through tax accountants and other tax experts whose function it is to know taxation rules. The third instance when tax-based tools are most effective is in the reform of perverse incentives within the fiscal system. Fourth, tax-based tools are particularly effective for engaging entrepreneurs in innovative change.[88]

Daly and Farley offer six general principles based on ecological economics for designing economic policy. The first has already been mentioned; the remaining five are new: (1) Every policy goal requires an independent policy instrument; (2) policies should strive to attain the necessary degree of macrocontrol with the minimal sacrifice of the microlevel freedom and variability; (3) policies should leave a margin of error when dealing with the biophysical environment; (4) policy must recognize that we always start from historically given initial conditions; (5) policies must be able to adapt to changed conditions; and (6) the domain of the policymaking unit must be congruent with the domain of the causes and effects of the problem with which the policy deals (also known as the *principle of subsidiarity*).[89]

5.2 Analytical Framework

In sum, there is a lot of general guidance but nothing uniform or concrete. This is not surprising, given that this is a complicated policy area with many interacting variables.[90]

used in this chapter. Thus for clarity and consistency, I have substituted *economic instruments* for *EFR* in the context of the NRTEE's literature on characteristics of instruments.

[86] *Id.* at 12.

[87] See Steve Hatfield-Dodds, Senior Policy Economist, CSIRO Division of Land and Water, Canberra, Australia, Address at the Fourth Annual Global Conference on Environmental Taxation, Sydney, Australia (7 June 2003).

[88] Entrepreneurs are likely to prefer tax initiatives to grants because the latter can be administratively complex and slow, and with grants an entrepreneur may have to reveal his or her idea too early, with the risk of the idea's being stolen. See *id.*

[89] Daly and Farley, *supra* note 2 at 362–363.

[90] There is a wealth of economic literature on assessing the cost-effectiveness of various policy instruments, mainly for pollution control, which reveals findings important to the discussion of instrument choice. For example, a recent bout of economics literature has identified a "tax interaction effect," which is a negative welfare impact that results from environmental taxes that do not take into account the distortions caused by preexisting taxes. This literature provides insight into the cost-effectiveness of

Table 29.1. Summary of analytical framework for selecting measures

Step one	Precisely define environmental goal.
Step two	Evaluate the impact of existing policy structure on goal.
Step three	Develop a short list of potential policy measures that could help achieve goal identified in step one.
Step four	Conduct cost–benefit and risk–return analyses of short-listed measures in order to select best measure.

Recognizing the challenge and complexity, I offer in this chapter a synthesis of the decision process for choosing among different instruments. In my opinion, it is better to have an imperfect analytical framework than none at all, since at least an imperfect model provides a basis upon which to build and improve. The framework is summarized in Table 29.1.

The starting point should be to define precisely what is the desired environmental policy objective.[91] What specifically is the behavior that should be changed? Which decisions should be impacted, and over what period? Understanding what changes are being sought is the most critical step in the analysis, since a policy instrument cannot be effectively designed without a clear direction. The articulation of the goal should include a clear definition of the scale at which the goal is to be pursued, the actors who are to be targeted, and the time frame within which change is desired. Ideally, it should include a mechanism for evaluating progress in achieving the objective.[92] Once the environmental objective is clearly defined, the next step is to evaluate the impact of the existing policy structure on the environmental goal.[93] Do existing policies create incentives that run counter to the environmental goal? Are there policy instruments working at cross-purposes that are undermining the goal? What, if any, changes should be made to the existing policy structure to help achieve the goal? Following on the results of the analysis of the impact of the existing policy structure, the final step is to evaluate the potential of various new policy measures, from economic instruments and EFR to more traditional command and control style regulation, to help achieve the goal identified in step one. The factors to be taken into account in selecting among

various policy instruments, considering a "second-best setting" (i.e., one that takes into account the impact of preexisting distortionary taxes). See, for example, Lawrence H. Goulder et al., "The Cost-Effectiveness of Alternative Instruments for Environmental Protection in a Second-Best Setting" (1999) 72 *Journal of Public Economics* 329–360.

[91] The starting point of this analytical framework is that of an environmental goal. This can be justified on the basis of the argument made by Daly and Farley that "sustainable scale" is the first priority in terms of policy design, since everything (from economic to social policy) is dependent upon a functioning biosphere.

[92] The International Institute for Sustainable Development (IISD) argues that the goal should be stated in such a way that is measurable so that the success of the initiative can be evaluated after a certain period to determine its success in shifting behavior. Causal connections between a measure and achievement of an environmental goal are often difficult to draw, so efforts to design evaluatory criteria are important. See Stephen Barg et al., International Institute for Sustainable Development, *Analysis of Ecological Fiscal Reform Activity in Canada* (2000) 3.

[93] This corresponds to Daly and Farley's fourth design principle, noted earlier, which is that policy must recognize initial conditions. See Daly and Farley, *supra* note 2 at 362–363.

various instruments include effectiveness, distributional impacts,[94] compliance costs, administrative ease,[95] and political support (including stakeholder support).[96] An effort should also be made to ensure that the proposed measure does not negatively impact another government policy objective.[97]

Once a short list of measures is identified, there are a number of analyses that should be conducted in order to assess the relative merits of each short-listed measure. In particular, the proponent should conduct a cost–benefit analysis that takes into account the broad array of costs and benefits for each short-listed measure (including environmental costs and benefits).[98] The proponent should also conduct a risk–return analysis to quantify the environmental risks to be addressed by the measures and the extent to which each measure will yield returns in terms of helping to mitigate the risk identified. Risk–return analysis is especially important for public expenditures, since it can help governments rationalize dedicating public resources to one activity versus another, on the basis of a risk assessment and potential return on investment from the public expenditure.[99] There are also a number of design principles that are relevant

---

[94] Fiscal policies such as an environmental tax will affect different households differently, because consumption patterns vary with income and demographic composition. It is very important to consider the distributional effects (both intra- and intergenerationally) of environmental fiscal measures to ensure that equity considerations are improved, or at least not worsened, by the measure. See Jorgen Aasness and Erling R. Larsen, "Distributional Effects of Environmental Taxes on Transportation" (2003) 26 *Journal of Consumer Policy* 279 (2003) (reviewing the distributional effects of environmental taxes on transportation). See also Daly and Farley, *supra* note 2 at 389–404 (for a discussion of just distribution from the perspective of ecological economics).

[95] It is important that an initiative can be fairly easily administered. It is not useful to implement an initiative that is very difficult and costly to administer. Related to the ease of an initiative's implementation is whether its compliance can be monitored. If it is very difficult to verify compliance with the initiative, the proposal could be taken advantage of; thus, instruments should be chosen and designed to ensure that they will help achieve the environmental goal at the lowest costs, considering costs of administering and enforcing the measure.

[96] Clearly, having stakeholder support for a measure will impact its success. Therefore, it is important to consult stakeholders when choosing and designing measures. There is often distrust of government claims that initiatives are not simply for revenue generation, but are in fact aimed at behavior modification. Therefore, it is important for proposals to be transparent in their objectives and means. The government should also consider a transition strategy for implementing the measure if necessary to achieve stakeholder support. Of course, every proposal will generate winners and losers, and few measures will generate complete support from stakeholders. It should be kept in mind that people tend to value losses more than gains (see Mark Jaccard, *The Role of Environmental Tax Shifting in the Slate of Sustainability Policies*, in 2nd Annual Global Conference on Environmental Taxation Issues, Experience and Potential 46 [2000]); therefore, those who will be negatively impacted by a measure will have the greatest motivation to resist. The health of the economy at the time will also impact the political appeal of an initiative. Also, if the measure is aimed at advancing a government policy goal, it will likely have much greater political support.

[97] As Tietenberg argues, replacing one distortionary measure with another is considered a government failure. It is important to screen any proposed measure against other valid policy objectives in order to ensure that the new measure (or reform of existing measures) will either be neutral or facilitate the other policy objective. If a proposed reform could undermine other policy goals, there would have to be a strong and clear justification for introducing that reform. See Tietenberg, *supra* note 6.

[98] As well, the impact of any changes, whether reform to the existing structure or a new measure, should be evaluated in terms of its potential impacts on other policy objectives. See Daily and Ellison, *supra* note 12 at 226–227 (2002).

[99] See Stewart, *supra* note 79 at 48 (2001) (explaining risk analysis in the environmental context and reviewing the United States' use of risk analysis).

once a fiscal instrument is selected.[100] I will not review them here in detail, though I will point out that they overlap in part with the selection criteria.[101]

5.3 Challenges for Applying the Analytical Framework

One of the major challenges to the methodology synthesized is that it is not easy to apply. It is no simple task, for instance, to evaluate the impact of existing policy on a given environmental goal. There is an enormous variety of policies that apply to any given situation, and it is extraordinarily complex to attempt to identify all of the relevant policies and tease out their incentive impacts. In addition, while there are economic tools and methodologies for conducting cost–benefit analysis of particular measures, these have their own limitations, and it is difficult to conduct such analysis for every given situation. In other words, the methodology proposed should be considered as a guideline for change in the right direction. One should not expect policymakers to complete full analyses of each step. That would be a recipe for policy paralysis. I argue instead that the methodology should be applied with the goal of improving upon existing, and implementing better, policies guided by a "best attempt" approach that takes into account time and resource constraints.

There are numerous other challenges in instrument selection. For instance, the information required to make an appropriate decision is often not available. The gap in information may be scientific or technical, but the policy analysis of existing conditions may also be missing. Teitenberg proposes that "government failure" is an important source of inefficiency[102] and a challenge in policymaking. Rent-seeking behavior (in which economic actors use resources to lobby governments to secure favorable policies)[103] by particular sectors poses a major policy challenge, since such behavior is often successful in influencing policy choices, resulting in suboptimal policy decisions. As public choice theory underlines, governments are motivated by a desire to maximize popular support.[104] "Accordingly, governments formulate policies in order to win elections rather than win elections to formulate policies."[105]

Another challenge is that ecosystem goods and services range dramatically in their spatial characteristics. For instance, some ecosystem services (such as water purification) are highly localized, while others (such as climate stabilization) have a global scale. The

---

[100] Stratos proposes a number of design principles, including that the measure should be simple; the incentive should promote innovation; monitoring and enforcement should be built into the design of the measure; the measure should deliver visible short-term results; the measure should be designed to mitigate adverse economic impacts (for instance, phasing in the measure or creating exceptions); and efforts should be made to coordinate efforts with adjacent jurisdictions, where appropriate. See Stratos Inc., *supra* note 80 at 23. In an advisory paper to the NRTEE, the International Institute for Sustainable Development (IISD) identified 12 issues relevant to the design and implementation of policy instruments, including administrative efficiency, stakeholder support, and respect for other policy initiatives. See Stephen Barg et al., International Institute for Sustainable Development, *Analysis of Ecological Fiscal Reform Activity in Canada* (2000) 3.

[101] For example, one might select an instrument because it can be administered relatively easily, but then commit more energy at the design stage to ensuring it is as administratively straightforward as possible.

[102] See Tietenberg, *supra* note 6 at 71.   [103] See *id.*

[104] See D. C. Meuller, *Public Choice II* (1989) 179.

[105] See Michael A. Geist, "Balanced Budget Legislation: An Assessment of the Recent Canadian Experience" (1998) 29 *Ottawa L. Rev.* 1 (referring to D. C. Meuller, *Public Choice II* [1989]).

variable spatial distribution of ecosystem goods and services makes it difficult to adhere to the idea of matching policy instruments to the scale of the environmental problem.[106] Daly and Farley note that many

> ecosystem services are global public goods, and most countries are free riders on the provision of those public goods. Although all nations in the world benefit from healthy ecosystems in other countries, they do little or nothing to help pay for their preservation.[107]

A related problem arises out of the context of globalization. Globalization expands the domain of much of the activity that impacts upon biodiversity to a worldwide scale. Public policy, on the other hand, remains at a national level.[108] The results are weakened public policy combined with an increase in private power.[109] And because of most countries' ongoing obsession with global economic growth, policy is watered down:

> Public efforts at the national level to deal with poverty, environmental degradation, public health, education and even macroeconomic goals of full employment without inflation are all automatically sacrificed to the overriding goal of growth in the global production of market goods as stimulated by free trade and free capital mobility.[110]

Lastly, the interdisciplinary aspect of the methodology is a major challenge. It requires drawing on ecology, economics, law, fiscal and tax policy, and political sciences, large disciplines that contain many discourses within them. I therefore reiterate my earlier comment that policymakers should use best efforts to design policy instruments in the context of various challenges. The context of a particular situation may require selecting instruments that appear suboptimal by certain disciplinary analyses (i.e., they may be the least cost-effective instrument in neoclassical economic terms), but that on balance, taking into account other factors such as political feasibility, are the best option. Policymakers should not seek perfect policies, but rather change in the right direction, taking into account all relevant considerations informed by multiple disciplines.

6 ECOLOGICAL FISCAL REFORM (EFR)

As noted earlier, EFR refers to the process of reforming fiscal policy to achieve an environmentally beneficial outcome. EFR is distinguished from fiscal instruments only insofar as the former refers to the overall process of reform, whereas the instruments are the tools of that reform. The foundation of EFR is a recognition that while governments

---

[106] See the subsidiarity principle, identified earlier. See Daly and Farley, *supra* note 2 at 417.

[107] Daly and Farley, *supra* note 2 at 419. They argue that a "beneficiary pays principle" that could be implemented via a global Pigouvian-style subsidy would help resolve this free-riding problem. They offer the example of the Brazilian ICMS *ecologico*, which is a tax on merchandise and services whereby some of the revenue from the tax is refunded to municipalities on the basis of the extent to which they met ecological goals such as watershed protection. It is a payment for ecological services and could be implemented globally (i.e., targeting payments at biodiversity hotspots). See *id* at 420–421. See also International Institute for Environment and Development, Fiscal Incentives for Biodiversity Conservation: *The ICMS Ecologico in Brazil* (2000).

[108] See Daly and Farley, *supra* note 2 at 386. While international law exists, and is growing, enforceable policy continues to be primarily a national creature.

[109] See *id.*

[110] *Id.* There is a vast body of literature examining the impacts of globalization and regulatory competition on environmental progress.

have little choice about using taxes to raise revenue, they do have a choice about what to tax and how to do so. What is subsidized, whether through the tax system or a direct expenditure, is also a matter of political choice. As the Canadian tax expert Vern Krishna says, "All tax law is policy. The [Income Tax] Act is a living document, a mirror that reflects the social, political, economic, and moral values of society."[111] The activities that are taxed and subsidized in many countries' fiscal systems (including Canada's) are largely the reflection of choices made given the circumstances of the early 20th century.[112] At that time, the environment was seemingly inexhaustible and labor was relatively scarce. The government wanted to encourage rapid exploitation of natural resources to stimulate economic growth, and so it avoided imposing taxes on natural resource use. Instead, the government applied the majority of taxes on income.[113] Although it has changed slowly over time, today's fiscal system continues to reflect the policy goals of a past era. Policy objectives have changed, but the evolution of the fiscal system has not kept pace.

Environmental taxes have "long been favoured by economists as mechanisms to internalize the external costs of pollution."[114] As discussed in the previous section, environmental taxes can be an efficient and effective policy response to correct for negative environmental externalities. In reality, however, efficiency and effectiveness are not the only factors that play into a government's choice about whether to apply such a tax. Political reality is such that governments are often unwilling to impose a corrective tax on economic actors to address environmental issues. A wide variety of political, economic, social, and other factors are at play, including fears of lost global competitiveness and institutional capture from rent-seeking behavior.

EFR includes not only environmental taxes, but also other fiscal instruments such as subsidies and grants, and instruments that combine taxes and spending. It can also involve changing existing fiscal policy, in addition to implementing new fiscal instruments. As in the case of policy instruments more broadly, there is no standard or consistent framework or lexicon for describing EFR or fiscal instruments. I therefore propose a simple one.

6.1 A Descriptive Framework for EFR

One of the most obvious ways to categorize fiscal instruments is by whether they are revenue-generating or expenditures. Revenue-generating measures include taxes, fees, and charges, while expenditure measures include subsidies, grants, and loans. However, a fiscal measure could incorporate revenue and expenditure components, such as a government-run fee-bate program that involves collecting revenue (such as a deposit) and rebating all or some of that revenue in the form of a rebate. Another characteristic that can be used to frame fiscal instruments is the delivery agent. Whether revenue-generating or expenditures, fiscal instruments can be delivered through the tax system or outside it. Thus, for instance, taxes and tax expenditures, such as tax credits

---

[111] Vern Krishna, *The Fundamentals of Canadian Income Tax* (6th ed., 2000) 1.
[112] See generally Paul Hawken et al., *Natural Capitalism: Creating the Next Industrial Revolution* (1999).
[113] See generally *id.*
[114] See William K. Jaeger, "Environmental Taxation Revisited" (Working Paper, Oregon State University, April 2003).

Table 29.2. Descriptive framework of EFR measures

	Delivered through tax system	Delivered through government programs outside of the tax system
Revenue generating	Taxes	Fees Charges

Expenditure	Tax expenditures
	Refundable and
	   nonrefundable tax credits
	Tax concessions
	Reductions in tax rates
	Tax deferrals
		Direct expenditures
		Grants
		Cash subsidies
		Loans
		Loan guarantees
		Preferential rates
		Direct provision of goods
		   and services

Neutral or not known	Tax shifts Changes to tax rules	Rebate programs Changes to program rules

or reduction in tax rates, can be delivered through income tax systems or other tax regimes such as sales or excise taxes. Fees, charges, loans, grants, or preferential interest rates, for example, can be delivered by government programs outside the tax system. This creates four main categories, as shown in Table 29.2.

Within each category, there are numerous types of instruments. Direct expenditures can be broken down into three main categories: direct public provision of goods or services, grants or cash subsidies, and loan subsidies, guarantees, or preferences.[115] There is no tax expenditure equivalent of direct public provision of goods or services, but there are many tax expenditures that are similar to grants and cash subsidies. In addition, tax deferrals are similar in function to loan subsidies or guarantees.[116] EFR is the process of manipulating these instruments in various combinations to achieve an environmental goal. So, for instance, it includes the removal, addition, or modification of fiscal instruments as well as tax and subsidy shifts. It also includes accelerated capital cost allowance and changes to tax rules, such as rollover provisions.

6.2 Environmental Tax Reform Distinguished

The terms *environmental tax reform* and *environmental tax shifting* are commonly used in the literature in this area, in addition to EFR and fiscal instruments. *Environmental tax reform* generally refers exclusively to reform delivered through the tax system.[117] It does not, in contrast to the broader term EFR, include reform of fees, charges, or spending policies outside the tax system. *Environmental tax shifting* generally refers to the process of levying taxes on the use of environmental resources, and then recycling the

---

[115] See Jonathan R. Kesselman, "Direct Expenditures versus Tax Expenditures for Economic and Social Policy," in *Tax Expenditures Government Policy* 283, 285 (Neil Bruce ed., 1988).

[116] See *id.*

[117] The Pembina Institute, a Canadian environmental nongovernmental organization (NGO), defines environmental tax reform as "adjusting existing taxes to make them sensitive to environmental impacts." See Pembina Institute, *Environmental Fiscal Reform: Glossary of EFR Terms*, at http://www.fiscallygreen.ca/efr5.html

revenue from such taxes to reduce other taxes, such as income taxes; using the revenue to fund other environmental programs; or simply applying the revenue to general public accounts.[118] A tax shift with revenue recycled back to reduce distortionary taxes such as payroll tax is said to produce a double dividend. The double-dividend hypothesis suggests that substituting environmental taxes for distortionary, revenue-motivated taxes will produce two benefits. First, it will correct the environmental externalities; second, it will improve the efficiency of the tax system.[119] Environmental tax shifting has been used most widely in Europe.

6.3 Instrument Choice within EFR

Although there is no definitive analytical framework for selecting among different policy measures, such as tradable permits versus regulation or fiscal instruments, there is a fair bit of literature to draw upon for guidance. Once the area of fiscal instruments is identified as the option going forward, there is not only no analytical framework for selecting among potential fiscal measures, but far less literature to guide the choice and design of the measure. The only area in which there is a research basis for differentiating between instruments is that of direct versus tax expenditures. Guidance on choosing between raising revenue through the tax system versus through an outside government program is far more sparse. One of the challenges to overcome is the fact that tax policy has tended to be developed in a vacuum, away from other policy processes.[120] Also, the principles of tax policy are at play in any discussion of taxes versus other fiscal instruments. In this section, I begin by providing a quick overview of the principles of tax policy, since they influence the politics of using the tax system to deliver policy instruments. Then, I discuss the characteristics of revenue-raising instruments (taxes versus charges, fees, and payments) and spending instruments (tax versus direct expenditures). Last, I offer some comments on ways to select among these instruments.

Tax Policy Principles

Most modern taxation systems were born of the need to finance wars.[121] The main source of revenue for Canada prior to World War I were customs and excise duties, but this quickly changed once the war started.[122] Canada began to collect a tax on

---

[118] The Pembina Institute defines an *environmental tax shift* as "leveling new ecological taxes to offer incentives to reduce environmental impacts and recycling the revenue from the new taxes." See *id*.

[119] See generally Lawrence H. Goulder, "Environmental Taxation and the Double Dividend: A Readers' Guide" (1995) 2 *International Tax and Public Finance* 157; William K. Jaeger, "Environmental Taxation Revisited" (Working Paper, Oregon State University, April 2003); Alan H. Sanstad and Gary H. Wolff, "Tax Shifting and the Likelihood of Double Dividends: Theoretical and Computational Issues," Address at the Fourth Annual Global Conference on Environmental Taxation, Sydney, Australia (7 June 2003). See also Lawrence H. Goulder and Ian W. H. Parry, "Green Tax Reform and the 'Double Dividend'" (2000), available at http://www.rff.org/~parry/Papers/Goulder-Parry%20AERE%20Newsletter.pdf and Thorsten Baymdir-Upmann and Matthias G. Raith, "Environmental Taxation and the Double Dividend: A Drawback for a Revenue-Neutral Tax Reform" (2003), available at http://www.wiwi.uni-bielefeld.de/~imw/Papers/files/imw-wp-274-revised.pdf (criticizing the double dividend theory).

[120] See G. Bruce Doern et al., *Taxing and Spending – Issues of Process* (1994) 37.

[121] For example, the British government introduced an income tax in 1803 to finance the Napoleonic Wars, and the U.S. introduced an income tax in 1862 to finance the Civil War. See David G. Duff, *Canadian Income Tax Law* (2003) 12.

[122] See Krishna, *supra* note 111 at 2. Two-thirds of the revenue was from customs duties and the rest from excise taxes. See Duff, *supra* note 121 at 12.

business profits in 1916.[123] This was followed by the enactment of the Income War Tax Act in 1917, which introduced a personal income tax.[124] This original 10-page statute was meant as a temporary measure to finance World War I.[125] However, the measure was never temporary, and the Income War Tax Act evolved over the course of the 20th century into the complex federal tax system whose rules are now embedded in the over-2,000-page Income Tax Act.[126]

The principal function of the modern tax system is still raising revenue to fund government expenditures. However, government expenditures are far more varied today than they were in the earlier part of the 20th century, when the main expenditure was to finance the two world wars.[127] The tax system is also used to implement a range of socioeconomic policies, an example of which is the use of an investment tax credit to stimulate research and development.[128] However, the extent to which the tax system can be used to achieve such policy objectives is limited by some of the theoretical underpinnings of the tax system.[129]

The main theoretical underpinnings of the Canadian federal income tax system are similar to those in many countries. Essentially, tax policy aims to create income tax rules that raise revenue in a way that is neutral, efficient, fair and equitable, certain, and administratively simple.[130]

Neutrality. The principle of neutrality essentially means that a tax system should not draw artificial distinctions between identical transactions merely on the basis of the form of a transaction or its source. As Vern Krishna states, "Neutrality implies a level playing field that does not favour or unfairly discriminate against taxpayers merely on the basis of their choice of entities or relationships to structure business and personal transactions."[131] Neutrality is important in order to impose constraints on governments who might otherwise "seek to reward their friends and punish their enemies"[132] through the tax system. While tax systems aim to be neutral, this is difficult to achieve in practice. Vern Krishna notes that "the Canadian tax system is far from neutral and invites behavioural responses from taxpayers that are often motivated purely by tax considerations."[133]

---

[123] See Duff, *supra* note 121 at 12.

[124] See Krishna, *supra* note 111 at 2; Duff, *supra* note 121 at 12. The provinces introduced income taxes in the 1920s and 1930s. See Duff, *supra*, at 13.

[125] See Krishna, *supra* note 111 at 2.

[126] R. S. C. 1985, c. 1 (5th Supp.) (hereafter Income Tax Act). In 1948, the federal government repealed the Income War Tax Act and passed the Income Tax Act. This was revised numerous times before consolidation in 1952, and again in 1972. The Act has been regularly revised since then. See Duff, *supra* note 121 at 14–15 (2003). See also Krishna, *supra* note 111 at 2.

[127] See, for example, Finance Canada, *Tax Expenditures and Evaluations 2003* (2003) 9; See also Krishna, *supra* note 111 at 8.

[128] See generally Krishna, *supra* note 111 at 8. Since major reform of the Canadian Income Tax Act (ITA) in 1972, the Act has been increasingly used as an instrument of federal economic and social policy, through the use of tax credits to encourage specific kinds of investments. Duff, *supra* note 121 at 16.

[129] See Neil Brooks, "Comment," in *Tax Expenditures and Government Policy* 324, 329 (1988).

[130] See Krishna, *supra* note 111 at 9. See also David G. Duff, *Canadian Income Tax Law* (2003).

[131] Krishna, *supra* note 111 at 10.

[132] Dan Usher, "The Concept of Neutrality as a Basis for Identifying and Classifying Tax Expenditures," in *Tax Expenditures Government Policy* 407 (Neil Bruce ed., 1988).

[133] Krishna, *supra* note 111 at 10.

Efficiency. Efficiency refers to the economic principle of efficient allocation of resources to maximize production and economic growth.[134] If a tax system causes business decisions to be based solely or primarily on tax considerations, this system can distort economic efficiency and capital flows.[135]

Equity and fairness. Equity in the context of tax law refers to the optimality of distribution of the tax burden.[136] In other words, an equitable tax system is one that offers equal treatment of taxpayers with equal ability to pay. Horizontal equity refers to a tax policy that treats similarly situated taxpayers in a similar manner.[137] Vertical equity refers to a fair distribution of income.[138] The principle is premised on the notion that individuals who have higher income should pay more tax than those who have less income.[139] The difficulty, of course, is to determine how much more the higher earners should pay. A proportional tax system uses flat tax rates, so that the tax payable is proportional to the amount that taxpayer earns. In a progressive tax system, deductions reduce the tax payable by a high-income taxpayer by a greater amount than the tax payable by a low-income taxpayer. The marginal tax rate thus becomes a very important factor in tax deduction decisions, because a lower-income taxpayer has a higher after-tax cost for deductions than a higher-marginal-rate taxpayer.[140]

Certainty and administrative simplicity. Certainty and administrative simplicity aim to ensure a tax system that is certain, is predictable, and does not impose unreasonable compliance costs.[141] Given that income tax rules rely upon self-assessment, the need for simplicity becomes quite important.

These well-developed principles have a very strong grounding in tax policy. While policies regularly diverge from the principles, proposing new measures to be delivered via the tax system requires adhering to the principles or justifying the deviation.

Revenue-Raising Instruments

Revenue-raising instruments include taxes, charges, and fees. How should a policymaker determine whether to impose a tax versus another sort of charge or fee? Part of the answer depends on the purpose of the measure. The OECD's definition of an environmental tax is helpful:

> [An environmental tax is] any compulsory, unrequited payment to the general government levied on tax bases deemed to be of particular environmental relevance (taxes are unrequited in the sense that benefits provided by government to taxpayers are not normally in proportion to their payments).[142]

---

[134] See Krishna, *supra* note 111 at 11.   [135] See *id.*

[136] See *id.* at 12.

[137] This relies upon an accurate measurement of income. A taxpayer's ability to pay may be different from that person's income in an accounting sense. See *id.*

[138] See *id.*   [139] See *id.*

[140] See *id.*

[141] See *id.* at 18 (6th ed. 2000); David G. Duff, *Canadian Income Tax Law* 52 (2003).

[142] OECD, *Environmentally Related Taxes in OECD Countries: Issues and Strategies* (2001). See also Jean Philippe Barde, Director of National Policies, Environment Directorate, OECD, Address to the Fourth Annual Global Conference on Environmental Taxation, Sydney, Australia (6 June 2003). The OECD emphasizes that the purpose of the tax is not important to its qualifying as an environmental tax. See *id.* Professor Krishna defines a *tax* as a "compulsory contribution levied on individuals, firms or property in order to fund government operations." Krishna, *supra* note 111 at 8.

In this definition, taxes are not tied to a specific benefit or service. A Canadian public finance textbook distinguishes between taxes and charges on the basis that the former is compulsory and the latter voluntary.[143] The same text also links charges and fees with the provision of particular services on a benefit basis.[144] Such direct charges can be appropriate when the goods or services being provided are private, because the benefit can be transferred to the user who has paid.[145] When the goods or services are public goods, direct fees and charges are less accurate since their value to a particular user cannot be calculated with any precision. In this case, it makes more sense to collect revenue via the tax system and use the revenue to finance public expenditures, without a direct link between the two.

The preceding discussion suggests that a policymaker should choose to collect revenue directly via fees and charges if the revenue will be used to compensate for provision of a service or specific benefit. If, on the other hand, the purpose of the instrument is to correct for an externality, the policymaker should select tax measures.[146]

A policymaker may also choose to use taxes rather than fees and charges if he or she is pursuing long-term, fundamental behavioral change among a large group, because delivering fiscal instruments through the tax system is effective and efficient in changing price signals at a systemic level. Changes in the tax system impact the economic decision making of all actors in the market, from corporate leaders to individual consumers to politicians. For example, if a tax raises the price of fossil fuel to reflect the full costs of fossil fuel use, the change will permeate the economy, affecting all energy-related economic decisions. Making price changes through the fiscal system is also administratively simple, as it eliminates the need for disseminating information about the measure. The signal is contained directly in the market price.

However, using the tax system to raise revenue has some disadvantages relative to fees and charges. The tax system relies upon self-assessment. While self-assessment can be an advantage in terms of dissemination of information of the measure, it can be a disadvantage in terms of verifying compliance and accuracy.[147] Of course, self-assessment may be considered an advantage since most individuals and businesses already file a tax report; that means that a new tax instrument does not require a new point of contact between the taxpayer and the government.[148]

A final consideration relates to tax policy. As noted in the section Tax Policy Principles, tax policy promotes neutrality, efficiency, equity, and administrative simplicity. Measures delivered through the tax system may be seen in some cases as conflicting with these basic principles of tax law and policy, or as introducing distortions into

---

[143] See Richard A. Musgrave et al., *Public Finance in Theory and Practice* 203 (1987).

[144] See *id.* at 212.

[145] The benefit principle can be pursued through tax measures as well, but only by earmarking the revenue from such taxes to be used to provide the benefit. See *id.*

[146] Tax measures have been used far more often than charges or fees to collect environmentally related revenue. See Michael Faure and Stefan Ubachs, "Comparative Benefits and Optimal Use of Environmental Taxes," in *Critical Issues in Environmental Taxation – International and Comparative Perspectives*, Volume I 27 (Janet Milne et al., eds., 2002). Perhaps this trend reflects that fact that so many environmental goods are public.

[147] See Neil Brooks, "Comment," in *Tax Expenditures and Government Policy* 324, 328 (G. Bruce Doern, ed., 1988).

[148] See Eric J. Toder, "Tax Cuts of Spending – Does It Make a Difference?" (2000) 53:3 *National Tax Journal* 361.

the system.[149] Recall that neutrality is aimed at ensuring the system does not provide preferential treatment to a particular group or groups of taxpayers or for particular activities.[150] Applying different rates to taxpayers in similar circumstances on the basis of environmental performance could be seen to violate neutrality principles. While such divergence would not be uncommon in the Income Tax Act, departing from neutrality would need to be justified since it is a fundamental democratic principle aimed at ensuring fair treatment.[151] To the extent that taxes are meant to internalize externalities, they should not be considered to compromise neutrality. They are rather helping to remove distortions and, where the degree of externalization is variable, level the playing field.

Expenditures

Tax expenditures involve using the "tax system as a policy tool to promote and induce desired kinds of economic and social behaviour or to prevent or limit undesired behaviour."[152] Such provisions are special preferences designed to favor particular industries, activities, or classes of persons.[153] Identifying a tax expenditure within the tax system involves identifying the benchmarks or norms within the system, and then identifying departures from the benchmarks, which are the tax expenditures.[154]

The identification of tax expenditures stems from the work of Stanley Surrey.[155] Surrey was one of the first to point out, in the 1960s, that there was little reflection about the government policies and programs delivered through the tax system compared with those delivered through government programs.[156] He pointed out that tax expenditures were somewhat hidden from visibility compared to policy discussions about direct program spending. Surrey and McDaniel noted that little was known about how governments chose between direct spending and tax expenditures and even suggested that governments may not have consciously realized that such a choice was possible.[157] Surrey's efforts culminated in the production by the U.S. Treasury Board in 1968 of a tax expenditure budget and the emergence of scholarship on tax expenditures.[158]

While the literature has evolved from Surrey's initial identification of the issue, however, many issues remain unresolved. There is ongoing debate about the difference

---

[149] See, for example, Neil Brooks, "Comment," in *Tax Expenditures and Government Policy* 324 (G. Bruce Doern, ed., 1988).

[150] See Krishna, *supra* note 111.

[151] See Dan Usher, "The Concept of Neutrality as a Basis for Identifying and Classifying Tax Expenditures," in *Tax Expenditures Government Policy* 407, 410 (Neil Bruce, ed., 1988).

[152] G. Bruce Doern, "Tax Expenditure Decisions and the Budgetary Process," in *Tax Expenditures and Government Policy* 105, 106 (Neil Bruce ed., 1998). See also Stanley S. Surrey and Paul R. McDaniel, *Tax Expenditures* 3 (1985) and OECD, *Tax Expenditures – a Review of the Issues and Country Practices* 36 (1984).

[153] See Stanley S. Surrey and Paul R. McDaniel, *Tax Expenditures* 3 (1985).

[154] See *id.* See also OECD, *Tax Expenditures – a Review of the Issues and Country Practices* (1984) 36. Benchmarks include the rate structure, accounting practices, deductibility of compulsory payments, provisions to facilitate tax administration, and international fiscal obligations. See Zhicheng Li Swift et al., "Tax Expenditures: General Concept, Measurement, and Overview of Country Practices," in *Tax Expenditures – Shedding Light on Government Spending through the Tax System – Lessons from Developed and Transitional Economies* 1, 3 (Hana Polackova Brixi et al., 2004).

[155] Stan Surrey was a senior official with the U.S. Treasury Department in the 1960s and 1970s. See Doern et al., *supra* note 120 at 36.

[156] See *id.*   [157] See Surrey and McDaniel, *supra* note 153 at 100.

[158] See Doern et al., *supra* note 120 at 36.

between tax and direct expenditures, and (assuming there is a difference) when, if at all, spending should take place via the tax system. For example, Surrey and McDaniel state:

> There appear to be no inherent differences between tax expenditures and direct expenditures, in terms of either tax policy or budget policy. A refundable, taxable credit and a direct grant program can produce identical results in terms of beneficiaries, distribution of benefits, and desired objectives. The same is true of direct loans and repayable, interest-bearing tax credits. The principle factors that remain to affect the choice between tax expenditures and direct spending programs are the agency that will run the program and the congressional committee that will exercise jurisdiction over the program.[159]

Similarly, and more recently, Eric Toder argues that tax incentives and direct spending are, in general, the same animal in different clothes.[160] Toder and others, however, point out many differences that could be very influential in the choice between the two beasts. Toder underlines the difference in the ways tax expenditures and direct spending initiatives are displayed in budgetary accounts and communicated to the public.[161] He also points out that the cost of administering direct spending initiatives is generally more transparent, because the administrative costs are generally included in the budgets of spending programs.[162] Thuronyi offers a persuasive argument in favor of direct spending versus tax initiatives, pointing out that the latter have a higher risk of clashing with other federal programs. Direct expenditures, on the other hand, are usually sufficiently transparent to alert policymakers about potential conflicts.[163] Christopher Howard states that tax expenditures are easier to enact than direct expenditures.[164] He also notes that tax expenditures shift the administrative burden onto taxpayers, rather than public administrators.[165]

While accepting that there are a number of problems with tax expenditures (such as the fact that they are less visible, are not always subject to regular review and control through budgetary processes, and may be unacceptable to the public), Surrey and McDaniel point out that these are not inherent problems but rather defects in the budgetary process or, in the latter case, an issue of public understanding.[166] One of the problems with tax expenditures that is not a defect in process or public understanding is the potential for creating undesired distributional impacts. In particular, tax expenditures can produce what is called an "upside-down effect," meaning that they

---

[159] Surrey and McDaniel, *supra* note 153 at 117.   [160] See Toder, *supra* note 148 at 361.

[161] See *id.* (who promotes including the analysis of tax expenditures in the overall budget process so that policymakers can evaluate the appropriateness of tax expenditures, compared to other instruments, for achieving a particular policy goal). See also Doern et al., *supra* note 120 at 37.

[162] See Toder, *supra* note 148 at 361. See also Zhicheng Li Swift et al., "Tax Expenditures: General Concept, Measurement, and Overview of Country Practices," in *Tax Expenditures – Shedding Light on Government Spending through the Tax System – Lessons from Developed and Transitional Economies* 1, 2 (Hana Polackova Brixi et al., eds., 2004).

[163] See Victor Thuronyi, "Tax Expenditures: A Reassessment" (1988) *Duke L. J.* 1155, 1207.

[164] Christopher Howard, "Testing the Tools Approach: Tax Expenditures versus Direct Expenditures" (1995) 55: 5 *Public Administration Review* 439.

[165] *Id.*

[166] See Jonathan R. Kesselman, "Direct Expenditures versus Tax Expenditures for Economic and Social Policy," in *Tax Expenditures Government Policy* 283 (Neil Bruce, ed., 1988). See also Stanley S. Surrey and Paul R. McDaniel, *Tax Expenditures* 117 (1985).

may generate greater financial benefits for taxpayers with higher gross income.[167] This problem can be addressed by designing the expenditure as a credit against tax payable, which reduces the tax liability dollar for dollar regardless of the taxpayer's marginal rate, eliminating the differentiation between lower- and higher-income earners.[168] Such a tax credit will only provide a benefit, however, if the taxpayer has taxable income against which to use the credit. To extend the benefit of the credit to taxpayers with low liability, the credit can be made refundable.[169]

Victor Thuronyi criticizes Surrey and McDaniel as having tried to accomplish too much with their efforts to rationalize tax expenditures and concentrate expenditures in the spending process.[170] Thuronyi argues that most tax expenditures can be replaced or substituted with a spending program.[171] To qualify as substitutable, however, the tax expenditure must be able to be replaced by a direct spending program at equal or lower costs (considering both administrative and compliance costs).[172] As an example, he suggests that accelerated depreciation on equipment cannot be adequately replaced with a non-tax spending initiative, since the direct subsidy would require greater administrative costs and the accelerated depreciation measure has the goal of compensating declines in real value of depreciation allowances.[173] Kesselman also points out the advantage of the tax system for delivering some forms of spending. He offers accelerated depreciation and capital gains preferences as examples, stating that these are so "general and sweeping in their coverage that one could not conceive of implementing them through a direct expenditure program."[174]

The OECD concluded in 1984 that there are no general rules to follow to determine whether direct or tax expenditures are more appropriate in a given case, but that each case must be examined individually.[175] However, Kesselman proposes that there are guiding principles. In addition to his comment (noted earlier) about favoring tax expenditures for initiatives of a sweeping nature, he notes that direct expenditures are preferable when the incentives require close monitoring of a firm (for instance, in areas that do not appear on financial or tax statements).[176] Kesselman also notes that fiscal incentives aimed at businesses to deal with externalities can be addressed through direct or tax expenditures. While he points out that tax administrators are unlikely to have the capacity to measure the behavior generating the externalities (such as emissions), an agency outside the department can certify the firm's performance for tax authorities.[177] Li Swift summarizes the advantages of tax expenditures as follows: (1) They encourage

---

[167] See Surrey and McDaniel, *supra* note 153 at 108.   [168] See *id.*

[169] See *id.* at 109 (1985). Surrey and McDaniel also argue that a refundable tax credit must be taxable as income in order to prevent a secondary "upside-down" effect. See *id.* at 110.

[170] See Victor Thuronyi, "Tax Expenditures: A Reassessment" (1988) *Duke L.J.* 1155, 1181.

[171] See *id.* at 1186.

[172] See *id.* He argues that the concept of substitutable tax provisions demonstrates that the dichotomy between tax expenditure and spending initiatives is "ultimately artificial for the purposes of policy analysis." See *id.* at 1197.

[173] See *id.*   [174] Kesselman, *supra* note 166 at 289.

[175] See OECD, *Tax Expenditures – a Review of the Issues and Country Practices* (1984) 15.

[176] See Kesselman, *supra* note 167 at 318.

[177] See *id.* at 317. Kesselman suggests that Pigouvian taxes and subsidies can be implemented by direct expenditure or tax expenditure, though he states that corrective taxes are better termed *tax penalties* rather than simply *additional taxes*. See *id.* at 286.

private sector participation in government programs; (2) they promote private decision making rather than government decision making; and (3) they reduce the need for close government supervision of spending.[178] Li Swift offers the following as disadvantages: (1) They are ineffective in overriding underlying economic forces; (2) they can cause inequity by being regressive; (3) they may erode revenue bases; (4) they provide open-ended government spending; (5) they add complexity to tax laws; (6) they make the size of government elusive; and (7) they are inefficient in that they can favor certain interest groups rather than dealing with actual needs.[179]

Li Swift's last point raises the issue of the tax policy goal of neutrality. Tax expenditures run counter to neutrality given that they allow taxpayers to deviate from the benchmark in specified cases. Avoiding any violations of the neutrality principle would require favoring direct spending; yet this leads to an unsatisfying result. As Eric Toder aptly points out:

> No general principles require that spending programs should treat all taxpayers with the same income equally or that they be neutral with respect to resource allocation. Instead, public spending programs explicitly aim to alter the allocation of resources and the distribution of income from what the market system would otherwise produce.[180]

If tax expenditures and direct spending are pursuing the same goal, why should measures delivered through the tax system be subject to neutrality principles while the same measure delivered through direct spending would not be? In the absence of other factors (such as the argument of transparency), the neutrality principle should not be a justification for favoring direct over tax expenditures.

7 CONCLUSION

Land and environmental resources are being degraded and lost as a result of a host of human activities that have accelerated dramatically in the last few decades. At the same time, local communities are often negatively impacted by policy efforts aimed at addressing environmental problems, such as the establishment of protected areas or regulations to safeguard endangered species. And yet the environmental policies are often ineffective, operating at the margins of the change required to achieve sustainable land management. In order to sustain the biosphere, we need to do more than apply bandages to hemorrhaging wounds. We need to change our economic system fundamentally so that economic activity takes place within the limits of the natural world. This chapter has attempted to frame the challenge in economic terms and to provide a discussion of the policy options available to decision makers to help them make land and resource management decisions that integrate economic and ecological values. These policy tools offer greater flexibility and can in many cases achieve the same ecological goal at lower economic cost, thereby making it easier for policymakers

---

[178] Zhicheng Li Swift et al., "Tax Expenditures: General Concept, Measurement, and Overview of Country Practices," in *Tax Expenditures – Shedding Light on Government Spending through the Tax System – Lessons from Developed and Transitional Economies* 1, 5 (Hana Polackova Brixi et al., eds., 2004).

[179] *Id*. See also Toder, *supra* note 148 at 361.

[180] Toder, *supra* note 148 at 361.

to apply in areas in which economic interests already dominate. These tools can and should also be used to integrate social and cultural values into land and resource management decisions. Implementing these new tools requires policymakers to show some courage and leadership. Without this leadership, our biosphere will continue to be degraded to the point where sustainable land use and development may no longer be an option.

30 The 2004 U.S. Ocean Report and Its Implications for Land Use Reform to Improve Ocean Water Quality

Linda A. Malone

1 INTRODUCTION

1.1 Background

In response to the increasing degradation of water quality in the nation's waterways and oceans, the United States Congress in 2000 mandated the first comprehensive review of ocean policy in over 30 years. That review resulted in the 1969 Stratton Commission report and led to the establishment of a legal and regulatory framework for ocean policy.[1] Since then, the growing coastal population and ad hoc governmental approach to environmental problems compelled Congress to create the United States Commission on Ocean Policy (Commission) to make recommendations for a coordinated and comprehensive national ocean policy.[2] Although the final report was delayed,[3] it was released in September 2004.[4] The report is a result of multiple regional public meetings held by the Commission with input from various federal and state governments, industry, interest groups, the academic community, the international community, and interested citizens.[5] Notably in November 2001, just as the Commission was beginning its public meetings, it unanimously passed a one-sentence resolution[6] urging the United States to accede immediately to the United Nations Convention on the Law of the Sea.[7]

---

[1] The original 1969 Stratton Commission report, *Our Nation and the Sea*, is available at http://www.lib.noaa.gov/edocs/stratton/title.html.

[2] Oceans Act of 2000, Pub. L. No. 106–256, 114 Stat. 644 (2001), amended by Pub. L. No. 107–206, 116 Stat. 833 (2003), Pub. L. No. 107–372, 116 Stat. 3096 (2003), available at http://www.oceancommission.gov/documents/oceanact.pdf.

[3] Because the members of the Commission were appointed in July 2001, the original statutory deadline for the final report was January 2003, later amended to June 2003. See § 3(f)(1), 114 Stat. 644, 647 (2001); § 3(f)(1), 116 Stat. 833 (2003).

[4] U.S. Commission on Ocean Policy, "An Ocean Blueprint for the 21st Century: Final Report of the U.S. Commission on Ocean Policy Policy – Pre-Publication Copy" (2004), available at http://www.oceancommission.gov/documents/prepub_report/pre_pub_fin_report.pdf. The full report, with appendices and supporting documents, was released in February 2005 (hereafter Final Report), is available at http://www.oceancommission.gov/documents/full_color_rpt/welcome.html.

[5] U.S. Commission on Ocean Policy, "Report Development Timeline as of April 5, 2004" (2004), at http://www.oceancommission.gov/calendar/timeline4_5_04.pdf.

[6] U.S. Commission on Ocean Policy, "United Nations Law of the Sea Convention Resolution" (2001), at http://www.oceancommission.gov/documents/los_resolution.pdf.

[7] 1982 United Nations Convention on the Law of the Sea (UNCLOS) (UN Doc A/CONF.62/122, reprinted in 21 ILM 1261 (1982) (signed 10 December 1982), available at http://www.un.org/Depts/los/convention_agreements/convention_overview_convention.htm.

As discussed in this chapter, the Commission's overall recommendation was to move quickly toward an ecosystem-based management approach to water quality. Achievement of this goal requires the creation of a National Ocean Council (NOC), composed of all cabinet secretaries and directors of federal agencies with ocean and coastal responsibilities, to advise the President regarding the national coordination of ocean policies.[8] The President must also receive advice from nonfederal interest groups such as state governments, tribes, local agencies, and private sector and nongovernmental agencies, in the form of a Council of Advisors.[9] Naturally, an ecosystem-based approach crosses political and geographic boundaries; thus, with the assistance of the NOC, the creation of voluntary regional ocean councils to "complement and enhance" efforts, not supplant other agency authority, is recommended to address the unique problems associated with coastal ocean waters and the respective watersheds that drain into them.[10]

The Commission recommended three stages for calibrating federal agencies and programs to end the ad hoc approach of the last 30 years and move toward an ecosystem-based management approach. "At last count, more than 60 congressional committees and subcommittees oversee some 20 federal agencies and permanent commissions in implementing at least 140 federal ocean-related statutes."[11] First, the United States National Oceanic and Atmospheric Administration (NOAA) must be strengthened to become the lead federal agency on ocean policy.[12] Second, the half-dozen or so federal area-based coastal programs should be consolidated under NOAA.[13] The two main nonpoint source pollution programs under the Coastal Zone Act Reauthorization Amendments and section 319 of the Clean Water Act should be strengthened on the basis of recommendations from the NOC.[14]

These changes are the foundation for addressing the most serious threats from land-based pollution sources. This chapter focuses on the Commission's proposals for further controlling point and nonpoint source pollution. It argues that although many recommendations are needed and have been suggested for many years, the most controversial aspects, particularly over nonpoint source pollution, did not go far enough.

1.2 The Scope of the Problem

The most significant threats to water quality in oceans and estuaries from land-based sources are the growing development of coastal areas and the accompanying increase in runoff, airborne pollutants, and toxic contamination. Nonpoint source pollution (NPS) is addressed in a coastal setting primarily in the nonpoint source provisions of the 1972

---

[8] Final Report, *supra* note 4, at 48–49.

[9] *Id.* at 50. The Commission noted its recommendations for establishing the National Ocean Council and the Presidential Council of Advisors on Ocean Policy are consistent with international trends, specifically the 2002 World Summit on Sustainable Development, which called for better coordination of environmental policy at the national level. In response, several nations have already established stronger national coordination of ocean and coastal policies. *Id.* at 48.

[10] *Id.* at 34. A watershed is a geographic area where water flows on its way to a larger water body, such as a river, estuary, lake, or ocean. See *id.* at 113.

[11] *Id.* at 25.   [12] *Id.* at 75.

[13] *Id.* at 115.

[14] *Id.* at 177. The original recommendation was for the consolidation of these two NPS pollution programs, but the Commission changed it so that consolidation would be an option considered by the National Ocean Council. See U.S. Commission on Ocean Policy, "Preliminary Report: Governor's Draft" (2004) 168.

Clean Water Act as amended and the Coastal Pollution Program established by the 1990 Coastal Zone Act Reauthorization Amendments. There are also a number of state, territorial, tribal, and local programs that address this issue. These include legislation surrounding agricultural waste, proper discharge of pesticides, and toxic chemicals.

The most common NPS pollutants in coastal areas are sediments and nutrients washed from agricultural lands, animal feeding operations, construction and industrial operations, urban runoff, and other areas of disturbance. Common nutrients are nitrates and phosphates, which wash from lawns and golf courses and threaten to become far more concentrated if the watersheds in coastal areas continue to develop as they have recently. Population increases in coastal areas also introduce more automobiles, which are another significant source of airborne pollution to coastal water. The increase in impervious surfaces (streets, parking lots, rooftops, etc.) produced by development significantly exacerbates runoff pollution. Recently, oil runoff from streets, driveways, and parking lots has become an additional area of concern.

These pollutants seriously affect rivers, streams, and watersheds, making them less productive, diverse, and stable. Furthermore, fish kills, unsafe drinking water, beach closures, and destroyed habitats in coastal areas have all been attributed to toxic chemicals and heavy metals in coastal waters, as well as surplus nutrients that cause bacterial and algal blooms that can cause illness in humans and marine and other creatures. Another type of pollution that is often overlooked is garbage and debris that find its way into the oceans from storm drain systems, beaches, wash from landfills and ill-maintained garbage receptacles, and littering.

Runoff pollution remains difficult to control because it is a classic transboundary problem with pollution traveling all the way from streamheads to coastal waters. There is a growing need to address the multiple sources of land-based runoff and airborne pollutants to impose substantive, enforced controls to reduce their pollution of the marine environment. The federal emphasis in controlling nonpoint source pollution and to a lesser extent in coastal zone management has been on mandatory procedures and planning at the state level rather than setting or achieving of substantive goals or criteria. Federal regulation of airborne pollutants has been focused on their impact on air quality with evolving consideration of their impact on water quality.

Despite these programs, overall water quality appears to be deteriorating. The latest *National Water Quality Inventory* concludes that "14 percent of ocean shoreline miles are impaired mostly from bacteria and low oxygen and 78 percent of the 92 percent of Great Lakes shoreline assessed were impaired largely from pollutants found in fish tissue that exceed standards to protect human health."[15] Mercury contamination is the leading cause of impairment in lakes and estuaries, causing 49 states to issue 2,618 fish advisories in 2001.[16] States have assessed only 19 percent of their rivers and streams and have found that 39 percent violated water quality standards.[17] The states assessed 43 percent of their lakes and 36 percent of their estuaries; of these 45 percent of lakes and 51 percent of estuaries did not meet their designated uses.[18] The lack of comprehensive monitoring by the states only underscores the difficulties in identifying causes and, in particular, sources of pollution in impaired waters.

---

[15] U.S. EPA, "2000 National Water Quality Inventory" (2000) http://www.epa.gov/305b/2000report.
[16] *Id.*   [17] *Id.*
[18] *Id.*

2 GOVERNING STATUTES

2.1 Clean Water Act

In response to the federal government's unsuccessful attempts at improving water quality standards, and the environmental awakening of the 1970s, the Federal Water Pollution Control Act of 1972 (commonly referred to as the Clean Water Act [CWA]) was passed.[19] Originally Congress required that all waters be made either "fishable" or "swimmable" by 1983 "wherever attainable" and that "the discharge of pollutants into navigable waters be eliminated by 1985."[20] In addition, the federal government was given the primary responsibility for ensuring the promulgation of these water pollution controls. Most important, the Act was also amended so that there would be federal, nationally uniform standards, requiring technology-based standards, which would be imposed on point sources through an "end-of-the-pipe" type of restriction on discharge. The technology-based standards were incorporated into permits under the National Pollutant Discharge Elimination System (NPDES), with which every point source that discharges a pollutant into the "navigable waters of the United States" must comply.[21] In 1972 the CWA required that all dischargers of pollutants (other than those from publicly owned treatment works [POTWs]) were to be treated with the "best practicable control technology" (BPT) by 1 July 1977, and with the "best available control technology" (BAT) by 1 July 1983.[22] The Act was amended in 1977, 1981, and 1987. The deadlines for industrial point source dischargers were extended in the 1987 amendments. BPT standards requiring substantially greater control or technology that was fundamentally different from that previously required had to be achieved no later than 31 March 1989. Compliance with BAT for toxic and nonconventional pollutants had to be achieved no later than 31 March 1989, and compliance with BPT for conventional pollutants no later than 31 March 1989.[23] As a result of controversies largely relating to wetlands and property rights issues, the CWA has not been reauthorized and amended since 1987.

Although successful in reducing "point source" pollution discharges into "navigable waters" by implementing technology-based standards, the CWA must be updated. Point source is broadly defined, even including urban storm water runoff, sewage discharges, and factory discharges. The definition excludes, however, "agricultural storm water and return flows from irrigated agriculture."[24] Not surprisingly, nonpoint source pollution from agricultural runoff is presently the largest source of pollution. Other significant limitations include the limitation of permits to discharge into surface waters – groundwater pollution is regulated by a number of other federal statutes aimed largely at hazardous and solid waste disposal.[25] The term navigable waters, defined to include the territorial sea, still contains the outdated 1958 treaty definition of the territorial sea as extending seaward 3 miles from the baseline, rather than 12 nautical miles, as currently recognized by the United States.[26] The Commission's proposals to improve the CWA are presented throughout this chapter.

---

[19] FWCPA (CWA), 33 U.S.C. §§ 1251–1387 (2002).   [20] CWA § 101, 33 U.S.C. § 1251 (2002).

[21] Id. at § 402, 33 U.S.C. § 1342 (2002).

[22] Id. at §§ 301(b)(1)-(A), (b)(2)(A), 33 U.S.C. §§ 1311(b)(1)(A), (b)(2)(A) (2002).

[23] Id.   [24] Id. at § 502(14), 33 U.S.C. § 1362(14).

[25] Linda A. Malone; "Environmental Regulation of Land Use" (2002) § 8.10.

[26] CWA §§ 502(7), (8), 33 U.S.C. §§ 1362(7), (8).

2.2 Coastal Zone Management Act

The Coastal Zone Management Act (CZMA) of 1972 was passed "to preserve, protect, develop, and where possible, to restore or enhance, the resources of the Nation's coastal zone for this and succeeding generations."[27] Enacted during the same period as the Clean Water Act and other major federal environmental legislation, the CZMA takes a different approach from the permit-based, regulatory style of the Clean Water Act and Clean Air Act. The CZMA program, administered by NOAA, provides funding to states for voluntary participation in coastal zone planning and requires, with certain exceptions, that federal agency activities be consistent with the enforceable policies of state-created and federally approved coastal management programs.[28] A useful provision of the CZMA that has proved effective in coordinating various federal programs is requiring state coastal management programs to incorporate the water quality standards of the CWA, as defined by the United States Environmental Protection Agency (EPA).[29]

"It is clear that the CZMA program has, in thousands of instances around the U.S. shoreline, prevented inappropriate coastal development, fostered public access to the coast, served to protect fragile coastal resources such as wetlands, and protected the public from coastal hazards."[30] Unfortunately, it has also become clear that the Act has not halted the overall degradation of our nation's coastal zones or made any significant progress in restoring degraded areas. Like the CWA, the CZMA fails to incorporate expressly a precautionary approach, allowing coastal development to increase in the last decade.[31] Although the flexibility states have in designing their coastal management programs is cited as a strength of the CZMA, the wide variety has led to differing program strengths and geographical scope.[32] Once a state's coastal program is approved, NOAA is limited to withholding funding or withdrawing approval if the state fails to achieve federal guidelines.[33] Federal funding has been capped at $2 million per year since 1992, significantly impeding program implementation.[34]

In February 2004, EPA rated the overall national coastal condition as being between "fair" and "poor."[35] Coastal water quality and the rate at which pollutants are accumulating in the tissues of marine organisms were generally considered "fair" overall.[36] Coastal habitats, however, were rated "poor."[37] The overall score for the benthic index and sediment quality for coastal waters was between "fair" and "poor."[38] The leading stressors on receiving waters are metals, pesticides, pathogens, oxygen-depleting substances, toxic chemicals, polychlorinated biphenyls (PCBs), and dissolved

---

[27] CZMA, 16 U.S.C. §§ 1451–1464 (2002).

[28] The nonpoint source pollution program established by section 6217 of the 1990 amendments to the CZMA is discussed *infra* in the section Nonpoint Source Pollution.

[29] Final Report, *supra* note 4, at 173.

[30] Biliana Cicin-Sain and Robert W. Knecht, *The Future of U.S. Ocean Policy* (2000) 127.

[31] Robin Kundis Craig, "Sustaining the Unknown Seas: Changes in U.S. Ocean Policy and Regulation Since Rio 92" (2002), 32 *Env't L. Rep.* 10,190. Although the Act prohibits federal flood insurance coverage or contribution from Housing and Urban Development (HUD) programs in certain costal areas and has removed many federal subsidiaries that formerly supported coastal construction (in the 1982 Coastal Barrier Resource Act), these efforts have not halted the trend toward coastal destruction. *Id.*

[32] Final Report, *supra* note 4, at 112.   [33] *Id.*

[34] *Id.*

[35] U.S. EPA, "Draft National Coastal Condition Report II" (2004) 2–1, available at http://www.epa.gov/owow/oceans/nccr2/downloads.html.

[36] *Id.*   [37] *Id.*

[38] *Id.*

solids.[39] The primary sources of these pollutants are municipal point sources, urban runoff or storm sewers, atmospheric deposition, industrial discharges, and agriculture.[40]

Coastal water quality will only further degrade because of increasing development. While coastal counties constitute only 17 percent of total land area, more than half the population of the United States lives in a coastal county.[41] It is expected that the coastal population will increase from 139 million people in 1998 to 165 million people by the year 2015 (an approximate 20 percent increase in total coastal population).[42]

The Commission recommended the CZMA program be strengthened by "developing strong, specific, measurable goals and performance standards" that reflect an ecosystem-based management approach.[43] Specifically, mechanisms to manage growth effectively should be included, and geographic boundaries expanded to include coastal watersheds (not just the coastal ocean waters).[44] Federal funding should be considerably increased and additional incentives provided for states that meet set national goals.[45] Finally, a "fallback mechanism is needed to ensure that national goals are realized when a state does not adequately participate or perform."[46]

3 ISSUE-BASED ANALYSIS

3.1 Point Source Pollution

Improving the National Pollutant Discharge Elimination System

The Commission on Ocean Policy noted that the National Pollutant Discharge Elimination System (NPDES) has led to significant reduction in point source pollution since its enactment in 1972, but many major offenders are subject to only light penalties or no enforcement at all.[47] EPA found that of the 6,652 major industrial facilities regulated by the NPDES program, approximately 1,670 (25 percent) are classified by EPA as being in "significant noncompliance" with the CWA. Significant noncompliance can include paperwork violations; however, in 2001 nearly half of the industries that violated their NPDES permits exceeded allowable levels by 100 percent, while 13 percent of violators discharged toxic pollutants that exceeded allowable levels by 1,000 percent.[48] This rate of noncompliance among major industrial facilities has remained constant since about 1994. Despite this noncompliance, the majority of major industrial facilities are not undergoing enforcement proceedings or receiving penalties from EPA. During 2002 and 2003, only 24 percent of major facilities listed as being in significant noncompliance

---

[39] *Id.* at ES–11.   [40] See generally *supra* note 35.

[41] Dana Beach, *Coastal Sprawl: The Effects of Urban Design on Aquatic Ecosystems in the United States* (2002) 1–2.

[42] *Id.*   [43] Final Report, *supra* note 4, at 112–113.

[44] *Id.*

[45] *Id.* The report issued prior to the final report actually recommended that federal funding be "considerably increased," but the final report deleted this language. See U.S. Commission on Ocean Policy, "Preliminary Report: Governor's Draft" (2004), 111.

[46] *Id.* at 112.   [47] *Id.* at 171.

[48] Susan Bruninga, "Most Large Industrial Sites Not Penalized for Violations of Their Discharge Permits" (19 June 2003), 34 *Env't Rep.* (BNA) 1339. EPA has indicated it has no plans to publish the report, entitled *A Pilot for Performance Analysis of Selected Components of the National Enforcement and Compliance Assurance Program*, as it was conducted as an internal assessment of compliance and enforcement issues. *Id.*

faced either formal or informal enforcement proceedings; 27 percent of "repeat signifi-cant noncompliance" facilities and 32 percent of "perpetual significant noncompliance" facilities faced similar proceedings.[49] To remedy these problems and accomplish fully the goals of the NPDES program, the Commission recommended more federal over-sight of states and more funding and enforcement personnel at the state level to achieve greater compliance from regulated industries.[50]

Another potential remedy is to expand the definition of point sources requiring a NPDES permit. Recently, the Ninth Circuit held that aircraft spraying insecticide directly over navigable streams was a point source discharge of a pollutant requiring a NPDES permit under the CWA.[51] The Forest Service had contended that the spraying was non-point source pollution for which no permit was required, or alternatively that it was an exempt point source under the regulatory and statutory exemption for silvicultural point sources.[52] The court stated that nonpoint source pollution, although undefined, "is widely understood to be the type of pollution that arises from many dispersed activ-ities over large areas, and is not traceable to any single discrete source."[53] The court also found that the regulatory exemption, particularly with its reference to "natural runoff," was inapplicable to spraying of a pesticide from aircraft directly over navigable waters.[54] The decision opens the door for EPA and the states to regulate airborne transmission of pollutants into navigable waters through the NPDES permit requirements of the CWA, as well as under its existing authority under the Clean Air Act (CAA). The advantage of requiring NPDES permits in addition to any required under the CAA is that the pollution source would have to comply with that Act's requirements directed toward improvement of *water* quality. So far, the EPA has maintained that pesticide applications are not considered a discharge of pollutant requiring an NPDES permit if they meet a four-part test, including whether the spraying has a public benefit. The question EPA is now struggling to address is how best to define a "public benefit."[55]

Publicly Owned Treatment Works and Sludge Disposal

Publicly owned treatment works (POTWs) are facilities that receive wastewater from domestic and industrial sources and remove the pollutants from the wastewater prior to releasing it into the environment. POTWs must obtain a permit to discharge wastewater and demonstrate that the wastewater meets a specific level of treatment. There are three conventional levels of treatment for wastewater: primary, secondary, and tertiary. The treatment levels are progressively more effective and expensive from primary to secondary to tertiary in removing pollutants from wastewater.

The Clean Water Act (CWA) originally required that all POTWs achieve a minimum of secondary treatment by 1977 to remove specific amounts of suspended solid waste and other waste that deplete the oxygen in water. Some large cities maintained the requirements for secondary treatment were unnecessary if a POTW discharged waste-water into deep oceanic waters with strong currents, allowing for greater dispersion of pollutants than POTWs that discharged into shallow fresh waters. In response, Congress

---

[49] *Id.*

[50] Final Report, *supra* note 4, at 171.

[51] *League of Wilderness Defenders/Blue Mountains Biodiversity Project v. Forsgren* (2002) 309 F.3d 1181 (9th Cir.).

[52] *Id.* at 1185.

[53] *Id.* at 1184.

[54] *Id.* at 1186.

[55] Karen L. Werner, "EPA to Release Guidance on Permits" (2 May 2003), 34 *Env't Rep.* (BNA) 1004.

amended section 301(h) of the CWA in 1977 (and again in 1981 and 1987) to allow for a case-by-case review of treatment requirements for POTWs that discharge into marine waters. After review, EPA can waive the secondary treatment requirement for pH, biochemical oxygen demand, and suspended solids if a POTW utilizes specified primary treatment and shows that discharges will not harm aquatic habitats and organisms.[56] POTWs have received waivers from EPA allowing them to operate at less than secondary treatment levels; however, there are few data generally on their long-term impact. Some coastal waters still suffering from nutrient overload, such as Tampa Bay and Chesapeake Bay, have begun to implement tertiary treatment.[57]

The Commission made three recommendations to improve POTW regulation. First, EPA and states should require tertiary treatment for POTWs that discharge into water bodies still impaired by nutrient pollution.[58] Second, the Commission reported that conventional levels of treatment are ineffective in removing household and industrial chemicals, such as pharmaceuticals, antibiotics, hormones, insecticides, and fire retardants; therefore, EPA should assess their impacts on aquatic habitats and organisms and support development of technologies to reduce their concentrations in wastewater.[59] Third, while current spending on wastewater treatment infrastructure is $13 billion per year, over $270 billion will be necessary over the next 20 years ($13.5 billion per year), plus another $265 billion for drinking water infrastructure.[60] To meet this goal Congress should adequately fund the State Revolving Fund Program.[61]

Although marine dumping of sludge (sludge is a by-product of wastewater treatment) is now prohibited, most sewage sludge continues to be disposed of through land application pursuant to regulations in 33 C.F.R. Part 503. These regulations have governed land application for over 10 years, and few data are currently available as to their effectiveness in protecting the environment, specifically with respect to runoff into coastal waters. Although the Commission made no recommendations regarding sludge disposal, a 2002 Report by the National Research Council stated there is a "critical need" to evaluate the water quality impacts for the land dumping of sludge.[62]

Sewer Overflows and Storm Water Runoff

POTWs accepting wastewater from combined storm and sewer systems are required under the CWA to treat the wastewater without allowing for a bypass.[63] Not until 1987 did Congress address discharges "entirely of storm water" in the CWA.[64] Storm water runoff collects oil, heavy metals, chemicals, pesticides, trash, and pet waste before being released into nearby waters and is considered nonpoint source pollution.[65] Despite the CWA regulations, EPA estimates at least 40,000 sewers overflow each year, causing

---

[56] See generally 40 C.F.R. part 125 subpart G.

[57] Final Report, *supra* note 4, at 167.

[58] *Id.* at 168.

[59] *Id.* at 168–169.

[60] *Id.* at 170.

[61] *Id.* at 171.

[62] National Research Council, "Biosolids Applied to Land: Advancing Standards and Practices" (2002), 3, available at http://www.epa.gov/waterscience/biosolids/nas/complete.pdf; see "Standards for the Use or Disposal of Sewage Sludge: Final Agency Response to the National Research Council Report on Biosolids Applied to Land and the Results of EPA's Review of Existing Sewage Sludge Regulations" (31 December 2003), 68 *Fed. Reg.* 75,531.

[63] Sheldon M. Novick et al. (eds.), *Law of Environmental Protection*; (1994) vol. 2, § 12.05[3][b]. For a discussion of the water quality impairment caused by combined sewer overflow (CSO), see Note, "The CSO Sleeping Giant: Combined Sewer Overflow or Congressional Stalling Objective" (1991), 10 *Va. Envtl. L.J.* 371.

[64] 33 U.S.C.A. § 1342(p)(2).

[65] Final Report, *supra* note 4, at 174.

direct discharges of untreated waste water and storm water runoff.[66] For combined storm and sewage systems, POTW infrastructure upgrades are necessary, as discussed previously. For storm water runoff, the Commission suggested EPA work with state and local officials to ensure best management practices are utilized by constructing detention basins, minimizing storm water flow over impervious surfaces, and taking preventive actions such as cleaning streets, reducing pesticide use, and educating the public.[67]

Concentrated Animal Feedlot Operations

Despite more than 25 years of regulation, concentrated animal feeding operations (CAFOs) have contributed to the serious and acute water quality problems throughout the United States. Animal feedlots produce an estimated 500 million tons of manure per year, which is more than three times the amount of sanitary waste produced by humans.[68] Water quality impairment from CAFOs arises through the improper management of manure, which results in discharge and runoff of manure and manure nutrients. In response, the EPA with U.S. Department of Agriculture (USDA) assistance issued a revised CAFO rule in February 2003, requiring all large CAFOs to obtain NPDES permits by 2006.[69] The new rule applies to an additional 11,000 livestock operations for a total of 15,500 and most notably eliminates the exception excusing CAFOs from obtaining permits if they discharge only during large storms.[70] Waste entering streams and coastal waters from CAFOs is expected to be greatly reduced.[71] The Commission suggested states should impose additional requirements beyond the federal requirements when necessary to meet water quality standards.[72]

There is more focus on research on methods to control air emissions from CAFOs. At the request of EPA, the National Research Council issued a report in 2002 that concludes that the current methods of estimating emissions on the basis of the number of animals or pounds of meat produced are inadequate because emissions can vary widely on the basis of other factors.[73] EPA will be using the report to determine whether it should regulate emissions from feedlots. Citing growth in emissions of ammonia, nitrogen oxides, methane, fine particles, and odors, the report calls for "a substantial long-term research program on the overall system of producing food from animal feedlot operations with the goal of eliminating the release of undesirable air and other emissions into the environment."[74] Specifically, given the impact of excess nitrogen on the environment, control strategies to decrease such emissions should be implemented

---

[66] *Id.* at 168.   [67] *Id.* at 180.

[68] "National Pollutant Discharge Elimination System Permit Regulation and Effluent Limitation Guidelines and Standards for Concentrated Animal Feeding Operations (CAFOs): Final Rule" (12 February 2003), 68 *Fed. Reg.* 7175, 7180 (to be codified at 40 C.F.R. pts. 9, 122, 123, 412), available at http://www.epa.gov/npdes/regulations/cafo_fedrgstr.pdf; see also EPA Press Release, "EPA and Agriculture Working Together to Improve America's Waters" (16 December 2002), http://www.epa.gov/epahome/headline_121602.htm.

[69] *Id. Large CAFOs* are defined in the final rule as animal operations confining more than 1,000 cattle, 700 dairy cows, 2,500 swine, 10,000 sheep, 125,000 chickens, 82,000 laying hens, or 55,000 turkeys. *Id.*

[70] *Id.*   [71] Final Report, *supra* note 4, at 170.

[72] *Id.*

[73] National Research Council, "Air Emissions from Animal Feeding Operations: Current Knowledge, Future Needs" (2003).

[74] William J. Weida, "Notes on the 2002 NAS Study: Air Emissions from Animal Feeding Operations: Current Knowledge, Future Needs" (2003), 20.

without delay.[75] The Commission addressed air emissions from CAFOs in the larger context of controlling atmospheric deposition from multiple sources, including agriculture, industry, motor vehicles, forest fires, lightning, and volcanoes,[76] and called on EPA, states, and watershed groups to explore regional approaches to reduce atmospheric deposition.[77] Air deposition is considered further in the next section.

3.2 Nonpoint Source Pollution

The United States has made tremendous advances in the past 25 years to clean up the aquatic environment by controlling pollution from industrial point sources and sewage treatment plants, but unfortunately less progress has been made in controlling pollution from diffuse, or nonpoint, sources. In addition to the TMDL program, during the last 10 years a number of programs are beginning to address NPS pollution. At the federal level, recent NPS control measures include the nonpoint source provisions established by section 319 of the 1987 Clean Water Act Amendments and the Coastal Nonpoint Pollution Program established by the 1990 Coastal Zone Act Reauthorization Amendments (CZARA). Other recent federal programs, as well as numerous state, territorial, tribal, and local programs, also tackle NPS problems. These programs, however, do not impose in most instances any mandatory, enforceable requirements on nonpoint sources, and no mandatory controls are imposed at the federal level by the Clean Water Act.

Today, nonpoint source pollution remains the nation's largest source of water quality problems. It is the main reason that approximately 40 percent of our surveyed rivers, lakes, and estuaries are not clean enough for basic uses such as fishing and swimming.[78] The latest *National Water Quality Inventory* indicates that agriculture is the leading contributor to water quality impairments, degrading 48 percent of the impaired river miles and 41 percent of the impaired lake acreage surveyed by states, territories, and tribes.[79] Although POTWs (point sources) are the leading contributor at 37 percent to water quality impairments in estuaries, runoff from urban areas is close behind, accounting for 32 percent of water quality impairments to surveyed estuaries (areas near the coast where seawater mixes with fresh water).[80]

The most common NPS pollutants are sediments and nutrients from agricultural lands, animal feeding operations, construction operations, urban runoff, and other areas of disturbance. Other common NPS pollutants include pesticides, pathogens (bacteria and viruses), toxic chemicals, and heavy metals. A recent National Academy of Sciences report indicates oil runoff into coastal waters from streets, parking lots, and industrial sources should be treated on the same threat level as nutrients, pesticides, and mercury.[81] Beach closures, destroyed habitat, unsafe drinking water, fish kills, and many other severe environmental and human health problems result from NPS pollutants. The pollutants also ruin the beauty of healthy, clean water habitats. Each year the United States spends millions of dollars to restore and protect the areas damaged by NPS pollutants.

---

[75] Steve Cook, "Research Council Calls for New Approach for Estimating Emissions from Farm Feedlots" (13 December 2002) 33 *Env't Rep.* (BNA) 2578.

[76] Final Report, *supra* note 4, at 182.   [77] *Id.* at 182–183.

[78] U.S. EPA, "2000 National Water Quality Inventory" (2000) at http://www.epa.gov/305b/2000report.

[79] *Id.* at 15, 22.   [80] *Id.* at 30–31.

[81] National Academy of Sciences, "Oil in the Sea III: Inputs, Fates, and Effects" (2003).

One of the most notorious examples of impairment due to nitrogen runoff is the "dead zone" in the Gulf of Mexico, where excess nitrogen, primarily from agricultural runoff, causes extensive algal growth off the mouth of the Mississippi River, triggering a hypoxic zone of 7,000 square miles that recurs every spring and summer. The Gulf of Mexico Hypoxia Action Plan, developed by federal and state officials, concludes that about 90 percent of the nitrate load to the Gulf is from nonpoint sources.[82]

Nonpoint Pollution Control Programs under CWA and CZARA

There are two main federal programs aimed at nonpoint source pollution control: section 319 of the Clean Water Act (CWA) and section 6217 of the Coastal Zone Amendment Reauthorization Act (CZARA). Congress enacted a watershed-based NPS pollution control program under section 319 of the 1987 CWA Amendments. First, states must prepare an assessment of navigable waters where the control of nonpoint source pollution is necessary to meet water quality standards and identify the significant sources of nonpoint pollution of these waters. Control measures must also be identified. Second, states prepare a management program that sets out the best management practices (BMPs) necessary to remedy the problems. EPA must approve both steps, but it can only adopt a state assessment as opposed to a management report if it disapproves a state program. Significantly, section 319 did not require that states actually mandate or enforce the BMPs or any other mandatory controls in their management programs. Although there is extensive literature and experience with BMPs, there are no minimal BMP guidelines at the federal level comparable to the technology-based effluent limitations set by EPA for point sources. Although EPA could complete nonpoint source assessments for noncomplying states under section 319(a), it lacks authority to develop and implement adequate control plans and measures if a state fails to comply. Moreover, section 319(h)(7) requires that section 319 funds could not be used for assistance to persons except for demonstration projects. EPA's only recourse was to withhold grant funds, but Congress's inadequate funding for section 319 grants, and the negligible consequences to the states for failure to adhere to section 319, resulted in the failure of section 319 to reduce significantly nonpoint source pollution. In short, under section 319, EPA lacked both the regulatory authority and the funding to impose any effective controls on nonpoint source pollution.

The 1990 congressional update of the Coastal Zone Management Act (CZMA), the Coastal Zone Amendment Reauthorization Act (CZARA), is an attempt to solve the problems surrounding nonpoint source pollution programs. CZARA section 6217 requires states that have approved coastal zone management programs to develop management programs to curb nonpoint source pollution in coastal waters that conform to EPA guidelines, including enforceable best management practices. In these programs, the coastal state identifies land uses that contribute to the degradation of coastal areas, identifies critical coastal areas, and implements best management practices. A major difference between CWA and CZARA is that under CZARA section 6217, if a state fails to implement its plan, EPA and NOAA can withhold CWA and CZMA funding.

---

[82] D. A. Goolsby, "Mississippi Basin Nitrogen Flux and Gulf Hypoxia" (2000) (unpublished document). See also Nancy N. Rabalais et al., "Hypoxia in the Gulf of Mexico" (2000), 30 *J. Envtl. Quality* 320–329; National Research Council, "Clean Coastal Waters: Understanding and Reducing the Effects of Nutrient Pollution" (2000).

The Commission made several recommendations regarding section 319 of the CWA and section 6217 of the CZARA. First, it noted withholding funding only exacerbates nonpoint source pollution in the failing state and instead recommended amending the CWA, CZARA, and other federal laws so EPA and NOAA would be able to withhold funding for programs that *contribute* to water quality degradation such as highway construction and agricultural subsidy programs.[83] Withholding funding should only occur when a state "chronically fails" to make progress toward controlling nonpoint source pollution, with consideration of the possibility that a state's failure is due to inland state pollution flowing into the coastal state.[84] In this manner the federal government continues to promote water quality standards. Second, the Commission found federal funding to the states insufficient to achieve the goals of CZARA, limiting the Act's effectiveness.[85]

The Commission recommended that the National Ocean Council should consider options to strengthen the section 6217 program of CZARA and the section 319 program of CWA, including possible consolidation.[86] National nonpoint pollution reduction goals should be set by the National Ocean Council (NOC) for all impaired coastal watersheds.[87]

Total Maximal Daily Load Program

Section 303(d) of the CWA establishes the total maximal daily load (TMDL) process to provide for more stringent water quality-based controls when technology-based controls are inadequate to achieve state water quality standards. Although implementing section 303(d) has proved difficult since its enactment in 1972, the TMDL process has provided valuable monitoring information of pollution in water bodies, allowing greater public awareness and leading to technically sound and legally defensible decisions for attaining and maintaining water quality standards. The controversy stems from the fact that the TMDL process provides a mechanism for regulating point *and* nonpoint pollution sources.

Section 303(d) requires states to ensure that their waters meet state water quality standards. A water quality standard consists of four basic elements: (1) designated uses of the water body (e.g., recreation, water supply, aquatic life, agriculture), (2) water quality criteria to protect designated uses (numeric pollutant concentrations and narrative requirements), (3) an antidegradation policy to maintain and protect existing uses and high-quality waters, and (4) general policies addressing implementation issues (e.g., low flows, variances, mixing zones).[88] A TMDL establishes the maximal allowable loadings of a pollutant, from all sources, for a water body and thereby provides the basis for states to establish water quality-based controls. These controls should provide the pollution reduction necessary for a water body to meet water quality standards, but mechanisms for establishing and enforcing TMDLs have proved ineffective so far.

Not until 1985 did an actual TMDL program exist. EPA was busy establishing point source standards and forcing states to set standards for all state waters that adequately

---

[83] Final Report, *supra* note 4, at 177–178. *See also supra* note 14 and accompanying text.

[84] *Id.* at 177.   [85] *Id.*

[86] *Id.* at 178.   [87] *Id.* at 177.

[88] For general information regarding state water quality standards, see EPA's Water Quality Standard Database (WQSDB), available at http://www.epa.gov/wqsdatabase.

protected existing water qualities and uses.[89] In the struggle to achieve these goals, EPA sidelined the TMDL program, delaying the identification of pollutants to be included in the program and trying to achieve loosely its goals through a basin planning initiative.[90] Although a court order finally forced EPA to identify the TMDL pollutants,[91] states essentially ignored their obligation to submit TMDLs.[92] After a series of citizen suits in the 1980s, courts ruled the continued nonsubmission of TMDLS by a state eventually becomes the submission of no TMDLs, thus requiring EPA to step in and promulgate acceptable TMDLs on the state's behalf.[93] Further litigation made it clear that EPA approval of inadequate TMDL submissions by states was not acceptable and triggered the necessity for EPA either to work with the state to reach a more acceptable solution or to step in with its own TMDL list.[94]

In the light of the nationwide TMDL litigation, EPA began taking a more aggressive approach to revise the program. In November 1996, EPA released a draft *TMDL Program Implementation Strategy*,[95] which recognized the importance of TMDL allocations in the watershed approach, extended the frequency of reporting obligations, combined report categories, and established many EPA resources for assistance in TMDL development.[96] Further review by a diverse committee established under the Federal Advisory Committee Act (FACA) achieved agreement on a number of difficult issues but failed to achieve agreement on whether the TMDL process should be used to address nonpoint source pollution.[97]

At about the same time Congress involved itself in the issue. The House Transportation Committee's Subcommittee on Water Resources and the Environment held hearings on the TMDL program and the proposed regulatory changes.[98] As a result of these hearings, Congress instructed the General Accounting Office (GAO) to address certain issues, primarily (1) whether sufficient data were available to determine scientifically which bodies of water are impaired and which TMDLs would be appropriate and (2) the economic impact of the new regulations.[99] The GAO expressed substantial

---

[89] Oliver A. Houck, "The Clean Water Act TMDL Program: Law, Policy, and Implementation" (1999), 49.

[90] *Id.* at 50.

[91] *Board of County Commissioners v. Costle* (20 June 1978), No. 78–0572, slip op. (D. D. C.).

[92] Houck, *supra* note 89, at 51.

[93] The rulings were established the doctrine of "constructive submission." See *Scott v. City of Hammond* (1981) 530 F. Supp. 288, (N. D. Ill.), aff'd in part, rev'd in part, 741 F.2d 992, 14 ELR 20,631 (7th Cir. 1984); *Alaska Center for the Environment v. Reilly* (1991) 762 F. Supp. 1422, 21 ELR 21,305, (W. D. Wash.), injunctive relief granted, 796 F. Supp. 1374, 22 ELR 21,204 (W. D. Wash. 1992), aff'd sub nom.; *Alaska Center for the Environment v. Browner*, 20 F.3d 981, 24 ELR 20,702 (9th Cir. 1994).

[94] See *Idaho Sportsmen's Coalition v. Browner* (1996) 951 F. Supp. 962, 27 ELR 20,771, (W. D. Wash.); *Sierra Club v. Hankinson* (1996) 939 F. Supp. 865, 27 ELR 20,280, (N. D. Ga.). See, e.g., *National Wildlife Federation v. Adamkus* (28 March 1991) No. 87 C 4196, 1991 WL 47374, (N. D. Ill.); *Sierra Club v. Browner* (1993) 843 F. Supp. 1304, 24 ELR 21,006, (D. Minn.). See also Diane K. Conway, "TMDL Litigation: So Now What?" (1997), 17 *Va. Envtl. L. J.* 83, 95; Michael M. Wenig, "How 'Total' Are Total Maximum Daily Loads? – Legal Issues Regarding the Scope of Watershed-Based Pollution Control under the Clean Water Act" (1998), 12 *Tul. Envtl. L. J.* 87, 110 n.103.

[95] U.S. EPA, "Draft TMDL Program Implementation Strategy" (1996).

[96] Houck, *supra* note 89, at 57.

[97] Oliver A. Houck, "TMDLs III: A New Framework for the Clean Water Act's Ambient Standards Program" (1998), 28 ELR 10,415, 10,422.

[98] Barclay Rogers and Anne Hazlett, "TMDLs: Are They Dead Letters?" (2001 August), *Agric. L. Update* 4.

[99] *Id.*

concerns on both issues, emphasizing uncertainties both in the available data and in EPA's economic analysis of the proposed regulations.[100]

Despite this negative input from Congress, EPA promulgated its revised TMDL rule in July 2000 and specifically included nonpoint sources of pollution.[101] States must schedule the establishment of TMDLs within 10 years of 10 July 2000, or the due date on the first list on which the water body appeared, although this schedule may be extended for five years if the original deadline cannot be met despite expeditious action.[102] Moreover, this regulation requires that all impaired water bodies, even those for which TMDLs are not yet required, be placed on a four-part list and prioritized.[103] States are further required to provide an implementation plan and a "reasonable assurance" that TMDL waste loads and load allocations will be met.[104]

Legal and political challenges resulted from the revised TMDL regulation, especially the inclusion of nonpoint sources and the revisions to the TMDL schedule.[105] The American Farm Bureau Federation, concerned about the implications of the inclusion of nonpoint sources in the TMDL program, immediately filed a petition to challenge the new regulation.[106] Other special interest groups have followed suit.[107] Interested parties have also managed to make themselves felt legislatively, persuading Congress not only to prohibit EPA from using any money from fiscal years 2000 or 2001 to fund the changes,[108] but also to require that the Agency hire the National Academy of Sciences (NAS) to analyze the TMDL program and the new regulation.[109] The NAS committee determined that there is enough scientific information available to begin the TMDL program because any uncertainty can be compensated for easily in the process of fulfilling the program's goals, although it emphasized that uncertainty should not be allowed to form the basis for unreasonable expectations.[110] The committee also made a number of recommendations that it believed would improve the TMDL program and expedite the achievement of its goals, such as designation of appropriate uses before development of the TMDL list, more periodic assessments of TMDL plans, and inclusion of more pollutants affecting water quality.[111] It stated, somewhat wryly, that success

---

[100] See U.S. General Accounting Office (GAO), "Water Quality, Key EPA and State Decisions Limited by Inconsistent and Incomplete Data" (2000) (GAO/RCED-00–54); U.S. GAO, "Review of Two EPA Proposed Regulations Regarding Water Quality Management" (2000) (GAO/RCED-00206R). In March 2000, GAO issued its first report highlighting a substantial lack of data available to determine which water bodies were impaired and to set appropriate TMDLs. *Id.* GAO published a second report in June 2000, which questioned the reasonableness of EPA's economic analysis of the proposed regulations. *Id.*

[101] "Revisions to the Water Quality Planning and Management Regulation and Revisions to the National Pollutant Discharge Elimination System Program in Support of Revisions to the Water Quality Planning and Management Regulation" (13 July 2000), 65 *Fed. Reg.* 43,586, 43,588.

[102] *Id.* at 43591.　　　　　　　　　　　　　　　[103] *Id.* at 43590.

[104] *Id.* at 43591.　　　　　　　　　　　　　　　[105] Rogers and Hazlett, *supra* note 98, at 5.

[106] *American Farm Bureau Federation v. Browner* (18 July 2000), No. 00–1320 (D. C. Cir.).

[107] See Susan Bruninga, "Nine Petitions Filed in Major Fight over Final Rule Revising TMDL Program" (15 December 2000), 31 *Env't Rep.* (BNA) 2618.

[108] Military Construction Appropriations Act, Pub. L. No.106–246, 114 Stat. 511, 567 (2000).

[109] Department of Veteran Affairs, Housing and Urban Development, and Independent Agencies Act, Pub. L. No. 106–377, 114 Stat. 1441, 1441A–3 (2000).

[110] National Research Council, Assessing the TMDL Approach to Water Quality Management: Committee to Assess the Scientific Basis of the Total Maximum Daily Load Approach to Water Pollution Reduction (2001).

[111] *Id.*

should be strictly predicated upon whether a water body can support its designated use so as to ensure that states do not lose sight of the ultimate goal.[112]

In response to these reactions, EPA postponed the effective date of the final TMDL regulation for 18 months, from 1 October 2001 to 1 March 2003.[113] The deadline for the submission of states' lists of impaired waters was extended from 1 April 2002 to 1 October 2002, with the extension to permit reconsideration of certain aspects of the revisions in light of the reactions to the revised rule and the NAS report.[114] EPA announced in 2002 development of a "water pollutant trading system" (generally for phosphorus and nitrogen nutrients) to be incorporated into the TMDL program, but that system has proved more difficult than air pollutant trading because water pollutant trading must occur within the same water body for the same pollutant.[115] While the pollutant trading policy is a voluntary, incentive-based approach, EPA remains hopeful that it will, through proper alignment with the CWA and implementing regulations, allow greater efficiency in the protection and restoration of impaired water bodies.[116] The Commission encouraged use of such incentive-based approaches.[117]

Thirty years in the making, an adequate and effective TMDL program has never seemed further from implementation. Consent decrees resulting from 40 legal challenges in 38 states have ordered states to finish preparing TMDLs in anywhere from 1 to 20 years.[118] The TMDLs that have been provided to EPA tend to avoid controlling nonpoint source pollution, do not calculate their share of the allocation load, or both.

---

[112] *Id.*

[113] "Delay of Effective Date of Revisions to the Water Quality Planning and Management Regulation and Revisions to the National Pollutant Discharge Elimination System Program in Support of Revisions to the Water Quality Planning and Management Regulations; and Revision of the Date for State Submission of the 2002 List of Impaired Waters" (9 August 2001), 66 *Fed. Reg.* 41,817.

[114] *Id.* Farm groups and industry generally supported the postponement; farm groups still objected to the regulation of nonpoint source pollution as a federal presumption of local land use policy, whereas environmental groups did not support the delay. See Susan Bruninga, "Environmental Advocates Oppose Delay in TMDL Rule; Industry, Ag Groups Supportive" (21 September 2001), 32 *Env't Rep.* (BNA) 1829 (hereafter Environmental Advocates Oppose Delay). The Federal Water Quality Coalition filed one of about a dozen petitions for review of the July 2000 rule. *American Farm Bureau Federation v. Browner* (18 July 2000), No. 00–1320, (D.C. Cir.). EPA subsequently circulated a draft report on the total estimated costs of the TMDL program, which stated that the costs to industry to implement the TMDL program could range from under $1 billion to $4.3 billion annually. U.S. EPA, "The National Costs of the Total Maximum Daily Load Program" (Draft Report) (2001) (EPA 841-D-01–003), at http://www.epa.gov/owow/tmdl/coststudy/coststudy.pdf.

[115] 33 *Env't Rep.* (BNA) S-19 (25 January 2002). On 15 May 2002, EPA proposed the water quality trading policy for comment. 67 *Fed. Reg.* 34,709 (15 May 2002). Various federal agencies, including EPA, the U.S. Department of the Interior, the U.S. Department of Agriculture, and the U.S. Department of Commerce, have agreed upon a final comprehensive science-based approach to watershed delineation and assessment on federal lands. See "Notice of Final Policy – Unified Federal Policy for a Watershed Approach to Federal Land and Resource Management" (18 October 2000), 65 *Fed. Reg.* 62,566, available at http://cleanwater.gov/ufp; factors affecting wetlands will be considered when determining the best management practices and priorities for both land and water uses. The agencies' watershed goals will involve minimizing adverse water quality impacts from management programs, minimizing the impairment of current and future uses, and restoring watersheds that do not reach water quality standards. *Id.*

[116] For the proposed rule, see 67 *Fed. Reg.* 34,709 (15 May 2002). EPA issued its final notice on 13 January 2003; see 68 *Fed. Reg.* 1608 (13 January 2003). A water pollutant trading system has been in place since the 1990s primarily for POTWs (i.e., point source to point source), but also in the Great Lakes and Long Island Sound areas.

[117] Final Report, *supra* note 4, at 171.   [118] 33 *Env't Rep.* 2424 (18 November 2002).

States in some cases also failed to submit inventories of impaired waters, rank them, promulgate TMDLs, and incorporate them into controls.[119] On 19 March 2003, EPA formally withdrew the July 2000 Total Maximum Daily Load rule.[120] Until a revised TMDL program is put into effect, the current TMDL program, promulgated in 1985 and amended last in 1992, remains in effect.[121]

The issue of EPA's authority to regulate nonpoint source pollution through TMDLs and section 303(d) was litigated in court. The Ninth Circuit recently affirmed EPA's authority to establish TMDLs even for water bodies impaired *solely* by nonpoint source pollution.[122] A California state agency issued a permit for timber harvesting to plaintiff-landowners with serious restrictions designed to reduce soil erosion into a nearby river. EPA stated the river was in violation of state water quality standards and imposed TMDLs when the state missed the deadline to establish its own TMDLs. Plaintiffs argued the permit restrictions were due to EPA's TMDL standard because the state feared losing federal funding and brought suit under the Administrative Procedure Act challenging EPA's interpretation that the CWA allowed EPA to establish TMDLs on rivers polluted solely by nonpoint source pollution.[123]

The Ninth Circuit noted that section 303 requires states to create EPA-approved water quality standards or to have EPA impose standards upon them and did not draw any distinction among navigable waters or their pollutants.[124] Furthermore, the mandatory planning process of section 303 required EPA to address nonpoint as well as point sources in approving or determining TMDLs, in order to ensure the adequate implementation of water quality standards for all navigable waters.[125] The court deferred to EPA's interpretation of the 1985 regulations without relying on the provisions of the delayed final rule.[126]

The Ninth Circuit's reasoning is consistent with the Tenth Circuit's approach to the issue of TMDL development, when the inability of EPA to address nonpoint sources directly is kept in mind. In *American Wildlands v. Browner*,[127] the plaintiff challenged EPA's approval of parts of Montana's TMDL plan to meet its water quality standards.

---

[119] Linda A. Malone, "The Myths and Truths That Threaten the TMDL Program" (2002) 32 *ELR* 11,133, 11,135.

[120] "Withdrawal of Revisions to the Water Quality Planning and Management Regulation and Revisions to the National Pollutant Discharge Elimination System Program in Support of Revisions to the Water Quality Planning and Management Regulation" (19 March 2003), 68 *Fed. Reg.* 13,607 (to be codified at 40 C.F.R. pts. 9, 122, 123, 124, 130). See also John Millett, "Final Withdrawal of 2000 TMDL Rule Takes Effect; Existing Rules Make Progress Cleaning Up Impaired Waters" available at http://yosemite.epa.gov/opa/admpress.nsf/b1ab9f485b098972852562e7004dc686/601385d1f25da12485256ce800824d38?OpenDocument.

[121] "Withdrawal of Revisions to the Water Quality Planning and Management Regulation and Revisions to the National Pollutant Discharge Elimination System Program in Support of Revisions to the Water Quality Planning and Management Regulation" (19 March 2003), 68 *Fed. Reg.* 13,607 (to be codified at 40 C.F.R. pts. 9, 122, 123, 124, 130).

[122] *Pronsolino v. Nastri* (2002) 291 F.3d 1123 (9th Cir.), *cert. denied*, 539 U.S. 926 (2003). See *id., Pronsolino v. Marcus* (2000) 91 F. Supp. 2d 1337, 30 ELR 20,460 (N.D. Cal.); David K. Bowles, Case Summary, "*Pronsolino v. Marcus*: EPA May Impose TMDLs for Substandard Rivers Impaired Solely by Nonpoint Sources" (June 2000), *ABA Special Comm'n on Agric. Mgmt. Newsl.* 15; Susan Bruninga, "Court Rules TMDL Program Can Apply to River Polluted by Nonpoint Sources" (7 April 2000), 31 *Env't Rep.* (BNA) 639.

[123] *Marcus,* 91 F. Supp. 2d. at 1339–1340.   [124] *Nastri,* 291 F.3d at 1127.

[125] *Id.* at 1132.   [126] *Id.* at 1131 n. 8.

[127] *American Wildlands v. Browner* (2001) 260 F.3d 1192, 31 ELR 20,860 (10th Cir.). See *American Wildlands v. Browner* (2000) 94 F. Supp. 2d 1150 (D. Colo.).

Under the CWA, a state must give each water body a "designated use," determine the degree to which various pollutants may be present considering the water body's designated use, then provide an "antidegradation review" consistent with the three-tiered federal antidegradation review to evaluate any activities that might further degrade water quality.[128] Furthermore, the states must establish a TMDL for any pollutant that does not meet water quality standards for a body of water.[129] EPA regulations, however, permit states to allow water quality requirements to be exceeded in certain areas where pollutant discharge initially meets a water body, the so-called mixing zone, if certain criteria are satisfied.[130] With EPA approval, Montana exempted existing nonpoint sources from part of the antidegradation review and further exempted subsequent nonpoint sources from review when reasonable conservation practices were employed and beneficial uses were protected.[131] Montana also exempted mixing zones from its antidegradation review policy, so long as the degradation to the water body at the periphery of the mixing zone was not significant, although it did develop a number of other strict requirements regarding mixing areas.[132] The Tenth Circuit affirmed the district court ruling that EPA's approval of these standards was proper.[133]

The Tenth Circuit first determined Congress had delegated authority to EPA to apply and interpret the CWA, both in general and in this specific instance, and EPA's interpretation would not be overturned unless its decision was arbitrary and capricious.[134] The court then turned to EPA's argument that antidegradation review requirements apply to a water body as a whole, rather than to a segment such as a mixing zone. The court found that this interpretation was reasonable, especially given the practical reality regarding mixing zones, and found that EPA was not arbitrary and capricious in approving Montana's exemption of mixing zones from antidegradation review so long as review of the water around such zones indicates that the overall water quality is not being damaged.[135]

Every environmental initiative of the past 30 years has had to grapple with scientific uncertainty, allocation of enforcement authority, inconsistencies in monitoring, and variances in state and federal approaches. The ultimate goal of the 1972 Clean Water Act remains the achievement of fishable and swimmable waters, yet there are no mandatory controls imposed at the federal level on nonpoint source pollution or sanctions for states who fail to meet their own water quality standards. Critics contend that nonpoint source pollution is not more varied, site-specific, or more technologically difficult to control than point source pollution.[136]

---

[128] *Id.* at 1194–1195 (citing 33 U.S.C. § 1313(c)(2)(A), ELR Stat. FWPCA § 303(c)(2)(A)); 40 C.F.R. §§ 130.3, 130.10(d)(4), 131.6, 131.10, 131.11).

[129] *Id.* (citing 33 U.S.C. §§ 1313(d), ELR Stat. FWPCA § 303(d)).

[130] *Id.* at 1195, 31 ELR at 20,861 (citing U.S. EPA, *Water Quality Standards Handbook* (2nd ed.) (1994) § 5.1.1, at 5–5).

[131] *Id.* at 1195, 31 ELR at 20,861 (citing Mont. Code Ann. § 75–5–317(2)(a) & (b)).

[132] *Id.* (citing Mont. Admin. R. §§ 17.30.715(1)(c), 17.30.505(1)(b) & (c), 17.30.506(1) & (2); Mont. Code Ann. § 75–5–301(4)).

[133] *Id.* at 1198–1199.

[134] *Id.* at 1197, 31 ELR at 20,861. The deferential standard was promulgated in *Chevron, U.S.A., Inc. v. Natural Resources Defense Council,* 467 U.S. 837, 14 ELR 20,507 (1984). *Id.*

[135] *Id.*

[136] Houck, *supra* note 89, at 87. For an ambitious article demonstrating how the TMDL program could remedy nonpoint source pollution, see Paula J. Lebowitz, "Land Use, Land Abuse, and Land Re-Use: A Framework for the Implementation of TMDL's for Nonpoint Source Polluted Water Bodies" (2001), 19

The controversy over the TMDL program has to be viewed against the backdrop of the problem of nonpoint source pollution, particularly from large-scale agriculture, and the history at the federal level of funding state and local programs that ordinarily do not impose mandatory requirements. As the GAO report concluded, many of the states' criticisms of the TMDL program stem not from scientific uncertainty but from the lack of consistency by the states in defining designated uses and various data utilized to evaluate impairment.[137] EPA guidelines can partially remedy the lack of consensus among states, but some states have vehemently objected to the possibility of EPA's requiring TMDLs with respect to a water body not within the states' designated use. Section 303(d) is regrettably silent on precisely how and when TMDL implementation should occur. The rather scant 1972 legislative history of state support of water quality standards is sufficient to demonstrate that the states feared the prospect of "federal land use" and fought to retain control by maintaining supervision of nonpoint source pollution. Land use is, however, determined at the federal level, in a number of ways through a variety of federal programs, most notably the CZMA.[138] Imposing some degree of mandatory controls, by assessing nonpoint sources' share of the load allocation and requiring some minimal level of control on those sources *only for impaired waters*, is one reasonable, moderate option in water quality improvement.

The focus now is clearly on regulation of nonpoint source pollution, but significantly the Commission failed to recommend further enforcement of the TMDL program. The Commission concluded, "Improving coastal water quality will require significant reductions in nonpoint sources" of pollution, the "majority" of which comes from agricultural and storm water runoff.[139] EPA has issued guidelines from a "watershed perspective" for managing agricultural nonpoint source pollution.[140] The voluntary guidelines cover all phases of runoff management from planning and development to program evaluation, and include both structural and nonstructural management practices that local and state agencies, landowners, developers, conservation groups, and other interested parties can use. Nonstructural practices include urban planning and zoning, minimizing of paved surfaces, pollution reduction and recycling techniques, and preservation of wetlands and other natural drainage systems. Guidance on structural practices pertains to storm water and wastewater treatment systems and runoff controls, such as silt fencing, retention ponds, and increased vegetation. The Commission recommendations echo the efforts of EPA but fail to mention the TMDL program in their proposals. However, the Commission did call for the National Ocean Council (NOC) to establish enforceable, national nonpoint pollution reduction goals for all impaired waters.

USDA Conservation Programs
The national agricultural policy to maintain farm income and subsidize food production has generally promoted monocultural agriculture and heavy inputs of nitrogen

---

Pace Envtl. L. Rev. 97. See also Oliver A. Houck, "The Clean Water Act TMDL Program V: Aftershock and Prelude" (April 2002), 32 *ELR* 10,385.

[137] See U.S. GAO, *supra* note 101.

[138] See generally Linda A. Malone, Environmental Regulation of Land Use (2002).

[139] Final Report, *supra* note 4, at 171, 173. For the Commission's recommendation regarding storm water runoff, see *supra* text accompanying notes 64–68.

[140] See "Nonpoint Source Program and Grants Guidelines for States and Territories" (23 October 2003), 68 *Fed. Reg.* 60,653, available at http://www.epa.gov/owow/nps.

fertilizer. As of 1985, there were over 27 federal programs under eight different agencies to control soil erosion.[141] All of these programs were voluntary and severely underfunded.[142] In addition there was no direction or "targeting" of funds to the most erosive soils.[143] The 1985 Farm Bill introduced three new conservation programs – the sodbusting, swampbusting, and conservation reserve programs – designed to pay farmers to remove highly erodible soils and wetlands from agricultural production for designated terms.[144] Under the agricultural conservation program, the Environmental Quality Incentives Program (EQIP),[145] technical assistance, cost sharing, incentive payments, and educational assistance are provided to producers who enter into contracts of approximately 5 to 10 years.[146] EQIP has expanded and was recently amended, establishing the reduction of nonpoint source pollution in impaired waters as the most important environmental need of EQIP.[147] The conservation ethic takes shape when EQIP and the 1985 Farm Bill are viewed together.

The 2002 Farm Bill quadrupled funding for the USDA conservation programs by providing $73.5 billion over six years.[148] The "conservation" characterization of some of these conservation programs has been questioned.[149] For example, conservation measures may include the construction of waste lagoons by large livestock producers. Also, none of the Farm Bill provisions require that funding be focused or "targeted" at the soil which would do the most good for water quality. Nevertheless, the increase in funding reflected a consensus that the conservation provisions first adopted in the 1985 Farm Bill were effective and successful in reducing nonpoint source pollution on agricultural land.[150] The Commission heralded the adequate funding and efforts at reducing nonpoint source pollution and encouraged further incentives-based approaches for farmers and ranchers to set aside areas of land, purchase better equipment, and employ best management practices.[151] A full range of incentives, such as tax breaks, insurance programs, and additional aid, should be used.[152] The Commission even suggested a market-based program for farmers, who would receive credits for reducing nutrient loads, which could then be sold to POTWs or other nutrient dischargers.[153]

---

[141] See generally Linda Malone, "The Renewed Concern over Soil Erosion: The Current Federal Programs and Proposals" (1989), 10 *J. Agric. Tax'n & L.* 310.

[142] *Id.*   [143] *Id.*

[144] *Id.*

[145] EQIP was a consolidation in the 1996 Federal Agricultural Improvement and Reform Act of the Agricultural Conservation Program, Great Plains Program, Water Quality Incentives Program, and Colorado River Salinity Program.

[146] For a complete history of soil conservation programs in the United States, see Linda Malone, "Reauthorization of the 1985 Farm Bill Conservation Provisions: Conservation at the Crossroads" (1989), 8 *Va. Envtl. L. J.* 215; Linda Malone, "The Renewed Concern over Soil Erosion: The Current Federal Programs and Proposals" (1989), 10 *J. Agric. Tax'n & L.* 310; Linda Malone, "A Historical Essay on the Conservation Provisions of the 1985 Farm Bill: Sodbusting, Swampbusting, and the Conservation Reserve" (1986), 34 *Kan. L. Rev.* 577.

[147] Final Report, *supra* note 4, at 173.

[148] Susan Bruninga, "Farm Bill Accord Would Boost Funding for Wetlands, Environmental Quality Projects" (3 May 2002), 33 *Env't Rep.* (BNA) 991.

[149] See John H. Davidson, "Sustainable Development and Agriculture in the United States" (May 2002), 32 *ELR* 10,543.

[150] Linda A. Malone, *Environmental Regulation of Land Use* (2002) § 5:8.

[151] Final Report, *supra* note 4, at 178.   [152] *Id.*

[153] *Id.*

3.3 Recognizing the International Transboundary Pollution Problem

The 1982 United Nations Convention on the Law of the Sea (UNCLOS)[154] is essentially the "constitution" for the oceans and covers six main sources of ocean pollution: land-based and coastal activities, continental-shelf drilling, potential seabed mining, ocean dumping, vessel-source pollution, and pollution from or through the atmosphere. Article 194 of the Convention provides that States shall take measures necessary to protect fragile ecosystems and the habitat of depleted and threatened species. States are also required to notify others in cases where the marine environment is in imminent danger of being damaged.

UNCLOS recognizes several zones of control over ocean waters. First the area beyond state control is the high seas, on which freedom of the seas is preserved. The coastal waters extending 12 nautical miles from the shore ("baseline") of a coastal nation make up the territorial sea, an expansion from the previously recognized limit of 3 nautical miles. A coastal state retains extensive control over the territorial sea, limited primarily by other states' right of innocent passage. The contiguous zone extends out an additional 12 nautical miles, or 24 nautical miles from the baseline. Within this zone, the coastal state has more limited authority than in the territorial sea, but that authority is still extensive. The exclusive economic zone (EEZ), which had not existed in the earlier 1958 law of the sea treaties, extends 200 nautical miles from the baseline. Within this zone the coastal state has "sovereign rights for the purpose of exploring and exploiting, conserving and managing the natural resources, whether living or nonliving."[155] The EEZ was an important innovation because in exchange for this sovereignty, coastal nations must attempt to "maintain or restore populations of harvested species at levels which can produce the maximum sustainable yield."[156] Coastal states also have the exclusive right to authorize and regulate drilling and other uses of the continental shelf as that term is delineated in the treaty.

The United States has not signed or ratified UNCLOS although the United States has recognized the territorial sea, contiguous zone, EEZ, and continental shelf boundaries as therein defined as customary international law.[157] The United States has claimed each of these jurisdictional zones through specific statutes and presidential proclamations, but its failure to ratify the treaty and the piecemeal assertions of jurisdiction have made the division of regulatory authority needlessly complicated and confusing. For example, in the Clean Water Act, which has not been amended since 1987, section 502 still defines navigable waters as extending seaward for three nautical miles, and "contiguous zone" as defined by the earlier 1958 treaty.[158] In addition, the states under the Submerged Lands Act of 1953 claim title to submerged lands and coastal waters out to three nautical miles.

---

[154] 1982 United Nations Convention on the Law of the Sea (UNCLOS) (UN Doc/CONF.62/122, reprinted in 21 ILM 1261 (1982) (signed 10 December 1982), available at http://www.un.org/Depts/los/convention_agreements/convention_overview_convention.htm.

[155] *Id.* at art. 56(1)(a).   [156] *Id.* at art. 61(3).

[157] The United States has not signed or ratified UNCLOS because of concern over deep seabed mining rights outside a nation's EEZ; however, a separate agreement was reached on the subject in 1994 that the United States has signed but has yet to ratify; see Final Report, *supra* note 4, at 385, 395.

[158] 33 U.S.C. §§ 502(7) & (9) (the 1958 treaty is specifically entitled *Convention of the Territorial Sea and Contiguous Zone*).

The Commission recommends all federal statutes, including the CWA, be updated and made consistent by establishing the territorial sea boundary as 12 nautical miles from the baseline and the contiguous zone as 24 nautical miles from the baseline.[159] Expanded federal jurisdiction of the territorial sea, however, does not compel extension of state claims beyond the three-nautical-mile limit.

UNCLOS declares that all states have an obligation to protect the marine environment, including regulating nonpoint source pollution. In the contiguous zone under both the 1958 and 1982 treaties, "sanitary" regulations are required, and the 1982 treaty more clearly contemplates the pollution controls necessary by coastal states, especially when read in conjunction with the newly created Part XII, "Protection and Preservation of the Marine Environment." Article 194(3)(a) specifically authorizes nonpoint source pollution control measures "designed to minimize to the fullest possible extent . . . the release of toxic, harmful, or noxious substances, especially those which are persistent, from land-based sources, from or through the atmosphere or by dumping." In addition, article 207(1) provides that "States shall adopt laws and regulations to prevent, reduce and control pollution of the marine environment from land-based sources, including rivers, estuaries, pipelines and outfall structures, taking into account internationally agreed rules, standards and recommended practices and procedures."

The Commission made it very clear there are "many compelling reasons for the United States to expeditiously accede to the Convention [UNCLOS]."[160] By not ratifying UNCLOS, the United States is unable to influence other nations' policies effectively to protect the United States' national interests, including the marine environment. Also, "[i]nternational bodies established under the Convention are in the process of making decisions that directly affect important U.S. interests," such as jurisdictional claims over resources on the continental shelf.[161] "In 2004, the Convention will be open for amendment by its parties for the first time. If the United States is to ensure that its interests as a maritime power and coastal state are protected, it must participate in this process."[162] It is clear in light of all of these factors that one significant step for an international approach to nonpoint source pollution is immediate ratification of the United Nations Convention on the Law of the Sea.

4 CONCLUSION: THE POLITICS OF REFORM

There is wide agreement that the last 30 years of environmental regulation have been successful in implementing technology-based controls on point source pollution, but the need now is for enforceable water quality standards regulating both point and nonpoint source pollution. The lack of enforcement mechanisms and water quality monitoring information has hampered efforts, as has lack of political will and federal funding. A recent report by the Pew Oceans Commission presaged many of the Commission's findings as to the need for stronger controls. Specific to nonpoint source pollution, the Pew Commission recommended effective implementation of the TMDL program: "States should determine the total maximum daily load (TMDL) of pollutants that a water body can accept and still attain water quality standards. The states should then

---

[159] Final Report, *supra* note 4, at 43.
[161] *Id.*

[160] *Id.* at 385.
[162] *Id.* at 386.

implement meaningful plans for achieving the point and nonpoint source pollution reductions indicated by TMDLs."[163]

The Oceans Act of 2000, passed by Congress and signed into law by the President on 7 August 2000, created the U.S. Commission on Ocean Policy to make recommendations for a coordinated and comprehensive national ocean policy.[164] The original timetable for submission of the final report to Congress and the President was January 2003,[165] later amended to June 2003.[166] After a preliminary report[167] received public comment, the Commission submitted the final report in September 2004, after which the President had 90 days to submit to Congress a statement of proposals to implement or respond to the Commission's recommendations.[168]

Congress established the Commission because of major changes since the 1969 Stratton Commission Report: the large migration of people to coastal areas; the increase of federal and state regulations, which often duplicated efforts and produced confusing and sometimes contradictory results; the increased use of the marine environment, leading to depletion of resources and degradation of habitats; the increased complexity of environmental threats; and the potential for economic and scientific opportunities using modern technology.[169] Congress mandated the Commission to review these issues and specify policy recommendations.[170]

After two initial public meetings in September and November of 2001, in which congressional members and various administrators testified, the Commission unanimously passed a resolution[171] urging the United States to accede immediately to the United Nations Convention on the Law of the Sea.[172] The Commission then held nine regional meetings across the country from January through September 2002, hearing testimony from various federal and state governments, industry interest groups, the academic community, the international community, and interested citizens.[173] On 24 September 2002, the Commission released its Mid-Term Report, summarizing the information gathered.[174] Four public deliberation meetings were held in Washington, D.C., from October 2002 to April 2003 to discuss possible policy recommendations further.[175] It was also

---

[163] Pew Oceans Commission, "America's Living Oceans: Charting a Course for Sea Change" (2004) 57–58.

[164] Oceans Act of 2000, Pub. L. No. 106–256, 114 Stat. 644 (2001), *amended by* Pub. L. No. 107–206, 116 Stat. 833 (2003), Pub. L. No. 107–372, 116 Stat. 3096 (2003), available at http://www.oceancommission.gov/documents/oceanact.pdf.

[165] § 3(f)(1), 114 Stat. 644, 647 (2001) ("Within 18 months after the establishment of the Commission," effective date of Act January 20, 2001 according to § 7 of Act), available at http://thomas.loc.gov/bss/d106/d106laws.html.

[166] § 3(f)(1), 116 Stat. 833 (2003).

[167] U.S. Commission on Ocean Policy, "Preliminary Report: Governor's Draft" (2004).

[168] § 4(a), 116 Stat. 3096 (2003).

[169] S. Rep. No. 106–301, at 2–5 (2000) (Comm. on Commerce, Science, and Transportation), at http://www.oceancommission.gov/documents/Senate_Report.pdf.

[170] § 3(f)(2), 114 Stat. 644, 647 (2001).

[171] U.S. Commission on Ocean Policy, "United Nations Law of the Sea Convention Resolution" (2001), at http://www.oceancommission.gov/documents/los_resolution.pdf.

[172] 1982 United Nations Convention on the Law of the Sea (UNCLOS) (UN Doc A/CONF.62/122, reprinted in 21 ILM 1261 (1982) (signed 10 December 1982), available at http://www.un.org/Depts/los/convention_agreements/convention_overview_convention.htm.

[173] U.S. Commission on Ocean Policy, "Report Development Timeline as of April 5, 2004" (2004), at http://www.oceancommission.gov/calendar/timeline4_5_04.pdf.

[174] U.S. Commission on Ocean Policy, "Developing a National Ocean Policy: Mid-Term Report" (2002), at http://www.oceancommission.gov/documents/midterm_report/ReportCovREV10_01_02.pdf.

[175] U.S. Commission on Ocean Policy, *supra* note 173.

during this time the date to submit the Commission's final report to Congress and the President was extended from "spring of 2003"[176] to "June 2003"[177] to "early fall of 2003."[178] Over the course of the Commission's 15 public meetings, 440 individuals testified, from ocean scientists and researchers to environmental organizations, industries, citizens, and government officials.[179] The Commission also received nearly 200 public comments from a similar cross section of interests.[180] In June 2003, the Commission released a draft Table of Contents for the forthcoming final report.[181] During the second half of 2003 and beginning of 2004, the Commission drafted its report; it released the Preliminary Report in April 2004 for public comments,[182] particularly from Governors of coastal states, whose comments must be included in the final report to Congress and the President.[183] The public comment period deadline was extended from 21 May 2004 to 4 June 2004.[184] Recommendations in the Preliminary Report include creation of a National Ocean Council; creation of a Presidential Council of Advisors on Ocean Policy; strengthening of the National Oceanic and Atmospheric Administration (NOAA) and federal agency coordination; implementation of the national Integrated Ocean Observing System; development of flexible and voluntary regional councils supported by the National Ocean Council; setting of measurable water pollution reduction goals, particularly for nonpoint sources; accession to the United Nations Convention on the Law of the Sea; doubling of the nation's investment in ocean research; increase in attention to ocean education; and establishment of an Ocean Policy Trust Fund based on revenue from offshore economic activities to pay for implementing the recommendations.[185] The final report was expected in August 2004.[186]

Although the final findings of the Commission on the need to control nonpoint source pollution are very forceful, the recommendations are much less so. The recommendations merely direct the yet to be established National Ocean Council to set a national goal of reducing nonpoint pollution in impaired coastal watersheds and to set specific, measurable objectives to meet water quality standards.[187] Its only directive to Congress is that it should authorize federal agencies to "impose financial disincentives

---

[176] Press Release, U.S. Commission on Ocean Policy, "Final Report to Congress and President Due in Spring 2003" (10 January 2002), at http://www.oceancommission.gov/newsnotices/jan10_chasmtg.html.

[177] U.S. Commission on Ocean Policy, *supra* note 174, at 1.

[178] Press Release, U.S. Commission on Ocean Policy, "U.S. Commission on Ocean Policy Sets Framework for New National Ocean Policy: Table of Contents Document Outlines Major Areas of Interest" (2 June 2003), at http://www.oceancommission.gov/newsnotices/jun2_03.html.

[179] *Id.*

[180] U.S. Commission on Ocean Policy, Public Comment Archive (public comments received through March 2004), at http://www.oceancommission.gov/publicomment/welcome.html.

[181] U.S Commission on Ocean Policy, "Working Table of Contents B Draft Final Report" (2003) (updated 26 June 2003), at http://www.oceancommission.gov/documents/working_toc6_26_03.pdf.

[182] Press Release, U.S. Commission on Ocean Policy, "U.S. Commission on Ocean Policy To Release *Preliminary Report* April 20 – Historic Report to be Reviewed by Governors and Stakeholders" (10 March 2004), at http://www.oceancommission.gov/newsnotices/mar10_04.html.

[183] Oceans Act of 2000, Pub. L. No. 106–256, § 3(g)(2), 114 Stat. 644, 648 (2001), *amended by* Pub. L. No. 107–206, 116 Stat. 833 (2003), Pub. L. No. 107–372, 116 Stat. 3096 (2003), available at http://www.oceancommission.gov/documents/oceanact.pdf.

[184] Press Release, U.S. Commission on Ocean Policy, "U.S. Commission on Ocean Policy Extends Comment Deadline to June 4, 2004" (14 May 2004), at http://www.oceancommission.gov/newsnotices/may14_04.html.

[185] U.S. Commission on Ocean Policy, *supra* note 167, at xvii.

[186] Press Release, U.S. Commission on Ocean Policy, *supra* note 182.

[187] Final Report, *supra* note 4, at 177.

and establish enforceable management measures to ensure action if a state does not make meaningful progress toward meeting water quality standards."[188] Significantly this recommendation does not direct Congress or EPA to *set* mandatory management measures, but only to authorize federal action if a state does not "make meaningful progress" toward meeting water quality standards.[189] This standard for federal intervention is essentially meaningless, given the vagueness of "meaningful progress" and that it need only be "progress" toward meeting in general water quality standards rather than any required best management practices.[190]

What then does the Report say as to setting some actual management measures for nonpoint pollution, and who is to set them? On both levels, the Report's recommendation is phrased in such a way as will ensure ineffectiveness. Recommendation 14–11 directs states and local governments to revise their codes and ordinances "to require land use planning and decision-making to carefully consider" the impacts of development on water quality.[191] In other words, after finding that nonpoint pollution from land-based activities is the most serious threat to coastal and ocean water quality, what does the Report recommend? That a yet-to-be established Council with no enforcement authority set objectives for meeting state water quality standards, whatever they might be, and that state and local governments make sure they "consider" the impacts of development on water quality, consideration they are already required to give under the Clean Water Act.[192] And if development continues to be authorized despite clearly detrimental impacts on water quality? Unlike the Pew Report, the preliminary Ocean Commission Report calls only for federal intervention if a state is not making "meaningful progress" toward meeting water quality standards, an ambiguous term that could allow for decades of unrestrained water quality impairment before federal intervention would be necessary.[193]

This discrepancy between the forcefulness of the findings and the tentativeness of the recommendations did not go unnoticed in the initial reactions of U.S. Senators from two Senate Committees, the Senate Commerce, Science, and Transportation Committee and the Senate Appropriations Committee, when presented with the preliminary Report.[194] Senator Fritz Hollings of South Carolina was the most outspoken in this regard.[195] He questioned the efficacy of an ocean council as opposed to a department that would have more direct access to the President.[196] He told James Watkins, who presented the Report, that he agreed with just about everything in the report but added, "You're passionate in your answers but tentative and almost a sissy in your recommendations."[197] Watkins agreed with Senator Hollings that the goals would not be met without a strong commitment to them by the President.[198]

Watkins also told the Senate Commerce Committee that climate change relates to "every single topic in the report" and that the "climate change issue alone is powerful enough to drive the recommendations all by itself."[199] The recommendations for

[188] *Id.* at 179.

[189] *Id.*

[190] *Id.*

[191] *Id.* at 180.

[192] *Id.*

[193] *Id.* at 179.

[194] See Susan Bruninga, "Senators Open to New Federal Policy Idea but Question Funding, Governance Structure" (30 April 2004), 35 *Env't Rep.* (BNA) 948–949.

[195] See *id.* at 948.

[196] See *id.*

[197] *Id.*

[198] *Id.*

[199] *Id.* at 949.

international policy, however, say nothing about the United States' failure to ratify the Kyoto Protocol or any other measures to control greenhouse gases. Chapter 29, "Advancing International Ocean Science and Policy," contains a chart that indicates that the United States has not ratified the Kyoto Protocol, the Protocol to the London Convention, Annexes IV (sewage) or VI (air emissions) to the International Convention for the Prevention of Pollution from Ships, the Convention on Biological Diversity, the Convention on Migratory Species of Wild Animals, or the Cartagena Protocol on Biosafety. Yet the only recommendation with respect to any of these treaties is that the National Ocean Council coordinate an expedited review and recommend to the State Department whether "from an ocean perspective, ratification of this treaty would be beneficial to U.S. interests" and that the United States ratify Annex VI. With respect to international efforts to control nonpont source pollution, favorable mention is made of the U.S. involvement in UNEP's 14 regional seas programs as part of the 1995 Global Program of Action [GPA] for the Protection of the Marine Environment from Land-Based Sources and UNEP's 2002 Hilltop to Oceans Initiative, and the 3 June 2003 G-8 statement declaring their intention to implement a global action plan for sustainable ocean development. The only recommendation, however, that relates to these deficiencies and potential corrective actions is Recommendation 29–8: "The United States should increase its efforts to enhance long-term ocean science and management capacity in other nations through funding, education and training, technical assistance, and sharing best practices, management techniques, and lessons learned."

The prospects for meaningful implementation of even the relatively timid recommendations of the Ocean Commission are bleak. Generally, the Report lays the most important burdens of implementation on the yet to be created Ocean Council for improvement at the federal level, and on the reluctant and financially strapped state and local governments for the remainder. With respect to control of nonpoint source pollution specifically, states and local governments are given a vague, unenforceable recommendation to make progress toward undefined goals, instead of a recommendation that Congress require compliance with TMDLs or mandate use of best management practices with sanctions (or withdrawal of funding) for failure to comply, or a recommendation of withdrawal of federal subsidies that directly encourage coastal development. As of mid-2004, only one-fifth of CAFOs were in compliance with the 2003 requirements, yet the Report says nothing about methods to ensure that CAFOs comply with the regulatory limitations.

The very creation of the Ocean Council has already prompted divergent criticism. In a public hearing on the preliminary Report on 28 July 2004, the last hearing before issuance of the Final Report, one of the most contentious issues was this creation of another level of bureaucracy, with some environmental NGOs, like Senator Hollings in the hearings, saying that the Council was too weak an instrument for change at the federal level, and state representatives insisting on more state influence in it and the regional ocean councils to be established. What timid control measures were recommended by the Report to control nonpoint pollution were questioned by the very state representatives charged with their oversight and implementation. Most states opposed the establishment of any form of disincentive or penalty as a mechanism for ensuring implementation of and compliance with federal program requirements. As a public summary of the state comments noted, "Most recognize nonpoint source pollution as a major problem facing the nation; however, there is not a consensus regarding the recommendation to merge the Coastal Zone Management Act Section 6217 program into the Clean Water Act Section 319 nonpoint program. In addition, most strongly disagree with the use of disincentives or penalties to facilitate the implementation of nonpoint programs." This longstanding unwillingness of states to require and enforce best management practices in land use is precisely why the most serious deficiency of the Report in this regard is its failure to mandate imposition of such requirements at the federal level.[200]

At the international level, even the state representatives indicated that too little attention was given in the Report to climate change and its effect on coastal resources and communities. No mention is made of the U.S. failure to ratify the Kyoto Protocol other than its inclusion in a chart. The Report's recommendations that the United States ratify the Law of the Sea Convention and Annex VI merely reflect ongoing processes already headed in that direction. The clear need for the United States to ratify the Biodiversity Convention to preserve marine resources results only in another directive to the Ocean Council to review the need for its ratification.

At the Senate hearings, James Watkins agreed with Senator Hollings that what was most necessary to national and international ocean policy was a commitment by the President to see that reform is effectuated. The President was given 90 days to respond to the Final Ocean Report, which expired on 20 December 2004. Instead of recommending action, on 17 December 2004, shortly before this chapter was finished, the President appointed yet another committee to review the recommendations of the U.S. Ocean Commission. On the forefront of issues to be addressed were expanding the use of fishing quotas and seeking ratification of UNCLOS. Conspicuously absent from the plan was any evaluation or decisions for control of nonpoint source pollution.

---

[200] See generally Linda A. Malone, *supra* note 119.

31 Historical Overview of the American Land Use System: A Diagnostic Approach to Evaluating Governmental Land Use Control

John R. Nolon

1 INTRODUCTION

This chapter explains, illustrates, and evaluates the legal system employed in the United States to regulate the use of privately owned land and provides an illustrative checklist of the components of the system. The checklist is intended to facilitate a comparison of the U.S. system with land use regimes in other countries. The chapter also describes how, in recent years, this system has evolved to meet the challenge of urban sprawl through innovative smart growth measures and how it has dealt with recent threats to local natural resources through the advent of local environmental laws and standards.

The U.S. system of land use control was based on English law precedents. The English system established strong private property rights that were limited initially by a few common law doctrines created and enforced principally by the courts. Gradually a system of regulating building construction and particularly noxious, or inappropriately located, land uses evolved at the local level. There was no "national" land use system in England at the time of the creation of the federal republic in the United States.

Under the U.S. system of government, states retained the power to define and limit property rights, including the right to use the land and its natural resources. From that reservoir of authority, states have delegated land use control principally to local governments, including the power to create land use districts that dictate how cities, towns, and villages and their surrounding regions develop. States began by empowering local governments to adopt land use plans, to establish uniform zoning districts, and to review and approve land subdivision and site development. In most states, local governments have been given additional powers by their states to achieve proper development patterns and to mitigate the adverse impacts of land development on natural resources and the environment. Some state and federal laws that limit local land use authority to ensure that statewide, regional, and federal interests are protected have been adopted.

The U.S. Constitution[1] gave the national Congress the power to regulate interstate commerce, including the authority to prevent sources of environmental pollution that enter navigable waters or travel across state lines in the air. This authority has been broadly interpreted, sustaining some federal regulation of private land, such as strip mining, when there is a rational basis for finding that the activity affects interstate

---

[1] The text of the United States Constitution is available online at http://www.house.gov/Constitution/Constitution.html.

The author gratefully acknowledges the assistance of Susan Moritz, Research Consultant.

commerce. Congress also has the authority to tax and spend, which it can use to discourage private pollution and to encourage positive state and local activity regarding the environment and land development.

This multijurisdictional approach has resulted in overlapping regimes, with all three levels of government establishing rules for some matters, such as wetlands and habitat protection, preservation of natural resources, transportation development, and prevention of environmental pollution. As a result, the contemporary challenge is to integrate some of the various governmental influences on private land use to limit waste and redundancy while preserving the need for flexibility in addressing diverse regional, state, and federal interests.

2 ENGLISH COMMON LAW ORIGINS

After the Battle of Hastings in 1066, the Norman system of governing England was based on feudal tenure, a method of land control under which trusted allies of King William were given rights in the land, which they held of the King, not privately or exclusively.[2] Those who held the land owed defined services to the sovereign, and the sovereign owed them protection in return. This form of land control was replaced by individual property ownership. This began with an early act of Parliament, the Statute of Quia Emptores, adopted in 1290, which gave those who held land the power to transfer it to the private ownership of others, subject to the state's right to tax, take, and control the land.

Under early English common law, private land ownership was regarded as sacred. In 1782, William Blackstone, one of the earliest commentators on the common law, referred to the right of property as "that sole and despotic dominion which one man claims over the external things of the world, in total exclusion of the right of any other individual in the universe."[3] Although few land use regulations existed by this time, Blackstone noted, even then, that property rights were to be enjoyed "without any control or diminution, save only by the laws of the land."[4] The right to exclude others from the land was protected by trespass actions brought in the common law courts. Any intentional incursion onto the land of another, whether actual damage occurred or not, was actionable. Liability for intentional trespass was absolute, regardless of motive or harm effected. Damages were assessed in proportion to actual injury caused to the property. Even when no actual damage resulted from a trespass, courts awarded nominal damages to settle property disputes.

The powerful right of individuals to use their land under the common law was balanced to a degree by the doctrine of nuisance, which established that private landowners could not use their property in a way that was injurious to property held by others.[5] Nuisance remedies were limited, by and large, to enjoining land uses that actually injured the owners or occupants of adjacent land, along with consequential damages. Offensive intrusions included the effects of smoke, dust, noise, or heat that interfered with or diminished the normal uses of nearby property. Nuisance rules limiting injurious land uses evolved slowly and only in response to one private party's dispute against another.

---

[2] See generally, A. W. B. Simpson, *A History of the Land Law* (Oxford) (1986).

[3] W. Blackstone, *Commentaries on the Laws of England* (1782) at 2.

[4] Ibid. at 138.   [5] See *Aldred's Case* [1611] 9 Coke R.D.F. 57b.

By the time cities matured in England, the private ownership of city lots made urban development easier – allowing individuals to build as they wished on their land in response to market demands. Unfettered landownership in urban areas, however, gave rise to dangerous overcrowding, impossible traffic congestion, and the rapid spread of disease and fire.[6]

In England, the great fire of 1666 in London led to the adoption of municipal building construction laws that required brick exteriors, wider streets, and open space along the Thames River for access to water for firefighting.[7] Land use was regulated to a minor degree, as well, as activities such as breweries and tanneries were prohibited in the central city. The law provided for compensation to be paid to any individual lot owner who was prohibited from building. These early land use rules were articulated first in a proclamation by King Charles II, supported by a report from an investigative committee established by the King, and formalized by the Act for the Rebuilding of London adopted by Parliament in 1667. The Act gave the municipality the power to regulate the construction of buildings: their size, height, and placement on the lot and the materials used.

England's principal legacies to the United States are, first, strong support for the private ownership of land, with uses limited by nuisance doctrines, and, second, the legitimacy of regulation of building construction and of the location of noxious land uses by the local municipality.[8] Land use regulation under the common law system relied on municipalities, not state, provincial, or national governments.

3 COLONIAL PERIOD

By the time of the development of the American colonies, individual property rights were well established. Individuals were thought to hold powerful control over their land – a concept that limited the power of the state to regulate that land.[9] Early colonial charter companies and towns allocated private ownership of land to each founding family. These grants were often subject to land use restrictions, such as requiring buildings to be perpendicular to the street and not to exceed 35 feet in height. In this early period, land uses were regulated more by conditions imposed on the land titles conveyed by colonial authorities than by governmental regulation. Lands granted to founding families were eventually subdivided by inheritance and transfer, creating lots for private use: agricultural, commercial, and residential. Colonial settlements evolved into cities, townships, and counties, which eventually achieved governmental status and the power to legislate.

These municipalities were regarded not as sovereign entities but as creatures of the state, authorized by state law to exercise a wide variety of powers affecting the health, safety, and welfare of their citizens. Most were deemed to have only those powers delegated by their state legislatures, and those additional powers fairly implied in that delegation. As early as 1787, the City of New York was granted power to enact laws

---

[6] See Rutherford H. Platt, *Land Use and Society: Geography, Law, and Public Policy*; revised edition (Island Press) (2004) at 82.

[7] See ibid. at 84.   [8] See ibid. at 81.

[9] See generally, John F. Hart, "Land Use Law in the Early Republic and the Original Meaning of the Takings Clause" [2000], *Zoning and Planning Law Handbook*, Chapter 3, reprinted from 94 *Nw. U. L. Rev.* 1099.

directing private landowners to arrange buildings uniformly in certain neighborhoods. In 1784, the Connecticut assembly had granted some cities authority to adopt laws regulating the placement and construction of private buildings. Similar laws were adopted in Virginia and Georgia at about the same time. By the end of the 18th century, postcolonial landowners had grown accustomed to governmental regulation of building on the land in the interests of public health, safety, and even aesthetics.[10]

4 FORMATION OF THE FEDERAL REPUBLIC

The U.S. system of government established formally in the 1780s, after the American Revolution, involved the creation by the people of sovereign states, vested with full powers, including the police power that permits state legislatures to enact laws to protect the public health, safety, welfare, and morals. States are governed by constitutions, adopted in conventions by representatives selected by local gatherings of the people of the state. The U.S. Constitution was drafted by delegates selected by the states and was signed by them in 1787. It created a federal government that has the power to legislate only within the parameters of the specific powers delegated to it in the Constitution. Notably, the full police powers of the states were not delegated to the federal government.

The principal power given to the federal government that affects private land use is the power to regulate interstate commerce, under Article I, § 8, of the U.S. Constitution. The courts have interpreted this power broadly to include the regulation of matters affecting two or more states regarding trade, and navigation, with appropriate regard for the welfare of the public. After adopting the National Environmental Policy Act of 1969,[11] Congress passed a number of federal laws that regulate private land use and business activity related to interstate commerce. These include the Clean Water Act of 1972,[12] the Coastal Zone Management Act of 1972,[13] the Endangered Species Act of 1973,[14] and the Comprehensive Environmental Response, Compensation and Liability Act of 1980.[15]

Article I, § 8, of the Constitution also gives Congress the power to raise revenue by taxation and to spend those resources for the public good. There was a vigorous debate at the time the Constitution was drafted regarding the breadth of this power to spend "to provide for the general welfare of the United States."[16] The debate continued into the 20th century, when congressional spending programs aimed at addressing the problems of the Great Depression were challenged. In upholding the constitutionality of the Social Security Act, the U.S. Supreme Court held that the federal power to spend was extremely broad.[17] The Court based its decision on the fact that the states, acting independently, could not deal effectively with problems such as relief for the elderly and unemployed. It defined the power to spend for the general welfare with these words: "Nor is the concept of general welfare static. Needs that were narrow or parochial a century ago may be interwoven in our day with the well-being of the nation. What is critical or urgent changes with the time."[18] Today, federal spending programs are used

---

[10] Ibid.

[12] 33 U.S.C. § 1251 *et seq.* (2004).

[14] 16 U.S.C. § 1531 *et seq.* (2004).

[16] U.S. Const. Art. I, § 8, cl. 1.

[18] Ibid. at 641.

[11] 42 U.S.C. §§ 4321 *et seq.* (2004).

[13] 16 U.S.C. §§ 1451 *et seq.* (2004).

[15] 42 U.S.C. §§ 9601 *et seq.* (2004).

[17] *Helvering v. Davis* [1935] 301 U.S. 619.

to provide incentives to state and local governments and private landowners to achieve environmental objectives that promote the general welfare of the nation in a time of heightened concern over critical environmental troubles.

Article VI of the Constitution grants the federal government the power to enter into international treaties that legally bind federal, state, and local governments in the United States. Under this authority, the United States has entered into many bilateral, regional, and international agreements that promote resource conservation and prevent environmental pollution.[19] An example of how a treaty may change the application of land use law is found in the expropriation provisions of the North American Free Trade Agreement (NAFTA). NAFTA allows foreign investors to arbitrate their claims that local, state, or federal laws constitute prohibited takings of investor property, using standards and adjudicatory forums quite different from those otherwise provided under domestic law.[20]

The Tenth Amendment of the U.S. Constitution reserves to the states all powers not delegated by the Constitution to the federal government. This power protects states against encroachments by Congress that are not justified by the power delegated to the federal government. The concept of dual sovereignty is dynamic and leaves room for flexibility in responding to challenges at the state and federal levels, with tensions resolved by the U.S. Supreme Court. Under Article VI of the Constitution, the laws and treaties of the United States are declared to be the supreme law of the land.

The power to control private land use is part of the states' police power, and it is regarded as a reserved power of the states, subject to Congress's power to regulate interstate commerce. Early attempts by the federal Environmental Protection Agency to reduce air pollution by intervening in local development matters were recognized as a threat to the power of the states to control land use, secured by the Tenth Amendment. Such concerns led to the 1977 amendments to the Clean Air Act, which stated that "[n]othing in this Act constitutes an infringement of existing authority of counties and cities to plan or control land use, and nothing in this Act provides or transfers authority over such land use."[21] In 2001, the efforts of the Army Corps of Engineers to prevent the construction of a landfill by a consortium of municipalities in the Chicago area were struck down by the U.S. Supreme Court. The Court held that the Army Corps lacked jurisdiction under the Clean Water Act to regulate development of intrastate, nonnavigable waters solely on the basis of the presence of migratory birds.[22]

The powers of the federal and state governments to regulate private matters such as trade and land use are limited by property and personal rights protected by the Constitution. The Fifth Amendment of the U.S. Constitution prohibits the federal government from taking title to property from private persons unless it is for a public purpose and only if just compensation is paid.[23] The Fourteenth Amendment incorporates Fifth Amendment guarantees and applies them to the states and their municipalities. Thus,

---

[19] See Celia Campbell-Mohn et al. (eds.), *Environmental Law: From Resources to Recovery* (West) (1993) 99–106.

[20] See Vicki Been, "Will International Agreements Trump Local Environmental Law?" [2003], *in* John R. Nolon (ed.), *New Ground: The Advent of Local Environmental Law* (Environmental Law Institute) at 73.

[21] 42 U.S.C. § 7431 (2004).

[22] *Solid Waste Agency of N. Cook County v. U.S. Corps of Eng'rs* [2001] 531 U.S. 159, 171.

[23] "No person . . . shall be . . . deprived of . . . property without due process of law; nor shall private property be taken for a public purpose, without just compensation." U.S. Const. amend. V.

states and their municipal corporations are prohibited from adopting land use regulations that deprive any person of property without due process of law or from denying
any person equal protection of the law.[24] Land use regulations that deny private property owners all use and enjoyment of their land are considered "regulatory takings."[25]
Courts will require governments that effect regulatory takings to compensate the private
landowners under the takings clause of the Fifth Amendment. Most state constitutions
have similar takings clauses.

The U.S. Constitution also protects individual freedom of speech, the right to assemble, and to worship.[26] These constitutionally protected freedoms limit local land use
regulations that are aimed at the content of signs, modes of personal expression in the
adult entertainment business, gatherings on land otherwise open to the public, and
construction of houses of worship and their related activities. Land use regulations that
affect these individual freedoms do not enjoy the usual presumption of constitutionality
that courts otherwise afford local laws.

These guarantees limit governmental land use authority. They require courts to
strike down land use laws that are unreasonable or arbitrary, that fail to accomplish a
legitimate public purpose, or that create land use categories that discriminate between
classes of landowners unless those categories serve a legitimate public purpose.

5 19TH-CENTURY LAND USE

During the 1800s, building on private lots in urban areas to respond to market demand
again caused a tangle of construction, poor traffic circulation, inadequate waste disposal,
and overcrowding. The spread of diseases such as tuberculosis and cholera was a result
of these conditions, as were serious fires in 1828 and 1835 in New York City. As modern
industrial cities emerged during the 19th century, the negative effects of uncontrolled
urbanization became clear.

This situation led to the birth of a movement of regulation of building construction
and location to prevent overcrowding, facilitate the fighting of fires, and forbid unsa-
vory or dangerous land uses in or near residential neighborhoods. During this period,
municipalities were given the power to regulate private activity to protect public health
and safety. This "police power" was used to prevent the spread of disease and the outbreak of fire. In 1866, the New York state legislature adopted the Metropolitan Health
Act, and its cities began to exert regulatory influence over unsanitary conditions on
privately owned property.[27]

---

[24] See *Chicago, Burlington & Quincy R.R. Co. v. City of Chicago* [1897] 166 U.S. 226: "[A] state may not, by
any of its agencies, disregard the prohibitions of the fourteenth amendment. . . . In determining what is
due process of law, regard must be had to substance, not to form. . . . In our opinion, a judgment of a
state court, even if it be authorized by statute, whereby private property is taken for the state or under
its direction for public use, without compensation made or secured to the owner, is, upon principle and
authority, wanting in the due process of law required by the fourteenth amendment of the constitution
of the United States, and the affirmance of such judgment by the highest court of the state is a denial by
that state of a right secured to the owner by that instrument."

[25] See John R. Nolon, "Footprints in the Shifting Sands of the Isle of Palms: A Practical Analysis of Regulatory
Takings Cases" [1992], 8 J. Land Use & Envtl. Law 1, at 23–44.

[26] "Congress shall make no law respecting an establishment of religion, or prohibiting the free exercise
thereof; or abridging the freedom of speech, or of the press; or the right of the people to peaceably
assemble." U.S. CONST. amend. I.

[27] See Rutherford H. Platt, *Land Use and Society: Geography, Law, and Public Policy, supra*, note 6, at 105.

This move toward regulatory intervention occurred in the United States, as it did in England, concurrently with the adoption of building regulations of a variety of types, including the regulation of height and location and some regulation of uses that were obnoxious to nearby residential owners or the public in general. In 1915, for example, the U.S. Supreme Court upheld a regulation by the City of Los Angeles to prevent the operation of a dangerous brick kiln within a part of the city.[28]

6 THE MODERN ERA OF ZONING

After the turn of the century more was needed in developing American communities.[29] In New York City, particularly, Fifth Avenue merchants were upset with the encroachment of other land uses, such as garment factories and offices, into their high-end retail neighborhood. There was broad sentiment that the City was becoming too densely settled, largely because of the spread of skyscrapers. In 1913, the City appointed a commission, which was told to investigate a completely new idea: the division of the city into land use districts.

On the basis of the commission's recommendations, the nation's first comprehensive zoning ordinance was adopted by New York City in 1916. It divided the City into multiple land use districts, or zones. These districts allowed private landowners to use their land only for the purposes permitted in the applicable district. This protected Fifth Avenue retailers, for example, from the incursion of garment factories – an industrial use – in that retail zone.

This concept spread quickly. By the mid-1920s, nearly 400 local governments had adopted comprehensive zoning laws. Their authority to do so was granted by enabling acts adopted by their state legislatures. In the United States, virtually all 50 states have adopted this method of land use regulation; their legislatures have passed relatively similar zoning enabling laws that delegate the authority to municipalities to regulate private land uses.

Local governments are regarded as legal instruments of their states. The states have created various types of local governments – cities, towns, townships, villages, boroughs, or counties – and delegated authority to them to legislate regarding specific interests. The legislative authority of municipalities is limited to that delegated by the state and extends only within their geographical boundaries.

Planning and zoning enabling laws specifically authorized municipal governments to control the use of the land by adopting land use plans and creating zoning districts. In most states, zoning regulations must conform to the locality's land use plan. In each zoning district, various building construction rules are established. These limit, for example, the heights and sizes of buildings and the amount of the building lot that can be built upon. Within each zoning district, each parcel of land is assigned at least one as-of-right land use, while permitting accessory uses typically associated with those principal uses. Variances of the standards may be awarded when landowners can prove that the zoning standards impose unnecessary hardships. Uses that do not conform to newly adopted zoning regulations may continue but may not be expanded or enlarged.

---

[28] *Hadacheck v. Sebastian* [1915] 239 U.S. 394.

[29] See Newman F. Baker, *Legal Aspects of Zoning* (University of Chicago) (1927). See generally, Seymour I. Toll, *Zoned American* (Grossman) (1969).

State enabling laws also authorized localities to create administrative and quasi-judicial agencies to review and adjudicate proposals for land development and petitions for relief from zoning regulations. Planning boards or commissions were established in most communities to review and approve individual development proposals. Zoning boards of appeal were created to hear applications to reverse adverse determinations of zoning enforcement officials or to provide relief from the strict application of zoning standards where they create unnecessary hardships regarding unique parcels of land. These agencies are required to hold public hearings on most proposals and petitions, to provide notice to affected parties of the hearings, to hold meetings open to the public, and to ensure that their voting members have no conflicts of interest that prevent their decisions from being objective.

The most controversial aspect of zoning was that it prohibited private landowners from using their land for activities of their own choosing. Building construction limits were firmly established and accepted under prior state and municipal law. But taking away the right of a private landowner to use his or her land to meet market needs was a new idea and more controversial.

In the state of Ohio, the constitutional authority of the Village of Euclid to adopt and enforce use limitations was challenged by Ambler Realty Company.[30] Ambler claimed that separating uses through zoning districts accomplished no legitimate governmental purpose and, on its face, was unconstitutional. The plaintiff's technical claim was that zoning violated its constitutional right to due process: to be protected from arbitrary or unreasonable laws that did not further a legitimate public purpose.

The U.S. Supreme Court disagreed. In 1926, it handed down its decision in *Euclid v. Ambler Realty Co.*,[31] holding that the separation of land uses among zoning districts did accomplish a legitimate public purpose, using nuisance limitations on private property use as an analogous doctrine. The Court reasoned that the effect of zoning was to create land use standards that protected neighbors from nuisance-like use of nearby land. Thereafter, establishing zoning districts that carefully prescribed authorized land uses within each zone became the principal method of controlling private land use in the interest of building communities that were safe and economically efficient. After this decision, the adoption of uniform building and use standards within various land use districts became known as "Euclidian Zoning."[32]

This system relied on local governments to make land use decisions. The role of the state was to establish the scope of local land use authority. Interestingly, during the early part of the 20th century, the role of the federal government was generally irrelevant to the creation of cities and towns and the control of private land use. The federal influence on metropolitan development began in earnest in 1934 with the adoption of the National Housing Act, which established a system of mortgage insurance through the Federal Housing Administration. In 1937, Congress created the public housing program, using its power to tax and spend to grant subsidies to local housing authorities to build low-income housing. In quick succession, it used this same authority to create the urban renewal program, offering planning and building grants

---

[30] *See Euclid v. Ambler Realty Co.* [1926] 272 U.S. 365.
[31] Ibid.
[32] See Charles Haar and Jerold Kayden (eds.), *Zoning and the American Dream: Promises Still to Keep* (APA Planners Press) (1989).

to local urban renewal agencies; to subsidize housing conservation and rehabilitation; to encourage the adoption of local housing codes provide funds to nonprofit housing companies for moderate- and middle-income housing; and eventually, in 1974, to provide block grants to localities, large and small, for community development activities.[33]

By the 1970s, state courts had determined that private nuisance actions were not competent, in the context of nuisance actions brought by a few affected landowners, to resolve regional air and water pollution problems resulting from commercial and industrial activities.[34] In response, Congress began a decade-long effort of adopting federal laws to control land, air, and water pollution, using its power under the interstate commerce clause. Curiously, this legislative initiative did not involve local governments or engage their potential to alter land development activities under their delegated land use authority.

At the inception of this era of federal environmental lawmaking, there was a reexamination of the wisdom of having delegated such extensive authority for controlling private land use to thousands of local governments in the 50 states, each making its own rules in the absence of any set of guidelines established by the states or the federal government.[35] Critics wondered how regional and statewide interests could be protected when local land use authority was confined to the borders of individual municipalities. Further, there were concerns that the delegation of land use power to localities was an ineffective method of controlling the underlying regional and national causes of environmental damage.[36]

Two responses followed: First, attempts were made to limit local control through preemptive measures, regional land use agencies, state directives, and other approaches. Local control of private land use began to be limited by state and federal laws adopted to deal with the negative effects of land use that were beyond the control, competence, or concern of local governments. Although these limitations on local control in a few states are noteworthy, they are not widespread and have not disturbed the primary reliance on municipal control in the U.S. land use system.

Second, many state legislatures gave greater power and flexibility to local governments to respond to development pressures. So-called neo-Euclidian zoning techniques such as planned unit development districts, floating zones, and special use permits evolved at the local level.[37] These allowed local governments more flexibility in locating development in appropriate places. In the modern era, additional techniques have been authorized such as the purchase of development rights, the transfer of development rights, and the recreation of traditional neighborhood districts to give even greater authority to local governments to marshal the forces of development and arrange buildings appropriately on the land.

---

[33] See John R. Nolon, "Reexamining Federal Housing Programs in a Time of Fiscal Austerity: The Trend toward Block Grants and Housing Allowances" [1982], 14 *Urb. Law.* 249, at 253–257.

[34] *Boomer v. Atlantic Cement Co.* [N.Y. 1970] 257 N.E. 2d 870.

[35] In 1972, there were about 38,500 general purpose local governments. See U.S. Census Bureau, Preliminary Report No. 1: The U.S. Census of Governments, http://www.census.gov/govs/www/cog2002.html

[36] Fred Bosselman and David Callies, *The Quiet Revolution in Land Use Control* (Council on Environmental Quality) (1972) at 1.

[37] See John R. Nolon, *Well Grounded: Using Local Land Use Authority to Achieve Smart Growth* (Environmental Law Institute) (2001) Chapters 6–8.

These responses – the minimal erosion of local land use discretion and the delegation of additional and flexible authority – are evidence that the traditional land use system is evolving.[38] It is interesting and instructive to examine how the federal and state governments have respected the centuries-old tradition of municipal control while confronting new challenges. The influential book *Land Use in America*[39] begins its agenda for land use in the 21st century with two critical recommendations. First, it states that "[l]ocal governments must take the lead role in securing good land use. Initiatives in land use planning and growth management need to be anchored in a community-based process that develops a vision for the future." Second, "State governments must help local governments by establishing reasonable ground rules and planning requirements . . . and providing leadership on matters that affect more than one local jurisdiction."[40] It is in the details of the limitation and expansion of local control that the ability of law to meet the changing exigencies of society is evident.

7 LIMITS AND INFLUENCES ON LOCAL LAND USE CONTROL

The seeds of the movement to limit and reshape local control were planted in the 1930s as planners dealt with the spread of land development beyond the borders of cities and urban villages.[41] After World War II, the search began for a higher level of government or administrative unit to define regional land use needs and shape development to meet them. The reformists of the 1970s called for state growth management laws, for regional governments to ensure that regional land use interests are met, and for further limits on local control of certain natural resources such as coastal areas and wetlands.

7.1 Regional Planning and Control

From its inception, the U.S. land use system has encouraged voluntary, grassroots approaches to intermunicipal and regional planning. The Standard City Planning Enabling Act, promulgated by the Hoover Commission in 1928, provided for regional planning by authorizing local planning commissions to petition their state's governor to establish a regional planning commission and to prepare a master plan for the region's physical development. Provisions were included in the planning enabling act for communication between the regional and municipal planning commissions with the objective of achieving a certain degree of consistency between local and regional plans.[42] In 1968, the Douglas Commission, the National Commission on Urban Problems, appointed by President Johnson, issued its report, *Building the American City*, which reinforced regional planning. The Commission recommended that each state create a state agency for land use planning and prepare state and regional land use plans. The

---

[38] See Charles M. Haar, "The Twilight of Land-Use Controls: A Paradigm Shift?" [1996], 30 *U. Rich. L. Rev.* 1011 at 1038.

[39] Henry L. Diamond and Patrick F. Noonan, *Land Use in America: The Report of the Sustainable Use of Land Project* (Island Press) (1996).

[40] Ibid. at 99–103.

[41] See Douglas R. Porter (ed.), *State and Regional Initiatives for Managing Development: Policy Issues and Practical Concerns* (Urban Land Institute) (1992) at 3.

[42] See Edward M. Bassett, *The Master Plan* (Russell Sage Foundation) (1938).

White House staff refused to accept the report.[43] A federal statute, the National Land-Use Planning Act, that would have provided a framework for federal, state, regional, and local land use planning was vigorously debated in the early 1970s but was not adopted.[44]

These examples illustrate that regional consciousness has been part of the land use system and regularly reaffirmed since the early days of American zoning. Much of the United States, at one time or another, has been brought within the jurisdiction of some form of voluntary regional planning organization as a result of a variety of influences. The most powerful of these forces was the promise of funding for regional efforts under housing, water, transportation, and other public works grant programs of the federal government. Predominant among the organizations formed were voluntary, areawide regional councils of government, multistate river basin compacts, and regional economic development and transportation organizations.

Three examples of responses to the need for extramunicipal land use control are the Adirondack Park Agency, the Oregon Growth Management Act, and Envision Utah. All took different strategic approaches.

Regulatory Regionalism

In 1971, the New York state legislature enacted the Adirondack Park Agency Act to focus the responsibility for land planning in one state agency and to provide a continuing role for local government.[45] The legislature found that the preservation of the park's resources was a matter of state, regional, and local concern. The nearly 2.5 million acres in the park that are owned by the state are protected from misuse by appropriate provisions of the state constitution.[46] In order to protect the area of the park that is privately owned, the state legislature created the Adirondack Park Agency (APA) and adopted the Adirondack Park Land Use and Development Plan in 1973.

The state statute creating the APA sets out the development plan in some detail. It requires the APA to prepare and file an official map, which is given specific planning and regulatory effects. The plan and map divide land within the park into several designated land use classifications.[47] The act describes the character of each classification, the policies and objectives to be achieved in the area, and the types and intensity of uses permitted. The APA has jurisdiction to review and approve all critical regional projects defined by their location in a critical environmental area or their impact as determined by their size and intensity of use. The APA may also review and approve other regional projects in any land use area not governed by an approved and validly enacted or adopted local land use program. It is directed to consult and work closely with local governments and county and regional planning agencies as part of the ongoing planning process and is empowered to review and approve or disapprove local land use plans. Once a local

[43] See P.L. 92–463, Federal Advisory Committee Act, H. REP. No. 92–1017 (25 April 1972).

[44] See Margaret Weir, "Planning, Environmentalism, and Urban Poverty: The Political Failure of National Land-Use Planning Legislation, 1970–1975," *in* Robert Fishman (ed.), *The American Planning Tradition: Culture and Policy* (Johns Hopkins University Press) (2000) at 193.

[45] N.Y. Exec. Law §§ 801–819 (Consol. 2004).

[46] N.Y.S. CONST. art. XIV, § 1.

[47] See *Helms v. Reid* [1977] 394 N.Y.S.2d 987, 90 Misc.2d 583 (holding that the division of lands in the Park into land use classifications was valid under the state constitution).

plan is approved, the locality assumes authority for reviewing and approving all but critical regional land use activities within its borders.

Urban Growth Boundaries

The Oregon growth management statute, adopted in 1973, creates a state agency known as the Land Conservation and Development Commission (LCDC), articulates a number of statewide land use planning goals, requires local governments to adopt comprehensive plans that contain urban growth boundaries, and requires local plans to be approved by the Commission.[48] The statute also created the Metropolitan Service District (Metro) to supervise the intermunicipal urban growth boundary in the greater Portland area. In 1979, the statute was amended to create the Land Use Board of Appeals (LUBA) to review local land use decisions.[49]

Goal 14 of the Oregon growth management statute – the urbanization goal – classifies land into three categories: rural, urbanizable, and urban.[50] Rural lands are agricultural, forest, or open space lands, or other land suitable for sparse settlement, with few public services. Urbanizable lands are to be contained within an urban growth boundary and are deemed suitable for future urban uses: lands that can be served by infrastructure and that are needed for the expansion of an urban area. Urban areas are within or adjacent to existing cities with concentrations of population and supporting public facilities and services. The statute provides for the orderly conversion of rural land to urban, based on the consideration of a number of factors including the need to accommodate population growth through the provision of housing, jobs, and infrastructure.

Voluntary Intermunicipal Strategies

With few exceptions, regional bodies in the United States have stopped far short of preemptive land use planning and regulation. They have become, however, effective vehicles for communication, education, collaboration, and networking. Among their most significant contributions is the effect they have of educating local land use officials.[51] In these regional bodies, local representatives learn about the common problems and interdependence of localities that share economic or housing markets or that have regulatory power over regional river basins and watersheds that cannot be protected without intermunicipal cooperation.

Envision Utah is a network of interest groups working at the regional level along a 100-mile corridor running north and south of Salt Lake City.[52] It comprises 88 local governments and 80 percent of the state's population. Assisted by state grants, Envision Utah is a nongovernmental alliance with significant private funding. Envision Utah conducted extensive opinion surveys of residents, who demonstrated a strong preference for walkable, transit-oriented development; infill strategies; and redevelopment of urbanized portions of the region. On the basis of grassroots-derived implementation strategies, the state legislature passed the Quality Growth Act in 1999, established a commission, and charged it with assisting local governments with grants and technical

---

[48] Or. Rev. Stat. §§ 197.005 et seq. (2004).

[49] See Or. Rev. Stat. §§ 197.540, 197.830–197.845 (2004).

[50] Or. Admin. R. 660–015–0000(14) (2004).

[51] See Nelson Wikstrom, *Councils of Governments: A Study of Political Incrementalism* (Burnham) (1977) at 131.

[52] See Envision Utah, at http://www.envisionutah.org.

assistance. The commission is also responsible for coordinating the work of six state agencies. Envision Utah developed a toolbox of techniques that can be used by local governments and intermunicipal councils to create their own visions and implement the regional vision.

7.2 Federal Environmental Control of Private Land Use

The federal environmental legal system was created in the late 1960s, beginning with the National Environmental Policy Act and followed rapidly by the Clean Air Act, the Clean Water Act, and a dozen other federal laws designed to prevent and clean up the pollution caused by the private sector and left unabated by the land use control system driven by local governments.[53] The signature approach of these federal laws is to create standards for pollution or protection that cannot be exceeded and to provide stiff criminal and civil penalties for violations.

Federal agencies are charged with the responsibility of enforcing these standards, and citizens are authorized to sue polluters under these statutes as well. The emphasis of federal environmental law is on the central role of the federal government as the standard setter and steward of a healthy environment. This focus all but obscures the importance of the role of local governments in land use control and environmental protection. Federal agencies have successfully reduced pollution that emanates from "point sources," such as smokestacks and water pipes. However, most environmental damage today is caused by "nonpoint source" pollution that results from land uses that are the legal responsibility of municipal governments. Federal attempts to influence local land use control in the interest of abating nonpoint source pollution have been thwarted by a variety of legal, political, and practical obstacles.

7.3 Federal and State Incentives, Assistance, Guidance, and Requirements

Federal and state legislatures have adopted a number of initiatives that encourage and influence local governments to regulate private land use. Under the National Flood Insurance Program of 1968,[54] the federal government provides private property owners insurance against damage caused by flooding, but only if local governments adopt and enforce building construction regulations in federally designated flood plains. Congress established land use policies for land development in coastal areas under the Coastal Zone Management Act of 1972.[55] It provides planning grants to states, which in turn grant funds to localities to adopt coastal development plans and regulations that comply with the federal and state coastal protection principles.

One interesting attempt to require localities to adopt environmental legislation is seen in the Phase II Storm water regulations issued by the federal Environmental Protection Agency (EPA).[56] Storm water runoff control is crucial to the success of the federal Clean Water Act. It is one of the most serious causes of water pollution in the United States, exceeding in many locales the contamination caused by sewage and industrial facility discharges. EPA, pursuant to its authority under the Clean Water

---

[53] See Celia Campbell-Mohn et al. (eds.), *Environmental Law: From Resources to* Recovery, *supra*, note 19.
[54] 42 U.S.C. §§ 4001 *et seq.* (2004).   [55] 16 U.S.C. §§ 1451 *et seq.* (2004).
[56] 40 C.F.R. § 9, 122, 123, and 124. See 64 Fed. Reg. 68,722 (8 December 1999).

Act, promulgated regulations establishing its Stormwater Management Program, which regulate municipalities that operate storm sewer systems, as do most U.S. municipalities of any size. These federal regulations require affected municipalities to implement a storm water management program as a means to control polluted discharges from their storm water systems: a form of point source regulation.

To ensure that these municipalities meet federal clean water standards, EPA set forth six minimal control measures that municipalities must meet, including programs to address storm water runoff from construction sites and postconstruction land uses. These regulations effectively direct municipalities to adopt procedures and regulations that affect private sector construction and development and that mitigate nonpoint source pollution. Local governments are required, for example, to adopt erosion and sediment control laws, to establish site plan review procedures for projects that will impact water quality, to inspect construction activities, and to adopt enforcement measures. Localities must adopt laws that result in improved clarity and reduced sedimentation of local water bodies and demonstrate increased numbers of sensitive aquatic organisms in their waters. Postconstruction runoff controls are also required for development and redevelopment projects. *Redevelopment* is defined to include any change in the footprint of existing buildings that disturbs more than one acre of land.

States, too, adopt laws that direct and influence local land use regulation. Nebraska state law requires that local governments adopt comprehensive land use plans before they are legally able to adopt any type of zoning regulation.[57] Under Minnesota law, local land use plans must contain a component regarding local open space protection.[58] The Minnesota state government assists its localities in land use regulation by providing them with model ordinances regarding the creation of urban growth boundaries and creating agricultural protection zones and subdivision ordinances that encourage sustainable development.[59] In Massachusetts, the state legislature has created a university-based program for providing technical assistance and training to local land use officials.[60] Under California's Environmental Quality Act, local governments must prepare an environmental impact report on any project that may have a significant impact on the environment.[61]

The Illinois legislature adopted the Local Planning and Technical Assistance Act in 2002. The law's purpose is to provide technical assistance to local governments for the development of local planning ordinances, promote and encourage comprehensive planning, promote the use of model ordinances, and support planning efforts in communities with limited funds.[62] The Department of Commerce and Community Affairs is authorized to provide technical assistance grants to be used by local governmental units to "develop, update, administer, and implement comprehensive plans, subsidiary plans, land development regulations . . . that promote and encourage the principles of comprehensive planning."[63] A particularly important tool is found in § 25, which sets forth

---

[57] NEB. REV. STAT. §. 23–114.03 (2004).

[58] MINN. STAT. ANN. §§ 422.351, 473.145 (West 2004).

[59] See http://www.mnplan.state.mn.us/pdf/2000/eqb/ModelOrdWhole.pdf.

[60] See The Center for Economic Development, University of Massachusetts at Amherst, http://www.umass.edu/larp/outreach_programs.html.

[61] CAL. PUB. RES. CODE §§ 21000 et. seq. (Deering 2004).

[62] 20 ILL. COMP. STAT. ANN. 662/5 (2004).   [63] Ibid. 662/15.

the specific elements that must be included in a plan for it to qualify for grant money.[64] The Local Planning and Technical Assistance Act does not mandate comprehensive planning. However, the grant money provides a strong incentive for communities to engage in planning.

7.4 State and Federal Preemption of Local Control

State and federal legislatures have adopted a few laws that fully or partially preempt local control of private land uses. Under the Telecommunications Act of 1996, for example, the federal government preempts local regulation of the location of cellular transmission facilities when such regulations are based on concerns over public health threats caused by the transmission of radio frequency emissions.[65] Localities are allowed to impose conditions on the location of such facilities based on aesthetic grounds, however. This is an example of partial preemption. Similarly, the Federal Aviation Act of 1958 preempts local regulation of federally approved flights, but not the height of airport buildings.[66] The Federal Fair Housing Act and its amendments prohibit localities from enforcing land use regulations that deny handicapped persons equal opportunity to use and enjoy the built environment.[67]

Another federal statute, the Religious Land Use and Incarcerated Persons Act (RLUIPA), partially preempts local land use control.[68] It prevents federal, state, and local governments from imposing or implementing land use regulations in a manner that imposes a substantial burden on religious exercise. RLUIPA applies to local land use decisions that involve individualized assessments of proposals by religious institutions for a variety of permits and approvals. It requires local governments to implement land use regulations in a manner that treats religious assembly or institution on equal terms, is nondiscriminatory, and does not exclude or unreasonably limit religious assembly.[69] When religious institutions bring a credible case of discrimination, the locality must demonstrate that its regulation furthers a compelling governmental interest and is the least restrictive measure for furthering that interest.

States adopt similar laws that preempt local action. The Colorado Land Use Act, for example, lists 21 areas of state interests, such as mineral exploitation, wildlife habitat areas, and flood hazards, and requires that when localities regulate such interests, they must follow state guidelines.[70] The New York Padavan Law mandates that local governments not deny applications by state-licensed nonprofit housing providers to establish group homes for developmentally disabled individuals in single-family zones.[71] New York law also provides for a state-controlled siting process for deciding on the location of electrical generation plants that preempts local control of them.[72]

---

[64] Ibid. 662/25(a)(1)–(10).
[66] 49 U.S.C. § 40101 (2004).
[68] 42 U.S.C. § 2000cc (2004).
[70] Colo. Rev. Stat. §§ 24–65.1–201–24–65.1–204 (2004).
[71] N.Y. Mental Hyg. Law § 41.34 (McKinney 2004).
[72] N.Y. Pub. Serv. Law art. X. See *Citizens for Hudson Valley v. New York State Bd. on Elec. Generation Siting and Envtl.* [3d Dep't. 2001] 281 A.D. 89, 723 N.Y.S.2d 532.

[65] 47 U.S.C. § 377 (2004).
[67] 42 U.S.C. § 3604 (2004).
[69] Ibid.

8 EXPANDING AND ENHANCING LOCAL CONTROL

By the middle of the 20th century, local zoning, subdivision, and site plan regulations had become traditional components of the land use system. Then, as the post–World War II building boom occurred, legislatures in many states began to give their local governments authority to adopt more complete, flexible, and diverse land use laws. They have been aided by liberal interpretations of delegated powers by state courts. Using these powers, localities in the United States have created two recent and dramatic movements: smart growth and local environmental protection.

8.1 Smart Growth Strategies

Smart growth is offered as a solution to the problems of urban sprawl, the deterioration of older cities and villages, and the failure of new development to create high-quality neighborhoods and to preserve natural resources. It provides a popular label for a growth strategy that addresses current concerns about traffic congestion, disappearing open space, nonpoint source pollution, the high cost of housing, increasing local property taxes, longer commutes, and the diminishing quality of community life. Under many suburban zoning laws and subdivision regulations, the densities and design features of traditional neighborhoods found in older urban areas can no longer be replicated.[73] Smart growth calls for a new type of land development pattern, one that is more concentrated, affordable, and environmentally sensitive and that creates a quality of neighborhood in which residents feel comfortable living.[74]

Smart growth also calls for the identification and preservation of critical environmental areas before land development occurs. By identifying critical environmental areas and protecting them via regulations and acquisition programs, communities can better define where to locate the development needed to accommodate population increases. The sustainable development movement taught that development and conservation are mutually supportive. Proper land conservation increases the quality of life, protects needed natural resources, stabilizes property values, and provides recreational and tourism benefits. Proper development, for its part, directs development pressures away from critical environmental areas, provides tax resources for municipal services, and can provide financial resources for land conservation.

Once municipal growth areas have been designated, local governments have a number of strategies to choose from in order to direct development into such areas. The following illustrative list, drawn from strategies local governments are authorized to use in New York State, is representative of local powers in most populous states:

- *Higher-density districts:* In a designated growth zoning district, the density of development can be increased as a matter of right. Municipalities can use their traditional zoning authority to create mixed-use neighborhoods with bulk, area, and use provisions that create the type of compact development pattern envisioned by the smart growth concept. Such districts provide sufficient density of mixed-use development

---

[73] Jonathan Barnett, "What's New about New Urbanism?" *in* Congress for the New Urbanism; *Charter of the New Urbanism* (McGraw-Hill) (2000) at 5.

[74] See Congress for the New Urbanism, *About New Urbanism,* at http://www.cnu.org/about/index.cfm.

to support the transportation and transit services needed to increase pedestrian traffic and reduce car travel.

- *Bulk and area requirements:* A designated growth zoning district can contain bulk, area, and parking provisions that encourage types of development that support smart growth principles. By establishing setback lines that require new buildings to be built up to the sidewalk and by requiring parking and garages in the rear, pedestrian use of streets can be encouraged and an attractive neighborhood design created. The number of parking spaces required can be fewer if real prospects of transit services exist. Design amenities such as front porches and traditional architectural styles can be included in the zoning provisions. In some parts of these designed zoning districts, narrower streets can be specified to discourage traffic and ease pedestrian use.

- *Incentive zoning:* Significant waivers of zoning requirements can be offered to developers, including increasing the density of development allowed, as a method of directing larger-scale development into designated growth areas.[75] Developers can be encouraged to provide public amenities such as transportation, parks, affordable housing, social service centers, or other infrastructure in exchange for the waivers.

- *Special permits:* Larger-scale developments providing for mixed uses may be approved by special permits issued by the planning board or other administrative body. This practice has been followed for decades by municipalities as a method of combining land uses in designated planned unit or planned residential zoning districts.[76]

- *Floating zones:* Large-scale developments can be permitted by amending the zoning code to provide for a special use zone, such as a mixed-use development district, that can be affixed to a large area upon the application of all or a majority of the landowners. That application, if successful, results in the amendment of the zoning map to redistrict the subject parcels and permit the new use.[77]

- *Generic environmental impact statements:* When any of these techniques is used to create a designated growth area, a generic environmental impact statement can be prepared to identify negative environmental impacts and provide for their mitigation.[78] When this happens, it is possible that developers of individual projects will not be required to prepare lengthy and costly environmental impact studies. This alone can provide a powerful incentive for developers to concentrate their projects in designated development areas.

- *Transfer of development rights:* State law allows New York municipalities to establish transfer of development rights programs that concentrate development in receiving districts and provide for the transfer of development rights from sending districts.[79]

---

[75] N.Y. Town Law § 261-b (McKinney 2004); N.Y. Gen. City Law § 81-d (McKinney 2004); N.Y. Village Law § 7–703 (McKinney 2004).

[76] N.Y. Town Law § 274-b (McKinney 2004); N.Y. Gen. City Law § 27-b (McKinney 2004); N.Y. Village Law § 7–725-b (McKinney 2004).

[77] In *Rodgers v. Village of Tarrytown* [N.Y. 1951] 96 N.E.2d 731, municipalities in New York learned that they have the authority to create novel zoning devices such as the floating zone to achieve the most appropriate use of land.

[78] See N.Y. Comp. Codes R. & Regs. Tit. 6, § 617.10 (2004).

[79] See N.Y. Town Law §261-a (McKinney 2004); N.Y. Village Law §7–701 (McKinney 2004); N.Y. Gen. City Law §20-f (McKinney 2004).

In smart growth terms, the receiving district is the designated growth area and the sending area is a conservation or natural resource protection area.

- *Intermunicipal agreements:* In New York, local governments have been given liberal legal authority to cooperate in the planning and zoning field.[80] Through intermunicipal agreements, they can designate shared or interlocking growth districts that create real market opportunities and a complementary range of housing types, retail services, office buildings, and needed amenities. This important technique is used most often when several communities share a transportation corridor.

8.2 Urban Revitalization and Community Building

A critical focus of smart growth strategies is to reverse the trend of "out migration" of affluent households from existing cities and urban areas and to aid their revitalization. This problem has been addressed aggressively by the federal government, using its spending power to provide grants to local governments and institutions. In the 1960s, Congress created the urban renewal program as the initial response to the question of how to accomplish urban revitalization. For a decade and a half, the federal Department of Housing and Urban Development awarded urban renewal planning and project grants to local urban renewal agencies to plan and execute slum clearance and redevelopment programs. States cooperated by passing laws enabling cities to establish urban renewal agencies and industrial development agencies empowered to enter into contracts with the federal government and issue municipal bonds to finance their activities.

The questionable results of slum clearance and redevelopment came under fierce attack in the late 1960s. The critics held that urban renewal fostered segregation, removed historic buildings, dislocated the urban poor, and wasted government resources. With the passage of the Housing and Community Development Act of 1974,[81] federal urban renewal planning and project grants were folded into the special revenue sharing formula of the Community Development Block Grant program. Under this program, localities were authorized to continue their urban renewal programs if they wished or to use the federal dollars for a much broader array of activities, such as street improvements, sidewalk repair, and housing rehabilitation grants, which were more popular with local citizens.[82]

A more recent attempt to encourage development in urban areas and prevent urban sprawl is brownfield redevelopment. In many communities, former industrial properties blight the landscape and remain unrealized economic opportunities. Generally known as *brownfields*, these properties are abandoned, idled, or underused industrial and commercial facilities where redevelopment is complicated because of the existence of hazardous or toxic substances in the soil or groundwater. Nationwide there are over 450,000 brownfields.[83]

Developers are often reluctant to purchase and redevelop brownfields because of the liability that may be imposed upon them under the Comprehensive Environmental

---

[80] N.Y. Town Law § 284 (McKinney 2004); N.Y. Gen. City Law § 20-g (McKinney 2004); N.Y. Village Law § 7–741 (McKinney 2004).

[81] 42 U.S.C. § 5301 *et seq.* (2004).

[82] See John R. Nolon, "Reexamining Federal Housing Programs in a Time of Austerity: The Trend toward Block Grants and Housing Allowances" [1982], 14 *Urb. Law.* 249.

[83] See U.S. Environmental Protection Agency, *Cleanup, at* http://www.epa.gov/ebtpages/cleanup.html.

Response, Compensation and Liability Act (CERCLA).[84] CERCLA and similar laws adopted by many states impose strict liability upon an owner or operator of a site where contamination is present, regardless of whether that person caused the pollution. Consequently, a developer could be liable for millions of dollars of remediation costs simply by purchasing a site with hazardous contamination. This potential liability causes most brownfield sites to lie fallow. As a means to encourage the redevelopment of brownfields, a number of states have enacted statutes to reduce liability and have created programs that provide financial incentives to redevelopers.

Brownfield redevelopment is an important smart growth technique for a variety of reasons. First, remediating contaminated properties reduces or eliminates, the environmental threat presented by these sites, thereby protecting the health of the community. Second, when redeveloped, the formerly abandoned sites generate tax revenue for the community. Third, developing brownfield sites, which are typically located in more urbanized areas, removes some development pressure from outlying greenfields. Fourth, communities can use brownfields to meet various planning objectives such as the creation of affordable housing or additional commercial development.

8.3 The Advent of Local Environmental Law

Slowly, during the past 30 years, local governments have developed a new body of local regulations designed to protect natural resources and prevent environmental pollution.[85] Today one can point to thousands of local laws that protect forests, freshwater and tidal wetlands, ridgelines, stream banks, vegetative cover, viewsheds, watersheds, wildlife habitats, and other natural resources that are threatened by land development. Equally numerous are local laws that prevent environmental contamination, notably nonpoint sources of water and air pollution that escape regulation under the Clean Air Act and the Clean Water Act enacted by the federal Congress. Local laws now regulate storm water runoff, soil erosion, and surface water sedimentation in an attempt to prevent further environmental degradation at the local level and to preserve the quality of community life.

Beginning in the 1960s, some communities used large-lot zoning as a crude way to protect open space and its associated natural resources. Up-zoning occurred in some suburban areas and was aimed principally at controlling population growth, maintaining residential property values, and containing the cost to the community of servicing development. Incidentally, it also limited water use, aquifer contamination, and nonpoint source pollution. As the environmental movement evolved and matured in the 1970s and 1980s, local lawmakers became increasingly sensitive to environmental issues. There were early signs forecasting the adoption of local environmental law. Of particular importance was the National Flood Insurance Program, which required local governments to adopt and enforce floodplain management programs as a prerequisite to local eligibility for national flood disaster assistance payments. Catastrophes had their role in the movement. Hurricanes, for example, led to storm water management regulations

---

[84] 42 U.S.C. § 9601 *et seq.* (2004).

[85] See John R. Nolon, "In Praise of Parochialism: The Advent of Local Environmental Law" [2002], 26 *Harv. Envtl. L. Rev.* 363.

and stringent setback requirements along the coasts of barrier islands, which are particularly vulnerable to tropical storm damage.

Contemporary local environmental laws take a number of forms. Environmental objectives can now be found in local comprehensive plans, the boundaries of conservation zoning districts can be drawn to correspond to and protect watershed areas, environmental standards can now be found in subdivision and site plan regulations, and localities can adopt stand-alone environmental laws to protect particular unique and threatened natural resources.[86] The clear purposes of these laws are to control nonpoint source pollution and preserve natural resources from the adverse impacts of land development. Although the majority of U.S. communities have not adopted numerous and sophisticated local environmental laws, the increasing number of these laws, in the aggregate, constitutes a significant body of land use practice.

9 EXPLORING MUNICIPAL AUTHORITY TO CONTROL PRIVATE LAND USE

Determining whether local governments in any particular state have the authority to adopt innovative land use laws of the type discussed requires a careful reading of the sources of delegated authority to control land use and an understanding of the rules of interpretation of these statutes in each state. Some state statutes and courts have adopted rules of strict construction, narrowly interpreting local power; others have interpreted the express, implied, and home rule authority of their municipalities more broadly.

In most states, it is understood that municipalities have no inherent powers but exercise only that authority expressly granted or necessarily implied from, or incident to, the powers granted to them by their state legislatures. The express authority to adopt land use plans and zoning regulations is delegated to local governments in most states through planning and zoning enabling acts. Many states have supplemental acts delegating land use authority to municipalities, such as the power to adopt subdivision and site plan regulations or to adopt transfer of development rights programs or protect particular environmental features such as wetlands, shorelines, and river corridors.

Land use enabling laws can be broadly construed to empower localities to adopt innovative and flexible land use regulations. One of the purposes of local zoning laws is to provide for "the most appropriate use of land," a broad objective indeed.[87] This phrase was contained in the original model zoning enabling act and is found in the law of most states.[88] State statutes may require all land use regulations, including zoning, subdivision and site plan regulations, and all other regulations affecting the use of private land, to conform to a comprehensive plan.[89] In North Carolina, the state legislature adopted

---

[86] Several hundred of these local laws are available on Gaining Ground Information Database, prepared and maintained by the Land Use Law Center, *at* http://landuse.law.pace.edu/SPT/SPT--Home.php.

[87] N.Y. Town Law § 263 (McKinney 2004); N.Y. Village Law § 7–704 (McKinney 2004).

[88] U.S. Department of Commerce, A Standard State Zoning Enabling Act, § 3 (1926), reprinted in Edward H. Ziegler, Jr. (ed.), *Rathkopf's The Law of Zoning and Planning* (West) (2003) Volume 5, Appendix A. See, e.g., Conn. Gen. Stat. § 8–2 (2003).

[89] N.Y. Town Law § 272-a(2)(b) (McKinney 2004); N.Y. Village Law § 7–222 (2)(b) (McKinney 2004); N.Y. Gen. City Law § 28-a(3)(b) (2004).

a legislative rule of broad construction of powers delegated to local governments.[90] Prior to that time, the courts had strictly construed specific grants of authority to local governments. A Raleigh, North Carolina, requirement that a developer create open space in a subdivision and convey title to it to a private homeowners' association was upheld, using the legislative rule of broad construction.[91] The New York statute delegating the power to adopt comprehensive plans states that local plans may have elements dealing with agricultural uses, cultural resources, coastal and natural resources, and sensitive environmental areas.[92] This at least implies that local land use regulations can be adopted to advance the "environmental elements" of a local comprehensive plan.

In most states, home rule authority is delegated to localities, giving them broader authority to adopt laws that affect local property, affairs, and government so long as those laws do not conflict with general or preemptive state laws. States utilize a variety of methods to grant home rule powers to their localities.[93] In most states, home rule authority is contained in the constitution. This authority, in some states, is self-executing and enables localities to adopt land use laws; in others, it requires the state legislature to adopt a home rule law and to delegate self-regulatory powers within a defined range of interests. Home rule provisions in state constitutions and statutes can delegate broad self-government authority or provide a rather narrow range of local legislation under home rule power. Where municipalities enjoy home rule authority, they may be able to exercise land use authority flexibly, outside the prescriptions and constraints of the zoning enabling laws. In other states, courts hold that localities must control private land use activity through discrete land use enabling laws and are limited to the techniques and procedures prescribed by them. At a minimum, local home rule power authorizes localities to legislate in matters related to their own property, affairs, and government, except where general or preemptive state laws operate. In nearly all states, home rule authority is not deemed to prevent the state from legislating in relation to legitimate state interests by guiding, directing, or preempting local land use control.

The South Dakota Constitution, for example, provides that "[a] chartered governmental unit may exercise any legislative power or perform any function not denied by its charter, the Constitution or the general laws of the state. . . . Powers and functions of home rule units shall be construed liberally."[94] In Illinois, the constitution states that "a home rule unit may exercise any power and perform any function pertaining to its government and affairs including, but not limited to, the power to regulate for the protection of the public health, safety, morals and welfare."[95] The California Constitution

---

[90] N.C. GEN. STAT. § 160A-4 (2004) (stating that "[i]t is the policy of the General Assembly that the cities of this State should have adequate authority to execute the powers, duties, privileges, and immunities conferred upon them by law. To this end, the provisions of this Chapter and of city charters shall be broadly construed and grants of power shall be construed to include any additional and supplementary powers that are reasonably necessary or expedient to carry them into execution and effect").

[91] *River Birch Assocs. v. City of Raleigh* [N.C. 1990] 388 S.E.2d 538, 542–544.

[92] N.Y. TOWN LAW § 272-a (McKinney 2004); N.Y. VILLAGE LAW § 7–222 (McKinney 2004); N.Y. GEN. CITY LAW § 28-a (McKinney 2004).

[93] See Daniel R. Mandelker, *Land Use Law*, 5th edition (LexisNexis Matthew Bender) (2003) § 4.24.

[94] S.D. CONST. art. IX, § 2.   [95] Ill. CONST. art. 7, § 6.

provides that a city "may make and enforce within its limits all local, police, sanitary, and other ordinances and regulations not in conflict with general laws."[96]

The home rule provisions of Article IX of the New York Constitution and legislation passed pursuant to it give local governments broad home rule powers.[97] The state legislature implemented Article IX with the enactment of the Municipal Home Rule Law (MHRL), the provisions of which are to be "liberally construed."[98] Under the MHRL, localities are given the authority to adopt laws for "the protection and enhancement of [their] physical and visual environment."[99] In *Ardizzone v. Elliot*,[100] the court stated that the municipality had the "power to regulate the freshwater wetlands within its boundaries under the Municipal Home Rule Law."[101]

10 FRAGMENTATION AND INTEGRATION

Under the modern American land use system, land ownership is held subject to the regulations of federal, state, and local governments. According to the U.S. Census Bureau, there are about 39,000 governments that have or can be given authority to regulate private land use.[102] In some areas, land developers must receive a permit to build near wetlands from the U.S. Army Corps of Engineers, the state department of environmental protection, and a local wetlands commission or planning board. In others, developers must comply with local erosion control regulations, meet state water quality standards, and comply with federal storm water regulations. Other examples of overlapping regulations that protect watersheds, habitats, surface waters, and other resources abound.[103]

There are certain inefficiencies that result from the current duplication of effort, undue costs, and delays that are imposed on some developments, and there is confusion about what are the appropriate roles. Since the federal government first regulated the habitats of endangered species, for example, states and local governments were slow to enter the field of habitat protection. State power over property and land use, however, is complete and comprehensive. Once states enter the field, the topic becomes biodiversity protection and their power to regulate extends far beyond the protection of federally listed threatened or endangered species. The same can be said for watershed planning and management, wetland protection, and natural resource protection of all types.

Although confusing in some cases and onerous in others, this duplicative jurisdiction is not altogether a bad thing. In New York, the state regulates wetlands that are larger than 12.4 acres. In many New York communities, the proper protection of the local environment can require the regulation of much smaller wetland areas, such as vernal pools, which are critical to the survival of certain species in the community. Federal wetland control is limited to wetlands connected to interstate or navigable waters. State

---

[96] CAL. CONST. art. 11, § 7.   [97] See N.Y. CONST. art. IX.

[98] N.Y. MUN. HOME RULE LAW § 51 (McKinney 2004).

[99] Ibid. § 10(1)(ii)(a)(11).   [100] 550 N.E.2d 906 (N.Y. 1989).

[101] Ibid. at 908.

[102] In addition to the federal government and 50 state governments, there are 38,971 general purpose local governments: 3,034 county governments, 19,431 municipal governments, and 16,506 township governments. A large percentage of these general purpose governments have some power to regulate private land use. See U.S. Census Bureau, Preliminary Report No.1: The 2002 Census of Governments, available at http://www.census/gov/govs/www/cog2002.html.

[103] See Peter A. Buchsbaum, "Permit Coordination Study by the Lincoln Institute of Land Policy" [2004], 36 Urb. Law. 191.

and local interests may dictate the regulation of wetlands that are located in areas beyond the geographical reach of federal law. Local, state, and federal interests may differ, and regulations that protect these interests must differ to some degree. Leaving this land use system flexible to respond to regional conditions allows citizens and their elected legislators to continue to adapt the system to meet their unique and changing conditions.

This is not to say, however, that the parts of the system could not be better linked or coordinated. The federal government has adopted a cooperative method of working with states on some environmental and land use issues such as coastal protection, storm water management, and point source pollution. States are encouraged by some federal regulations to develop their own permitting systems for polluters and by some federal spending programs to involve local governments in protecting coasts, preventing the development of areas prone to natural disasters, limiting storm water runoff, and reducing the pollution of navigable waters. Within the U.S. system of dual sovereignty and cooperative federalism more of this type of integration and cooperation is merited and should be encouraged.

11 CONCLUSION

Local governments, empowered and guided by their states, have considerable authority to effect comprehensive and complete solutions. If properly guided and assisted, they can create strong local communities, while meeting regional and statewide needs. They can become effective partners of the federal government in protecting federal waters, the air, and other matters of interstate importance.

Many states draft model local land use and environmental laws that localities may be allowed or required to adopt. State agencies provide technical assistance to municipalities regarding the adoption and enforcement of these models and sponsor educational programs to encourage more local governments to become involved. Some states also provide incentives, such as bonus eligibility points for discretionary grant programs to local governments that have adopted effective land use and environmental laws.

The federal government can encourage states to delegate authority to promote smart growth and protect natural resources to local government by sponsoring the preparation of model state acts that enable municipalities to adopt flexible and innovative land use laws. It was the model act promulgated by the U.S. Department of Commerce in the 1920s that led to the rather rapid adoption of state zoning enabling acts and of local zoning ordinances. Providing federal funding to support the emerging efforts of states to prepare smart growth policies and plans helps create a framework for state and local action to protect environmental resources in critical areas.

Further efforts in this direction are warranted. Federal and state funding also can be provided for the identification of critical watersheds, habitats, and forests and the development of local inventories of natural resources. With federal support, states can encourage local governments to create natural resource inventories and protect critical environmental assets by providing financial incentives to localities that comply with state smart growth programs. Federal and state incentives can also be provided to facilitate efforts to link transportation planning with intermunicipal land use planning. To the extent that the federal government builds on state and local action, its legal and geographical influence is broadened.

Beyond these municipally focused initiatives, additional strategies for integrating governmental land use regulations are possible. These include coordinated project review and joint permitting systems of the federal and state agencies; delegation of the administration of federal wetland, storm water, and habitat permitting authority to state governments; and, importantly, cross-certification of compatible state and federal land use plans and programs. This coordinated approach to land use regulation was evident 30 years ago in the Coastal Zone Management Act of 1972, under which federal incentives for state and local cooperation were applied. This cooperative approach is also reflected in the Disaster Mitigation Act of 2000, a federal law that requires states, in conjunction with their localities, to create and submit plans for more intelligently regulating development in disaster-prone areas and that rewards those that cooperate with enhanced eligibility for federal disaster relief payments.[104]

Although the U.S. land use system is fragmentary and still uncoordinated in many respects, it shows signs of coherence. Further integration of the system can be achieved by focusing on and reinforcing the role of municipalities. United States law and practice emphasize the role of local government in land use control for a number of important reasons. First, it is the historical approach, emanating from the medieval municipal corporation and surviving today, despite many attempts to loosen the local grip. Second, local economic markets and environments differ – they are not readily susceptible to generic statewide and national solutions. Third, local citizens and politicians are intimately familiar with local circumstances and have a great stake in economic success and protection of the quality of community life. Fourth, emphasizing a strong local role organizes state and federal political, legal, and financial energies by giving them a focal point.

Respecting the role of municipalities in land use and environmental regulation reminds policymakers that conditions and interests differ greatly from place to place. It suggests, too, that the legal system must remain open to invention. As Justice Brandeis observed over 70 years ago, "a single courageous state may, if its citizens choose, serve as a laboratory; and try novel social and economic experiments without risk to the rest of the country."[105] By enabling, encouraging, guiding, and directing local government experimentation in land use matters, the 50 states empower thousands of local partners in society's perpetual search for the creation of livable, affordable, and environmentally sound communities.

12 ILLUSTRATIVE CHECKLIST OF LAND USE CONTROLS IN THE UNITED STATES

The general characteristics of this diverse and detailed system of laws and an illustrative list of the techniques employed by each level of government follows:

1. Private property rights are protected by federal and state constitutions.
2. Market demand for housing, retail, industrial, commercial, and other land uses drives landowners and developers to propose particular uses of the land in compliance with local, state, and federal land use and environmental laws.

---

[104] P.L. 106–390 (30 October 2000).
[105] *New State Ice Co. v. Liebmann* [1932] 285 U.S. 262, 31 (Brandeis, J., dissenting).

3. The use of land is subject to reasonable government restrictions that accomplish a legitimate governmental purpose and that permit some economically viable use of the land.

4. The general power to regulate land use to protect the public interest is retained by state governments.

5. State legislatures delegate to municipal governments the power to regulate the use of land by the private sector. States vary with respect to the extent of land use authority they delegate to municipalities and of guidance they provide localities in exercising that authority.

6. The federal government is a government of delegated powers that include the authority to regulate interstate commerce, the power upon which most environmental regulations are based. Federal environmental laws regulate significant private land use activity in the interest of preventing point source pollution and cleaning up hazardous and toxic deposits.

7. States and the federal government have created only a few regional land use agencies that dictate land use standards or policies to local regulators; some state and federal laws encourage or require localities to take certain desirable actions and prevent them from taking others that interfere with state and federal interests.

8. Municipalities adopt comprehensive plans that lay the foundation for the adoption of local land use laws. In a few states, these local plans must be consistent with regional or statewide land use plans.

9. Municipalities also adopt traditional land use laws such as zoning ordinances and standards that regulate land subdivision and site plan development.

10. Local governments are empowered to adopt innovative local land use laws that promote smart growth – more balanced land use patterns – and that protect natural resources and prevent environmental pollution.

11. Procedures for adopting land use plans and laws provide for citizen participation in the process with varying degrees of input and effectiveness.

12. Local administrative review agencies are established to review and approve individual development proposals. These agencies are required to hold public hearings on most proposals, to provide notice to affected parties of the hearings, to hold meetings open to the public, and to ensure that their voting members have no conflicts of interests that prevent their decisions from being objective.

13. The two consistent standards that all land use laws must meet are that they accomplish a legitimate public objective and that they allow the landowner some economically viable use of the land.

14. The judicial branch of government mediates disputes among landowners, affected citizens, environmental organizations, and governmental regulators.

15. Courts tend to defer to the judgment of land use regulators and impose a heavy burden on those who challenge land use regulations to prove that such regulations are arbitrary, capricious, not within the scope of local authority, deny owners an economical use of the land, or violate other constitutional protections such as equal protection of the law.

16. Some land use projects are subject to permitting standards by multiple agencies and levels of government. This overlap reveals some redundancy and inefficiency in the national land use system that could be reduced.

17. Land use and environmental controls exist at the federal, state, and local levels and are not organized or guided by commonly accepted policies and principles. Local and regional land use controls vary considerably from place to place. This fragmentation of authority and policy could be ameliorated by forging an agreement on a framework for intergovernmental policies and procedures for decision making.

18. Because of the size of the United States and the great diversity of geography, population, and political views, however, a single system of land use law and practice will not serve the unique needs and realities of every region.

12.1 The Role of the National Government

Constitutional Provisions
- Interstate commerce clause
- Power to tax and spend
- Powers reserved to the states
- Protection of individual rights and freedoms
- Protection of property rights

Regulatory Acts
- Clean Air Act
- Clean Water Act
- Coastal Zone Management Act
- Comprehensive Environmental Response, Compensation, and Liability Act
- Endangered Species Act
- Resource Conservation and Recovery Act
- Surface Mining Control and Reclamation

Funding and Other Programs
- Environmental protection
- Housing and urban development
- Natural resource protection
- Technical assistance, data, studies, training
- Transportation

Treaties and Conventions
- Endangered species
- Natural resources
- Tariffs and trade

12.2 The Role of the State Government

Constitutional Provisions
- Protection of natural resources
- Protection of property rights

- Protection of religious freedoms
- Protection of the environment

Laws That Allow and Direct Local Land Use Control
- Traditional techniques
- Smart growth
- Local environmental and resource protection
- Urban revitalization and community building
- Character and patrimony
- Home rule

Laws That Restrict Local Land Use Control
- Affordable housing appeals laws
- Control of regional-impact projects
- Creation of regional agencies with land use authority
- Development of state projects (eminent domain)
- Growth management laws
- Location of public utilities
- Regional compacts with other states

Funding and Other Programs
- Environmental protection
- Housing and urban development
- Natural resource protection
- Technical assistance, data, studies, training
- Transportation

12.3 The Role of Municipal Governments[106]

Traditional Land Use Controls
- Land use plans
- Zoning laws
- Land uses: as-of-right, accessory, or specially permitted
- Building construction and use of the lot
- Subdivision and site plan controls
- Special use permits
- Variances and nonconforming uses
- Official map

Smart growth[107]
- Affordable housing zoning
- Clustered subdivisions

---

[106] For a glossary that defines most of these terms and techniques, See John R. Nolon, *Well Grounded: Using Local Land Use Authority to Achieve Smart Growth, supra*, note 35, at 446–457.

[107] See ibid.

- Floating zones
- Growth limits
- Incentive zoning
- Intermunicipal planning and regulation
- Moratoria
- Overlay zones
- Performance zoning
- Planned unit development
- Purchase of development rights
- Regulatory plans
- Traditional neighborhood districts
- Transfer of development rights

Local Environmental and Natural Resource Protection Laws[108]

- Aquifer protection
- Conservation area zoning
- Conservation easements
- Environmental impact review procedures
- Erosion and sediment control
- Floodplain protection
- Large landscape protection zones
- Ridgeline protection
- Scenic resource protection
- Steep slope protection
- Storm water management
- Timber harvesting
- Tree preservation
- Watercourse protection
- Waterfront management laws
- Watershed planning
- Wetlands protection
- Wildlife habitat protection

Urban Revitalization and Community Building

- Brownfield redevelopment
- Housing development and rehabilitation
- Infrastructure provision
- Urban renewal

Protection of Character and Patrimony

- Adult entertainment laws
- Design control
- Historic preservation

---

[108] See John R. Nolon, *Open Ground: Effective Local Strategies for Protecting Natural Resources* (Environmental Law Institute) (2003) 193–518.

- Landmark preservation
- Protection of cultural resources and patrimony

Home Rule
- Constitutional
- Statutory
- Broad
- Limited

Index